Coding for Pediatrics 2015

A Manual for Pediatric Documentation and Payment

For use with AMA CPT 2015

20th Edition

Author

Committee on Coding and Nomenclature (COCN)
American Academy of Pediatrics

Edward A. Liechty, MD, Editor

Cindy Hughes, CPC, CFPC, Consulting Editor
Becky Dolan, MPH, CPC, CPEDC, Staff Editor

American Academy of Pediatrics
141 Northwest Point Blvd
Elk Grove Village, IL 60007-1019

ISBN: 978-1-58110-880-4
eBook: 978-1-58110-900-9
ISSN: 1537-324X
MA0720

Quantity prices on request. Address all inquiries to
American Academy of Pediatrics
Division of Marketing and Sales
141 Northwest Point Blvd
Elk Grove Village, IL 60007-1019

The recommendations in this publication do not indicate an exclusive course of treatment or serve as a standard of medical care. Variations, taking into account individual circumstances, may be appropriate.

Products are included for informational purposes only. Inclusion in this publication does not imply endorsement by the American Academy of Pediatrics.

Fee schedules, relative value units, conversion factors, and/or related components are not assigned by the AMA, are not part of *CPT*, and the AMA is not recommending their use. The AMA does not directly or indirectly practice medicine or dispense medical services. The AMA assumes no liability for data contained or not contained herein.

CPT is a registered trademark of the AMA.

This publication has prior approval of the American Academy of Professional Coders (AAPC) for 4.0 continuing education units. Granting of this approval in no way constitutes endorsement by AAPC of the publication content or publication sponsor.

Disclaimer

||||||||||

Every effort has been made to include the new and revised 2015 *Current Procedural Terminology (CPT®); International Classification of Diseases, Ninth Revision, Clinical Modification (ICD-9-CM); International Classification of Diseases, 10th Revision, Clinical Modification (ICD-10-CM);* and Healthcare Common Procedure Coding System (HCPCS) codes, their respective guidelines, and other revisions that might have been made. Due to our publishing deadlines and the publication date of the American Medical Association *CPT,* additional revisions and/or additional codes may have been published subsequent to the date of this printing. It is the responsibility of the reader to use this manual as a companion to the *CPT, ICD-9-CM, ICD-10-CM,* and HCPCS publications. Vignettes are provided throughout this publication to illustrate correct coding applications. They are not intended to offer medical advice on the practice of medicine. *ICD-10-CM* codes are used for reference purposes only. Do not report *ICD-10-CM* codes until its published implementation date. Further, it is the reader's responsibility to access the American Academy of Pediatrics Web site (www.aap.org/cfp) routinely to find any corrections due to errata in the published version.

Copyright Acknowledgment

Current Procedural Terminology (CPT®) is a listing of descriptive terms and 5-digit numeric identifying codes and modifiers for reporting medical services and procedures performed by physicians. This presentation includes only the *CPT* descriptive terms, numeric identifying codes, and modifiers for reporting medical services and procedures that were selected by the American Academy of Pediatrics (AAP) for inclusion in this publication. The inclusion of a *CPT* service or procedure description and its code number in this publication does not restrict its use to a particular specialty group. Any procedure or service in this publication may be used to report the services provided by any qualified physician or, when appropriate, other qualified health care professional.

The American Medical Association (AMA) and the AAP assume no responsibility for the consequences attributable to or related to any use or interpretation of any information or views contained in or not contained in this publication.

Any 5-digit numeric *CPT* code, service descriptions, instructions, and/or guidelines are copyright 2014 (or such other date of publication of *CPT* as defined in the federal copyright laws) AMA. All rights reserved.

The most current *CPT* is available from the AMA.

No fee schedules, basic unit values, relative value guides, conversion factors or scales, or components thereof are included in *CPT.*

Contents

||||||||||

Foreword

The American Academy of Pediatrics (AAP) is pleased to publish this, the 20th edition of *Coding for Pediatrics*—an instructional manual and reference tool for use by primary care pediatricians, pediatric subspecialists, and others involved in the provision of care to children. The purpose of this manual is to support the delivery of quality care to children by providing the pediatric practitioner with the knowledge to best support appropriate business practices. Many changes have been made to this edition, including updating the 2015 *Current Procedural Terminology (CPT®)* codes with guidelines for their application, a new chapter on coding for perinatal counseling and care of the newborn, and a new chapter on coding for nontraditional evaluation and management services and non-physician services. For several years, *Coding for Pediatrics* has included information on *International Classification of Diseases, 10th Revision, Clinical Modification (ICD-10-CM)* in anticipation of the transition, which was scheduled for October 1, 2014. On April 1, 2014, this transition was delayed to October 1, 2015, by the enactment of the Protecting Access to Medicare Act of 2014. In response to this delay, *Coding for Pediatrics 2015* includes *ICD-9-CM* and *ICD-10-CM* codes in clinical vignettes, providing *ICD-10-CM* education in anticipation of the pending transition. Coding tips include key documentation elements to support specific and accurate *ICD-10-CM* code selection. In addition, the AAP is pleased to provide *Coding for Pediatrics 2015* as an eBook.

Any corrections that may be necessary subsequent to the publication of the manual will be available to readers of *Coding for Pediatrics 2015* by accessing www.aap.org/cfp. *Coding for Pediatrics 2015* does not replace *CPT, ICD-9-CM, ICD-10-CM,* or Healthcare Procedure Coding System (HCPCS); rather, it supplements those manuals. Every effort has been made to include the 2015 codes and their respective guidelines; however, revised codes and/or guidelines may have been published subsequent to the date of this printing. Updates to this manual will be posted on the *Coding for Pediatrics* Web site (www.aap. org/cfp).

The AAP actively works with the American Medical Association (AMA) *CPT* Editorial Panel and the AMA/Specialty Society Relative Value Scale Update Committee (RUC) to develop pediatric specialty codes and assign them appropriate relative value units. Since 1995, the AAP has contributed to the process that evaluates and reviews changes to the Medicare Resource-Based Relative Value Scale (RBRVS). Pediatricians have been actively involved in the AMA RUC Practice Expense Advisory Committee to review direct practice expenses for all existing codes. As importantly, the AAP is represented on the AMA *CPT* Editorial Advisory Panel and on the *ICD-10-CM* Editorial Advisory Board. The AAP continues to be involved in all areas of payment. The AAP Committee on Coding and Nomenclature oversees all areas of coding as they relate to pediatrics, including *CPT* procedure coding, *ICD-9-CM* and *ICD-10-CM* diagnosis coding, and the valuation of *CPT* services through the Medicare RBRVS.

The AAP will continue to request new code changes and attempt to expeditiously notify membership of changes through various means. The *AAP Pediatric Coding Newsletter™*—a monthly newsletter available in print and online—provides members and their office personnel with up-to-date coding and payment information. The newsletter and other online resources can be accessed through the AAP newsletter Web site (http://coding.aap.org). Other resources include coding seminars presented at the AAP National Conference & Exhibition; webinars sponsored by the AAP (www.aap.org/webinars/coding); instructional materials in *AAP News,* including the Coding Corner; *Pediatric Code Crosswalk: ICD-9-CM to ICD-10-CM* and the forthcoming *Pediatric*

ICD-10-CM: A Manual for Provider-Based Coding; and various quick reference cards. A list of these and other resources can be found in Appendix D of this manual. The use of these resources should provide the membership with the skills needed to report their services appropriately. The Division of Health Care Finance and Practice Improvement at the AAP headquarters stands ready to assist with problem areas not adequately covered in this manual. The AAP Coding Hotline can be accessed through e-mail at aapcodinghotline@aap.org.

Acknowledgments

Coding for Pediatrics, 20th Edition, is the product of the efforts of many dedicated individuals. My work has been made immeasurably easier and the final edition dramatically improved by the dedicated work of my collaborators. First and foremost, I must thank Cindy Hughes, CPC, CFPC, consulting editor, for her professional input and particularly for her ongoing work to make it more user-friendly and readable, a goal she and I share. Additionally, I must thank the Committee on Coding and Nomenclature (COCN) support staff at the American Academy of Pediatrics (AAP), particularly Becky Dolan, MPH, CPC, CPEDC, staff editor, for her many excellent suggestions as well as for reviewing major portions of the project. Thank you also to Teri Salus, MPA, CPC, CPEDC, for her review of new *Current Procedural Terminology (CPT®)* codes and suggestions for changes to content. I would also like to thank the members of the COCN and the AAP Coding Publications Editorial Advisory Board. The members of those committees have each contributed extensive time in reviewing and updating content of the manual.

I would like to particularly acknowledge those COCN members who have devoted their time and expertise to national committees, providing a breadth of knowledge not otherwise possible:

Margie C. Andreae, MD, AAP representative to the American Medical Association/ Specialty Society Relative Value Scale Update Committee (RUC); Eileen D. Brewer, MD, AAP alternate RUC representative; Steven E. Krug, MD, AAP RUC advisor; Joel F. Bradley, MD, AAP *CPT* advisor and former *CPT* Editorial Panel member; Sanjeev Y. Tuli, MD, AAP alternate *CPT* advisor; Julia M. Pillsbury, DO, *CPT* Editorial Panel member; Jeffrey F. Linzer Sr, AAP *International Classification of Diseases, 10th Revision, Clinical Modification* Editorial Advisory Board representative and *ICD-11* Pediatric Topic Advisory Group chairperson; and Richard A. Molteni, MD, former AAP *CPT* advisor and former *CPT* Editorial Panel member.

I am most grateful to the invaluable input of the following AAP committees and individuals: the Committee on Medical Liability and Risk Management, specifically Stephan Paul, MD, JD, FAAP, and AAP staff Julie Ake, senior health policy analyst; the Private Payer Advocacy Advisory Committee, specifically Sue Kressly, MD, FAAP, and AAP staff Lou Terranova, senior health policy analyst; Samuel D. Smith, MD, liaison for the American Pediatric Surgical Association; and the Section on Perinatal Pediatrics coding trainers. I appreciate the information on emerging payment methodologies provided to me by Edward P. Zimmerman, director, AAP Department of Practice, and by the AAP Committee on Child Health Financing, particularly Thomas Long, MD, FAAP.

This project would not have been completed were it not for the outstanding work of the AAP staff. In the Department of Marketing and Publications, Alain Park, senior product development editor; Jason Crase, manager of editorial services; Peg Mulcahy, manager of graphic design and production; Leesa Levin-Doroba, manager of publishing and production services; and Marirose Russo, brand manager for practice management and professional publications, deserve special recognition for their outstanding skill and dedication to this project. In the Division of Health Care Finance and Practice Improvement, I am especially appreciative of the support and professional expertise of Linda Walsh, MAB, division director, and AAP staff support to the AAP COCN, a dedicated advocate for all of us who provide medical care to children.

Edward A. Liechty, MD
Editor

||¦||¦||¦||

CHAPTER 1

New and Revised *CPT®* and *ICD-9-CM* Codes for 2015

||¦||¦||

Current Procedural Terminology (CPT®*)* is published annually by the American Medical Association (AMA). It is used by national carriers and is designated as the official procedure code set under the Health Insurance Portability and Accountability Act of 1996. *Current Procedural Terminology* codes are known as Level I codes of the broader-based Healthcare Common Procedure Coding System, termed HCPCS. The HCPCS coding system includes Level I codes *(CPT-4)*, Level II codes (Centers for Medicare & Medicaid Services national codes), and Level III codes (local codes assigned and used by Medicare carriers).

Current Procedural Terminology Category I codes are updated annually. New or revised codes are effective on January 1 of each year. The symbols on page 4 are used to assist physicians in recognizing the annual revisions made in *CPT*. Exceptions are the vaccine product and emerging technology codes, which are updated twice annually (January and July).

Current Procedural Terminology includes specific guidelines that are located at the beginning of each section and throughout the *CPT* manual. Always read the applicable instructions and guidelines before selecting a code.

New, Revised, and Deleted *CPT* Codes for 2015

The following new codes, revisions, and code deletions are effective with services provided on or after January 1, 2015. We have made every effort to include those procedures and services that are applicable to pediatric practices. However, revisions and/or additional codes may have been published subsequent to the date of this printing. This list does not include all changes made to *CPT 2015*. Please note that in the interest of efficiency, we will follow the established format of the *CPT* Editorial Panel meeting minutes; therefore, sections without any revisions will include only the first few italicized words of the section followed by an ellipsis (eg, *In the instance where a physician is on call…*). This represents the sections that were unchanged in the *CPT 2015* manual to more easily direct you toward the revised text within the guidelines. Always refer to *CPT 2015* for a complete listing of new codes, complete descriptions, and revisions.

New text is underlined, deleted text is indicated with a ~~strikethrough~~, new codes are identified with the bullet (●) symbol, and revised codes are identified with the triangle (▲) symbol.

A few of the changes presented in this chapter include

- A new code to describe chronic care management services has been added. *Current Procedural Terminology* code **99488,** describing complex chronic care management services with a face-to-face visit, has been deleted because these evaluation and management (E/M) visits would be reported separately.

- A new code has been added for total body and selective head hypothermia. The codes published in 2014 have been deleted and replaced with a single code representing initiation of hypothermia.

- News codes have been added for reporting services related to advance directive plan discussions with patients.

- A new series of codes replace codes **33960, 33961,** and **36822** for reporting services involving prolonged extracorporeal membrane oxygenation (ECMO) and extracorporeal life support (ECLS) services.

- A new code, **96127,** has been added for reporting brief emotional or behavioral assessment. In addition, code **96110** was revised to create consistency in the language used in this code and code **96127.**

❂ Codes for nonavalent human papillomavirus (HPV) and intradermal quadrivalent influenza vaccines, previously published online, are included in the 2015 manual.

❂ New Category III codes have been implemented for behavior assessments and adaptive behavior treatments. The codes will be published in *CPT 2015.*

Symbols	Description
●	A bullet at the beginning of a code means that the code is a new code for the current year. For example, ●99184 Initiation of selective head or total body hypothermia in the critically ill neonate, includes appropriate patient selection by review of clinical, imaging and laboratory data, confirmation of esophageal temperature probe location, evaluation of amplitude EEG, supervision of controlled hypothermia, and assessment of patient tolerance of cooling
▲	A triangle means that the code descriptor has been revised. For example, ▲96110 Developmental screening, (eg, developmental milestone survey, speech and language delay screen), with scoring and documentation interpretation and report, per standardized instrument form
+	A plus sign means that the code is an *add-on* code. For example, +90461 each additional vaccine or toxoid component administered
Ø	A null sign means that the code is a "modifier **51** exempt" code and therefore does not require modifier **51** (multiple procedures) even when reported with other procedures. For example, Ø31500 Intubation, endotracheal, emergency procedure
►◄	Arrows enclose new or revised text in the current edition of *CPT.* For example, ►(To report bilateral procedure, report **69210** with modifier **50**)◄
⊙	The target means that the code includes moderate sedation. For example, ⊙36557 Insertion of tunneled centrally inserted central venous catheter, without subcutaneous port or pump; younger than 5 years of age
⚡	The lightning bolt identifies codes for vaccines that are pending US Food and Drug Administration approval. For example, ⚡90630 Influenza virus vaccine, quadrivalent (IIV4), split virus, preservative free, for intradermal use
#	The pound symbol is used to identify resequenced codes that are out of numerical sequence. This allows related codes to be placed in an appropriate location, making it easier to locate a procedure or service. For example, #99485 Supervision by a control physician of interfacility transport care of the critically ill or critically injured pediatric patient, 24 months of age or younger, includes 2-way communication with transport team before transport, at the referring facility and during the transport, including data interpretation and report; first 30 minutes
O	The O symbol precedes codes that are recycled or reinstated. Within revised codes, the deleted language appears with a strikethrough, while new text appears underlined.

Category I

Evaluation and Management

►*Advance Care Planning*

The following codes are used to report the face-to-face service between a physician or other qualified health care professional and a patient, family member or surrogate in counseling and discussing advance directives, with or without completing relevant legal forms. An advance directive is a document appointing an agent and/or recording the wishes of a patient pertaining to his/her medical treatment at a future time should he/she lack decisional capacity at that time. Examples of written advance directives include, but are not limited to, Health Care Proxy, Durable Power of Attorney for Health Care, Living Will and Medical Orders for Life-Sustaining Treatment (MOLST).

When using these codes, no active management of the problem(s) is undertaken during the time period reported.

These codes may be reported separately if these services are performed on the same day as another Evaluation and Management service (**99201–99215, 99217–99220, 99221–99223, 99224–99226, 99231–99233, 99234–99239, 99241–99245, 99251–99255, 99281–99285, 99304–99318, 99324–99337, 99341–99350, 99381–99397, 99495–99496).◄**

●**99497**   Advance care planning including the explanation and discussion of advance directives such as standard forms (with completion of such forms, when performed), by the physician or other qualified health-care professional; first 30 minutes, face-to-face with the patient, family member(s) and/or surrogate

+●**99498**   each additional 30 minutes (List separately in addition to code for primary procedure)

(Use **99498** in conjunction with **99497**)

(Do not report **99497** and **99498** on the same date of service as critical care services codes **99291, 99292** and neonatal and pediatric critical care codes **99468–99476, 99477–99480**)

Inpatient Neonatal Intensive Care Services and Pediatric and Neonatal Critical Care Services

Newborn Care Services

Inpatient Neonatal Intensive Care Services and Pediatric and Neonatal Critical Care Services

Inpatient Neonatal and Pediatric Critical Care

●**99184**   Initiation of selective head or total body hypothermia in the critically ill neonate, includes appropriate patient selection by review of clinical, imaging and laboratory data, confirmation of esophageal temperature probe location, evaluation of amplitude EEG, supervision of controlled hypothermia, and assessment of patient tolerance of cooling

(Do not report **99184** more than once per hospital stay.)

This code replaces now deleted codes **99481** and **99482**. For more information on reporting initiation of hypothermia in the critically ill neonate, see Chapter 10.

►~~Complex Chronic Care Coordination~~ Management Services

~~Complex chronic c~~Care ~~coordination~~ management services are ~~patient centered~~ management and support services provided by ~~physicians, other qualified health care professionals, and~~ clinical staff, under the direction of a physician or other qualified health care professional, to ~~an individual who~~ patient resid~~es~~ing at home or in a domiciliary, rest home, or assisted living facility. Services may include establishing, implementing, revising, or monitoring the care plan, coordinating the care of other professionals and agencies, and educating the patient or caregiver about the patient's condition, care plan, and prognosis. ~~These services typically involve clinical staff developing, substantially revising, and implementing a care plan under direction of the physician or other qualified health care professional. Substantial revision to a care plan typically occurs when the patient's clinical condition changes sufficiently (eg, identification of a new problem requiring additional interventions, introduction of new interventions because existing interventions are deemed ineffective, exacerbation of an existing problem requiring new interventions) to require more intensive staff monitoring, changes in the treatment regimen, and additional time to educate the patient and/or caregiver about the patient's condition and/or change in treatment plan and prognosis. These services address the coordination of care by multiple professionals, disciplines, and/or community service agencies.~~ The physician or other qualified health care professional ~~reporting individual~~ provides or oversees the management and/or coordination of services, as needed, for all medical conditions, psychosocial needs, and ~~instrumental and basic~~ activities of daily living ~~(IADL/ADL)~~.

~~Patients who require complex chronic care coordination services may be identified by practice-specific or other published algorithms that recognize multiple illnesses, multiple medication use, inability to perform activities of daily living, requirement for a caregiver, and/or repeat admissions or emergency department visits. Typical adult patients take or receive three or more prescription medications and may also be receiving other types of therapeutic interventions (eg, physical therapy, occupational therapy) and have two or more chronic continuous or episodic health conditions expected to last at least 12 months, or until the death of the patient, that place the patient at significant risk of death, acute exacerbation/decompensation, or functional decline.~~

~~Typical pediatric patients receive three or more therapeutic interventions (eg, medications, nutritional support, respiratory therapy) and have two or more chronic continuous or episodic health conditions expected to last at least 12 months, or until the death of the patient, that place the patient at significant risk of death, acute exacerbation/decompensation, or functional decline. Because of the complex nature of their diseases and morbidities, these patients commonly require the coordination of a number of specialties and services. In some cases, due to inability to perform IADL/ADL and/ or cognitive impairment the patient is unable to adhere to the treatment plan without substantial assistance from a caregiver. For example, patients may have medical and psychiatric behavioral co-morbidities (eg, dementia and chronic obstructive pulmonary disease or substance abuse and diabetes) that complicate their care. Social support requirements or access to care difficulties may cause a need for these services. Medical, functional, and/or psychosocial problems that require medical decision making of moderate or high complexity and extensive clinical staff support are required. Medical decision making as defined in the Evaluation and Management (E/M) guidelines is not only applied to the face-to-face services, but is determined by the nature of the problems addressed by the reporting individual during the month.~~

A plan of care must be documented and shared with the patient and/or caregiver. A care plan is based on a physical, mental, cognitive, social, functional, and environmental ~~(re)~~assessment ~~and an inventory of resources and supports~~. It is a comprehensive plan of care for all health problems. It typically includes, but is not limited to, the following elements: problem list, expected outcome and prognosis, measurable treatment goals, symptom management, planned interventions, medication management, community/social services ordered, how the services of agencies and specialists unconnected to the practice will be directed/coordinated, identification of the individuals responsible for each intervention, requirements for periodic review, and, when applicable, revision of the care plan.

Codes **99487–99489 99490** are reported only once per calendar month and ~~include all non-face-to-face complex chronic care coordination services and none or 1 face-to-face office or other outpatient, home, or domiciliary visit. Physicians or other qualified health care professionals may not report care coordination services if the care plan is unchanged or requires minimal change (eg, only a medication is changed or an adjustment in a treatment modality is ordered). Codes **99487-99489**~~ may only be reported by the single physician or other qualified health care professional who assumes the care ~~coordination~~ management role with a particular patient for the calendar month.

~~Code selection is as follows:~~

~~Code **99487** is reported when, during the calendar month, there is no face-to-face visit with the physician or other qualified health care professional and at least 31 minutes of clinical staff time is spent in care coordination activities. **99488** is reported when, during the calendar month, there is a face-to-face visit with the physician or other qualified health care professional and at least 31 minutes of clinical staff time is spent in care coordination activities.~~

The face-to-face and non-face-to-face time spent by the clinical staff in communicating with the patient and/or family, caregivers, other professionals and agencies; revising, documenting and implementing the care plan; or teaching self-management is used in determining the ~~complex chronic~~ care ~~coordination~~ management clinical staff time for the month. Only the time of the clinical staff of the reporting professional is counted. Only count the time of one clinical staff member when two or more clinical staff members are meeting about the patient. Note: Do not count any clinical staff time ~~on the date of the first visit or~~ on a day when the physician or qualified health care professional reports an E/M service (office or other outpatient services **99211 99201–99215,** domiciliary, rest home services **99334 99324–99337,** home services **99347 99341–99350**).

Care ~~coordination~~ management activities performed by clinical staff typically include:
- communication and engagement with patient, family members, guardian or caretaker, surrogate decision makers, and/or other professionals regarding aspects of care;
- communication with home health agencies and other community services utilized by the patient;
- collection of health outcomes data and registry documentation;
- patient and/or family/caregiver ~~taker~~ education to support self-management, independent living, and activities of daily living;
- assessment and support for treatment regimen adherence and medication management;
- identification of available community and health resources;
- facilitating access to care and services needed by the patient and/or family;
- management of care transitions not reported as part of transitional care management (**99495, 99496**);
- ongoing review of patient status, including review of laboratory and other studies not reported as part of an E/M, noted above;
- development, communication, and maintenance of a comprehensive care plan.

The care ~~coordination~~ management office/practice must have the following capabilities:

* provide 24/7 access to physicians or other qualified health care professionals or clinical staff including providing patients/caregivers with a means to make contact with health care professionals in the practice to address urgent needs regardless of the time of day or day of week;
* provide continuity of care with a designated member of the care team with whom the patient is able to schedule successive routine appointments;
* provide timely access and management for follow-up after an emergency department visit or facility discharge;
* utilize an electronic health record system so that care providers have timely access to clinical information;
* use a standardized methodology to identify patients who require ~~chronic complex~~ care ~~coordination~~ management services;
* have an internal care ~~coordination~~ management process/function whereby a patient identified as meeting the requirements for these services starts receiving them in a timely manner;
* use a form and format in the medical record that is standardized within the practice;
* be able to engage and educate patients and caregivers as well as coordinate care among all service professionals, as appropriate for each patient.

~~If a face-to-face visit was provided during the month by the physician or other qualified health care professional, report~~ **99488.** ~~Additional~~ E/M services ~~beyond the first visit~~ may be reported separately by the same physician or other qualified health care professional during the same calendar month. ~~Complex~~ care ~~coordination~~ management services include care plan oversight services (**99339, 99340, 99374–99380**), prolonged services without direct patient contact (**99358, 99359**), anticoagulant management (**99363, 99364**), medical team conferences (**99366–99368**), education and training (**98960–98962, 99071, 99078**), telephone services (**98966–98968, 99441–99443**), on-line medical evaluation (**98969, 99444**), preparation of special reports (**99080**), analysis of data (**99090, 99091**), transitional care management services (**99495, 99496**), medication therapy management services (**99605–99607**) and, if performed, these services may not be reported separately during the month for which **99487–99489** are reported. All other services may be reported. Do not report **99487–~~99489~~99490** if reporting ESRD services (**90951–90970**) during the same month. If the ~~complex chronic~~ care ~~coordination~~ management services are performed within the postoperative period of a reported surgery, the same individual may not report **99487–~~99489~~99490**.

~~Complex chronic c~~Care ~~coordination~~ management ~~can~~ may be reported in any calendar month during which the clinical staff time requirements are met. If care ~~coordination~~ management resumes after a discharge during a new month, start a new period or report Transitional Care Management Services (**99495, 99496**) as appropriate. If discharge occurs in the same month, continue the reporting period or report Transitional Care Management Services. Do not report **99487–~~99489~~99490** for any post-discharge ~~complex chronic~~ care ~~coordination~~ management services for any days within 30 days of discharge, if reporting **99495, 99496.**

~~Total Duration of Staff Care Coordination Services~~	~~Code(s)~~
~~Less than 30 minutes~~	~~Not reported separately~~
~~31 to 74 minutes~~ ~~(31 minutes—1 hr. 14 min.)~~	~~**99487** or **99488** × 1~~
~~75—104 minutes~~ ~~(1 hr. 15 min.—1 hr. 44 min.)~~	~~**99487** or **99488** × 1 and **99489** × 1~~
~~5 minutes or more~~ ~~(1 hr. 45 min. or more~~	~~**99487** or **99488** × 1 and **99489** × 2 or more for each additional 30 minutes~~

Chronic Care Management Services

Chronic care management services are provided when medical and/or psychosocial needs of the patient require establishing, implementing, revising, or monitoring the care plan. Patients who receive chronic care management services have two or more chronic continuous or episodic health conditions that are expected to last at least 12 months, or until the death of the patient, and that place the patient at significant risk of death, acute exacerbation/decompensation, or functional decline. Code **99490** is reported when, during the calendar month, at least 20 minutes of clinical staff time is spent in care management activities.

●**99490**   Chronic care management services, at least 20 minutes of clinical staff time directed by a physician or other qualified health care professional, per calendar month, with the following required elements:
   ☀ multiple (two or more) chronic conditions expected to last at least 12 months, or until the death of the patient,
   ☀ chronic conditions place the patient at significant risk of death, acute exacerbation/decompensation, or functional decline,
   ☀ comprehensive care plan established, implemented, revised, or monitored
   (Chronic care management services of less than 20 minutes duration, in a calendar month, are not reported separately)

Complex Chronic Care Management Services

Complex chronic care management services are provided during a calendar month that includes criteria for chronic care management services as well as establishment or substantial revision of a comprehensive care plan; medical, functional, and/or psychosocial problems requiring medical decision making of moderate or high complexity; and clinical staff care management services for at least 60 minutes, under the direction of a physician or other qualified health care professional. Physicians or other qualified health care professionals may not report complex chronic care management services if the care plan is unchanged or requires minimal change (eg, only a medication is changed or an adjustment in a treatment modality is ordered). Medical decision making as defined in the Evaluation and Management (E/M) guidelines is determined by the problems addressed by the reporting individual during the month.

   Patients who require complex chronic care management services may be identified by practice-specific or other published algorithms that recognize multiple illnesses, multiple medication use, inability to perform activities of daily living, requirement for a caregiver, and/or repeat admissions or emergency department visits. Typical adult patients who receive complex chronic care management services are treated with three or more prescription medications and may be receiving other types of therapeutic interventions (eg, physical therapy, occupational therapy). Typical pediatric patients receive three or more therapeutic interventions (eg, medications, nutritional support, respiratory therapy). All patients have two or more chronic continuous or episodic health conditions that are expected to last at least 12 months, or until the death of the patient, and that place the patient at significant risk of death, acute exacerbation/decompensation, or functional decline. Typical patients have complex diseases and morbidities and, as a result, demonstrate one or more of the following:

- need for the coordination of a number of specialties and services;
- inability to perform activities of daily living and/or cognitive impairment resulting in poor adherence to the treatment plan without substantial assistance from a caregiver;
- psychiatric and other medical co-morbidities (eg, dementia and chronic obstructive pulmonary disease or substance abuse and diabetes) that complicate their care; and/or
- social support requirements or difficulty with access to care.

Total Duration of Staff Care Management Services	Complex Chronic Care Management
Less than 60 minutes	Not reported separately
60 to 89 minutes (1 hour—1 hr. 29 min.)	99487
90—119 minutes (1 hr. 30 min.—1 hr. 59 min.)	99487 and 99489 × 1
120 minutes or more (2 hours or more)	99487 and 99489 × 2 and 99489 for each additional 30 minutes

99487   Complex chronic care ~~coordination~~ management services,~~,~~ with the following required elements:
- multiple (two or more) chronic conditions expected to last at least 12 months, or until the death of the patient,
- chronic conditions place the patient at significant risk of death, acute exacerbation/decompensation, or functional decline,
- establishment or substantial revision of a comprehensive care plan,
- moderate or high complexity medical decision making;
- ~~first hour~~ 60 minutes of clinical staff time directed by a physician or other qualified health care professional ~~with no face-to-face visit~~, per calendar month

(Complex chronic care management services of less than 60 minutes duration, in a calendar month, are not reported separately)

(**99488** has been deleted. To report one or more face-to-face visits by the physician or other qualified health care professional that are performed in the same month as **99487,** use the appropriate E/M code(s).)

Total Duration of Staff Care Coordination Services	Code(s)
Less than 30 minutes	Not reported separately
31 to 74 minutes (31 minutes—1 hr. 14 min.)	99487 or 99488 × 1
75—104 minutes (1 hr. 15 min.—1 hr. 44 min.)	99487 or 99488 × 1 and 99489 × 1
105 minutes or more (1 hr. 45 min. or more)	99487 or 99488 × 1 and 99489 × 2 or more for each additional 30 minutes

99488   first hour of clinical staff time directed by a physician or other qualified health care professional with one face-to-face visit, per calendar month

+99489   each additional 30 minutes of clinical staff time directed by a physician or other qualified health care professional, per calendar month (List separately in addition to code for primary procedure)

(Report **99489** in conjunction with **99487, 99488**)

(Do not report **99489** for care management services of less than 30 minutes additional to the first 60 minutes of complex chronic care management services during a calendar month)

(Do not report **99487–99489 99490** during the same month with **90951–90970, 98960–98962, 98966–98969, 99071, 99078, 99080, 99090, 99091, 99339, 99340, 99358, 99359, 99363, 99364, 99366–99368, 99374–99380, 99441– 99444, 99495, 99496, 99605–99607**)

Coding Tip

Time of care ~~coordination~~ management with the emergency department is reportable using **99487–99489 99490,** but time while the patient is inpatient or admitted as observation is not.

If the physician personally performs the clinical staff activities, his or her time may be counted toward the required clinical staff time to meet the elements of the code. ◄

Please see Chapter 11 for more information on reporting chronic care management services.

Surgery

Surgery Guidelines

CPT Surgical Package Definition

►By their very nature, the services to any patient are variable. The *CPT* codes that represent a readily identifiable surgical procedure thereby include, on a procedure-by-procedure basis, a variety of services. In defining the specific services "included" in a given *CPT* surgical code, the following services related to the surgery when furnished by the physician or other qualified health care professional who performs the surgery are ~~always~~ included in addition to the operation per se:

- ❋ Evaluation and Management (E/M) service(s) subsequent to the decision for surgery on the day before and/or day of surgery (including history and physical)
- ❋ *Local infiltration, metacarpal/metatarsal/digital block or topical anesthesia*

- ~~Subsequent to the decision for surgery, one related Evaluation and Management (E/M) encounter on the date immediately prior to or on the date of procedure (including history and physical)~~
- *Immediate postoperative care, including dictating operative notes, talking with the family and other physicians or other qualified health care professionals*
- *Writing orders*
- *Evaluating the patient in the post-anesthesia recovery area*
- *Typical postoperative follow-up care*

Cardiovascular System

Heart and Pericardium

Heart (including Valves) and Great Vessels

►*Patients receiving major cardiac procedures may require simultaneous cardiopulmonary bypass insertion of cannula(e) into the venous and arterial vasculatures with support of circulation and oxygenation by a heart-lung machine. Most services are described by codes in dyad arrangements to allow distinct reporting of procedures with or without cardiopulmonary bypass. Cardiopulmonary bypass is distinct from support of cardiac output using devices (eg, ventricular assist or intra-aortic balloon). For cardiac assist services, see* ~~**33960**~~**33946–33949, 33967–33983, 33990, 33991, 33992, 33993.**◄

Cardiovascular System

►*Extracorporeal Membrane Oxygenation (ECMO) or Extracorporeal Life Support (ECLS) Services*

Prolonged extracorporeal membrane oxygenation (ECMO) or extracorporeal life support (ECLS) is a procedure that provides cardiac and/or respiratory support to the heart and/or lungs that allows them to rest and recover when sick or injured. ECMO/ECLS supports the function of the heart and/or lungs by continuously pumping some of the patient's blood out of the body to an oxygenator (membrane lung) where oxygen is added to the blood, carbon dioxide is removed, and the blood is warmed before it is returned to the patient. There are two methods that can be used to accomplish ECMO/ECLS. One method is veno-arterial extracorporeal life support, which will support both the heart and the lungs. Veno-arterial ECMO/ECLS requires that two cannula(e) are placed—one in a large vein and one in a large artery. The other method is veno-venous extracorporeal life support. Veno-venous ECMO/ECLS is used for lung support only and requires one or two cannula(e), which are placed in a vein.

Services directly related to the cannulation, initiation, management, and discontinuation of the ECMO/ECLS circuit and parameters (**33946–33949**) are distinct from the daily management of the patient. The daily management of the patient is a factor that will vary greatly depending on the patient's age, disease process, and condition. Daily management of the patient may be separately reported using the relevant hospital observation services, hospital inpatient services, or critical care evaluation and management codes (**99218–99220, 99221–99223, 99231–99233, 99234–99236, 99291, 99292, 99468–99476**).

Services directly related to the ECMO/ECLS involve the initial cannulation and repositioning, removing, or adding cannula(e) while the patient is being supported by the ECMO/ECLS. Initiation of the ECMO/ECLS circuit and setting parameters (**33946, 33947**) is performed by the physician and involves determining the necessary ECMO/ECLS device components, blood flow, gas exchange, and other necessary parameters to manage the circuit. The daily management of the ECMO/ECLS circuit and monitoring parameters (**33948, 33949**) requires physician oversight to ensure that specific features of the interaction of the circuit with the patient are met. Daily management of the circuit and parameters includes management of blood flow, oxygenation, CO_2 clearance by the membrane lung, systemic response, anticoagulation and treatment of bleeding, and cannula(e) positioning, alarms and safety. Once the patient's heart and/or lung function has sufficiently recovered, the physician will wean the patient from the ECMO/ECLS circuit and finally decannulate the patient. The basic management of the ECMO/ECLS circuit and parameters are similar regardless of the patient's condition.

ECMO/ECLS is a complex process and commonly involves multiple physicians and supporting non-physician personnel to manage each patient. Different physicians may insert the cannula(e) and initiate ECMO/ECLS, manage the ECMO/ECLS circuit, and decannulate the patient. In addition, it would be common for one physician to manage the ECMO/ECLS circuit and related patient issues (eg, anticoagulation, complications related to the ECMO/ECLS devices), while another physician manages the overall patient medical condition and underlying disorders, all on a daily basis. The physicians involved in the patient's care are commonly of different specialties, and significant physician team interaction may be required. Depending on the type of circuit and the patient's condition, there is substantial non-physician work by ECMO/ECLS specialists, cardiac perfusionists, respiratory therapists and specially trained nurses who provide long periods of constant attention.

If the same physician performs the ECMO/ECLS initiation, and provides the daily management of the ECMO/ECLS circuit for the remainder of that day, the initiation code (**33946** or **33947**) and the daily management code (**33948** or **33949**) may both be reported. Patient management provided by the physician who initiates and/or provides the daily management of the ECMO/ECLS circuit may also report the level of patient management provided with the appropriate E/M service (**99218–99220, 99221, 99223, 99231–99233, 99234–99236, 99291, 99292, 99468–99476**). If the same physicians provides all of the services for placing a patient on an ECMO/ECLS circuit they may report the appropriate codes for the cannula(e) insertion (**33951–33956**), ECMO/ECLS initiation (**33946** or **33947**), daily ECMO/ECLS management (**33948** or **33949**) and the patient management code (**99218–99220, 99221–99223, 99231–99233, 99234–99236, 99291, 99292, 99468–99476**). If different physicians provide parts of the service, each physician may report the correct code(s) for the service(s) they provided.

Repositioning of the ECMO/ECLS cannula(e) (**33957–33964**) at the same session as insertion (**33951–33956**) is not separately reportable. Replacement of ECMO/ECLS cannula(e) in the same vessel should be reported using the insertion code (**33951–33956**) only. If cannula(e) are removed from one vessel and new cannula(e) are placed in a different vessel, report the appropriate cannula(e) removal (**33965–33986**) and insertion (**33951–33956**) codes. Extensive repair or replacement of an artery may be additionally reported (eg, **35226, 35286, 35371** and **35665**). Fluoroscopic guidance used for cannula(e) repositioning (**33957–33964**) is included in the procedure when performed and should not be separately reported. ◄

33960 ~~Prolonged extracorporeal circulation for cardiopulmonary insufficiency; initial day~~

(**33960** has been deleted. To report, see **33946–33949**)

⊘~~**33961** each subsequent day~~

(~~Do not report modifier **63** in conjunction with **33960, 33961**~~)

(~~For insertion of cannula for prolonged extracorporeal circulation, use **36822**~~)

(**33961** has been deleted. To report, see **33948, 33949**)

●**33946**   Extracorporeal membrane oxygenation (ECMO)/extracorporeal life support (ECLS) provided by physician; initiation, veno-venous

(Do not report modifier **63** in conjunction with **33946–33949**)

(For insertion of cannula(e) for extracorporeal circulation, see **33951–33956**)

●**33947**   initiation, veno-arterial

(Do not report modifier **63** in conjunction with **33946–33949**)

●**33948**   daily management, each day, veno-venous

(Do not report modifier **63** in conjunction with **33946–33949**)

●**33949**   daily management, each day, veno-arterial

●**33951**   insertion of peripheral (arterial and/or venous) cannula(e), percutaneous, birth through 5 years of age (includes fluoroscopic guidance when performed)

●**33952**   insertion of peripheral (arterial and/or venous) cannula(e), percutaneous, 6 years and older (includes fluoroscopic guidance when performed)

●**33953**   insertion of peripheral (arterial and/or venous) cannula(e), open, birth through 5 years of age

●**33954**   insertion of peripheral (arterial and/or venous) cannula(e), open, 6 years and older

●**33955**   insertion of central cannula(e) by sternotomy or thoracotomy, birth through 5 years of age

●**33956**   insertion of central cannula(e) by sternotomy or thoracotomy, 6 years and older

●**33957**   reposition peripheral (arterial and/or venous) cannula(e), percutaneous, birth through 5 years of age (includes fluoroscopic guidance when performed)

●**33958**   reposition peripheral (arterial and/or venous) cannula(e), percutaneous, 6 years and older (includes fluoroscopic guidance when performed)

●**33959**   reposition peripheral (arterial and/or venous) cannula(e), open, birth through 5 years of age (includes fluoroscopic guidance when performed)

●**33962**   reposition peripheral (arterial and/or venous) cannula(e), open, 6 years and older (includes fluoroscopic guidance when performed)

●**33963**   reposition of central cannula(e) by sternotomy or thoracotomy, birth through 5 years of age (includes fluoroscopic guidance when performed)

●**33964**   reposition central cannula(e) by sternotomy or thoracotomy, 6 years and older (includes fluoroscopic guidance when performed)

●**33965**   removal of peripheral (arterial and/or venous) cannula(e), percutaneous, birth through 5 years of age

●**33966**   removal of peripheral (arterial and/or venous) cannula(e), percutaneous, 6 years and older

●**33969**   removal of peripheral (arterial and/or venous) cannula(e), open, birth through 5 years of age

●**33984**   removal of peripheral (arterial and/or venous) cannula(e), open, 6 years and older

●**33985**   removal of central cannula(e) by sternotomy or thoracotomy, birth through 5 years of age

●**33986**   removal of central cannula(e) by sternotomy or thoracotomy, 6 years and older

●+**33987**   Arterial exposure with creation of graft conduit (eg, chimney graft) to facilitate arterial perfusion for ECMO/ECLS (list separately in addition to code for primary procedure)

●**33988**   Insertion of left heart vent by thoracic incision (eg, sternotomy, thoracotomy) for ECMO/ECLS

●**33989**   Removal of left heart vent by thoracic incision (eg, sternotomy, thoracotomy) for ECMO/ECLS

Cardiac Assist

►*The insertion of a ventricular assist device (VAD) can be performed via percutaneous* (**33990, 33991**) *or transthoracic* (**33975, 33976, 33979**) *approach. The location of the ventricular assist device may be intracorporeal or extracorporeal.*

~~For surgical insertion of cannula(s) for prolonged extracorporeal circulation for cardiopulmonary insufficiency (ECMO), use 36822.~~

Open arterial exposure when necessary...◄

Arteries and Veins

Hemodialysis Access, Intervascular Cannulation for Extracorporeal Circulation, or Shunt Insertion

~~36822~~   ~~Insertion of cannula(s) for prolonged extracorporeal circulation for cardiopulmonary insufficiency (ECMO) (separate procedure)~~

For more information on ECMO/ECLS services, please see Chapter 10.

Medicine

Vaccines, Toxoids

A new vaccine product code for Human Papillomavirus vaccine (HPV) to protect against nine (nonavalent) types of HPV (6, 11, 16, 18, 31, 33, 45, 52, 58) was approved and posted online for implementation.

●**90651**   Human Papillomavirus (HPV) vaccine types 6, 11, 16, 18, 31, 33, 45, 52, 58 (nonavalent), 3 dose schedule, for intramuscular use

Another new code was established for a quadrivalent influenza vaccine to be administered using a proprietary ID microinjection system to individuals 18–64 years of age. Existing code **90654** was revised to indicate it represents a trivalent influenza vaccine administered via an intradermal microinjection system.

▲**90654**   Influenza virus vaccine, <u>trivalent (IIV3),</u> split virus, preservative free, for intradermal use

#●**90630**   Influenza virus vaccine, quadrivalent (IIV4), split virus, preservative free, for intradermal use

●**90697**   Diphtheria, tetanus toxoids, acellular pertussis vaccine, inactivated poliovirus vaccine, *Haemophilus influenzae* type b PRP-OMP conjugate vaccine, and hepatitis B vaccine (DTaP-IPV-HibHepB), for intramuscular use

Central Nervous System Assessments/Tests

▲**96110**   Developmental screening <u>(eg, developmental milestone survey, speech and language delay screen), with scoring and documentation</u> ~~interpretation and report~~, per standardized instrument ~~form~~
<u>(For an emotional/behavioral assessment, use **96127**)</u>

●**96127** Brief emotional/behavioral assessment (eg, depression inventory, attention-deficit/hyperactivity disorder (ADHD) scale), with scoring and documentation, per standardized instrument
<u>(For developmental assessment screening, use **96110**)</u>

Hydration, Therapeutic, Prophylactic, Diagnostic Injections and Infusions...

Therapeutic, Prophylactic, and Diagnostic Injections and Infusions

A change was made to editorially revise the parenthetical that follows code **96372** to reflect the deletion of codes **96365** and **96366** (IV infusion procedures included in error) and addition of code **90460** and **90461** to correctly reference the immunization administration codes.

96372 Therapeutic, prophylactic, or diagnostic injection (specify substance or drug); subcutaneous or intramuscular
(For administration of vaccines/toxoids, see <u>**90460, 90461,** </u>**90471, 90472,** ~~**96365,**~~ ~~**96366**~~)

●**99188** Application of topical fluoride varnish by a physician or other qualified health care professional

Category III Emerging Technology

These codes were released on the *CPT®* Category III Web site for implementation on July 1, 2014. The codes will be published in *CPT®* 2015. Refer to Chapter 13, page 333 for a listing of all newly added Category III codes.

Pediatric *ICD-10-CM* Codes for 2015

International Classification of Diseases, 10th Revision, Clinical Modification (ICD-10-CM) codes are scheduled for implementation on October 1, 2015. No major updates to the *ICD-9-CM* code set have been considered since October 1, 2011. The *ICD-10-CM* Coordination and Maintenance Committee is currently expected to issue the first major annual update to *ICD-10-CM* on October 1, 2016.

There are no new or revised pediatric *ICD-10-CM* codes for 2015. However, some revisions were made to the code set to correct errors and to reflect changes made to the *ICD-10* classification by the World Health Organization.

You can access the *ICD-10-CM* code set and guidelines at the National Center for Health Statistics Web site at www.cdc.gov/nchs/icd/icd10cm.htm or by contacting the American Academy of Pediatrics (AAP) Coding Hotline at aapcodinghotline@aap.org.

If you have any suggestions for new codes or changes to existing *ICD-10-CM* codes, please submit your suggestions to the AAP Coding Hotline at aapcodinghotline@aap.org

Diagnosis Coding: *ICD-9-CM* and *ICD-10-CM*

International Classification of Diseases (ICD)

The *International Classification of Diseases (ICD)* is published by the World Health Organization (WHO) for epidemiologic tracking and the collection of mortality statistical data worldwide. The *ICD* is currently in its 10th revision. The United States currently uses a clinical modification of the ninth revision of *ICD*. Implementation of the *International Classification of Diseases, 10th Revision, Clinical Modification (ICD-10-CM)* has been postponed in the United States with implementation set for October 1, 2015. The World Health Organization is currently working on the next revision, *International Classification of Diseases, 11th Revision (ICD-11)*, which is expected to be presented to the World Health Assembly for initial approval in 2017. The current US version, *International Classification of Diseases, Ninth Revision, Clinical Modification (ICD-9-CM)*, is the official system for reporting morbidity and mortality associated with health care data. The clinical modifications in the US version are generally proposed by specialty medical societies to improve injury and illness tracking and are reviewed by the *ICD-10-CM* Coordination and Maintenance Committee. For diagnosis codes, this process is coordinated by the National Center for Health Statistics (NCHS) of the Centers for Disease Control and Prevention, which then publishes new and revised codes in the public domain after approval by the secretary of the US Department of Health and Human Services. Oversight and resolution of coding questions related to the US version of *ICD* is performed by the *Coding Clinic* Editorial Advisory Board and the public-private "cooperating parties": the Centers for Medicare & Medicaid Services (CMS), NCHS, American Hospital Association (AHA), and American Health Information Management Association. The increased granularity and specificity in *ICD-10-CM* are also at the specific request of certain medical societies. No clinical diagnosis codes are added for payment purposes.

The American Academy of Pediatrics (AAP) holds a seat on the editorial advisory board. Findings are published quarterly by the AHA in *Coding Clinic*. *ICD-10-CM* codes and accompanying guidelines and findings by the editorial advisory board are part of the standard transaction code sets under the Health Insurance Portability and Accountability Act of 1996 (HIPAA) and must be recognized by all payers. For *ICD-9-CM* and *ICD-10-CM*, the hierarchy of official coding guidelines and instructions is as follows:

1. Alphabetic index and tabular list
2. Official Guidelines for Coding and Reporting
3. AHA *Coding Clinic* advice

Another code set, *ICD-10-Procedure Coding System (PCS)*, will be implemented in addition to *ICD-10-CM* but is only used to show hospital inpatient resource utilization and is not intended to show physician or other outpatient services. Physicians continue to report services and resources provided through use of *Current Procedural Terminology®* and Healthcare Common Procedure Coding System codes.

Transitioning to 10

Although the transition to *International Classification of Diseases, 10th Revision, Clinical Modification (ICD-10-CM)* has been delayed until October 1, 2015, *Coding for Pediatrics 2015* continues to provide tips, including important documentation elements, to support code selection in *ICD-10-CM*.

Is ICD-11-CM Coming Soon?

There have been concerns about the adoption of *ICD-10-CM* when WHO is currently developing *ICD-11*. However, as was the case with *ICD-10-CM*, it is expected to take 5 to 6 years for development and testing of a clinical modification for use in the United States following WHO release of *ICD-11*. In its 2009 final rule adopting *ICD-10-CM* as a replacement of *ICD-9-CM* for diagnosis coding, the US Department of Health and Human Services noted that had *ICD-11* been released by WHO in 2014, the earliest projected date to begin rule making for implementation of a US clinical modification of *ICD-11* would be 2020. At the time of this publication, the WHO Web site indicates that development of *ICD-11* is expected to continue until 2018. Given this, physicians may expect to report *ICD-10-CM* codes well beyond 2020.

ICD-9-CM

Coding for Pediatrics 2015 continues to include *ICD-9-CM* codes in clinical vignettes because these codes must be reported for all services prior to the date of transition to *ICD-10-CM*. However, this chapter will focus more on the conventions and guidelines of *ICD-10-CM*. Though delayed for several years now, the transition to *ICD-10-CM* on October 1, 2015, is likely. Many health care professionals and other health care entities have invested heavily in transition planning, education, and testing and must maintain these activities during the extended delay. In recognition of this, *ICD-9-CM* codes included in all clinical vignettes are followed by *ICD-10-CM* codes for the same conditions. Physicians will report only the appropriate codes based on the date of service before or on and after the date of transition to *ICD-10-CM*.

The official conventions for *ICD-9-CM* are outlined in sections that include descriptions of symbols, abbreviations, and other instructional notes. The guidelines are organized into 4 sections. Only sections I and IV pertain to physicians reporting services. Sections II and III relate to hospital or facility technical services and are not discussed here. *ICD-9-CM* guidelines can be found in the *ICD-9-CM* manual or at www.cdc.gov/nchs/data/icd/icd10cm_guidelines_2014.pdf. Most *ICD-9-CM* guidelines are the same as *ICD-10-CM* guidelines for the same conditions (described as follows). The authors have made an effort to include clinical vignettes and coding tips throughout this manual to describe where the guidelines for *ICD-9-CM* and *ICD-10-CM* differ for reporting of conditions commonly managed in pediatrics.

ICD-10-CM

In preparation for the transition to *ICD-10-CM*, it is important to learn the terminology used with this code set and the guidelines for accurate reporting. In some cases, *ICD-10-CM* codes are more specific than *ICD-9-CM* codes for the same conditions. This increased specificity will allow health care professionals to better identify specific conditions, enabling tailored disease management programs (eg, diabetes, hypertension, asthma). It will also allow for better communication of active diagnoses, staging, and severity of chronic conditions, with better specificity for meaningful use and quality indicators. The increase in the number of pre-coordinated codes (eg, laterality, stage of care) was done to decrease the number of diagnosis codes that will need to be reported.

Transitioning to 10

Current plans call for the replacement of *ICD-9-CM* with *ICD-10-CM* beginning with claims for dates of service on October 1, 2015.

ICD-10-CM *Terminology*

To correctly select codes in *ICD-10-CM*, it is important to know how the reference is structured and the terminology used in the code set. The following terms describe the structure and some of the key conventions used in this code set as listed in the *ICD-10-CM Official Guidelines for Coding and Reporting:*

Code: A code is a complete set of alphanumeric characters for which there are no further subdivisions, 3 to 7 characters long, describing a condition or reason for an encounter or related factors such as external causes. The first character of each code is a letter ranging from A to T or V to Z. The second through seventh characters may be letters or numbers.

Alphabetic index: Like *ICD-9-CM*, code selection in *ICD-10-CM* begins in the alphabetic index. The main portion of the alphabetic index consists of an alphabetic list of terms for diseases, injuries, and other reasons for encounters with their corresponding codes or code categories. The alphabetic index also includes an index to external causes of injuries, a table of neoplasms, and a table of drugs and chemicals.

Tabular list: The tabular list is the end point for code selection. It is an alphanumeric list of *ICD-10-CM* codes structured as an indented list of 21 chapters with further divisions including blocks, categories, subcategories, and codes. Chapters are based on condition, body system, consequences of external causes, external causes, and other factors influencing health status or contact with health services.

Character: A letter or number that serves as the building block of *ICD-10-CM* codes, sometimes referred to as digits as a holdover of the term used in *ICD-9-CM*.

Category: A 3-character unit that may be a complete code when no further subcategories exist but often serves as the base for building a 4- to 7-character code. Categories are the main entries of the tabular list.

Subcategory: A further defined category of 4 to 6 characters that may or may not be a complete code.

Placeholder: *ICD-10-CM* uses the letter X as a placeholder. When a subcategory of fewer than 6 characters requires 7 characters for a complete code, an X must be used as a placeholder filling in for any undefined characters.

And: Means *and/or* in *ICD-10-CM*.

NEC: Not elsewhere classifiable. Indicates a code for other specified conditions that is reported when the medical record provides detail that is not captured in a specific code.

NOS: Not otherwise specified. Indicates a code for an unspecified condition that is reported when the medical record does not provide sufficient detail for assignment of a more specific code.

With. Means *with* or *due to* in *ICD-10-CM*.

First-listed diagnosis: For reporting of professional services, the diagnosis, condition, problem, or other reason for the encounter or visit shown in the medical record to be chiefly responsible for the services provided.

Combination code: A single code that represents multiple conditions or a single condition with an associated secondary process or complication.

Sequela: A late effect of an illness or injury that is no longer in the acute phase.

These terms are used throughout the *ICD-10-CM* code set and are further defined in the guidelines for its use.

ICD-10-CM *Code Structure*

As indicated by the previously given definition, codes in *ICD-10-CM* begin with a letter. All alphabetic characters are used except for the letter U. For codes that extend beyond 3 characters, the first 3 characters are found to the left of a decimal with the remaining characters to the right.

Pattern: XXX.XXXX

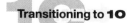

Transitioning to 10

When a seventh character is required to complete a code that has fewer than 6 characters, the placeholder X must be used to complete the undefined characters.

Chapter 2: Diagnosis Coding: *ICD-9-CM* and *ICD-10-CM*

Although typically illustrated in capital letters, the alphabetic characters are not case sensitive. Each 3-character code category may then be further expanded with etiology, severity, site, manifestations, or intent within the fourth through sixth characters. When required, a seventh character is an extension to further define the episode of care, status of fracture healing, number of the fetus in obstetric conditions, or site of recording of the Glasgow Coma Scale.

Examples of complete codes include

R05	Cough
J06.9	Acute upper respiratory infection
H65.04	Acute recurrent serous otitis media, right ear
Z00.129	Encounter routine child health examination without abnormal findings
W07.XXXA	Fall from chair, initial visit

Note the letter X is used as a placeholder in code **W07.XXXA.** The tabular listing for this code is **W07** with no further subcategories but with an instruction that the appropriate seventh character A, D, or S must be added to code **W07** to indicate the initial encounter, subsequent encounter, or encounter for a sequela of the fall from chair. The placeholder must be used to complete the code so that the seventh character is in the appropriate position. If **W07.A** were submitted, the associated claim would likely be rejected because this is not a valid *ICD-10-CM* code. The letter X is also embedded in some codes to provide for future expansion of a code category (eg, **H60.8X1**, other otitis externa of the right ear).

ICD-10-CM Guidelines

The official conventions found in the *ICD-10-CM Official Guidelines for Coding and Reporting* are outlined in sections that include descriptions of symbols, abbreviations, and other instructional notes. The guidelines are organized into 4 sections. Only sections I and IV pertain to physicians reporting services. Sections II and III relate to hospital or facility technical services and are not discussed here. *ICD-10-CM* guidelines can be found in *ICD-10-CM* manuals or at www.cdc.gov/nchs/data/icd/icd10cm_guidelines_2014.pdf. The following Table provides an overview of the information pertinent to pediatric care as provided in each section of the guidelines. Please note that the 2015 guidelines have not changed from the 2014 guidelines.

ICD-10-CM Guidelines

Section I—Conventions, General Coding Guidelines, and Chapter-Specific Guidelines

A. Conventions

Punctuation

[ ] In the alphabetic index, brackets identify manifestation codes. Brackets are used in the tabular list to enclose synonyms, alternative wording, or explanatory phrases.

( ) Parentheses are used in the alphabetic index and tabular list to enclose supplementary words (ie, nonessential modifiers) that may be included in the medical record but do not affect code selection. If a nonessential modifier is mutually exclusive to a sub-term of the main term, the sub-term is given priority.

Notes

- **Includes:** Further defines or gives examples of the content of a category.
- **Excludes 1:** Not coded here—used to indicate codes for conditions that would not occur in conjunction with the code category where the note is found.
- **Excludes 2:** Not included here—used to indicate codes for conditions not included in the code category where the note is found but that may be additionally reported when both conditions are present.
- **Code first:** A sequencing rule in the tabular list to report first a code for an underlying cause or origin of a disease (etiology).
- **Code also:** An instruction that another code may be necessary to fully describe a condition.
- **See:** In the alphabetic index, this instructs that another term should be referenced to find the appropriate code.
- **See also:** In the alphabetic index, this instructs that another term may provide additional entries that may be useful.
- **Use an additional code:** A sequencing rule often found at the listing of an etiology code, this instruction directs to also report a code for the manifestation.

B. General Coding Guidelines

- First and foremost, begin by finding a term in the alphabetic index and then turn to the tabular list to be sure you are selecting a complete code and follow code instructions for that chapter and code category.
- Assign a code for signs and symptoms when no definitive diagnosis has been reached at an encounter.
- Do not report additional codes for conditions that are inherent or routinely associated with a disease process.
- When the same condition is documented as acute and chronic, codes for both conditions are reported if the alphabetic index lists the conditions at the same indentation level. The acute condition is sequenced first.
- When a combination code describes 2 diagnoses, or a diagnosis and its associated manifestation or complication, report only the combination code. If a manifestation or complication is not identified in a combination code, it may be separately reported.
- When reporting a sequela (late effect) of an injury or illness, report first the current condition and then the sequela code.
- If both sides are affected by a condition and the code category does not include a code for the bilateral condition, assign codes for right and left.
- Coders may not assume a complication of care without documentation of the cause and effect relationship (eg, complications of diabetes, infection in a patient with a central venous line).
- Unspecified codes are appropriately selected when information to support a more specific code was not available at the time of the encounter (eg, type of pneumonia is not known).

C. Chapter-Specific Guidelines

- See these guidelines for specific diagnoses and/or conditions found in each chapter.
- When selecting electronic coding applications, look for inclusion of chapter-specific guidelines when using the code search functionality.
- Chapter 16: Certain Conditions Originating in the Perinatal Period (**P00–P96**)
  - ❖ For conditions that originate in the perinatal or neonatal period, the provider selects diagnostic codes from Chapter 16 in *ICD-10-CM,* **P00–P96.** For coding and reporting purposes, the perinatal period is defined as before birth through the 28th day following birth. Should a condition originate in the perinatal period and continue to have health care implications throughout the life of the patient, the Chapter 16 code should continue to be used regardless of the patient's age. If the reason for a particular encounter is a perinatal or neonatal condition (ie, originated in the perinatal or neonatal period), the Chapter 16 code may be sequenced

first (exception: the **Z38** series type of delivery code ranks as primary at the initial hospital episode of birth). *ICD* coding guidelines allow for exclusive use of perinatal or neonatal period codes to characterize a patient's clinical condition on an encounter claim so long as the condition(s) originated in the perinatal or neonatal period and so long as the condition(s) continue to have clinical implications for the care of the patient. Typical scenarios that may require exclusive use of perinatal or neonatal codes beyond the perinatal period are often found in neonatal intensive care unit settings where early gestational ages and evolving maturation extend diagnostic impact—such as in drug withdrawal syndrome of infant of dependent mother (**P96.1**), chronic respiratory disease arising in the perinatal period (**P27.-**), necrotizing enterocolitis (**P77.-**), and prematurity (**P07.-**).

Section IV—Diagnostic Coding and Reporting Guidelines for Outpatient Services

Selecting a code
- The coding conventions and guidelines of Section I take precedence over these outpatient guidelines.
- Never assign a code for a condition that is unconfirmed (eg, probable obstruction). Instead, assign codes for signs and symptoms.
- Use codes in categories **Z00–Z99** when circumstances other than a disease or injury are recorded as the reason for encounter.

Sequencing of diagnosis codes
- Physicians and other providers of professional services should list first the condition, symptom, or other reason for encounter that is chiefly responsible for the services provided. List also any coexisting conditions. (Note: Some codes and chapters have specific guidelines with regard to sequencing.)

Reporting previously treated conditions
- Do not code conditions that have been previously treated but no longer exist. History codes **Z80–Z87** may be used to identify historical conditions or family history that impacts current care.
- Report codes for chronic or recurring conditions as many times as the patient receives care for each condition.

Reporting diagnoses for diagnostic examinations
- The condition, symptoms, or other reason for a diagnostic examination or test should be linked to the service. For laboratory or radiology testing in the absence of related conditions, signs, or symptoms, report code **Z01.89**, encounter for other specified special examinations.
- When diagnostic tests have been interpreted by a physician and the final report is available at the time of coding, code any confirmed or definitive diagnosis(es) documented in the interpretation. Do not code related signs and symptoms as additional diagnoses.

Reporting preoperative evaluations
- When the reason for an encounter is a preoperative evaluation, a code from subcategory **Z01.81-**, encounter for pre-procedural examinations, is reported first followed by codes for the condition that is the reason for surgery and codes for any findings of the preoperative evaluation.

Reporting health examinations (preventive care)
- Codes for pediatric health examinations are found in subcategory **Z00.1-**. Encounters for routine child health examinations are reported based on findings—with or without abnormal findings. When reporting an encounter with abnormal findings, report also codes to describe the findings.

Application of the Guidelines and Conventions of *ICD-10-CM*

Formatting and Reporting Instructions for ICD-10-CM

In addition to the guidelines, it is important to recognize and follow instructions found in the alphabetic index and tabular list. The indentation and instructions in the alphabetic index guide the user to the correct chapter and category of the tabular list. The alphabetic index may include many sub-terms for a single main entry. The indentation of each term directs to the appropriate listing.

Example

Otitis

…(entries omitted)

- media (hemorrhagic) (staphylococcal) (streptococcal) **H66.9-**

… (entries omitted)

- - nonsuppurative **H65.9-**

- - - acute or subacute NEC **H65.19-**

- - - - allergic **H65.11-**

- - - - - recurrent **H65.11-**

- - - - recurrent **H65.19-**

- - - - secretory—see Otitis, media, nonsuppurative, serous

- - - - serous **H65.0-**

- - - - - recurrent **H65.0-**

- - - chronic **H65.49-**

- - - - allergic **H65.41-**

- - - - mucoid **H65.3-**

- - - - serous **H65.2-**

- - post-measles **B05.3**

- - purulent—see Otitis, media, suppurative

Notes

1. Attention to the level of indentation is necessary for accurate selection. The 4 hyphens that precede "recurrent **H65.19-**" indicate the pathway to this entry is otitis, -media, --nonsuppurative, ---acute, ----recurrent.

2. Note how the index listings for otitis media start with an unspecified code category (**H66.9-**). This is the default entry that is followed only if no further specification is provided in the medical record.

3. The alphabetic index uses a dash (**H66.9-**) to indicate code subcategories and incomplete codes. Although subcategory **H66.9-** represents an unspecified type of otitis media, the tabular list will provide additional specificity, such as laterality. In contrast, the alphabetic list entry for otitis, -media, --post-measles directs to a complete code, **B05.3,** and the tabular list is consulted to verify the code selection and any additional coding instruction.

4. A *see* note is also illustrated for the diagnosis of acute secretary otitis media directing to otitis, -media, --nonsuppurative, ---acute, ----serous.

In the tabular list, instructions are found at many levels, starting with chapter instructions and following down through the block, category, and subcategory levels. These instructions provide important details on the use of the codes that follow each instruction. For instance, the following notes are found in Chapter 16:

Example of Chapter-Level Note

Chapter 16

Certain conditions originating in the perinatal period (**P00–P96**)

Note: Codes from this chapter are for use on newborn records only, never on maternal records.

Includes: conditions that have their origin in the fetal or perinatal period (before birth through the first 28 days after birth) even if morbidity occurs later

Excludes 2:

congenital malformations, deformations and chromosomal abnormalities (**Q00–Q99**)

endocrine, nutritional, and metabolic diseases (**E00–E88**)

injury, poisoning, and certain other consequences of external causes (**S00–T88**)

neoplasms (**C00–D49**)

tetanus neonatorum (**A33**)

Notes

> ||ı|ı||ı|| **Coding Pearl** ||ı|ı||ı||
>
> *Excludes 2* notes in *ICD-10-CM* mean that the code and the excluded code can both be reported when appropriate.

1. The first note advises that codes from Chapter 16 are never used on the maternal record.
2. The inclusion note further defines that codes in this chapter represent conditions that originate in the newborn period but may be reported even if morbidity occurs later.
3. The Excludes 2 note provides information on potentially coexisting conditions that may be separately reported but are not included in this chapter.

Example of Block-Level Note

Newborn affected by maternal factors and by complications of pregnancy, labor, and delivery (P00–P04)

Note: These codes are for use when the listed maternal conditions are specified as the cause of confirmed morbidity or potential morbidity which have their origin in the perinatal period (before birth through the first 28 days after birth). Codes from these categories are also for use for newborns who are suspected of having an abnormal condition resulting from exposure from the mother or the birth process, but without signs or symptoms, and, which after examination and observation, is found not to exist. These codes may be used even if treatment is begun for a suspected condition that is ruled out.

Note

1. This note provides important context to codes in this block by making clear that codes **P00–P04** may be reported when an abnormal condition is suspected to have passed to the newborn from the mother or in the birth process but after examination and observation is ruled out. These diagnosis codes then support the necessity of services that may have been provided in observing for and ruling out the suspected condition.

Example of Category-Level Note: Asthma

J45   **Asthma**

           Includes: allergic (predominantly) asthma

                    allergic bronchitis NOS

                    allergic rhinitis with asthma

                    atopic asthma

                    extrinsic allergic asthma

                    hay fever with asthma

                    idiosyncratic asthma

                    intrinsic nonallergic asthma

                    nonallergic asthma

Use additional code to identify

exposure to environmental tobacco smoke (**Z77.22**)

exposure to tobacco smoke in the perinatal period (**P96.81**)

history of tobacco use (**Z87.891**)

occupational exposure to environmental tobacco smoke (**Z57.31**)

tobacco dependence (**F17.-**)

tobacco use (**Z72.0**)

Excludes 1:   detergent asthma (**J69.8**)

eosinophilic asthma (**J82**)

lung diseases due to external agents (**J60–J70**)

miners' asthma (**J60**)

wheezing NOS (**R06.2**)

wood asthma (**J67.8**)

Excludes 2:   asthma with chronic obstructive pulmonary disease (**J44.9**)

chronic asthmatic (obstructive) bronchitis (**J44.9**)

chronic obstructive asthma (**J44.9**)

J45.2   Mild intermittent asthma

J45.20   Mild intermittent asthma, uncomplicated

Mild intermittent asthma NOS

J45.21   Mild intermittent asthma with (acute) exacerbation

J45.22   Mild intermittent asthma with status asthmaticus

J45.3   Mild persistent asthma

J45.30   Mild persistent asthma, uncomplicated

Mild persistent asthma NOS

J45.31   Mild persistent asthma with (acute) exacerbation

J45.32   Mild persistent asthma with status asthmaticus

J45.4   Moderate persistent asthma

J45.40   Moderate persistent asthma, uncomplicated

Moderate persistent asthma NOS

J45.41   Moderate persistent asthma with (acute) exacerbation

J45.42   Moderate persistent asthma with status asthmaticus

J45.5   Severe persistent asthma

J45.50   Severe persistent asthma, uncomplicated

Severe persistent asthma NOS

J45.51   Severe persistent asthma with (acute) exacerbation

J45.52   Severe persistent asthma with status asthmaticus

J45.9   Other and unspecified asthma

J45.90   Unspecified asthma

Asthmatic bronchitis NOS

Childhood asthma NOS

Late-onset asthma

Chapter 2: Diagnosis Coding: ICD-9-CM and ICD-10-CM

J45.901   Unspecified asthma with (acute) exacerbation

J45.902   Unspecified asthma with status asthmaticus

J45.909   Unspecified asthma, uncomplicated

Notes

1. Format: The indented format directs the coder to the more specified code.
2. Excludes 1 notes: Indicate that the code excluded should never be used at the same time as codes in the category that includes the Excludes 1 note. Used when 2 conditions cannot occur together.
3. Excludes 2 notes: Indicate that the condition excluded is not part of the condition represented by the code, but a patient may have both conditions at the same time. The code and excluded code can be reported when appropriate.
4. Abbreviations: The designation of NOS means that the information available does not allow a more specific code.
5. Use additional code: Used to show sequencing for certain codes that are not part of an etiology/manifestation combination. Note that the instructions to use additional codes for tobacco use or exposure apply to all codes in categories **H66** and **J45.**

Examples of Subcategory-Level Note

R06.1   Stridor
    Excludes 1:
    congenital laryngeal stridor (**P28.89**)
    laryngismus (stridulus) (**J38.5**)

R06.2   Wheezing
    Excludes 1:
    Asthma (**J45.-**)

Notes

1. Note that these subcategories of category **R06** include exclusion notes to direct to an appropriate code or category for conditions that are not reported at the same encounter as the codes for stridor and wheezing. The exclusion notes indicate that stridor and wheezing may occur in the excluded conditions but are not separately reported (eg, wheezing is considered inherent to asthma).
2. Each of the subcategories are also complete codes with no further subdivisions.

Who Assigns the Codes?

The clinician (pediatrician, pediatric nurse practitioner, or physician assistant) should assign a primary diagnosis that best explains the reason with the highest risk of morbidity or mortality for the patient encounter unless the tabular instructions direct to "code first" a specific condition (eg, code first cystic fibrosis [**E84.-**] in a patient with secondary diabetes [**E08.-**] due to cystic fibrosis). Assignment of the specific diagnosis code by a nonphysician provider or administrative staff should be done under the physician's or reporting provider's supervision. For those practices using a printed encounter form, including 50 to 100 of the most commonly used diagnoses *and* their respective codes on the outpatient encounter form allows the physician or health care professional to mark the appropriate code(s), indicating which is primary. All contributing (secondary) diagnoses that help explain the medical necessity for the episode of care should also be listed. Only those conditions that specifically affect the patient's encounter should be listed. If a specific diagnosis code is not included on your form, write it in! Do not select a diagnosis code that is "closest to" your diagnosis. Refer to Chapter 15 for tips on designing an encounter form.

Linking the Diagnosis

- Every encounter and physician service must be linked to the appropriate *ICD-10-CM* code on the billing form.
- The diagnosis code may be the same for each service performed. For example, if a child is diagnosed with a urinary tract infection (UTI), the code for a UTI *(ICD-10-CM* code **N39.0**) should be linked to the E/M service and the urinalysis ordered.

  The diagnoses may differ for each service or procedure. For example, when the physician reports a significant, separately identifiable problem-oriented (sick) visit and a preventive medicine visit during the same encounter, he or she must link the appropriate diagnosis codes to each service. *ICD-10-CM* code **Z00.110** (health examination for newborn under 8 days old), **Z00.111** (health examination for newborn 8 to 28 days old), or **Z00.121** (routine child health examination with abnormal findings) would be linked to the preventive medicine visit and the appropriate abnormal finding or "sick" diagnosis code would be linked to the sick visit.

- Physicians and qualified nonphysician professionals should clearly designate the primary diagnosis on the encounter form (superbill) or use another method that easily sequences the diagnoses and links them to the appropriate service or procedure. For example, when using an electronic health record (EHR), physicians should list the primary diagnosis in the EHR first and make certain that the software knows that it should be reported as the first listed. In addition, the EHR should be able to link diagnosis codes to the appropriate services.

- Appropriate information should be documented in the medical record to support the principal and contributing diagnoses. Just listing them in a problem list is not sufficient.

- Diagnosis code assignment by a non-clinician should be done only by trained personnel and with clinician supervision. Remember that coders are not medical professionals and cannot make presumptions as to a diagnosis if the documentation is unclear to them. Coding professionals are instructed to "query the physician" whenever there is a question as to a diagnosis. Ultimately, the clinician in whose name the service is reported is responsible for the code assignment and linkage.

- The primary diagnosis code should best identify the condition carrying the highest risk or that is the main reason for the encounter (procedure, service, or visit) unless otherwise instructed by the coding guidelines or tabular instructions.

Examples

> **A child who had an incision and drainage of a leg abscess on the left calf 2 days ago is seen in the pediatrician's office for a wound check.** The pediatrician reviews the emergency department record and current medication and inspects the wound for signs of improvement. The culture report shows the patient has methicillin-resistant *Staphylococcus aureus* (MRSA) that is sensitive to the current antibiotic. The plan is to continue the current antibiotic and have the child return at the end of therapy. You would report the service and diagnosis as

9921X	(evaluation and management [E/M])	**L02.416**	(cutaneous abscess left lower limb)
		Z48.817	(aftercare following surgery of the skin and subcutaneous tissue)
		B95.62	(MRSA)

➤ **During a recheck for otitis media (resolved), the physician recommends the influenza vaccine to a patient who is accompanied by the nanny.** The nanny is unsure of whether the parent would really want the child to receive the vaccine so refuses the administration until such time that the parent can consent. You would report the service and diagnoses as

9921X	(E/M)	**Z09**	(follow-up examination after completed treatment for conditions other than malignant neoplasm)
		Z23	(encounter for immunization)
		Z28.82	(immunization not carried out because of caregiver refusal)

Additional examples of *ICD-10-CM* code assignment are included in each chapter of this manual with specific documentation elements and code reporting instructions highlighted in coding tips.

Diagnosis Coding Tips

- Physicians and other practitioners should become familiar with the documentation elements that are captured in *ICD-10-CM* code categories for conditions commonly seen in their practice. For example, when documenting care for otitis media, key documentation elements include whether the condition affects the right, left, or both ears; is acute, acute recurrent, or chronic; is suppurative or nonsuppurative; and is with or without spontaneous rupture of the tympanic membrane. Exposure to or use of tobacco is also reported in conjunction with otitis media.
- Pay close attention to the terminology for nonspecific diagnoses. For example, the diagnosis "reactive airway disease" is to be coded as asthma per the guidelines. In children treated for an asthma-like condition who have not been diagnosed with asthma, it may be more appropriate to report the signs or symptoms as the primary diagnosis.
- When testing is performed to rule out or confirm a suspected diagnosis or condition on a patient with a sign(s) or symptom(s) it is considered a diagnostic examination and is not screening. Therefore, the code that explains the reason for the test (ie, sign or symptom) should be reported. Screening codes may be reported as the primary code if the reason for the visit is specifically for the screening examination or test.
- When routine vision, developmental, and/or hearing screening services are performed in conjunction with a preventive medicine visit, the diagnosis code for a routine infant or child health check should be linked to the appropriate screening service.
- Codes for reporting live-born neonates according to type of birth (*ICD-10-CM* codes **Z38.0–Z38.8**) are reported as the first-listed diagnosis for a newborn at the time of birth and for the duration of the birth admission as long as the baby is consuming health care (eg, crib or bassinet occupancy). This includes reporting for a neonate kept in the normal newborn nursery (eg, awaiting adoption) or mother's room (awaiting a mother's discharge) and those neonates who stay in the birth hospital for a prolonged time.
- Codes in Chapter 16, Conditions Originating in the Perinatal Period, are used when the diagnosis is made on a fetus or a neonate who is 28 days or younger. The World Health Organization defines the day of birth as day of life 0 (zero). A baby reaches 28 days of life on day 29 of age. These codes are only to be reported when the condition originates in this time but can be reported beyond the perinatal period if the conditions causes morbidity or is the primary reason for or contributing to why the patient is receiving health care.

Diagnosis Coding Tips, continued

If, after evaluation and study of a suspected condition, there is no diagnosis or no signs or symptoms that are appropriate, report the codes for observation and evaluation for suspected conditions not found. Codes for observation and evaluation for suspected conditions not found in a neonate that are related to a maternal condition or birth process (*ICD-10-CM* codes **P00.0–P04.9**) are distinct from those for reporting suspected conditions not found in older children and adults (*ICD-10-CM* code **Z03.89**).

* Use aftercare codes (**Z42–Z49, Z51**) for patients who are receiving care to consolidate treatment or managing residual conditions.

* Conditions that were previously treated and no longer exist cannot be reported. Therefore, it is correct coding to report care following completed treatment with *ICD-10-CM* code **Z09,** encounter for follow-up examination after completed treatment for conditions other than malignant neoplasm. Personal history codes (**Z86.-, Z87.-**) may be used to provide additional information on follow-up care. If a payer does not accept follow-up care codes as primary and requires that the service be reported with the diagnosis code that reflects the condition that had been treated, report the follow-up care codes as secondary. However, get the payer's policy in writing and inquire why it is not following coding guidelines.

* Do not select a diagnosis code that is "closest to" the diagnosis or condition documented in the medical record. If a specific diagnosis code is not included on your encounter form, write it in. For example, do not report unspecified joint pain (**M25.50**) if the diagnosis is right knee pain (**M25.561**).

* Pay attention to age factors within certain code descriptors. For example, *ICD-10-CM* code **R10.83** is used to report infantile colic. Colic in the child older than 12 months is reported with *ICD-10-CM* code **R10.84.**

* There is no limit to the number of diagnosis codes that can be reported. Although space is only allotted for up to 4 codes on the CMS-1500 claim form, you may submit as many claim forms as necessary to report the diagnoses. Electronic claims in Health Insurance Portability and Accountability Act version 5010 may include up to 12 diagnosis codes and each service line may be connected to 1 to 4 of the included codes.

* "Unspecified" codes can still be reported if, at the time of the encounter, more information cannot be obtained. However, it will be important to not report "unspecified" for conditions or information that should be documented, such as laterality.

* "Recurrent" is not defined by the *International Classification of Diseases.* Therefore, to use a recurrent code, the documentation should reflect that a practitioner believes it to be a recurrence.

* "Confirmed" influenza or other conditions do not require a positive laboratory or other test. What is requires is that the practitioner, through training and experience, believes that the patient has the condition based on clinical assessment and documents the condition in the chart.

Requesting New *ICD-10-CM* Codes

The *ICD-10-CM* Coordination and Maintenance Committee typically meets in March and September of each year to consider proposals for new codes or revisions to existing codes or instructions. The first annual update of *ICD-10-CM* is scheduled for October 1, 2016.

Pediatricians with suggestions for new or changes to existing *ICD-10-CM* codes related to pediatric care are encouraged to forward their suggestions to coding staff at the AAP headquarters. The AAP staff and advisor who are involved in the process can be of great assistance. E-mail the coding staff at aapcodinghotline@aap.org.

Resources

The AAP *Pediatric ICD-10-CM: A Manual for Provider-Based Coding* will be a condensed version of the entire *ICD-10-CM* manual and will provide only the guidelines and codes that are applicable and of importance to pediatric practitioners. This publication is currently expected to be available in early 2015.

The AAP *Pediatric Code Crosswalk: ICD-9-CM to ICD-10-CM* can serve as a resource for supporting your transition to *ICD-10-CM*. It is formatted as a crosswalk to assist practices in identifying the most commonly reported *ICD-10-CM* codes.

An AAP guidebook to *ICD-10-CM* coding, *Principles of Pediatric ICD-10-CM Coding*, provides the pediatric-specific knowledge and know-how your staff will need to successfully implement the new code set. The guidebook was designed for use in conjunction with the complete *ICD-10-CM* code set. The *ICD-10-CM* codes are found at www.cdc.gov/nchs/icd/icd10cm.htm.

The *AAP Pediatric Coding Newsletter*™ will continue to provide articles on diagnosis coding for pediatric conditions.

Modifiers and Coding Edits

Modifiers Reviewed in This Chapter

Modifiers		Used With E/M Services	Used With Surgical or Other Procedures
22	Increased procedural services		•
24	Unrelated E/M service by the same physician or other qualified health care professional during a postoperative period	•	
25	Significant, separately identifiable E/M service by the same physician or other qualified health care professional on the same day of the procedure or other service	•	
26	Professional component		•
32	Mandated services	•	•
33	Preventive services	•	•
47	Anesthesia by surgeon		•
50	Bilateral procedure		•
51	Multiple procedures		•
52	Reduced services		•
53	Discontinued procedure		•
54, 55, 56	Surgical care, pre- and postoperative management only		•
57	Decision for surgery	•	
58	Staged or related procedure or service by the same physician or other qualified health care professional during the postoperative period		•
59	Distinct procedural service		•
62	Two surgeons		•
63	Procedure performed on infants less than 4 kg		•
66	Surgical team		•
76	Repeat procedure or service by same physician or other qualified health care professional		•
77	Repeat procedure or service by another physician or other qualified health care professional		•
78	Unplanned return to the operating/procedure room by the same physician or other qualified health care professional following initial procedure for a related procedure during the postoperative period		•
79	Unrelated procedure or service by the same physician or other qualified health care professional during the postoperative period		•
80, 81, 82	Assistant surgeon, minimum assistant surgeon, assistant surgeon (when qualified resident surgeon not available)		•
91	Repeat clinical diagnostic laboratory test		•

Chapter 3: Modifiers and Coding Edits

Modifiers		Used With E/M Services	Used With Surgical or Other Procedures
HCPCS Modifiers			
QW	CLIA-waived tests		•
TC	Technical component		•
RT, LT	Right and left side		•
JW	Drug amount discarded/not administered to any patient		•

Current Procedural Terminology (CPT®) defines a *modifier* as a means to indicate that a service or procedure has been altered by some specific circumstance but not changed in its basic code definition. Because a modifier is used to report a service or procedure that was altered, medical record documentation must always support the use of the modifier.

In addition to the *CPT* modifiers, the Centers for Medicare & Medicaid Services (CMS) maintains a list of modifiers for use with Healthcare Common Procedure Coding System (HCPCS) and *CPT* codes. Most state Medicaid programs and many commercial payers follow CMS guidelines and may recognize the HCPCS modifiers as well.

Some modifiers are used exclusively with evaluation and management (E/M) services, and others are reported only with surgical or other procedures. Refer to the previous table.

The Health Insurance Portability and Accountability Act of 1996 requires recognition of all *CPT* modifiers, but payers may have their own payment and billing policies for the use of modifiers that can vary from *CPT* guidelines. Know and understand their policies. When payment is denied inappropriately because of nonrecognition or the incorrect application of a modifier, appeal the denied services. For more information, contact the AAP Coding Hotline (aapcodinghotline@aap.org).

22   INCREASED PROCEDURAL SERVICES

- Modifier **22** is used to report procedures when the work required to provide a service is substantially greater than typically required.
- Modifier **22** is only appended to anesthesia, surgery, radiology, laboratory, pathology, and medicine codes.
- Documentation must support the substantial additional work and the reason for the additional work (eg, increased intensity, time, technical difficulty of procedure, severity of patient's condition, physical and mental effort required).
- Most payers will require that a copy of the medical record documentation be sent with the claim when modifier **22** is reported. Make certain that the procedure or progress note clearly reflects the complexity of the procedure and/or the increased time that was required. Report additional diagnoses that contributed to the increased work.
- For an electronic claim, indicate "additional documentation available on request" in the claim level loop (2300 NTE) or in the line level loop (2400 NTE) segment. If the payer allows electronic claim attachments, follow the payer's instructions to submit the procedure note and, if necessary, a physician statement about the increased difficulty of the procedure.

||||||| *Coding Pearl* |||||||

When reporting a procedure with modifier **22**, the procedure or progress note must clearly reflect the complexity and/or increased time required.

Chapter 3: Modifiers and Coding Edits

Examples—Modifier 22

> **The physician needs 45 minutes to perform a simple repair of a 1-cm laceration on a 2-year-old because the child was combative and several stops and starts were required.**
>
>   **12011 22** (simple repair superficial wound of face; ≤2.5 cm)

> **An appendectomy is performed on a morbidly obese 12-year-old.** The surgery is complicated and requires additional time because of the obesity.
>
>   **44950 22** (appendectomy)

24   **UNRELATED E/M SERVICE BY THE SAME PHYSICIAN OR OTHER QUALIFIED HEALTH CARE PROFESSIONAL DURING A POSTOPERATIVE PERIOD**

*   Modifier **24** is appended to an E/M code when the physician or other qualified health care professional who performed a procedure provides an unrelated E/M service during the postoperative period.
*   The CMS has its own system for definition of global periods, and some payers will follow those guidelines or assign a specific number of follow-up days for surgical procedures. (See Chapter 12 for information on global surgery guidelines.)

> ||||||| **Coding Pearl** |||||||
>
> When reporting modifier **24**, link the appropriate diagnosis code for that encounter, not the surgical diagnosis.

Link the appropriate *International Classification of Diseases, 9th Revision, Clinical Modification (ICD-9-CM)* or *International Classification of Diseases, 10th Revision, Clinical Modification (ICD-10-CM)* code to the E/M visit to support that the service was unrelated to the surgical procedure. Do not report the surgical diagnosis code if it was not the reason for the encounter.

Example—Modifier 24

> **The physician sees a 6-year-old established patient for swimmer's ear (right ear) and performs a problem-focused history and physical examination.** Eight days prior to this visit the physician had performed a removal of a subcutaneous foreign body (by incision) not involving the fascia, from the foot. The CMS has assigned a 10-day global postoperative period to code **10120** (removal foreign body subcutaneous tissues, simple), indicating that payment for all follow-up visits within that period related to that surgical service is included under the code. Many payers will follow the CMS global period.
>
> **99212 24** (established office/ outpatient E/M)   } *ICD-9-CM*
>   **380.12** (acute swimmers' ear)
>   *ICD-10-CM*
>   **H60.331** (acute swimmer's ear, right ear)

25   **SIGNIFICANT, SEPARATELY IDENTIFIABLE E/M SERVICE BY THE SAME PHYSICIAN OR OTHER QUALIFIED HEALTH CARE PROFESSIONAL ON THE SAME DAY OF THE PROCEDURE OR OTHER SERVICE**

*   Modifier **25** is used when a procedure or service identified by a *CPT*® code is performed by the same physician or other qualified health care professional or physician or other health care professional of the same specialty and group and the patient's condition requires a significant, separately identifiable E/M service above and beyond the other service

Chapter 3: Modifiers and Coding Edits

provided or beyond the usual preoperative and postoperative care associated with the procedure that was performed.

☀ Different diagnoses are not required for reporting of the E/M service on the same date.

☀ Separate documentation is required for the E/M service and the procedure or other service. Documentation for both services may be on one progress note. The performed and documented E/M components must support the level of service reported and be separately identifiable from the procedure or other service documentation.

☀ *Current Procedural Terminology* procedure codes include evaluation services routinely performed prior to the procedure and the routine postoperative care. An assessment of the problem with an explanation of the procedure to be performed is considered inherent to the procedure and should not be reported separately with an E/M service code. (See Chapter 12 for information on global surgery guidelines.)

☀ When appropriate, modifier **25** may be reported on more than one E/M service for a single encounter. An example would be if you performed and reported a preventive medicine service (eg, **99393 25**) along with a problem-oriented service (eg, **99212 25**) in addition to giving the patient vaccines with counseling (eg, **90460**).

☀ Do not use modifier **25**

 Ø When the medical record does not support both services.

 Ø When a problem encountered during a preventive medicine visit is insignificant or incidental (eg, minor diaper rash, renewal of prescription medications, minor cold, stable chronic problem) or did not require additional work to perform the key components (history, physical examination, medical decision-making, or time) of the E/M service.

 Ø When the E/M service is a routine part of the usual preoperative and postoperative care.

 Ø When modifier **57** is more appropriate. The ultimate decision on whether to use modifier **25** or **57** requires knowledge of payer policies. (See modifier **57**).

CMS Versus *CPT* Guidelines: Reporting a Significant, Separately Identifiable E/M Service and Minor Procedures

The CMS allows modifier **25** to be used when a significant, separately identifiable E/M service is provided by the same physician or other qualified health care professional on the same day as a minor procedure (eg, suturing, removal of foreign bodies, endoscopy) but not with a major procedure. (See modifier **57**.) The CMS defines a *minor procedure* as one with a 0- to 10-day Medicare global period.

 Current Procedural Terminology does not define global periods, but some commercial payers will assign their own definition of a global service period for minor procedures. Medical record documentation must clearly support the care as distinct or over and above the usual preoperative care associated with the procedure.

Examples—Modifier 25

➤ **A 2-year-old established patient is seen in the office for a preventive medicine visit. The mother reports that he had vomiting and diarrhea since last evening.** An expanded-level history and physical examination are performed and the patient is treated for acute gastroenteritis. The work performed for the illness (history, physical examination, and medical decision-making) is documented in addition to the preventive medicine service.

99392 (preventive medicine visit, established patient, 1–4 years of age)

99213 25 (established office/outpatient E/M)

} *ICD-9-CM*
V20.2 (routine infant or child health check)
558.9 (acute gastroenteritis)

ICD-10-CM
Z00.121 (routine child health examination with abnormal findings)
K52.9 (unspecified noninfective gastroenteritis and colitis)

Teaching Point: See Chapter 5 for additional examples and guidelines for reporting a preventive medicine visit and a problem-oriented visit on the same day of service. Be aware of certain circumstances in which there is no patient co-payment for preventive medicine visits, yet there is for office visits. The use of modifier **25** in such instances may result in a co-payment required from the family for the additional E/M service.

➤ **A patient is scheduled for an office encounter for excision of ingrown toenail.** The physician takes a problem-focused history from the patient who has no other complaints, examines the affected nail, and agrees with excision, explaining the procedure, risks, and benefits. The ingrown nail is corrected by wedge excision of the nail fold.

11765 (wedge excision of skin of nail fold)

} *ICD-9-CM*
703.0 (ingrowing nail)

ICD-10-CM
L60.0 (ingrowing nail)

Teaching Point: An E/M service with modifier **25** is not reported. A separate charge for an E/M service is reported only when the E/M service is significant and separately identifiable from the preservice work of a procedure reported on the same date.

➤ **An E/M service is performed on a 6-year-old established patient.** He is given 600,000 units of Bicillin by intramuscular injection for strep throat.

99212–99215 25 (established patient E/M visit, office)
J0561 × 6 units (injection penicillin G benzathine, 100,000 units)
96372 (administration therapeutic injection)

} *ICD-9-CM*
034.0 (streptococcal sore throat)

ICD-10-CM
J02.0 (streptococcal pharyngitis)

Teaching Point: *Current Procedural Terminology* requires that modifier **25** be appended to an E/M service when also reporting the administration of a therapeutic injection.

➤ **An established patient is seen for evaluation after falling from a tree in her backyard.** An expanded history and physical examination are performed. She has a 1-cm laceration (repaired) on the left forearm and abrasions on her right elbow and right hand.

99213 25 (established patient office visit)

12001 (simple repair superficial wound of forearm; ≤2.5 cm)

}

ICD-9-CM
913.0 (abrasion without mention of infection, elbow)
914.0 (abrasion without mention of infection, hand)
881.00 (open wound without mention of complication, forearm)
E884.9 (fall from tree)
E849.0 (place of occurrence, home)

ICD-10-CM
S50.311A (initial encounter for abrasion right elbow)
S60.511A (initial encounter for abrasion right hand)
S51.812A (initial encounter for laceration without foreign body, left forearm)
W14.XXXA (fall from tree)
Y92.017 (injury occurred in the yard of a private residence)
Y93.39 (injury occurred while climbing)

Transitioning to 10

Place of occurrence (category **Y92**) and activity (category **Y93**) codes are used only once, at the initial encounter for treatment. These codes do not require seventh characters.

---

26 **PROFESSIONAL COMPONENT**

- Modifier **26** is used to indicate that only the physician or other qualified health care professional component (supervision and interpretation) is being reported on a procedure that includes a technical and professional (physician) component.

- Some codes were developed to distinguish between the technical and professional components (eg, routine electrocardiogram codes **93000–93010**). Modifier **26** is not appropriate when reporting codes that distinguish the professional and technical components.

Examples—Modifier 26

➤ **A physician interprets an x-ray of the foot that was taken at the outpatient department of the hospital.**

73620 26 (x-ray foot, 2 views)

The physician reports modifier **26** indicating professional component only because the hospital provided the technical component.

➤ **A surgeon reprograms a cerebrospinal fluid shunt in the radiology department of the hospital.**

The surgeon would report code **62252 26** (reprogramming of programmable cerebrospinal shunt) and the hospital would report code **62252 TC.**

Reporting Procedures With Modifier 26 or TC

CPT® does not have a modifier for reporting only the technical component. However, most payers recognize the HCPCS modifier **TC** (technical component only). If a service includes a professional and technical component and the physician owns the equipment, employs the staff to perform the service, and interprets the test, the procedure is reported without a modifier. The physician who does not own the equipment but performs the written interpretation and report should report the service with modifier **26** appended to the appropriate *CPT* code. The facility or provider who owns the equipment and is responsible for the overhead and associated costs would report the same procedure code with modifier **TC** appended.

32   **MANDATED SERVICES**

☀ Modifier **32** is appended to services (eg, second opinion) that are mandated by a third-party payer or governmental, legislative, or regulatory requirements.

☀ The modifier is not limited to E/M services.

☀ Modifier **32** would be used when, for example, radiologic services are requested from a worker's compensation carrier, laboratory testing (eg, drug tests) is requested by a court system, or a physical therapy assessment is requested by an insurer.

Example—Modifier 32

➤ **A developmental pediatrician is asked by the managed care organization (MCO) to provide a second opinion on a family physician's patient for selected treatment services for autism spectrum disorder.** A comprehensive history and physical examination with high medical decision-making are performed and documented and a report is sent back to the MCO.

99245 32 (office/outpatient consultation)
}
    ICD-9-CM
    299.00 (autistic disorder)
    ICD-10-CM
    F84.0 (autistic disorder)

33   **PREVENTIVE SERVICES**

☀ Modifier **33** was added in response to the Patient Protection and Affordable Care Act, which prohibits member cost sharing for defined preventive services for non-grandfathered policies.

☀ The appropriate use of modifier **33** will reduce claim adjustments related to preventive services and corresponding refunds to members.

☀ Modifier **33** should only be appended to codes represented in one or more of the following 4 categories:

  ❖ Services rated A or B by the US Preventive Services Task Force[1]

  ❖ Immunizations for routine use in children, adolescents, and adults as recommended by the Advisory Committee on Immunization Practices of the Centers for Disease Control and Prevention

  ❖ Preventive care and screenings for children as recommended by Bright Futures (AAP) and newborn testing (American College of Medical Genetics and Genomics)

[1] For more information, refer to the American Medical Association Web site at www.ama-assn.org.

Chapter 3: Modifiers and Coding Edits

❖ Preventive care and screenings provided for women supported by the Health Resources and Services Administration

☀ More information on modifier **33** is included in Chapter 5.

47   **ANESTHESIA BY SURGEON**

☀ Modifier **47** is used when a physician performing a procedure also personally performs the regional and/or general anesthesia.

    The physician may also report the regional nerve blocks but may not report anesthesia codes **00100–01999.**

☀ Do not use modifier **47**

Ø When administering local anesthesia because that is considered to be inherent to the procedure

Ø When performing moderate (conscious) sedation

Example—Modifier 47

➤ **The surgeon performs a nerve block on the brachial plexus (64415) and removal of a ganglion cyst on the wrist (25111).**

    25111 47 and **64415**

The regional anesthesia is separate from the procedure.

50   **BILATERAL PROCEDURE**

☀ Modifier **50** is used to identify bilateral procedures that are performed at the same session.

☀ It is used only when the services and/or procedures are performed on identical anatomic sites, aspects, or organs.

☀ Modifier **50** is not appended to any code with a descriptor that indicates that the procedure includes "one or both" or "unilateral or bilateral."

☀ The Medicare Physician Fee Schedule includes a column (Column Z, BILAT SURG) that identifies codes that may be reported with modifier **50.** Procedures with a 1 indicator can be reported with modifier **50.**

☀ When the *CPT*® code descriptor indicates a bilateral procedure and only a unilateral procedure is performed, modifier **52** (reduced services) should be appended to the procedure code.

☀ For Medicaid claims that require the use of modifier **50,** only report one unit of service on the line item for the bilateral procedure.

Coding Conundrum: Modifier 50

Current Procedural Terminology guidelines and Medicaid National Correct Coding Initiative (NCCI) edits require that bilateral procedures be reported with modifier **50** and 1 unit of service. Some payers may require that the procedure be reported with modifier **50** appended to the second code. Other payers may require that HCPCS modifiers **RT** (right) and **LT** (left) be appended to the code.

    For example: Foreign bodies are removed from both ears.

• Report with code **69200 50** with 1 unit, or

• **69200 50** with 2 units, or

• **69200** and **69200 50,** or

• **69200 RT** and **69200 LT**

Know payer guidelines and report services accordingly.

Examples—Modifier 50

➤ **A physician performs an incision and drainage of abscesses on both legs.**
10060 50 (incision and drainage of abscess; simple or single)
Report based on payer guidelines. (See Coding Conundrum: Modifier **50.**)

➤ **A physician performs bilateral computerized corneal topography.**
Modifier **50** would not be appended to code **92025** (computerized corneal topography, unilateral or bilateral, with interpretation and report) because the code descriptor indicates a unilateral or bilateral procedure.

51 MULTIPLE PROCEDURES

❖ Modifier **51** is appended to the additional procedures(s) or service(s) when multiple procedures are performed at the same session by the same individual or individual in the same group practice. The primary procedure or service is reported first without a modifier.

❖ The CMS identifies those procedures that are eligible for modifier **51** and therefore are subject to payment reductions. Most payers that follow CMS guidelines will also adhere to this and will apply payment reductions for multiple procedures. Therefore, it is important that the primary procedure reported is the one with the highest relative value.

❖ Some payers, including some Medicare administrative contractors, have advised against reporting of this modifier because their systems automatically assign multiple service reductions to the appropriate services. In these cases, the system ignores the **51** modifier. Check payer policies prior to reporting services with this modifier.

❖ When multiple procedures are reported, payers usually reduce the payment for the second code by 50% because there is some resource cost duplication when both are done at the same visit or session. Medicare and some state Medicaid programs follow this policy.

❖ The Medicare Physician Fee Schedule includes a column (Column S, MULT PROC) that identifies codes that are subject to multiple procedure payment adjustment. The numerical indicators for multiple procedures are

— 0: Procedure is not subject to multiple procedure payment adjustment.

— 2: Procedure is subject to standard multiple procedure payment adjustment if reported on the same date as other procedures with indicators of 2 or 3.

— 3: Procedure is subject to special rules for endoscopy when reported on the same date as another procedure in the same endoscopy family.

— 4: Procedure is subject to special rules for diagnostic imaging when reported on the same date as another procedure in the same diagnostic imaging family (affects technical component only).

— 5: The practice expense component for certain therapy services is subject to 20% reduction (25% reduction for services rendered in an institutional setting—effective for services January 1, 2013, and after).

> ||||||| **Coding Pearl** |||||||
> When reporting multiple procedures, always report the code that has the highest relative value as primary procedure without the modifier.

Chapter 3: Modifiers and Coding Edits

— 6: The technical component of a diagnostic cardiovascular service is subject to 25% reduction (effective for services January 1, 2013, and after).

— 7: The technical component of a diagnostic ophthalmology service is subject to 20% reduction (effective for services January 1, 2013, and after).

— 9: Concept does not apply.

For more information on multiple surgery indicators and adjustments, see Chapter 12, Section 40.6, of the *Medicare Claims Processing Manual* at www.cms.gov/Regulations-and-Guidance/Guidance/Manuals/Downloads/clm104c12.pdf.

☀ Do not use modifier **51**

Ø When reporting add-on procedures (Codes identified with the + symbol are exempt from the need to report this modifier because the services are performed in addition to a primary procedure or service.)

Ø When reporting *CPT* codes identified with the symbol Ø (exempt from modifier **51**) because they have no associated or already reduced work relative value units (RVUs) (See Appendix E in *CPT* for a list of these codes.)

Ø When different providers perform the procedures

Ø When 2 or more physicians perform different and unrelated procedures (eg, multiple trauma) on the same patient on the same day (unless one of the physicians performs multiple procedures)

Ø When reporting E/M services, physical medicine and rehabilitation services, or provision of supplies (eg, vaccines)

Examples—Modifier 51

➤ **A simple repair of a 1.5-cm laceration on the left forearm and an intermediate repair of a 2.0-cm laceration on the head are performed on a child who has fallen while in-line skating at the local park.**

12031 (layer closure of wound of scalp; ≤2.5 cm)
12001 51 (simple repair of superficial wound of extremity; ≤2.5 cm)

}

ICD-9-CM
873.0 (open wound of scalp, without mention of complication)
881.00 (open wound without mention of complication, forearm)
E885.1 (fall from roller skates)
E849.4 (place for recreation and sport)

ICD-10-CM codes
S01.01XA (initial encounter for laceration without foreign body of scalp)
S51.812A (laceration without foreign body of left forearm)
V00.111A (fall from in-line roller skates)
Y93.51 (injury occurred while in-line skating)
Y92.830 (place of occurrence, public park)

Teaching point: Code **12031** is reported without the modifier because it carries the highest work RVUs.

> **Incision and removal of a foreign body of the left foot in the fascia and cryotherapy wart removal were performed for common warts at an office visit.**

28190 (removal foreign body, foot, subcutaneous)

17110 51 (destruction of benign lesions other than skin tags or cutaneous vascular proliferative lesions; up to 14 lesions)

ICD-9-CM
917.6 (superficial foreign body without major open wound and mention of infection)
078.19 (other specified viral warts)

ICD-10-CM
S90.852A (superficial foreign body, left foot)
B07.8 (other viral warts)

52   REDUCED SERVICES

* Modifier **52** is used when a service or procedure is partially reduced or eliminated (ie, procedure started but discontinued) at the discretion of the physician or other qualified health care professional.

* Modifier **52** is not used when a procedure is canceled prior to the induction of anesthesia and/or surgical preparation in the operating room.

* A payer may require that a letter of explanation and/or copy of the procedure or operative report be submitted with the claim.

* The diagnosis code linked to the procedure reported with modifier **52** should reflect why the procedure was reduced.

* When reporting a reduced service or a procedure code with modifier **52,** do not reduce your normal fee. Let the payer reduce the payment based on its policy and review of the submitted progress note.

Examples—Modifier 52

> **Evoked otoacoustic emissions; limited test is performed on one ear due to a congenital deformity.**

92587 52 (distortion product evoked otoacoustic emissions; limited)

ICD-9-CM
744.00 (unspecified anomaly of ear with impairment of hearing)

ICD-10-CM
Q16.9 (congenital malformation of ear causing impairment of hearing, unspecified)

Teaching Point: Code **92587** includes testing of both ears. Therefore, modifier **52** would be appended.

> **A developmental pediatrician performs a series of developmental tests but shortens the diagnostic session because the child's attention wanes.**
> **96111 52** (developmental testing)

53   DISCONTINUED PROCEDURE

- ☀ Modifier **53** signifies that a procedure was terminated (ie, started but discontinued) due to extenuating circumstances or circumstances in which the well-being of the patient was threatened (eg, patient is at risk or has unexpected, serious complications such as excessive bleeding, hypotension) during a procedure.
- ☀ It is not used to report the elective cancellation of a procedure prior to the patient's anesthesia induction and/or surgical preparation in the operating suite.
- ☀ The diagnosis code should reflect the reason for the termination of the procedure.
- ☀ Most payers will require that operative or procedure reports be submitted with the claim.

Examples—Modifier 53

➤ **An unsuccessful attempt is made to place a central line in the right subclavian vein. The line is successfully placed in the left subclavian vein.**

36555 53 RT (insertion non-tunneled centrally inserted central venous catheter; younger than 5 years)

36555 LT

Note: Some payers do not recognize modifiers **RT** and **LT.** See the descriptions and use of these modifiers at the end of this chapter.

Coding Conundrum: Modifier 52 or 53?

The main distinction between modifiers **52** (reduced services—service was started but the physician elected to reduce the scope or even eliminate the procedure or service) and **53** (discontinued procedure—reason for terminating the procedure is due to extenuating circumstances or because complications arise that place the patient at risk) is the basis for the decision to alter the procedure. Modifier **52** is often used when the physician plans to reduce the scope or extent of the procedure as noted, whereas **53** is used for situations such as unexpected events that occur in the course of the procedure (eg, cardiac arrest, profuse bleeding, arrhythmia). The following examples demonstrate the appropriate application of these modifiers when a physician performs a routine circumcision:

52: A physician begins a circumcision (**54150**) on a 3-day-old male. The physician elects to perform the circumcision without a dorsal penile or ring block. In this circumstance modifier **52** would be reported with code **54150** to indicate that the service was reduced from its full descriptor based on the physician's discretion.

53: A physician begins a circumcision (**54150**) on a 3-day-old male. During the procedure, the physician notices that the baby is showing signs of respiratory distress. The physician determines that the procedure needs to be discontinued to assess the baby. Due to the severity of the situation, the physician decides not to continue with the procedure. In this circumstance the physician would append modifier **53** to code **54150**, linking it to *ICD-9-CM* codes **V50.2** (encounter for routine male circumcision) and **770.89** (respiratory problems after birth) or *ICD-10-CM* codes **Z41.2** (encounter for routine and ritual male circumcision) and **P22.9** (respiratory distress newborn) to indicate why the procedure was discontinued. When reporting a procedure with modifier **53,** it is important to indicate why the procedure was discontinued.

➤ **During a right heart catheterization the child experienced ventricular arrhythmia and the procedure is discontinued.**

93451 53 (right heart catheterization)

54   **SURGICAL CARE ONLY**

       ❋   Modifier **54** is appended to the surgery procedure code when the physician does the procedure but another physician or other qualified health care professional (not of the same group practice) accepts a transfer of care and provides preoperative and/or postoperative management.

55   **POSTOPERATIVE MANAGEMENT ONLY**

       ❋   Modifier **55** is appended to the surgical code to report that only postoperative care is performed because another physician or other qualified health care professional of another group practice has performed the surgical procedure and transferred the patient for postoperative care.

56   **PREOPERATIVE MANAGEMENT ONLY**

       ❋   Modifier **56** is appended to the surgical code when only the preoperative care and evaluation are performed because another physician or other qualified health care professional of another group practice has performed the surgical procedure.

Coding Conundrum: Modifiers 54, 55, and 56

Modifiers **54, 55,** and **56** typically are used to report surgical procedures that have a global period of 10 to 90 days. They are not reported with procedures that have 0-day global periods. It is important to learn which guidelines are followed by your major payers. When reporting these modifiers, coordination and communication between the physicians and their billing staff is imperative.

Examples—Modifiers 54, 55, and 56

➤ **An infant undergoes a repair of tetralogy of Fallot.** The patient's pediatric cardiologist provides the postoperative management.

     The surgeon reports code **33692** (complete repair tetralogy of Fallot without pulmonary atresia) with modifier **54** appended, and the cardiologist reports code **33692 55** for the postoperative care services.

     These split care arrangements will usually require a manual review by payers, with some variable amount of the global fee being carved out for the 2 physicians. Check with your payers for their payment policy if this is typical for your practice.

➤ **A child is admitted to the hospital by the pediatrician for intravenous antibiotics for a deep abscess on the right leg.** On the second day of the hospital stay a surgeon is called in and performs an incision and drainage of the abscess. The child is discharged on day 3 and seen in follow-up by the pediatrician.

Surgeon reports

27603 54 (incision and drainage)   }   *ICD-9-CM*
682.6 (abscess, leg)
ICD-10-CM
L02.415 (cutaneous abscess of right lower limb)

Chapter 3: Modifiers and Coding Edits

Pediatrician reports

27603 55 (incision and drainage) } *ICD-9-CM* **682.6** (abscess, leg)

ICD-10-CM **L02.415** (cutaneous abscess of right lower limb)

57   DECISION FOR SURGERY

☀ Modifier **57** is appended to an E/M service that resulted in the initial decision to perform the surgery or procedure.

☀ Appending modifier **57** to the E/M service indicates to the payer that the E/M service is not part of the global period. The global period for surgical procedures is assigned by the CMS, private payers, or state Medicaid and not by the American Medical Association.

☀ Many payers will follow the CMS Medicare payment policy that allows reporting of modifier **57** only when the visit on the day before or day of surgery results in a decision to perform a surgical procedure that has a 90-day global period (major procedure). Know commercial and state Medicaid policies, maintain a written copy of the policy, and adhere to the policy. Refer to Chapter 12 for more detail on surgical package guidelines.

Examples—Modifier 57

➤ **A 10-year-old is seen by the pediatrician for the evaluation of pain in her foot.** X-ray reveals a metatarsal fracture, and the decision is made to treat the closed fracture.

The appropriate E/M code (**99201–99215 57**) based on the medical necessity and performance and documentation of the required key components would be reported in addition to code **28470** (closed treatment, metatarsal fracture; without manipulation). Code **28470** has an assigned global surgery period of 90 days.

➤ **A circumcision is performed on a 2-day-old born in the hospital, delivered vaginally, on the day of discharge.**

The procedure has a 0-day global period. Per CMS guidelines, modifier **25** would be appended to the E/M service instead of modifier **57**.

99238 25 (hospital discharge management)

54150 (circumcision using clamp/device with dorsal penile or ring block)

} *ICD-9-CM*
V30.00 (single liveborn, born in hospital, delivered without mention of cesarean delivery)
V50.2 (encounter for routine male circumcision)

ICD-10-CM
Z38.00 (single liveborn infant, delivered vaginally)
Z41.2 (encounter for routine male circumcision)

Transitioning to 10

Report first a code from category **Z38,** liveborn infant, based on type of delivery for services performed during the birth admission at the birth hospital.

Chapter 3: Modifiers and Coding Edits

58 **STAGED OR RELATED PROCEDURE OR SERVICE BY THE SAME PHYSICIAN OR OTHER QUALIFIED HEALTH CARE PROFESSIONAL DURING THE POSTOPERATIVE PERIOD**

- Modifier **58** is used to indicate that a procedure or service performed during the postoperative period was planned or anticipated (ie, staged), was more extensive than the original procedure, or was for therapy following a surgical procedure.
- Modifier **58** is a recognized modifier under the NCCI.
- Typically, payers recognize modifier **58** only when there is a global surgical period associated with the procedure code.
- Do not report modifier **58**
  - Ø When treatment of a problem requires a return to the operating/procedure room (eg, unanticipated clinical condition) (See modifier **78.**)
  - Ø When reporting procedures that include as part of their *CPT*® descriptor "one or more visits" or "one or more sessions"

Examples—Modifier 58

➤ **An excision of a malignant lesion (1 cm) on the leg is performed.** The pathology report indicates that the margins were not adequate and a re-excision is performed 1 week later. The excised diameter is less than 2 cm.

11602 58 (excision, malignant lesion including margins, leg; excised diameter 1.1–2.0 cm) for the second excision

Note: The first excision would be reported using code **11600** (margin diameter 0.5 cm or less) or **11601** (margin diameter 0.6–1.0 cm).

➤ **Closure of a perineal urethrostomy, 5 weeks post-hypospadias repair is performed as planned.**

53520 58 (closure of urethrostomy)

59 **DISTINCT PROCEDURAL SERVICE**

- Modifier **59** indicates that a procedure or service was distinct or independent from other non-E/M services performed on the same day.
- It is used to identify procedures/services, other than E/M services, that are not normally reported together but are appropriate under the circumstances.
- Documentation must support a different session, different procedure or surgery, different site or organ system, separate incision/excision, separate lesion, or separate injury (or area of injury in extensive injuries) not ordinarily encountered or performed on the same day by the same individual.
- Only use modifier **59** if it best explains the circumstances and no other, more descriptive modifier is available. Modifier **59** is the modifier of last resort.
  - ❖ Never use modifier **59** on an E/M code and do not use it in place of modifier **25.** For example, it would not be appropriate to report this scenario: **9921X** (established patient office visit) with **69210 59** (removal of cerumen). The correct way to report those services is with modifier **25** appended to the E/M service code.

|||||||| *Coding Pearl* ||||||||

Never use modifier **59** in place of modifier **25** or on an E/M service.

Chapter 3: Modifiers and Coding Edits

* Modifier **59** is recognized as an approved modifier under the NCCI. Append modifier **59** to the NCCI component codes (column 2) when clinically appropriate. (See Appropriate NCCI Modifiers on page 58 for more on NCCI edits.) Refer to the Medicaid NCCI Web site, www.medicaid.gov/Medicaid-CHIP-Program-Information/By-Topics/Data-and-Systems/National-Correct-Coding-Initiative.html, for further details on the proper use of modifier **59** to override an edit.

* Payers may require medical record documentation prior to payment of services. A pattern of excessive use of modifier **59** may also prompt a post-payment audit.

Coding Conundrum: Modifier 51 (Multiple Procedures) or 59 (Distinct Procedure)?

Modifier **51** is most often used on surgical procedures that are performed during the same session and through the same incision. This modifier identifies potentially overlapping or duplicative RVUs related to the global surgical package or the technical component of certain services (eg, radiology services).

Modifier **59** is used to identify distinct and independent procedures that are not normally reported together but are appropriate to the clinical circumstances. They are typically unrelated procedures or services performed on the same patient by the same provider on the same day on different anatomic sites or at different encounters. This is a modifier of last resort. When another modifier, such as **51**, is more appropriate, it should be reported in lieu of modifier **59**.

Examples—Modifier 59

➤ **The mother, teacher, and nanny each complete the Parents' Evaluation of Developmental Status.** The screens are scored and interpreted.

96110 59 (developmental screen) with 3 units of service

Remember that payers may have different reporting requirements for these services.

➤ **Influenza A and B tests (87804) were performed. In this case, the rapid influenza test provides the physician with 2 distinct results.**

87804 (infectious agent antigen detection by immunoassay with direct optical observation; influenza)

87804 59

Modifier **59** would be appended to the second test to reflect that 2 distinct tests were performed.

62   TWO SURGEONS

* Modifier **62** is used when 2 surgeons work together as primary surgeons performing a distinct part(s) of a procedure.

* Each surgeon should report his or her distinct operative work by adding modifier **62** to the procedure code and any associated add-on code(s) for that procedure as long as both surgeons continue to work together as primary surgeons.

* Each surgeon should report the co-surgery once using the same procedure code.

- If an additional procedure(s) (including an add-on procedure[s]) is performed during the same surgical session, a separate code(s) may also be reported without modifier **62** added.
- Column AB (CO SURG) of the Medicare Physician Fee Schedule (Resource-Based Relative Value Scale [RBRVS]) identifies procedures that may or may not be performed by co-surgeons. Indicator 1 is assigned to those procedures for which co-surgery is allowed under the Medicare program. See www.cms.hhs.gov/PhysicianFeeSched.

Example—Modifier 62

➤ **A neurosurgeon and general surgeon work together to place a ventriculoperitoneal shunt.**

Both physicians would report code **62223 62** with the same diagnosis code. The operative note must include the name of each surgeon, specific role of each surgeon, and necessity for 2 surgeons. Each surgeon should dictate his or her own operative report. Most payers will require authorization prior to the procedure.

63   **PROCEDURE PERFORMED ON INFANTS LESS THAN 4 KG**

- Modifier **63** is used to report procedures performed on neonates and infants up to a present body weight of 4 kg that involve significantly increased complexity and physician work commonly associated with these patients.
- Unless otherwise designated, this modifier may only be appended to procedures/services listed in the **20000–69999** code series.
- Use of modifier **63** may require submission of an operative note with the claim. The operative note should include the patient's weight. It is also beneficial to report the patient's weight on the claim.
- Do not report modifier **63**
   - Ø When the code descriptor indicates the procedure is performed on young infants or neonates because the relative value for those procedures reflects the additional work (eg, code **49491** for repair initial inguinal hernia on preterm infant)
   - Ø With any *CPT®* code listed in Appendix F of the *CPT* manual

> ||||||| *Coding Pearl* ||||||||
> When reporting a procedure with modifier **63**, include the infant's weight on the operative note.

Examples—Modifier 63

➤ **A premature neonate weighing 2.1 kg requires a physician's skill for central venous access.**
36568 63 (insertion of peripherally inserted central venous catheter [PICC] without subcutaneous port or pump; <5 years of age)

➤ **A repair of patent ductus arteriosus by ligation is performed on an infant weighing less than 4 kg.**
33820 63

Chapter 3: Modifiers and Coding Edits

66   **SURGICAL TEAM**

- Modifier **66** is appended to the basic procedure code when highly complex procedures (requiring the concomitant services of several physicians or other qualified health care professionals, often of different specialties, plus other highly skilled, specially trained personnel and various types of complex equipment) are carried out under the surgical team concept.
- Each surgeon reports modifier **66.**
- Each surgeon should dictate his or her own operative report, and it should reflect the medical necessity for team surgery.
- Column AC (TEAM SURG) of the Medicare Physician Fee Schedule (RBRVS) identifies procedures that may or may not be performed by a team of surgeons. Indicator 1 is assigned to those procedures for which team surgery is allowed under the Medicare program.
- The operative notes are usually required by the payer.
- If a surgeon is assisting another surgeon, modifier **80, 81,** or **82** would be more applicable.

Example—Modifier 66

➤ **Multiple surgeons perform different portions of an organ transplant.**

Each physician would report his or her services with modifier **66** appended to the procedure code.

76   **REPEAT PROCEDURE OR SERVICE BY SAME PHYSICIAN OR OTHER QUALIFIED HEALTH CARE PROFESSIONAL**

- Modifier **76** is used when a procedure or service is repeated by the same physician or other qualified health care professional subsequent to the original procedure or service. Use of this modifier may prevent denial as a duplicate service line.
- The repeat procedure may be performed on different days. (Payer guidance may vary.)
- This modifier is appended to procedure codes only and is not reported when the code definition indicates a repeat procedure.
- The use of this modifier advises the payer that this is not a duplicate service.
  - ❖ See modifier **91** for repeat clinical diagnostic laboratory services.
- The CMS only recognizes this modifier on electrocardiograms and x-rays or when a procedure is performed in an operating room or other location equipped to perform procedures. State Medicaid programs or other commercial payers may follow this guideline. Check with payers to determine their policy on use of the modifier.

Examples—Modifier 76

➤ **The physician has to place a central venous catheter on a 2-year-old 2 times on 1 calendar day because the first catheter clotted.**

36555 and **36555 76** (insertion non-tunneled centrally inserted central venous catheter; <5 years of age)

➤ **You see a patient in your office with severe asthma, giving 3 nebulized albuterol treatments and steroids over the course of the visit.**

Report **94640** three times with modifier **76** appended to the second and third codes or, if required by payers, report **94640 76** with 3 units.

(The Medicare and Medicaid NCCI manuals contradict *CPT* instruction for code **94640,** stating that *CPT* code **94640** should only be reported once during a single patient encounter regardless of the number of separate inhalation treatments that are administered.)

➤ **A repeat x-ray is performed following insertion of a chest tube by the pulmonologist in the emergency department.**

71020 76, 26   (chest x-ray, 2 views)

77   **REPEAT PROCEDURE OR SERVICE BY ANOTHER PHYSICIAN OR OTHER QUALIFIED HEALTH CARE PROFESSIONAL**

- ❉ Modifier **77** is used when a procedure or service is repeated by another physician or health care professional subsequent to the original procedure or service.
- ❉ Payers may require documentation to support the medical necessity of performing the same service or procedure on the same day or during the global surgical period (if applicable).

Examples—Modifier 77

➤ **A simple repair of a 3-cm laceration of the knee is performed by the pediatrician.** Later that day the child falls on the knee and opens the wound. A physician at the urgent care center performs another simple repair.

The second physician should report the service with code **12002 77.**

Remember that the diagnosis code selected must provide the medical necessity for the duplicate procedure. Payers may require a copy of the medical record.

➤ **A physician on call replaces a central venous catheter that had been put in earlier that day by the child's regular pediatrician.**

36555 77

Remember that the diagnosis code selected must provide the medical necessity for the duplicate procedure, and at times documentation must be submitted.

78   **UNPLANNED RETURN TO THE OPERATING/PROCEDURE ROOM BY THE SAME PHYSICIAN OR OTHER QUALIFIED HEALTH CARE PROFESSIONAL FOLLOWING INITIAL PROCEDURE FOR A RELATED PROCEDURE DURING THE POSTOPERATIVE PERIOD**

- ❉ Modifier **78** is used when another procedure is unplanned and related to the initial procedure, requires a return to the operating or procedure room, and is performed during the postoperative period of the initial procedure by the same physician.
- ❉ The related procedure might be performed on the same day or anytime during the postoperative period. (For repeat procedures, see modifier **76.**)
- ❉ Link the appropriate diagnosis code(s) that best explains the reason for the unplanned procedure.

Chapter 3: Modifiers and Coding Edits

Examples—Modifier 78

> **A pediatric surgeon returns to the operating room to stop bleeding from an abdominal procedure performed earlier in the day.**
>
> **35840 78** (exploration for postoperative hemorrhage, thrombosis, or infection; abdomen)
>
> The second procedure will usually be paid only for the intraoperative service, not the preoperative or postoperative care already paid in the original procedure.

> **An incision and drainage of a deep abscess in the pelvis area 6 days following excision of a lipoma is performed.**
>
> **26990 78** (incision and drainage, pelvis area; deep abscess)

79 **UNRELATED PROCEDURE OR SERVICE BY THE SAME PHYSICIAN OR OTHER QUALIFIED HEALTH CARE PROFESSIONAL DURING THE POST-OPERATIVE PERIOD**

- The physician may need to indicate that the performance of a procedure or service during the postoperative period was unrelated to the original procedure. This circumstance may be reported by using modifier **79**.
- The diagnosis must identify the reason for the new procedure. (For repeat procedures by the same physician on the same day, see modifier **76**.)

Example—Modifier 79

> **A patient had closed treatment of a shoulder dislocation with manipulation and 2 months later requires open treatment of a humeral shaft fracture.**
>
> **24515 79**

80 **ASSISTANT SURGEON**

- Modifier **80** is used when the assistant surgeon assists the surgeon during the entire operation.
- The primary surgeon reports the appropriate *CPT*® code for the procedure and the assistant surgeon reports the same code with modifier **80** appended.
- Payers vary on payment rules. The CMS establishes guidelines for payment of assistant surgery for each procedure code. Most payers, including the CMS, will not pay for nonphysician surgery technicians in this role.
- Many payers require documentation to support the necessity of an assistant surgeon.

> ||||||| **Coding Pearl** |||||||
>
> The Medicare Physician Fee Schedule includes indicators identifying procedures that may or may not be billed by an assistant surgeon, co-surgeon, or team surgeon.

81 **MINIMUM ASSISTANT SURGEON**

- Modifier **81** is used when an assistant surgeon is required for a short time and minimal assistance is provided.
- The assistant surgeon reports the same procedure code as the surgeon with modifier **81** appended.
- Many payers require documentation to support the use of an assistant surgeon for only a portion of a procedure.

82   **ASSISTANT SURGEON (WHEN QUALIFIED RESIDENT SURGEON NOT AVAILABLE)**

☀ Modifier **82** is used in teaching hospitals when a resident surgeon is not available to assist the primary surgeon.

☀ The unavailability of a qualified resident surgeon is a prerequisite for the use of modifier **82** appended to the usual procedure code number(s).

Modifiers 80, 81, and 82

☀ The Medicare Physician Fee Schedule includes in column AA (ASST SURG) indicators identifying procedures that may or may not be billed by an assistant surgeon. Indicator 1 is assigned to those procedures for which an assistant surgeon is allowed under the Medicare program. Note that a payer may require use of HCPCS modifier **AS** (physician assistant, nurse practitioner, or clinical nurse specialist services for assistant-at-surgery) for surgical assistance performed by a nonphysician qualified health care professional.

91   **REPEAT CLINICAL DIAGNOSTIC LABORATORY TEST**

☀ Modifier **91** is used to indicate that it is necessary to repeat the same laboratory test on the same day to obtain subsequent test results.

☀ Modifier **91** is only reported when the laboratory test is performed more than once on the same patient on the same day.

☀ Modifier **91** cannot be reported when repeat tests are performed to confirm initial results, because of testing problems with the specimen or equipment, or for any reason when a normal one-time, reportable result is all that is required.

> |||||||| **Coding Pearl** |||||||
>
> Report modifier **91** only when a laboratory test is performed on the same day to obtain subsequent results and not to confirm results.

Example—Modifier 91

➤ **In the course of treatment for hyperkalemia, a patient had 2 serum potassium determinations (84132) done on the same day in the same office.** The second was performed after a series of enemas was performed to increase elimination of potassium.

   84132 91 with 2 units of service

HCPCS Modifiers

The HCPCS modifiers most often reported by pediatric practices are **QW** (tests waived by Clinical Laboratory Improvement Amendments [CLIA]), **TC** (technical component), and anatomic-specific modifiers such as **RT** (right side) and **E1** (upper left eyelid). The anatomic-specific modifiers are designated as appropriate modifiers under the NCCI edits and are listed on page 58. Be sure to review the list of HCPCS modifiers in your manual.

QW   **CLIA-WAIVED TESTS**

☀ The CLIA-waived tests are those commonly done in a laboratory or an office.

☀ One common test in the *CPT*® **80000** series that is CLIA-waived is the rapid strep test (**87880**).

- Laboratories and physician offices performing waived tests may need to append modifier **QW** to the *CPT* code for CLIA-waived procedures. The use of modifier **QW** is payer specific.
- Some of the CLIA-waived tests are exempt from the use of modifier **QW** (eg, **81002, 82272**).

To review the list of CLIA-waived procedures, go to http://cms.gov/CLIA.

RT and LT RIGHT AND LEFT SIDE

> **||||||||| Coding Pearl |||||||||**
>
> Modifiers **RT** and **LT** are for information only and are not used in place of modifier **50** unless directed by a payer.

- Modifiers **RT** and **LT** are used for information only and do not affect payment of a procedure.
- Used to identify procedures performed on the left or right side of the body.
- Modifiers **RT** and **LT** are not used in place of modifier **50** but may be used in association with modifier **50.**

Example—Modifiers RT and LT

➤ **The physician removes a subcutaneous foreign body from the left elbow and a deep foreign body from the right elbow.**

24200 LT (removal of a subcutaneous foreign body from the elbow)

24201 RT (removal of a deep foreign body from the elbow)

Some payers may require that modifier **59** (distinct procedure) be reported.

JW   DRUG AMOUNT DISCARDED/NOT ADMINISTERED TO ANY PATIENT

- May be used as tool to internally track wasted drugs/vaccines.
- This modifier is reported on claims only when required by certain payers.
- When required by payer policy, report only when the full amount of a single-dose vial is not used due to patient indications.
  - ❖ Report only when the amount of drug wasted is equal to at least 1 billing unit.
- Never report for discarded amounts from a multidose vial.
- Use for internal tracking purposes only (ie, do not report) when
  - ❖ A parent decides to forego an immunization after the vaccine had been drawn up.
  - ❖ The vial is dropped and the medication must be discarded.
  - ❖ A vaccine is discarded due to temperature out of range during storage.

Coding Edits

NCCI Edits

The NCCI edits were developed for use by the CMS in adjudicating Medicare claims, but they also are used by many private payers, and all Medicaid programs now implement their own NCCI edits. The NCCI edits frequently form the basis for proprietary claims software.

The NCCI edits

- Have been developed based on *CPT®* code descriptors and instructions, coding guidelines developed by national medical societies (eg, AAP), Medicare billing history, local and national Medicare carrier policies and edits, and analysis of standard medical and surgical practice.
- Identify code pairs that normally should not be billed by the same physician for the same patient on the same date of service.
- Are used by payers to translate payment policies into the claims processing system for physician services as well as to promote correct coding.
- Include edits based on services that are mutually exclusive based on code descriptor or anatomic considerations, services that are considered to be inherent to each other, and edits based on coding instructions.
  - ❖ If 2 codes of an edit are billed by the same provider for the same patient for the same date of service without an appropriate modifier, the column 1 code is paid.
  - ❖ If clinical circumstances justify appending the appropriate modifier to the column 2 code, payment of both codes may be allowed.

Medicaid and Medicare NCCI edits are updated quarterly. Each Medicare NCCI version ends with .0 (point zero), .1, .2, or .3 indicating their effective dates.

- Versions ending in .0 (point zero) are effective from January 1 through March 31 of that year.
- Versions ending in .1 are effective from April 1 through June 30 of that year.
- Versions ending in .2 are effective from July 1 through September 30 of that year.
- Versions ending in .3 are effective from October 1 through December 31 of that year.

The CMS releases the Medicare NCCI edits free of charge on its Web site (www.cms. gov/NationalCorrectCodInitEd/NCCIEP/list.asp). Medicaid NCCI files are published separately free of charge at http://bit.ly/1mvdrGj. Although many of the Medicaid edits mirror Medicare edits, this is not always the case. The CMS has instructed that use of the appropriate NCCI file is important to correct coding. Online NCCI edits are posted in spreadsheet form, which allows users to sort by procedure code and effective date. Further, there is a "Find" tool that allows users to look for a specific code. The edit files are indexed by procedure code ranges for simplified navigation. Policy manuals that explain the rationale for edits and correct use of NCCI-associated modifiers are published to the Web pages listed previously. Updated manuals for the year ahead are published annually in late fall. Be sure to update your NCCI edit files quarterly.

> **|||||||| Coding Pearl ||||||||**
>
> Medicaid NCCI files are published separately from Medicare files at http://bit.ly/1mvdrGj.

Examples of Medicaid NCCI Edits

Column 1	Column 2	Modifier Indicator	Effective Date
99149 (moderate sedation services; 5 years of age or older, first 30 minutes intra-service time)	**99148** (younger than 5 years, first 30 minutes intra-service time)	0	10/1/2010
The NCCI edits preclude any payment for the component code because they are mutually exclusive due to age definitions.			
94640 (pressurized/non-pressurized inhalation treatment)	**94664** (demonstration and/ or evaluation patient use of nebulizer)	1	10/1/2010

Examples of Medicaid NCCI Edits, continued

Column 1	Column 2	Modifier Indicator	Effective Date
The comprehensive code (94640) would be paid and the component code (94664) would be denied unless modifier 59 (distinct procedural service) is appended to the component code (94664). Please note that under current CMS payment policy, modifier 59 could only be used if the nebulizer treatment and demonstration occurred at separate encounters. Please refer to the CMS NCCI edit site for more information (http://bit.ly/1mvdrGj).			
94060 (bronchodilation responsiveness, spirometry as in 94010, pre- and post-bronchodilator administration)	94010 (spirometry)	0	10/1/2010
The NCCI edits preclude any payment for the component code (ie, column 2 code 94010).			
90460 (immunization administration through 18 years of age, first or only component, with counseling by physician)	99392 (preventive medicine service, established patient age 1–4)	1	01/1/2013
The comprehensive code (90460) would be paid and the component code (99392) would be denied unless modifier 25 (significant, separately identifiable E/M service) is appended to the component code (99392).			

Appropriate NCCI Modifiers

Modifier indicators are assigned to every code pair identified in the NCCI. They dictate whether modifiers are needed or will be accepted to override the edit. These indicators are

0: Under no circumstance may a modifier be used to override the edit.

1: An appropriate modifier may be used to override the edit.

9: This edit was deleted prior to its effective date or there is essentially no edit.

Only certain modifiers can be used to override edits when the service/procedure is clinically justified, and they may be used only on the code pairs that are assigned the 1 indicator. For overrides of mutually exclusive edits or correct coding edits, the appropriate modifier always is appended to the code that appears in column 2 because that is considered the bundled procedure. To append the appropriate modifier and override an edit, it is imperative that the conditions of that modifier are met.

Modifiers that can be used to override NCCI edits

24	Unrelated E/M service by the same physician or other qualified health care professional during a postoperative period
25	Significant, separately identifiable E/M service by the same physician or other qualified health care professional on the same day of the procedure or other service
57	Decision for surgery
58	Staged or related procedure or service by the same physician or other qualified health care professional during the postoperative period
59	Distinct procedural service

78	Unplanned return to the operating/procedure room by the same physician or other qualified health care professional following initial procedure for a related procedure during the postoperative period
79	Unrelated procedure or service by the same physician or other qualified health care professional during the postoperative period
91	Repeat clinical diagnostic laboratory test
E1	Upper left, eyelid
E2	Lower left, eyelid
E3	Upper right, eyelid
E4	Lower right, eyelid
FA	Left hand, thumb
F1	Left hand, second digit
F2	Left hand, third digit
F3	Left hand, fourth digit
F4	Left hand, fifth digit
F5	Right hand, thumb
F6	Right hand, second digit
F7	Right hand, third digit
F8	Right hand, fourth digit
F9	Right hand, fifth digit
LC	Left circumflex, coronary artery
LD	Left anterior descending coronary artery
LM	Left main coronary artery
RC	Right coronary artery
RI	Ramus intermedius coronary artery
LT	Left side
RT	Right side
TA	Left foot, great toe
T1	Left foot, second digit
T2	Left foot, third digit
T3	Left foot, fourth digit
T4	Left foot, fifth digit
T5	Right foot, great toe
T6	Right foot, second digit
T7	Right foot, third digit
T8	Right foot, fourth digit
T9	Right foot, fifth digit

Reviewing and Using These Edits

1. Be aware of all of the coding edits that are applicable to your specialty; as each update replaces the former edits, it is important to review them quarterly. Always look for new or deleted edits. Updated files can be found at www.aap.org/coding under the NCCI edit tab.

2. Pay close attention to the modifier indicator because it may have changed from the last quarterly update. For example, a code set that initially would not allow override with a modifier may now subsequently allow one, or vice versa.

3. Pay attention to the effective date and deletion date of each code set. The edits are applicable only if they are effective. The effective date is based on the date of service, not the date the claim was submitted. Sometimes a pair is retroactively terminated. If so, you may resubmit claims for payment if the date of service is within the filing time frame of the payer.

4. Use modifiers as appropriate. Modifiers should be used only *when applicable* based on coding standards, when medically justified or necessary, and when supported by medical record documentation (progress notes, operative notes, procedure notes, diagrams, or pictures), or, as previously mentioned, when dictated by payers. Refer to the CMS written guidelines (because they are very explicit about billing surgical procedures) or to your payer's provider manual.

5. When billing surgical procedures, you may need to look at several different codes for possible edits. Be sure to always use the code that is reflective of the total service performed.

6. If you are denied payment for services for which there is no edit, for which a reported modifier should have allowed payment, and/or for which the edit is inconsistent with *CPT* guidelines, you need to appeal the denial. Having knowledge of how this system works is to your benefit when appealing the denial.

7. Some payers have developed or adopted coding edit programs that are different from and often more comprehensive than the NCCI. If a payer policy differs from the CMS/NCCI policy and is not clearly defined in its provider manual, refer to the Web site. Make sure that you get the policies in writing for the services you commonly perform.

8. Report the services provided correctly based on *CPT* code guidelines (unless a payer has clearly stated otherwise). Remember that these edits are based on Medicare and Medicaid guidelines, and not all private payers follow all of these edits.

Evaluation and Management Documentation and Coding Guidelines*: Incident-To, PATH Guidelines, and Scope of Practice Laws

Evaluation and Management (E/M) Documentation and Coding Guidelines

Three versions of evaluation and management (E/M) guidelines exist, including

◉ *Current Procedural Terminology (CPT®)*

❖ The most vague of all versions

❖ Includes specialty-specific clinical examples in Appendix C of the American Medical Association (AMA) *CPT 2015*

The AMA clinical examples are only examples and should not be used as a basis for coding patient encounters with the same diagnosis because the selection of a code must be based on the medically necessary services performed and documented and may include clinical variations.

◉ The Centers for Medicare & Medicaid Services (CMS) *Documentation Guidelines for Evaluation and Management Services*

❖ Two sets of guidelines, 1995 and 1997 (see Appendix A or online at www.aap.org/cfp, access code AAPCFP20).

❖ Guidelines are more specific than those of the AMA.

❖ Followed by the Medicare program, most private payers, and state Medicaid programs.

❖ The CMS documentation guidelines were based on the adult population because few children are covered under the Medicare program. However, both the 1995 and 1997 guidelines state that a history and/or examination performed on a pediatric patient may vary from the adult standard and yet be appropriate when considering the selection of an E/M code. As noted in the 1997 guidelines, under Section III: Documentation of E/M Services, paragraph 5:

"These Documentation Guidelines for E/M services reflect the needs of the typical adult population. For certain groups of patients, the recorded information may vary slightly from that described here. Specifically, the medical records of infants, children, adolescents, and pregnant women may have additional or modified information recorded in each history and examination area.

As an example, newborn records may include under history of the present illness (HPI) the details of mother's pregnancy, and the infant's status at birth; social history will focus on family structure; family history will focus on congenital anomalies and hereditary disorders in the family. In addition, the content of a pediatric examination will vary with the age and development of the child. Although not specifically defined in these documentation guidelines, these patient group variations on history and examination are appropriate."

Pediatric clinical vignettes are presented throughout this manual. These too are only examples, and the associated *CPT®* codes should not be used for every patient with the same diagnosis.

Coding E/M Services From a Clinical Perspective

The definitions of the levels of service and requirements for each key component (ie, history, physical examination, and medical decision-making [MDM]) are ambiguous, and the steps defined in the requirements for selection of the code are not consistent with a physician's approach to addressing and treating an illness or problem. A physician does not enter a room and perform first a history, then a physical examination, and finally MDM. Rather, the key components of an E/M service are performed in conjunction with one another. The MDM typically supports the level of history and/or physical examination medically necessary and is derived from the following:

- The documented chief complaint (CC) helps to formulate the presenting problem or nature of the patient presentation.
- The level of history obtained and documented is based on the nature of the patient presentation. Concurrently, the physician is forming his or her impression of the problem's severity, possible diagnoses, other factors that require consideration in patient management, and a potential plan of care.
- The level of the performed physical examination is based on the presenting problem(s) and history. From the moment the physician observes the patient and while obtaining the history, the physician simultaneously is starting his or her physical assessment and examination (eg, general appearance). Additional history may be obtained concurrently with the examination. While performing the examination the physician again is determining the severity or risk, need for diagnostic testing, differential diagnosis(es), and treatment plan.
- The documentation of the history, physical examination, ordered and performed diagnostic studies, assessment, and plan infer and support the complexity of MDM.

Categories of E/M Codes

There are 20 categories of E/M codes (eg, office or outpatient services, consultations, prolonged physician services, newborn care). Specific guidelines for reporting codes within these categories are described in detail in chapters 5 through 11. Most E/M codes require the performance and documentation of key components. Those E/M services that do not require the key components as the basis for code selection include those services that are

- Bundled as a daily care code (eg, pediatric and neonatal critical care)
- Bundled as a period of care (eg, transitional care management)
- Based on specific guidelines (eg, normal newborn care, preventive medicine visits)
- Based on time (eg, hourly critical care, discharge services, prolonged services)

E/M Code Components

Seven components are considered when selecting the level of E/M service code.

Overarching Component	Description	Components
Key Components	Used to select a level of E/M service	1. History
		2. Examination
		3. Medical decision-making
Contributory Factor	May contribute to, but are not required for the selection of a code. However, they usually affect the extent of the key components that are performed.	4. Counseling
		5. Coordination of care
		6. Nature of presenting problem
Explicit Component	Used to select a level of E/M service when time becomes the controlling factor	7. Time

Key Components

Most E/M services require the performance and documentation of the key components (history, physical examination, and MDM).

Contributory Factors

Current Procedural Terminology® *(CPT)* defines a presenting problem as "a disease, condition, illness, injury, symptom, sign, finding, complaint or other reason for encounter, with or without a diagnosis being established at the time of the encounter." This may be better described as patient presentation and may include psychosocial issues or ethical considerations determined by the physician or other qualified health care professional to require consideration in patient management. The nature of the patient presentation may be more extensive or different from the patient's CC (eg, adolescent girl states her reason for visit is headaches but also presents with anxiety about possible unwanted pregnancy). It is the nature of the presenting problem that generally determines the level of history and physical examination performed and documented and supports MDM. For example, an infant with high fever and wheezing warrants a more comprehensive history and/or examination to determine the diagnosis or condition than an infant presenting with a diaper rash. This does not mean that all elements of examination, for example, require individual justification.

|||||||| **Coding Pearl** ||||||||

The nature of the presenting problem is defined by severity, risk, and probability of functional impairment.

Levels of presenting problems are defined as follows:

Nature of Presenting Problem		
Problem/Severity	**Risk of Morbidity or Mortality Without Treatment**	**Probability of Functional Impairment**
Minimal physician supervision required, presence not required		
Self-limited or minor	Problem runs a definite and prescribed course, is transient in nature.	Not likely to permanently alter health status Good prognosis with management/compliance
Low	Risk of morbidity or mortality without treatment is low.	Full recovery without functional impairment is expected.
Moderate	Risk of morbidity or mortality without treatment is moderate.	Uncertain prognosis or increased probability of prolonged functional impairment
High	Risk of morbidity without treatment is high to extreme. Moderate risk of mortality without treatment	High probability of severe, prolonged functional impairment

Explicit Component—Time

Time shall be used as the key or controlling factor in the selection of some E/M services (those that are assigned a typical time) when more than 50% of the physician face-to-face patient and/or family encounter is spent in counseling and/or coordination of care.

Key Components Defined

The 3 key components are further defined in 4 levels of service described as problem focused, expanded problem focused, detailed, and comprehensive. To select the proper E/M service code, the service must meet or exceed the level required for the appropriate key items.

Chapter 4: Evaluation and Management Documentation and Coding Guidelines

History

The history component includes a CC, HPI, review of systems (ROS), and past, family, and social history (PFSH).

To meet a particular level of history, all of the elements of HPI, ROS, and PFSH listed under each level must be met (ie, an expanded problem-focused history requires that a CC, 1–3 elements of the HPI, and review of one system be performed and documented).

Documentation Requirements and Tips

The nature or severity of the problem(s) should determine the level of history obtained, documented, and counted. *Only the history that is pertinent* to the problem(s) addressed at that visit should be used to establish the level of history in the code selection process.

> **||||||| Coding Pearl |||||||**
>
> Only elements of history that are pertinent to the presenting problem or patient presentation are used in code selection. Electronic health records may carry forward or otherwise include history beyond what is pertinent.

- The CC, HPI, ROS, and PFSH may be documented as separate items or in a summary format.
- A CC must be documented on every encounter. If the purpose of the visit is for follow-up of a previously addressed problem, the documentation should state the problem or diagnosis responsible for the visit (eg, follow-up of pneumonia).
- The HPI *must be obtained and documented by the physician.* Documentation guidelines do not state this; however, it is inferred. If the HPI is documented only by ancillary staff, it is not used in determining the level of history for code selection.

> **||||||| Coding Pearl |||||||**
>
> Documentation of the ROS and PFSH must reflect the physician's review of the information by confirmation or supplemental information.

- If the HPI summarizes the status of chronic conditions, include information such as current medications and their effects, a description of the patient's present condition, and patient compliance with treatment plans.
- The ROS and PFSH may be documented by the patient, family, or ancillary staff; however, documentation must reflect the physician's review of the information by confirmation or supplemental information. Documentation should clarify any conflicting information between the ROS completed by patient, family, or ancillary staff and the physician's documentation of the patient presentation (eg, ROS is negative for musculoskeletal complaints but HPI says patient has pain in right knee).
- The ROS must be pertinent to the problem(s), and pertinent negative and positive responses must be documented.
- Appropriate documentation for a complete ROS (at least 10 of 14 systems) might include a checklist with documentation of "negative" or the pertinent response for each system. If a checklist is not used, documentation might indicate pertinent responses and "otherwise negative or unremarkable for all systems," pertinent responses and "all other systems reviewed and negative," or "complete ROS unchanged from previous review dated _____." Documentation of "ROS negative" is not sufficient.
- An ROS and/or PFSH does not have to be recorded again on a subsequent encounter if there is documentation that the physician reviewed and/or updated a previous version. Documentation to reflect the subsequent review might be "ROS unchanged from most recent visit dated _____."
- If a separate patient history form is used (eg, new patient history), the physician must sign and date the form to reflect his or her review. Pertinent responses to the ROS and/or PFSH may be documented on a separate history form, a progress note, or the signed history form.

- If the physician is unable to obtain a history, the record must describe the circumstance that precludes obtaining the history. In that circumstance, the history may be considered as comprehensive. For example, a child is transferred to the emergency department of a children's hospital and her parents are transferred to another facility following an accident. In this circumstance, if the accepting physician documents this limitation and any history obtained from available past medical records or the medical transport team, the history is considered comprehensive.

- The distinction between an HPI and ROS is often confusing. The HPI and ROS are obtained for different reasons and both contribute to the level of history performed in the selection of an E/M service code. Documentation guidelines do not directly state that a comment made under the HPI cannot be counted again in the ROS when it is repeated. However, most coders and payers will refer to this as "double-dipping."

  - Example: HPI: "abdominal pain for 3 days"; ROS: "abdominal pain." Think about the context in which the information was obtained. If the information was gathered as a description of the development of the problem, consider it as HPI. If the information was obtained to help further define the scope of the problem, consider the information as part of the ROS. Example: HPI: "lower abdominal pain for 3 days without nausea, vomiting, constipation"; ROS: "not associated with eating or exercise; intermittent dysuria; denies fever."

- Histories obtained on infants and newborns will vary. For example, a history obtained on a newborn might include details of the mother's pregnancy, the newborn's status at birth, family and social history, and an ROS appropriate to the age of the newborn. In young children, all or part of the history is typically obtained from the parent and/or caregiver. This should not be confused with obtaining additional history with summarization in the medical record which may increase the level of MDM (ie, increased amount and complexity of data).

- Examples of elements used to describe an HPI

  - Location—right ear, big toe, head, right lower abdomen
  - Duration—2 days, since last night, 1 week
  - Timing—persistent, occasionally, twice a week, recurrent, daily, 15 minutes after…
  - Quality—dull, clear, cloudy, thick, throbbing
  - Severity—moderate, pain scale (1–10), low grade, progressive, improving, worsening
  - Context—occurred when awoke from nap, while playing soccer, fell from tree
  - Modifying factors—took acetaminophen without relief, improved with albuterol treatment
  - Associated signs and symptoms—blurred vision with headache, coughing with runny nose, nausea with vomiting

Establishing the Level of History Performed

To select a particular level of history, all of the elements of CC, HPI, ROS, and PFSH required for that level must be met.

Thirteen-year-old established patient

- *Problem focused*
  "Here for stomachache. Stomach has hurt for 2 days."
- *Expanded problem focused*
  "Here for stomachache. Stomach has hurt for 2 days. No diarrhea or constipation."

Chapter 4: Evaluation and Management Documentation and Coding Guidelines

- *Detailed problem focused*

  "Here for stomachache. Stomach has hurt on and off for a few months. Pain occurs primarily after eating, worsening over the last few days. No fever, diarrhea, or vomiting; last menstrual period 2 weeks ago and normal. Takes no medication; no known allergies."

- *Comprehensive*

  "Here for stomachache. Stomach has hurt on and off for a few months. Pain occurs primarily after eating, worsening over the last few days. No fever, diarrhea, or vomiting; last menstrual period 2 weeks ago and normal; no rashes; no injuries; all other systems negative. Takes no medication, no known allergies, no exposure to illness, has excellent grades and enjoys school. Family history negative for abdominal problems or headaches."

The Elements of History

History Components	Description	Elements
Chief complaint (CC)	The stated purpose or reason for the encounter (usually a quote of the patient's or parent's words)	Though not a defined element, a CC is required as part of the history documentation.
History of present illness (HPI)	Description of the development of the present illness from the onset of the problem or symptom or from the previous encounter to the present; described with 8 specified elements or a summary of the status of 3 or more chronic or inactive conditions	<ul><li>Location (specific anatomic site)</li><li>Duration (period from onset of sign/symptom to present)</li><li>Timing (number or frequency of occurrences of sign/symptom within the time patient has experienced the sign/symptom)</li><li>Quality (characterizations of sign/symptom)</li><li>Severity (acuteness or intensity of sign/symptom)</li><li>Context (circumstances or situation in which sign/symptom occurred)</li><li>Modifying factors (effort taken to change the sign/symptom and its effect)</li><li>Associated signs and symptoms (other related or additional signs/symptoms)</li></ul>
Review of systems (ROS)	A series of questions asked in an attempt to identify signs or symptoms experienced by the patient and to more clearly define the problem to help in establishing a diagnosis(es) and management options	<ul><li>Constitutional (eg, fever, weight loss)</li><li>Eyes</li><li>Ears, nose, mouth, and throat</li><li>Cardiovascular</li><li>Respiratory</li><li>Gastrointestinal</li><li>Genitourinary</li><li>Musculoskeletal</li><li>Integumentary (skin or breast)</li><li>Neurologic</li><li>Psychiatric</li><li>Endocrine</li><li>Hematologic/lymphatic</li><li>Allergic/immunologic</li></ul>

The Elements of History, continued

History Components	Description	Elements
Past, family, and social history (PFSH)	Review of medical/surgical history	Illnesses, injuries, treatments, surgeries, hospitalizations, current medications, allergies, age-appropriate immunization status, age-appropriate feeding or dietary status, pregnancy and birth history (weight, Apgar score), developmental history
	Review of medical events in the patient's family that may place a patient at risk	Health status or cause of death of family members, specific diseases of family members, hereditary disorders in the family
	Age-appropriate review of activities	Living arrangements; use of drugs, alcohol, and tobacco by patient or caregiver; education level; sexual history; domestic violence; other relevant social factors

Four Levels of History Defined

Level of History	CPT® Guidelines	1995 Guidelines	1997 Guidelines
Problem focused	CC Brief HPI	CC Brief HPI (1–3 elements)	Same as 1995
Expanded problem focused	CC Brief HPI Problem-pertinent system review	CC Brief HPI (1–3 elements) Problem-pertinent system review (one system)	Same as 1995
Detailed	CC Extended HPI Problem-pertinent system review to include a review of a limited number of additional systems Pertinent PFSH directly related to the patient's problems	CC Extended HPI (4 elements or status of 3 chronic conditions) Extended system review to include a review of a limited number of additional systems (2–9 systems) Pertinent PFSH directly related to the patient's problems (requires one item from past, family, or social history)	Same as 1995
Comprehensive	CC Extended HPI ROS directly related to the problem(s) identified in the HPI plus a review of all additional body systems Complete PFSH	CC Extended HPI ROS directly related to the problem(s) identified in the HPI plus a review of all additional body systems (at least 10 of 14 systems) Complete PFSH **Established patient** Office/outpatient/home, nursing home visits, subsequent hospital visits, or emergency department visits require one item from 2 areas of PFSH. **New patient** Office/outpatient/home, nursing facility visits, initial outpatient/inpatient hospital visits, consultations, or comprehensive nursing facility assessments require one item from all 3 areas of PFSH.	Same as 1995

Chapter 4: Evaluation and Management Documentation and Coding Guidelines

Physical Examination

Most payers follow the 1995 and 1997 CMS guidelines. The major difference between *CPT*® and the 1995 and 1997 CMS guidelines is the definition of the physical examination component.

- ☀ A general multisystem examination or a single organ system examination is not specialty-specific.
- ☀ The 1995 guidelines
  - ❖ Are easier to follow and less complex with no bullet points and, therefore, are perceived as more "forgiving."
    - ☀ The 1997 guidelines
      - ❖ Are very specific with regard to the performance of specific elements of a physical examination and documentation requirements.
      - ❖ An element is defined as a description of the examination or assessment of a specified site or area. To "count" as part of an examination component, the documentation has to be very specific.
      - ❖ Specific elements have been developed for general multisystem and specialty examinations. The elements are described under each body area and organ system recognized by *CPT*. The lists of examination elements are included in the 1997 documentation guidelines (see Appendix A).
  - ❖ Pediatric subspecialists in particular may find them more applicable.
  - ❖ Recognized body areas
    - — Head, including the face
    - — Neck
    - — Chest, including breasts and axilla
    - — Abdomen
    - — Genitalia, groin, and buttocks
    - — Back
    - — Each extremity
  - ❖ Recognized organ systems
    - — Constitutional (vital signs, general appearance)
    - — Eyes
    - — Ears, nose, mouth, and throat
    - — Cardiovascular
    - — Respiratory
    - — Gastrointestinal
    - — Genitourinary
    - — Musculoskeletal
    - — Skin
    - — Neurologic
    - — Psychiatric
    - — Hematologic, lymphatic, and immunologic

The extent of the examination performed depends on clinical judgment and the nature of the presenting problem(s). There are 4 levels of physical examination defined.

> ||||||||| *Coding Pearl* |||||||||
>
> The extent of the examination performed depends on clinical judgment and the nature of the presenting problem(s) or patient presentation.

Levels of Physical Examination

Level of Examination	CPT® Guidelines	1995 Guidelines	1997 Guidelines[a]
Problem focused	Limited examination of the affected area or system	Limited examination of the affected area or system	Performance and documentation of 1–5 elements identified by a bullet (●) in one or more areas or systems
Expanded problem focused	Limited examination of the affected body area or organ system and other symptomatic or related organ system(s)	Limited examination of the affected body area or organ system and other symptomatic or related organ system(s)	Performance and documentation of at least 6 elements identified by a bullet (●) in one or more areas or systems
Detailed problem focused	Extended examination of the affected body area(s) and other symptomatic or related organ system(s)	Extended examination of the affected body area(s) and other symptomatic or related organ system(s)	Performance and documentation of at least 2 elements identified by a bullet (●) in at least 6 areas or systems or at least 12 elements identified by a bullet (●) in at least 2 areas or systems
Comprehensive	General multisystem examination or a complete examination of a single organ system	General multisystem examination (requires 8 or more organ systems) or a complete examination of a single organ system	Multisystem examination—Examination of at least 9 organ systems or body areas with performance of all elements identified by a bullet (●) in each area/system examined Documentation is expected for at least 2 elements identified by a bullet (●) of each area(s) or system(s). Single organ system examination—Performance of all elements identified by a bullet (●) and documentation of every element in each box with a shaded border and at least one element in a box with an unshaded border

[a]These examination requirements may be different depending on the specialty.

Documentation Requirements and Tips

- All body areas and organ systems examined must be documented individually with relevant positive or negative findings appropriate to that area or system.
- Documentation of "normal" or "negative" is acceptable on any examined body area(s) or system(s) with the exception of the area(s) and/or system(s) that is symptomatic or affected. Pertinent findings from the physical examination must be documented for each affected or symptomatic area or system.
- All abnormal findings must be documented.
- The medical record must clearly indicate the areas/systems examined.
- Documentation of a comprehensive-level examination should include specific findings of at least 8 organ systems (based on the 1995 guidelines).

||||||| **Coding Pearl** |||||||

Pertinent findings from the physical examination must be documented for each affected or symptomatic area or system.

Chapter 4: Evaluation and Management Documentation and Coding Guidelines

- Use of a checklist is acceptable. If a checklist is used to document the examination, written descriptions with positive or negative findings should be documented for any area or system related to the problem or complaint.
  - A checklist without any specific findings, whether negative or normal for symptomatic systems, does not truly constitute a comprehensive (eg, thorough) level examination.
- Documentation of "normal" or "negative" or a simple check mark denoting normal examination findings is accepted documentation for examination of an unaffected body area or asymptomatic organ system under the 1995 and 1997 CMS guidelines. However, this method of documentation is only counted as one element when following the 1997 CMS guidelines.
  - Example: If a check mark is used to document a normal examination of the abdomen, it would count as one element unless further documentation indicates that, for example, the liver and spleen were normal, no masses or tenderness was noted, and there was no hernia. This more complete documentation would support the performance of 3 elements under the 1997 guidelines.

Following are 2 examples of acceptable documentation using different styles:

Acceptable Documentation of Examination of a Patient With Vomiting and Fever			
	Normal	**Abnormal**	**Findings**
Gen appearance		x	Sick appearing, fussy, temperature 102.8°F
Eyes	x		
Head	x		
ENT	x		Tympanic membranes normal, nasopharynx normal
Neck	x		Without tenderness or masses
Respiratory		x	Tachypnea, wheezing, rhonchi bilaterally, subcostal retractions
Cardio		x	Tachycardia
GI/Abdomen	x		Soft, non-tender; liver and spleen normal
GU	x		
Skin	x		

OR

PE: sick appearing; fussy; temperature 102.8°F; head: normal; eyes: normal; ENT: tympanic membranes normal; neck: without tenderness or masses; cardio: tachycardia; lungs: tachypnea, wheezing, rhonchi bilaterally, subcostal retractions; GI: normal; GU: normal; skin: normal

What level examination is this?

1995 Guidelines—This example would be considered a comprehensive-level examination (examination of 8 organ systems). Documentation reflects specific findings on the pertinent areas and systems.

1997 Guidelines—This example would be considered a detailed-level examination. A detailed examination in the 1997 guidelines requires documentation of at least 2 elements identified by a bullet (●) from at least 6 areas or systems or at least 12 elements identified by a bullet in at least 2 areas or systems.

This example demonstrates the importance of clear, concise, and thorough documentation. It is not meant to discourage any physician from using the 1997 guidelines because these guidelines are very beneficial to the specialist. Physicians may use the 1995 or 1997 documentation guidelines to justify a level of E/M coding. It's your decision.

Medical Decision-making

Medical decision-making typically determines the level of an E/M service because it supports the level of history and physical examination, medical necessity, and severity of illness. Some payers and audit contractors are now requiring MDM as one of the 2 key components supporting the level of service for established patient E/M services in response to conceived issues of over-documentation of history and examination in electronic health records (EHRs).

The descriptions in the levels of MDM are vague. The ambiguity is deliberate because of the variability within and between specialties. Physicians must use their best judgment in selecting the level of MDM. Medical decision-making is based on the complexity of establishing a diagnosis and/or selecting the management or treatment plan. There are 3 elements used to determine the level of MDM.

> ||||||| **Coding Pearl** |||||||
>
> Physicians must document the complexity of establishing a diagnosis and selecting the management plan.

1. Number of possible diagnoses and/or management options

Considerations	Circumstances That May Increase Complexity When Determining Treatment Management
☀ The number and types of problems or conditions that are addressed ☀ The number of management options that are considered in the treatment of the patient ☀ The complexity involved in establishing the diagnosis and plan (referral, prescriptions, diagnostic tests) ☀ The nature of the presenting problem	☀ There is an undiagnosed problem. ☀ A problem or condition is unresponsive to treatment. ☀ A number of problems or conditions are being addressed. ☀ One problem or condition may have several management options. ☀ The risk of morbidity without treatment is moderate or high. ☀ There is a need for advice from others. ☀ There is a need for ordering or reviewing a number of tests or medical records.

2. Amount and/or complexity of data ordered and/or reviewed

Considerations	Circumstances That May Increase Complexity
☀ The number of diagnostic tests ordered and/or reviewed ☀ The complexity of the tests and/or procedures and their review ☀ Nature of the presenting problem	☀ The combination of types of diagnostic tests (pulse oximetry, chest x-ray, pulmonary function test) that are required usually constitutes a higher level of complexity in this category, while performing 1 or 2 tests within a category of service (eg, hematocrit and urinalysis) usually constitutes a minimal level. ☀ Review and summarization of old medical records. ☀ Results discussed with another physician. ☀ Order or review of invasive or complex diagnostic tests (eg, lumbar puncture, magnetic resonance imaging, computed tomography, imaging studies). ☀ Obtaining additional history with summarization in the medical record. ☀ Poor historian or no history. ☀ Problems or complaints are vague. ☀ Obtaining advice from others.

Chapter 4: Evaluation and Management Documentation and Coding Guidelines

3. Risk of significant complications, morbidity, and/or mortality

Considerations	Circumstances That May Increase Complexity
• The overall risk associated with the patient's presenting problem(s) (ie, comorbidities, underlying diseases or factors) • Risk related to the disease process that is anticipated between the present encounter and the next one • Risk during and immediately following any diagnostic tests and/or procedures • Risk associated with the treatment and/or management options • Nature of the presenting problem	• Poor patient compliance • Uncertain prognosis • Increased probability of functional impairment • Need for invasive procedure or surgery • Need for prescription drug management • Need for intravenous therapy • Need for intensive or critical care • Surgical risk factors

Four Levels of Medical Decision-making Defined
(2 of 3 components must be met or exceeded.)

Level of Medical Decision-making	Number of Diagnoses or Management Options	Amount and/or Complexity of Data	Risk of Complications and/or Morbidity and Mortality
Straightforward	Minimal	Minimal or none	Minimal
Low complexity	Limited	Limited	Low
Moderate complexity	Multiple	Moderate	Moderate
High complexity	Extensive	Extensive	High

CMS Table of Risk

- Developed as part of the 1995 and 1997 documentation guidelines for E/M services to help physicians select level of risk using clinical examples.
- Level of risk can be determined by selecting the highest level of risk from any of the 3 categories in the table.
- Level of risk alone does not determine the complexity of MDM. It is only 1 of the 3 elements of MDM. For example, prescription drug management alone does not constitute moderate-level MDM because it is only 1 of the 3 components of MDM.
- While some items in the CMS Table of Risk may not necessarily focus on items relevant to infants and children, pediatricians can extrapolate and apply the relative hierarchy of principles and concepts embedded within the table to their own population of patients.

CMS Table of Risk

Level of Risk	Presenting Problem(s)	Diagnostic Procedure(s) Ordered	Management Options Selected
Minimal	• One self-limited or minor problem (eg, cold, insect bite, tinea corporis)	• Laboratory tests requiring venipuncture • Chest x-rays • Electrocardiogram/ electroencephalogram • Urinalysis • Ultrasound (eg, echocardiography)	• Rest • Gargles • Elastic bandages • Superficial dressings

CMS Table of Risk, continued

Level of Risk	Presenting Problem(s)	Diagnostic Procedure(s) Ordered	Management Options Selected
Low	• Two or more self-limited or minor problems • One stable chronic illness (eg, well-controlled hypertension, non–insulin-dependent diabetes, cataract, benign prostatic hyperplasia) • Acute uncomplicated illness or injury (eg, cystitis, allergic rhinitis, simple sprain)	• Potassium hydroxide preparation • Physiological tests not under stress (eg, pulmonary function tests) • Non-cardiovascular imaging studies with contrast (eg, barium enema) • Superficial needle biopsies • Clinical laboratory tests requiring arterial puncture • Skin biopsies	• Over-the-counter drugs • Minor surgery with no identified risk factors • Physical therapy • Occupational therapy • Intravenous fluids without additives
Moderate	• One or more chronic illnesses with mild exacerbation, progression, or side effects of treatment • Two or more stable chronic illnesses • Undiagnosed new problem with uncertain prognosis (eg, lump in breast) • Acute illness with systemic symptoms (eg, pyelonephritis, pneumonitis, colitis) • Acute complicated injury (eg, head injury with brief loss of consciousness)	• Physiological tests under stress (eg, cardiac stress test, fetal contraction stress test) • Diagnostic endoscopies with no identified risk factors • Deep needle or incisional biopsy • Cardiovascular imaging studies with contrast and no identified risk factors (eg, arteriogram, cardiac catheterization) • Obtain fluid from body cavity (eg, lumbar puncture, thoracentesis, culdocentesis)	• Minor surgery with identified risk factors • Elective major surgery (open, percutaneous, or endoscopic) with no identified risk factors • Prescription drug management • Therapeutic nuclear medicine • Intravenous fluids with additives • Closed treatment of fracture or dislocation without manipulation
High	• One or more chronic illnesses with severe exacerbation, progression, or side effects of treatment • Acute or chronic illnesses or injuries that pose a threat to life or body function (eg, multiple trauma, acute myocardial infarction, pulmonary embolus, severe respiratory distress, progressive severe rheumatoid arthritis, psychiatric illness with potential threat to self or others, peritonitis, acute renal failure) • An abrupt change in neurologic status (eg, seizure, transient ischemic attack, weakness, sensory loss)	• Cardiovascular imaging studies with contrast with identified risk factor • Cardiac electrophysiological tests • Diagnostic endoscopies with identified risk factors • Discography	• Elective major surgery (open, percutaneous, or endoscopic) with identified risk factors • Emergency major surgery (open, percutaneous, or endoscopic) • Parenteral controlled substances • Drug therapy requiring intensive monitoring for toxicity • Decision not to resuscitate or to deescalate because of poor prognosis

Chapter 4: Evaluation and Management Documentation and Coding Guidelines

Establishing the Level of Medical Decision-making Performed

- To meet the level of complexity of MDM, 2 of the 3 elements described must be met.
- The number of diagnoses or associated risk alone does not determine the level of MDM. For example, the patient with fever and no findings on examination may require an increased complexity of decision-making to try to establish a differential diagnosis or manage the condition (combination of tests or diagnostic procedures, discussion with another physician).
  - The descriptors listed in the CMS Table of Risk are vague and often difficult to quantify.
  - There are no defined parameters for the number of diagnoses or management options that are necessary to satisfy the requirement for each level of MDM.
  - A good guide to follow is to use the nature of the presenting problem in association with the examples listed under the presenting problem(s) in the CMS Table of Risk, with good supporting documentation.

> |||||||| **Coding Pearl** ||||||||
>
> Documentation to support MDM may be found throughout a progress note.

Documentation Requirements and Tips

Management options are supported with documentation of the problems or conditions being addressed, the patient's progress and response to treatment, and the resulting plan of care. Documentation to support MDM may be found throughout a progress note in the history and physical examination portion of the encounter as well as in the assessment and plan. Documentation should include

- Specific findings on examination that support the risk (eg, increased work of breathing, rebound tenderness)
- Elements of a patient's history that support risk (eg, a newborn whose mother used drugs while pregnant)
- That a problem or condition is stable, resolving, worsening, well controlled, or not responding to treatment (eg, diabetes under control, pneumonia resolving, otitis media resolved)
- The diagnoses and/or management options being considered (eg, will determine need for ultrasound)
- An impression, differential diagnoses (eg, viral vs bacterial or differential diagnoses include…)
- The level of uncertainty and patient risk (eg, abdominal pain of unclear etiology, fever with neutropenia)
- Response to treatment (eg, resolved after antibiotics)
- Patient compliance with the treatment plan (eg, noncompliant with diet plan)
- Psychosocial or cognitive factors that increase the effort to obtain information or that affect management options (eg, access to care)
- Support for ordering tests and procedures (eg, rule out urinary tract infection, hydronephrosis on prenatal ultrasound)
- Review of test results (eg, strep test negative, urinalysis shows ++ketones)
- Initiation or revision of treatment plans (eg, renew medication, albuterol as needed)
- Instructions for prescription management, home care, and follow-up care (eg, return for follow-up in 2 weeks, over-the-counter medications)
- Need for consultations (eg, persistent otitis media—will consult otolaryngologist)
- Insight into what the thought processes were that lead to the diagnosis(es) and management options, ordering/review of data, and level of risk (eg, patient complains of burning on urination; examination: listless, skin turgor poor; assessment: reflux likely due to overfeeding)

Examples of Levels of Medical Decision-making

Minimal—*One self-limited or minor problem*
Examples
Diagnosis: uninfected bug bite, wart, resolved upper respiratory infection (URI)/otitis media (OM), sore throat
Documented management options: no treatment necessary, rest, gargle
Nature of the presenting problem/risk: minimal or self-limited

Limited—*Two or more self-limited or minor problems, one stable chronic illness, acute uncomplicated illness or injury*
Examples
Diagnoses: minor feeding problem, umbilical drainage, stable attention-deficit/hyperactivity disorder (ADHD), asthma, URI, OM, acute gastroenteritis without systemic symptoms, tonsillitis
Documented management options: prescription drug management versus over-the-counter drugs, rule out allergy, rhinitis versus URI
Nature of the presenting problem/risk: low

Moderate—*One or more chronic illnesses with mild exacerbation progression or side effect of treatment; 2 or more stable chronic illnesses; undiagnosed new problem with uncertain prognosis; acute illness with systemic symptoms; 3 or more self-limited problems (Although not specified on the risk table, this would be appropriate based on the extent of problems or conditions addressed.)*
Examples
Diagnoses: exacerbation of asthma, increased behavioral issues associated with ADHD, persistent asthma, chronic eczema, cystic fibrosis or diabetes, acute gastroenteritis with mild to moderate dehydration, bronchiolitis, pyelonephritis, abdominal pain, pneumonia, chronic OM with fever
Documented management options: prescription drug management versus over-the-counter therapy, diagnostic testing, referrals, discussion with other physicians, observation or inpatient hospital admission, rule out respiratory syncytial virus (RSV) versus bronchiolitis, appendicitis versus pelvic inflammatory disease
Nature of the presenting problem/risk: moderate

High—*One or more chronic illnesses with severe exacerbation, progression, or side effects of treatment; acute or chronic illnesses or injuries that pose a threat to life or bodily function; abrupt change in neurologic status; 4 or more stable or chronic illnesses (Although not specified on the risk table, this would be appropriate based on the extent of problems or conditions addressed.)*
Examples
Diagnoses: seizure, exacerbation of asthma with respiratory distress, cyanotic heart disease, RSV, child abuse, meningitis, sickle cell crisis
Documented management options: admission to inpatient hospital, major surgery, invasive diagnostic tests
Nature of the presenting problem/risk: high

General documentation requirements are noted throughout the CMS 1995 and 1997 guidelines.

Time

Key guidelines for using time as the controlling factor in the selection of an E/M service include

❖ Time shall be used as the key component in the selection of an E/M code if there is an assigned typical time *and* counseling and/or coordination of care account for more than 50% of the physician face-to-face time (for outpatient) or floor/unit time (for inpatient) with the patient and/or family.

|||||||| **Coding Pearl** ||||||||

Only physicians or other qualified health care professionals with their own National Provider Identifier may report services using time as the key component.

Chapter 4: Evaluation and Management Documentation and Coding Guidelines

- The time spent in counseling and/or coordination of care may be with the patient, family, and/or those who may have assumed responsibility for the care of the patient (eg, foster parents, legal guardian, person acting in loco parentis).
- The term *counseling* is broadly defined by *CPT®* as most activities that are not procedures and includes discussions about a condition and/or its management. Per *CPT,* counseling includes
  - Diagnostic results, impressions, and/or recommended diagnostic studies
  - Prognosis
  - Risks and benefits of management (treatment) options
  - Instructions for management (treatment) and/or follow-up
  - Importance of compliance with chosen management (treatment) options
  - Risk factor reduction
  - Patient and family education
- Time spent on a particular calendar day does not have to be continuous.
- Only physicians or qualified health care professionals with their own National Provider Identifier (NPI) may report services using time as the key component. Keep in mind that the "incident-to" requirements are Medicare policy, and commercial payers may have their own policies. Please refer to the Medicare Incident-To Requirements section in this chapter.
- When time is used as the controlling factor in the selection of an E/M code and the service is provided by a resident, the time reported is based on the face-to-face time (for outpatient) or floor/unit time (for inpatient) spent by the teaching physician with the patient or caregiver. Refer to the Physicians at Teaching Hospitals (PATH) Guidelines section in this chapter.
- When selecting an E/M code based on time and the actual time is between 2 typical times, select the code with a typical time that is closest to the total physician time spent and documented. For example, if a physician spent 35 minutes face-to-face with an established patient in the office (and if the visit met the conditions for time-based coding), the physician would report the service with *CPT* code **99215** (typical time of 40 minutes). Note that this is a *CPT* guideline and some payers may not allow "rounding up."

CPT Definition of Face-to-Face Time

Office/Outpatient	Inpatient Hospital, Observation Setting, Nursing Home
Direct physician to patient and/or family member/other with responsibility for care of the patient	Floor/unit time dedicated to the one patient Includes the time spent at the patient's bedside, counseling the family/patient, and on the floor documenting and coordinating care with the patient's care team members

Documentation of Time Spent in Counseling and/or Coordination of Care

According to the guidelines as specified in the AMA publication *Principles of CPT® Coding,* when selecting a code based on time, the medical record documentation must reflect

1. The amount of time and extent of counseling and/or coordination of care services provided
2. Distinguishing of that time from time spent performing key components by reporting time separately
3. The total time spent face-to-face (for outpatient) or floor/unit (for inpatient)
4. A summary of the discussion items and/or the coordination of care efforts

If the entire face-to-face encounter is spent in counseling only, the total time spent and a summary of the discussion items must be clearly documented.

In distinguishing the time and extent of counseling and/or coordination of care services for a service that includes time spent performing key components, physicians may document the estimated number of minutes or the percentage of the documented total face-to-face time that was spent in counseling and coordination of care. See Examples for Documenting Time box.

The summary of discussion items and/or coordination of care efforts should be sufficient in detail to support the selection of a code based on time (eg, include options discussed, patient/caregiver concerns addressed, summary of patient and family education).

Coding Conundrum: Child Is Not Present

It is common in pediatrics to have a parent come into the office to discuss a child's condition or problem without the child present. *Current Procedural Terminology®* clarifies that counseling and/or coordination of care can be provided to those who have assumed responsibility for the care of the patient or decision-making even if they are not family members (eg, foster parents, legal guardians, persons acting in loco parentis). Therefore, counseling of those responsible for the care of the patient without the patient present is reported with the various levels of E/M service. It does not matter if the patient is a new or an established patient, although typically counseling and/or coordination of care with family members alone is performed for established patients. The pediatrician can report this E/M service using time as the key factor even if the child is not present. However, some payers require that the patient be present. Be aware of payer-specific requirements. These services are performed on behalf of the patient and reported under the patient's name, not the parent's name.

Examples for Documenting Time

Counseling in the office might be documented as follows:
- Spoke with xxxxx about, and
- 40-minute visit with approximately 25 minutes spent discussing xxxxx, or
- T = # minutes; C = # minutes; Counseled regarding xxxxx, or
- Total face-to-face time was 40 minutes with greater than 50% spent in counseling and/or coordination of care

If you choose to use the second method for documentation of time, be sure to include a description of T (total time) and C (counseling time) in your office policy. Otherwise, the documentation should state "total time" or "counseling time."

Hospital/observation care progress notes might be documented as follows:
- 25 minutes spent on floor with patient, nursing staff, and physical therapy regarding xxxxx or document time in and time out.
- Timed chart entry in the progress notes or orders may be enough to support floor time. Caseworkers, physical therapists, etc, may document the time spent communicating with the physician. All of these documented entries may support total floor time.

If you use a template for your progress notes, include space for reporting face-to-face time, counseling time, and a summary of discussion items. If you are using EHRs, make software changes to accommodate the documentation requirements. Do not just use the "office time" as shown in your EHR because that does not reflect face-to-face time.

New Versus Established Patient

For some encounters (office, home, and preventive medicine), a distinction is made between new and established patients. *Current Procedural Terminology®* defines a new patient as "one who has not received any face-to-face professional services from the physician or another physician of the *exact* same specialty *and subspecialty* who belongs to the same group practice, within the past three years" (ie, if a patient's only practice contact for the past 3 years has been non–face-to-face, such as telephone or online services, the patient would be considered a new patient on return for a face-to-face service).

The complexity of care required for a new patient visit does not equal the complexity of care required for an established patient visit. New patient codes require that all 3 key components be met, while established patient visit codes only require that 2 of the 3 key components be met, unless coding is based on counseling and/or coordination of care time.

Examples

> ‖‖‖‖‖‖ **Coding Pearl** ‖‖‖‖‖‖
>
> If a physician is covering for another physician of the same specialty, the patient's encounter is reported as it would have been by the physician who is not available.

- If a physician of a different specialty is covering for another physician (eg, pediatrician covering for a family physician) and has the first face-to-face contact with the other physician's established patient, the encounter is considered new. If a physician is covering for another physician of the same specialty, the patient's encounter is coded as it would have been by the physician who is not available. For example, an established patient for a pediatrician is seen by the on-call pediatrician. The on-call pediatrician should report that patient as established.
- When a new physician joins a group of other pediatricians, patients who follow the physician to the new practice are considered to be established patients to any of the pediatricians in the new practice because the patients were seen by a physician of the same specialty in the group within the past 3 years.
- If the physician has moved to a different location or changed his or her tax identification number, patients would still be considered established if they were established patients before these changes took place.
- When a newborn or child is examined in the hospital (eg, in the emergency department) and is subsequently examined in the office by the same physician or member of the same group and same specialty, the newborn or child is considered an established patient.
- A nonphysician provider (NPP) who may report E/M services is considered to be working in the exact same specialty and subspecialty as the supervising physician. (Medicare assigns different specialty designations to NPPs and does not consider the specialty of the physician providing supervision in new patient determination. Medicaid and private plans may follow Medicare practices.)

More Than One E/M Service on the Same Calendar Day

Current Procedural Terminology guidelines specify that one E/M service can be reported for services provided to a patient by the same physician (or another physician of the same specialty in the same group practice with the same tax identification number) on the same day of service. However, if the problems for which the services were required are unrelated, both E/M services may be reported.

- Services are related.
  - ❖ One E/M service is reported based on the combined services of both physicians.
- Services are unrelated.
  - ❖ Each service is reported based on the performance and documentation of the required key components.
  - ❖ Each service is reported with the diagnosis or condition that was addressed.
  - ❖ Modifier **25** is appended to the second service to indicate that a significant, separately identifiable service was performed.
    - — The National Correct Coding Initiative (NCCI) edits developed for the CMS Medicare program may have edits or coding pairs that will require the use of modifier **25** on a particular E/M service to override the edit.
    - — Prior to reporting 2 E/M services on the same day of service for the same patient, check the NCCI edits. (See Chapter 3 to learn about the NCCI.)

Be prepared to submit a copy of the medical record to payers.

> ||||||||| *Coding Pearl* |||||||||
>
> If reporting 2 unrelated E/M services on the same day, be prepared to submit a copy of the medical record to payers.

More E/M Documentation and Coding Tips

- When using an EHR system that copies the ROS and PFSH from one visit to the next, the physician must document his or her review of the copied information. Only the history that is pertinent to the problem addressed at that visit and reviewed should be used to determine the level of history for the selection of a code. (Please see Coding Conundrum: Pitfalls of EHR Coding on page 346 of Chapter 14 for more on this topic.)
- A pertinent PFSH may be indicated for an area that is related to the problem or condition. A complete PFSH may be required when a more comprehensive assessment is indicated.
- Although *CPT*® currently requires that documentation support any 2 of 3 key components for established patient and subsequent encounters in a facility, some payers require that 1 of the 2 key components is MDM.
- Determine which set of guidelines best serves your practice and document which set of guidelines is used by your practice in your policies and procedures manual.
- Using a line drawn down a physical examination checklist is not sufficient unless the documentation clearly defines the exact area or system examined. Most coders and auditors will advise physicians and physician extenders not to use lines but to define the area or system examined more clearly by using individual check marks or circles.
- Ideally, physicians in a group practice should be consistent in their documentation policies. However, if documentation practices differ between physicians, have those differences documented in the practice's written policies.
- Although it may be a physician's preference to perform a detailed or comprehensive examination at every visit, only the level of physical examination that is medically indicated should be used in the selection of the code.
- Counseling about a condition emerging as part of the information gathering for the primary diagnosis may appropriately be included in total time of counseling (eg, discussing ways to increase caloric intake in a patient with anorectic effects of medication for ADHD).

* The code selected for a new patient will often be one level lower than for an established patient for the same amount of work. However, the Medicare relative value units are higher for new patient visits, compensating the physician for the extra work required.

* If using a template for progress notes, include space for reporting face-to-face time, counseling time, and summary of the discussion. If using an EHR system, make software changes to accommodate documentation requirements. Do not use "office time" because that is not a reflection of face-to-face time.

* The AAP has developed forms that promote good documentation of office or outpatient visits. Examples are included in Appendix B-3 and can be found online at www.aap.org/cfp (access code AAPCFP20). They can also be ordered from the AAP by calling 888/227-1770 or by visiting http://shop.aap.org.

Scope of Practice Laws

Many *CPT*® codes and modifiers include reference to the performance of a service or procedure by a physician or other qualified health care professional (eg, pediatric immunization administration, modifier **76**).

Scope of practice is terminology that is used by state licensing boards for various professions to define the procedures, actions, and processes that are permitted for a licensed individual.

The level of medical responsibility or health services (boundaries within which a health care professional may practice) or range of activities that a practitioner is legally authorized to perform is based on his or her specific education and experience.

Physicians, registered nurses, clinical nurse practitioners, physician assistants, licensed practical nurses (LPNs), physical therapists, and nutritionists are among some of the professions for which scope of practice laws are defined. However, it can vary by state.

Every state has laws and regulations that describe the requirements of education and training for health care professionals. However, some states do not have different scope of practice laws for every level of professional (eg, LPN).

The *CPT* definition of a "qualified health care professional" is as follows:

A "physician or other qualified health care professional" is an individual who is qualified by education, training, licensure/regulation (when applicable), and facility privileging (when applicable) who performs a professional service within his or her scope of practice and independently reports that professional service. These professionals are distinct from "clinical staff." A clinical staff member is a person who works under the supervision of a physician or other qualified health care professional and who is allowed by law, regulation, and facility policy to perform or assist in the performance of a specified professional service but who does not individually report that professional service. Other policies may also affect who may report specific services.

||||||||| *Coding Pearl* |||||||||

Incident-to provisions apply only in the office or other out-patient setting.

Medicare Incident-To Requirements: Supervision of Nonphysician Health Care Professionals

Billing for care provided by allied health professionals (AHPs) requires careful attention to state licensure and local payer requirements. Most state Medicaid programs and commercial payers follow these Medicare payment rules. Some have their own policies addressing incident-to provisions and certified NPP billing. Please see Medicare Requirements for Incident-To Services on page 85 for detailed requirements. Please see Chapter 12, section 30.6, of the *Medicare Claims Processing Manual* and Chapter 15, section 60, of the *Medicare Benefit Policy Manual* at http://cms.gov/manuals for detailed information on incident-to services. Check with your payers and obtain a copy of their specific policies.

* The CMS defines *incident to* as "services incident to the service of a physician or other professional permitted by statute to bill for services incident to their services when those services meet all of the requirements applicable to the benefit."

* Incident-to services are always provided as a continuation of a physician's services and do not address new problems (eg, a nursing visit performed at patient/caregiver request and not based on a physician's recommendation is not an incident-to service).

* Although licensed NPPs and AHPs otherwise may bill for their services under their own NPI when they provide medically necessary services (within their state's scope of practice without direct physician supervision), the incident-to provision allows for reporting under the name and NPI of a supervising physician when the requirements of incident-to billing are met. Payment for NPPs billing under the incident-to provision may be 100% of the physician payment versus 85% when reporting under the NPP's individual NPI.

* Nonphysician providers without their own NPI must report services incident to a physician and must meet the entire incident-to requirements, including physician presence in the office suite and continuation of a physician's previously established plan of care.

* Physicians and qualified NPPs billing under their own NPI may

   1. Bill directly for services that they have personally performed.
   2. Bill for the services that are performed by any employee, leased employee, or contracted employee (eg, nurse practitioners, physician assistants, therapists, nurses, medical assistants, technicians). Any services performed by an employee who does not have his or her own individual NPI must be reported as incident to (when provided within the incident-to requirements).

The medical assistant, as allowed under state scope of practice laws, administers a nebulizer treatment that was ordered, documented, and directly supervised by the physician. The treatment (**94640**) would be reported under the physician's NPI. If the certified pediatric nurse practitioner (CPNP) had ordered the treatment, the service would be reported under the CPNP's NPI.

Split/Shared Evaluation and Management Services

A split/shared E/M service is one in which a physician and an NPP from the same group practice each personally perform a medically necessary and substantive portion of one or more face-to-face E/M encounters on the same date. A portion of the key components of the service must be provided face-to-face by the physician to report under the physician's NPI. Split/shared services were defined and implemented for services to Medicare beneficiaries. Private payers may adopt the same or a similar policy. The split/shared concept is applied differently for inpatient services than for services in the office or clinic setting.

* In the office or clinic setting, split/shared E/M services must meet incident-to

requirements for the service to be reported under the physician's NPI.

❖ The patient history and a portion of the examination are provided in the office by a nurse practitioner for an established patient in continuation of a physician's previously documented plan of care. The physician also sees the patient face-to-face and performs a more detailed examination and documents the assessment and plan of care. The total service may be reported under the physician's NPI because incident-to provisions have been met and both professionals provided face-to-face services.

◉ Split/shared services provided in the emergency department, outpatient departments, observation, or inpatient floor/unit of a facility may be reported by the physician (which may result in higher payment) or the NPP. This often occurs when the NPP and physician provide face-to-face hospital visits at different times on the same date.

The following apply to all split/shared services:

◉ The physician and NPP must document and sign their portion of the service. A physician cannot merely sign off on the documentation of the NPP's work.

◉ If the E/M service is reported based on counseling and/or coordination of care, only the physician's time is used to select the level of service. The physician must document his or her total time spent in counseling and/or coordination of care and a summary of the issues discussed or coordination of care provided.

◉ Critical care is never a split/shared service because critical care services reflect the work of only one individual.

◉ Split/shared billing does not apply in the nursing or skilled nursing facility settings.

Documentation Requirements and Tips When Reporting Incident-To Services

◉ Ancillary staff can document a CC, ROS, and PFSH. However, the physician must document the HPI. If the HPI is documented by ancillary staff, the physician must document his or her actual review of the HPI.

◉ Physicians must document their order for a service or treatment (eg, injection) that will be performed as incident to or document their plan for a follow-up visit in the treatment plan (eg, follow-up visit in 1 week for weight check). Medical record documentation must reflect the identity of the person providing the service.

◉ The supervising physician must document his or her supervision of the encounter and must cosign the encounter note when services are provided by ancillary staff (eg, nurse, medical assistant). Documentation may be as simple as "service performed/provided under the direct supervision of Dr X." The supervising physician's signature must be legible.

Medicare Requirements for Incident-To Services[a]

- Services must be related to the physician service and must be of a type commonly furnished in a physician office or clinic (physician owned and independent of a hospital or other facility), commonly performed without charge, or included in the physician/NPP service (eg, vital signs, assistance with dressing change).
- Services performed must be reasonable and medically necessary.
- Services performed must be within the employee's state scope of practice and require direct physician supervision. Direct supervision of auxiliary personnel requires that the physician (ie, any physician in the group practice) be on the premises (eg, in the office or facility) and be immediately available to provide assistance or direction. The supervising physician who is reporting the service (his or her name is on the claim form) must be the one who was providing the direct supervision.
- Services can only be provided to an established patient after the physician has performed the initial visit, established the plan of care, and established the physician-patient relationship. The physician must evaluate and initiate the treatment of new problems. The physician is not required to be involved in each subsequent patient encounter. Subsequent patient encounters and services must be incidental and integral to the initial service. They do not require physician involvement, but the physician must remain actively involved in a patient's treatment and must personally see the patient. Review of the medical record alone does not constitute active management of the patient.
- Time cannot be used as the controlling factor when counseling and/or coordination of care is performed incident to the physician. Therefore, when an E/M service is provided as incident to the physician (physician is not involved in the service) and time is the key factor (ie, history, physical examination, and MDM requirements are not met), only code 99211 (minimal office/outpatient E/M service) may be reported.
- Services provided in a home are covered only if there is direct supervision by the physician.
- Inpatient hospital services can be reported only if the physician sees the patient face-to-face. The physician must perform some portion of the required key components (history, physical examination, MDM) to report the encounter under his or her name. If the E/M encounter is reported based on time, only the physician face-to-face time is considered.
- Incident-to services cannot be billed for E/M services performed in the inpatient or outpatient hospital (unless a split/shared service is performed under the requirements of Transmittal 1776 for a nursing facility or home).
- Although diagnostic tests do not fall under incident-to provisions, the CMS requires certain levels of physician supervision for covered diagnostic tests. The Medicare Physician Fee Schedule database includes an indicator on each *CPT*® and Healthcare Common Procedure Coding System (HCPCS) code to define the level of supervision required. The 3 levels of physician supervision include general supervision (ie, the procedure is performed under the physician's overall direction and control but the physician's presence is not required during the performance of the test and the physician is responsible for personnel training and maintenance of the equipment and supplies), direct supervision (ie, the physician must be on the premises and immediately available to provide assistance or direction), or personal supervision (ie, the physician must be in the room while the test is being performed). Medicare regulations do not allow supervision of diagnostic tests by NPPs.
- Some payers may require the use of HCPCS codes and/or modifiers to identify services provided by AHPs.

[a]Note that the term physician *also includes qualified NPPs billing under their own NPI.*

Physicians at Teaching Hospitals (PATH) Guidelines

Physicians who supervise residents or other students in a teaching facility or their office need to have a clear understanding of the CMS Physicians at Teaching Hospitals (PATH) guidelines. Many state Medicaid programs and commercial payers have adopted the standards that were developed for Medicare services. A copy of the PATH guidelines can be found online at www.aap.org/cfp (access code AAPCFP20) and http://cms.gov/manuals/downloads/clm104c12.pdf, section 100.

Guidelines for Reporting E/M Services Under PATH Guidelines

- A teaching physician may bill for resident or fellow services if the teaching physician (1) personally performs the key components (history, physical examination, and MDM) of the service, (2) performs the key components jointly with a resident, or (3) personally observes the resident performing the key or critical components.

  - The level of service billed will be dependent on the level of work performed and documented by the resident and the teaching physician in combination or by the teaching physician if seen independent of the resident.

  - The teaching physician must document that he or she personally performed the service or was physically present (in the same room as the patient) during the key or critical portions of the service performed by the resident and participated in the management of the patient. The selected key or critical portion of the visit is at the discretion of the physician.

> **||||||| Coding Pearl |||||||**
>
> The only student (eg, medical student, NPP in training) obtained documentation that may be used for billing purposes is the ROS and/or PFSH.

- Medical students and other students (eg, physician assistants in training) are not considered or treated as interns or residents. Therefore, the only student documentation that may be used for billing purposes is the ROS and/or PFSH. Any other documentation recorded by a student cannot be used in the selection of the E/M code. The teaching physician must verify and personally document the HPI; indicate review of the ROS and PFSH; and perform and document the physical examination, assessment, and plan.

- Time-based services (eg, face-to-face prolonged services, critical care, and hospital discharge management) can only be billed when the teaching physician is present for the time required by the description of service. This also applies to E/M visits when time is considered the key component in the selection of the E/M code (>50% of the total face-to-face visit was spent counseling or coordinating care). The total time spent by the teaching physician must be documented.

- The teaching physician must document the key or critical part of the service personally performed, link his or her documentation back to the resident's note, and document that the care plan was reviewed and approved. It is not necessary to repeat the resident's documentation. However, the teaching physician documentation must be linked to the resident's note and all exceptions to the resident's findings must be documented. A signature alone is not acceptable documentation.

- Medicare guidelines stipulate that when documenting in an EHR, the teaching physician may use a macro (eg, predetermined text) as the required personal documentation if it is personally entered by the teaching physician. The resident or teaching physician must enter customized information to support medical necessity. If the resident and teaching physician use macros, the documentation is not sufficient.

Examples

- The resident admits a 2-month-old at 10:30 pm. The teaching physician's initial visit is performed the following morning at 8:00 am. The teaching physician reports an initial hospital care service based on the work personally performed that morning. See Chapter 8 for more information on reporting inpatient teaching physician services.

- The teaching physician sees the same patient for follow-up inpatient care subsequent to the resident's visit.

- The teaching physician and resident jointly admit or perform a subsequent visit on the same patient.

- The teaching physician performs the subsequent inpatient visit jointly with the resident.

Unacceptable	Minimal Documentation Acceptable
Countersignature	**Minimal documentation required**—"I performed a history and physical exam of the patient. Findings are consistent with Resident's note. Discussed patient's management with Resident and agree with his documented findings and plan of care." Signature
"Agree with above." Signature "Rounded, reviewed, agree." Signature	**Minimal documentation required**—"I saw and evaluated the patient. I agree with the findings and the plan of care as documented in Resident's note." Signature
"Patient seen with resident and evaluated." Signature "Seen and agree." Signature	**Minimal documentation required**—"I saw the patient with Resident and agree with Resident's findings and plans as written." Signature
"Discussed with resident." Signature	**Minimal documentation required**—"I was present with Resident during the history and exam. I discussed the case with Resident and agree with the findings and plan as documented in Resident's note." Signature

Primary Care Exception Rule (PCER)

The primary care exception rule (PCER) in the PATH guidelines allows teaching physicians to bill for services provided by residents under their supervision who have completed at least 6 months of approved graduate medical education (GME).

- To qualify for this exception, services must be provided in a teaching hospital ambulatory care center or clinic.
  - If the services are provided outside a hospital, there must be a written agreement with the teaching hospital that includes a contract outlining the payment for the teaching services or written documentation that the services will be "donated." In general, this exception cannot be applied in a private physician's office.

- Preventive medicine visit codes are not included in the Medicare exception at this time. Some state Medicaid programs have granted the exemption for preventive medicine services to established patients.

- No more than 4 residents can be supervised at a time by a teaching physician.

  This may include one resident with fewer than 6 months in a GME-approved residency program in the mix of 4 residents under the teaching physician's supervision. However, the teaching physician must be physically present for the critical or key portions of services furnished by the resident with fewer than 6 months in a GME-approved residency program. That is, the primary care exception does not apply in the case of the resident with fewer than 6 months in a GME-approved residency program.

- Patients seen should consider this practice as their primary location for health care.

> |||||||| **Coding Pearl** ||||||||
>
> Preventive medicine visit codes are not included in the Medicare PCER at this time despite continued advocacy from the AAP.

Chapter 4: Evaluation and Management Documentation and Coding Guidelines

- The teaching physician
  - ❖ Must be physically present in the clinic or office and immediately available to the residents and may not have other responsibilities (including supervising other personnel or seeing patients).
  - ❖ Must review the care provided (history, findings on physical examination, assessment, and treatment plan) during or immediately after each visit. The documentation must reflect the teaching physician's participation in the review and direction of the services performed.
  - ❖ May only report codes **99201–99203** for new patient visits or **99211–99213** for established patient visits. If a higher-level E/M service is necessary and performed, the teaching physician must personally participate in the care of the patient as outlined in the guidelines. As always, code selection is based on the E/M code descriptions and documentation guidelines.

The AAP continues to advocate for the preventive medicine service codes (**99381–99385** and **99391–99395**) to be included under the primary care exception. Look for updates in the *AAP Pediatric Coding Newsletter*™.

You can access the updated guidelines addressing the PCER at www.aap.org/cfp (access code AAPCFP20) or www.cms.gov/transmittals/downloads/R2247CP.pdf.

Example

➡ The teaching physician is supervising the resident in the clinic under the primary care exception. A child is diagnosed with acute otitis media. An expanded-level history and physical examination are performed with MDM of low complexity.

Unacceptable	Acceptable
Countersignature	"I reviewed Resident's note and agree with Resident's findings and plans as written." Signature
	"I reviewed Resident's note and agree but will refer to ENT for consultation." Signature

Reporting Procedures Under PATH Guidelines

Refer to Chapter 12, page 273, for the PATH guidelines for billing surgical, high-risk, or other complex procedures.

Preventive Services

Preventive Medicine Services

Preventive care is the hallmark of pediatrics. The Patient Protection and Affordable Care Act (PPACA) recognized the importance of preventive care for children, a critical provision of which ensures that the majority of health care plans cover *without cost sharing* the gold standard of pediatric preventive care—the American Academy of Pediatrics (AAP) *Bright Futures: Guidelines for Health Supervision of Infants, Children, and Adolescents,* 3rd Edition.

Coverage of and appropriate payment for these pediatric preventive services should, at a minimum, reflect the total relative value units outlined for the current year under the Medicare Resource-Based Relative Value Scale (RBRVS) Physician Fee Schedule, inclusive of all separately reported codes for these services. Section 2713 of the PPACA includes the following 2 sets of services that must be provided to children without cost sharing:
1. The standard set of immunizations recommended by the Advisory Committee on Immunization Practices (ACIP) of the Centers for Disease Control and Prevention (CDC) with respect to the individual involved
2. Evidence-informed preventive care and screenings provided for in the comprehensive guidelines supported by the Health Resources and Services Administration (HRSA), which include
   i. Bright Futures recommendations for preventive pediatric health care
   ii. Recommendations of the secretary's Discretionary Advisory Committee on Heritable Disorders in Newborns and Children

The Bright Futures interactive "Recommendations for Preventive Pediatric Health Care" (periodicity schedule) is a great tool to identify recommended age-appropriate services. In addition, it can be used to identify those services that can and should be reported with their own *Current Procedural Terminology (CPT®)* or Healthcare Common Procedure Coding System (HCPCS) code, and it identifies appropriate diagnosis coding. This tool can be accessed online at www.aap.org/periodicityschedule.

Preventive Medicine Services (99381–99397)

Well-child or preventive medicine services are a type of evaluation and management (E/M) service and are reported with codes **99381–99397.** Most health plans provide a 100% benefit (no patient out-of-pocket cost) for the 31 recommended preventive medicine service encounters when provided by network providers. The selection of the pediatric-specific codes **99381–99395** is based simply on the age of the patient and whether the patient is new or established (Table 5-1). In brief, an established patient has been seen by a physician or another physician of the same specialty and group practice within the last 3 years. Refer to Chapter 4 for more information about *new* versus an *established* patient.

- Preventive medicine services include counseling, anticipatory guidance, and risk-factor reduction interventions. No average or typical times are assigned to these services, unlike the times found in many other E/M codes.
- Immunizations, laboratory tests, and other special procedures or screening tests (eg, vision, hearing, developmental screening) that have their own specific *CPT* codes are reported separately *in addition to* preventive medicine E/M services.

> ||||||||| **Coding Pearl** |||||||||
>
> A comprehensive history performed as part of a preventive medicine visit does not require a chief complaint or history of present illness.

- A comprehensive history and physical examination must reflect an age- and gender-appropriate history/examination and are *not* synonymous with the "comprehensive" history and examination described in the E/M documentation guidelines from the Centers for Medicare & Medicaid Services (CMS) (see Chapter 4).

- The comprehensive history performed as part of a preventive medicine visit does not require a chief complaint or history of present illness. It does require a comprehensive age-appropriate review of systems with an updated past, family, and social history (PFSH). The history should also include a comprehensive assessment or history of age-pertinent risk factors.

- Routine management of contraception is considered part of the comprehensive preventive medicine E/M service when it is provided during the well visit.

- A comprehensive physical examination is a multisystem examination that may include a routine pelvic and breast examination (when performed in the absence of specific symptoms of a separate problem) depending on the age of the patient and/or sexual history.

- State Medicaid programs have requirements for performing, documenting, and reporting certain services in their Early Periodic Screening, Diagnosis, and Treatment (EPSDT) programs. Review your state Medicaid policies for the specific documentation and reporting requirements for services to patients in these programs.

- Most payers will require reporting modifier **25** with the preventive medicine service when immunizations or other services are also performed and reported.

Table 5-1. New and Established Preventive Medicine Codes

Code Description	New Patient Code	Established Patient Code
Comprehensive preventive medicine evaluation and management; infant (age <1 year)	99381	99391
early childhood (age 1–4 years)	99382	99392
late childhood (age 5–11 years)	99383	99393
adolescent (age 12–17 years)	99384	99394
age 18–39 years	99385	99395

Coding Conundrum: Pelvic and Breast Examinations Performed at the Preventive Medicine Service and Problem-Oriented Visit

A pelvic examination (with or without obtaining a Papanicolaou [Pap] test) and a breast examination are components of the preventive medicine examination. Code **99000** (handling and/or conveyance of specimen for transfer from the physician's office to a laboratory) may be reported in addition to the preventive medicine visit when a Pap test is obtained. Medicare requires reporting HCPCS code **Q0091** (screening Papanicolaou, obtaining, preparing, and conveyance of cervical and vaginal smear to laboratory) in addition to the E/M service. Some state Medicaid programs and commercial payers may also recognize obtaining a Pap test as a separate service. If reporting code **Q0091,** do not report **99000.**

If the pelvic examination is performed because of a gynecologic problem during a routine preventive medicine service, it may be appropriate to report a problem-oriented E/M service in addition to the preventive medicine service if this required additional physician work and required key components of the E/M code are met.

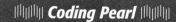

Reporting a Preventive Medicine Visit With a Problem-Oriented Visit

When a problem or abnormality is addressed *and requires significant additional work* (eg, symptomatic atopic dermatitis, exercise-induced asthma, migraine headache, poor academic performance in a patient with attention-deficit/hyperactivity disorder [ADHD]) to perform the required key components and is medically necessary, it may be reported using the office or other outpatient services code (**99201–99215**) in addition to the preventive medicine services code.

> |||||||| **Coding Pearl** ||||||||
>
> There should be additional documentation for preventive medicine and problem-oriented services when performed on the same calendar day.

When reporting both E/M services

- The levels of history and examination performed and documented relative to the problem or abnormality may be limited by the work already included in the preventive medicine service (ie, elements that are included in the preventive service cannot be counted toward the level of service for the problem-oriented service).

  - An age- and gender-appropriate examination is included in the preventive medicine service, but an extended examination of the affected body area(s) and other symptomatic or related organ system(s) would be separately considered in determining the level of E/M service provided to address the problem.

  - Because *CPT®* states that the comprehensive history of a preventive medicine service includes a comprehensive or interval PFSH, the level of problem-oriented history on the same date may be limited to expanded problem focused unless you can show that elements of the PFSH were obtained only in relation to the problem being addressed.

  - Payers may require medical decision-making (MDM) as 1 of the 2 key components met (ie, history and MDM or examination and MDM) to support an established patient visit.

- Documentation for each service should be maintained in the medical record. That documentation may be on a separate progress note or, if included on the same progress note, must clearly reflect the additional work performed. If the problem-oriented visit is reported based on time, documentation must clearly reflect (1) the total time spent in the face-to-face encounter addressing the issue(s) or problem(s), (2) the total time spent in counseling and/or coordination of care, and (3) a summary of the issues discussed.

- Well-care *International Classification of Diseases, Ninth Revision, Clinical Modification (ICD-9-CM)* diagnosis code **V20.31** (health supervision for newborn <8 days), **V20.32** (health supervision for newborn 8–28 days old), **V20.2** (routine infant or child check), or **V70.0** (general medical examination for older patients) should be linked to the appropriate preventive medicine code (**99381–99395**) and the sick care diagnosis code linked to the problem-oriented service code (**99201–99215**).

  - After transition to *International Classification of Diseases, 10th Revision, Clinical Modification (ICD-10-CM)*, well-care diagnosis code **Z00.110** (health supervision for newborn <8 days), **Z00.111** (health supervision for newborn 8–28 days old), **Z00.121** or **Z00.129** (routine child health examination with or without abnormal findings), or **Z00.00** or **Z00.01** (encounter for general adult medical examination without or with abnormal findings) should be linked to the appropriate preventive medicine code (**99381–99395**) and the sick care diagnosis code linked to the problem-oriented service code (**99201–99215**).

Transitioning to **10**

Chapter 5: Preventive Services

- The presence of a chronic condition(s) in and of itself does not change a preventive medicine visit to a problem-oriented visit, nor does it unilaterally support a separate problem-oriented E/M service (**99201–99215**) with the well visit, unless it is significant and has been separately addressed.
- An insignificant problem or condition (eg, minor diaper rash, stable chronic problem, renewal of prescription medications) that does not require additional work to perform the required key components cannot be reported.
  - Modifier **25** (significant, separately identifiable E/M service by the same physician on the same day of the procedure or other service) should be appended to the problem-oriented service code (eg, **99212**).
  - Some patients will be required to provide a co-payment for the non-preventive medicine visit code under the terms of their plan benefit even when there is no co-payment required for the preventive medicine visit. Legally this co-payment cannot routinely be written off.
  - The AAP has developed forms that promote good documentation of preventive medicine services. Examples are included in Appendix B and can be ordered from the AAP by calling 888/227-1770 or visiting http://shop.aap.org. Additionally, some state Medicaid programs have developed documentation templates for preventive services delivered in their EPSDT program.

Transitioning to 10

Although a separate E/M service is not reported when a minor problem or chronic condition requires less than significant additional work, code **Z00.121** (well-child check with abnormal findings) may be reported in addition to the code for the problem or chronic condition.

Coding Conundrum: Reporting 2 New Patient Codes on the Same Day

When a preventive medicine visit and problem-oriented E/M service are performed on the same day to a new patient, both codes may be reported with the appropriate new patient codes (eg, **99381** and **99203 25**).

Before reporting 2 new patient codes on the same patient on the same day of service, consider the following:

- A new patient office/outpatient visit requires that 3 of the 3 key components (history, physical examination, and MDM) or typical time (if more than 50% of the total face-to-face encounter is spent in counseling and/or coordination of care) be met.
- If only 2 of the 3 required key components are met (eg, the physical examination was part of the comprehensive preventive medicine service), the code selection would have to be based on an established patient code (**99212–99215**).
- In clinical situations in which the examination component of the problem-oriented visit for a new patient would be considered as distinct or in addition to what is normally performed during the preventive medicine examination, the physical examination component can be counted as a key element.

Examples

➤ **A mother of a new patient who presents for a well-child examination reports that her 6-year-old has been very disruptive at home and school since their move to the community.** In addition to the preventive medicine service, a total of 20 minutes is specifically spent by the physician counseling the mother and child on the disruptive behavior. Diagnosis for the problem-oriented service is adjustment disorder with conduct disturbance.

Preventive medicine visit

99383

ICD-9-CM

V20.2 (well-child check)

ICD-10-CM

Z00.121 (well-child check with abnormal findings)

Problem-oriented visit } **99202 25**
20 minutes spent
counseling

ICD-9-CM

309.3 (adjustment disorder with disturbance of conduct)

ICD-10-CM

F43.24 (adjustment disorder with disturbance of conduct)

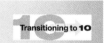
Transitioning to 10

Teaching Point: The level of service for the problem-oriented E/M service was selected based on time spent counseling and/or coordinating care. Coders should not assign a diagnosis of conduct disorder for disruptive behavior as specific diagnostic criteria are used in diagnosing behavior disorders. **Consult the physician or other qualified health care professional with questions about the appropriate code assignment.**

➤ **A 12-month-old girl is seen for a new patient preventive medicine visit.**
Mother states that she has been crying when voiding for 2 days and her urine "smells bad." Review of systems reveals that she had a fever of 100°F last night, is voiding more frequently, and is irritable. A comprehensive physical examination is performed. Urinalysis is consistent with a urinary tract infection (UTI). A urine culture is ordered. She is placed on antibiotics for 10 days. Mother is advised to follow up in 2 weeks.

Preventive medicine visit

99382

ICD-9-CM

V20.2 (well-child check)

ICD-10-CM

Z00.121 (well-child check with abnormal findings)

Problem-oriented visit } **99213 25**

MDM: Moderate complexity

History: Expanded problem focused

Physical examination: Included in preventive medicine visit

ICD-9-CM

599.0 (UTI)

ICD-10-CM

N39.0 (UTI)

Transitioning to 10

Teaching Point: Because the physical examination was included as part of the preventive medicine visit, only 2 of the required 3 components needed to select the code for a new office/outpatient visit were provided and considered in the selection of the problem-oriented service. Therefore, the problem-oriented service is reported using the established patient visit code **99213.**

➤ **A 2-year-old boy with history of macrocephaly is seen for a preventive medicine visit.** He is referred to an ophthalmologist because of strabismus noted by photoscreening.

Chapter 5: Preventive Services

Preventive medicine visit
Photoscreening

}

New Patient
99382

Established Patient
99392

99174 (instrument-based ocular screening, bilateral)

ICD-9-CM
V20.2 (well-child check)
378.9 (strabismus)
756.0 (macrocephaly)

ICD-10-CM
Z00.121 (well-child check with abnormal findings)
H50.9 (strabismus, unspecified)
Q75.3 (macrocephaly)

Teaching Point: Because this scenario includes no additional workup of the strabismus, only the preventive medicine and photoscreening services are reported. The diagnosis code for strabismus discovered during the preventive medicine service is reported as an additional diagnosis to the code for the well-child check.

➤ **A 13-month-old with special health care needs is referred from a family practitioner to a pediatrician for ongoing care.** The child is a new patient and has not yet had his annual preventive medicine service.

Preventive medicine visit

}

99382

ICD-9-CM
V20.2 (well-child check)

ICD-10-CM
Z00.129 (well-child check without abnormal findings)

Teaching Point: If a problem or abnormality was addressed and required significant additional work to perform required key components, code **99201–99215 25** could also be reported.

Coding Conundrum: Sports/Camp Physicals

Current Procedural Terminology® guidelines recommend that preventive medicine codes (**99381–99397**) be reported when possible because they most accurately describe the services performed in that they are preventive and age-appropriate in nature and physicians offer counseling on, for example, appropriate levels of exercise or injury prevention. However, the need for these services often arises after the child has had a yearly preventive medicine service, thereby rendering this service uncovered by health plans, which allow only one preventive service per year. In this case, the parent may be billed if the payer contract allows because the service is non-covered. Office visit codes (**99211–99215**) may be used if a problem is discovered during the service. Outpatient consultation codes (**99241–99245**) might be considered if the coach or school nurse requested the physician's opinion of a suspected problem (ie, exercise cough associated with reduced performance in cold weather). The medical record must include documentation of the written or verbal request and a copy of the written report with the physician's opinion and/or advice sent back to the coach or school nurse. *ICD-9-CM* code **V70.3** (other medical examination for administrative purposes) would be reported for these services. Any problems or conditions that are addressed during the course of the visit would also be reported. If the school physical is incorporated into the annual well visit, use code **V20.2**. Following transition to *ICD-10-CM,* code **Z02.5** is reported for an encounter for examination for participation in sports. If the school physical is incorporated into the annual well visit, use code **Z00.121** or **Z00.129.**

When reporting sports or camp physicals for patients with Medicaid or Medicaid managed care plans, check the plan's policy on payment for these services and instructions for coding and billing.

Counseling Risk-Factor Reduction and Behavior Change Intervention (99401–99412)

Codes **99401–99412** are used to report risk factor reduction services and behavior change interventions provided for the purpose of promoting health and preventing illness or injury. Behavior change interventions are for persons who have a behavior that is often considered an illness itself, such as tobacco use and addiction or substance abuse/misuse. Behavior change services may be reported when performed as part of the treatment of condition(s) related to or potentially exacerbated by the behavior or when performed to change the harmful behavior that has not yet resulted in illness.

Table 5-2 lists the codes for counseling individuals and groups.

- Counseling, anticipatory guidance, and risk-factor reduction interventions provided at the time of the initial or periodic comprehensive preventive medicine examination are not separately reported.

- Risk-factor reduction and behavior change interventions may be reported separately with other E/M services.

  - Evaluation and management services reported on the same day must be separate and distinct.

  - Time spent in the provision of behavior change intervention or risk-factor reduction may not be used as a basis for the selection of the other E/M code.

  - When reporting a distinct E/M service, append modifier **25** to the risk counseling/behavior change code.

- Codes **99401–99404, 99411,** and **99412** are used for the purpose of promoting health and preventing illness and/or injury.

  - Services will vary with age and address issues such as diet, exercise, sexual activity, dental health, injury prevention, and family problems.

  - Services are reported based on time.

- Behavior change intervention codes **99406–99409** are reported when

  - Services are provided by a physician or other qualified health care professional for patients who have a behavior that is often considered an illness (ie, tobacco use and addiction, substance abuse or misuse).

  - Services involve specific validated interventions, including assessing readiness for change and barriers to change, advising change in behavior, providing specific suggested actions and motivational counseling, and arranging for services and follow-up care.

- Services may be reported when they are performed as part of the treatment of the condition(s) related to or potentially exacerbated by the behavior or when provided in an effort to change the behavior that has not yet resulted in an illness.

- Medical record documentation supports the total time spent in the performance of the service, and a detail of the behavior change intervention is provided.

- Behavior change intervention services cannot be performed on a parent or guardian of a patient and reported under the patient's name.

- Code **99078** is reported when a physician counsels groups of patients with symptoms or an established illness. This service is reported for each participating child. (See Coding for Children With Special Health Care Needs on page 252 for an example of how code **99078** is used.)

> ||ıı|ı|ı| **Coding Pearl** ı|ıı||ı|ı|
>
> Codes **99401–99404** are time-based codes. Once the midpoint is passed, you may report the code with the closet time. To report code **99401,** the midpoint to pass is 7.5 minutes.

Chapter 5: Preventive Services

Table 5-2. Preventive Medicine Counseling and/or Risk-Factor Reduction and Behavior Change Intervention

Code	Description
99401	Preventive medicine counseling and/or risk-factor reduction intervention(s) provided to an individual (separate procedure); approximately 15 minutes
99402	approximately 30 minutes
99403	approximately 45 minutes
99404	approximately 60 minutes
99406	Smoking and tobacco use cessation counseling visit; intermediate, >3 minutes up to 10 minutes
99407	intensive, >10 minutes
99408	Alcohol and/or substance (other than tobacco) abuse structured screening (eg, AUDIT, DAST), and brief intervention services; 15–30 minutes
99409	>30 minutes
99411	Preventive medicine counseling and/or risk-factor reduction intervention(s) provided to individuals in a group setting; approximately 30 minutes
99412	approximately 60 minutes

Abbreviations: AUDIT, Alcohol Use Disorder Identification Test; DAST, Drug Abuse Screening Test.

Examples

➤ **Parents of a 2-month-old patient come to their physician's office to discuss immunizations.** To date they have refused to have their child immunized. Although the physician has discussed the need for vaccines during the child's previous visits, the parents indicate that they have further questions. The physician spends 25 minutes counseling the parents about current recommendations, safety and efficacy of vaccines, and their importance in preventing disease.

Risk-factor reduction counseling } **99402**

ICD-9-CM	*ICD-10-CM*
V65.49 (other specified counseling)	**Z71.89** (other specified counseling)
V15.83 (personal history of under-immunization status)	**Z28.3** (personal history of under-immunization status)
V03–V06 (specific vaccine product)	**Z28.82** (vaccination not carried out because of caregiver refusal)
V64.05 (vaccination not carried out because of caregiver refusal)	

Coding Conundrum:
Report the *CPT* or HCPCS Code for Smoking Cessation Counseling?

Current Procedural Terminology codes **99406** and **99407** are used to report smoking and tobacco use cessation counseling. The CMS requires that these codes be reported when smoking/tobacco use cessation counseling is performed on Medicare patients who have symptoms of tobacco-related diseases. Healthcare Common Procedure Coding System codes **G0436** (smoking and tobacco cessation counseling visit for the asymptomatic patient; intermediate, >3 minutes, up to 10 minutes) and **G0437** (smoking and tobacco cessation counseling visit for the asymptomatic patient; intensive, >10 minutes) are used to report tobacco cessation counseling services for Medicare patients who use tobacco who are asymptomatic of tobacco-related conditions when counseling is performed by a qualified physician or other Medicare-recognized practitioner.

According to HCPCS guidelines, the *CPT* code should be reported when the *CPT* and HCPCS codes have virtually identical narratives for the procedure or service. The HCPCS code should be reported if the narratives are not identical (eg, the *CPT* narrative is generic and the HCPCS code is more specific).

Note that not all payers recognize HCPCS codes. Therefore, before reporting codes **G0436** and **G0437** instead of codes **99406** and **99407,** check with payers about coverage and payment policies.

➤ **During an office visit for a 14-year-old new patient for an unrelated problem, it is learned that he has been smoking for 2 years.** After counseling him about the dangers and potential health problems associated with smoking, he and his mother express interest in assistance to help him stop using tobacco. The physician spends 10 minutes discussing specific methods to overcome barriers, pharmacologic options, behavioral techniques, and nicotine replacement. The patient is referred to a community support group and a follow-up visit is scheduled in 2 weeks to provide additional encouragement and counseling as needed. Diagnosis is tobacco use.

New patient office or other outpatient visit

Smoking and tobacco use cessation counseling, 3–10 minutes
}

99201–99205
(based on service performed and documented)

diagnosis code appropriate for problem addressed

99406 25

ICD-9-CM
305.1 (tobacco use disorder)

ICD-10-CM
Z72.0 (tobacco use)
Z71.6 (tobacco abuse counseling)

Transitioning to 10

Teaching Point: If only general advice and encouragement to stop smoking had been provided, it would be considered part of the new patient office visit.

➤ **A group of 4 overweight patients attend a session in the physician's office to discuss diet and exercise.** The physician conducts the counseling session.

Risk-factor reduction counseling, group $\Big\}$

99411

ICD-9-CM
V65.3 (dietary surveillance and counseling)
Use additional code to identify body mass index (BMI), if known (**V85.0–V85.54**).
V65.41 (exercise counseling)

ICD-10-CM
Z71.3 (dietary counseling and surveillance)
Use additional code from category **Z68** to identify BMI.
Z71.89 (other specified counseling)

Teaching Point: Services are documented in each patient's medical record and are reported for each child. Services provided to a group of patients may not be reported as individual office E/M visits (**99201–99215**) because only face-to-face time spent counseling the individual patient may be reported based on time spent counseling and/or coordinating care when reporting office or other outpatient E/M visits.

Other Preventive Medicine Services (99420–99429)

❂ Code **99420** is reported for administration and interpretation of a health risk assessment instrument (eg, health hazard appraisal). Examples include lead or tuberculosis exposure questionnaires. Code **99420** cannot be used in conjunction with codes **99408** and **99409.**

❂ Code **99429** (unlisted preventive medicine service) may be reported if these options are not suitable. If the unlisted code is used, most payers will require a copy of the progress notes filed with the claim.

Immunizations

Vaccine services are reported using 2 families of *CPT* codes—one for the vaccine serum (the product) and one for the services associated with the administration of the vaccine.

Vaccines and Toxoids

❂ Codes **90476–90748** are used to report the vaccine/toxoid product only. They do not include the administration of a vaccine.

❂ The exact vaccine product administered needs to be reported to meet the requirements of immunization registries, vaccine distribution programs, and reporting systems (eg, the Vaccine Adverse Event Reporting System), as well as for payment.

   ❂ Codes may be specific to the product manufacturer and brand, schedule (number of doses or timing), chemical formulation, dosage, appropriate age guidelines, and/or route of administration.

   ❂ Codes for combination vaccines (eg, **90707,** measles, mumps, and rubella virus vaccine) are available, as are separate codes for single component vaccines (eg, **90705,** measles vaccine).

   ❂ It is not appropriate to code each component of a combination vaccine separately using separate vaccine product codes when a combination vaccine is administered. However, if a combination vaccine is commercially available but a physician elects to administer the component

Transitioning to 10

Because *CPT* codes identify each vaccine/toxoid, *ICD-10-CM* includes only one code for need for prophylactic immunization. Code **Z23,** encounter for immunization, is reported when immunizations are provided.

vaccines due to nonavailability or other clinical reason, each vaccine product administered would be separately reported. See Appendix B-5 for a list of vaccine product codes.

New Vaccines/Toxoids

The *CPT* Editorial Panel, in recognition of the public health interest in vaccine products, has chosen to publish new vaccine product codes prior to US Food and Drug Administration (FDA) approval. The American Medical Association (AMA) uses its *CPT* site (www.ama-assn.org/ama/pub/physician-resources/solutions-managing-your-practice/coding-billing-insurance/cpt/about-cpt/category-i-vaccine-codes.page) to provide updates of *CPT* Editorial Panel actions on new vaccine products. Once approved by the *CPT* Editorial Panel, vaccine/toxoid product codes will be made available for release on a semiannual basis (July 1 and January 1). As part of the electronic distribution, there is a 6-month implementation period from the initial release date (ie, codes released on January 1 are eligible for use on July 1; codes released on July 1 are eligible for use on January 1). These codes are indicated with a lightning bolt symbol (⚡) and will be tracked by the AMA to monitor FDA approval status. The symbol will be removed once the FDA status changes to "approved." Refer to the AMA Web site indicated earlier for the most up-to-date information on codes with this symbol.

Before administering any new vaccine product or product with new recommendations, make certain the CDC in the *Morbidity and Mortality Weekly Report* or the AAP in *Pediatrics* has endorsed the use or recommendations of the vaccine. You may also want to verify with your carriers if the vaccine will be covered.

If a vaccine enters the market this year and is FDA approved, recommendations for use are published by the CDC or AAP, and no code exists for the specific vaccine, use code **90749** (unlisted vaccine/toxoid) and list the specific vaccine given.

> |||||||| **Coding Pearl** ||||||||
>
> The administration of immune globulins (including Synagis) is not reported using the immunization administration codes. See codes **96365–96368**, **96372**, **96374**, and **96375**.

Immunization Administration (IA)

Current Procedural Terminology codes **90460** and **90461** *or* **90471–90474** are reported *in addition* to vaccine/toxoid code(s) **90476–90749**. If a significant, separately identifiable E/M service (eg, office or other outpatient services, preventive medicine services) is performed, the appropriate E/M service code appended with modifier **25** should be reported in addition to the vaccine and toxoid administration codes.

Codes **90460** and **90461**

90460   Immunization administration through 18 years of age via any route of administration, with counseling by physician or other qualified health care professional; first or only component of each vaccine or toxoid administered

+90461   each additional vaccine or toxoid component administered
(List separately in addition to code for primary procedure.)

When reporting codes **90460** and **90461**

☀ Physicians or qualified health care professionals must provide *face-to-face* counseling for the patient (aged ≤18 years) and/or family at the time of the encounter for the administration of a vaccine.

❖ *Current Procedural Terminology* defines a physician or other qualified health care professional as follows: A *"physician or other qualified health care professional" is an individual who by education, training, licensure/regulation, facility credentialing (when applicable), and facility privileging (when applicable) performs a professional service within his/her scope of practice and independently reports that professional service. These professionals are distinct from "clinical staff." A clinical staff member is a person who works under the supervision of a physician or other qualified health care professional and who is allowed by law, regulation, and facility policy to perform or assist in the performance of a specified professional service, but who does not individually report that professional service. Other policies may also affect who may report specific services.*

❖ Therefore, although nurses may be allowed by state scope of practice laws to explain risks and benefits of vaccines, their counseling does not fall under the description of code **90460** or **90461,** and codes **90471–90474** must be reported.

◉ When a private payer contract does not allow qualified health care professionals to report services under their own name and National Provider Identifier (NPI), check with the payer to determine eligibility of these professionals to report immunization counseling (**90460–90461**) and report under the name and number of the supervising physician.

◉ Code **90460** is reported for the *first (or only) component of each vaccine administered* (whether single or combination) on a day of service and includes the related vaccine counseling.

◉ Code **90461** is only reported in conjunction with **90460** and is used to report the work of counseling for *each additional component(s) beyond the first* in a given combination vaccine.

❖ Combination vaccines are those vaccines that contain multiple vaccine components. Refer to Appendix B-5 for the number of components in the most commonly reported pediatric vaccines.

◉ The IA codes include provider (ie, physician or other qualified health care professional) work of discussing risks and benefits of the vaccines, providing parents with a copy of the appropriate CDC Vaccine Information Statement (VIS) for each vaccine given, the cost of clinical staff time to record each vaccine component administered in the medical record and statewide vaccine registry, giving the vaccine, observing and addressing reactions or side effects, and cost of supplies (eg, syringe, needle, bandages).

> ||||||| *Coding Pearl* |||||||
>
> The word *component* refers to an antigen in a vaccine that prevents disease(s) caused by one organism.

For each individual vaccine administered, report code **90460** because every vaccine will have at minimum one vaccine component. Depending on the specific vaccine, code **90461** is additionally reported for counseling on each additional component of each combination vaccine. The following examples illustrate how some of the more common pediatric vaccines are classified (ie, single or combination component vaccine) and how codes **90460** and **90461** (when applicable) will be applied to each vaccine:

Examples

▶ **A patient receives the diphtheria, tetanus toxoids, acellular pertussis;** *Haemophilus influenzae* **type b; and inactivated poliovirus (DTaP-Hib-IPV) vaccine and an influenza vaccine.**

Report **90460** for each vaccine given (2 units) and **90461** with 4 units for counseling related to additional components of the combination vaccine (DTaP-Hib-IPV).

▶ **You administer a measles, mumps, rubella (MMR) vaccine and a varicella vaccine at the same encounter.**

Report codes **90460** with 2 units for each vaccine given (2), and **90461** with 2 units for counseling related to additional components of the combination vaccine.

Codes 90471–90474

Codes **90471–90474** will be reported when criteria for reporting the 2 pediatric IA codes (**90460** and **90461**) have not been met (ie, physician or qualified health care professional does not counsel patient/family or does not document that the counseling was personally performed, or when the patient is ≥19 years).

90471   Immunization administration includes percutaneous, intradermal, subcutaneous, or intramuscular injections; one vaccine (single or combination vaccine/toxoid)

+90472   each additional vaccine (single or combination vaccine/toxoid) (List separately in addition to code for primary procedure.) (Use code **90472** in conjunction with **90460, 90471,** or **90473.**)

90473   Immunization administration by intranasal or oral route; one vaccine (single or combination vaccine/toxoid)

+90474   each additional vaccine (single or combination vaccine/toxoid) (List separately in addition to code for primary procedure.) (Use code **90474** in conjunction with **90460, 90471,** or **90473.**)

When reporting codes **90471–90474**

☀ Codes **90471–90474** are reported for each vaccine administered whether single or combination vaccines.

☀ *Only one* "first" IA code (**90471** or **90473**) may be reported on a calendar day.

The "first" IA code can be reported from either family or either route of administration (eg, when a patient receives an immunization via injection and second one via intranasal route, IA services can be reported with codes **90471** and **90474** or with codes **90473** and **90472**).

☀ The Medicare National Correct Coding Initiative (NCCI) pairs code **90460** with codes **90471** and **90473,** not allowing codes from both sets to be reported on the same day of service by the same physician or physician of the same group and specialty. If a physician personally performs counseling on one vaccine but not on another when given during the same encounter, IA will be reported using codes **90460** (and **90461** if appropriate) and either **90472** (IA, each additional vaccine via injection) or **90474** (each additional vaccine via intranasal or oral route).

For more information on vaccine administration, please see the following examples and Appendix B-4, found at www.aap.org/cfp (access code AAPCFP20).

Examples

➤ **A 15-year-old patient receives the human papillomavirus (HPV) vaccine (quadrivalent) from her physician.** The ordering physician discusses risks of the vaccine and the disease for which it provides protection. The parent/guardian is given the CDC VIS. The parent/guardian consents; the nurse prepares the vaccine. The patient receives the vaccine by a single injection, and the nurse charts the required information and accesses and enters vaccine data into the statewide immunization registry. The patient is discharged home after the nurse confirms that there are no serious immediate reactions.

90649 (HPV, quadrivalent)   *ICD-9-CM*
90460   **V04.89** (need for prophylactic vaccination—other viral diseases)

                                   ICD-10-CM
                                   Z23 (encounter for immunization)

Teaching Point: Because the physician personally performed the counseling, code **90460** is reported for this single component vaccine. No other services are reported because the purpose of the visit was for the administration of the vaccine only.

➤ **A 4-month-old established patient receives the DTaP-Hib-IPV combination vaccine, rotavirus vaccine, and pneumococcal conjugate vaccine from her physician at the time of her preventive medicine visit.** The ordering physician discusses the risks of each additional vaccine component (eg, tetanus, pertussis) and the diseases for which each additional vaccine component provides protection. The parent/guardian is given the CDC VIS for each vaccine component and consents for each of the additional vaccine components. The nurse charts the required information and enters data into the statewide immunization registry for each additional vaccine component.

99391 25 (preventive medicine visit; younger than 1 year)

90698 (DTaP-Hib-IPV)

90480 (rotavirus vaccine, pentavalent)

90669 (pneumococcal conjugate vaccine, 7-valent)

90460 with 3 units for counseling for first component of each of 3 vaccines

90461 with 4 units for counseling for additional components (eg, tetanus, pertussis, *H influenzae* type b, inactivated polio)

ICD-9-CM

V20.2 (routine infant or child check)

ICD-10-CM

Z00.129 (routine infant or child check without abnormal findings)

Teaching Point: *Current Procedural Terminology* code **90460** is reported for each vaccine administered and includes the work of counseling for the first component of each vaccine administered (diphtheria, rotavirus, and pneumococcal). Code **90461** is reported in conjunction with **90460** for each additional component that is part of the combination vaccine DTaP-Hib-IPV. Payers who have adopted the Medicare and Medicaid NCCI edits will require that modifier **25** be appended to code **99391** to signify that it was significant and separately identifiable. (For more information on NCCI edits, see Chapter 3.) The encounter for routine infant or child exam (*ICD-9-CM* code **V20.2** or *ICD-10-CM* code **Z00.129**) encompasses routine vaccines.

➤ **A 12-year-old established patient is seen for his preventive medicine visit by the certified pediatric nurse practitioner (CPNP), who bills under her own NPI.** The patient complains of an increasingly severe itchy rash on his hands, arms, and legs for 3 days. A problem-focused history related to the complaint is performed. He is diagnosed and treated for a moderately severe case of poison ivy, requiring a prescription for a topical steroid. He has not yet received his tetanus, diphtheria, and acellular pertussis (Tdap) or meningococcal vaccines. The CPNP counsels the parents on the risks and protection from each of the diseases. The CDC VISs are given to the parents and the nurse administers the vaccines.

99394 25 (preventive medicine visit, established patient, age 12 through 17 years)

90715 (Tdap, 7 years or older, intramuscular)

90734 (meningococcal conjugate vaccine, quadrivalent, intramuscular)

90460 with 2 units

90461 with 2 units

99212 25 (office/outpatient E/M, established patient)

ICD-9-CM
V20.2 (routine infant or child check)

ICD-10-CM
Z00.121 (well-child check with abnormal findings)

ICD-9-CM
692.6 (allergic dermatitis due to plants)

ICD-10-CM
L23.7 (allergic contact dermatitis due to plants, except food)

Teaching Point: Medical record documentation supports a significant, separately identifiable E/M service was provided and is reported in addition to the preventive medicine service. Modifier **25** is appended to code **99212** to signify that it is significant and separately identifiable from the preventive medicine service. Modifier **25** is also appended to code **99394** to signify that it is significant and separately identifiable from IA. Because the child is younger than 18 years and vaccine counseling was performed by the CPNP with her own NPI, codes **90460** and **90461** may be reported as appropriate.

Coding Conundrum: Vaccine Counseling on Day Different From Administration

Current Procedural Terminology states that codes **90460** and **90461** are reported when the physician or qualified health care professional provides face-to-face counseling of the patient and family during the administration of a vaccine. However, there are situations in which the vaccine counseling is performed on a day different from the actual administration. For example, the physician or qualified health care professional might provide vaccine counseling during an encounter, but because the child is ill, the vaccines are deferred to a later date. Or the physician/other qualified health care professional may counsel the patient/parent on all vaccines needed during the annual preventive medicine service visit, but the parent refuses multiple vaccines on the same day and some of the vaccines are given over a series of encounters for vaccine administration only. How would a physician then report IA?

Because these circumstances split the actual administration from vaccine counseling, codes **90460** and **90461** cannot be reported. In these situations, IA is reported using codes **90471–90474** on the day that the vaccines are administered.

➤ **A 4-year-old patient had a high fever and an ear infection at her preventive medicine visit 2 weeks ago. The physician has the patient return for a follow-up in 2 weeks. She now returns to see the nurse to have her ear checked and is also due for her influenza vaccine.** The nurse performs an interval history and very brief examination and finds the symptoms from the earlier illness have resolved. After assessing that the patient is in good health, she confirms that there are no contraindications to the immunization per CDC guidelines. Next, the nurse reviews the VIS with the father, reviews the antipyretic dosage for weight, and obtains the father's consent for the immunization. The nurse then administers the influenza vaccine and observes for immediate reactions.

99211 25 (E/M service)

ICD-9-CM
V67.59 (follow-up examination; following other treatment; other)

ICD-10-CM
Z09 (encounter for follow-up examination after completed treatment for conditions other than malignant neoplasm)

90660 (influenza virus vaccine, trivalent, live, intranasal)

ICD-9-CM
V04.81 Need for prophylactic vaccination and inoculation against influenza

ICD-10-CM
Z23 (encounter for immunization)

90473 (IA, intranasal)   Same diagnosis codes as those linked to **90660**

Teaching Point: If the payer follows NCCI edits, *CPT* code **99211** will never be paid for separately from vaccine administration (eg, **90473**), even with modifier **25.**

➤ **A 5-year-old established patient presented 2 weeks ago for her 5-year check and vaccines.** Her mom asked that the vaccines be split, so the DTaP and IPV were given at that encounter. The patient returns today for a nurse-only visit to get the MMR and varicella vaccines.

90707 (MMR, live)
90471 (IA, first injection)

90716 (varicella virus vaccine)
90472 (IA, subsequent injection)

ICD-9-CM
V06.4 (MMR)
V05.4 (varicella)

ICD-10-CM
Z23 (encounter for immunization)

Teaching Point: Because counseling for all vaccines occurred at the last encounter and all VISs were handed out, only administration occurred today. *Current Procedural Terminology* codes **90460** and **90461** would be reported with the appropriate codes for DTaP and IPV vaccines that were administered during the previous encounter. (See Coding Conundrum: Vaccine Counseling on Day Different From Administration on page 105.)

National Drug Code (NDC)

Some payers, specifically Medicare, Medicaid, and other government payers (eg, Tricare), require the use of the National Drug Code (NDC) when reporting vaccine product codes. The NDCs are universal product identifiers for medications, including vaccines. These codes are 10-digit, 3-segment numbers that identify the product, labeler, and trade package size. The Health Insurance Portability and Accountability Act of 1996 standards require an 11-digit code. If you are not currently reporting vaccines with NDCs, be sure to coordinate the requirements with your billing software company. For more information on NDCs, visit www.fda.gov/Drugs/InformationOnDrugs/ucm142438.htm or link through www.aap.org/cfp.

Vaccines for Children (VFC) Program

The Vaccines for Children (VFC) program makes vaccines available to children up to 19 years of age who meet any of the following criteria: are enrolled in the Medicaid program, do not have health insurance, have no coverage of immunizations under their

Transitioning to 10

Chapter 5: Preventive Services

health plan, or are American Indians or Alaska Natives. Vaccines are provided at no cost to the participating physician or patient and payment is made only for administration of the vaccine.

If reporting the VFC vaccine with administration codes and not the product code, you need to capture data for the vaccine products administered for registry and quality initiatives. This can be accomplished by entering the vaccine codes with a $0 charge (if your billing system allows) and appending modifier **SL** (state-supplied vaccine) to the vaccine code. However, follow your individual payer rules for reporting.

According to the VFC Web site, providers are encouraged to use code **90460** for administration of a vaccine under the VFC program. If code **90461** is used for a vaccine with multiple antigens or components, it should be given a $0 value for a child covered under the VFC program. This applies to Medicaid-enrolled VFC-entitled children as well as non–Medicaid-enrolled VFC-entitled children (ie, uninsured, underinsured, and American Indian or Alaska Native children not enrolled in Medicaid). Please be aware that some state Medicaid programs do have reporting rules that differ from VFC. *Be sure to get this policy in writing from your state Medicaid program* and follow it to avoid denied payment. The AAP continues to advocate to the CMS to allow for recognition and payment for component-based vaccine counseling and administration (ie, code **90461**). Under the current statute, administration can only be paid "per vaccine" and not component.

Participants in the VFC program should be aware of program-specific guidance, including storage of VFC vaccine separate from privately purchased vaccines. For more information on the VFC program, visit www.cdc.gov/vaccines/programs/vfc/index.html.

Coding Conundrum: Reporting E/M Services With IA

Evaluation and management services most often reported with the vaccine product and IA include new and established patient preventive medicine visits (*CPT* codes **99381–99395**), problem-oriented visits (**99201–99215**), and preventive medicine counseling services (**99401–99404**).

The E/M service must be medically indicated, significant, and separately identifiable from the IA.

Payers may require modifier **25** (significant, separately identifiable E/M service by the same physician on the same day of the procedure or other service) to be appended to the E/M code to distinguish it from the administration of the vaccine.

If a patient is seen for the administration of a vaccine only, it is not appropriate to report an E/M visit if it is not medically necessary, significant, and separately identifiable.

Current Procedural Terminology code **99211** (established patient E/M, minimal level, not requiring physician presence) *should not* be reported when the patient encounter is for vaccination only because Medicare RBRVS relative values for IA codes include administrative and clinical services (ie, greeting the patient, routine vital signs, obtaining a vaccine history, presenting the VIS and responding to routine vaccine questions, preparation and administration of the vaccine, and documentation and observation of the patient following administration of the vaccine). However, if the service is medically necessary, significant, and separately identifiable, it may be reported with modifier **25** appended to the E/M code (**99211**). The medical record must clearly state the reason for the visit, brief history, physical examination, assessment and plan, and any other counseling or discussion items. The progress note must be signed with the physician's countersignature. For more information and clinical vignettes on the appropriate use of code **99211** during IA, visit www.aap.org/cfp, access code AAPCFP20. Payers who do not follow the Medicare RBRVS may allow

---

Coding Conundrum: Reporting E/M Services With IA, continued

payment of code **99211** with IA. Know your payer guidelines, and if payment is allowed, make certain that the guidelines are in writing and maintained in your office. Be aware that a co-payment will be required when the "nurse" visit is reported. The same guidelines apply to physician visits (**99201–99215**).

Hearing Screening

Audiometric tests require the use of calibrated electronic equipment, recording of results, and a written report with interpretation. Services include testing of both ears. If the test is applied to one ear only, modifier **52** (reduced services) must be appended to the code.

> **Transitioning to 10**
>
> Report hearing tests conducted following a failed hearing screening with code **Z01.110** if results are normal. If findings are abnormal, report code **Z01.118** and a code to identify the abnormality.

- Code **92551** (screening test, pure tone, air only) is used when earphones are placed on the patient and the patient is asked to respond to tones of different pitches and intensities. This is a limited study.
- Code **92552** (full pure tone audiometric assessment) is used when earphones are placed on the patient and the patient is asked to respond to tones of different pitches and intensities. The threshold, which is the lowest intensity of the tone that the patient can hear 50% of the time, is recorded for a number of frequencies. Bone thresholds are obtained in a similar manner. The air and bone thresholds are compared to differentiate among conductive, sensorineural, or mixed hearing losses.
- Code **92583** (select picture audiometry) is typically used for younger children. The patient is asked to identify different pictures with the instructions given at different sound intensity levels.
- Other commonly performed procedures include codes **92567** (tympanometry [impedance testing]) and **92568** (acoustic reflex testing, threshold portion).
- Automated audiometry testing is reported with Category III codes **0208T–0212T**. See Chapter 13 for a listing of these codes.

Vision Screening

99173	Screening test of visual acuity, quantitative, bilateral
99174	Instrument-based ocular screening (eg, photoscreening, automated-refraction), bilateral
0333T	Visual evoked potential, screening of visual acuity, automated

- Screening test of visual acuity (**99173**) must use graduated visual stimuli that allow a quantitative estimate of visual acuity (eg, Snellen chart).
- Medical record documentation must include a measurement of acuity for both eyes, not just a pass or fail score.
- Code **99173** is only reported when vision screening is performed in association with a preventive medicine visit. It is not reported when it is performed as part of an evaluation for an eye problem or condition because the assessment of visual acuity is considered an integral part of the eye examination.
- Instrument-based ocular screening (**99174**) is used to report screening for a variety of conditions, including esotropia, exotropia, isometropia, cataracts, ptosis, hyperopia, myopia, and others, that affect or have the potential to affect vision. This test is especially useful for screening infants, preschool patients, and those older patients whose ability to participate in traditional acuity screening is limited or very time intensive. It cannot be reported with codes **92002–92700** (general ophthalmologic

services), **99172** (visual function screening), or **99173** (screening test of visual acuity, quantitative) because ocular screening is inherent to these services. An AAP policy statement on instrument-based pediatric vision screening is available online at http://pediatrics.aappublications.org/content/130/5/983.full.

☀ Vision screening performed using an automated visual evoked potential system is reported with code **0333T.** This code applies to automated screening using an instrument-based algorithm with a pass/fail result. Report code **95930** only for comprehensive visual evoked potential testing with physician interpretation and report.

Developmental Screening

Structured screening for developmental delay is a universal recommendation of the "Recommendations for Preventive Pediatric Health Care" at 18-month and 2-year visits for autism spectrum disorder–specific screening (eg, Modified Checklist for Autism in Toddlers [M-CHAT]) and at 9-month, 18-month, and 2- or 2½-year visits for other developmental screening (eg, Ages & Stages Questionnaire [ASQ]). When reporting these screenings, code **96110** represents developmental screening with scoring and documentation per standardized instrument. (Note that screening results should be included in the patient medical record.)

Code **96110** (developmental screening with scoring and documentation, per standardized instrument)

☀ Is reported for standardized developmental screening instruments. It is not reported when the pediatrician conducts an informal survey or surveillance of development as part of a comprehensive preventive medicine service (which is considered to be part of the history and is not separately billed).

☀ May be reported for each standardized developmental screening instrument administered.

☀ Includes standardized screening tools such as ASQ, Australian Scale for Asperger's Syndrome, M-CHAT, or Parents' Evaluation of Developmental Status (PEDS). Other tools are also used for developmental screening.

Code **96127** (brief emotional/behavioral assessment [eg, depression inventory, ADHD scale], with scoring and documentation, per standardized instrument)

☀ Like developmental screening (**96110**), represents the practice expense of administering, scoring, and documentation of each standardized instrument. No physician work value is included. Physician interpretation is included in a related E/M service.

☀ Is not reported in conjunction with **99401–99404, 96101–96103,** or **96118–96120.**

☀ Can involve 2 separately reported completions (eg, by teacher and by parent) of the same form.

Examples

➤ **A 20-month-old girl presents to her primary physician with a complaint of pulling at her ears and signs suggesting an upper respiratory infection.** She missed her 18-month well-child checkup. Her mother is given the PEDS and M-CHAT (a standardized screening instrument for autism in children 16–30 months of age) by the nursing assistant, who explains why the instruments are given and how they should be completed. After the child's mother completes both forms, the

Transitioning to 10

ICD-10-CM code **Z13.4,** encounter for screening for certain developmental disorders in childhood, is not reported for routine developmental testing of infant or child at the time of a preventive service. An Excludes 1 note directs to codes in subcategory **Z00.1-.**

nursing assistant scores and attaches them to the child's medical chart. The physician interprets and records the results in the medical record.

Code **96110** is reported with 2 units of service and modifier **59,** or **96110** and **96110 59** are reported, depending on payer requirements. *ICD-9-CM* code **V79.3** (developmental handicaps in early childhood) or *ICD-10-CM* code **Z13.4** may be reported to indicate screening for developmental handicap in children when the screening is not performed in conjunction with a well-child visit.

➤ **The mother of a 7-year-old boy is concerned about the child not paying atten-tion at school and complaints from teachers that he does not stay on task.** The parent version of a behavior assessment system for children is administered to the mother and scored for the physician's review. The physician recommends that an additional behavioral assessment be completed by the boy's teachers to confirm or rule out ADHD.

The appropriate E/M service code (preventive medicine visit, new or established patient office visit, or consultation) would be reported in addition to code **96127.** Because the physician did not diagnose ADHD, symptoms of attention and concentra-tion deficit are reported with diagnosis code **R41.840.**

Application of Fluoride Varnish

A new code is added in *CPT 2015* for application of fluoride varnish by a physician or other qualified health care professional.

99188   Application of topical fluoride varnish by a physician or other qualified health care professional

☀ *Code on Dental Procedures and Nomenclature (CDT®)* codes also exist for topical application of fluoride varnish and fluoride. In addition, *CDT* codes exist for nutri-tion counseling to prevent dental disease, oral hygiene instruction, and oral evaluations.

☀ Coverage and payment of topical fluoride application is likely to be payer specific. With the AAP focus on oral health, several state Medicaid programs are now paying for topical fluoride varnish application. Specific benefits, physician and provider edu-cational requirements, and billing requirements may vary across Medicaid standard and managed care plans.

Some payers will provide coverage for oral evaluation and health risk assessment or other dental preventive services when provided on the same day as a preven-tive medicine visit; other payers will allow services only when they are provided at an encounter separate from a preventive medicine visit. Know payer requirements for reporting.

❖ Preventive counseling for oral health may be included as part of the preventive medicine service (**99381–99397**) or, if performed at a separate encounter, reported under the individual preventive medicine counseling service codes (**99401–99404**) or with an office/outpatient E/M service code (**99201–99215**). *ICD-9-CM* code **V82.89** or *ICD-10-CM* code **Z13.84** may be reported for encounter for screening for dental disorders.

❖ For those carriers (particularly state Medicaid plans under EPSDT) that cover oral health care, some will require a modifier. These modifiers are payer specific and should only be used as directed by your state Medicaid agency or other private payer.

SC   Medically necessary service or supply
EP   Services provided as part of Medicaid EPSDT program
U5   Medicaid Level of Care 5, as defined by each state

❖ The AAP Section on Oral Health and chapter oral health advocates have gathered resources online to assist practices in learning about their state Medicaid coverage as well as a variety of other practice resources. Go to www2.aap.org/oralhealth/COHA.html for more information.

Screening Laboratory Tests

☀ A test performed in the office's laboratory should be billed using the appropriate laboratory code and, if performed, the appropriate blood collection code (**36400–36416**).

☀ Codes **36415** (collection of venous blood by venipuncture) and **36416** (collection of capillary blood specimen [eg, finger, heel, ear stick]) are used for any age child when the physician is not needed to perform the procedure.

☀ When a physician's skill is required to perform venipuncture (eg, access is too difficult for other staff to attain) on a child younger than 3 years, codes **36400–36406** are reported based on the anatomic site of the venipuncture. Report code **36400** when performed on femoral or jugular vein, code **36405** when on the scalp vein, or code **36406** when another vein is accessed.

❖ When a physician's skill is required to perform venipuncture on a child 3 years or older, code **36410** (venipuncture, age 3 years and older, necessitating physician's skill, for diagnostic or therapeutic purposes [not to be used for routine venipuncture]) is reported.

❖ If the physician performs the venipuncture as a convenience or because staff is not trained in the procedure, code **36415** is reported because the physician's skill was not required.

☀ Though typically not required, some payers will require that modifier **25** be appended to the E/M code if a separate and significant E/M service is reported on the same day of service.

☀ Laboratories and physician offices performing waived tests may need to append modifier **QW** to the *CPT* code for Clinical Laboratory Improvement Amendments (CLIA)-waived procedures. The use of modifier **QW** is payer specific. To review the list of CLIA-waived procedures, go to http://cms.hhs.gov/Regulations-and-Guidance/Legislation/CLIA/Categorization_of_Tests.html.

Screening for Anemia

85014   Blood count; hematocrit
85018   Blood count; hemoglobin

☀ Screening for anemia is reported with *ICD-9-CM* code **V78.0** or *ICD-10-CM* code **Z13.0,** encounter for screening for diseases of the blood and blood-forming organs and certain disorders involving the immune mechanism.

Lead Testing

83655   Lead, quantitative analysis

☀ This test does not specify the specimen source or method of testing. Alternative tests sometimes (though now rarely) used for lead screening are **82135** (aminolevulinic acid, delta), **84202** (protoporphyrin, red blood cell count, quantitative), and **84203** (protoporphyrin, red blood cell count, screen).

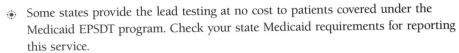

- Some states provide the lead testing at no cost to patients covered under the Medicaid EPSDT program. Check your state Medicaid requirements for reporting this service.

- Report *ICD-9-CM* code **V82.5** or *ICD-10-CM* code **Z13.88** (encounter for screening for disorder due to exposure to contaminants) when performing lead screening.

Tuberculosis (TB) Skin Test (Mantoux)

86580 Tuberculosis, intradermal (includes administration)

- The tuberculosis (TB) skin test (Mantoux) using intradermal administration of purified protein derivative (PPD) is the recommended diagnostic skin test for TB. (This is not the bacille Calmette-Guérin TB vaccine.)
- Code **99211** is the appropriate code to report when the patient returns for the reading of a PPD test. In the case of a positive test result, when the physician sees the patient and forms a further diagnostic or treatment plan, the complexity may lead to a higher-level code. The appropriate *ICD-9-CM* code is **V74.1** or for *ICD-10-CM* **Z11.1** (encounter for screening for respiratory TB).

- There is not a separate administration code reported when the TB test is performed.

Dyslipidemia Screening

80061 Lipid panel (must include total serum cholesterol, lipoprotein by direct measurement high-density cholesterol [HDL], and triglycerides) *or*

82465 Cholesterol, serum, total

83718 Lipoprotein, direct measurement, high-density cholesterol (HDL cholesterol)

84478 Triglycerides

- The appropriate *ICD-9-CM* and *ICD-10-CM* codes for dyslipidemia screening are **V77.91** and **Z13.220,** respectively (encounter for screening for lipoid disorders).

Screening for Sexually Transmitted Infection

86701 Antibody; HIV-1

G0433 QW Infectious agent antibody detection by enzyme-linked immunosorbent assay (ELISA) technique, HIV-1 and/or HIV-2, screening

- Screening laboratory tests for chlamydia, gonorrhea, and syphilis require more than waived testing laboratory certification. These include
  - ❖ **86631** Antibody; chlamydia
  - ❖ **86632** Antibody; chlamydia, IgM
  - ❖ **86703** Antibody; HIV-1 and HIV-2; single assay
  - ❖ **87081** Culture, presumptive, pathogenic organisms, screening only
  - ❖ **87110** Culture, chlamydia, any source
  - ❖ **87205** Smear, primary source with interpretation; Gram or Giemsa stain for bacteria, fungi, or cell types
- *ICD-9-CM* codes supporting screening laboratory tests are **V73.88** (chlamydia) and **V74.5** (venereal disease). Code **V69.8,** other problems related to lifestyle, may also be reported to support screening of a sexually active adolescent.

- *ICD-10-CM* codes supporting screening laboratory tests are **Z11.8,** encounter for screening for other infectious and parasitic diseases (eg, chlamydia); **Z11.3,** encounter for screening for infections with a predominantly sexual mode of transmission (eg, syphilis and gonorrhea); and **Z11.4,** encounter for screening for HIV. Codes in category **Z72,** problems related to lifestyle, may also be required to support screening of a sexually active adolescent.

Quality Initiatives and Preventive Care

Certain preventive services, such as measuring height, weight, and BMI, are components of the preventive medicine service and require no additional procedure coding. However, diagnosis codes may be required for quality reporting initiatives. For instance, a group practice may decide to participate in a quality improvement program that requires calculation and reporting of BMI percentiles at all well-child visits for children aged 2 to 17 years. *ICD-9-CM*, and later *ICD-10-CM*, codes (Table 5-3) may be used in support of this effort.

Certain procedure codes are not specific to a quality measure. Code **99420** is reported for use of a standardized health risk assessment tool. Examples of risk assessment instruments include those for alcohol abuse screening and maternal depression screening.

Table 5-3. Diagnosis Codes for Body Mass Index Percentile		
BMI	***ICD-9-CM***	***ICD-10-CM***
BMI <5th percentile	**V85.51**	**Z68.51**
BMI 5th to <85th percentile	**V85.52**	**Z68.52**
BMI 85th–95th percentile	**V85.53**	**Z68.53**
BMI ≥95th percentile	**V85.54**	**Z68.54**

Abbreviations: BMI, body mass index; ICD-9-CM, International Classification of Diseases, Ninth Revision, Clinical Modification; ICD-10-CM, International Classification of Diseases, 10th Revision, Clinical Modification.

Preventive Medicine Services Modifier

As a result of the PPACA, the *CPT* Editorial Panel created a modifier to communicate with payers that a preventive medicine service (defined by the PPACA provisions listed as follows) was performed on a patient enrolled in an individual and group non-grandfathered health care plan and therefore should not be subject to cost sharing.

- The appropriate use of modifier **33** will reduce claim adjustments related to preventive services and corresponding payments to members.
- Modifier **33** should only be appended to codes represented in one or more of the following 4 categories:
  - ❖ Services rated A or B by the US Preventive Services Task Force
  - ❖ Immunizations for routine use in children, adolescents, and adults as recommended by ACIP of the CDC
  - ❖ Preventive care and screenings for children as recommended by Bright Futures (AAP) and newborn testing (American College of Medical Genetics)
  - ❖ Preventive care and screenings provided for women supported by HRSA
- Do not use modifier **33**
  - Ø When the *CPT* code(s) is identified as inherently preventive (eg, preventive medicine counseling)
  - Ø When the service(s) is not indicated in the categories noted previously
  - Ø With an insurance plan that continues to implement the cost-sharing policy on preventive medicine services

Chapter 5: Preventive Services

Check with your payers before fully implementing the use of modifier **33** to verify any variations in reporting requirements.

Examples

➤ **A 9-month-old patient presents for her age-appropriate preventive medicine service.** The physician completes the age-appropriate history and physical examination and provides anticipatory guidance. While reviewing immunization history, the physician notes that the patient is behind on her Hib because of a recent shortage from the manufacturer. The physician counsels the mother on the vaccine (ActHIB) and orders it. The physician also reviews the periodicity schedule and notes that the patient is due for a developmental screening as part of the Bright Futures recommendations. The nurse administers the screening to the mother and scores it. The physician reviews the unremarkable results with the mother and the next routine visit is scheduled for 12 months.

99391   **Z00.129**
96110 33 (developmental screen)   **Z23**
90648 33 (ActHIB)
90460 33

Teaching Point: Append modifier **33** to those services that fall within the 4 listed categories. In this case, the developmental screening fell under Bright Futures recommendations for a 9-month-old and the vaccine product and administration fall under routine immunizations recommended by ACIP. Note that the modifier does not have to be appended to code **99391** because that service is inherently preventive.

➤ **An 11-year-old is seen for an established patient office visit on Monday for a rash.** The physician provides an E/M service with a problem-focused history and physical examination and straightforward MDM. The physician notes that the patient is scheduled for a preventive medicine service one afternoon next week and has not been screened for dyslipidemia. The physician orders a fasting lipid panel to be performed prior to the preventive service. The patient returns the next morning, and the in-office laboratory performs the lipid panel test. The results are reported to the physician.

Monday: **99212**   *ICD-9-CM*
                               782.1 (rash)

                               ICD-10-CM
                               R21 (rash)

Tuesday: **80061 QW 33**   *ICD-9-CM*
                               V77.91 (encounter for screening for lipid disorders)

                               ICD-10-CM
                               Z13.220 (encounter for screening for lipoid disorders)

Teaching Point: Append modifier **33** to code **80061** to indicate that the test was performed as a preventive service, even though it is ordered and performed on a date when no preventive medicine service was provided. Modifier **QW** is also appended when required by the payer to indicate the test is CLIA-waived.

Evaluation and Management Services in the Office, Outpatient, Home, or Nursing Facility Setting

Codes Reviewed in This Chapter

99201–99215	Office/outpatient E/M services, new and established patient
99241–99245	Office/outpatient consultations
99291, 99292	Critical care (outpatient setting)
99050–99060	After-hours and special services
99354, 99355	Prolonged services, direct patient contact, office/outpatient
99341–99350	Home visits, new and established patients
99304–99318	Nursing facility care, new and established patients
99324–99337	Domiciliary, rest home, custodial care, new and established patients

Selecting the Appropriate Evaluation and Management (E/M) Codes

This chapter includes tables with descriptions of the required key components (ie, history, physical examination, medical decision-making [MDM], and, if appropriate, time) for all of the evaluation and management (E/M) services that are reported in the office, outpatient, home, nursing facility and domiciliary, and rest home settings. The following key provides the specific detail of required elements within each level of history and physical examination (eg, problem focused, expanded) and MDM (eg, straightforward, moderate) of an E/M code. Refer to this key when using some of the tables in this chapter. These tables can be downloaded at www.aap.org/cfp (access code AAPCFP20).

NOTE: All E/M code descriptors and their specific instructions reflect the exclusion of references to provider/professional type, whenever not essential, throughout the code set. The codes also reflect the inclusion of a qualified health care professional when the word "physician" is included.

See Chapter 4 for a detailed description of the guidelines and components of E/M services with documentation requirements and tips.

Chapter 6: Evaluation and Management Services in the Office, Outpatient, Home, or Nursing Facility Setting

E/M Key Components				
History (must meet or exceed HPI, ROS, and PFSH)	**Problem focused** HPI: 1–3 elements ROS: 0 PFSH: 0	**Expanded** HPI: 1–3 elements ROS: 1 PFSH: 0	**Detailed** HPI: 4+ elements or status of 3 chronic or inactive conditions ROS: 2–9 PFSH: 1	**Comprehensive** HPI: 4+ elements or status of 3 chronic or inactive conditions ROS: 10+ PFSH: 2 (established patient) or 3 (new patient)
Examination	**Problem focused** 1995: 1 body area/organ system 1997: Performance and documentation of 1–5 elements identified by a bullet (●) in one or more areas or systems	**Expanded** 1995: Limited exam affected body area/organ system and other related areas/systems 1997: Performance and documentation of at least 6 elements identified by a bullet (●) in one or more areas or systems	**Detailed** 1995: Extended exam—affected body area(s) and other symptomatic or related organ system(s) 1997: Performance and documentation of at least 2 elements identified by a bullet (●) in at least 6 areas or systems or at least 12 elements identified by a bullet (●) in at least 2 areas or systems	**Comprehensive** 1995: 8+ organ systems or complete exam of a single organ system 1997: Multisystem exam—9 systems or areas with performance of all elements identified by a bullet (●) in each area/system examined Documentation of at least 2 elements identified by a bullet (●) of each area(s) or system(s) Single organ system exam—Performance of all elements identified by a bullet (●) and documentation of every element in box with shaded border and at least one element in box with unshaded border
Medical Decision-making (must meet 2 of diagnoses/options, data, and risk)	**Straightforward** # diagnoses/options: Minimal Data: Minimal Risk: Minimal Presenting problem: Usually self-limited or minor severity	**Low complexity** # diagnoses/options: Limited Data: Limited Risk: Low Presenting problem: Usually moderate severity	**Moderate complexity** # diagnoses/options: Multiple Data: Moderate Risk: Moderate Presenting problem: Usually moderate to high severity	**High complexity** # diagnoses/options: Extensive Data: Extensive Risk: High Presenting problem: Usually moderate to high severity

Abbreviations: HPI, history of present illness; PFSH, past, family, and social history; ROS, review of systems.

Office and Other Outpatient Services (99201–99215)

- Codes are reported when services are provided in an outpatient setting (eg, physician office, outpatient hospital clinic, walk-in urgent care clinic, or health department clinic).
- Codes are subcategorized into new patient and established patient visits.
- New patient E/M visits (**99201–99205**) require the performance and documentation of all 3 key components, unless billing based on time. See Chapter 4 for information on new versus established patient.
- Established patient visits (**99212–99215**) are reported based on the performance and documentation of 2 of the 3 key components, unless billing based on time. Some payers require performance and documentation of MDM and either history or examination.

⚛ Code **99211** is used to report E/M services that do not require a physician's presence but are usually performed incident to the physician. There are no required key components. Physicians and other qualified health care professionals should not report **99211** for face-to-face encounters with patients.

⚛ Any service with its own code (eg, immunizations, laboratory procedures) should be reported in addition to E/M visit codes when performed as a separate service and documented. (Modifiers may be necessary; see Chapter 3 for more information.)

⚛ Time may be used as the key controlling factor in the selection of the code, when appropriate, in lieu of key components. (See Chapter 4 for specific guidelines to follow when reporting an E/M service based on time.)

Use tables 6-1 and 6-2 to guide you in the selection of the appropriate codes in the following clinical examples. Clinical vignettes are provided to illustrate correct coding applications and not intended to offer advice on the practice of medicine.

Table 6-1. Office Visit Codes: New Patient

Key Components (For a description of key components, see page 118.)
3 of 3 key components must be performed to at least the degree specified for the code.

CPT Code/ Time[a]	Medical Decision-making	History	Examination
99201 10 min	Straightforward PP: Usually self-limited or minor severity	Problem focused	Problem focused
99202 20 min	Straightforward PP: Usually low to moderate severity	Expanded	Expanded
99203 30 min	Low complexity PP: Usually moderate severity	Detailed	Detailed
99204 45 min	Moderate complexity PP: Usually moderate to high severity	Comprehensive	Comprehensive
99205 60 min	High complexity PP: Usually moderate to high severity	Comprehensive	Comprehensive

Abbreviations: CPT®, Current Procedural Terminology; *PP, presenting problem.*

[a]*Typical time is an average and represents a range of times that may be higher or lower depending on clinical circumstances. The presenting problem is considered to be a contributory factor and does not need to be present to the degree specified.*

Table 6-2. Office Visit Codes: Established Patient

Key Components (For a description of key components, see page 118.)
2 of 3 key components must be performed to at least the degree specified for the code. Some payers may require medical decision-making as 1 of the 2 components performed and documented.

99211 5 min	Not required; may not require the presence of a physician PP: Usually minimal severity	Not required	Not required
99212 10 min	Straightforward PP: Usually self-limited or minor severity	Problem focused	Problem focused
99213 15 min	Low complexity PP: Usually moderate severity	Expanded	Expanded
99214 25 min	Moderate complexity PP: Usually moderate to high severity	Detailed	Detailed

Chapter 6: Evaluation and Management Services in the Office, Outpatient, Home, or Nursing Facility Setting

Table 6-2. Office Visit Codes: Established Patient, continued

Key Components (For a description of key components, see page 118.)
2 of 3 key components must be performed to at least the degree specified for the code. Some payers may require medical decision-making as 1 of the 2 components performed and documented.

CPT® Code/Time[a]	Medical Decision-making	History	Examination
99215 40 min	High complexity PP: Usually moderate to high severity	Comprehensive	Comprehensive

Abbreviations: CPT, Current Procedural Terminology; *PP, presenting problem.*

[a]*Typical time is an average and represents a range of times that may be higher or lower depending on clinical circumstances. The presenting problem is considered to be a contributory factor and does not need to be present to the degree specified.*

The examples included here and throughout the chapter are based on the 1995 E/M documentation guidelines. *International Classification of Diseases, Ninth Revision, Clinical Modification (ICD-9-CM)* and *International Classification of Diseases, 10th Revision, Clinical Modification (ICD-10-CM)* diagnosis codes are included for reference. ICD-10-CM codes will be reported only on and after the final date of transition from ICD-9-CM to ICD-10-CM.

Examples

➤ **A 2-year-old patient is seen with chief complaint of vomiting and diarrhea.**

History: Vomiting and watery diarrhea since last evening, fussy. No fever.

Physical examination: 4 organ systems documented (constitutional, cardiovascular, respiratory, abdomen)

Assessment/plan: Acute noninfectious gastroenteritis. Mother is told to give fluids and watch for dehydration. Call if no improvement or condition worsens.

MDM: Low
(acute uncomplicated illness and low risk)

History: Expanded (brief history of present illness [HPI] including timing, quality, and associated signs/symptoms; review of 1 system)

Physical examination: Expanded (limited examination of the affected organ systems or body areas)

	New Patient	Established Patient
}	**99202**	**99213**

ICD-9-CM
446.19 (noninfectious gastroenteritis)

ICD-10-CM
K52.9 (noninfectious gastroenteritis and colitis, unspecified)

➤ **A 6-month-old is seen for a follow-up 2 weeks after a visit for an ear infection and cough.**

History: No fever or cough. Acting fine.

Physical examination: 3 organ systems documented (constitutional; ears, nose, and throat; respiratory)

Assessment: Resolved otitis media, right ear. Follow up as necessary.

MDM: Straightforward

History: Problem focused

Physical examination: Expanded problem focused

}

New Patient   **Established Patient**
99201   **99212**

ICD-9-CM
V67.59 (other follow-up examination)

ICD-10-CM
Z09 (encounter for follow-up examination after complete treatment for conditions other than malignant neoplasm)

Teaching Point: Otitis media should not be reported because it is resolved. If your payers require this, remind them that *ICD* guidelines stipulate that resolved conditions are not reported in the outpatient setting or by providers. *ICD* guidelines are part of the Health Insurance Portability and Accountability Act of 1996 (HIPAA) standard code set and any violation of *ICD* guidelines is a direct HIPAA violation.

➤ **A 12-year-old boy presents for management of medications prescribed for predominantly hyperactive attention-deficit/hyperactivity disorder (ADHD).**

History: No improvement was seen after starting medication, continues to disrupt class, fidgeting more, and unable to focus on work; no weight loss, occasional trouble sleeping, loss of appetite, and no diarrhea. No changes in his school or home environment.

Behavioral rating scales: Parent Vanderbilt ADHD scale showed 8/9 level 3 responses for inattention and hyperactivity; teacher Vanderbilt showed 9/9 level 3 responses for inattention and hyperactivity. Neither rating scale by either observer showed changes from pretreatment behaviors.

Physical examination: 3 organ systems documented (constitutional, cardiovascular, gastrointestinal)

Assessment/plan: New medication is prescribed, old discontinued; follow up in 2 months. Twenty-five minutes is spent discussing side effects of the medication, behavior modifications, changes at school, and when psychiatric referral may be needed.

> **Coding Pearl**
>
> Code **96127** is new in 2015. This code may be reported for structured screening for mood disorders and other behavioral and emotional disorders. For more information, see Chapter 5.

The physician documents that 35 minutes was spent face-to-face with the child and guardian and 25 minutes of that was spent on counseling. A summary of the issues discussed is documented. Time (35 minutes face-to-face) is the key controlling factor.

}

New Patient   **Established Patient**
99203 25 (30 minutes)   **99215 25** (40 minutes)
96127 × 2 (brief behavioral and emotional assessment, with scoring and documentation, per instrument [2 scales reviewed])

ICD-9-CM
314.01 (ADHD)

ICD-10-CM
F90.1 (ADHD, predominantly hyperactive)

Teaching Point: When the actual time is between 2 typical times, select the code with a typical time closest to the total physician time spent. Code **99214** has a typical time of 25 minutes. The actual time spent in this encounter (35 minutes) is closer to the 40 minutes assigned to code **99215.** (Some state Medicaid programs may require that the typical time assigned to a code be met or exceeded.)

Chapter 6: Evaluation and Management Services in the Office, Outpatient, Home, or Nursing Facility Setting

➤ **A 5-year-old is seen by an office nurse in follow-up to a physician office visit 3 days earlier at which nonbullous impetigo was diagnosed and a topical anti-biotic was prescribed. The area of infection shows improvement and the child's temperature is normal. Based on the physician's orders, the nurse advises the parents to continue the antibiotic until the skin is clear and completes a form provided by the child's school indicating that the child has improved sufficiently to return to class.**

History: Here for follow-up of nonbullous impetigo per Dr Good's order. Started anti-biotic ointment on Monday evening. Mother reports no fever and feels the sores are healing quickly. Needs form completed for return to school.

Physical examination: Small area of sores remains. Temperature 36.8°C.

Assessment/plan: Discussed with Dr Good. Mother is told to continue antibiotic oint-ment until all sores are gone. Form completed. Call if no improvement or condition worsens.

Office or other outpatient visit for the E/M of an established patient that may not require the presence of a physician or other qualified health care professional. Usually, the presenting problem(s) are minimal. Typically, 5 minutes are spent performing or supervising these services.

} **99211**

ICD-9-CM
684 (impetigo)

ICD-10-CM
L01.01 (non-bullous impetigo)

➤ **A 13-year-old female is seen with complaints of severe headaches.**

History: Throbbing headaches on left side of face and head a few times over the last few months, each lasting about 24 hours. Has nausea but no vomiting. Over-the-counter pain medication does not relieve the pain. No family history of migraines, doing well in school, no known allergies. Last menstrual period 2 weeks ago, no specific triggers noted.

Physical examination: Detailed examination of the neurologic system with additional 4 organ systems documented

Assessment/plan: Headaches, possible migraine. Given headache diary to complete and counseled on triggers and treatment of migraines. Follow-up visit scheduled.

MDM: Low

History: Comprehensive

Physical examination: Detailed

}

New Patient
99203

Established Patient
99214

ICD-9-CM
784.0 (headache)

ICD-10-CM
R51 (headache)

Office or Other Outpatient Consultations (99241–99245)

Codes **99241–99245** are used to report consultations provided in the physician's office or in an outpatient or other ambulatory facility, including hospital observation services, home services, domiciliary, rest home, custodial care, or emergency department (ED). (See Chapter 8 to learn the reporting guidelines for inpatient consultations.)

The Medicare program no longer covers consultation codes **99241–99245** but has guidelines for reporting the services with the office/outpatient E/M codes **99201–99215.** Check with your state Medicaid program and commercial payers to learn their coding policies.

Consultations are defined by *Current Procedural Terminology (CPT®)* as services provided by a physician at the request of another physician or "other appropriate source" to provide advice or opinion about the management or evaluation of a specific problem or to determine whether to accept responsibility for ongoing management of the patient's entire care or for the care of a specific condition/problem. The "other appropriate source" is not explicitly defined in *CPT.* It may mean any interested source (eg, schools, juvenile court, attorney, psychologist, dentist, physician extender, occupational therapist).

Guidelines for reporting consultations include

- A physician or other appropriate source must request the consultation for opinion and/or advice. Consultations may be requested of a child's primary care physician by other physicians or sources such as a school counselor or coach.
- Documentation must include
  - The request (written or verbal; if verbal, still must be documented).
  - Name of the requesting physician or other appropriate source who requested the consultation.
  - Reason or need for the consultation (advice or opinion requested).
  - Opinion, recommendations, and services performed or ordered.
  - Written report back to the requesting physician or other appropriate source. A copy of the report must be maintained in the medical record. The report may be in letter form, a copy of the progress note, or a completed form (eg, preoperative form, consultation report). In a large group practice with shared medical records, it is acceptable to include the consultant's report as part of the documentation and a separate letter or report is not required.
  - The requesting physician or other appropriate source must also document the request (even if it is a verbal request) for consultation in his or her patient medical record.
- The consultant may initiate diagnostic or therapeutic services at the same or subsequent visit. Any identifiable procedures performed on or after the date of initial consultation (eg, endoscopy, cardiac catheterization, biopsy) should be reported separately.
- The management of the patient remains with the requesting or attending physician and is released in whole or in part only by the written notation of the requesting or attending physician in the medical record.
- Physicians in a group practice can provide consultations at the request of another member of the same practice if they are a different specialty or have an expertise in a specific medical area. For example, you may refer a patient to your partner who has expertise in the treatment of asthma and is an allergist.
- Consultations for preoperative clearance may be reported when the surgeon requests an opinion and/or advice and a written report is sent to the requesting physician. Be aware of Medicaid program and commercial payer guidelines—some do not allow preoperative clearance consultations.
- Follow-up visits that are initiated by the physician consultant are reported using codes for established patients appropriate to the place of service (office, home, domiciliary, rest home, custodial care).

|||||||| *Coding Pearl* ||||||||

A patient and/or family member is not an appropriate consultation request source.

Chapter 6: Evaluation and Management Services in the Office, Outpatient, Home, or Nursing Facility Setting

- If an additional request for an opinion or advice on the same or a new problem is received from the attending physician and documented, the office consultation codes may be used again.
- Consultations mandated by a third party (eg, payer, regulatory authority) are reported with modifier **32.**

Guidelines Used by Payers That Follow Medicare Consultation Guidelines

It is important that you check with your major payers to determine if they have adopted the Medicare policy or if they have established their own policy and guidelines for reporting consultations. You can access the American Academy of Pediatrics (AAP) position on Medicare consultation policy at www.aap.org/cfp (access code AAPCFP20) and the letter to major payers and their responses at www.aap.org/en-us/professional-resources/practice-support/financing-and-payment/Pages/Private-Payer-Advocacy-Letters-to-Carriers.aspx (AAP login required).

- See Chapter 8 for Medicare requirements for reporting consultations performed in the hospital setting.
- Consultations performed on patients in the office/outpatient setting are reported with the office/outpatient E/M codes **99201–99215.**
- If the patient is new to the consulting physician (has not received any face-to-face professional services from the physician or another physician of the same specialty who belongs to the same group practice within the past 3 years), code **99201–99205** is reported based on the performance and documentation of the required key components or time if appropriate.
- If the patient does not meet the requirements of a new patient, an established patient office/outpatient E/M code (**99211–99215**) is reported.
- If the service is provided in the ED, ED codes **99281–99285** are reported.
- The referring physician must document the request for consultation in his or her medical record and the consulting physician must document the request and communicate the results back to the referring physician.

Table 6-3. New or Established Office/Outpatient (99241–99245) Consultation Codes

Key Components (For a description of key components, see page 118.)
3 of 3 key components must be performed to at least the degree specified under the code.

CPT® Code/ Time[a]	Medical Decision-making	History	Examination
99241 15 min	Straightforward PP: Usually self-limited or minor	Problem focused	Problem focused
99242 30 min	Straightforward PP: Usually low to moderate severity	Expanded	Expanded
99243 40 min	Low complexity PP: Usually moderate severity	Detailed	Detailed
99244 60 min	Moderate complexity PP: Usually moderate to high severity	Comprehensive	Comprehensive
99245 80 min	High complexity PP: Usually moderate to high severity	Comprehensive	Comprehensive

Abbreviations: CPT, Current Procedural Terminology; PP, presenting problem.

[a]Typical time is an average and represents a range of times that may be higher or lower depending on clinical circumstances. The presenting problem is considered to be a contributory factor and does not need to be present to the degree specified.

Examples

Use Table 6-3 to determine the appropriate consultation codes in the following examples:

➤ **A 3-month-old with a right indirect inguinal hernia is seen by the pediatric general surgeon for evaluation of the need for repair at the request of the primary care physician.** A comprehensive history and detailed physical examination are performed. Assessment/plan: Surgery is scheduled. A letter with these recommendations is sent to the primary care physician.

MDM: Moderate

History: Comprehensive

Physical examination: Detailed

} **99243**

or, if payer does not recognize consultations,
99203 (new patient E/M) or
99214 (established patient E/M)

ICD-9-CM
550.90 (inguinal hernia, without mention of obstruction or gangrene, unilateral or unspecified)

ICD-10-CM
K40.90 (inguinal hernia, without mention of obstruction or gangrene, unilateral or unspecified)

Teaching Point: When a decision for surgery is made during an E/M service on the day before or day of a procedure, it may be necessary to append modifier **57,** decision for surgery, to indicate that the service should not be included in the global period for the procedure. (See Chapter 3 for more information on modifier **57** and the global period for procedures.)

➤ **A 5-year-old boy is referred from his family physician for opinion and recommendations for the treatment of sickle cell anemia.** A comprehensive history and physical examination are performed with moderate-level MDM. A written report is sent back to the referring family physician with recommendations of treating the anemia and preventing vaso-occlusive crises.

MDM: Moderate

History: Comprehensive

Physical examination: Comprehensive

} **99244**

or, if payer does not recognize consultations,
99204 (new patient E/M) or
99215 (established patient E/M)

ICD-9-CM
282.60 (sickle cell anemia)

ICD-10-CM
D57.1 (sickle cell disease without crisis)

➤ **A 6-year-old is seen at the request of his surgeon for preoperative clearance prior to an adenoidectomy and tonsillectomy.** The child has had 6 episodes of streptococcal pharyngitis in the past 15 months with one episode that resulted in a peritonsillar abscess that required surgical drainage. He has a history of seasonal allergies and intermittent asthma, takes montelukast and inhaled corticosteroids daily, and is allergic to penicillin. A comprehensive history and physical examination are performed and the results of the complete blood cell count and coagulation profile that was ordered by the surgeon are reviewed. The child is healthy and determined to be at standard anesthetic risk for the surgery. Medical record documentation includes the request for the consultation, findings, and a copy of the written report that is sent to the requesting physician.

MDM: Low

History: Comprehensive

Physical examination: Comprehensive

}

99243

or, if payer does not recognize consultations,

99203 (new patient E/M) or

99214 (established patient E/M)

ICD-9-CM

V72.84 (preoperative examination, unspecified)

493.00 (asthma)

V12.69 (personal history of diseases of respiratory system)

ICD-10-CM

Z01.811 (preoperative examination, unspecified)

J45.20 (mild intermittent asthma, uncomplicated)

Z87.09 (personal history of diseases of respiratory system)

Teaching Point: In this scenario, if the patient did not have a history of a chronic (respiratory) problem or other preexisting risk factors, some payers may not allow the consultation.

Coding Conundrum: Consultation or Transfer of Care?

Consultation codes should not be reported by the physician who has agreed to accept transfer of care (ie, takes over the responsibility of management of the patient's entire care or the care of a specific condition/problem at the request of another physician) before an initial evaluation. Consultation codes are appropriate to report if the decision to accept transfer of care cannot be made until after the initial consultation evaluation, regardless of site of service. Any services that constitute transfer of care are reported with the appropriate new or established patient codes for office or other outpatient visits, domiciliary services, rest home services, or home services. The medical record should reflect the transfer of care to the service of the receiving physician.

Examples

Consultation

Primary Care Pediatrician to Specialist
"Consultation requested for opinion regarding treatment of 8-year-old with joint pain, limited range of motion, malaise, and fatigue."

Specialist to Pediatrician
Written summary of findings and recommended treatment plan for the treatment of juvenile arthritis sent.
Consulting physician is unable to accept the responsibility of ongoing management for the specific condition or problem until he or she has performed an E/M service.

Pediatrician to Specialist
"Consultation requested for consideration of assuming management of juvenile arthritis on this 8-year-old patient."

Specialist to Pediatrician
Written summary of findings and agreement to assume ongoing care of the problem.

Transfer of Care

Pediatrician to Endocrinologist
"Please accept ongoing care of uncontrolled diabetes in this 4-year-old."

Subsequent to a consultation, the physician accepts the responsibility of ongoing management of the patient or care for the specific condition or problem.

Endocrinologist to Pediatrician
"Thank you for referring this patient to us for the management of her diabetes."
Transferring physician no longer provides care for the management of a patient or for those problems for which another physician has agreed to accept.

Interprofessional Telephone/Internet Consultation (99446–99449)

A consultation by a patient's attending or primary physician or other qualified health care professional requesting opinion and/or treatment advice by telephone or Internet from a physician with specialty expertise (consultant) is reported by the consultant with inter-professional consultation codes **99446–99449** (see Table 11-1). This consultation does not require face-to-face contact with the patient by the consultant and often takes place when a timely face-to-face service with the consultant is not feasible (eg, consultant is geographically distant). See Chapter 11 for codes, examples, and guidelines for reporting.

The requesting physician or qualified health care professional may report time spent in discussion with the consultant with an appropriate E/M service code according to site of service (when the patient is present for service) and/or prolonged service codes.

Critical Care

Critical care services provided in the office or outpatient setting are reported with hourly critical care codes (**99291** and **99292**) regardless of the patient's age. If the same patient requires outpatient and inpatient critical care services on the same day, the physician or a physician of the same group and specialty would report his or her services based on where the services were provided as well as the patient's age. Refer to Table 6-4 for more information, and see Chapter 10 for reporting guidelines.

Table 6-4. Critical Care by Setting and Age		
Critical Care Provided in	**Age**	**Report**
Outpatient setting only	Any	**99291–99292** (minimum of 30 min) or **99205** or **99215** (<30 min)
Outpatient and inpatient setting	≤5 years	Initial inpatient neonatal or pediatric critical care (**99468, 99471, 99475**) only.
Outpatient and inpatient setting	6 years	**99291–99292** (minimum of 30 min) Combine inpatient and outpatient time. Report **99291** only once per day.

Note: This chart references the same physician or same physician group practice providing care only.

Example

➤ **A 3-year-old girl is seen with complaints of shortness of breath and wheezing.** She has a history of moderate persistent childhood asthma. The patient goes into respiratory distress and vital signs are deteriorating. The physician initiates critical care. After working for 10 minutes to stabilize the critical patient, an ambulance is called when the patient responds too slowly. The physician continues critical care services for another 25 minutes before the ambulance arrives. The total time for critical care services provided in the office was 35 minutes. The patient is admitted to the pediatric intensive care unit at the local university hospital under a pediatric intensivist. The pediatrician provides no more hands-on care for the patient that day and reports outpatient critical care services with a diagnosis of status asthmaticus.

99291 (critical care, first 30–74 minutes)

ICD-9-CM
493.01 (extrinsic asthma with status asthmaticus)

ICD-10-CM
J45.42 (moderate persistent asthma with status asthmaticus)

Transitioning to 10

Chapter 6: Evaluation and Management Services in the Office, Outpatient, Home, or Nursing Facility Setting

Teaching Point: If the same physician or physician group of the same specialty provided outpatient and inpatient critical care services, due to the patient's age only the per-day critical care code (**99475**) would be reported. Had the patient been 6 years or older, the time spent in outpatient critical care would be combined with time spent in the inpatient setting.

After-hours Services

Codes **99050–99060** are used to report services that are provided after hours or on an emergency basis and are an adjunct to the basic E/M service provided.

Third-party payers will have specific policies for coverage and payment. Some carriers pay practices for extended hours because they recognize the cost benefit they realize from decreased urgent care and ED visits. Communicate with individual payers to understand their definition or interpretation of the service and their coverage and payment policies. As part of this negotiation and education process, it is important to demonstrate the cost savings recognized by the payer for these adjunct services. If appropriate, more than one adjunct code may be reported on the same day of service (eg, **99058** and **99051**). However, most payers will pay only for the use of a single special services code per encounter and may manually review, question, or deny payment for a claim with stacked codes.

After-hours service codes are used by physicians or other qualified health care professionals (under their state scope of practice and when billing with their own provider number) to identify the services that are adjunct to the basic services rendered. These codes

- Describe the special circumstances under which a basic procedure is performed.
- Are only reported in addition to an associated basic service (eg, E/M, fracture care).
- Are reported without a modifier appended to the basic service because they only further describe the services provided.

99050 Services provided in office at times other than regularly scheduled office hours, or days when the office is normally closed (eg, holidays, Saturday, Sunday), in addition to basic service

- Office hours must be posted. *Current Procedural Terminology* does not define a holiday or posted office hours.
- Code **99050** is *not* reported when a physician or other qualified health care professional is behind schedule and sees patients after posted office hours.
- The service must be requested by the patient, and the physician or other qualified health care professional must agree to see the patient.
- Documentation must indicate the time and date of the encounter and the request to be seen outside of normal posted hours.

99051 Service(s) provided in the office during regularly scheduled evening, weekend, or holiday office hours, in addition to basic service

- Regularly scheduled office hours must be posted.
- Documentation must include the time and date of the encounter.
- Evenings and holidays are not defined by *CPT®*.

99053 Services(s) provided between 10:00 pm and 8:00 am at 24-hour facility, in addition to basic service

❋ Emergency department physicians who are scheduled during these hours will not typically report code **99053,** although they are not precluded by *CPT*.

❋ Documentation must include the time and date of the encounter.

❋ Use the appropriate place of service code.

99056 Services typically provided in the office, provided out of the office at request of patient, in addition to basic service

❋ It is not appropriate for an ED physician to report code **99056.**

❋ Documentation should include the patient's request to be seen outside of the office.

99058 Service(s) provided on an emergency basis in the office, which disrupts other scheduled office services, in addition to basic service

❋ Report when an office patient's condition, in the clinical judgment of the physician, warrants the physician interrupting care of another patient to deal with the emergency.

❋ Code **99058** may not be reported when patients are fit into the schedule.

❋ Document that the patient was seen immediately and the reason for the emergent care.

Example

➤ **A child is seen for severe exacerbation of moderate persistent asthma on a Saturday at 9:00 am.** The child arrives and is immediately taken to an examination room by the triage nurse and the physician disrupts his schedule to see the child urgently. The office is open on Saturday mornings from 8:00 am to 12:00 noon.

99201–99215 (new or established office E/M)
99058 (service provided on an emergency basis in office, disrupting other scheduled services)
99051 (service provided in office during regularly scheduled weekend hours)

ICD-9-CM
493.02 (extrinsic asthma, acute with exacerbation)

ICD-10-CM
J45.41 (moderate persistent asthma with acute exacerbation)

   Teaching Point: If the Saturday hours were for walk-in visits only (ie, no scheduled appointments), code **99058** would not also be reported.

99060 Service(s) provided on an emergency basis, out of office, which disrupts other scheduled office services, in addition to basic service, hospital unit, on an emergency basis

Documentation should indicate that the physician was called away during scheduled office hours to attend to a patient in another location (eg, ED).

Prolonged Services

Prolonged service codes are used to report 30 minutes or more of prolonged service provided on the same date as designated E/M services that have a typical or designated time published in *CPT*®. See Table 6-5 for a list of the codes and descriptors used to report prolonged services when provided in the office or outpatient setting. Chapter 8 addresses reporting prolonged services performed in the observation and inpatient hospital setting.

Table 6-5. Prolonged Services Descriptors	
Code	**Description of Face-to-Face Prolonged Services**
+**99354**	Prolonged service in the office or other outpatient setting requiring direct patient contact beyond the usual service; first hour (List separately in addition to code for office or other outpatient E/M service.) (Use code **99354** in conjunction with codes **90837, 99201–99215, 99241–99245, 99324–99337, 99341–99350.**)
+**99355**	each additional 30 minutes (List separately in addition to code for prolonged service.) (Use code **99355** in conjunction with **99354.**)
Code	**Description of Non–Face-to-Face Prolonged Services**
99358	Prolonged evaluation and management service before and/or after direct patient care; first hour
+**99359**	each additional 30 minutes (List separately in addition to code for prolonged service.) (Use code **99359** in conjunction with code **99358.**) (Do not report **99358, 99359** during the same month with **99487–99489.**) (Do not report **99358, 99359** when performed during the service time of codes **99495–99496.**)

Prolonged Services With Direct Patient Contact (99354–99355)

Codes **99354** and **99355** are reported when a physician provides prolonged face-to-face service beyond the usual service in the office or other outpatient setting.

> ||||||| **Coding Pearl** |||||||
>
> Codes **99354** and **99355** may not be reported with initial- or subsequent-day observation care services (**99218–99220** and **99224–99226**).

These codes may *not* be reported with initial- or subsequent-day observation care services (**99218–99220** and **99224–99226**). The American Medical Association has clarified that although observation care services are performed in an "outpatient" setting, intra-service times for the observation care codes are defined as unit/floor time rather than face-to-face time as required in the office/outpatient setting.

Following are guidelines for reporting direct (face-to-face) physician or other qualified health care professional prolonged services when performed in the office or outpatient setting:

- ⚬ Use codes **99354** and **99355** in conjunction with E/M codes **99201–99215, 99241–99245, 99324–99337,** and **99341–99350.**
- ⚬ Only the time spent face-to-face between the physician or other qualified health care professional and the patient/family may be reported.
- ⚬ Time does not have to be continuous but is reported for services provided in a calendar day.
- ⚬ Reported with any level E/M service that is assigned a typical time.
- ⚬ When an E/M service is reported using time as the key or controlling factor (>50% of the total face-to-face time was spent in counseling and/or coordination of care), prolonged service can be reported only when the prolonged service exceeds 30 minutes beyond the highest level of E/M service (eg, **99205, 99245**).
- ⚬ The total time of and medical necessity for the service must be documented.
- ⚬ The first-hour prolonged service code (**99354**) is reported for the total duration of prolonged service of 30 (minimum) to 74 minutes' duration on a given day of service. Prolonged service of less than 30 minutes is included in the E/M service performed (eg, **99203**) and may not be reported separately. See Table 6-6.
- ⚬ Each additional 30 minutes beyond the first hour (**99355**) is reported. Code **99355** may be used to report the final 15 to 30 minutes of prolonged service on a given date.

☀ Less than 15 minutes beyond the first hour or less than 15 minutes beyond the final 30 minutes is not reported separately.

Table 6-6. How to Code Prolonged Services (Office/Outpatient)	
Total Duration of Prolonged Services, min	**Code(s)**
<30	Not reported separately
30–74	**99354** or **99358** × 1
75–104	**99354** or **99358** × 1 AND **99355** or **99359** × 1
>105 (>1 hour and 45 minutes)	**99354** or **99358** × 1 AND **99355** or **99359** × 2 or more for each additional 30 minutes

Examples

➤ **A 9-month-old previously healthy child is seen in follow-up for failure to gain weight and increasing irritability with recurrent bouts of constipation.** A comprehensive history and detailed physical examination are performed. Medical decision-making is moderate. Because of a family history of gluten intolerance, the physician wants to refer the child to a pediatric gastroenterologist. The parents are resistant to the referral. A total of 35 minutes was spent providing the face-to-face E/M service and another 30 minutes was spent counseling the parents.

Office/outpatient visit
Prolonged service of 30 minutes

} **99214** (25 minutes average time)
99354 (additional 40 minutes)

ICD-9-CM
783.41 (failure to thrive)
564.00 (constipation)
799.22 (irritability)

ICD-10-CM
R62.51 (failure to thrive, child)
K59.00 (constipation, unspecified)
R45.4 (irritability and anger)

Transitioning to 10

For failure to thrive in a child younger than 28 days, see code **P92.6**.

➤ **A 6-year-old established patient is seen for acute exacerbation of mild persistent asthma.** An expanded history and physical examination are performed and MDM is moderately complex. He receives 2 nebulizer treatments and is reexamined by the physician after each treatment. The physician spends a total of 20 minutes providing face-to-face care. The child returns later that afternoon and is examined, and 2 additional nebulizer treatments are administered. The physician documents the initial care, each subsequent reevaluation following treatments, the subsequent care, the assessment, and the plan. A total of 60 minutes is spent in face-to-face care.

Office/outpatient visit
Prolonged service of 30 minutes

} **99214** (25 minutes average time)
99354 (additional 35 minutes)
94640 76 × 4 (nebulizer treatments)

ICD-9-CM
493.02 (acute exacerbation of asthma)

ICD-10-CM
J45.31 (acute exacerbation of mild persistent asthma)

Teaching Point: *Current Procedural Terminology*® stipulates that modifier **76** (repeat procedure) be used to report multiple nebulizer treatments. At the time of publication, Medicaid National Correct Coding Initiative policy does not allow for the reporting of multiple **94640** codes for the same encounter.

Prolonged Services Without Direct Patient Contact (99358 and 99359)

Prolonged service without direct patient contact (ie, non–face-to-face) is reported when a physician provides prolonged service that does not involve face-to-face care. Please see Chapter 11 for more information, code descriptors, and a coding vignette.

Home Care Services (99341–99350)

- Home visits are reported with place of service code **12** (home location, other than hospital or other facility, where patient receives care in a private residence).
- Do not report home visit codes for visits to patients in residential facilities or group homes. See codes for domiciliary, rest home, or custodial care services (**99324–99328** and **99334–99337**).
- Code selection is based on the performance and documentation of the required key components or time if more than 50% of the time is spent in counseling and/or coordination of care, as seen in tables 6-7 and 6-8.
- Travel time to and from a patient's home is assumed to be in the level of care, just as travel time to and from the hospital is included in hospital care codes and is not counted in the time spent. However, if escorting a patient to a medical facility becomes necessary, code **99082** (unusual travel) is available.
- Services provided by a nonphysician provider (NPP) who does not have his or her own provider number may not be billed unless the physician provides direct supervision. Refer to Chapter 4, page 83.
- Any procedures performed by the physician may be separately reported.
- Payers may have varied policies on coverage and reporting requirements for home visits and may not use Medicare incident-to guidelines. Check with them prior to reporting this service.

Table 6-7. Home Visits for New Patients

Key Components (For a description of key components, see page 118.)
3 of 3 key components must be performed to at least the degree specified under the code.

CPT® Code/ Time[a]	Medical Decision-making	History	Examination
99341 20 min	Straightforward PP: Usually low severity	Problem focused	Problem focused
99342 30 min	Low complexity PP: Usually moderate severity	Expanded	Expanded
99343 45 min	Moderate complexity PP: Usually moderate to high severity	Detailed	Detailed
99344 60 min	Moderate complexity PP: Usually high severity	Comprehensive	Comprehensive
99345 75 min	High complexity PP: Usually patient is unstable or has developed a new problem requiring immediate physician attention	Comprehensive	Comprehensive

Abbreviations: CPT®, Current Procedural Terminology; PP, presenting problem.

[a]Typical time is an average and represents a range of times that may be higher or lower depending on clinical circumstances. The presenting problem is considered to be a contributory factor and does not need to be present to the degree specified.

Table 6-8. Home Visits for Established Patients

Key Components (For a description of key components, see page 118.)

2 of 3 key components must be performed to at least the degree specified under the code. Some payers may require medical decision-making as 1 of the 2 components performed and documented.

CPT® Code/ Time[a]	Medical Decision-making	History	Examination
99347 15 min	Straightforward PP: Usually self-limited or minor	Problem focused	Problem focused
99348 25 min	Low complexity PP: Usually low to moderate severity	Expanded	Expanded
99349 40 min	Moderate complexity PP: Usually moderate to high severity	Detailed	Detailed
99350 60 min	Moderate to high complexity PP: Usually moderate to high severity	Comprehensive	Comprehensive

Abbreviations: CPT, Current Procedural Terminology; PP, presenting problem.

[a]*Typical time is an average and represents a range of times that may be higher or lower depending on clinical circumstances. The presenting problem is considered to be a contributory factor and does not need to be present to the degree specified.*

Initial Nursing Facility Care (99304–99306)

- The level of service reported is dependent on performance and documentation of the 3 key components (history, physical examination, and MDM) or time if more than 50% of the floor/unit time is spent in counseling and/or care coordination. Refer to Table 6-9.
- Services are reported for a new or an established patient.
- When the patient is admitted to the nursing facility in the course of an encounter at another site of service (eg, hospital ED, physician's office), all E/M services provided by that physician in conjunction with that admission are considered part of the initial nursing facility care when performed on the same date as the admission or readmission.
- The nursing facility care level of service reported by the admitting physician should include services related to the admission he or she provided in the other sites of service on the same date.
- Hospital discharge or observation discharge services performed on the same date of nursing facility admission or readmission may be reported separately. When a patient is discharged from inpatient or observation status on the same date of nursing facility admission or readmission, hospital discharge services (**99238, 99239,** or **99217**) should be reported in addition to the initial nursing facility care. (For a patient admitted and discharged from observation or inpatient status on the same date, see codes **99234–99236.**)
- For nursing facility care discharge, see codes **99315** and **99316.**
- Prolonged services provided in conjunction with a face-to-face nursing facility service are reported with codes **99356–99357.** For more information on these codes, see Chapter 8.

Chapter 6: Evaluation and Management Services in the Office, Outpatient, Home, or Nursing Facility Setting

Table 6-9. Initial Nursing Facility Care: New or Established Patient

Key Components (For a description of key components, see page 118.)
3 of 3 key components must be performed to at least the degree specified under the code.

CPT® Code/Time[a]	Medical Decision-making	History	Examination
99304 25 min	Straightforward or low PP: Usually low severity	Detailed	Detailed
99305 35 min	Moderate complexity PP: Usually moderate severity	Comprehensive	Comprehensive
99306 45 min	High complexity PP: Usually high severity	Comprehensive	Comprehensive

Abbreviations: CPT, Current Procedural Terminology; *PP, presenting problem.*

[a]*Typical time is an average and represents a range of time that may be higher or lower depending on clinical circumstances. The presenting problem is considered to be a contributory factor and does not need to be present to the degree specified.*

Subsequent Nursing Facility Care (99307–99310)

- ❋ Codes are used to report services provided to residents of nursing facilities who do not require a comprehensive assessment and/or who have not had a major, permanent change of status.
- ❋ Code selection is based on the performance and documentation of 2 of the 3 key components or time if more than 50% of the floor/unit time is spent in counseling and/or coordination of care. (See Table 6-10.)
- ❋ All levels of service include reviewing the medical record and results of diagnostic studies, noting changes in the resident's status and response to management since the last visit, and reviewing and signing orders.

Table 6-10. Subsequent Nursing Facility Care

Key Components (For a description of key components, see page 118.)
2 of 3 key components must be performed to at least the degree specified under the code. Some payers may require medical decision-making as 1 of the 2 components performed and documented.

CPT® Code/Time[a]	Medical Decision-making (meets 2 of 3)	History (meets all 3)	Examination
99307 10 min	Straightforward PP: Usually stable, recovering, or improving	Problem focused	Problem focused
99308 15 min	Low complexity PP: Usually responding inadequately to therapy or minor complication	Expanded	Expanded
99309 25 min	Moderate complexity PP: Usually patient develops significant complication or new problem	Detailed	Detailed
99310 35 min	High complexity PP: Usually patient unstable or new problem requiring immediate attention	Comprehensive	Comprehensive

Abbreviations: CPT, Current Procedural Terminology; *PP, presenting problem.*

[a]*Typical time is an average and represents a range of times that may be higher or lower depending on clinical circumstances. The presenting problem is considered to be a contributory factor and does not need to be present to the degree specified.*

Nursing Facility Discharge Services (99315 and 99316)

☀ The nursing facility discharge day management codes (Table 6-11) are used to report the total time spent by a physician for the final nursing facility discharge of a patient, even if the time spent by the physician on that date is not continuous.

☀ The codes include, as appropriate, final patient examination and discussion of the nursing facility stay. Instructions are given to all relevant caregivers for continuing care, preparation of discharge records, prescriptions, and referral forms.

☀ If the work of performing the discharge management is more than 30 minutes, the total time must be documented in the medical record.

Table 6-11. Nursing Facility Discharge Services	
99315	Nursing facility discharge day management; 30 minutes or less
99316	more than 30 minutes

Annual Nursing Facility Assessment (99318)

Code **99318** is used to report a comprehensive annual assessment that includes a detailed interval history, comprehensive physical examination, and minimum data set/resident assessment instrument evaluation. The patient's and family's goals for care and preferences for medical interventions are assessed including, if applicable, reassessment of advance directives and updates of contact information for surrogate decision-makers. Table 6-12 describes the 3 key components for code **99318.**

Table 6-12. Annual Nursing Facility Assessment			
Key Components (For a description of key components, see page 118.) 3 of 3 key components must be performed to at least the degree specified under the code.			
CPT® Code/ Time[a]	**Medical Decision-making**	**History**	**Examination**
99318 30 min	Low–moderate complexity PP: Usually stable, recovering, or improving	Detailed interval history	Comprehensive

Abbreviations: CPT, Current Procedural Terminology; *PP, presenting problem.*

[a]*Typical time is an average and represents a range of times that may be higher or lower depending on clinical circumstances. The presenting problem is considered to be a contributory factor and does not need to be present to the degree specified.*

Domiciliary, Rest Home, or Custodial Care Services (99324–99328 and 99334–99337)

These services are provided in a facility that provides room and board and other personal assistance services (eg, assisted living facility) (tables 6-13 and 6-14).

☀ These codes are not reported for patients residing in a private residence (see codes **99341–99350**).

☀ Codes **99324–99328** and **99334–99337** are reported for services provided in facilities assigned the following place of service codes: **13** (assisted living) and **14** (group home), **33** (custodial care facility), and **55** (residential substance abuse facility).

☀ Prolonged services provided in a domiciliary, rest home, or custodial care are reported with codes **99354–99355.**

Table 6-13. Domiciliary, Rest Home, or Custodial Care Services: New Patient

Key Components (For a description of key components, see page 118.)
3 of 3 key components must be performed to at least the degree specified under the code.

CPT® Code/ Time[a]	Medical Decision-making (meets 2 of 3)	History (meets all 3)	Examination
99324 20 min	Straightforward PP: Usually low severity	Problem focused	Problem focused
99325 30 min	Low complexity PP: Usually moderate severity	Expanded	Expanded
99326 45 min	Moderate complexity PP: Usually moderate to high severity	Detailed	Detailed
99327 60 min	Moderate complexity PP: Usually high severity	Comprehensive	Comprehensive
99328 75 min	High complexity PP: Usually patient unstable or developed new problem requiring immediate physician attention	Comprehensive	Comprehensive

Abbreviations: CPT, Current Procedural Terminology; *PP, presenting problem.*

[a]*Typical time is an average and represents a range of times that may be higher or lower depending on clinical circumstances. The presenting problem is considered to be a contributory factor and does not need to be present to the degree specified.*

Table 6-14. Domiciliary, Rest Home, or Custodial Care Services: Established Patient

Key Components (For a description of key components, see page 118.)
3 of 3 key components must be performed to at least the degree specified under the code. Some payers may require medical decision-making as 1 of the 2 components performed and documented.

CPT® Code/ Time[a]	Medical Decision-making (meets 2 of 3)	History (meets all 3)	Examination
99334 15 min	Straightforward PP: Usually self-limited to minor	Problem focused	Problem focused
99335 25 min	Low complexity PP: Usually low to moderate severity	Expanded	Expanded
99336 40 min	Moderate complexity PP: Usually moderate to high severity	Detailed	Detailed
99337 60 min	Moderate complexity PP: Usually moderate to high severity; patient may be unstable or develop new problem requiring immediate attention	Comprehensive	Comprehensive

Abbreviations: CPT, Current Procedural Terminology; *PP, presenting problem.*

[a]*Typical time is an average and represents a range of times that may be higher or lower depending on clinical circumstances. The presenting problem is considered to be a contributory factor and does not need to be present to the degree specified.*

Nontraditional E/M Services and Care of Children With Special Health Care Needs

As electronic communications and adoption of the principles of the medical home have increased, so has the need for codes that capture services beyond the traditional face-to-face visit. Please see Chapter 11 for more information on reporting nontraditional E/M services and services by NPPs. Chapter 11 includes information on services such as

- Telehealth consultations (**G0406–G0408, G0425–G0427**)
- Chronic care management (**99487, 99489, 99490**)
- Transitional care management services (**99495** and **99496**)
- Medical team conferences (**99366–99368**)
- Care plan oversight (**99339–99340, 99374–99380**)

Continuum Models for Otitis Media, Attention-Deficit/Hyperactivity Disorder (ADHD), and Asthma

Chapter 6: Evaluation and Management Services in the Office, Outpatient, Home, or Nursing Facility Setting

Chapter 6: Evaluation and Management Services in the Office, Outpatient, Home, or Nursing Facility Setting

Continuum Model for Otitis Media

CPT Code Vignette	History	Physical Examination	Medical Decision-making
99211* Nursing evaluations Follow-up on serous fluid or hearing loss with tympanogram (Be sure to code tympanogram [92567] and/or audiogram [92551 series] in addition to **99211**.) **There are no required key components; however, the nurse must document his or her history, physical examination, and assessment to support medical necessity.*	1. Chief complaint 2. History of treatment		1. Completion of medication 2. No need for further therapy 3. No need for further follow-up
99212 Follow-up otitis media, uncomplicated with primary examination being limited to ears	Problem focused 1. Chief complaint 2. History of treatment 3. Difficulties with medication 4. Hearing status	Problem focused 1. Ears	Straightforward 1. Completion of medication 2. No need for further therapy 3. No need for further follow-up

99213
 	
 2-year-old presents with pinkeye and recent upper respiratory infection
	Problem focused
	 1. Chief complaint
	 2. Brief history of present illness (HPI) plus pertinent review of systems (ROS)
	   a. Symptoms
	   b. Duration of illness
	   c. Home management, including over-the-counter medications, and response
	   d. Additional symptoms from ROS
		Expanded problem focused
		 1. Ears
		 2. Nose
		 3. Throat
		 4. Conjunctiva
		 5. Overall appearance
			Moderate or low complexity
			 1. Observation and nonprescription analgesics

Continuum Model for Otitis Media, continued

CPT Code Vignette	History	Physical Examination	Medical Decision-making

99214
An infant presents for suspected third episode within 2–3 months Infant presents with fever and cough
	Detailed
	1. Chief complaint
	2. Detailed HPI plus pertinent ROS and pertinent past, family, and social history (PFSH)
	  a. Symptoms of illness
	  b. Fever, other signs
	  c. Any other medications
	  d. Allergies
	  e. Frequency of similar infection in past and response to treatment
	  f. Environmental factors (eg, tobacco exposure, child care)
	  g. Immunization status
	  h. Feeding history
		Detailed
		1. Overall appearance
		2. Hydration status
		3. Eyes
		4. Ears
		5. Nose
		6. Throat
		7. Lungs
		8. Skin
			Moderate complexity
			1. Treatment including antibiotics and supportive care.
			2. Consider/discuss tympanocentesis (**69420** or **69421**).
			3. Hearing evaluation planned.
			4. Discuss possible referral to an allergist or otolaryngologist for tympanostomy.
			5. Discuss contributing environmental factors and supportive treatment.

99215
3-month-old presents with high fever, vomiting, irritability
	Detailed
	1. Chief complaint
	2. Detailed HPI plus pertinent PFSH and pertinent ROS and pertinent PFSH
	  a. Symptoms of illness
	  b. Fever, other signs
	  c. Any other medications
	  d. Allergies
	  e. Frequency of similar infection in past and response to treatment
	  f. Environmental factors (eg, tobacco exposure, child care)
	  g. Immunization status
	  h. Feeding history
		Detailed
		1. Overall appearance
		2. Hydration status
		3. Eyes
		4. Ears
		5. Nose
		6. Throat
		7. Lungs
		8. Skin
			High complexity
			1. Laboratory tests: Consider a complete blood cell count with differential, blood culture, blood urea nitrogen, creatinine, electrolytes, urinalysis with culture, chest x-ray, and possible lumbar puncture based on history and clinical findings.
			2. Antibiotic therapy: Consider parenteral antibiotics.
			3. Consider hospitalization based on history, physical findings, and laboratory studies.
			4. Determine need for follow-up (eg, reassess later in same day by phone or follow-up visit as well as later follow-up).
			5. Attempt oral rehydration in office.

Chapter 6: Evaluation and Management Services in the Office, Outpatient, Home, or Nursing Facility Setting

Continuum Model for Otitis Media, continued

CPT Code Vignette	History	Physical Examination	Medical Decision-making
99214 or 99215 **NOTE:** Depending on the variables (ie, time), this example could be reported as **99214** or **99215**. Extended evaluation of child with chronic or recurrent otitis media **NOTE:** Time is the key factor when counseling and/or coordination of care are more than 50% of the face-to-face time with the patient. For **99214**, the total visit time would be 25 minutes; for **99215**, the total time is 40 minutes. You must document time spent on counseling and/or coordination of care and list the areas discussed.	Detailed History with extended HPI as in **99214**, but complete ROS and PFSH	Detailed or comprehensive General or single organ system (ears, nose, mouth, and throat)	Moderate or high complexity Tests: audiometry and/or tympanometry Extensive discussion of treatment options including but not limited to 1. Continued episodic treatment with antibiotics 2. Myringotomy and tube placement 3. Adenoidectomy 4. Allergy evaluation 5. Steroid therapy with weighing of risk-benefit ratio of various therapies

Continuum Model for Attention-Deficit/Hyperactivity Disorder (ADHD)

CPT Code Vignette	History	Physical Examination	Medical Decision-making
99211* Nurse visit to follow up growth or blood pressure prior to renewing prescription for psychoactive drugs *There are no required key components; however, the nurse must document his or her history, physical examination, and assessment to support medical necessity.*	1. Chief complaint 2. Brief HPI, existing medications, and desired/undesired effects	1. Weight, blood pressure 2. Overall appearance	1. Refill existing prescription.
99212 Follow-up visit to recheck prior weight loss in patient with established ADHD otherwise stable on stimulant medication	Problem focused 1. Chief complaint 2. Document brief HPI, existing medications, and desired/undesired effects	Problem focused 1. Weight, blood pressure 2. Overall appearance	Straightforward 1. Refill existing prescription.

Continuum Model for Attention-Deficit/Hyperactivity Disorder (ADHD), continued

CPT Code Vignette	History	Physical Examination	Medical Decision-making
99213 3- to 6-month follow-up of child with ADHD who is presently doing well using medication and without other problems	Expanded problem focused 1. Reason for the visit 2. Review of medications 3. Effect of medication on appetite, mood, sleep 4. Quality of schoolwork (eg, review report cards) 5. Absence of tics 6. Problem-pertinent ROS	Expanded problem focused 1. General multisystem examination or single organ system examination with special reference to neurologic examination 2. Rating scale review: teacher Vanderbilt ADHD rating scale results reviewed	Low complexity 1. Review rating scale results and feedback materials from teacher. 2. Discuss 6-month treatment plan with adjustment of medication. 3. Plan for further monitoring.
99214 Follow-up evaluation of an established patient with ADHD with failure to improve on medication and/or weight loss	Detailed All data implicit in **99213** expanded plus pertinent review of PFSH and extended ROS including gastrointestinal and psychiatric	Detailed 1. General multisystem examination or detailed single organ system examination of the neurologic system 2. Rating scale review: parent and teacher Vanderbilt ADHD rating scale results reviewed	Moderate complexity Discussion of possible interventions including but not limited to 1. Educational intervention 2. Alteration in medications 3. Obtaining drug levels 4. Psychiatric intervention 5. Behavioral modification program
99215 Initial evaluation of an established patient experiencing difficulty in classroom, home, or social situation and suspected of having ADHD This could be billed as a consultation if the established patient is referred by school for opinion or advice (not transfer of care) and the criteria for reporting a consultation are met.	Comprehensive 1. Chief complaint 2. History of the problem, extended 3. Complete PFSH 4. Complete ROS	Comprehensive 1. General multisystem examination with special attention to neurologic examination and mental health status 2. Rating scale review: parent and teacher Vanderbilt ADHD rating scale results reviewed	High complexity Review of Vanderbilt scales, school record, any other formal evaluations completed to date; discussion of differential diagnoses; possible interventions including but not limited to 1. Educational interventions 2. Initiation of medications 3. Obtaining drug levels or rule out substance abuse, if appropriate 4. Laboratory tests as indicated (eg, complete blood cell count and iron studies, serum lead levels) 5. Psychological and/or psychiatric interventions 6. Behavioral modification program 7. Consideration of neurology consultation 8. Coordination of care services with school, family, and other providers

Chapter 6: Evaluation and Management Services in the Office, Outpatient, Home, or Nursing Facility Setting

Continuum Model for Asthma

CPT Code Vignette	History	Physical Examination	Medical Decision-making
99211* Nurse reviews inhaler technique (94664) and obtains a peak expiratory flow rate for a well 10-year-old established patient. Nurse reviews a disease management protocol with mother and child and teaches child home monitoring. **There are no required key components. The nurse, however, must document the history, physical examination, and assessment to support medical necessity.*			
99212 Follow-up visit for an 8-year-old with stable asthma who is in good health	Problem focused 1. Chief complaint 2. Brief HPI a. Cough b. Wheeze c. Labored breathing	Problem focused 1. Limited to respiratory system. 2. A peak expiratory flow rate may be obtained.	Straightforward 1. Continue current medications. 2. Routine follow-up.
99213 Follow-up visit for a child with stable chronic asthma who is using a metered-dose steroid inhaler with beta-agonist as needed	Expanded problem focused 1. Chief complaint 2. Brief HPI a. Cough, including nocturnal symptoms b. Wheeze c. Respiratory distress d. Exercise tolerance e. Frequency of rescue medication use f. Peak flow monitoring at home g. Associated illnesses and problem-pertinent review of systems	Expanded problem focused 1. Examination of respiratory system including lungs, nose, throat, and other pertinent organ systems. 2. A peak expiratory flow rate may be obtained.	Low complexity 1. Review of home peak flow data 2. Evaluation of medications 3. Alteration of medications 4. Criteria for urgent follow-up care 5. Plans for routine follow-up care
99214 An 8-year-old with known unstable asthma is examined because of an acute exacerbation of the disease; already receiving inhaled albuterol and inhaled steroids by metered-dose inhaler.	Detailed 1. Chief complaint 2. Extended HPI 3. Pertinent PFSH	Detailed 1. General appearance 2. Ears, nose, throat 3. Neck, lymph 4. Lymph 5. Respiratory 6. Cardiovascular	Moderate As in 99213 plus 1. Treatment with a nebulized beta-agonist in office and at home 2. Use of oral steroids 3. Discussion of effects of medications 4. Limitations on physical activity

Continuum Model for Asthma, continued

CPT Code Vignette	History	Physical Examination	Medical Decision-making
99215 A 1-year-old known to have recurrent wheezing following respiratory syncytial virus bronchiolitis has had increasingly frequent attacks during the past 2 months. New infiltrates are revealed by chest radiograph. Laboratory evaluation since last visit documented a positive sweat test. A diagnosis of cystic fibrosis is made.	Comprehensive 1. Chief complaint 2. Extended HPI 3. Complete ROS 4. Complete PFSH	Comprehensive As in **99214**, plus 1. Eyes 2. Skin 3. Gastrointestinal	High complexity 1. Review laboratory data and radiology results. 2. Consult with pulmonologist by telephone. 3. Initiate therapy with review of adverse effects and their duration. 4. Plan for alternatives if deterioration occurs. 5. Discuss implications of positive sweat test with parent(s).

Chapter 6: Evaluation and Management Services in the Office, Outpatient, Home, or Nursing Facility Setting

Perinatal Counseling and Care of the Neonate

Codes Reviewed in This Chapter

99401–99404	Preventive medicine counseling
99464, 99465	Attendance at delivery and delivery/birthing room resuscitation
99460–99463	Normal newborn care
99221–99223	Initial hospital care
99231–99233	Subsequent hospital care
99238, 99239	Hospital discharge day management
99354–99359	Prolonged services

This chapter focuses on coding for care of the normal newborn and those with conditions not requiring intensive monitoring or critical care. See Chapter 10 for intensive or critical care services provided to a neonate.

The American Academy of Pediatrics (AAP) Section on Perinatal Pediatrics, in conjunction with state chapters and councils of the AAP, has developed strategies that have been successful in addressing payment concerns for neonatal care. Contact your state chapter, its pediatric council, section district AAP Executive Committee representative, neonatal trainer, or AAP Committee on Coding and Nomenclature for assistance in addressing any payment inequities for neonatal services in your state.

Definition of Perinatal Period

For coding purposes, the *perinatal period* is defined as before birth through the 28th day following birth. Based on this definition, the perinatal period continues through the completed 28th day of life, ending on the 29th calendar day after birth. The day of birth is considered day 0. Therefore, the day after birth is considered day 1. This definition is important to diagnosis code selection for conditions that originate in the perinatal period.

Prenatal Counseling and Consultation Codes

Preventive Medicine, Individual Counseling Codes (99401–99404)

Codes **99401–99404** may be reported if a family is seen by the physician to discuss a risk-reduction intervention (ie, seeking advice to avoid a future problem or complication). If a family is referred by its obstetrician for an existing problem, the outpatient consultation should be reported using office-based consultation codes (**99241–99245**) or other appropriate evaluation and management (E/M) codes as directed by payer policy. (See chapters 6 and 8.)

International Classification of Diseases, Ninth Revision, Clinical Modification (ICD-9-CM) code **V65.11** (person consulting on behalf of another person [pre-birth visit]) would be reported in addition to other relevant *ICD-9-CM* codes as applicable. Following transition to *International Classification of Diseases, 10th Revision, Clinical Modification (ICD-10-CM)*, code **Z76.81** (expectant parent[s] pre-birth pediatrician visit) would be reported in addition to other relevant *ICD-10-CM* codes as applicable.

Codes **99401–99404** are reported based on time (the time closest to the typical time published for the code in *Current Procedural Terminology [CPT®]*) spent providing counseling. The medical record must include documentation of the total counseling time and a summary of the issues discussed.

When counseling and risk-reduction interventions are provided to a mother or her fetus prior to delivery, report them under the mother's insurance. Verification of the payer's benefit policy for these services is recommended prior to service; if non-covered, an advance beneficiary notice should be signed by the patient.

Preventive Medicine Individual Counseling Code	Time[a]	Documentation Examples
99401	~15 min	15 minutes spent with parents reviewing the risks of recurrent congenital heart disease; assured low risk of recurrence in next pregnancy
99402	~30 min	30 minutes spent in discussion with parents considering in vitro fertilization; discussed potential risks of multiple gestations and preterm delivery, types of problems, and hospital stay associated with preterm delivery; parents understand risks
99403	~45 min	45 minutes spent with parents who request counseling on the fetal/maternal risks due to mother having insulin-dependent diabetes; reviewed maternal risks for infection, poor glucose control, and operative delivery; reviewed risks of fetal anomaly risk, macrosomia, and preterm delivery; postnatal risk for hypoglycemia, respiratory problems reviewed
99404	~60 min	60 minutes spent with parent(s) and maternal grandparents reviewing the hospital records and autopsy results of a previous child who died shortly after birth from congenital skeletal dysplasia and pulmonary hypoplasia; reviewed genetics, risk factors for recurrence, and screening studies that would be used to identify risk or recurrence

[a]*Unless* CPT *instructs otherwise for a code or code range, time is met when the midpoint is passed. Payers following Medicare policy may require that time be met or exceeded.*

Consultations

||||||||| ***Coding Pearl*** |||||||||

Consultations are *not* reported when they are requested by a patient or family member; office codes are used. See Chapter 6.

A consultation is reported when a physician or other appropriate source requests an opinion and/or advice from another physician or appropriate source. The consulting physician renders advice, records it, and returns a report to the requesting physician or appropriate source. Chapters 6 and 8 detail the specific reporting, documentation, and coding requirements for the selection of consultation codes or other E/M service codes when consultation codes are not recognized. See Table 6-3 for the key components of consultation codes used in reporting outpatient (eg, office or observation) and inpatient consultations.

Examples

➤ **At the request of the obstetrician, you counsel a family that was just informed that its fetus has an enlarged bladder and dilated ureter.** You meet with the family in your office and spend 28 minutes counseling the family about the condition. The time spent in counseling and a summary of the issues discussed is documented in your medical record. Your consultation report is sent to the requesting physician and a copy is maintained in your medical record.

Time (30 minutes face-to-face) is the key controlling factor.

} **99242** (average 30 minutes)
or, if payer does not recognize consultations,
99203 (new patient, average 30 minutes), or
99214 (established patient, average 25 minutes)

ICD-9-CM
V65.11 (pre-birth visit)

ICD-10-CM
Z76.81 (expectant parent pre-birth visit)

➤ **At the request of a primary care physician, a neonatologist evaluates a 35-week neonate with recurrent hypoglycemia.** A detailed history is obtained from the mother, documenting hyperglycemia during pregnancy but she was not overtly diabetic. Family history is negative for previous neonates with hypoglycemia or other metabolic diseases. Review of labor and delivery records is unremarkable. After birth, the newborn had 3 documented preprandial blood glucose concentrations less than 40 mg/dL and responded well to oral feeding. On physical examination, the neonate's earlobes showed no abnormal creases, the liver size was normal, and a complete neurologic examination was normal. Gestational age assessment by physical examination was consistent with 35 weeks' gestation. The neonatologist recommends more frequent feeding and rechecking blood glucose before feeds until 4 consecutive preprandial glucose concentrations are greater than 60 mg/dL. The neonatologist spends 10 minutes explaining the findings and reassuring the baby's parents. She writes a detailed chart note and discusses her recommendations with the pediatrician by phone.

Medical decision-making (MDM): Low complexity

History: Detailed

Physical examination: Detailed

} **99253**
or, if payer does not recognize consultations,
99221 (initial hospital care)

ICD-9-CM
775.6 (hypoglycemia, newborn)

ICD-10-CM
P70.4 (hypoglycemia, newborn)

Transitioning to **10**

Attendance at Delivery and Newborn Resuscitation (**99464** and **99465**)

Attendance at delivery (**99464**) is only reported when the physical presence of the provider is requested by the delivering physician and indicated for a newborn who may require immediate intervention (ie, stabilization, resuscitation, or evaluation for potential problems). Code **99464** is not reported when hospital-mandated attendance is the only underlying basis for providing the service. When physician on-call services are mandated

Chapter 7: Perinatal Counseling and Care of the Neonate

by the hospital (eg, attending specific types of deliveries, such as all repeat cesarean deliveries) and are not physician requested, report code **99026** (hospital-mandated on-call service; in hospital, each hour) or **99027** (hospital-mandated on-call service; out of hospital, each hour). See Chapter 12 for guidelines regarding use of codes **99026** and **99027.**

Attendance at delivery (**99464**)

- Service is only reported when requested by the delivering physician.
- Medical record documentation must include the request for attendance at the delivery and substantiate the medical necessity of the services performed. If there is no documentation by the delivering physician for attendance at delivery, the verbal request and the reason for the request should be documented in the attendance note.
- Includes initial drying, stimulation, suctioning, blow-by oxygen, or continuous positive airway pressure (CPAP) without positive-pressure ventilation; a cursory visual inspection of the neonate; assignment of Apgar scores; and discussion of the care of the newborn with the delivering physician and parents.

- Any medically necessary procedures to complete the resuscitation that are provided in the delivery room may be reported separately (eg, direct laryngoscopy without intubation).
- May be reported in addition to the initial normal newborn (**99460**), initial sick newborn (**99221–99223**), initial intensive care of the neonate (**99477**), or critical care (**99468; 99291–99292**) codes.

When qualifying resuscitative efforts are provided, code **99465** (delivery/birthing room resuscitation) is reported instead. Codes **99464** and **99465** cannot be reported on the same day of service.

Code **99465**

- Includes bag-and-mask or bag-to-endotracheal tube ventilation (positive-pressure ventilation) with or without CPAP, and/or cardiac compressions.
- Other life support procedures that are performed as a necessary part of the resuscitation may be reported separately. For example
  - ❖ **31500** Intubation, endotracheal, emergency procedure
  - ❖ **31515** Laryngoscopy, direct, for aspiration
  - ❖ **36510** Catheterization of umbilical vein for diagnosis or therapy, newborn
  - ❖ **94610** Surfactant administration
- May be reported in addition to any initial care service, including initial critical care (**99468; 99291–99292**) or initial neonatal intensive care (**99477**).

> **Coding Pearl** ||||||||
>
> Attendance at delivery is reported only when the service is requested by the delivering physician and is medically indicated.

Examples

➤ **A physician attends a repeat cesarean delivery.** The services are provided because they are mandated by hospital policy. The delivering physician did not request the services.

Code **99026** (hospital-mandated on-call service; in hospital, each hour) is reported.

➤ **A physician is called to stand by during a delivery and spends 30 minutes waiting for the delivery before she attends the delivery of the normal newborn and admits him to her service.**

Codes **99464** (attendance at delivery) and **99460** (initial hospital or birthing center care, per day, for the E/M of normal newborn infant) are reported. Standby services are not reported in addition to attendance at delivery or newborn resuscitation services per *CPT®* guidelines.

➤ **A physician provides brief resuscitation services, including positive-pressure ventilation, to a neonate with mild primary apnea who recovered quickly and is later released to the newborn nursery for close monitoring over the next 4 hours.** The neonate shows no further signs of distress.

Codes **99465** and **99460** (initial newborn care) are reported. (Neonatal resuscitation is likely followed by initial neonatal intensive or critical care more often than normal newborn care.)

➤ **A neonatologist is asked to be present at delivery by the delivering physician.** The neonatologist documents a comprehensive examination of the infant, in addition to the maternal and fetal history, and provides all the elements required for reporting of attendance at delivery. The neonate is normal and admitted to the newborn nursery under the orders of her general pediatrician.

Coding Conundrum: When a Physician Arrives After Delivery, What Service Can Be Reported?

There are no specific time requirements for reporting attendance at delivery. Remember, this service requires a request for attendance at delivery by the delivering physician and includes physician work to perform the initial drying, stimulation, suctioning, blow-by oxygen, or CPAP without positive-pressure ventilation; a cursory visual inspection of the neonate; assignment of Apgar scores; and discussion of the care of the newborn with the delivering physician and parents. When a physician arrives in the delivery room after the delivery and some or all of this work has been performed, should attendance at delivery be reported? Physicians might want to consider the following:

- When the newborn continues to require intervention or stabilization in the delivery room, code **99464** (attendance at delivery) may be reported if the physician work and medical necessity are related to the delivery, not a component of a sick, intensive, or critical admission, and the nature of the intervention is documented in the medical record.
- When the work provided in the delivery room is related more to the initial hospital care (neonate is examined and the physician sends him to the well-baby nursery), only the initial normal newborn code (**99460**) is reported.

For example, attendance at delivery was requested by the delivering physician and the physician arrives after the delivery.

→ The 1-minute Apgar score has been assigned and the neonate has been dried, stimulated, and suctioned and is ready to be sent to the newborn nursery. The physician will report initial normal newborn care (**99460**) after completing his or her initial examination of the newborn. However, if the physician is not the attending pediatrician, no service can be reported.

→ A second Apgar score is assigned, a cursory examination is performed, and the physician discusses the care of the newborn with the delivering physician and parents. Code **99464** can be reported because the basic elements of the attendance at delivery were performed and documented in the medical record.

A stillborn neonate for whom resuscitation services are provided will be billed to the mother's insurer.

A stillborn neonate examined after birth at the request of the obstetrician should be reported on the mother's insurance as a consultation, with a report sent to the obstetrician.

Chapter 7: Perinatal Counseling and Care of the Neonate

Code **99464** is the only code reported by the neonatologist. Although a history and examination were performed, this does not equate to initial hospital care of the newborn, which is reported by the attending physician who provides a comprehensive history and examination, ordering of screening tests and prophylactic interventions, and counseling the family on topics such as infant feeding, sleep, and safety.

Normal Newborn Care (99460–99463, 99238, 99239)

||||||| Coding Pearl |||||||

Normal newborn codes can be reported for care provided to neonates who are acting normally but recovering from a low Apgar score or being observed for a potential problem but are asymptomatic.

Codes **99460, 99462–99463, 99238,** and **99239** are used to report E/M services provided to the healthy newborn in a hospital setting (including birthing room deliveries). They are reported when the neonate is cared for in the mother's room (rooming-in), a labor and delivery room, a postpartum floor, or a traditional newborn nursery and when a normal neonate is cared for after the mother is discharged. Normal newborn codes are also used to report services to neonates who are being observed for onset of jaundice or other conditions or problems but are presently asymptomatic.

Guidelines for reporting include

- The neonate is considered admitted at the time of arrival to the nursery.
- Code **99460** (history and examination of the normal newborn, initial service) is reported only once on the first day that the physician provides a face-to-face service in the facility. This date may not necessarily correlate with the date the patient is born.
- Code **99462** (subsequent hospital care, normal newborn) is reported once per calendar date on the date(s) subsequent to the initial normal newborn care service but not on the discharge date.
- Any additional procedures (eg, lumbar puncture, arterial puncture, circumcision, bladder tap) should be reported in addition to normal newborn care codes. Modifier **25** (significant, separately identifiable E/M service) should be appended to the E/M code when a procedure is performed on the same day of service.
- Discharge management services performed on a day subsequent to initial newborn care are reported with code **99238** (hospital discharge day management; 30 minutes or less) or **99239** (hospital discharge day management; more than 30 minutes), when discharging a normal newborn. Include time spent in final examination of the patient, discussion of the hospital stay, instructions for continuing care, and preparation of discharge records, prescriptions, and referral forms. Chapter 8 provides more information on these codes.
- Code **99463** (history and examination of the normal newborn, including discharge) should be reported when an initial history and physical examination and the discharge management are performed on the same calendar date for a normal newborn.
- Code **99461** (normal newborn care in other than hospital and birthing room) is reported when newborn care is provided in a setting other than the hospital or birthing room (eg, home, freestanding birthing center). The service includes a prenatal history, family and social history, the initial physical examination, and conference with the parent(s).
  - ❖ Do not report **99461** for the initial office encounter of a newborn when the baby was seen in the hospital setting by any provider.

❖ *ICD-9-CM codes from categories* **V30–V39** *are used to report live-born neonates according to type of birth and are the first-listed codes for care during the birth admission. Likewise, ICD-10-CM codes from category* **Z38**, *live-born infants, are the first-listed codes for care during the birth admission. When a healthy newborn continues to receive daily visits pending discharge of the mother, adoption, or other reasons, ICD-9-CM code* **V20.1** *(healthy infant receiving care) or ICD-10-CM code* **Z76.2** *(encounter for health supervision and care of other healthy infant and child) may be reported in addition to the appropriate code for the live-born neonate.*

Examples

➤ **The physician is not present at a repeat cesarean delivery of a healthy term male neonate.** The nursery calls the office and relates that the newborn has been admitted and seems fine. The physician's standing admission orders are followed and the physician examines the newborn the following morning. The physician reviews the record, examines the neonate, and speaks to the mother. The newborn and his mother remain in the hospital 2 additional days, when both are then discharged home. Discharge management takes 25 minutes.

Day 1 of hospital stay	No charge (no face-to-face services provided)
Day 2	**99460** (initial normal newborn care)
Day 3	**99462** (subsequent normal newborn care)
Day 4	**99238** (hospital discharge day management; 30 minutes or less)
Diagnosis code for all days	*ICD-9-CM*
	V30.01 (single liveborn by cesarean section)
	ICD-10-CM
	Z38.01 (single liveborn by cesarean section)

Transitioning to **10**

➤ **A baby is born vaginally in the hospital on March 3 at 4:00 pm.** The pediatrician first sees the baby on March 4 and determines after the initial hospital assessment that the newborn is ready for discharge. A history and examination of the newborn, discussion of the hospital stay with the parents, instructions for continuing care, family counseling, and preparation of the final discharge records are performed.

99463 (initial normal newborn care and discharge)	*ICD-9-CM*
	V30.00 (single liveborn without cesarean section)
	ICD-10-CM
	Z38.00 (single liveborn without cesarean section)

Transitioning to **10**

➤ **A subsequent hospital visit is performed in the well-baby nursery on a 2-day-old who is being observed for the progression of jaundice; however, no interventions are noted and baby is doing well.**

Code **99462** (subsequent normal newborn care) is reported.

➤ **A physician provides initial newborn care in her office to a neonate who was born at home earlier that day.**

Code **99461** (normal newborn care in other than hospital and birthing room) is reported.

Chapter 7: Perinatal Counseling and Care of the Neonate

> **A neonate fails a routine hearing examination.** During a subsequent newborn care visit, the attending physician spends 15 minutes discussing the results with the parents and refers to an audiologist for testing to confirm or rule out hearing abnormality.

99462 (subsequent normal newborn care)

ICD-9-CM
V30.00 (single liveborn without cesarean section)
794.15 (abnormal auditory function studies)

ICD-10-CM
Z38.00 (single liveborn without cesarean section)
R94.120 (abnormal auditory function study)

Diagnosis Codes for Perinatal Conditions

There are some important guidelines for reporting conditions that originate in the perinatal period. In *ICD-9-CM*, these conditions are classified to Chapter 15 and codes **760–779.** Codes in this chapter are used only on the neonate's record and not that of the mother. Other important guidelines include

- Perinatal condition codes are assigned for any condition that is clinically significant.
- In addition to clinical indications for reporting codes from other chapters, perinatal conditions are considered clinically significant if the condition has implications for future health care needs. Other clinical indications that apply to all conditions are those requiring
    - Clinical evaluation
    - Therapeutic treatment
    - Diagnostic procedures
    - Extended hospital stay
    - Increased nursing care and/or monitoring
- Should a condition originate in the perinatal period and continue throughout the life of the patient, the perinatal code should continue to be used regardless of the patient's age.
- If a newborn has a condition that could be due to the birth process or community acquired and documentation does not indicate which it is, the condition is reported as due to the birth process. Community-acquired conditions are reported with codes other than those in Chapter 15.
- Codes for prematurity in categories **764–765** are assigned only if the physician has documented prematurity and are not based on a coder's interpretation of the recorded birth weight or estimated gestational age. As with other perinatal conditions, prematurity and low birth weight codes may be assigned beyond 28 days of age when documented by the physician as clinically significant.
- Codes in categories **760–763**, maternal causes of perinatal morbidity and mortality, may be reported only when the maternal condition has actually affected the fetus or newborn. A code from category **V29,** observation and evaluation of newborns and infants for suspected conditions not found, is reported when a healthy newborn is evaluated for a suspected condition that is determined after study not to be present. Do not use a code from category **V29** when the patient has identified signs or symptoms of a suspected problem; in such cases, code the sign or symptom.

Transitioning to 10

The ordering of codes for neonates at the birth hospital are as follows:
1. Birth outcome (**Z38-**)
2. Codes from the perinatal chapter (**P00–P96**)
3. Codes from the congenital anomalies chapter (**Q00–Q99**)
4. All other chapters

ICD-10-CM Coding Guidelines for Perinatal Conditions

In *ICD-10-CM*, these conditions are classified to Chapter 16 and codes **P00–P96.** *ICD-10-CM* guidelines for perinatal conditions are mostly the same as *ICD-9-CM*. A few exceptions are

- Codes in categories **P00–P04,** newborn affected by maternal factors and by complications of pregnancy, labor, and delivery, may be reported when the conditions are suspected but, after examination, ruled out.

- Codes from category **P07,** disorders of newborn related to short gestation and low birth weight, are reported based on the recorded birth weight and estimated gestational age to indicate these conditions as the cause of morbidity or additional care of the newborn.

  - When both are documented, weight is sequenced before age.

  - These codes may be reported for a child or adult who was premature or had a low birth weight as a newborn and this is affecting the patient's current health status.

  - Codes in category **P07** are not reported in conjunction with codes in category **P05,** disorders of the newborn due to slow fetal growth and fetal malnutrition.

Hospital Care of the Ill Neonate (99221–99223 and 99231–99239)

Initial Hospital Care (99221–99223)

Codes **99221–99223** are used to report the initial hospital care of a sick neonate who does not require intensive observation and monitoring or critical care services. Refer to Chapter 8 and Table 8-1 for the specific coding and documentation requirements for reporting initial hospital care.

Examples

> **The neonatologist sees a newborn male admitted to the well-baby nursery.**
He was born to a mother with O+ blood type who has a history of 2 previous newborns with jaundice secondary to ABO incompatibility. Umbilical cord blood sent for blood typing and direct antibody (Coombs) test shows that the baby is A+ DAT+. At 8 hours of age the neonate appears jaundiced. A bilirubin and complete blood cell count with a reticulocyte count are ordered, results are evaluated, newborn's risks for kernicterus are discussed with the family, and phototherapy is started. The neonatologist performs a comprehensive history and physical examination. Medical decision-making is of moderate complexity.

MDM: Moderate

History: Comprehensive

Physical examination: Comprehensive

} **99222**

ICD-9-CM

V30.00 (single liveborn without cesarean section)
773.1 (hemolytic disease due to ABO isoimmunization)

ICD-10-CM

Z38.00 (single liveborn without cesarean section)
P55.1 (hemolytic disease due to ABO isoimmunization)

Teaching Point: When reporting initial hospital care, all 3 key components (history, physical examination, MDM), or average total floor/unit time if more than 50% of time spent is in counseling and/or coordination of care, must be met. If the minimum key components are not sufficiently met (eg, an expanded history is performed), the initial care must be reported using subsequent hospital care codes (**99231–99233**). See Chapter 8.

➤ **The pediatrician admits a 3,500-g term neonate born vaginally to a mother who developed a low-grade fever during labor.** The neonate is hypothermic. A comprehensive history, including review of the maternal, prenatal, labor, and delivery history; history of present illness; and social and family history, are performed. A comprehensive examination is performed. Complete blood cell count and blood cultures are obtained and antibiotics are started.

MDM: Moderate complexity **99222**

History: Comprehensive

Physical examination: Comprehensive

ICD-9-CM

V30.00 (single liveborn without cesarean section)

778.3 (other hypothermia of newborn)

V29.0 (observation and evaluation of newborns for suspected conditions not found)

ICD-10-CM

Z38.00 (single liveborn without cesarean section)

P80.8 (other hypothermia of newborn)

P00.2 (newborn [suspected to be] affected by maternal infectious and parasitic diseases)

Transitioning to **10**

Teaching Point: If test results are positive, use a diagnosis code appropriate to the findings.

Subsequent Hospital Care and Discharge Management (99231–99233, 99238, 99239)

Subsequent hospital care codes (**99231–99233**) are reported for each day of service subsequent to initial care for the newborn who continues to be sick (ie, not a normal neonate but is not in critical condition and not requiring intensive care). Code **99238** or **99239** (hospital day discharge management) is reported on the day the newborn is discharged (when on a separate day from the initial hospital care).

❄ When a neonate is not treated but only observed for the potential development of illness, normal newborn codes would be reported.

❄ If the neonate is sick but improves and requires no more care than a normal newborn, the subsequent normal newborn care code (**99462**) should be reported.

❄ Codes **94780** and **94781** (car seat testing) may be reported in addition to the subsequent hospital or discharge day management codes when performed and documented. Time spent in car sear testing would not be counted as time spent in discharge day management.

Refer to Chapter 8 for detailed coding and documentation requirements for codes **99231–99233** (see Table 8-2). Chapter 8 also includes more information on codes **99238** and **99239.**

Examples

➤ **A neonate was born to a mother who had a temperature of 39.5°C during labor but no other signs of chorioamnionitis.** The newborn appeared normal in the delivery room and was admitted to the newborn nursery. A comprehensive maternal history and physical examination with review of intrapartum laboratory values were performed. Complete blood cell count and blood cultures are performed, but the physician determines that there is no indication to begin antibiotics. On day 2, the pediatrician reviews the neonate's chart and performs a problem-focused interval history and an expanded-level physical examination including examination of the heart, lungs, and abdomen. Laboratory findings are reviewed and the normal findings are discussed with the mother.

Day 1
99460

ICD-9-CM
V30.00 (single liveborn without cesarean section)
V29.0 (observation and evaluation of newborn for suspected infectious condition)

ICD-10-CM
Z38.00 (single liveborn without cesarean section)
P00.2 (newborn [suspected to be] affected by maternal infectious and parasitic diseases)

Day 2
99462

ICD-9-CM
V30.00 (single liveborn without cesarean section)
V29.0 (observation and evaluation of newborn for suspected infectious condition)

ICD-10-CM
Z38.00 (single liveborn without cesarean section)
P00.2 (newborn [suspected to be] affected by maternal infectious and parasitic diseases)

Transitioning to **10**

Teaching Point: Initial and subsequent newborn care codes are reported because the neonate was not treated but observed.

➤ **The physician performs an expanded problem-focused history and physical examination on a term neonate born via cesarean delivery who is experiencing mild tachypnea on a subsequent day.** The newborn requires intermittent low-flow oxygen by nasal cannula but is alternately nipple and gavage feeding. The physician then speaks with the mother.

MDM: Moderate complexity

History: Expanded problem focused

Physical examination: Expanded problem focused

} **99232**

ICD-9-CM
V30.01 (single liveborn by cesarean section)
770.6 (transitory tachypnea)

ICD-10-CM
Z38.01 (single liveborn by cesarean section)
P22.1 (transitory tachypnea of newborn)

Transitioning to **10**

➤ **Follow-up visit for neonate who was on intravenous antibiotics until this morning, breastfeeding well, with no further fevers. Vital signs and general appearance and examination of the heart, lungs, abdomen, and skin are performed. Blood and urine cultures remain negative after 48 hours. Intravenous antibiotics are discontinued. Patient is discharged home with instructions for home care and follow-up. Thirty-five minutes were spent on the floor reviewing**

Chapter 7: Perinatal Counseling and Care of the Neonate

the hospital course, expected follow-up, and signs and symptoms of possible sepsis or infection with mother.

Time (35 minutes unit/floor time dedicated to the patient) is the key controlling factor. If time spent in discharge day management is not documented, code **99238** must be reported.

} **99239** (more than 30 minutes)

Prolonged Services (99354–99359)

⊛ If direct (face-to-face) prolonged services (**99354–99357**) are required on the same day as a consultation (**99241–99245, 99251–99255**), initial hospital service (**99221–99223**), or subsequent hospital service (**99231–99233**), they may be reported in addition to the basic E/M service (an add-on code).

⊛ Direct prolonged services are not reported with normal newborn codes, intensive care codes, or neonatal/pediatric critical care codes because these services do not include an assigned typical time.

The specific coding guidelines for reporting face-to-face (**99354–99357**) and non–face-to-face (**99358** and **99359**) prolonged service codes are detailed in chapters 6 and 8. See tables 6-5 and 8-5 for the list of prolonged service codes.

Examples

➤ **An infant is transferred from a Level III neonatal intensive care unit, following a 30-day hospital stay, to a community Level II unit to complete her recovery before home discharge.** A large volume of records accompany the infant. A comprehensive history and physical examination are performed on admission; MDM is moderately complex. The provider spends another 1 hour and 20 minutes reviewing the extensive transfer records while off the unit.

MDM: Moderate complexity

History: Comprehensive

Physical examination: Comprehensive

} **99222**
99358 (prolonged non–face-to-face services, first hour)
99359 (each additional 30 minutes)

Teaching Point: This service included 80 minutes of prolonged services. Code **99358** represents the first 60 minutes. Code **99359** is reported for the final 15 to 30 minutes of prolonged services; in this example, the final 20 minutes. If fewer than 75 minutes of prolonged services were provided, code **99359** would not be reported because this code is reported for time that goes at least 15 minutes beyond the first hour or final 30 minutes.

➤ **The physician performs an expanded problem-focused history and physical examination on a term neonate born via cesarean delivery who is experiencing mild tachypnea on a subsequent day.** The physician obtains and reviews a chest x-ray and complete blood cell count and requests that an oxygen saturation (Spo_2) monitor be placed on the neonate for 5 minutes. The chest x-ray and complete blood cell count are normal and the Spo_2 is persistently greater than 95%. The physician spends 65 minutes of total time on the floor with the patient, speaking with the mother and reviewing the chart.

MDM: Low complexity

History: Expanded problem focused

} **99232** (average time is 25 minutes)
99356 (direct prolonged services, first 30–74 minutes)

Physical examination:
Expanded problem focused

Teaching Point: In addition to code **99232,** code **99356** will be reported based on total documented time spent on the floor or unit dedicated to the one patient. Time is not the controlling factor in selection of the subsequent hospital care code because there is no documentation of time spent counseling and coordinating care.

Coding for the Newborn Who Transitions to a Higher Level of Care

During a hospital stay, a newborn or readmitted neonate may require different levels of care. A normal newborn may end up becoming sick, intensively ill, or critical during the same hospital stay.

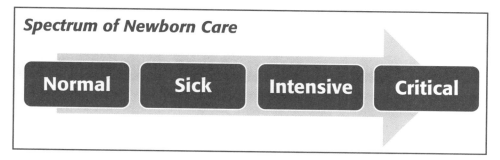

Spectrum of Newborn Care

Normal → Sick → Intensive → Critical

It is important to remember that

* Normal newborn care (**99460** or **99462**) may be reported in addition to hospital care (**99221–99223**), initial intensive care (**99477**), or initial critical care (**99468**) or time-based critical care (**99291–99292**) on the same day when a patient requires normal newborn care and, at a subsequent encounter, a different level of service.

* Once an initial-day care code for a higher service level has been reported, an initial code for a lower service level within the same hospital stay will not be reported. For example, a patient is critical and a physician reports code **99468.** Two days later, when the patient requires intensive care, do not report **99477;** rather, report subsequent intensive care (**99478–99480**) provided the patient meets the weight criteria.

* Once an initial-day care code for a level of service (eg, **99468**) is reported, do not report that code again during the same hospital stay, even if the patient recovers and is stepped up again to that higher level of care.

Post-discharge Newborn Care

Physicians often see a newborn in the office for a well-child visit (preventive medicine service) within 3 to 5 days after birth. In keeping with the *CPT*® guidelines on new and established patients, a physician, or physician of the same group practice and same specialty and subspecialty of the physician who provided care during the birth admission, has established a professional relationship with the newborn (ie, provided a professional service within the past 3 years). All office and other outpatient services, including preventive medicine services, provided to the newborn would be reported with established patient codes (**99211–99215** and **99391–99397**). This guideline also applies to nurse practitioners and physician assistants who work in the same group practice as a physician who has provided professional services to the newborn, as these professionals are considered to be working in the same specialty and subspecialty as the physician. Code **99381** is limited to reporting an initial preventive medicine service to a patient younger than 1 year who meets the definition of a new patient.

ICD-9-CM codes for newborn health examinations are

| **V20.31** | Health supervision for newborn under 8 days old |
| **V20.32** | Health supervision for newborn 8 to 28 days old |

ICD-10-CM codes for newborn health examinations are

| **Z00.110** | Health examination for newborn under 8 days old |
| **Z00.111** | Health examination for newborn 8–28 days old |

Codes for any abnormal findings (eg, underfeeding of newborn) should be reported in addition to the code for newborn health examination.

The appropriate level of office or other outpatient E/M service (**99212–99215**) may be reported in addition to a preventive medicine service when a significant and separately identifiable service is necessary to address a problem or abnormal finding. Modifier **25** is appended to codes **99212–99215** to indicate the separately reportable service.

Coding Conundrum: 3- to 5-Day Visit Post-discharge Encounter

The AAP "Recommendations for Preventive Pediatric Health Care" or periodicity schedule is the gold standard of care for preventive services. The Patient Protection and Affordable Care Act has adopted the recommendations under its required benefits for all non-grandfathered plans. On the schedule is the 3- to 5-day post-discharge visit. Therefore, this service should be included in the number of preventive medicine services a patient is allowed in the first year of life. However, the AAP is often asked how to code for this encounter because many times, this visit addresses follow-up of a problem or a new problem. The AAP recommends coding for the services provided and documented. If the visit is strictly a problem-oriented encounter because of a new or existing problem, report an office/outpatient encounter code (eg, **99213**). If, however, the focus of the encounter is growth, feeding, anticipatory guidance, and preventive counseling, report a preventive medicine service (ie, **99381** or **99391**). For more information on the recommendations, visit www.aap.org/periodicityschedule.

Newborn Metabolic Screening

ICD-9-CM code **V72.62**, laboratory examination ordered as part of a routine general medical examination, does not have an exact code match in *ICD-10-CM*. The alphabetic index directs to the codes for a general adult medical examination (**Z00.00–Z00.01**) for laboratory tests as part of a general medical examination.

Early preventive services may include state-mandated metabolic screening panels and recommended second screenings. Healthcare Common Procedure Coding System code **S3620** reports use of a test kit specific to state requirements.

| **S3620** | Newborn metabolic screening panel, includes test kit, postage and the laboratory tests specified by the state for inclusion in this panel (eg, galactose; hemoglobin, electrophoresis; hydroxyprogesterone, 17-D; phenylalanine (phenylketonuria [PKU]); and thyroxine, total) |

Collection of venous (**36415**) or capillary (**36416**) blood may be separately reported. States may have program-specific guidelines for reporting initial, secondary, and repeat screenings.

Diagnosis code **V20.31** or **V20.32** reported with **V72.62**, laboratory examination ordered as part of a routine general medical examination, is typically sufficient to support the reason for this testing. After transition to *ICD-10-CM*, code **Z00.110** or **Z00.111** reported with **Z13.228,** encounter for screening for other metabolic disorders (includes inborn errors), or **Z13.0,** encounter for screening for diseases of the blood and blood-forming organs and certain disorders involving the immune mechanism, may be reported. However, a payer may require reporting of individual codes supporting each included screening.

Transitioning to **10**

ICD-9-CM Codes for Newborn Metabolic Screening	*ICD-10-CM* Codes for Newborn Metabolic Screening
V20.31 Health supervision, newborn, <8 days old	**Z00.110** Health supervision, newborn, <8 days old
V20.32 Health supervision, newborn, 8–28 days old	**Z00.111** Health supervision, newborn, 8–28 days old
V72.62 Laboratory examination ordered as part of a routine general medical examination	**Z13.29** Encounter for screening for other suspected endocrine disorder (except diabetes)
V77.0 Special screening for thyroid disorders	**Z13.228** Encounter for screening for other metabolic disorders (eg, galactosemia, cystic fibrosis, phenylketonuria)
V77.3 Special screening for PKU	
V77.4 Special screening for galactosemia	
V77.7 Special screening for other inborn errors of metabolism	**Z13.0** Encounter for screening for diseases of the blood and blood-forming organs and certain disorders involving the immune mechanism (eg, sickle cell trait)
V78.2 Special screening for sickle cell disease	
V78.3 Special screening for other hemoglobinopathies	

Lactation Counseling

Breastfeeding support, supplies, and counseling are preventive services when not provided in response to maternal or newborn/infant problems. These may be covered without out-of-pocket costs to the patient under coverage through a non-grandfathered health plan. (See Chapter 5 for more information on coverage of preventive services.) Coverage may vary by health plan, with some considering breastfeeding support and counseling bundled to the well-woman preventive service, while others allow separate benefits.

When medically necessary, a standard medical benefit may apply along with deductible, coinsurance, or co-payment costs to the patient. The service may be provided to address a feeding problem of the newborn/infant or a lactation disorder of the mother. Services to address a mother's condition should be documented in a separate chart from that of her infant and reported to her health plan. Verification of benefits prior to service is recommended.

ICD-9-CM code **V24.1** is reported for care and examination of the lactating mother. When addressing lactation disorders such as cracked nipple, suppressed lactation, or agalactia, see codes in category **676.** It is important to verify benefits and bill for services to the mother separately from services to address a condition of the newborn. For feeding problems in a newborn, see code **779.31.**

After transition to *ICD-10-CM*, code **Z39.1** is reported for encounter for care and examination of lactating mother. When addressing lactation disorders such as cracked nipple, suppressed lactation, or agalactia, see codes in category **O92.** Diagnosis codes for feeding difficulty in the newborn are found in category **P92.**

Chapter 7: Perinatal Counseling and Care of the Neonate

Examples

➤ **A 1-month-old presents for a scheduled preventive medicine visit.** The child appears to be thriving without problems. Mother indicates that she is supplementing breastfeeding with formula because she felt the baby was not satisfied with breastfeeding alone. The physician spends about 5 minutes discussing the mother's concerns and benefits of exclusive breastfeeding and recommends a lactation consultation.

Code **99391** is reported. The brief counseling is not a significant, separately reported service.

➤ **A 6-day-old is seen by a nurse following the physician's instruction to perform a weight check in follow-up to the newborn's well-baby visit 3 days earlier.** The nurse consults the physician because the newborn's weight is only slightly higher than the previous encounter. An interim history indicates a fussy newborn who feeds every 1 to 2 hours. The physician spends 30 minutes face-to-face with the patient and parents examining the newborn, observing a feeding, counseling the parents, and arranging a referral for a lactation consultation. Counseling and coordination time is documented as 18 of 30 minutes. Diagnosis is feeding problem of newborn.

Code **99214** is reported based on time spent counseling and coordinating care, with *ICD-9-CM* code **779.31** or, after implementation of *ICD-10-CM*, **P92.9,** unspecified feeding problems of newborn.

➤ **A newborn is seen in the office for a 5-day well-baby visit.** The mother expresses anxiety about breastfeeding her baby and wishes to receive lactation support and counseling services. The pediatrician completes the well-baby examination confirming that the newborn appears healthy and thriving. Mother and baby are also referred to a lactation class offered by the practice's registered nurse, a certified lactation counselor. Mother and baby return for a class 2 days later.

Code **99391** is reported by the physician for the 5-day well-baby visit along with *ICD-9-CM* code **V20.31** or *ICD-10-CM* code **Z00.110** for health examination for newborn younger than 8 days. The lactation class is reported according to payer specifications that may require specific certification in lactation counseling and credentialing of the counselor as a nonphysician provider. Payer policies vary and should be confirmed prior to providing these services. Healthcare Common Procedure Coding System code **S9443** may be accepted by some payers for this service. *ICD-9-CM* code **V24.1** or *ICD-10-CM* code **Z39.1** is reported for an encounter for care and examination of a lactating mother.

CHAPTER 8

Noncritical Hospital Care

Codes Reviewed in This Chapter

99217	Observation services discharge day
99218–99220	Initial observation care
99224–99226	Subsequent observation care
99234–99236	Admission and discharge same day
99221–99223	Initial hospital care
99231–99233	Subsequent hospital care
99238, 99239	Hospital discharge day management
99241–99245	Consultations—observation setting
99251–99255	Consultations—inpatient setting
99356–99359	Prolonged services

Evaluation and management (E/M) codes for noncritical hospital care services require adherence to the 1995 or 1997 Centers for Medicare & Medicaid Services (CMS) *Documentation Guidelines for Evaluation and Management Services.* (See Chapter 4 for specific documentation requirements.) This chapter includes tables with descriptions of the required key components (ie, history, physical examination, medical decision-making [MDM], and time) for all of the E/M services that are reported in the observation and inpatient hospital setting.

Here are basic guidelines for reporting noncritical observation and inpatient hospital E/M services.

- There are no distinctions between new and established patients.
- Codes are reported based on the cumulative services (performance of the required key components and/or time when appropriate) provided by an individual physician (or physicians or other qualified health care professionals of the same specialty within a group with the same tax identification number) during a calendar day.
- Time in the observation and inpatient setting is defined as floor/unit time (dedicated to the one patient) and includes the time spent
  - ❖ At the patient's bedside
  - ❖ Counseling family or patient (or those who may have assumed responsibility for the care of the patient, eg, foster parents, legal guardian, person acting in loco parentis)
  - ❖ On the floor documenting care, performing the history and examination, and reviewing diagnostic tests
  - ❖ Coordinating care with care team members
- When time is used as the controlling factor in the selection of the code, the time spent and the notation that more than half of the time was spent in counseling and/or coordination of care *must be documented* in the medical record. See the reporting guidelines for using time as the controlling key component in Chapter 4, page 79.
- Services may be performed and reported by any physician of any specialty (eg, hospitalist, primary care physician, specialist).
- Any procedure or other service with a *Current Procedural Terminology (CPT®)* code may be reported separately when performed by the reporting provider or group and documented.

E/M Key Components provides the specific detail of required elements within each level of history and physical examination (eg, problem focused, expanded) and MDM (eg, straightforward, moderate) of an E/M code. Services may be reported using either the 1995 or 1997 documentation guidelines. The nature of the presenting problem (ie, reason for the encounter) is included as a contributory factor for levels of MDM but is not 1 of the 3 required elements.

E/M Key Components[a]

History (must meet or exceed HPI, ROS, and PFSH)	Problem focused	Expanded	Detailed	Comprehensive
	HPI: 1–3 elements ROS: 0 PFSH: 0	HPI: 1–3 elements ROS: 1 PFSH: 0	HPI: 4+ elements or status of 3 chronic or inactive conditions ROS: 2–9 PFSH: 1	HPI: 4+ elements or status of 3 chronic or inactive conditions ROS: 10+ PFSH: 3
Examination	**Problem focused** 1995: 1 body area/organ system 1997: Performance and documentation of 1–5 elements identified by a bullet (●) in one or more areas or systems	**Expanded** 1995: Limited exam affected body area/organ system and other related areas/systems 1997: Performance and documentation of at least 6 elements identified by a bullet (●) in one or more areas or systems	**Detailed** 1995: Extended exam—affected body area(s) and other symptomatic or related organ system(s) 1997: Performance and documentation of at least 2 elements identified by a bullet (●) in at least 6 areas or systems or at least 12 elements identified by a bullet (●) in at least 2 areas or systems	**Comprehensive** 1995: 8+ organ systems or complete exam of a single organ system 1997: Multisystem exam—9 systems or areas with performance of all elements identified by a bullet (●) in each area/system examined Documentation of at least 2 elements identified by a bullet (●) of each area(s) or system(s) Single organ system exam—Performance of all elements identified by a bullet (●) and documentation of every element in box with shaded border and at least one element in box with unshaded border
MDM (must meet 2 of diagnoses/ options, data, and risk)	**Straightforward** # diagnoses/ options: Minimal Data: Minimal Risk: Minimal Presenting problem: Usually self-limited or minor severity	**Low complexity** # diagnoses/ options: Limited Data: Limited Risk: Low Presenting problem: Usually moderate severity	**Moderate complexity** # diagnoses/options: Multiple Data: Moderate Risk: Moderate Presenting problem: Usually moderate to high severity	**High complexity** # diagnoses/options: Extensive Data: Extensive Risk: High Presenting problem: Usually moderate to high severity

Abbreviations: E/M, evaluation and management; HPI, history of present illness; MDM, medical decision-making; PFSH, past, family, and social history; ROS, review of systems.

[a]See Chapter 4 for a detailed description of the guidelines and components of E/M services with documentation requirements and tips.

Observation Care (99217–99220 and 99224–99226)

- Hospital observation services are provided to patients who require monitoring for possible inpatient admission. For example, a patient with dehydration who requires hydration and is not quite sick enough to be at an inpatient level of care in the hospital would be admitted to observation.
- Hospitals do not need to designate a separate area for these patients; rather, designation of observation versus inpatient status is dependent on the patient's diagnosis(es) and severity of illness.
- Initial observation care is reported by the admitting physician or qualified health care professional using codes **99218–99220.** Subsequent-day observation care is reported with codes **99224–99226** and observation care discharge management with code **99217.**
- Physicians of specialties other than the supervising physician (ie, attending physician) who provide care in the observation setting report outpatient consultation (**99241–99245**) or subsequent observation care codes. (See Coding Conundrum: 2 Physicians Providing Initial Observation or Inpatient Hospital Day Services on page 169 for Medicare and *CPT®* guidance.)
- Admission (ie, initial care) and discharge services (observation or inpatient status) provided on the same day are reported with codes **99234–99236.**
- When the patient's status changes from observation to inpatient status or the reverse (eg, physician is asked by utilization review staff to change status from inpatient to observation), the physician should write an order to reflect the change and report the code consistent with the type of service.
- Typical times have not been established for code **99217,** so time is not a factor in the selection of this code.

Initial Observation Care (99218–99220)

Initial observation care codes are reported

- On the first day that the admitting physician provides face-to-face services to the patient in the observation setting
- Using the code that reflects the overall care provided to the patient on that calendar date (see Unique Considerations for Hospital Services on page 179 for further details about coding for initial observation care initiated elsewhere [eg, office, emergency department (ED)].)
  - ❖ When "observation status" is initiated in the course of an encounter in another site of service (eg, ED, physician's office), all E/M services performed by the same physician (or physicians of the same specialty in the same group practice) are considered part of the initial observation care when performed on the same calendar date.

Important guidelines to remember include

- If the patient is admitted for observation and subsequently formally admitted to the hospital on the same day, only the initial inpatient hospital code (**99221–99223**) is reported.
- Physicians from other groups providing services on the same date will report other appropriate outpatient E/M services based on the services provided and on payer requirements. Chapter 6 addresses the guidelines for selection of codes **99241–99245** and **99201–99215.**
- Place of service code **22** (outpatient hospital) is reported with these codes.

- Selection of the code is dependent on the performance and documentation of all 3 key components. Time may be used as the key controlling factor in the selection of the code if more than 50% of the total face-to-face encounter (eg, floor/unit time) is spent in counseling and/or coordination of care.
- Observation care codes are not reported for initial care of hospital-born neonates.

Use Table 8-1 to help you in the selection of the appropriate codes in the following clinical examples. The examples included here and throughout the chapter are coded based on the 1995 E/M documentation guidelines.

Table 8-1. Initial Observation Care (99218–99220), Inpatient Hospital Care (99221–99223), and Observation or Inpatient Care Admission and Discharge Same Day (99234–99236)

Key Components (For a description of key components, see page 166.)
3 of 3 key components must be performed to at least the degree specified for the codes in each row.

CPT Code/Time[a]	Medical Decision-making	History	Examination
99218 30 min 99221 30 min 99234 40 min	Straightforward to low Presenting problem: Usually low severity	Detailed	Detailed
99219 50 min 99222 50 min 99235 50 min	Moderate complexity Presenting problem: Usually responding inadequately to therapy or minor complication	Comprehensive	Comprehensive
99220 70 min 99223 70 min 99236 55 min	High complexity Presenting problem: Usually patient is unstable or develops significant complication or new problem	Comprehensive	Comprehensive

Abbreviation: CPT, Current Procedural Terminology.

[a]*Typical time is an average and represents a range of times that may be higher or lower depending on clinical circumstances. The presenting problem is considered to be a contributory factor and does not need to be present to the degree specified.*

Coding Conundrum: 2 Physicians Providing Initial Observation or Inpatient Hospital Day Services

When Payers Follow Medicare Rules

Initial observation services: The admitting physician will report the initial observation care codes (**99218–99220**). Other physicians (ie, physicians belonging to a different group practice or of a different specialty) providing initial services to a patient in observation will report a new or established office/outpatient E/M code (**99201–99215**) based on the performance and documentation of the required key components.

Initial inpatient hospital services: Initial inpatient hospital care codes (**99221–99223**) may be reported by every physician that performs initial hospital care. The admitting physician will append modifier **AI** (principal physician of record) to code **99221–99223**.

When Payers Do Not Follow Medicare Rules

Initial observation services: The admitting physician will report the initial observation care codes (**99218–99220**). The office/outpatient consultation codes (**99241–99245**) may be reported by other physicians if the service was requested by a physician or other appropriate source, opinion and/or advice was rendered by the consulting physician, and a written report was generated from the consulting physician to the referring physician. When the criteria for reporting a consultation are not met, the subsequent observation E/M codes (**99224–99226**) would be reported based on the level of care provided and documented.

Initial inpatient hospital services: The admitting physician will report the initial hospital care codes (**99221–99223**). Inpatient consultation codes (**99251–99255**) may be reported by other physicians if the requirements for reporting the services are met (ie, requested, opinion/advice rendered, written report to requesting source). Otherwise, subsequent hospital care E/M codes (**99231–99233**) are reported.

Examples

➤ **A 3-year-old female is admitted to observation for vomiting and diarrhea with dehydration.**

History: Parents report vomiting and diarrhea for 2 days, and the patient is not keeping liquids down. She has had a fever to 102°F and is sluggish with decreased urine output. She has no respiratory symptoms or rashes and remainder of a complete system review is negative. She attends child care. Past and family histories are noncontributory. Immunizations including rotavirus are up-to-date.

Physical examination: Detailed-level examination includes vital signs, general appearance, and examination of the mouth, neck, heart, lungs, abdomen, and skin.

Assessment/plan: Moderate dehydration secondary to acute viral gastroenteritis. Will rehydrate with intravenous (IV) fluids and monitor electrolytes, urine output, and weight. Stool to be tested for rotavirus. Appropriate infection precautions.

Transitioning to 10

Report code **A08.4,** viral intestinal infection, unspecified, as the infectious agent had not been identified at the end of this encounter.

Chapter 8: Noncritical Hospital Care

MDM: Moderate complexity

History: Comprehensive

Physical examination: Detailed

}

99218 (requires at least detailed history and examination and MDM that is straightforward or low)

International Classification of Diseases, Ninth Revision, Clinical Modification (ICD-9-CM)

008.8 (viral gastroenteritis, other organism, not elsewhere classified)

276.51 (dehydration)

International Classification of Diseases, 10th Revision, Clinical Modification (ICD-10-CM)

A08.4 (viral intestinal infection, unspecified)

E86.0 (dehydration)

Teaching Point: Remember, all 3 key components must be met for the level of initial observation care reported. The detailed examination limits reporting of this service to code **99218** even though the history and MDM meet or exceed requirements for code **99219**.

➤ **A 3-year-old girl is admitted to observation for vomiting and diarrhea with dehydration.**

History: Parents report that she has vomited about 10 times over the last 24 hours with frequent watery, non-bloody stools. She has become sluggish and has a decreased urinary output. She is unable to keep any liquids down. Fever to 102°F last night; given acetaminophen but vomited it back up.

Physical examination: Comprehensive-level examination includes vital signs, general appearance, and examination of the mucous membranes, neck, lymph nodes, ears, eyes, heart, lungs, gastrointestinal system, and skin.

Assessment/plan: Moderate dehydration secondary to acute viral gastroenteritis. Will rehydrate with IV fluids and monitor electrolytes, urine, and weight. Stool to be tested for rotavirus. Appropriate infection precautions.

MDM: Moderate complexity

History: Comprehensive

Physical examination: Comprehensive

}

99219

ICD-9-CM

008.8

276.51

ICD-10-CM

A08.4

E86.0

Transitioning to 10

The documentation in this example supports code **N12,** tubulointerstitial nephritis, not specified as acute or chronic. When specified as acute, pyelonephritis is reported with code **N10,** acute tubulointerstitial nephritis. An additional code for infectious agent is required when known.

➤ **An established patient presents to her physician's office on Monday.** During the evaluation of the patient, the physician decides to admit to observation care for further treatment and monitoring for pyelonephritis and dehydration. The physician does not see the patient in the observation setting until the next morning (Tuesday) but phones in orders and keeps in touch with the nursing staff. On Tuesday the physician performs an initial observation care service (detailed history and examination, moderate-complexity MDM) on the patient and determines that the patient is not improving enough to be discharged.

Monday's visit   **99212–99215** (office E/M, established patient)

ICD-9-CM

276.51 (dehydration)

590.80 (pyelonephritis, unspecified)

ICD-10-CM

E86.0

N12 (tubulointerstitial nephritis, not specified as acute or chronic)

Tuesday's visit   **99218** (initial observation care)

Same diagnosis codes as Monday's visit

➤ **Same patient; however, the physician sees the patient in the hospital on Monday.** The combined E/M service in the office and hospital results in a comprehensive history and physical examination with moderately complex MDM.

Monday's services   **99219** (initial observation care)

Subsequent Observation Care (99224–99226)

- Codes include all E/M services by a physician or physician group provided on a given day.
- Level of service reported will be dependent on the total services provided and documented.
- Codes require that 2 of the 3 key components be performed and documented. Some payers may require MDM as 1 of the 2 key components performed and documented.
- Time may be used as the key controlling factor in the selection of the code if more than 50% of the total face-to-face encounter (ie, floor/unit time) is spent in counseling and/or coordination of care.
- The history component required for subsequent observation visits is considered interval history (ie, new history obtained since the last physician assessment, including history of present illness and problem-pertinent system review). A past, family, and social history is not required.
- Because the individual documentation for each encounter should contain all information necessary to determine the level of service provided, it is important to document the chief complaint and other factors of the patient presentation that affect management at each encounter.
- Use Table 8-2 to help you select the appropriate codes in the following clinical example:

Example

➤ **7:00 am: A 3-year-old female is seen for subsequent observation care for vomiting and diarrhea with dehydration.** Occasional diarrhea and vomiting but now tolerating sips of liquids. Low-grade fever without abdominal discomfort. Vital signs stable and examination of skin, heart, lungs, and abdomen normal. Diagnostic tests negative. Will continue IV fluids until vomiting and diarrhea decrease and patient is eating soft foods.

Chapter 8: Noncritical Hospital Care

MDM: Low complexity

History: Expanded problem focused

Physical examination: Expanded problem focused

} **99225**

ICD-9-CM

267.51 (dehydration)

ICD-10-CM

E86.0 (dehydration)

Table 8-2. Subsequent Observation and Inpatient Hospital Care

Key Components (For a description of key components, see page 166.)
2 of 3 key components must be performed to at least the degree specified for the codes in each row.

CPT Code/ Time[a]	Medical Decision-making[b]	History[c]	Examination
99224 15 min **99231** 15 min	Straightforward to low Presenting problem: Usually stable, recovering, or improving	Problem focused	Problem focused
99225 25 min **99232** 25 min	Moderate complexity Presenting problem: Usually responding inadequately to therapy or minor complication	Expanded	Expanded
99226 35 min **99233** 35 min	High complexity Presenting problem: Usually patient is unstable or develops significant complication or new problem	Detailed	Detailed

Abbreviation: CPT, Current Procedural Terminology.

[a]*Typical time is an average and represents a range of times that may be higher or lower depending on clinical circumstances. When counseling and/or coordination of care dominates the encounter, time shall be the controlling factor.*

[b]*The presenting problem is considered to be a contributory factor and does not need to be present to the degree specified.*

[c]*Past, family, and social history are not required for interval history.*

Observation Care Discharge Day Management (99217)

Code **99217** is to be used to report all services provided to a patient on discharge from "observation status" (ie, final examination of the patient, discussion of the hospital stay, counseling, instructions for continuing care, and preparation of discharge records) if the discharge is on a day other than the initial date of observation status.

⁘ Performance of the key components is not required.

⁘ Observation care discharge services are not assigned a typical time.

Example

Transitioning to 10

A code for viral gastroenteritis is not assigned because terms such as "most likely" do not support assignment of a diagnosis for physician services.

➤ **Same patient as previous example (ie, patient with dehydration).** Patient fully alert and interactive. No vomiting overnight; diarrhea decreased. Low-grade fever; no abdominal pain. Tolerating fluids and had cereal this morning. Parents are now comfortable with discharge home.

    Physical examination: Vital signs and examination of skin, heart, lungs, and abdomen.

    Assessment/plan: Resolving gastroenteritis, most likely viral. Instructions for home care and follow-up given.

99217 (observation care discharge management)

ICD-9-CM

558.9 (acute gastroenteritis)

ICD-10-CM

K52.9 (acute gastroenteritis)

Observation or Inpatient Hospital Care Services (Including Admission and Discharge Services) (99234–99236)

When a patient is admitted and discharged from observation or inpatient services on the *same date of service,* report codes **99234–99236.**

⚬ Selection of the code is based on the performance and documentation of all 3 key components and includes the combined services provided by the same physician or physician of the same specialty within a group during a calendar day.

⚬ Time may be used as the key controlling factor in the selection of the code if more than 50% of the total face-to-face encounter (eg, floor/unit time) is spent in counseling and/or coordination of care.

Use Table 8-1 to review the required components used to select level of service in the following examples:

Examples

➤ **6:00 am: A 3-year-old girl is admitted to observation for vomiting and diarrhea with dehydration.** Physician returns to the hospital at 7:00 pm.

7:00 pm: Occasional diarrhea without vomiting and now tolerating sips of liquids. Low-grade fever without abdominal discomfort. Vital signs stable and examination of skin, heart, lungs, and abdomen normal. Diagnostic tests negative. Resolving viral gastroenteritis. Parents are comfortable with taking child home. Discharge instructions given.

Face-to-face services performed include initial care and discharge management. A code from the **99234–99236** series would be reported because observation admission and discharge services were provided on the same date.

MDM: Moderate complexity

History: Comprehensive

Physical examination: Comprehensive

99235

ICD-9-CM

008.8 (viral gastroenteritis, other organism, not elsewhere classified)

ICD-10-CM

A08.4 (viral gastroenteritis)

Transitioning to 10

➤ **On Monday evening a physician admits a 4-year-old patient by phone to observation care for acute viral laryngotracheitis (croup).** On Tuesday morning the physician performs a face-to-face service in the observation setting. The physician performs a comprehensive history and physical examination with low-complexity MDM. Later that day the physician determines that the patient has improved enough to be discharged and performs the discharge service.

Monday's service

There is no *CPT*® code to report for this service.

Transitioning to 10

If known, a code from categories **B95–B97** identifying the infectious agent should be reported in addition to code **J05.0.**

Chapter 8: Noncritical Hospital Care

Tuesday's visit

MDM: Low complexity

History: Comprehensive

Physical examination: Comprehensive

99234 (observation care, same-day admission and discharge)

ICD-9-CM
464.4 (croup)

ICD-10-CM
J05.0 (croup)

➤ **An established patient is seen in the physician's office with acute viral laryngo-tracheitis (croup) and admitted for observation at 6:00 pm on Tuesday.** The attending physician telephones the observation admission orders and does not see the child again until the next morning (Wednesday). On Wednesday the physician completes a history and physical examination and discharges the child.

Tuesday's visit

99211–99215 (office E/M, established patient)

ICD-9-CM
464.4 (croup)

ICD-10-CM
J05.0 (croup)

Wednesday's visit

99234–99236 (observation care, same-day admission and discharge)

Same diagnosis code as was reported for Tuesday's visit.

➤ **A 4-year-old patient with croup is admitted from the ED at 6:00 am on Monday.** A physician from a different group than the ED physician sees the child that morning and performs the initial history and physical examination. Another physician from the same group practice returns to the hospital at 5:00 pm and after evaluation of the child, discharges the patient home. The combined service is a comprehensive history and physical examination with moderate-level MDM.

MDM: Moderate complexity

History: Comprehensive

Physical examination: Comprehensive

}

99235 (observation care, same-day admission and discharge)

ICD-9-CM
464.4 (croup)

ICD-10-CM
J05.0 (croup)

➤ **A 14-year-old patient is seen in the ED at 8:00 am on Monday after falling while riding his skateboard to school.** Witnesses reported brief loss of consciousness and the emergency medical technician reported disorientation at the time of transport. The ED physician consults the patient's pediatrician, who orders observation care to rule out clinically significant brain injury. The pediatrician visits the patient and provides initial observation care, including a comprehensive history and physical examination with moderate-level MDM, finding the patient has a moderately severe headache and mild nausea. Later the same day, the patient experiences seizures and repeated vomiting. After reexamining the patient, the pediatrician orders admission, computerized tomography, and a neurologic consultation. The pediatrician's combined services include a comprehensive history and examination and high-complexity MDM. Assessment is closed head injury with concussion.

MDM: High complexity

History: Comprehensive

Physical examination: Comprehensive

} **99223** (initial hospital care)

ICD-9-CM

850.11 (concussion; with loss of consciousness of 30 minutes or less)

E885.2 (fall from skateboard)

ICD-10-CM

S06.0X1A (initial encounter for concussion with loss of consciousness of 30 minutes or less)

V00.131A (initial encounter for fall from skateboard)

Teaching Point: Observation care is not separately reported when initial hospital care is provided on the same date by the same physician or physicians of the same group and specialty.

Inpatient Hospital Care

Initial Inpatient Hospital Care (99221–99223)

✷ Initial inpatient hospital service codes are used to report initial face-to-face services provided to a hospital inpatient.

✷ Initial inpatient encounters by more than one physician must be reported based on payer guidelines. (See Coding Conundrum: 2 Physicians Providing Initial Observation or Inpatient Hospital Day Services on page 169.)

✷ Selection of the code is based on performance and documentation of the 3 key components or time if more than 50% of the encounter is spent in counseling and/or coordination of care (Table 8-1).

✷ If the level of history and physical examination performed and documented is expanded or problem focused, initial inpatient hospital care must be reported using subsequent hospital visit codes **99231–99233** because the required key components for code **99221** (ie, at least a detailed history and detailed examination) have not been met.

✷ The code is reported on the first day that a face-to-face (physician-patient) service is provided.

✷ The date of initial hospital care that the physician reports does not need to correlate with the facility's date of admission.

✷ Report only an initial hospital care code when a patient is admitted to inpatient status from observation status.

Examples

➤ **An 8-week-old is seen in the ED and admitted by physician A.** Over the past 2 days, the mother reported that the infant seemed warm to the touch, fed much less than normal, and had been harder to arouse. The mother had noticed only 2 wet diapers and one stool in the past 24 hours.

Review of systems: Fever, no history of heart murmur, no apnea or cyanosis, no wheeze or respiratory distress.

Past, family, and social history: Full-term male, no reported problems with pregnancy or delivery, delivered by repeat cesarean section. No maternal complications with delivery; rupture of membranes at the time of cesarean section, no fever prior

Chapter 8: Noncritical Hospital Care

Transitioning to 10

to cesarean section; no prior ED visits or hospitalizations since birth hospitalization, no sick contacts at home, and lives with parents and 2 older female siblings. Two-month well-child vaccinations received last week.

Physical examination: Comprehensive examination including vital signs and general appearance with examination of head, mucous membranes, clavicles, heart, lungs, abdomen, hips, genitalia, and skin.

Assessment: Laboratory evaluation: complete blood cell count with white blood cells 12,000, no left shift on differential; urinalysis normal or negative with pH 7.0, specific gravity 1.020; fever, concern for sepsis or serious bacterial infection, doubt pyelonephritis given normal urinalysis, less likely meningitis given normal exam and not ill appearing, doubt bronchiolitis given lack of viral symptoms.

Plan: Admit for IV antibiotics, pending culture results. Continue breastfeeding ad lib. Discussed differential diagnoses, working diagnosis, current diagnostic and treatment plans, and anticipated hospital course with parents.

MDM: Moderate complexity

History: Detailed

Physical examination: Comprehensive

} **99221**

ICD-9-CM
780.60 (fever, unspecified)

ICD-10-CM
R50.9 (fever, unspecified)

Transitioning to 10

➤ **Later that same calendar day, Physician B from the same group practice sees the infant.** She performs a more comprehensive history, examines the infant, and spends 20 minutes talking with the parents.

MDM: Moderate complexity

History: Comprehensive

Physical examination: Comprehensive

} **99222**

ICD-9-CM
780.60

ICD-10-CM
R50.9

Transitioning to 10

Teaching Point: The total E/M services provided on this date now meet the guidelines for a comprehensive history. Physician B may now report the service with code **99222.** Physician A would submit no bill for his work that day.

➤ **Physician A performed a comprehensive history and physical examination with moderate-level complexity MDM at the initial hospital visit and documents that he spent 25 minutes on the floor with the patient and family.** The service would be reported with code **99222.** However, later that same calendar day, physician B (same specialty and from the same practice) sees the patient. She documents that 35 of her 40 minutes spent on the floor were spent counseling the parents and coordinating the patient's care. The code for all of the care provided on that calendar day would now be reported using code **99223** based on the documented floor/unit time (total of 65 minutes between the 2 physicians with 35 minutes spent in counseling/coordination of care). Physician A would submit no bill and physician B would submit the bill for the calendar day's service.

Subsequent Hospital Care (99231–99233)

◉ Codes include all E/M services by a physician or physician group provided on a given subsequent day.

◉ The level of service reported will be dependent on the total services provided and documented.

◉ Selection of the code is based on performance and documentation of 2 of the 3 key components or time if more than 50% of the encounter is spent in counseling and/or coordination of care (Table 8-2).

◉ The history component required for subsequent hospital visits is considered interval history (ie, new history information obtained since the last physician assessment, including chief complaint, history of present illness, and problem-pertinent system review).

||||||| *Coding Pearl* |||||||

Past, family, and social history is not required as part of an interval history.

Use Table 8-2 to help you in the selection of the appropriate codes in the following clinical examples:

Examples

➤ **No reported problems overnight; breastfeeding well, continues to have low-grade fever (100.7°F max) overnight, no reported apnea or cyanosis, no respiratory distress.**

Physical examination: Expanded-level examination including vital signs and general appearance, heart, lungs, and skin.

Laboratory: No growth in blood or urine cultures at less than 24 hours.

Assessment/plan: Continued fever; concern for sepsis, suspect viral etiology given negative workup so far for common serious bacterial infections such as pyelonephritis and bacteremia. Continue IV antibiotics until cultures are negative for 48 hours; continue breastfeeding ad lib. Spoke with mom and reviewed overnight events, morning laboratory results, current plan, and possible discharge home tomorrow.

MDM: Low complexity

History: Expanded interval history

Physical examination: Expanded

} **99232**

ICD-9-CM
780.60 (fever, unspecified)

ICD-10-CM
R50.9 (fever)

Transitioning to **10**

Teaching Point: Time cannot be used as the controlling factor in selection of the code because the documentation does not indicate the total floor/unit time and time spent in counseling and/or coordination of care.

➤ **Same progress note as in previous vignette but with additional documentation.**

Spoke with mom for 30 minutes and reviewed overnight events, morning laboratory results, and current plan; anticipate discharge home tomorrow. Total visit time: 40 minutes.

Time would be used as the controlling factor in selection of the code because a total of 40 minutes was spent on the unit/floor with the patient and more than 50% of the time was spent in counseling. The appropriate code would be **99233.**

Hospital Discharge Day Management (99238, 99239)

99238   Hospital discharge day management; 30 minutes or less
99239   more than 30 minutes

 *Coding Pearl* |||||||||

If the total time spent in performing discharge management is not documented in the medical record, report code **99238** instead of **99239**.

Codes **99238** (≤30 minutes) and **99239** (>30 minutes) are reported by the attending physician providing discharge services on a day subsequent to the date that the admission service was provided.

* A face-to-face physician-patient encounter in the hospital is required.
* Reporting is based on the total time (time does not have to be continuous) spent performing all final discharge services including, as appropriate, examination of the patient, discussion of the hospital stay, patient and/or family counseling, instructions for continuing care to all relevant caregivers, and preparation of referral forms, prescriptions, and records.
* May be used to report discharge services provided to patients who die during their hospital stay.
* Services are reported on the day that the physician sees the patient and performs discharge services, even if the patient leaves the hospital on a different day.
* Only the attending physician or physician providing services on behalf of the attending physician (eg, covering physician, physician of same group and same specialty) may report discharge management services. If another physician is providing concurrent care, his or her services would be reported using subsequent hospital visit codes (**99231–99233**).
* Time spent in discharge services must be documented in the medical record when reporting code **99239.** If the total time spent performing the discharge management is not documented in the medical record, report code **99238** instead of **99239.** Only time spent on the day of discharge may be counted.
* Time spent on the day of discharge performing separately reported services (eg, car seat testing) is not included in the discharge day management time.

Example

> **Continued on IV antibiotics until this morning, breastfeeding well, no further fevers.** Vital signs and general appearance and examination of the heart, lungs, abdomen, and skin are performed. Blood and urine cultures remain negative after 48 hours. Intravenous antibiotics discontinued. Patient discharged home with instructions for home care and follow-up. Spent 35 minutes on the floor reviewing the hospital course, expected follow-up, and signs and symptoms of possible sepsis or infection with mother.

This visit would be reported with code **99239** because 35 minutes was spent in the provision of discharge management services and the time was documented in the medical record.

Unique Considerations for Hospital Services

Admission to the hospital after a visit in the office and hospital rounds by more than one physician can create unusual circumstances. Proper coding in these situations will be contingent on whether the attending physician and colleagues provide coverage, bill under the same group name and tax identification number, or bill independently using individual tax identification numbers.

Office Visit and Initial Hospital Care Same Day of Service

The primary care physician examines the patient in the office and a colleague admits the patient to the hospital later the same day for the same problem. If using independent billing numbers, each physician would submit a separate bill (ie, the primary care physician would bill for the office visit, the colleague would bill for the observation or inpatient hospital admission). If using the same billing number, services should be combined into one initial hospital care code encompassing the combined work of the 2 encounters. If the 2 encounters are not related and have different diagnoses, there is a legitimate reason to submit a claim for 2 distinct E/M services on the same day, even by the same provider, but be prepared to justify payment. Alternatively, bundle the 2 encounters, including all appropriate *ICD-9-CM* or *ICD-10-CM* codes. If 2 distinct E/M services are reported on the same day of service by the same provider, append modifier **25** to the second service.

Two Hospital Visits on Same Day of Service

The primary care physician admits the patient to the hospital in the morning and a colleague is called to see the patient in the evening. If using independent identification numbers, separate bills are submitted. If using the same identification number, the services are combined.

When office/outpatient E/M and hospital admissions occur on the same calendar day, coding will depend on whether the admitting physician and/or physician of the same group and specialty provides face-to-face care in the hospital setting.

Office Visit Without Face-to-Face Encounter in Hospital

The primary care physician examines an established patient in the office and determines that the patient needs admission. The admission history and physical examination are performed, and a treatment plan and orders are sent to the hospital. The physician remains in communication with the hospital nurses that night as the child improves and sees him the next morning on rounds—he is stable but not ready for discharge. The office visit on day 1 would be reported with code **99212–99215** (office/outpatient E/M service, established patient) based on the performance and documentation of the required key components. The second day's work is reported using initial hospital care or observation care codes (**99221–99223** or **99218–99220**) based on the level of work (ie, history, physical examination, and MDM or time) performed on the hospital floor on that day of service. If the work performed on the second day did not meet the required key components, the service would be reported using subsequent-day codes (**99224–99226, 99231–99233**).

Office Visit and Inpatient Encounter Same Day of Service

The physician (or physician of the same group) provides face-to-face services in the hospital later that same day. The level of initial hospital care service will then be based on the combination of the E/M services provided during that calendar day.

Coordinating billing is important. The office billing manager should have all hospital charges for each patient by the end of the next business day to coordinate billing and avoid delays in claims submissions.

Unique Considerations for Hospital Services, continued

Teaching Physician Encounter on Day After Admission
If a resident provides the only face-to-face encounter on the date a patient is admitted to inpatient or observation status and the attending physician provides an initial face-to-face encounter on the next day, the encounter is reported based on the extent of work performed. If documentation clearly supports the work of an initial encounter (**99221–99223** or **99218–99220**), this service may be reported because these services are reported for the initial encounter without regard to the date of admission. However, if the encounter involves a more limited interval assessment, subsequent encounter services (**99231–99233** or **99224–99226**) or same-day admission and discharge services (**99234–99236**) are likely more appropriate.

Discharge Versus Subsequent Hospital Services

Codes **99238** and **99239** are underused and often reported incorrectly. Subsequent hospital visit codes should not be reported on the day of discharge alone or in addition to the discharge code. Code **99239** is one of the most underreported *CPT®* codes even though it often more accurately reflects the service performed! Physicians often spend more than 30 minutes in discharge management, especially when the patient is seen several times that day. Time spent in charting *on the day of discharge* is counted in the total unit/floor time.

The relative value units (RVUs) for discharge service codes reflect the additional services provided on the day of discharge. *Note:* The 2015 RVUs were not available at the time of publication.

CPT Code	2014 Medicare RVUs
99231	1.1
99232	2.02
99233	2.91
99238	2.03
99239	3.0

Teaching Point: The RVUs for discharge service codes reflect the additional services provided on the day of discharge.

Consultations (99241–99245, 99251–99255)

Current Procedural Terminology defines *consultations* as services provided by a physician at the request of another physician or "other appropriate source" to provide advice or opinion about the management or evaluation of a specific problem. Medicare does not recognize consultation codes but pays for the services using codes for other E/M services. Detailed information on the *CPT®* and CMS Medicare guidelines for reporting consultations are described for office and outpatient consultations in Chapter 6. Please review those guidelines carefully for general guidelines that apply for all consultations.

Consultation codes are not used when a transfer of care occurs. See Chapter 6, page 126, for the definition of *transfer of care* versus consultation.

Guidelines Used by Payers That Do Not Follow Medicare Consultation Guidelines

Consultations for Patients in Observation

99241–99245   Office consultation for a new or established patient (includes consultations in other outpatient settings)

- Level of care is determined by performing and documenting the required 3 key components (history, physical examination, and MDM) or time (Table 8-3) as described for other E/M services that are assigned a typical time.

- Follow-up visits that are initiated by the physician consultant are reported using codes for subsequent observation care services (**99224–99226**).

- If an additional request for an opinion or advice on the same or a new problem is received from the attending physician and documented in the medical record, office/outpatient consultation codes, unlike inpatient consultation codes, may be used again.

- When reporting prolonged physician care with consultations that are performed in the observation care setting, report the office or other outpatient setting prolonged services code (**99354, 99355**) in addition to the appropriate outpatient consultation code (**99241–99245**) or appropriate other outpatient service code (**99201–99205, 99212–99215**). See Chapter 6 for more information.

> **Coding Pearl**
>
> Consultation codes are not reported when a transfer of care occurs before the patient is seen.

Table 8-3. Observation (99241–99245) and Inpatient (99251–99255) Consultation Codes

Key Components (For a description of key components, see page 166.)
3 of 3 key components must be performed to at least the degree specified under the code.

CPT Code/Time[a]	Medical Decision-making	History	Examination
99241 15 min 99251 20 min	Straightforward	Problem focused	Problem focused
99242 30 min 99252 40 min	Straightforward	Expanded	Expanded
99243 40 min 99253 55 min	Low complexity	Detailed	Detailed
99244 60 min 99254 80 min	Moderate complexity	Comprehensive	Comprehensive
99245 80 min 99255 110 min	High complexity	Comprehensive	Comprehensive

Abbreviation: CPT, Current Procedural Terminology.

[a]*Typical time is an average and represents a range of times that may be higher or lower depending on clinical circumstances. The presenting problem is considered to be a contributory factor and does not need to be present to the degree specified.*

Chapter 8: Noncritical Hospital Care

Example

➤ **A 14-year-old is admitted to observation for closed head trauma and possible concussion after a fall from his skateboard with brief loss of consciousness.** The attending physician consults a pediatric neurologist for her opinion and advice. The neurologist performs a detailed history and physical examination, reviews computerized tomography images, and orders additional diagnostic studies. Documentation of the written report is included in the shared medical record. Assessment is concussion with brief loss of consciousness. The neurologist reports the service with

MDM: Moderate

History: Detailed

Physical examination: Detailed

} **99243**

or, if payer does not recognize consultations,

99214 (office/outpatient E/M, established patient) or

99203 (new patient)

ICD-9-CM

850.11 (concussion; with loss of consciousness of 30 minutes or less)

E885.2 (fall from skateboard)

ICD-10-CM

S06.0X1A (initial encounter for concussion with loss of consciousness of 30 minutes or less)

V00.131A (initial encounter for fall from skateboard)

Inpatient Consultations (99251–99255)

❋ Codes **99251–99255** are to be used only once by the reporting physician for an individual hospital patient for a particular admission. There are no specific guidelines for the length of stay.

❋ Follow-up visits provided in the hospital by the same physician must be reported using subsequent care codes (**99231–99233**). Examples of a follow-up visit might be to complete the initial consultation when test results become available or in response to a change in the patient's status.

❋ If a consultation is requested by the attending physician for the same patient on a completely different problem during the same hospital stay, subsequent hospital care codes (**99231–99233**) must be reported. The subsequent role of a consultant in the ongoing care of the patient must be made clear in the medical record by the attending physician. If the attending physician turns over the care of the patient to the consultant, the consultant, now the new attending physician, should use subsequent hospital care codes (**99231–99233**) to indicate the level of service provided.

❋ The attending physician and consultant may continue to provide care to the patient. Each would code for subsequent hospital care as long as the problems that they manage are different. (The attending and consulting physicians should use different *diagnosis* codes to indicate that they are managing different problems. However, sometimes the diagnosis will be the same.)

❋ If a patient is readmitted for the same or different problem (a new hospital stay), an initial inpatient consultation code may be reported if it meets the definition and requirements for reporting a consultation.

❖ When an inpatient consultation is performed on a date that a patient is admitted to the hospital, all E/M services provided by the consultant (including any outpatient encounters) related to the admission are reported with the inpatient consultation service code. If a patient is admitted after an outpatient consultation (eg, office, ED) and the patient is not seen on the unit on the date of admission, only the outpatient consultation code is reported.

Example

➤ **A 3-month-old patient is seen by the pediatrician in the ED and is subsequently admitted for bilious vomiting, dehydration, and possible bowel obstruction.** A gastroenterologist is consulted and following workup diagnoses volvulus. He documents his written report in the medical record, speaks to the parents, and agrees to follow the patient. The gastroenterologist reports his consultation service with

MDM: High complexity
History: Comprehensive
Physical examination:
Comprehensive

} **99255**
or, if payer does not recognize consultations,
99223 (initial hospital visit)

ICD-9-CM
560.2 (volvulus)

ICD-10-CM
K56.2 (volvulus)

Teaching Point: Follow-up visits by the gastroenterologist are reported using the appropriate-level subsequent inpatient hospital codes (**99231–99233**). Had the volvulus been documented as congenital, *ICD-9-CM* code **751.5** (other anomalies of intestine) or, after transition to *ICD-10-CM*, code **Q43.8** (other specified congenital malformation of the intestine) would be reported.

Interprofessional Telephone/Internet Consultation

A consultation by a physician with specialty expertise (consultant) conducted by telephone or Internet in response to a request by the patient's attending or primary physician or other qualified health care professional for an opinion and/or treatment advice is reported by the consultant with interprofessional consultation codes **99446–99449.** This consultation does not require face-to-face contact with the patient by the consultant and often takes place when a timely face-to-face service with the consultant is not feasible (eg, consultant practices at a distant site). Please see Chapter 11 for more detailed code and reporting information for these consultations.

Guidelines Used by Payers That Follow Medicare Consultation Guidelines

Medicare guidelines require that consultations provided to patients in observation status will be reported with office/outpatient E/M codes **99201–99215.** If the patient is new to the physician (ie, has not received any face-to-face professional services from the physician or another physician of the same specialty who belongs to the same group practice within the past 3 years), codes **99201–99205** are reported based on the performance and documentation of the required key components. If the patient does not meet the requirements of a new patient, an established patient office/outpatient E/M code is reported.

Transitioning to **10**

Chapter 8: Noncritical Hospital Care

Consultations provided to inpatient hospital patients are reported using initial inpatient hospital care codes (**99221–99223**). The admitting physician must report the initial hospital care services with modifier **AI** (principal physician of record) appended to the appropriate code to distinguish the services from the consulting physician. Subsequent face-to-face services, including new consultations within the same admission, are reported with subsequent hospital care codes **99231–99233.**

Check with your commercial payers to learn if they follow the Medicare consultation guidelines or if they have adopted consultation guidelines that differ from *CPT.*

Concurrent Care

Concurrent care is defined by *CPT*® as the provision of similar services to the same patient by more than one physician on the same day. Concurrent care may be provided by physicians from different practices or physicians of the same practice but different specialties. When concurrent care is provided, the diagnosis code(s) that is (are) reported by each physician should reflect the medical necessity for the provision of services by more than one physician on the same *date* of service. Although it is easier to justify concurrent care when each treating physician reports different diagnoses, if the *diagnosis* code is reported for the same condition, it does not prevent billing for the services.

Example

> ➤ **The attending physician wants the consultant to provide ongoing management of one problem (eg, heart failure) while the attending physician provides ongoing management for other active problems (eg, pneumonia, inadequate weight gain).**

Both physicians would report subsequent hospital care codes and link the *CPT* codes to the appropriate *diagnosis* codes.

Prolonged E/M Services Provided in the Inpatient Setting (99356–99359)

According to *CPT*, the prolonged services inpatient add-on codes **99356** and **99357** may be reported in addition to observation codes (**99218–99220, 99224–99226, 99234–99236**) because, although observation care services are performed in an "outpatient" setting, the intra-service times for the codes are defined as unit/floor time rather than face-to-face time as required in the office/outpatient setting. Prolonged service codes (tables 8-4 and 8-5) are reported when a physician provides services that are beyond the usual service duration described in an E/M code or other codes with a published maximum time. The codes for prolonged service are subdivided into the following categories: service with direct (ie, face-to-face) patient contact and service without direct patient contact.

Refer to Chapter 6 for details of the specific requirements for reporting physician prolonged services in the office/outpatient setting.

- ☀ Direct prolonged services (**99356** and **99357**) may only be reported in conjunction with the following codes:
  - ❖ **90837** (psychotherapy without E/M, 60 minutes)
  - ❖ **99221–99223** (initial hospital care)
  - ❖ **99218–99220** (initial observation care)
  - ❖ **99234–99236** (admission/discharge same day)

|||||||| *Coding Pearl* ||||||||

When an E/M service is reported using time as the key or controlling factor, prolonged services can be reported only when the prolonged service exceeds 30 minutes beyond the highest level of E/M service (eg, **99223, 99220**).

❖ **99224–99226** (subsequent observation care)

❖ **99231–99233** (subsequent hospital care)

❖ **99251–99255** (inpatient consultations)

❖ **99304–99310** (nursing facility services)

⦿ Direct prolonged services (**99356** and **99357**) may not be reported in conjunction with observation or inpatient discharge management (**99217, 99238,** or **99239**), critical care (**99291, 99292; 99466, 99467; 99468–99476**), or intensive care (**99477–99480**) because none of these E/M services has an assigned typical time.

⦿ Direct patient contact time in the inpatient facility is defined as floor or unit time dedicated to the patient.

⦿ The medical record must reflect the total time of the service and the medical need for the service.

⦿ Non-direct prolonged physician services (**99358** and **99359**) may be reported on a different date than the related primary service. The related primary service may be an E/M service (with or without an assigned typical time), a procedure, or other service.

⦿ Non-direct prolonged E/M services must relate to a face-to-face service that has occurred or will occur and must be relative to ongoing care.

Examples

➤ **The pediatrician spends 40 minutes reviewing extensive medical records that are received the day after a patient is admitted.**

Code **99358** would be reported.

Table 8-4. Prolonged Services in the Hospital Setting

Code	Description of Prolonged Services
+99356	Prolonged service in the inpatient or observation setting, requiring unit/floor time beyond the usual service; first hour (30–74 min) (List separately in addition to the code for inpatient E/M service.) (Use code **99356** in conjunction with codes 90837, 99218–99220, 99221–99223, 99224–99226, 99231–99233, 99234–99236, 99251–99255, 99304–99310.)
+99357	each additional 30 minutes (List separately in addition to the code for prolonged physician service.) (Use code **99357** in conjunction with code **99356**.)
99358	Prolonged evaluation and management service before and/or after direct patient care; first hour
+99359	each additional 30 minutes (Use code **99359** in conjunction with code **99358**.)

Table 8-5. Coding Direct Prolonged Services for Inpatient and Observation Care

Total Duration of Prolonged Services, min	Code(s)
>30	Not reported separately
30–74	**99356** × 1
75–104	**99356** × 1 and **99357** × 1
≥105 (≥1 hour and 45 minutes)	**99356** × 1 and **99357** × 2 or more for each additional 30 minutes

Chapter 8: Noncritical Hospital Care

➤ **A 10-year-old patient is admitted to the care of a neurologist following a first-time seizure that occurred shortly after waking in the morning.** The neurologist completes a comprehensive history and physical examination. Results of an electro-encephalogram are reviewed. The diagnosis is juvenile myoclonic epilepsy. Later that same day, the neurologist visits the patient and spends 60 minutes discussing the patient's test results and the anticipated plan of care with the parents and documents the total unit/floor time of 120 minutes in the medical record.

The neurologist reports her services with codes **99223** and **99356**.

Teaching Point: The neurologist reports initial inpatient hospital code **99223** based on the key components of comprehensive history and examination and high-complexity MDM. The typical time assigned to code **99223** is 70 minutes. This leaves an additional 50 minutes of unit/floor time that may be appropriately reported with prolonged services code **99356.**

Critical Care and Continuing Intensive Care Services

Specific guidelines for reporting hourly and inpatient neonatal and pediatric critical care are provided in Chapter 10.

Medical Team Conferences (99366–99368)

Codes **99366–99368** are used to report participation by physicians or nonphysician health care professionals in conferences to coordinate or manage care and services for established patients with chronic or multiple health conditions (eg, cerebral palsy) or with congenital anomalies (eg, craniofacial abnormalities). Code **99367** is the only code that may be reported by a physician, and it can only be reported when the patient and/or family is not present at the team conference. When the physician participates in a medical team conference with the patient and/or family present, the appropriate-level E/M code (eg, **99231–99233**) will be reported based on the place of service and total face-to-face time spent in counseling and/or coordination of care.

See Chapter 11 for a complete summary of the reporting requirements.

Teaching Points: Progression of Care

Selecting the appropriate level of service from the appropriate family of codes will be dependent on the child's condition, type of service (observation vs inpatient), and intensity of the service provided and documented on a particular day of service. The following scenarios indicate the category of codes that should be reported based on the progression of care provided. Remember that the level of service reported is based on all of the face-to-face care provided during the calendar day. See the progression of care when reporting daily hospital care and neonatal and pediatric critical care or neonatal intensive care in Chapter 10.

One Physician or Physicians of the Same Specialty and Group

1. *The patient receives E/M services in the office and is sent to the hospital on the same day.*

   If the patient is examined in the office or outpatient department, admitted to the hospital for observation or as an inpatient, and not seen in the hospital on the same day, report the appropriate office/outpatient code (**99201–99215**).

   If the patient is examined in the office or outpatient department, admitted to the hospital for observation or as an inpatient, and seen in the hospital on the same day, report the appropriate initial observation or inpatient hospital code (**99218–99220** or **99221–99223**) based on all of the E/M services provided on that calendar day.

   If the patient is admitted by physician A and discharged on the same day by physician B (from same practice and of same specialty), a code for same-day admission and discharge observation or inpatient services (**99234–99236**) is reported based on the combined services.

2. *The patient receives an initial face-to-face E/M service in the observation setting.*

   If the patient is admitted to observation, the appropriate initial observation code (**99218–99220**) is reported.

   If the patient is admitted and discharged on the same day, a code for admission and discharge observation or inpatient services (**99234–99236**) is reported.

   If the patient is admitted for observation and subsequently formally admitted to the hospital on the same day, the initial inpatient hospital code (**99221–99223**) is reported.

   If the patient was admitted to observation care status and is seen the following day and not discharged, codes **99224–99226** are reported for the subsequent day encounter.

   If the patient is placed in observation status and then admitted as an inpatient the next day, initial observation (**99218–99220**) and initial hospital care (**99221–99223**) codes are reported with the appropriate dates of service. If the level of service performed during the initial hospital care does not meet the requirements for the initial hospital care (meet all 3 key components or time requirements), report the appropriate subsequent hospital care code (**99231–99233**).

   If the patient is discharged from observation status on a day subsequent to the admission, observation care discharge management (**99217**) is reported.

3. *The patient receives face-to-face E/M services in the inpatient hospital setting.*

   If the patient is evaluated in the hospital, the appropriate initial hospital care code (**99221–99223**) is reported for first face-to-face E/M service.

   If the patient is followed on subsequent days, codes **99231–99233** are reported for each subsequent day of service.

   If the patient's condition declines and he or she requires intensive care services, see Chapter 10 for specific details about coding intensive care services for infants weighing 5,000 g or less.

   If the patient's condition deteriorates and he or she requires critical care services, coding will be dependent on the age of the child. If the child is 6 years or older, hourly critical care services will be reported (**99291** and **99292**) in addition to codes **99231–99233.** See Chapter 10 for guidelines used to report critical care.

   If the patient is discharged on a day subsequent to the initial service, discharge code **99238** or **99239** is reported.

Transfer of Service

If the patient is examined by physician A in the office or outpatient department and sent to the hospital to be admitted by physician B from a different group or specialty (eg, hospitalist or other physician from a group with a different tax identification number than physician A), physician A will report all E/M and other services that he or she provided in the office (**99201–99215**). Physician B will report the appropriate initial hospital observation or inpatient service code (**99218–99220, 99221–99223,** or **99234–99236**).

If a patient is admitted by physician A and care is transferred to another physician from a different group or specialty (physician B), physician B will report subsequent hospital care services (**99231–99233**).

If physician A requests an opinion or advice from physician B, who may be from the same or different group or specialty, and the requirements for a consultation are performed, physician B will report the appropriate consultation code (**99241–99245** or **99251–99255**). If subsequent to the consultation both physicians provide E/M services, both will report subsequent observation or hospital care codes (**99224–99226** or **99231–99233**). If both physicians are from the same group, additional justification may be required to support payment for services by both physicians. See Chapter 10 for guidelines for reporting concurrent critical care or transfer of care of the critically ill infant or child.

Chapter 8: Noncritical Hospital Care

Emergency Department Services

Codes and/or Services Reviewed in This Chapter

99281–99285	Emergency department visit for the evaluation and management (E/M) of a patient
99288	Physician direction of emergency medical systems (EMS) emergency care, advanced life support
99291, 99292	Critical care, E/M of the critically ill or critically injured patient
99053, 99056, 99060	Special services

Emergency Department (ED) Evaluation and Management (E/M) Codes (99281–99285)

- Evaluation and management (E/M) codes **99281–99285** are only reported when care is provided in an emergency department (ED) that is an organized hospital-based facility for the provision of unscheduled episodic services to patients who present for immediate medical attention. The facility must be available 24 hours a day.

- Services performed in an urgent care center, nonhospital facility, or a facility that is not open for 24 hours a day should be reported with the appropriate *Current Procedural Terminology* (*CPT*®) office/outpatient visit codes (**99201–99215**) with the appropriate place of service code (eg, **20** for urgent care facility).

- Selection of the appropriate E/M code is primarily driven by the risk involved in the presenting problem, evaluation measures, and/or treatment options.

- Performance and documentation of all 3 key components (history, physical examination, and medical decision-making [MDM]) are used to select the level of an ED E/M code.

- Because of the unpredictability and inconsistency in the intensity of these services, there are no time values assigned to this family of codes. Therefore, time spent in counseling and/or coordination of care *cannot* be used as a key or controlling factor in the selection of the code, nor can prolonged services be reported with ED codes.

> ||||||||| *Coding Pearl* |||||||||
>
> Services provided in an urgent care center or nonhospital-based facility are not reported with codes **99281–99285**.

- There is no differentiation between new or established patients for ED encounters. All problems for encounters in the ED are considered new to the attending physician for purposes of determining MDM.

- The ED codes are not reported if the physician admits the patient to his or her service for observation or inpatient status on the same date of service as the ED encounter. Only the appropriate initial observation (**99218–99220**), initial hospital care (**99221–99223**), or initial observation or inpatient hospital admission and discharge same day (**99234–99236**) codes are reported instead of ED codes. All of the E/M work performed in the ED should be combined with any additional work performed for admission (and when appropriate, discharge) when selecting the correct code and level of care.

Table 9-1 summarizes the key components required for each ED E/M code based on the 1995 and 1997 Centers for Medicare & Medicaid Services *Documentation Guidelines for Evaluation and Management Services*. Also refer to Chapter 4 for more detail on E/M coding guidelines.

Table 9-1. Emergency Department Services

Key Components

3 of 3 key components must be performed to at least the degree specified for each code. All patients in the emergency department are considered new patients.

Code	Medical Decision-making	History	Physical Examination
99281	**Straightforward** # diagnoses/options: Minimal Data: Minimal Risk: Minimal	**Problem focused** HPI: 1–3 elements ROS: 0 PFSH: 0	**Problem focused** **1995:** One body area/organ system **1997:** Performance and documentation of 1–5 elements identified by a bullet (●) in one or more areas or systems
99282	**Low complexity** # diagnoses/options: Limited Data: Limited Risk: Low	**Expanded problem focused** HPI: 1–3 elements ROS: 1 PFSH: 0	**Expanded problem focused** **1995:** Limited exam—affected body area/organ system and other related areas/systems **1997:** Performance and documentation of at least 6 elements identified by a bullet (●) in one or more areas or systems
99283	**Moderate complexity** # diagnoses/options: Multiple Data: Moderate Risk: Moderate	**Expanded problem focused** HPI: 1–3 elements ROS: 1 PFSH: 0	**Expanded problem focused** **1995:** Limited exam—affected body area/organ system and other related areas/systems **1997:** Performance and documentation of at least 6 elements identified by a bullet (●) in one or more areas or systems
99284	**Moderate complexity** # diagnoses/options: Multiple Data: Moderate Risk: Moderate	**Detailed** HPI: 4+ elements or status of 3 chronic or inactive conditions ROS: 2–9 PFSH: 1	**Detailed** **1995:** Extended exam—affected body area(s) and other symptomatic or related organ system(s) **1997:** Performance and documentation of at least 2 elements identified by a bullet (●) in at least 6 areas or systems or at least 12 elements identified by a bullet (●) in at least 2 areas or systems
99285	**High complexity** # diagnoses/options: Extensive Data: Extensive Risk: High	**Comprehensive** HPI: 4+ elements or status of 3 chronic or inactive conditions ROS: 10+ PFSH: 2 Or clinical condition or mental status did not permit performance of history	**Comprehensive** **1995:** 8+ organ systems or complete exam of a single organ system **1997:** Multisystem exam—at least 9 organ systems or body areas with performance of all elements identified by a bullet (●) in each area/system examined Documentation is expected for at least 2 elements identified by a bullet (●) of each area(s) or system(s) Single organ system exam—Performance of all elements identified by a bullet (●) and documentation of every element in each box with a shaded border and at least one element in a box with an unshaded border Or clinical condition or mental status did not permit performance of exam

Abbreviations: HPI, history of present illness; PFSH, past, family, and social history; ROS, review of systems.

Chapter 9: Emergency Department Services

ED Caveat: Code 99285

The ED E/M code **99285** allows an exception to the 3 key components rule (Level 5 caveat) for patients whose clinical condition, mental status, or lack of available history may not permit obtaining a comprehensive history and/or physical examination. Therefore, code **99285** may be reported in patients presenting with a high-severity condition that requires a high level of MDM when circumstances prevent the physician from obtaining a comprehensive history and/or completing a comprehensive physical examination. When such urgency exists, the physician must document the condition or reason why a comprehensive history and/or physical examination could not be obtained.

Reporting the Diagnosis Code for ED Visits

While several symptoms may be listed as the "chief complaint" as part of the ED triage process, the physician must designate only one sign, symptom, disease, or injury as the chief complaint. The hospital depends on the physician's designation of the chief complaint because only one diagnosis code may be reported for this category on the hospital claim form. This diagnosis is used to help support the urgency of the ED visit under prudent layperson guidelines. This may be different from conditions that are "present on admission" that must now be tracked by hospitals.

Comanagement of ED Patients

Only one physician should report an ED E/M service for a patient who receives care in the ED. In general, this will be the emergency physician or pediatric emergency medicine specialist staffing the ED. At times, other physicians (eg, generalists, specialists) may have to provide care for a patient in the ED. When this occurs, the code(s) used by each physician will depend on several factors.

> ||||||||| *Coding Pearl* |||||||||
>
> Only one physician may report an ED E/M code (**99281– 99285**) for a patient who receives care in the ED.

1. Is the physician managing the patient in the ED or was the physician called in by the ED physician?
2. Did the physician personally perform any procedures in the ED or only direct the ED staff?
3. Was the patient sent home, transferred to another facility, or kept at the hospital for observation or admission?
4. Was the patient stable or critically ill or injured?

   Follow these guidelines to determine which codes will be reported.

➤ **You are the primary physician managing the patient in the ED (ie, ED physician or physician meeting his or her patient in the ED).**

Codes **99281–99285** (ED E/M service) will be reported.

➤ **You are the primary physician managing the patient in the ED (ie, ED physician or physician meeting his or her patient in the ED) and you call in another physician to see the patient.**

The type of service reported will depend on whether the other physician is providing consultative services, a specific intervention (eg, diagnostic or therapeutic procedure), or primary management of the patient. The ED physician will typically report the ED E/M code and the other physician will report services as follows:

- *Consultation:* An outpatient consultation (**99241–99245**) may be reported when the ED physician requests the opinion of and/or advice from the other physician (and the request is documented in the medical record), the consulting physician provides an opinion and/or advice (including the initiation of diagnostic and/or therapeutic services), and a written report is documented (may be part of the ED medical record). If a payer follows Medicare guidelines and does not cover consultations, services should be reported using the office/outpatient E/M codes (**99201–99215**). See Chapter 6 for detailed requirements for reporting consultations. No matter which code set you report, place of service code **23** (ED) would be used.

- *Procedure:* The second physician may report the diagnostic and/or therapeutic procedure requested by the ED physician that is provided to the patient in the ED (eg, fracture reduction by an orthopedic surgeon; wound repair by a plastic surgeon; echocardiogram performed by a cardiologist; lumbar puncture performed by a pediatrician, hospitalist, or neonatologist).

- *Assume management:* If the second physician is called in to take over management of the patient (not a consultation) and the patient is sent home, an office/outpatient code (**99201–99215**) would be reported with place of service code **23** (ED). This would also be the case when an insurance carrier does not recognize consultation codes and the patient is sent home.

- *Observation or inpatient admission:* If the other physician admits the child to the hospital for observation or inpatient services after stabilization and/or provision of care in the ED, he or she would report only the appropriate initial observation, hospital inpatient, or pediatric critical or intensive care code (**99218–99220, 99221–99223, 99468, 99471, 99475, 99477**) as appropriate based on all of the E/M services provided in the ED and as part of the initial service. That could also apply if

  - ❖ The admitting physician is a member of the same physician group as the ED physician, but the admitting physician is providing different services and is not considered the exact same specialty.

  - ❖ The other physician transferred the child to another facility where the child would be under his or her care (or a member of his or her group and same specialty).

- *Critical care:* If the patient is critically ill or injured, the physicians managing the patient's care may report their services using time-based critical care codes **99291** and **99292** (see Table 10-2 in Chapter 10).

➤ **You are the primary physician managing the patient in the ED (ie, ED physician or physician meeting his or her patient in the ED) and you treat a patient and request an opinion and/or advice from another physician who provides consultative services, and a third physician admits the child to the hospital.**

Each physician will report the appropriate service (ie, ED physician reports code **99281–99285,** consulting physician reports code **99241–99245** [or **99201– 99215** if the payer follows Medicare rules], and admitting physician reports an appropriate initial code [eg, **99218–99220** or **99221–99223**]) so long as the physicians are not in the same group practice and of the exact same specialty.

Examples

Use Table 9-1 to help you in the selection of the appropriate level of ED E/M service in the following examples:

➤ **The ED physician is managing a 6-year-old who was struck by a car while riding a bicycle.** The patient is brought in by EMS from the scene with head trauma (no know loss of consciousness [LOC] is reported), a friction burn on her right shoulder, multiple abrasions on her forearm and elbow, and large contusions on her left hip and thigh. The child is not accompanied by a parent. While initially there was a concern that the child might be in imminent risk of a life-threatening condition, following further assessment, the ED physician determines that there is no risk of deterioration and that the child is clinically stable. No history, other than that obtained from EMS, is available prior to the trauma service evaluation. There was high-complexity MDM. No separately billable procedures were performed. The child is admitted for observation by a hospitalist for a concussion. On discharge, the patient is noted to have a concussion.

The ED physician reports **99285** (ED visit code)	*ICD-9-CM* **959.01** (closed head trauma) **919.0** (abrasion/friction burns, multiple sites) **924.4** (contusions, multiple sites of lower limb) **E812.6** (other motor vehicle traffic accident with motor vehicle, pedal cyclist) *ICD-10-CM* **S09.90XA** (head injury, no other symptoms) **T22.151A** (friction burn, first degree, right shoulder) **S50.811A** (abrasion, right forearm) **S50.311A** (abrasion, right elbow) **S70.02XA, S70.12XA** (contusions, left hip and thigh) **V13.4XXA** (pedal cycle driver injured in collision with car in traffic accident)
The hospitalist reports **99218–99220** (initial observation care)	*ICD-9-CM* **850.0** (concussion with no LOC) **919.0, 924.4,** and **E812.6** *ICD-10-CM* **S06.0X0A** (concussion with no LOC) **T22.151A, S50.811A, S50.311A, S70.02XA, S70.12XA, V13.4XXA**

Teaching Point: The Level 5 caveat would apply because this patient's condition was initially felt to be unstable and no other history, other than that from EMS, was available. If included in the scenario, a diagnosis code indicating the place of occurrence of the accident would also be reported by each physician for the initial episode of care.

➤ **The ED physician evaluates a 10-month-old for fever, vomiting, and lethargy.** A comprehensive history and physical examination are performed and there is high-complexity MDM. Because of the concern for meningitis, the on-call pediatrician is consulted and is asked to perform the lumbar puncture and to determine the child's disposition. The pediatrician does the procedure, confirms the course of treatment by the ED physician, and admits the infant as an inpatient to his or her service.

Chapter 9: Emergency Department Services

The ED physician reports
99285 (ED visit code)

The pediatrician reports
99221–99223 25 (initial inpatient
hospital care)
62270 (lumbar puncture)

Both physicians report

ICD-9-CM	ICD-10-CM
780.60 (fever)	**R50.9** (fever)
787.03 (vomiting)	**R11.10** (vomiting)
780.79 (lethargy)	**R53.83** (lethargy)

Teaching Point: A code for meningitis is not reported because this condition is not confirmed.

Directing Emergency Medical Technicians (99288)

> ||ᴵ||||ᴵ|| **Coding Pearl** ||ᴵ||||ᴵ||
>
> Code **99288** may be reported on the same day as ED E/M or hourly critical care services.

- Report code **99288** (physician direction of EMS) when
  - ❖ The physician directing the services is in the hospital and in 2-way communication with EMS personnel who are in the prehospital setting providing advanced life support that requires direct or online medical control.
  - ❖ The documentation includes the times of all contacts, any orders provided, and/or directions provided to the EMS team.
- Code **99288** may be reported on the same day as ED E/M or hourly critical care services. Modifier **25** would be appended to code **99288** to alert payers that this was a significant and separately identifiable service from ED E/M (**99281–99285**) or the critical care (**99291–99292**) service provided.
- The supervising physician cannot report the actual procedures and interventions performed by the EMS team because he or she is not physically present during the transport.
- Code **99288** is designated as a bundled procedure by Medicare. There are no relative values assigned under the Medicare Resource-Based Relative Value Scale. Check with your major payers and negotiate for coverage of this service.
- For information on supervision of interfacility transport of a critically ill or injured patient, 24 months or younger, via direct 2-way communication with a transport team, see codes **99485–99486** in Chapter 10.

Critical Care in the ED (99291 and 99292)

A critical illness or injury is defined in *CPT®* as one that acutely impairs one or more vital organs such that there is a high probability of imminent or life-threatening deterioration of the patient's condition. Guidelines for reporting critical care codes **99291** (critical care, E/M of the critically ill or injured patient; first 30–74 minutes) and **99292** (each additional 30 minutes) are described in detail in Chapter 10.

> ||ᴵ||||ᴵ|| **Coding Pearl** ||ᴵ||||ᴵ||
>
> Critical care is only reported when the patient's condition meets the specific *CPT* definition of a critically ill or injured patient.

- Time-based critical care codes (**99291, 99292**) should be used to report the provision of critical care when performed in the ED. The patient's condition must meet the specific *CPT* definition of a critically ill or injured patient. The global codes for pediatric or neonatal critical care should not be reported by a physician providing critical care in the ED unless that physician (eg, an intensivist) will continue to provide critical care services in the inpatient setting.

Chapter 9: Emergency Department Services

- Critical care may be reported on the same day as an ED E/M code when provided by the same physician when 2 independent services are provided. Modifier **25** should be appended to the ED E/M code when this occurs. Following are examples of critical care and ED E/M services that may be separately reportable when provided on the same date:
  - ❖ A child injured in an accident arrives at the ED. The ED physician evaluates the child's injuries and orders a surgical consultation. While the surgeon is in route to the facility, the patient's condition deteriorates and the ED physician provides 40 minutes of critical care before the patient is transferred to the surgeon's care.
  - ❖ A child arrives to the ED in critical condition. The ED physician provides 45 minutes of critical care services. After the child's condition improves, the ED physician obtains a comprehensive history, completes a detailed examination, and arranges admission to the intensive care unit by a hospitalist.
- Time spent providing critical care does not need to be continuous and includes time at the bedside as well as time in the ED reviewing data specific to the patient, discussing the patient with other physicians, and discussing the patient's management or condition with the patient's family.
- Time reported for critical care must be devoted to the critically ill or injured patient. Therefore, the "critical care clock" stops when attention is turned to the care of another patient or the physician is not readily available in the ED.
- Those procedures not bundled with codes **99291** and **99292** and when personally performed by the reporting provider may be reported separately (eg, starting an intravenous line on a child younger than 3 years, placing an intraosseous or central venous line, endotracheal intubation, cardiopulmonary resuscitation, cardioversion). Time spent performing these separately reported services must be subtracted from the critical care time calculated and reported. See Table 9-2 for a list of services and procedures that are included in hourly critical care codes.

Examples

▶ **The ED physician performs a comprehensive history and physical examination on a 13-month-old patient with severe stridor and respiratory distress believed to be secondary to croup.** Medical decision-making is highly complex. The patient's condition does not improve with nebulized epinephrine and then worsens due to progressive lethargy. The patient goes into respiratory failure and 45 minutes of critical care is provided. Endotracheal intubation is performed.

99285 25 (ED visit code)   *ICD-9-CM*
99291 (critical care, first 30–74 minutes)   **518.81** (acute respiratory failure)
31500 (emergency endotracheal intubation)   **464.4** (croup)

                                                          ICD-10-CM
                                                         J96.00 (acute respiratory failure)
                                                         J05.0 (croup)

Transitioning to **10**

    Teaching Point: This endotracheal intubation is not bundled with critical care; therefore, time spent in the provision of the service is not considered in the total critical care time. Modifier **25** is appended to code **99285** to indicate that it was a significant and separately identifiable service.

Chapter 9: Emergency Department Services

➤ **The ED physician saw a 10-year-old for moderate asthma exacerbation in the morning.** The child responded well to an aerosol bronchodilator treatment and was discharged home. The child returns to the ED a few hours later with a more severe exacerbation and is seen by the same physician. The child now has very poor air movement and significant hypoxia and hypercapnia. The child receives oxygen, a continuous bronchodilator nebulizer treatment, and subsequently a parenteral bronchodilator. The child improves enough to be admitted to a monitored medical ward bed with diagnosis of severe exacerbation of moderate persistent asthma. The ED physician spends a total of 60 minutes in patient-directed critical care.

99284 25
99291

ICD-9-CM
493.92 (unspecified asthma with acute exacerbation)

ICD-10-CM
J45.41 (moderate persistent asthma with acute exacerbation)

Teaching Point: The patient received oxygen, continuous inhalation treatment, and parenteral bronchodilator in the ED. However, these services include no professional component. The facility will report the services because the cost of supplies and clinical staff time are an expense to the facility.

➤ **A 1-year-old with apparent sepsis and hypotension is brought to the ED.** The child requires placement of an intraosseous needle to achieve vascular access and subsequently receives parenteral fluids, antibiotics, and vasopressors. The child suffers cardiopulmonary arrest, prompting the ED physician to intubate the child. Cardiopulmonary resuscitation is performed for 20 minutes. The child is in the ED for a total of 45 minutes before transfer to the intensive care unit.

99285 25
92950 (cardiopulmonary resuscitation)
36680 (placement of intraosseous needle)
31500 (emergency endotracheal intubation)

ICD-9-CM
427.5 (cardiac arrest)

ICD-10-CM
I46.9 (cardiac arrest)

> **Transitioning to 10**
>
> If septic shock was specified as the cause of cardiac arrest, codes **A41.9,** sepsis, unspecified organism; **R65.21,** severe sepsis with septic shock; and **I46.8,** cardiac arrest due to other underlying condition, would be reported.

Critical care time does not accrue during the performance of non-bundled, separately billable procedures. Because cardiopulmonary resuscitation is a separately billable, non-bundled procedure, the ED physician did not spend a minimum of 30 minutes providing critical care.

Reporting Procedures in the ED

Many procedures performed in the ED have an associated global period assigned by payers. (See Chapter 12 for the definition of the *CPT*® surgical package and Medicare global period.) Physicians need to understand when it is appropriate to report the ED E/M code with modifiers **25** (significant, separately identifiable E/M service), **57** (decision for surgery), and **59** (distinct procedural service). See Chapter 3 for more information on modifiers.

See Table 9-2 for a list of procedures (with assigned Medicare global periods) commonly performed in the ED.

Table 9-2. Common Emergency Department Procedures

Procedure	CPT Code	Global Period (days)
Arterial puncture	36600	NA
Bladder aspiration	51100	0
Burn care, >10% TBSA	16030	0
Burn care, 5%–10% TBSA	16025	0
Burn care, <5% TBSA	16020	0
Cardiopulmonary resuscitation	92950	0
Cardioversion	92960	0
Chest tube insertion	32551	0
Dislocation, shoulder, reduction	23650	90
Emergency childbirth, vaginal delivery	59409	NA
Endotracheal intubation	31500	0
Foreign body removal, conjunctiva	65205	0
Foreign body removal, ear	69200	0
Foreign body removal, nose	30300	10
Foreign body removal with incision, subcutaneous, simple	10120	10
Fracture, clavicle	23500	90
Fracture, finger distal, each	26750	90
Fracture, finger shaft, each	26720	90
Gastric intubation and aspiration(s), therapeutic, including lavage (if performed)	43753	0
Incision and drainage, abscess, simple	10060	10
Incision and drainage, finger, complicated (eg, felon)	26011	10
Incision and drainage, perianal abscess	46050	10
Intraosseous needle placement	36680	0
Laceration repair, simple ≤2.5 cm, face/ears/lips	12011	0
Repair, simple ≤2.5 cm, scalp/trunk/extremities	12001	0
Repair, simple 2.6–5.0 cm, face/ears/lips	12013	0
Repair, simple 2.6–7.5 cm, scalp/trunk/extremities	12002	0
Laceration repair, intermediate ≤2.5 cm, face/ears/lips	12051	10
Repair, intermediate ≤2.5 cm, hands/feet/neck	12041	10
Repair, intermediate ≤2.5 cm, scalp/trunk/arms/legs	12031	10
Repair, intermediate 2.6–5.0 cm, face/ears/lips	12052	10
Repair, intermediate 2.6–7.5 cm, hands/feet/neck	12042	10
Repair, intermediate 2.6–7.5 cm, scalp/trunk/extremities	12032	10
Lumbar puncture	62270	0

Chapter 9: Emergency Department Services

Table 9-2. Common Emergency Department Procedures, contiued

Procedure	CPT Code	Global Period (days)
Nursemaid's elbow	24640	10
Puncture aspiration of abscess, hematoma, bulla, or cyst	10160	10
Repair, nail bed	11760	10
Splint, finger	29130	0
Splint, short arm	29125	0
Splint, short leg	29515	0
Strap, ankle	29540	0
Strap, knee	29530	0
Strap, shoulder	29240	0
Subungual hematoma evacuation	11740	0
Thoracentesis	32554	0
Venipuncture, >3 y requiring physician skill	36410	NA
Venipuncture, requiring physician skill, femoral/jugular <3 y	36400	NA

Abbreviations: CPT, Current Procedural Terminology; NA, not applicable; TBSA, total body surface area.

Procedures noted with global period NA have an X or M status in the Medicare Physician Fee Schedule.

||||||| **Coding Pearl** |||||||

Hydration, infusion, and/or injection procedures cannot be reported by the physician because physician work involves only confirmation of the treatment plan and direct supervision of the staff.

Any separately identifiable procedure that is personally performed by the physician may be reported, with the exception of

- Procedures that are bundled in timed-based critical care codes
- Services performed by hospital personnel because they are billed by the hospital facility (If a nurse or allied health care professional assists in part of a procedure, the ED physician may bill for the professional services if he or she provides the primary or key component of the procedure.)
- Hydration, infusion, and/or injection procedures (**96360–96379**) because the physician work associated with the procedures involves only confirmation of the treatment plan and direct supervision of staff
- Procedures involving use of hospital-owned equipment (eg, pulse oximetry) unless the procedure includes a technical and professional component (The professional component may be reported if performed and documented with modifier **26** [professional component] appended to the procedure code.)

Modifiers Used With ED Codes

In addition to modifiers **25, 26,** and **57,** physicians providing care in the ED should be familiar with several other modifiers. See Table 9-3 for a list of modifiers commonly used in the ED. (See Chapter 3 for more detail on the use of modifiers.)

Coding Conundrum: Follow-up Care for Procedures Performed in the ED

It is common for the ED physician to repair lacerations and to refer these patients to their primary care physician for removal of sutures. Although suture removal is considered part of the *CPT®* surgical package or Medicare global period for intermediate and complex laceration repair, payers have recognized this practice and will typically pay the ED physician for the repair and another physician for the E/M visit required to remove the sutures. The physician removing the sutures will report the appropriate-level office/outpatient E/M code (**99201–99215**).

In general, however, procedures are considered global services, and payment includes preoperative care, surgical procedure, and associated postoperative care. If the ED physician will not be providing post-procedure care, there are several options for reporting global procedures performed in the ED.

Using fracture care as an example, the following options can be used to report global procedures performed in the ED:

- If the ED physician performs the fracture care and follow-up management, the fracture care code can be reported.
- The ED physician can report the fracture care code with modifier **54** (surgical care only) to show performance of procedure (eg, closed reduction) but no post-procedure care.
- The ED physician can report an ED E/M service and splinting (if performed personally by the physician), allowing the orthopedic surgeon to report the fracture care. (See Chapter 3 for guidelines when reporting services with modifier **54**.)

If the ED physician does not report the fracture care with modifier **54**, the physicians providing follow-up care may find that their claims for services are denied. They will need to contact the ED physician to have a corrected claim filed (and to educate the ED physician in the appropriate use of modifier **54**).

Table 9-3. Common Modifiers Used in the Emergency Department

Modifier	When to Use
24	An unrelated E/M service is provided during the global period of a previously performed procedure by the same physician or group.
25	A significant, separately identifiable E/M service is performed by the same physician on the same day of the procedure or other service.
26	Reporting professional component only of a service for which payment includes equipment (or technical services) cost (eg, x-ray).
32	A service is mandated by third-party payer, regulation, or governmental entity.
51	Multiple procedures are performed on the same day other than E/M, physical medicine and rehabilitation services, or provision of supplies (eg, vaccines).
54	Only the surgical care component of a procedure was provided. Another physician will provide postoperative care.
57	Decision for surgery was made. Some payers may require this appended to the E/M code only with procedures with 90-day global periods.
59	Distinct procedural service (non-E/M) was performed on the same day as another procedural service and was at a different encounter or a different surgery or procedure, or performed on a different body site or organ system.
63	Procedures (**20000–69999**) performed on an infant weighing <4 kg if the code descriptor does not include a descriptor of "young infant or neonate."

Table 9-3. Common Modifiers Used in the Emergency Department, continued

Modifier	When to Use
76	The same physician repeats a procedure or service on the same date of service.
77	Another physician repeats a procedure or service already performed by another physician on the same day of service.
79	An unrelated procedure is performed during the global period of a previously provided procedure by the same physician or group.

Examples

> **A child is seen for left shoulder pain that occurred following a fall while playing soccer.** The child is examined for additional injuries (expanded problem-focused history, detailed examination). X-ray reveals a mid-shaft clavicle fracture. The physician places the patient in a sling and refers the patient to another physician for follow-up care.

99283 25
23500 54 (closed treatment of clavicular fracture, without manipulation)

ICD-9-CM
810.00 (fracture of clavicle, closed)
E888.9 (fall on same level, not otherwise specified)
E007.5 (activity, soccer)

ICD-10-CM
S42.022A (displaced fracture of left clavicle)
W18.30XA (unspecified fall on same level)
Y93.66 (activity, soccer)

Transitioning to 10

A fracture not specified as displaced or non-displaced should be reported as displaced.

The use of modifier **54** (surgical care only) alerts payers that another physician will report postsurgical care.

Alternatively, the ED physician may report the ED E/M code based on the level of service performed and documented and allow another physician to report the global fracture care.

> **The ED physician evaluates a 6-year-old with a small (<2.5 cm) simple laceration on her right cheek that occurred when she fell, striking her face on the edge of a table at home.** The wound is clean, there is no concern for other associated injury, and her immunization status is up-to-date. The parents are concerned about scarring and request a plastic surgeon to do the repair. The on-call surgeon is consulted and responds to the ED. The surgeon evaluates the child and repairs the wound with sutures in the ED. The ED physician documents a detailed history and physical examination.

Although the ED physician documented a detailed history and physical examination, the MDM would only rise to moderate complexity (potential associated head injury). The surgical consultation was at the request of the family and not the ED physician.

ED physician reports
99283 25
Surgeon reports
12011 (laceration repair)

ICD-9-CM
873.41 (open wound, cheek, without mention of complication)
E888.1 (fall resulting in striking against other object)
E849.0 (occurred at home)

ICD-10-CM
S01.411A (laceration without foreign body, right cheek)
W01.190A (fall on same level from slipping, tripping, and stumbling with subsequent striking against furniture)
Y92.009 (occurred at home)

➤ **The ED physician is caring for a 9-year-old who has a 4-cm–long, deep laceration of the leg from broken glass in his backyard.** The physician performs a detailed history and physical examination. An x-ray of the extremity shows no retained radiopaque foreign bodies. The child's immunizations are current, with the last tetanus booster less than 5 years previously. The physician irrigates, carefully explores the wound, and performs a 2-layer repair. The child is discharged with appropriate follow-up plans.

The E/M service should meet moderate-complexity MDM but is not a high-severity presenting problem. The determination as to the need for surgery (laceration repair) by the ED physician or possibly by a consultant was influenced by the x-ray results. Therefore, the pre-procedure period did not begin until that point.

99283 25
12032 (layered closure of the extremities, 2.6–7.5 cm)

ICD-9-CM
891.0 (open wound leg, without mention of complication)

ICD-10-CM
S71.119A or **S81.819A** (Coders must query the physician for information on the site of the laceration—upper or lower leg—to assign an *ICD-10-CM* diagnosis code.)

➤ **A 14-year-old unconscious male is brought into the ED after having ingested drugs.** The physician is unable to obtain additional history and documents this in the record. A comprehensive physical examination and high-level MDM are performed. The physician performs gastric intubation and lavage.

99285 25
43753 (gastric lavage)

ICD-9-CM
977.9 (unspecified drug or medicinal substance)

ICD-10-CM
T50.901A (poisoning, unspecified drug or medicinal substance, accidental intent)

> **Transitioning to 10**
>
> *ICD-10-CM* codes for poisoning include intent. If intent is unknown, assign a code for accidental intent.

Moderate Sedation (99143–99150)

Moderate sedation (**99143–99150**) is a drug-induced depression of consciousness during which patients may respond purposefully to verbal commands, alone or accompanied by light tactile stimulation. This may be necessary when performing some procedures in

Chapter 9: Emergency Department Services

the ED. Coding and documentation requirements for reporting this service are detailed in Chapter 12.

Special Service Codes (99053, 99056, 99060)

The following special service codes may be used to report services that are an adjunct to the basic service provided. *Current Procedural Terminology* guidelines do not restrict the reporting of adjunct special service codes in the ED. However, third-party payers will have specific policies for coverage and payment. Communicate with individual payers to understand their definition or interpretation of the service and coverage and payment policies.

These codes are intended to describe services that are provided outside the normal time frame and location.

99053	Service(s) provided between 10:00 pm and 8:00 am at 24-hour facility, in addition to basic service
99056	Service(s) typically provided in office, provided out of office at request of patient, in addition to basic service
99060	Service(s) provided on an emergency basis, out of office, which disrupts other scheduled office services, in addition to basic service

Code **99053** would be reported when services are provided between the designated time limits in an ED.

Current Procedural Terminology does not restrict reporting of any procedure or service to any specific specialty. However, it would be inappropriate for an ED physician to report code **99056** or **99060** for services provided in the ED.

If appropriate, a non-ED physician could report *CPT*® code **99056** or **99060** when he or she provides services in the ED in addition to an outpatient office/clinic, ED visit, or consultation E/M code.

> |||||||| **Coding Pearl** ||||||||
>
> It would not be appropriate for an ED physician to report code **99056** or **99060** for services provided in the ED.

Continuum Models for Asthma, Head Injury, and Laceration

Three common conditions seen in the ED follow in a teaching tool called the Coding Continuum Model. Each condition—asthma, head injury, and laceration—is described across the continuum of codes **99281–99285** plus critical care. Although the actual assignment of a code for an individual patient may vary from the examples, members of the American Academy of Pediatrics Committee on Coding and Nomenclature have generally agreed that these examples provide an accurate representation of how one condition typically flows across the family of codes.

Continuum Model for Asthma

CPT Code Vignette	History	Physical Examination	Medical Decision-making

99281
Stable asthma, concern about potential, but not active problems 8 days later
	Problem focused
	1. Chief complaint
	2. Problem-focused HPI
	  a. Cough
	  b. Wheeze
		Problem focused
		Limited respiratory system
			Straightforward
			Anticipatory guidance
			Recommend routine follow-up

99282 Stable asthma, out of medication	**EPF** 1. Chief complaint 2. Brief HPI plus pertinent ROS Cough Wheeze Respiratory distress Home peak flow data Frequency of rescue medication Associated signs and symptoms	**EPF** Examination of respiratory system including lungs, ENT, and other pertinent organ systems	**Low** Review and evaluation of home medications Alteration in medication regimen Refills Criteria for urgent/emergent follow-up Plan for follow-up care
99283 Known asthmatic with URI symptoms or mild exacerbation	**EPF** 1. Chief complaint 2. Brief HPI plus pertinent ROS Cough Wheeze Respiratory distress Home peak flow data Frequency of rescue medication Associated signs and symptoms	**EPF** Examination of respiratory system including lungs, ENT, and other pertinent organ systems A peak expiratory flow rate may be obtained.	**Moderate complexity** Same as 99282 plus 1 respiratory treatment and reassessment (Pulse oximetry and peak flow may be included.)
99284 Known asthmatic with moderate exacerbation	**Detailed** 1. Chief complaint 2. Extended HPI and ROS 3. Problem-pertinent PFSH	**Detailed** Constitutional, ENT, neck, respiratory, cardiovascular, and other pertinent systems A peak expiratory flow rate may be obtained.	**Moderate complexity** Same as 99283 plus 1–3 respiratory treatments (or 1 continuous treatment) Systemic (oral or parenteral) steroids Multiple reassessments (Pulse oximetry and peak flow may be included.) CXR may be obtained. May be admitted for observation

Continuum Model for Asthma, continued

CPT Code Vignette	History	Physical Examination	Medical Decision-making
99285 Known asthmatic with moderate to severe exacerbation	**Comprehensive** 1. Chief complaint 2. Extended HPI 3. Complete ROS 4. 2 of 3 PFSH	**Comprehensive** Constitutional, eyes, ENT, respiratory, cardiovascular, GI, neurologic, skin A peak expiratory flow rate may be obtained.	**High complexity** Same as **99284** plus 4 respiratory treatments (or 2 continuous treatments or 1 continuous with 1 intermittent treatment) Multiple reassessments (Pulse oximetry and peak flow may be included.) CXR may be obtained. Blood gas or end-tidal CO_2 monitoring may be obtained.
99291, 99292 Critical care Known asthmatic unstable with marked distress and (impending) respiratory failure Critically ill, unstable patient; requires >30 minutes of directed patient care (bedside, review of data, consultation with other specialist, discussion with family members, documentation)			**High complexity** Same as **99285**. Usually requires use of additional therapies such as ketamine, magnesium sulfate, parenteral adrenergic agents, and/or heliox; ET intubation; or BiPAP.

Abbreviations: BiPAP, bi-level positive airway pressure; CPT, Current Procedural Terminology; CXR, chest x-ray; ENT, ear, nose, throat; EPF, expanded problem focused; ET, endotracheal; GI, gastrointestinal; HPI, history of present illness; PFSH, past, family, and social history; ROS, review of systems; URI, upper respiratory infection.

Continuum Model for Head Injury

CPT Code Vignette	History	Physical Examination	Medical Decision-making
99281 Repaired scalp laceration, well healed, presents for suture removal	**Problem focused** 1. Chief complaint 2. Problem-focused HPI a. Signs of infection, poor healing	**Problem focused** Limited skin	**Straightforward** Suture removal
99282 Minor head trauma without local bruising, swelling, or laceration, no neurologic changes	**EPF** 1. Chief complaint 2. Injury mechanism Associated signs and symptoms	**EPF** Examination of skin and neurologic system and other pertinent organ systems	**Low** May recommend OTC analgesic or local care Anticipatory guidance Criteria for urgent/emergent follow-up Plan for follow-up care
99283 Minor head trauma with local bruising, swelling, or laceration, no neurologic changes	**EPF** 1. Chief complaint 2. Injury mechanism Associated signs and symptoms	**EPF** Eyes, ENT, skin, and neurologic system and other pertinent organ systems	**Moderate complexity** Same as 99282 May require laceration repair
99284 Head trauma with signs of concussion including loss of recall, brief LOC (<5 minutes), and/or emesis but no focal neurologic changes	**Detailed** 1. Chief complaint 2. Extended HPI and ROS 3. Problem-pertinent PFSH	**Detailed** Eyes, ENT, neck, respiratory, cardiovascular, skin, neurologic, and other pertinent systems	**Moderate complexity** Same as 99283 plus multiple reassessments C-spine films may be obtained. Head CT may be obtained. Laboratory tests may be obtained. Neurology or neurosurgical consultation may be obtained.
99285 Head trauma with signs of concussion including LOC (>5 minutes), brief seizure, and/or persistent emesis; closed skull fracture and/or focal neurologic changes may be present; GCS >8	**Comprehensive** 1. Chief complaint 2. Extended HPI 3. Complete ROS 4. 2 of 3 PFSH	**Comprehensive** Constitutional, eyes, ENT, respiratory, cardiovascular, GI, neurologic, skin	**High complexity** Same as 99284 plus anticonvulsant(s) may be administered

Chapter 9: Emergency Department Services

Continuum Model for Head Injury, continued

CPT Code Vignette	History	Physical Examination	Medical Decision-making
Critical Care Head trauma with persistent LOC and/or seizures; open or closed skull fracture and/or focal neurologic changes may be present; GCS ≤8 Critically ill, unstable patient; requires >30 minutes of directed patient care (bedside, review of data, consultation with other specialist, discussion with family members, documentation)			**High complexity** Same as **99285** May require additional interventions such as ET intubation

Abbreviations: CT, computed tomography; CPT, Current Procedural Terminology; ENT, ear, nose, throat; EPF, expanded problem focused; ET, endotracheal; GCS, Glasgow coma score; GI, gastrointestinal; HPI, history of present illness; LOC, loss of consciousness; OTC, over the counter; PFSH, past, family, and social history; ROS, review of systems.

Continuum Model for Laceration

These codes reflect E/M services only and not any procedure that the same physician may provide. The physician needs to be aware that the pre-procedural and intra-procedural global period may include some of the medical decision-making indicated with each code, thus reducing the level of E/M service provided, and that any E/M service reported with a procedure must meet the requirement for a significant, separately identifiable service.

CPT Code Vignette	History	Physical Examination	Medical Decision-making
99281 Patient with this condition in the ED usually does not meet the criteria for this level. Patient presenting for removal of sutures not placed at that facility			
99282 Uncomplicated laceration of single body area or organ system	**EPF** 1. Chief complaint 2. Mechanisms Timing Foreign body risk Associated signs and symptoms	**EPF** Examination of affected body area and other pertinent organ systems	**Low** Laceration repair Sedation with or without analgesia Criteria for urgent/emergent follow-up Plan for follow-up care
99283 Uncomplicated laceration of single body area or organ system with minor associated injury (eg, minor head injury) OR Uncomplicated lacerations of >1 body area or organ system OR Minimally complicated laceration (eg, small foreign body, delay in seeking care) of single body area or organ system	**EPF** 1. Chief complaint 2. Mechanisms Timing Foreign body risk Associated signs and symptoms	**EPF** Examination of affected body area(s) and other pertinent organ systems	**Moderate complexity** Same as **99282** X-ray of affected area may be obtained. Oral pain medication may be administered. Antibiotics may be administered and/or prescribed. Sedation with or without analgesia may be given.

Continuum Model for Laceration, continued

These codes reflect E/M services only and not any procedure that the same physician may provide. The physician needs to be aware that the pre-procedural and intra-procedural global period may include some of the medical decision-making indicated with each code, thus reducing the level of E/M service provided, and that any E/M service reported with a procedure must meet the requirement for a significant, separately identifiable service.

CPT Code Vignette	History	Physical Examination	Medical Decision-making
99284 Uncomplicated laceration of single body area or organ system with other associated injury (eg, mild concussion) OR Minimally complicated laceration (eg, small foreign body) >1 body area or organ system OR Complicated laceration (eg, infection, GSW, deep knife wound) of single body area or organ system without immediate threat to life or limb	**Detailed** 1. Chief complaint 2. Extended HPI and ROS 3. Problem-pertinent PFSH	**Detailed** ENT, neck, respiratory, cardiovascular, musculoskeletal, neurologic, and other pertinent systems	**Moderate complexity** Same as **99283** Parenteral pain medication may be administered. Surgical consultation may be obtained. Sedation with or without analgesia provided for another service May be admitted for observation
99285 Uncomplicated laceration of ≥1 body area or organ system with significant associated injury (eg, multiple trauma) OR Complicated laceration (eg, GSW, deep knife wound) >1 body area or organ system without immediate threat to life or limb	**Comprehensive** 1. Chief complaint 2. Extended HPI 3. Complete ROS 4. 2 of 3 PFSH	**Comprehensive** Constitutional, eyes, ENT, respiratory, cardiovascular, GI, neurologic, skin	**High complexity** Same as **99284** plus may require operating room for repair
Critical Care Uncomplicated or complicated laceration of ≥1 body area or organ system with or without significant associated injury (eg, multiple trauma) with immediate threat to life or limb Critically ill, unstable patient; requires >30 minutes of directed patient care (bedside, review of data, consultation with other specialist, discussion with family members, documentation)			**High complexity** Same as **99285** Usually requires use of additional therapies such as cardiovascular support

Abbreviations: CPT, Current Procedural Terminology; ED, emergency department; E/M, evaluation and management; ENT, ear, nose, throat; EPF, expanded problem focused; GI, gastrointestinal; GSW, gunshot wound; HPI, history of present illness; LOC, loss of consciousness; PFSH, past, family, and social history; ROS, review of systems.

||ₗ||ₗ||

Critical and Intensive Care

||ₗ||ₗ||

Codes Reviewed in This Chapter

99291, 99292	Hourly critical care
99468, 99469	Initial and subsequent critical care, neonate 28 days of age or less
99471, 99472	Initial and subsequent critical care, 29 days through 24 months of age
99475, 99476	Initial and subsequent critical care, 2 through 5 years of age
0188T, 0189T	Remote real-time interactive video conferenced critical care, evaluation and management (E/M) of the critically ill or critically injured patient
99477	Initial neonatal intensive care
99478–99480	Subsequent intensive care, low birth weight or recovering infant, present body weight 5,000 g or less
99464, 99465	Attendance at delivery and delivery/birthing room resuscitation
99288	Physician direction of emergency medical systems (EMS) care (non–face-to-face)
99466, 99467	Pediatric critical care patient transport
99485, 99486	Supervision by a control physician of interfacility transport care of the critically ill or critically injured pediatric patient, 24 months of age or younger
99184	Initiation of selective head or total body hypothermia in the critically ill neonate, includes appropriate patient selection by review of clinical, imaging and laboratory data, confirmation of esophageal temperature probe location, evaluation of amplitude electroencephalogram (EEG), supervision of controlled hypothermia, and assessment of patient tolerance of cooling
33946–33989	Extracorporeal membrane oxygenation (ECMO) or extracorporeal life support (ECLS) services
94780, 94781	Car seat/bed testing

This chapter focuses on coding for critical and intensive care including hourly critical care, critical care of the neonate and children younger than 6 years, and intensive care of the neonate and recovering or low birth weight infants. Services commonly reported before and after intensive or critical care services, such as care during emergency transport, consultations, attendance at delivery, neonatal resuscitation, and medical team conferences, are included.

Evaluation and management of the child who no longer requires intensive or critical care are discussed in Chapter 8.

Critical Illness or Injury

- A *critical illness or injury* is defined by *Current Procedural Terminology (CPT®)* as one that acutely impairs one or more vital organs such that there is a high probability of imminent or life-threatening deterioration of the patient's condition.
- Critical care involves high-complexity medical decision-making (MDM) to assess, manipulate, and support vital organ system function(s); treat single or multiple organ system failure; and/or prevent further life-threatening deterioration of the patient's condition.
- Immaturity alone, or any of the specific procedures, equipment, or therapies associated with care of the immature neonate, does not define critical care.

- Coding critical care is not determined by the location in which the care is delivered but by the nature of the care being delivered and the condition of the patient requiring care.
- Services qualify as critical care *only if both* the injury or illness *and* the treatment being delivered meet the following criteria:
    - The illness or injury acutely impairs one or more vital organs as defined previously.
    - The treatment delivered involves high-complexity MDM to prevent life-threatening deterioration of the patient's condition.
- Critical care is not limited to an inpatient setting or a critical care area, and a physician of any specialty can provide these services.
    - Services must be provided directly by the physician or other qualified health care professional.

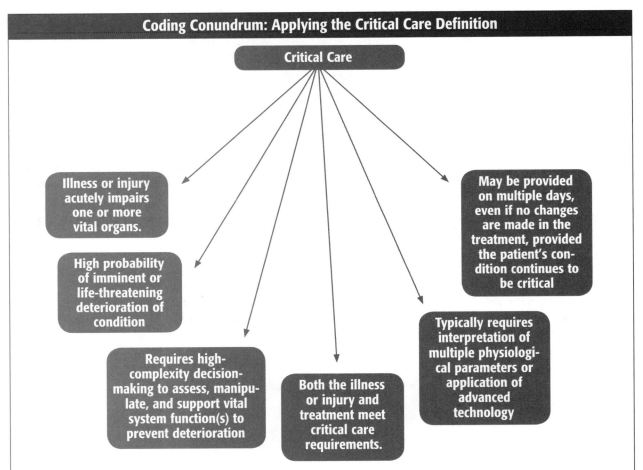

Coding Conundrum: Applying the Critical Care Definition

Critical Care

Illness or injury acutely impairs one or more vital organs.

High probability of imminent or life-threatening deterioration of condition

Requires high-complexity decision-making to assess, manipulate, and support vital system function(s) to prevent deterioration

Both the illness or injury and treatment meet critical care requirements.

Typically requires interpretation of multiple physiological parameters or application of advanced technology

May be provided on multiple days, even if no changes are made in the treatment, provided the patient's condition continues to be critical

The physician must use his or her judgment in assigning the *CPT* definition of critical care (see above). In summary, these are patients at clear risk of death or serious morbidity requiring close observation and frequent interventions and assessments and where the high-complexity MDM is apparent in the medical record documentation. No one criterion places a patient in this category, and the patient is not required to demonstrate all of the characteristics. The most convincing way to demonstrate the appropriate application of a critical care code is to clearly document in the medical record the child's condition with the risks to the patient, the frequency of needed assessment and interventions, the degree of the type of organ failure the patient is presently experiencing, and the complexity of the MDM. Despite the fact that immaturity will increase the risk of a critical illness in a newborn, neither immaturity alone nor any of the specific procedures or therapies associated with care of the immature neonate/infant qualifies alone for reporting critical care.

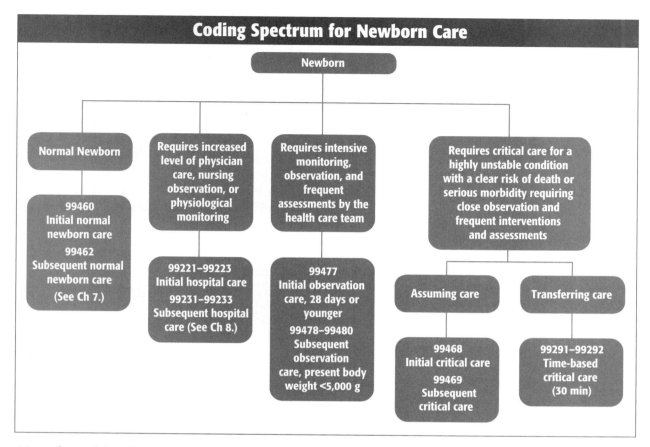

Coding Spectrum for Newborn Care

Newborn

- Normal Newborn
  - **99460** Initial normal newborn care
  - **99462** Subsequent normal newborn care
  - (See Ch 7.)

- Requires increased level of physician care, nursing observation, or physiological monitoring
  - **99221–99223** Initial hospital care
  - **99231–99233** Subsequent hospital care (See Ch 8.)

- Requires intensive monitoring, observation, and frequent assessments by the health care team
  - **99477** Initial observation care, 28 days or younger
  - **99478–99480** Subsequent observation care, present body weight <5,000 g

- Requires critical care for a highly unstable condition with a clear risk of death or serious morbidity requiring close observation and frequent interventions and assessments
  - Assuming care
    - **99468** Initial critical care
    - **99469** Subsequent critical care
  - Transferring care
    - **99291–99292** Time-based critical care (30 min)

Hourly Critical Care (99291, 99292)

99291   Critical care, E/M of the critically ill or critically injured patient; first 30 to 74 minutes

+99292   each additional 30 minutes (Use in conjunction with **99291.**)

Guidelines for reporting codes **99291–99292**

☀ Reported when critical care is provided

- ❖ In the outpatient setting (eg, emergency department [ED], office) regardless of age
- ❖ To an inpatient 6 years or older (Daily critical care of a child younger than 6 years is discussed later in this chapter.)
- ❖ Concurrently by a second physician from a different practice/specialty to a critically ill or injured child aged 5 years or younger
- ❖ To an inpatient aged 5 years or younger when the patient is being transferred to another facility where receiving physician of same specialty but different medical group will be reporting the daily inpatient critical care service codes (**99468–99469, 99471–99472,** and **99475–99476**)
- ❖ By the physician physically transporting a critically ill child older than 2 years

☀ These are bundled codes (include many procedures in the work valuation of the code that cannot be reported separately). See Table 10-1.

☀ Procedures not included as bundled may be reported separately (eg, lumbar puncture, endotracheal intubation). The reported time cannot include any time spent performing procedures or services that are reported separately.

|||||||||| *Coding Pearl* ||||||||||

Codes **99291** and **99292** are used to report critical care when provided concurrently by a second physician from a different practice/specialty to a critically ill or injured child aged 5 years or younger (ie, another physician is reporting **99468** or **99469**).

|||||||||| *Coding Pearl* ||||||||||

The time spent performing non-bundled, separately reportable procedures must be subtracted from the time reported for critical care services.

- Reported based on the total floor/unit time devoted to the patient in the provision of critical care. Critical care time includes physician-patient face-to-face time or time spent on the patient's unit or floor directly related to the patient's care (eg, care at the bedside, reviewing test results, discussing the care with other medical staff or family, documenting services in the medical record).
- Time spent in the provision of critical care does not need to be continuous.
- The physician must be immediately available to the patient during time reported as critical care. No time spent in activities that take place out of the unit or off of the patient's floor are included in critical care time.
- Code **99291** is reported once on a given date of service when 30 to 74 minutes of critical care is performed. If less than 30 minutes of critical care is provided, an appropriate E/M service (eg, **99201–99215** for office services, **99221–99233** for inpatient hospital care) is reported.
- Code **99292** is reported for each additional 30 minutes (beyond the first 74 minutes) of critical care provided. See Table 10-2 for reporting the correct codes based on the total duration of critical care.
    - Time spent providing critical care services must be documented in the medical record.

When inpatient and outpatient critical care services are provided to a neonate or child younger than 6 years on the same date by the same physician (or physician of same group and specialty), only the inpatient critical care codes are reported (**99468–99476**).

Table 10-1. Neonatal and Pediatric Critical Care Bundled Services

Procedures	*CPT* Code	Hourly Critical Care 99291, 99292	Pediatric Transport 99466, 99467	Neonatal/Pediatric Critical and Intensive Care 99468–99476, 99477–99480
Invasive, Noninvasive Electronic Monitoring				
Cardiac output measurements	93561, 93562	×	×	×
Chest x-rays	71010, 71015, 71020	×	×	×
Information/data stored in computers, ECG, BP, hematologic data	99090	×	×	×
Oral or nasogastric intubation	43752, 43753	×	×	×
Temporary transcutaneous pacing	92953	×	×	×
Endotracheal intubation	31500			×
Ventilatory management, CPAP	94002–94003	×	×	×
	94004	×		×
	94660, 94662	×	×	×
Surfactant administration	94610			×
Vascular Access Procedures				
Centrally inserted central vessel catheterization	36555			×
Umbilical catheterization	36510, 36660			×

Table 10-1. Neonatal and Pediatric Critical Care Bundled Services, continued

Procedures	CPT Code	Hourly Critical Care 99291, 99292	Pediatric Transport 99466, 99467	Neonatal/Pediatric Critical and Intensive Care 99468–99476, 99477–99480
Vascular Access Procedures, continued				
Other arterial catheterization	36140, 36620			×
Vascular access procedures	36000	×	×	×
	36400		×	×
	36405		×	×
	36406		×	×
	36410	×		×
	36415	×	×	×
	36591	×	×	×
Vascular punctures	36420			×
	36600	×	×	×
Transfusion blood components	36430, 36440			×
Other Procedures				
Pulse oximetry	94760–94762	×	×	×
Pulmonary function testing	94375			×
Lumbar puncture (diagnostic)	62270			×
Suprapubic bladder aspiration	51100			×
Bladder catheterization	51701, 51702			×
Car seat testing	94780, 94781			×

Abbreviations: BP, blood pressure; CPAP, continuous positive airway pressure; CPT, Current Procedural Terminology; ECG, electrocardiogram.

Table 10-2. Reporting Hourly Critical Care Services

Duration of Face-to-Face Critical Care	CPT Codes
<30 min	Do not report as critical care; included in the reported E/M service.
30–74 min	99291
75–104 min	99291 × 1 unit plus 99292 × 1 unit
105–134 min	99291 × 1 unit plus 99292 × 2 units

Abbreviations: CPT, Current Procedural Terminology; E/M, evaluation and management.

Chapter 10: Critical and Intensive Care

Examples

> ➤ **A 3-week-old is seen in the ED for respiratory distress.** The ED physician provides an hour of critical care before the neonate is admitted to the neonatal intensive care unit (NICU) by the neonatologist.
>
> Code **99291** with 1 unit of service is reported by the ED physician.

> ➤ **A 4-month-old is admitted with bronchiolitis.** During the night, the infant decompensates and develops impending respiratory failure. The pediatrician returns to the bedside; 4 hours are spent at the hospital stabilizing the infant, directing nursing staff, discussing management options with the tertiary care facility, speaking with the parents, and monitoring the infant while awaiting the transport team to take the infant to a hospital where the pediatrician does not practice.
>
> Codes **99291** and **99292** with 6 units of service would be reported.

> ➤ **A 3-year-old girl is seen in the physician's office with complaints of shortness of breath and wheezing.** She has a history of moderate persistent childhood asthma. The patient goes into respiratory distress and vital signs are deteriorating. The physician initiates critical care. After working for 10 minutes to stabilize the critical patient, an ambulance is called when the patient responds too slowly. The physician continues critical care services for another 25 minutes before the ambulance arrives. The total time for critical care services provided in the office was 35 minutes. The patient is admitted to the pediatric intensive care unit at the local university hospital under a pediatric intensivist. The pediatrician provides no more hands-on care for the patient that day and reports outpatient critical care services with a diagnosis of status asthmaticus.
>
> Code **99291** with 1 unit of service is reported.
>
> **Teaching Point:** If the same physician or physician group of the same specialty provided outpatient and inpatient critical care services, due to the patient's age only the pediatric critical care code (**99475**) would be reported. Had the patient been 6 years or older, the time spent in outpatient critical care by the same physician or group providing inpatient and outpatient services would be combined. Keep in mind that **99291** is only reported once per day.

Neonatal and Pediatric Critical Care (99468–99476)

Codes are
- ☀ Global—encompass all E/M services by a single provider (or provider of the exact same specialty in the same group) on one calendar date.
- ☀ Bundled—have commonly performed procedures included in the E/M codes.
- ☀ Not time-based.
- ☀ Not based on typical E/M rules and the performance and documentation of key components (history, physical examination, MDM, and/or time).
- ☀ Reported based on age (see Definition of Perinatal Period on page 220) and initial or subsequent care (see Table 10-3).

Table 10-3. Neonatal and Pediatric Global Critical Care

Inpatient Neonatal Critical Care	28 Days or Younger	29 Days Through 24 Months of Age	2 Through 5 Years of Age
Initial inpatient neonatal critical care, per day, for the E/M of a critically ill neonate, infant, or young child	99468	99471	99475
Subsequent inpatient neonatal critical care, per day, for the E/M of a critically ill neonate, infant, or young child	99469	99472	99476

Abbreviation: E/M, evaluation and management.

Guidelines for reporting neonatal or pediatric inpatient critical care

- The physician (or neonatal nurse practitioner [NNP] if independent billing is allowed in a state, services are within scope of practice, and NNP has hospital privilege credentials for the service) primarily responsible for the patient should report the neonatal or pediatric critical care codes.

- Includes all E/M services and bundled procedures provided on a calendar day. If critical care is provided in the outpatient and inpatient setting by the same physician or physician of the same specialty and group, only the inpatient code is reported.

- May be reported in addition to normal newborn care (**99460** or **99462**) when the patient receives normal newborn care and then, at a subsequent separate encounter the same day, requires critical care.

- Codes are reported only once per day, per patient.

- Initial critical care codes (**99468, 99471, 99475**) are only reported once, per day, per hospital stay for a given patient. If the patient has to be readmitted to critical care during the same hospital stay, report a subsequent critical care code (**99469, 99472, 99476**).

- Subsequent critical care may be reported on multiple days even if there is no change in the patient's condition as long as the patient continues to require critical care.

- Procedures bundled in these codes should not be reported separately. The services and procedures that are included with the neonatal critical care codes are identified in Table 10-1. Examples of procedures that are not bundled with the critical care services include

  - Thoracentesis
  - Thoracostomy
  - Exchange transfusion
  - Abdominal paracentesis
  - Subdural or shunt tap
  - Bone marrow aspiration
  - Circumcision
  - Cardiopulmonary resuscitation
  - Peripherally inserted central catheter (PICC) (National Correct Coding Initiate [NCCI] edits do bundle the PICC code [**36568**] with all neonatal and pediatric critical care codes. However, a modifier can override. See Chapter 3 for more information on NCCI edits.)

- Care may be provided on any unit in a hospital facility.

- Care must be provided by the reporting physician but also includes care provided by the team under the direct supervision of the physician or an advanced nurse practitioner who is employed by the physician or physician group and when allowed under state licensure requirements. See Critical and Intensive Care Supervision Requirements on the next page or Appendix B-6.

❋ Medical record documentation must support the need for critical care (eg, complex MDM, high probability of imminent or life-threatening deterioration, organ system failure).

Subsequent-day neonatal and pediatric intensive care codes (**99478–99480**) are reported when critical care is no longer required; however, intensive care is required and the infant weighs 5,000 g or less on the day that the code is reported. Once the infant weighs at least 5,001 g and critical care services are no longer required, report subsequent-day inpatient hospital visit codes (**99231–99233**).

Critical and Intensive Care Supervision Requirements

The American Medical Association/Specialty Society Relative Value Scale Update Committee (RUC) makes valuation recommendations based on surveys in which physicians who perform services are presented with a vignette describing the typical patient and face-to-face physician work. The neonatal, pediatric critical and intensive care code vignettes describe care by the attending physician (intra-service) as well as the preservice and post-service work associated with this service. Neither the vignette nor the intent of the codes was to imply that 24-hour in-house attendance was a requirement of this code set. However, it is assumed that the physician is physically present and participating directly in the patient's care for at least a significant portion of the service. Documentation in the patient's chart should reflect this active participation, including documentation of a personal physical examination. Supervision of all of the care from a distance without face-to-face care is not reported with these services. (Refer to Appendix B-6).

The vignettes also include the phrase "repeated examinations over a 24-hour period," which was included to indicate that these neonates or infants do not receive "continuous" care but rather may be evaluated during numerous intervals over a 24-hour period depending on the clinical needs of the patient. In some cases, the neonate's or infant's level of illness requires in-house attending presence for extended periods, while in other situations, only daytime and evening presence is required. Overnight in-house care is determined by the complexity of the population of neonates cared for in a nursery or the changes in a specific neonate's or infant's condition that cannot be adequately assessed or managed over the telephone.

Under the heading Inpatient Neonatal and Pediatric Critical Care Service, *CPT*® states that codes **99468, 99469,** and **99471–99476** are used to report services provided by a physician "directing the inpatient care" of a critically ill neonate or child through 5 years of age. The medical record documentation must support the physician's presence and supervision of the team. The directing physician is not required to be present or in the facility for the total 24 hours of daily care. Rather, because neonatal and pediatric critical and intensive care may require numerous encounters to reevaluate and manage the patient each day, neonatal and pediatric critical and intensive care codes encompass all of the sick care provided within a calendar day.

Definition of Perinatal Period

For coding purposes, the *perinatal period* is defined as before birth through the 28th day following birth. Based on this definition, the perinatal period continues through the 28th day of life, ending on the 29th calendar day after birth. The day of birth is considered day 0. Therefore, the day after birth is considered day 1.

This definition affects reporting of the initial- and subsequent-day neonatal and pediatric critical care codes **99468–99472** and code **99477** for the initial hospital care of the neonate, 28 days or younger, who requires intensive observation, frequent interventions, and other intensive care services.

Examples

➤ **A term 3,500-g neonate is born cyanotic following a vaginal delivery.** He has minimal respiratory distress and appears otherwise vigorous. He is brought to the NICU where a chest x-ray shows dramatic cardiomegaly and a marked increase in pulmonary markings. An umbilical artery catheter and umbilical vein catheter are inserted to determine blood gases. An electrocardiogram is performed and a pediatric cardiologist is consulted to obtain an emergency echocardiogram.

Code **99468** would be reported for initial neonatal critical care services. Depending on the findings on the echocardiogram and a need for cardiac intensive care, the cardiologist may be permitted to report hourly critical care for any additional time beyond the echocardiogram. If the neonate were transferred to a cardiac center by the neonatologist, the neonatologist would report time-based critical care codes (**99291, 99292**) for the care provided prior to the transfer.

➤ **A 22-month-old with developmental delays and a seizure disorder is initially treated by the ED physician for status epilepticus.** Although seizures were initially controlled, the child became apneic and hypotensive. She was admitted to the pediatric intensive care unit at 11:00 pm that evening by the critical care attending physician, who intubated her, placed her on a ventilator, began a volume infusion and dobutamine to control her blood pressure, and made arrangements for a bedside electroencephalogram (EEG).

The ED physician would report 1 hour of critical care (**99291**). The pediatrician or intensivist would report his or her services with the initial inpatient pediatric critical care code (**99471**) for that calendar day.

➤ **A 3-day-old recovering from respiratory distress syndrome with a present body weight of 1,600 g is still unstable but is weaned off the ventilator to continuous positive airway pressure (CPAP).** He is continued on total parenteral nutrition by central vein and intravenous (IV) antibiotics.

Code **99469** is reported because the neonate continues to require critical care.

Coding Conundrum: Apnea in Neonates

Apnea in neonates may be an expected component of prematurity and may be effectively managed by manual stimulation, pharmacologic stimulation, high-flow nasal oxygen, or CPAP. At other times this symptom will be associated with a serious underlying problem(s) and is a reflection of the instability of a critically ill neonate or child and will require one or more of the same interventions. The physician must employ his or her best clinical judgment and clearly document the factors that make the patient's present condition critical. The same requirements for organ failure, the risk of imminent deterioration, and complex MDM apply. With apnea and many other conditions, it is the total picture of the neonate with the diagnosis, clinical presentation, and immediate threat to life as well as the level of intervention needed to manage that neonate's problems on a given day that drives the correct code selection. In all cases, when critical care codes are reported, the documentation must support the physician's judgment that the patient is critically ill and that services provided are commensurate with the condition on that day of service on which critical care codes are reported.

Patients Critically Ill After Surgery

Postoperative care of a surgical patient is included in the surgeon's global surgical package. For some neonatal surgical care (eg, code **39503** [repair of diaphragmatic hernia], **43314** [esophagoplasty, thoracic approach; with repair of tracheoesophageal fistula], or **49605** [repair of large omphalocele or gastroschisis; with or without prosthesis]), critical care days are included in the work values assigned these surgical procedures.

However, if

- A second physician provides care for the routine postoperative patient, the surgeon must append modifier **54** (surgical care only) to the surgical code.

- The surgeon provides and reports the complete surgical care package, a request for consultation from another specialist may be made.

- The patient's course is not typical and an unexpected complication occurs that requires the concurrent care of another specialist, both may report their service. For example, if the surgeon first requests a consultation, an initial consultation code (or other appropriate E/M code based on the payer's payment policy for consultations) would be reported. If the surgeon requests concurrent care for a specific medical problem, time-based critical care (**99291–99292**) or subsequent hospital care (**99231–99233**) codes would be reported dependent on the child's condition and the care provided. The diagnosis code representing the condition or symptom being treated should be reported with the concurrent *CPT®* code. The rationale for the need for concurrent care must be documented in the surgeon's notes.

Remote Critical Care Services (0188T, 0189T)

Remote critical care is the direct delivery by a physician(s) of medical care for a critically ill or critically injured patient from an off-site location (ie, when a critically ill or injured patient requires additional critical care resources that are not available on-site). To report remote critical care, the following conditions must exist:

- The patient's condition must fall under the strict *CPT®* definition of critically ill or critically injured.

- The physician(s) in the remote location must have real-time access to the patient's medical record, including progress notes, nursing notes, current medications, vital signs, clinical laboratory test results, other diagnostic test results, and radiographic images.

- The physician(s) must have real-time capability to enter electronic orders; document the remote care services provided in the hospital medical record; videoconference with the on-site health care team in the patient room; assess patients in their individual room using high-fidelity audio and video capabilities, including but not limited to clear observation of the patient, monitors, ventilators, and infusion pumps; and speak with the patient and family members.

- The total duration of time spent providing remote critical care on a given day should be reported, regardless of whether the time is continuous. The time reported includes time spent on work directly related to the patient's care (eg, time reviewing test results or imaging studies, discussing the patient's care with other medical staff, documenting remote critical care services in the medical record, talking with the patient and/or family or surrogate decision-makers to obtain history and/or discuss the management and prognosis of the patient). Any time spent away from the remote site when the physician does not have the real-time capabilities described previously or time is spent on activities that do not directly contribute to the treatment of the patient may not be reported.

❖ The first hour (**0188T**) of remote critical care can only be reported once on a given date of service and only if 30 minutes or more of critical care is performed. Remote critical care cannot be reported if less than 30 minutes of remote critical care is provided. Each additional 30 minutes beyond the first 74 minutes of remote critical care is reported with code **0189T**. (See Table 10-4.)

❖ Medical record documentation must include the actual time spent providing remote critical care services and support the critical nature of the patient's condition and interactions with the patient, family, and other providers.

❖ Category III codes are not assigned relative values under the Medicare Resource-Based Relative Value Scale (RBRVS). Payment for remote critical care services is based strictly on payer policies. Work with your payers to determine their coverage, educate payers, and provide them with information that demonstrates the value of the service.

Table 10-4. Reporting Remote Critical Care Services

Duration of Remote Critical Care	*CPT* Codes
<30 min	Do not report.
30–74 min	**0188T**
75–104 min	**0188T** × 1 unit plus **0189T** × 1 unit
105–134 min	**0188T** × 1 unit plus **0189T** × 2 units

Abbreviation: CPT, Current Procedural Terminology.

Neonatal and Pediatric Intensive Care (99477–99480)

Code **99477** is used for initial hospital care, per day, for the E/M of the ill neonate, 28 days or younger, who requires intensive observation and monitoring. See Table 10-5 for code descriptions for subsequent-day neonatal and pediatric intensive care services (**99478–99480**). Neonatal intensive care codes (**99477–99480**) may be used to report care for neonates or infants who are not critically ill; who were previously classified as critically ill and are no longer in critical condition but have a need for intensive monitoring, observation, and frequent assessments by the health care team; or require intensive but not critical care services from birth. These neonates often have a continued need for oxygen, parenteral or gavage enteral nutrition, treatment for apnea of prematurity, and thermoregulatory needs for an isolate or radiant warmer. The intensive services described by these codes include intensive cardiac and respiratory monitoring, continuous and/or frequent vital sign monitoring, heat maintenance, enteral and/or parenteral nutritional adjustments, and laboratory and oxygen saturation monitoring.

Table 10-5. Neonatal and Pediatric Subsequent-Day Intensive Care

Description	Present Weight <1,500 g	Present Weight 1,500–2,500 g	Present Weight 2,501–5,000 g	Present Weight 5,001 g+
Subsequent intensive care, per day, for the E/M of the recovering low birth weight infant	99478	99479	99480	99231–99233

- Code **99477** is used to report the more intensive services that an ill but not critically ill neonate (28 days or younger) requires on the day of admission to intensive care services.
- Services are typically provided in a NICU or special care unit and require a higher intensity of care than would be reported with codes **99221–99223** (initial hospital care of sick patient).
- Patients are under constant observation by the health care team under direct physician supervision.
  - These are global codes and include all of the E/M services provided to the neonate on that date of service, excluding normal newborn care (**99460–99462**) if performed.
  - These are bundled services and include the same procedures that are bundled with neonatal and pediatric critical care services (**99468–99476**). Table 10-1 lists all of the services and procedures that are included.
  - Code **99477** should also be used to report readmission to a facility of an ill neonate (aged 28 days or younger) if the neonate requires intensive (not critical) care services.
  - If the infant is older than 28 days at admission but weighs less than 5,000 g, code **99223** should be used for initial care and **99478–99480** for subsequent days, as long as the infant continues to require intensive care.
- Codes **99478–99480** are reported once per day of subsequent intensive (but not critical) care for the E/M of the recovering infant weighing 5,000 g or less. Selection of the code will be dependent on the *present* body weight of the infant, not the infant's age, on the date of service. Therefore, code selection may change from one day to the next depending on the infant's present body weight and condition.
- Once the baby's weight exceeds 5,000 g, subsequent hospital care codes (**99231–99233**) are reported.

> ||||||||| **Coding Pearl** |||||||||
>
> Continuing intensive care services provided to an infant weighing more than 5,000 g (approximately 11.2 lb) are reported with subsequent hospital care codes (**99231–99233**).

Examples

➤ **A 1,500-g neonate has mild respiratory distress.** She is on 30% oxygen by nasal cannula and on a cardiorespiratory monitor and continuous pulse oximetry. Laboratory tests and x-rays are ordered, and IV fluids and antibiotics are started. Frequent monitoring and observation are required and ordered.

Code **99477** (initial hospital care for the ill neonate, 28 days of age or less, who requires intensive observation and monitoring) would be reported by the admitting physician.

➤ **A 1,150-g neonate, now 5 days old, is receiving 30% oxygen and continues on IV fluids, small trophic feeds, and caffeine for apnea.**

Code **99478** would be reported.

➤ **A 15-day-old, 1,600-g neonate remains in an Isolette for thermoregulation and is on methylxanthines for intermittent apnea and bradycardia for which the neonate requires continuous cardiorespiratory and pulse oximetry monitoring.** The physician adjusts the neonate's continuous gavage feeds based on tolerance and weight.

Code **99479** would be reported.

In these examples, the neonate is not critically ill but continues to require intensive monitoring and constant observation by the health care team under direct physician supervision.

> **A baby requires intensive care and weighs 2,500 g on Monday.** The following day she continues to require intensive care and her weight is 2,504 g.
>
> Code **99479** would be reported for the care provided on Monday. Code **99480** would be reported for the continuing intensive care provided the following day.

Consultation Codes (99241–99245, 99251–99255, 99446–99449)

Pediatric hospital care may at times begin prior to birth with services provided to the mother during the peripartum period. Although it is atypical for pediatric claims to be submitted for services to adult patients, these services rendered to the mother are an exception.

A consultation (**99241–99245, 99251–99255**) is reported when a physician or other appropriate source requests an opinion and/or advice from another physician or appropriate source. The consulting physician renders his or her opinion and advice, records it, and returns a report to the requesting physician or appropriate source. Chapters 6 and 8 detail the specific reporting, documentation, and coding requirements for the selection of consultation codes or other E/M service codes when consultation codes are not recognized. See Table 8-3 for the key components of consultation codes used in reporting outpatient (eg, office or observation) and inpatient consultations.

Codes **99446–99449** for interprofessional telephone/Internet consultations were introduced in 2014. These codes are discussed in detail in Chapter 11.

> |||||||| ***Coding Pearl*** ||||||||
>
> Consultations are not reported when they are requested by a patient or family member; office codes are used. See Chapter 6.

Examples

> **At the request of the obstetrician, you counsel a family who was just informed that its fetus has an enlarged bladder and dilated ureter.** You meet with the family in your office and spend 30 minutes counseling the family about the condition. The time spent in counseling and a summary of the issues discussed is documented in your medical record. Your consultation report is sent to the requesting physician and a copy is maintained in your medical record.

Time (30 minutes face-to-face) is the key controlling factor. }

99242 (average 30 minutes)
or, if payer does not recognize consultations,
99203 (new patient, average 30 minutes) or
99214 (established patient, average 25 minutes)

ICD-9-CM
V65.11 (pre-birth visit)

ICD-10-CM
Z76.81 (expectant parent[s] pre-birth pediatrician visit)

Chapter 10: Critical and Intensive Care

➤ **A 2-day-old hospitalized newborn develops poor feeding and tachypnea and is diagnosed with group B streptococcal septicemia.** The patient's primary care physician telephones an infectious disease specialist located several hours away for treatment advice. The physicians spend 8 minutes discussing the child's condition and treatment options. The infectious disease specialist reports this service with

99446 (interprofessional consultation, 5–10 minutes)

ICD-9-CM
771.81 (septicemia of newborn)
041.02 (streptococcus B infection in diseases classified elsewhere)

ICD-10-CM
P36.0 (sepsis of newborn due to streptococcus, group B)

The attending physician will include this work in the per diem charge for intensive or critical care services based on the type of care rendered.

➤ **A neonatologist is asked by an obstetrician to consult with a mother in preterm labor with triplets at 23 weeks' gestation.** She is being treated with steroids and magnesium sulfate. The neonatologist reviews the maternal prenatal and hospital record, interviews the mother, and meets with both parents to discuss the fetal and neonatal risks and likely hospital course and complications if delivered in the next few days. The neonatologist spends a total of 65 minutes of floor/unit time devoted to this patient's consultation, which is dominated by discussing the morbidity and mortality risks and resuscitation and possible treatment.

Inpatient floor/unit time (65 minutes) is the key controlling factor.
}
99253 (typical time 55 minutes)
or, if payer does not recognize consultations,
99223 (average 70 minutes)

ICD-9-CM
644.2 (premature labor)
651.13 (triplet pregnancy, antepartum condition or complication)

ICD-10-CM
O60.02 (preterm labor without delivery, second trimester)
O30.102 (triplet pregnancy, unspecified number of placenta and unspecified number of amniotic sacs, second trimester)

Attendance at Delivery and Newborn Resuscitation (99464 and 99465)

||||||| *Coding Pearl* |||||||

Attendance at delivery is reported only when the service is requested by the delivering physician and is medically indicated.

Attendance at delivery (**99464**) is only reported when the physical presence of the provider is requested by the delivering physician and indicated for a newborn who may require immediate intervention (ie, stabilization, resuscitation, or evaluation for potential problems). Code **99464** is not reported when hospital-mandated attendance is the only underlying basis for providing the service. When physician on-call services are not requested by the delivering physician but rather are mandated by the hospital (eg, attending specific types of deliveries without physician request, such as all repeat cesarean deliveries), report code **99026** (hospital-mandated on-call service; in hospital, each hour) or **99027** (hospital-mandated on-call service; out of hospital, each hour). See Chapter 12 for guidelines on the use of codes **99026** and **99027.**

Attendance at delivery (**99464**)

⚙ Service is only reported when requested by the delivering physician.

⚙ Medical record documentation must include the request for attendance at the delivery and substantiate the medical necessity of the services performed. If there is no documentation by the delivering physician for attendance at delivery, the verbal request and the reason for the request should be documented in the attendance note.

⚙ Includes initial drying, stimulation, suctioning, blow-by oxygen, or CPAP without positive-pressure ventilation; a cursory visual inspection of the neonate; assignment of Apgar scores; and discussion of the care of the newborn with the delivering physician and parents.

⚙ Any medically necessary procedures to complete the resuscitation that are provided in the delivery room may be reported separately (eg, direct laryngoscopy without intubation).

⚙ May be reported in addition to the initial normal newborn (**99460**), initial sick newborn (**99221–99223**), initial intensive care of the neonate (**99477**), or critical care (**99468; 99291–99292**) codes.

When qualifying resuscitative efforts are provided, code **99465** (delivery/birthing room resuscitation) is reported instead. Codes **99464** and **99465** cannot be reported on the same day of service.

Code **99465**

⚙ Includes bag-and-mask or bag-to-endotracheal tube ventilation (positive-pressure ventilation) with or without CPAP, and/or cardiac compressions.

⚙ Other life support procedures that are performed as a necessary part of the resuscitation may be reported separately. For example

  ❖ **31500** Intubation, endotracheal, emergency procedure

  ❖ **31515** Laryngoscopy, direct, for aspiration

  ❖ **36510** Catheterization of umbilical vein for diagnosis or therapy, newborn

  ❖ **94610** Surfactant administration

⚙ May be reported in addition to any initial care service, including initial critical care (**99468; 99291–99292**) or initial neonatal intensive care (**99477**).

⚙ Medically necessary procedures (eg, intubation, umbilical line placement) that are essential to successful resuscitation (and not performed as a convenience before admission to the NICU) that are performed in the delivery room prior to admission may also be reported in addition to code **99468** or **99477.** Medical record documentation must clearly support that the services are provided as part of the preadmission or pre-global service.

Example

➤ **A neonatologist attends the cesarean delivery of a 27-week neonate at the request of an obstetrician who suspects an abruption.** The neonate has no spontaneous activity. The resuscitation includes positive-pressure ventilation, intubation, and placement of an umbilical vein catheter. The newborn is stabilized and admitted to the NICU, where the neonatologist administers surfactant and performs an umbilical artery catheterization.

Chapter 10: Critical and Intensive Care

Chapter 10: Critical and Intensive Care

The intubation and umbilical vein catheterization are separately reported procedures provided as part of the resuscitation and not as a convenience to the physician prior to admission.

} **99465** (delivery/birthing room resuscitation)
31500 (endotracheal intubation)
36510 (catheterization of umbilical vein for diagnosis or therapy, newborn)
99468 25 (initial neonatal critical care)

Teaching Point: Modifier **25** is appended to code **99468** to signify a significant, separately identifiable E/M service provided in addition to codes **31500** and **36510** because these services are bundled by NCCI edits (for more on edits, see Chapter 3). Codes **99465** and **99468** are not bundled by NCCI edits, but individual payers may require modifier **25** to designate separately identifiable critical care services on the same date.

Emergency Medical Services Supervision and Patient Transport

Direction of Emergency Medical Services Care (99288) by Physician or Qualified Health Care Professional

Guidelines for reporting code **99288** (direction of emergency medical systems [EMS] emergency care, advanced life support) by physician or qualified health care professional

* May be reported by any physician of any specialty or qualified health care professional when advanced life support services are provided via 2-way voice communications (eg, cardiac and/or pulmonary resuscitation; administration of IV fluids, antibiotics, or surfactant).
* This code reflects all of the services provided by the directing physician and is not based on any time requirements. Code **99288** may be reported when less than 16 minutes is spent in physician non–face-to-face supervision of interfacility transport of a critically ill or injured pediatric patient (ie, requirements for reporting **99485** are not met).
* The directing physician should maintain documentation of the times of all contacts, orders, and/or directions for treatment or management of the patient.
* Services or procedures performed by EMS personnel are not reported by the physician because he or she was not physically present.
* The appropriate diagnoses are linked to the service.
* If, after directing EMS emergency care, the physician performs the initial critical care, code **99468** (initial inpatient neonatal critical care) would also be reported with modifier **25** appended to indicate that 2 separate and distinct E/M services were provided by the same physician on the same day of service.

There is no assigned Medicare relative value unit (RVU) to this service, so it is "carrier priced" and payments will vary by payer.

Medicare considers code **99288** a bundled service and does not pay separately for the service. Check with your state Medicaid program and other payers to determine their coverage policy.

See page 230 for discussion of physician non–face-to-face supervision of interfacility transport of a critically ill or injured pediatric patient 24 months or younger (**99485–99486**).

Pediatric Critical Care Patient Transport (99466 and 99467, 99485 and 99486)

Face-to-Face Critical Care Patient Transport (99466 and 99467)

Codes **99466** (critical care services delivered by a physician or qualified health care professional, face-to-face, during an interfacility transport of a critically ill or critically injured pediatric patient, 24 months of age or less; first 30 to 74 minutes of hands-on care during transport) and **99467** (each additional 30 minutes) are used to report the physical attendance and direct face-to-face care provided by a physician during the interfacility transport of a critically ill or injured patient aged 24 months or younger.

- The patient's condition must meet the *CPT* definition for critical care.
- Face-to-face time begins when the physician or practitioner assumes primary responsibility for the patient at the referring hospital or facility and ends when the receiving hospital or facility accepts responsibility for the patient's care. Only the time the physician spends in direct face-to-face contact with the patient during transport should be reported.
- Less than 30 minutes' face-to-face time cannot be reported.
- Code **99466** is used to report the first 30 to 74 minutes of physician face-to-face time with the critically ill or injured patient during the transport.
- Code **99467** is used to report each additional 30 minutes of physician face-to-face time of critical care provided on the same day of service.
- Codes include the bundled services listed in Table 10-1. Codes **99466** and **99467** may be reported separately from any other procedures or services that are not bundled and performed on the date of transfer.
  - ❖ The time involved in performing any procedures that are not bundled and reported separately should not be included in the face-to-face transport time.
- Procedures or services that are performed by other members of the transport team with the physical presence, participation, and supervision of the accompanying physician may be reported by the physician.
  - ❖ Documentation must support the physician's participation.
- Medical record documentation must include the total face-to-face time spent with the patient, the critical nature of the patient's condition, and any performed procedures that are not bundled.
- The pediatric critical care transport codes are preadmission codes and may be reported in addition to neonatal (**99468**) or pediatric (**99471**) initial-day critical care codes.
- Face-to-face critical care services provided during an interfacility transport to a child older than 24 months are reported with hourly critical care codes (**99291** and **99292**).
- If an NNP employed by the neonatal group is on the transport team, the NNP may report codes **99466** and **99467** if independent billing by an NNP is allowed by the state and the activities are covered in the scope of practice. The neonatologist from that same group would not report codes **99485–99486** (physician direction of pediatric critical care transport) or **99288** (physician direction of EMS emergency care). The facility (hospital) could also report these services if the NNPs are employed by the hospital. In this case, the neonatologist would report codes **99485–99486.**

Chapter 10: Critical and Intensive Care

Example

➤ **A 3,000-g 38-week neonate born at a community hospital with meconium aspiration syndrome requires ventilator care and transport to a Level III unit.** The receiving neonatologist accompanies the transport nurse and therapist. Ground transport takes 40 minutes one way. On arrival, the neonatologist spends 60 minutes face-to-face evaluating and stabilizing the newborn. The newborn is intubated, surfactant is administered, umbilical venous and arterial catheters are inserted, and parents are counseled. The neonatologist spends 5 minutes intubating and administering the surfactant and 10 minutes placing the umbilical venous and arterial catheters. The newborn is then transferred to the neonatal transport van and back to the receiving nursery. Total time from bedside back to the receiving nursery is 60 minutes. Frequent assessments and alterations in drugs, fluids, and ventilator settings are performed on the transport back. The neonatologist spent a total of 120 minutes of face-to-face critical care time with the neonate; 25 minutes is subtracted for the performance of non-bundled procedures. The neonatologist continues care of the newborn in the NICU.

99466 25
99467 25 with 1 unit
31500 (endotracheal intubation)
94610 (surfactant administration)
36510 (catheterization of umbilical vein)
36660 (catheterization of umbilical artery)
99468 25 (initial neonatal critical care)

Non–Face-to-Face Pediatric Critical Care Patient Transport (99485 and 99486)

Code **99485** is used to report the first 30 minutes of a control physician's non–face-to-face supervision of interfacility critical care transport of a patient 24 months or younger, which includes all 2-way communication between the control physician and the specialized transport team prior to transport, at the referring facility, and during transport to the receiving facility. Each additional 30-minute period of communication is reported with add-on code **99486.** These codes do not include communication between the control physician and referring facility before or following patient transport.

❋ The patient's condition must meet the *CPT®* definition for critical care.
❋ Only report for patients 24 months or younger who are critically ill or injured.
❋ The control physician does not report any services provided by the specialized transport team.
❋ The control physician only reports cumulative time spent communicating with the specialty transport team members during an interfacility transport.
❋ Reportable time begins with the initial discussions with the transport team, including discussions of best mode of transport and strategies for therapy on arrival. Time ends when the patient's care is handed over to the receiving facility team.
❋ Code **99485** is used to report the first 16 to 45 minutes of direction on a given date and should only be used once even if time spent by the physician is discontinuous.
❋ Code **99486** is used in conjunction with **99485** for each additional 30 minutes.
❋ Do not report **99485** or **99486** for services of 15 minutes or less or any time when a provider from the same group is also reporting **99466–99467.**

☀ Time spent with the individual patient's transport team and reviewing data submissions should be recorded. Time spent discussing the patient with the referring physician or facility is not counted.

Example

➤ **A community pediatrician asks to refer a newborn with severe meconium aspiration.** The neonatologist dispatches the transport team consisting of a hospital-employed nurse and respiratory therapist. On the trip to the referring hospital, the neonatologist converses by telephone for 10 minutes with the team, explaining the newborn's condition and formulating an initial treatment plan. After arrival, the nurse evaluates the neonate and telephones the neonatologist to discuss the findings. The decision is made to intubate the neonate and give surfactant. Because of the critical nature of the newborn, the neonatologist elects to remain on the telephone until surfactant therapy is completed—15 minutes. The team then leaves the referring hospital. On the return trip, SpO_2 falls to 80%. Telephone contact is again made and the neonatologist instructs the team to begin inhaled nitric oxide; this call lasts for another 10 minutes. The team then completes the transport without further incident.

The neonatologist spent a total of 35 minutes in direct 2-way telephone communication with the team in 3 discrete episodes. The neonatologist carefully documents in the medical record the time spent and what decisions were made in each contact.

Code **99485** is used to report this service.

Total Body Systemic and Selective Head Hypothermia (99184)

The procedure codes implemented in *CPT® 2014* for total body systemic (**99481**) and selective head hypothermia (**99482**) have been deleted for 2015. The new code for reporting either service is

99184　　Initiation of selective head or total body hypothermia in the critically ill neonate, includes appropriate patient selection by review of clinical, imaging and laboratory data, confirmation of esophageal temperature probe location, evaluation of amplitude EEG, supervision of controlled hypothermia, and assessment of patient tolerance of cooling

(Do not report **99184** more than once per hospital stay)

When total body systemic or selective head hypothermia is used in treatment of a critically ill neonate, this code represents the work of initiating the service. Documentation for use of total body systemic hypothermia and selective head hypothermia should include the neonatal criteria that support initiating this service.

☀ During either cooling approach, monitoring includes
  ❖ Radiographic confirmation of core temperature probe
  ❖ Continuous core temperature assessment and adjustment
  ❖ Repeated assessment of skin integrity
  ❖ Recurrent objective evaluation of evolving neurologic changes (eg, Sarnat score), which may also include assessment of continuous amplitude EEG monitoring

☀ In addition, cooling-related laboratory evaluations are required to monitor for cooling-specific complications, including metabolic and coagulation alterations.

Examples

➤ **A term neonate is born following severe in utero hypoxemia, is admitted to the NICU, and receives critical care services.** Laboratory, EEG, blood gas, and imaging studies confirm the neonate meets objective criteria for total body cooling. Continuous total body cooling is undertaken.

   Code **99184** is reported for total body systemic hypothermia in addition to **99468,** initial day of neonatal critical care.

➤ **A term neonate is born following severe in utero hypoxemia, is admitted to the NICU, and receives critical care services.** Laboratory, EEG, blood gas, and imaging studies confirm the neonate meets objective criteria for selective head cooling. Continuous selective head cooling is undertaken.

   Code **99184** is reported for selective head hypothermia in addition to **99468,** initial day of neonatal critical care.

Extracorporeal Membrane Oxygenation or Extracorporeal Life Support Services

Prolonged extracorporeal membrane oxygenation (ECMO) and extracorporeal life support (ECLS) services provide cardiac and/or respiratory support, allowing the heart and/or lungs to rest and recover when sick or injured. These services commonly involve multiple physicians and supporting health care personnel to manage each patient. *CPT®* *2015* includes an entirely new code set for initiation and management of ECMO and ECLS, along with new prefatory language to help differentiate components of initiation and daily management of ECMO and ECLS from daily management of a patient's overall medical condition.

   These services include cannula(e) insertion (**33951–33956**), ECMO or ECLS initiation (**33946** or **33947**), daily ECMO or ECLS management (**33948** or **33949**), repositioning of the ECMO or ECLS cannula(e) (**33957–33964**), and cannula(e) removal (**33965–33986**). Do not report modifier **63** (procedure performed on infants less than 4 kg) when reporting codes **33946–33949**.

   Initiation of the ECMO or ECLS circuit and setting parameters (**33946, 33947**) involves determining the necessary ECMO or ECLS device components, blood flow, gas exchange, and other necessary parameters to manage the circuit.

●**33946**   Extracorporeal membrane oxygenation (ECMO)/extracorporeal life support (ECLS) provided by physician; initiation, veno-venous

●**33947**   initiation, veno-arterial

   Daily care for a patient on ECMO or ECLS includes managing the ECMO or ECLS circuit and related patient issues. These services may be performed by one physician while another physician manages the overall patient medical condition and underlying disorders. Regardless of the patient's condition, the basic management of ECMO and ECLS is similar.

⁕ The physician reporting daily ECMO or ECLS oversees the interaction of the circuit with the patient, management of blood flow, oxygenation, CO_2 clearance by the membrane lung, systemic response, anticoagulation and treatment of bleeding, cannula(e) positioning, alarms and safety, and weaning the patient from the ECMO or ECLS circuit when heart and/or lung function has sufficiently recovered.

☀ Daily management of the patient may be separately reported using the relevant hospital observation services, hospital inpatient services, or critical care evaluation and management codes (**99218–99220, 99221–99223, 99231–99233, 99234–99236, 99291, 99292, 99468–99476**).

☀ If the same physician performs the ECMO or ECLS initiation, and provides the daily management of the ECMO or ECLS circuit for the remainder of that day, the initiation code (**33946** or **33947**) and the daily management code (**33948** or **33949**) may be reported.

●**33948**   Extracorporeal membrane oxygenation (ECMO)/extracorporeal life support (ECLS) provided by physician; daily management, each day, veno-venous

●**33949**   daily management, each day, veno-arterial

Codes for insertion, repositioning, and removal of ECMO and ECLS are reported based on the patient's age with separate codes for procedures on newborn through 5 years of age and on patients 6 years and older. Codes for these services are shown in tables 10-6, 10-7, and 10-8.

☀ Do not separately report repositioning of the ECMO or ECLS cannula(e) (**33957–33964**) at the same session as insertion (**33951–33956**).

☀ Fluoroscopic guidance used for cannula(e) repositioning (**33957–33964**) is included in the procedure when performed and should not be separately reported.

☀ Report replacement of ECMO or ECLS cannula(e) in the same vessel using the insertion code (**33951–33956**) only.

☀ If cannula(e) are removed from one vessel and new cannula(e) are placed in a different vessel, report the appropriate cannula(e) removal (**33965–33986**) and insertion (**33951–33956**) codes.

☀ Extensive repair or replacement of an artery may be additionally reported (eg, **35226, 35286, 35371, 35665**).

☀ Direct anastomosis of a prosthetic graft to the artery sidewall to facilitate arterial perfusion for ECMO or ECLS is separately reported with code **33987** in addition to codes **33953–33956.**

+**33987**   Arterial exposure with creation of graft conduit (eg, chimney graft) to facilitate arterial perfusion for ECMO/ECLS (List separately in addition to code for primary procedure)

❖ Do not report **33987** in conjunction with **34833** (open iliac artery exposure with creation of conduit for delivery of aortic or iliac endovascular prosthesis, by abdominal or retroperitoneal incision, unilateral).

Table 10-6. Insertion of ECMO or ECLS Cannula(e)

Extracorporeal membrane oxygenation (ECMO)/extracorporeal life support (ECLS) provided by physician	Birth through 5 years of age	6 years and older	Not reported in conjunction with
Insertion of peripheral (arterial and/or venous) cannula(e), percutaneous (includes fluoroscopic guidance when performed)	●33951	●33952	N/A
Insertion of peripheral (arterial and/or venous) cannula(e), open	●33953	●33954	34812, 34820, 34834
Insertion of central cannula(e) by sternotomy or thoracotomy	●33955	●33956	32100, 39010

Table 10-7. Repositioning ECMO or ECLS Cannula(e)

Extracorporeal membrane oxygenation (ECMO)/extra-corporeal life support (ECLS) provided by physician	Birth through 5 years of age	6 years and older	Not reported in conjunction with
Reposition peripheral (arterial and/or venous) cannula(e), percutaneous (includes fluoroscopic guidance when performed)	33957	33958	34812, 34820, 34834
Reposition peripheral (arterial and/or venous) cannula(e), open (includes fluoroscopic guidance when performed)	33959	33962	34812, 34820, 34834
Reposition of central cannula(e) by sternotomy or thoracotomy (includes fluoroscopic guidance when performed)	33963	33964	32100, 39010

Table 10-8. Removal of ECMO or ECLS Cannula(e)

Extracorporeal membrane oxygenation (ECMO)/extra-corporeal life support (ECLS) provided by physician	Birth through 5 years of age	6 years and older	Not reported in conjunction with
Removal of peripheral (arterial and/or venous) cannula(e), percutaneous	33965	33966	
Removal of peripheral (arterial and/or venous) cannula(e), open	33969	33984	34812, 34820, 34834, 35201, 35206, 35211, 35216, 35226
Removal of central cannula(e) by sternotomy or thoracotomy	33985	33986	35201, 35206, 35211, 35216, 35226

Car Seat/Bed Testing (94780 and 94781)

Neonates who required critical care during their initial hospital stay are most often those patients who require monitoring to determine if a neonate may be safely transported in a car seat or must be transported in a car bed. While these codes are bundled under the neonatal and pediatric critical and intensive care codes, these services most often take place when a neonate is about to go home and therefore can be reported if hospital care services (**99231–99233**) or hospital discharge services (**99238, 99239**) are being reported instead. See Table 10-9 for further description of the codes.

To report codes **94780** and **94781,** the following conditions must be met:

- ☀ Continual nursing observation with continuous recording of pulse oximetry, heart rate, and respiratory rate is required.
- ☀ Inpatient or office-based services are reported.
- ☀ Vital signs and observations must be reviewed and interpreted and a written report generated by the physician.
- ☀ Codes are reported based on the total observation time spent and documented.
- ☀ These codes may be reported with discharge day management (**99238–99239**), normal newborn care services (**99460, 99462, 99463**), or subsequent hospital care codes (**99231–99233**).
- ☀ Codes **94780** and **94781** may not be reported with neonatal or pediatric critical or intensive care services (**99468–99472, 99477–99480**).
- ☀ If less than 60 minutes is spent in the procedure, code **94780** may not be reported.
- ☀ Each additional full 30 minutes (ie, not less than 90 minutes) is reported with code **94781.**

Table 10-9. Car Seat/Bed Testing in the Neonate	
94780	Car seat/bed testing for airway integrity, neonate, with continual nursing observation and continuous recording of pulse oximetry, heart rate and respiratory rate, with interpretation and report; 60 minutes (Do not report **94780** for less than 60 minutes.)
+94781	each additional full 30 minutes (List separately in addition to the code for primary procedure.) (Use **94781** in conjunction with **94780**.)

Examples

➤ **A neonate born at 35 weeks' gestation requires a car seat test on the date of discharge from the hospital.**

Code **94780** is reported with hospital discharge management code **99238** or **99239**.

➤ **A neonate born at 35 weeks' gestation requires a car seat test prior to discharge from the hospital.** The newborn has received 60 minutes of testing reported with **94780** and now receives an additional 30 minutes.

Codes **94780** and **94781** are reported with a subsequent hospital care code (**99231–99233**) or a discharge day management code (**99238–99239**).

Medical Team Conferences (99366–99368)

99367   Medical team conference with interdisciplinary team of health care professionals, patient and/or family not present, 30 minutes or more; participation by physician

A detailed explanation of the requirements for a physician and nonphysician provider to report medical team conference codes **99366–99368** is provided in Chapter 11. Only code **99367** is reported for physician participation in a team conference and then only for when the patient is not present at the conference.

No separate code is presently available to report physician participation in a medical team conference when the patient or family is present. The physician will report his or her services with the appropriate E/M service based on the total face-to-face time of counseling and/or coordination of care provided and documented or as part of the global critical or intensive care service.

Sedation

Refer to Chapter 12 for specific guidelines for reporting sedation services, including moderate conscious sedation (**99143–99150**).

Some examples of procedures commonly performed on neonates or infants that include sedation are venous cutdown, arterial cutdown, tube or line removal, cryotherapy, echocardiography, and central line placement.

Chapter 10: Critical and Intensive Care

Hospital Care of the Ill Child

Initial Hospital Care (99221–99223)

Codes **99221–99223** are used to report the initial hospital care of a sick neonate who does not require intensive observation and monitoring or critical care services. Refer to Chapter 8 and Table 8-1 for the specific coding and documentation requirements for reporting initial hospital care.

Example

> **The neonatologist sees a newborn male admitted to the well-baby nursery.** He was born to an O+ mother who has a history of 2 previous newborns with jaundice secondary to ABO incompatibility. Umbilical cord blood sent for blood typing and direct antibody (Coombs) test shows that the baby is A+ DAT+. At 8 hours of age, the neonate appears jaundiced. A bilirubin and complete blood cell count with a reticulocyte count are ordered, results are evaluated, the newborn's risks for kernicterus are discussed with the family, and phototherapy is started. The neonatologist performs a comprehensive history and physical examination. Medical decision-making is of moderate complexity.

Transitioning to 10

Report first a code from category **Z38** (liveborn infants according to place of birth and type of delivery) when care is provided during the birth admission. Codes for conditions such as ABO isoimmunization are reported secondary to the code for live birth.

MDM: Moderate

History: Comprehensive

Physical examination: Comprehensive

} **99222**

ICD-9-CM

V30.00 (single liveborn without cesarean section)

773.1 (hemolytic disease due to ABO isoimmunization)

ICD-10-CM

Z38.00 (single liveborn without cesarean section)

P55.0 (ABO isoimmunization of a newborn)

 Teaching Point: When reporting initial hospital care (**99221–99223**), all 3 key elements (history, physical examination, MDM), or typical total floor/unit time if more than 50% of time spent is in counseling and/or coordination of care, must be met. If the key components are not sufficiently met for even the lowest level, **99221** (eg, an expanded history is performed), the initial care must be reported using subsequent hospital care codes (**99231–99233**). See Chapter 8.

Subsequent Hospital Care and Discharge Management (99231–99233, 99238, 99239)

When a neonate is not treated but only observed for the potential development of illness, normal newborn codes would be reported. Report initial hospital care codes (**99221–99223**) when an intensively ill patient is admitted whose age is 29 days or older.

 Subsequent hospital care codes (**99231–99233**) are reported for each day of service subsequent to initial care for the newborn who continues to be sick (ie, not a normal neonate but is not in critical condition and not requiring intensive care). Code **99238** or **99239** (hospital day discharge management) is reported on the day the neonate is discharged (when on a separate day from the initial hospital care).

- When a neonate is not treated but only observed for the potential development of illness, normal newborn codes would be reported.
- If the neonate is sick but improves and requires no more care than a normal newborn, the subsequent normal newborn care code (**99462**) should be reported.
- Codes **94780** and **94781** (car seat testing) may be reported in addition to the subsequent hospital or discharge day management codes when performed and documented.

Subsequent hospital care (**99231–99233**) is reported for an intensively ill patient whose present body weight is over 5,000g.

Refer to Chapter 8, Table 8-2, for detailed coding and documentation requirements for codes **99231–99233.** Chapter 8 also includes more information on codes **99238** and **99239.**

Prolonged Services (99354–99359)

- If direct (face-to-face) prolonged services (**99354–99357**) are required on the same day as a consultation (**99241–99245, 99251–99255**), initial hospital service (**99221–99223**), or subsequent hospital service (**99231–99233**), they may be reported in addition to the basic E/M service (an add-on code).
- Direct prolonged services are not reported with normal newborn codes, intensive care codes, or critical care codes because these services do not include an assigned typical time.

The specific coding guidelines for reporting face-to-face (**99354–99357**) and non–face-to-face (**99358** and **99359**) prolonged service codes are detailed in chapters 6, 8, and 11.

Selecting the Appropriate Code

Selection of the appropriate code will depend on the newborn's or infant's condition and the intensity of the service provided and documented on a particular day of service.

Coding Conundrum: Selecting the Appropriate Code

Many diagnoses or conditions, such as respiratory distress, infection, seizures, mild to moderate asphyxia, and metabolic disorders, can be reported with codes **99468, 99477,** or **99221–99223.** The patient's clinical status, required level of monitoring and observation, and present body weight will determine which of these code sets is chosen. Selection of the service must be justified by medical record documentation.

In some situations, the neonate will be normal at birth and many hours later will show signs of an illness. *Current Procedural Terminology®* guidelines specify that only one initial hospital service may be reported for the same patient on the same day of service by the same physician or physician of the same specialty within the same group. However, if 2 distinct, medically necessary services are provided, both services may be reported. Each service should be reported with the appropriate diagnosis code to support the service (eg, diagnosis codes for well newborn and the defined illness). In other situations, a newborn's illness or condition progresses during the hospital stay, requiring a higher intensity of service by the same physician or another physician from a different group or specialty. When all of the neonate's care on the same date of service is related to the same condition or disease but the level of illness and required care progresses through the day, only a single code representing the highest level of service performed and documented is reported. However, when the intensity of care progresses over the day and services are provided by physicians from different groups or specialties or the patient is transferred to another facility, coding becomes more complicated.

Resources

RBRVS

The 2014 RVUs for the services described in this chapter are included in the RBRVS brochure found at www.aap.org/cfp. Or go to www.cms.hhs.gov to find the current year RVUs and Medicare conversion factor. At the time of publication, the 2015 RVUs were not available; they are typically published in November for the upcoming year. The RBRVS brochure is updated accordingly.

Physician Work

The times for E/M services most commonly provided to newborns (typical time for neonatal services) based on RUC survey results for 2011 are provided in Table 10-10. Though not exact or applicable for every patient, they are the average times (in minutes) spent by neonatologists for the typical or average patient. This is an excellent and quick internal audit mechanism to judge the adequacy of your coding or nursery coverage.

Table 10-10. RUC Survey Times for Subsequent Hospital Care and Critical Care (in minutes)

Code	Preservice	Intra-service	Post-service	Total RUC Time
99231	5	10	5	20
99232	10	20	10	40
99233	10	30	15	55
99291	15	40	15	70
99292	–	30	–	30
99468	45	180	48.8	274
99469	–	128	–	128
99471	30	180	30	240
99472	20	90	30	140
99477	30	77.5	40	147.5
99478	10	30	20	60
99479	10	30	15	55
99480	15	30	15	60
99475	30	105	30	165
99476	20	65	20	105

Abbreviation: RUC, American Medical Association/Specialty Society Relative Value Scale Update Committee.

Coding Education

American Academy of Pediatrics (AAP) Section on Perinatal Pediatrics (SoPPe) coding trainers are available to provide coding education through local educational seminars and continuing education events. At least one coding trainer is appointed in each district. Each trainer is equipped with educational materials that can be used as an important resource for your state or hospital. Contact SoPPe Manager Jim Couto (jcouto@aap.org) for additional information about these valuable services.

The AAP SoPPe, in conjunction with state chapters and councils of the AAP, has developed strategies that have been successful in addressing payment concerns for neonatal care. Contact your state chapter, its pediatric council, section district AAP Executive Committee representative, neonatal trainer, or AAP Committee on Coding and Nomenclature for assistance in addressing any payment inequities for neonatal services in your state.

Most of the codes used to report services for the intensive and critically ill neonate are reported based on the severity of the condition of the neonate and the intensity of the services that are required and performed. It is important to remember that specific therapies or diagnoses do not always equate to a specific level of care, and therefore documentation of the critical status of the newborn is required.

Chapter 10: Critical and Intensive Care

Evolving Evaluation and Management and Nonphysician Services

Codes Reviewed in This Chapter

99446–99449	Interprofessional telephone/Internet consultations
99358, 99359	Prolonged services without direct patient contact
99441–99443 99966–98968	Physician telephone services Nonphysician telephone services
99444 98969	Online medical evaluation by physician Online medical evaluation by nonphysician
G0406–G0408 G0425–G0427	Telehealth consultation
99487, 99489, 99490	Chronic care management (CCM)
99495–99496	Transitional care management (TCM)
99366–99368	Medical team conferences
99339, 99340	Care plan oversight in home, domiciliary, or rest home
99374–99380	Care plan oversight for home health, hospice, or nursing facility patient
97802–97804	Nonphysician medical nutrition therapy
96150–96155	Nonphysician health behavior assessment
98960–98962	Nonphysician education and training for patient self-management
96040	Nonphysician genetic counseling
S9441–S9470	Patient education Healthcare Common Procedure Coding System (HCPCS) codes
99502–99600	Home health procedures/services

Chapter 11: Evolving Evaluation and Management and Nonphysician Services

Evolving Evaluation and Management Services

Increasing use of technology and recognition of the need to support care management services has led to significant changes in care delivery and, in some cases, coverage of services by public and private payers. Codes for services such as interprofessional consultations and transitional care management (TCM) offer a means of reporting services that include care beyond the traditional face-to-face encounter.

Codes and payment policy for many of these services continue to evolve as the value and intensity of care beyond the traditional face-to-face physician encounter is recognized. Awareness of the codes for these services and the related coding instructions may offer physicians new opportunities for providing and/or coordinating comprehensive care for all children.

Interprofessional Telephone/Internet Consultation (99446–99449)

A consultation by a patient's attending or primary physician or other qualified health care professional requesting opinion and/or treatment advice by telephone or Internet from a physician with specialty expertise (consultant) is reported by the consultant with interprofessional consultation codes **99446–99449** (Table 11-1). This consultation does not require face-to-face contact with the patient by the consultant and often takes place when a timely face-to-face service with the consultant is not feasible (eg, consultant is geographically distant).

Guidelines for the consultant reporting interprofessional telephone/Internet consultations include

- Telephone/Internet consultations of less than 5 minutes are not reported. The majority of time reported as interprofessional consultation must have been spent in medical consultative discussion (verbal or Internet).

- A single interprofessional consultation code is reported for the cumulative time spent in discussion and information review regardless of the number of telephone or Internet contacts.

- Time spent in telephone or online consultation with the patient and/or family may be reported using codes **99441–99444** or **98966–98968.**

- When the purpose of communication is to arrange a transfer of care or face-to-face patient encounter, interprofessional consultation codes are not reported.

- Interprofessional consultation services are not reported if the consultant has provided a face-to-face service to the patient within the past 14 days or when the consultation results in scheduling of a face-to-face service within the next 14 days or at the consultant's next available appointment date.

- Time spent by the consultant reviewing pertinent medical records, studies, or other data is included in the telephone/Internet consultation and not separately reported.

- As with all consultations, the request for advice or opinion should be documented in the patient record. A verbal opinion report and a written opinion report from the consultant must also be documented.

The requesting physician or qualified health care professional may report time spent in discussion with the consultant with prolonged service codes if the total time of discussion exceeds 30 minutes beyond the typical time of the associated evaluation and management (E/M) service. Prolonged service codes **99354–99355** may be reported when the patient is present and accessible to the requesting physician in the office or other outpatient setting during the time of service. Prolonged services without the patient present are reported with codes **99358–99359.** For more information on prolonged services, please see Chapter 6 for prolonged services in an outpatient setting or Chapter 8 for prolonged services in an inpatient setting.

Table 11-1. Interprofessional Telephone/Internet Consultation	
99446	Interprofessional telephone/Internet assessment and management service provided by a consultative physician including a verbal and written report to the patient's treating/requesting physician/qualified health care professional; 5–10 minutes of medical consultative discussion and review
99447	11–20 minutes of medical consultative discussion and review
99448	21–30 minutes of medical consultative discussion and review
99449	31 minutes or more of medical consultative discussion and review

Examples

➤ **A 10-year-old boy with attention-deficit/hyperactivity disorder (ADHD) has become increasingly aggressive at home and school.** The child's pediatrician arranges a telephone consultation with a child and adolescent psychiatrist and forwards the child's history records prior to the telephone consultation. The pediatrician and psychiatrist spend a total of 16 minutes in discussion. The child and mother are present in the pediatrician's office and included in the discussion. A new care plan is developed for achieving better control of the child's predominantly hyperactive ADHD and agreed to by the mother. The total face-to-face time for the pediatrician is approximately 25 minutes.

| The consultant reports **99447** (11–20 minutes of medical discussion and review) | The pediatrician reports **99214** (16 of 25 minutes [face-to-face] spent in counseling/coordination of care) | Both physicians report *International Classification of Diseases, Ninth Revision, Clinical Modification (ICD-9-CM)* **314.01** (ADHD) *International Classification of Diseases, 10th Revision, Clinical Modification (ICD-10-CM)* **F90.1** (ADHD, predominantly hyperactive type) |

Transitioning to 10

Teaching Point: In this vignette, the patient and mother are present and are counseled on the revised care plan, allowing the pediatrician to report the encounter based on time spent counseling and/or coordinating care. If time had not been the controlling factor of the visit, the pediatrician would report the encounter based on key components of the E/M service rendered and, if applicable, prolonged service codes **99354–99355**.

➤ **A physician at a rural hospital admits a child with acute lymphoblastic leukemia who developed a *Streptococcus pneumoniae* infection.** The physician communicates with the child's hematologist, who is located several hours away, via a secure health information exchange for advice about treatment. The hematologist spends a total of 25 minutes reviewing hospital records and communicating with the attending physician.

Transitioning to 10

The categories for leukemia have codes indicating whether or not the leukemia has achieved remission. Coders are instructed to ask the physician for status if documentation is unclear.

| The consultant reports **99448** (21–30 minutes of medical consultative discussion and review) | The pediatrician reports **99221–99223** (appropriate level of initial hospital care) | Both physicians report *ICD-9-CM* **041.9** (pneumococcus infection of unspecified site) **204.00** (acute lymphoid leukemia without mention of having achieved remission) *ICD-10-CM* **A49.1** (streptococcal infection, unspecified site) **C91.00** (acute lymphoblastic leukemia not having achieved remission) |

Chapter 11: Evolving Evaluation and Management and Nonphysician Services

Teaching Point: The attending physician will report the appropriate level of hospital care (eg, **99223**); if the unit/floor time spent caring for this patient exceeds the typical time of the hospital care service by at least 30 minutes, the attending physician will also report inpatient prolonged services (**99356–99357**).

Prolonged Services Without Direct Patient Contact (99358 and 99359)

Guidelines for Reporting Non-direct Physician Prolonged Services

- Reported when a physician provides prolonged service that does not involve face-to-face care.
- Must be related to another physician or other qualified health care professional service. The primary service may be an E/M service (with or without an assigned average time), a procedure, or other non–face-to-face service codes that have a published maximum time (eg, telephone services). However, it must relate to a service or patient where direct (face-to-face) patient care has occurred or will occur and relate to ongoing patient management.
  - May be reported on a different date than the related primary service.
  - Cannot be reported for time spent in medical team conferences, online medical evaluations, care plan oversight services, chronic care management (CCM) services, TCM services, or other non–face-to-face services that have more specific codes and no upper time limit assigned.
  - The first-hour prolonged service code (**99358**) is reported for the total duration of prolonged service of 30 to 74 minutes' duration on a given day of service, and code **99359** is used to report each additional 30 minutes beyond the first hour, regardless of the place of service. Code **99359** may be used to report the final 15 to 30 minutes of prolonged service on a given date.
- Less than 30 minutes' total duration on a given date cannot be reported.
- Less than 15 minutes beyond the first hour or less than 15 minutes beyond the final 30 minutes is not reported separately.

Please see chapters 6 and 8 for discussion of face-to-face prolonged services in the outpatient and inpatient settings.

> ||||||| **Coding Pearl** |||||||
>
> Codes **99358** and **99359** must be related to an E/M service, procedure, or other non–face-to-face service with a published maximum time.

Code	Description of Non–Face-to-Face Prolonged Services
99358	Prolonged evaluation and management service before and/or after direct patient care; first hour
+99359	each additional 30 minutes (List separately in addition to code for prolonged service.) (Use code **99359** in conjunction with code **99358**.) (Do not report **99358**, **99359** during the same month with **99487–99489**.) (Do not report **99358**, **99359** when performed during the service time of codes **99495–99496**.)

Example

➤ **The physician requested and has received medical records from the former physician of a 6-year-old who is developmentally delayed and has an intractable chronic seizure disorder.** The patient has been cared for at a children's hospital on several occasions for breakthrough seizures. On a day separate from any face-to-face service, the physician spends 35 minutes reviewing and summarizing the medical records and documents his time in the medical record.

Prolonged physician services without direct patient contact (30–74 minutes)

}

99358

ICD-9-CM
345.91 (epilepsy, unspecified, with intractable epilepsy)
78340 (lack of normal physiological development, unspecified)

ICD-10-CM
G40.911 (epilepsy, unspecified, intractable, with status epilepticus)
R62.50 (unspecified lack of expected normal physiological development in childhood)

After-hours and Special Services

Codes **99050–99060** are used to report services that are provided after hours or on an emergency basis and are an adjunct to the basic E/M service provided. Refer to Chapter 6 for further details on after-hours and special services codes.

Telephone Calls (99441–99443, 98966–98968)

Telephone services (**99441–99443**) are non–face-to-face E/M services provided to a patient using the telephone by a physician or other qualified health care professional, who may report E/M services. Codes **98966–98968** are used to report telephone assessment and management services by health care professionals who may not report E/M services.

Guidelines for reporting of telephone services by the qualified health care professional are the same as those for physician telephone management.

Codes 99441–99443 *may* be reported when	Codes 99441–99443 are *not* reported when
The call was initiated by an established patient or guardian of an established patient (Table 11-2).	The call results in a face-to-face encounter within 24 hours.
They include physician management of a new problem that does not result in an office visit within 24 hours from the telephone call or at the next available urgent visit appointment.	There was a face-to-face encounter related to the problem in the previous 7 days from the telephone call.

Chapter 11: Evolving Evaluation and Management and Nonphysician Services

Codes 99441–99443 *may* be reported when, continued	Codes 99441–99443 are *not* reported when, continued
They include physician management of an existing problem for which the patient was not seen in a face-to-face encounter in the previous 7 days from the telephone call (physician requested or unsolicited patient follow-up) or within the postoperative period of a performed and reported procedure.	The call occurs within the postoperative period of a reported procedure.
The physician documentation of telephone calls includes the date of the call, name and telephone number of the patient, name of person and relationship of the caller, type of service provided (eg, provide consultation or medical management, initiate or adjust therapy, report results), and the time spent in the encounter.	The call occurs within 7 days of a previously reported telephone management service.
	Domiciliary, rest home, or home care plan oversight services codes (**99339** and **99340**) or care plan oversight services codes (**99374–99380; 99487–99489; 99495** and **99496**) are reported and the calls are reported as part of these services.
	Non–face-to-face communication is between the physician and other health care professionals. If applicable, the services may be reported using non–face-to-face prolonged physician service codes **99358** and **99359** or as part of care plan oversight services (**99339** and **99340; 99374–99380; 99487–99489; 99495** and **99496**).
	Anyone other than a physician or other certified non-physician professional (NPPs) (under their state's scope of practice and with their own NPI) performs the service.

Table 11-2. Telephone Calls

Code	Description
99441	Telephone E/M service provided by a physician to an established patient, parent, or guardian not originating from a related E/M service provided within the previous 7 days nor leading to an E/M service or procedure within the next 24 hours or soonest available appointment; 5–10 minutes of medical discussion
99442	11–20 minutes of medical discussion
99443	21–30 minutes of medical discussion
98966	Telephone assessment and management services provided by a qualified nonphysician health care professional to an established patient, parent, or guardian not originating from related assessment and management service provided within the previous 7 days nor leading to an assessment and management service or procedure within the next 24 hours or soonest available appointment; 5 to 10 minutes of medical discussion
98967	11 to 20 minutes of medical discussion
98968	21 to 30 minutes of medical discussion

Examples

➤ **A 6-month-old was seen in the office 3 days ago for treatment of otitis media. Mom calls to discuss problems with diarrhea.** The discussion of antibiotic-associated diarrhea, probiotics, and symptoms that may require change in treatment lasts for 10 minutes.

    Code **99441** cannot be reported because it is related to the E/M visit performed within the previous 7 days.

➤ **Mom calls because her 12-year-old has poison ivy after being in the woods 2 days ago.** Physician spends 10 minutes confirming poison ivy and prescribing a treatment plan.

    Code **99441** is reported with the diagnosis code.

Physician telephone E/M, 5–10 minutes }

99441

ICD-9-CM
692.6 (contact dermatitis and other eczema due to plants)

ICD-10-CM
L23.7 (allergic contact dermatitis due to plants, except food)

Transitioning to **10**

➤ **Dad calls to discuss son's anxiety since his mother left for a tour of duty.** Physician spends 20 minutes discussing how the father can deal with the child's anxiety.

Physician telephone E/M, 11–20 minutes }

99442

ICD-9-CM
309.24 (adjustment disorder with anxiety)
V61.01 (family disruption due to family member on military deployment)

ICD-10-CM
F43.22 (adjustment disorder with anxiety)
Z63.31 (absence of family member due to military deployment)

Transitioning to **10**

Online Medical Evaluation (99444, 98969)

An online electronic medical evaluation (**99444**) is a non–face-to-face E/M service by a physician or other qualified health care professional who may report E/M services to a patient using Internet resources in response to a patient's online inquiry. Code **98969** is used by a qualified NPP to report an online assessment and management service. The reporting guidelines for code **98969** are the same as those required for online services provided by the physician. See Table 11-3.

    The Centers for Medicare & Medicaid Services (CMS) has not assigned relative value units to online medical evaluation codes and considers them non-covered services. As a result, most third-party payers do not pay for them.

    Before providing online medical services, understand local and state laws, ensure that communications will be Health Insurance Portability and Accountability Act of 1996 compliant, establish written guidelines and procedures, educate payers and negotiate for payment, and educate patients.

Chapter 11: Evolving Evaluation and Management and Nonphysician Services

Code 99444 *may* be reported	Code 99444 is *not* reported
When Internet resources are used by a physician to an established patient (including parent or guardian) in response to a patient's or guardian's online inquiry	When the online medical evaluation refers to an E/M service previously performed and reported by the physician within the previous 7 days (physician requested or unsolicited patient follow-up) or within the postoperative period of the previously completed procedure; the service(s) is considered inherent to the previous E/M service or procedure.
When the service involves the physician's personal timely response to the patient's inquiry and there is permanent documentation (electronic or hard copy) of the encounter	When it had been reported in the previous 7 days
Only once for the same episode of care during a 7-day period, although multiple physicians could report their exchange with the same patient	When domiciliary, rest home, or home care plan oversight service codes (**99339** and **99340**) or care plan oversight service codes (**99374–99380; 99487–99489; 99495** and **99496**) are reported and include the online service
Only one time and encompasses the sum of communication (eg, related telephone calls, prescription provision, laboratory orders) pertaining to the online patient encounter	When the patient is new or for established patients with an emergent medical issue (eg, seizure, severe exacerbation) or condition that requires a face-to-face encounter to appropriately treat the condition (eg, atypical or complex rash)

Table 11-3. Online Medical Evaluation

Code	Description
99444	Online E/M service provided by a physician to an established patient or guardian not originating from a related E/M service provided within the previous 7 days, using the Internet or similar electronic communications network
98969	Online assessment and management service provided by a qualified nonphysician health care professional to an established patient or guardian not originating from a related assessment and management service provided within the previous 7 days, using the Internet or similar electronic communications network

Telehealth

Many states have enacted or have pending legislation to increase coverage of telehealth services to bring a specialist in a distant location to a patient's bedside or clinic right in the patient's own community without the need for either party to physically travel. *Telehealth* is one term used to describe the provision of face-to-face services through the use of technology. Telehealth may also be referred to as *telemedicine*; definitions for each vary by state and payer. Without any consideration of state law or payer policies, telehealth services might be loosely defined as technology-enabled patient-specific services provided by a physician or practitioner in a distant geographic location to a patient who requires medical expertise not otherwise available at their location.

Although the federal Medicaid statute does not recognize telehealth as a distinct service, states may choose to cover these services, and many do. However, there is wide variation in how private payers and state Medicaid plans define and cover telehealth services, making it important to identify the applicable definition and payment policies prior to delivery of services. Many states limit coverage to that delivered via interactive systems using multimedia communications equipment that includes, at minimum, audio and video equipment permitting 2-way, real-time communication between the patient and the distant site practitioner. Asynchronous or store-and-forward technology may be allowed in some areas or for certain services.

From a coding perspective, telehealth services are face-to-face services reported using the same procedure codes that would be appropriate for encounters where the services are provided in person.

- ☀ Usually these are consultation services (eg, **99251–99255**) with the place of service determined by the location of the patient (eg, hospital inpatient, rural health clinic).
- ☀ As with many services, there are combinations of *CPT*® and Healthcare Common Procedure Coding System (HCPCS) codes and modifiers that may apply.
- ☀ An understanding of coverage, payment policies, and coding requirements is essential to establishing a successful telehealth service.
- ☀ See Chapter 10 for information on reporting remote real-time interactive video-conferenced critical care services (**0188T** and **0189T**).

Healthcare Common Procedure Coding System modifiers that identify telehealth services are

- ❖ **GT** via interactive audio and video telecommunications system
- ❖ **GQ** via asynchronous telecommunications system

Under some plans, additional codes may be reported for overhead expenses of providing telehealth services.

- ❖ **Q3014** Telehealth originating site facility fee
- ❖ **T1014** Telehealth transmission, per minute, professional services bill separately

While *CPT* codes are accepted by most plans covering telehealth services, payers may require HCPCS codes that are used in the Medicare program.

- ❖ **G0425** Telehealth consultation, emergency department or initial inpatient, typically 30 minutes communicating with the patient via telehealth
- ❖ **G0426** typically 50 minutes communicating with the patient via telehealth
- ❖ **G0427** typically 70 minutes or more communicating with the patient via telehealth
- ❖ **G0406** Follow-up inpatient consultation, limited, physicians typically spend 15 minutes communicating with the patient via telehealth
- ❖ **G0407** intermediate, physicians typically spend 25 minutes communicating with the patient via telehealth
- ❖ **G0408** complex, physicians typically spend 35 minutes communicating with the patient via telehealth

Example

➤ **A consultation is requested of a rheumatologist at a teaching facility for an inpatient in a rural hospital 75 miles away.** Through interactive technology, the physician performs a consultation including a comprehensive history, comprehensive examination (assisted by clinical staff of the facility), and medical decision-making (MDM) of moderate complexity. The total time of the interactive communication is 30 minutes. A written report to the requesting physician is transmitted via secure electronic health information exchange.

MDM: Moderate

History: Comprehensive

Physical examination: Comprehensive

}

99254 GT
Or if payer requires HCPCS codes
G0425 GT (telehealth consultation, emergency department or initial inpatient, typically 30 minutes communicating with the patient via telehealth)

Teaching Point: If payer policy allows payment for overhead expenses related to telehealth services, also report **T1014,** telehealth transmission, per minute, professional services bill separately. Because this is billed per minute, 30 units are reported. The rural hospital, as the originating facility, may also report **Q3014,** telehealth originating site facility fee.

Coding for Children With Special Health Care Needs

Children with special health care needs are patients who require greater levels and amounts of medical, psychosocial, rehabilitation, and habilitation services than their same-aged peers. The child with special health care needs will require extra services, such as prolonged services, home care visits, and care management, with an increased frequency of E/M visits. In recent years, new *CPT®* codes have been developed to capture services such as chronic care management (CCM) and transitional care management (TCM).

In addition, medical team conferences may be performed on occasion to coordinate or manage care and services or to present findings and recommendations that are used to develop or revise a plan of care that includes coordination of care. Several different types of non–face-to-face E/M services may be performed within the same calendar month, so practices must be cognizant of *CPT* coding guidelines.

Chronic Care Management Services (99487, 99489, 99490)

Chronic care management services (Table 11-4), formerly known as complex chronic care coordination services, are management and support services that are provided under the direction of a physician or other qualified health care professional by clinical staff to individuals with 2 or more chronic conditions who reside at home or in a domiciliary, rest home, or assisted living facility. The care management provider provides or oversees the management and/or coordination of services, as needed, for all of the patient's medical conditions, psychosocial needs, and activities of daily living. A comprehensive care plan for all health problems is created, monitored, and revised as needed. *CPT 2015* includes several changes to CCM service codes and the instructions for reporting these services; see Table 11-4 for an overview of these changes. Codes in Table 11-5 represent 2 levels of care management. Codes **99487** and **99489** require additional elements of service and greater clinical staff time than code **99490.** The appropriate CCM code is reported once per calendar month by only one physician or other qualified health care professional who has assumed a management role for the patient's care. Evaluation and management services may be separately reported by the same physician or qualified health care professional during the same calendar month. See Appendix B-7 for an example of a worksheet for tracking CCM services and online at www.aap.org/cfp (access code AAPCFP20).

Table 11-4. Comparison of Chronic Care Services 2014 to 2015

2014 Complex Chronic Care Coordination	2015 Chronic Care Management
Codes are **99487–99489**.	Codes **99487** and **99489** are revised. Code **99488** is deleted. Code **99490** is added. (Codes descriptors are included in Table 11-5.)
Codes **99487–99489** included the terms *complex* and *coordination*.	Changes reflect many statements made by the CMS about proposed coverage of chronic care services. Based on these comments, codes **99487, 99489,** and **99490** now include the term *management* rather than *coordination* to indicate active management of a patient's care. Also, the term *complex* was noted as confusing and not included in the descriptor of code **99490**.
Codes **99487–99489** are reported only once per calendar month and include all non–face-to-face complex chronic care coordination services and none or one face-to-face office or other outpatient, home, or domiciliary visit.	Codes **99487, 99489,** and **99490** are reported once per calendar month. Face-to- face E/M services may be reported separately by the same physician or other qualified health care professional during the same calendar month.
Physicians or other qualified health care professionals may not report care coordination services if the care plan is unchanged or requires minimal change (eg, only a medication is changed, an adjustment in a treatment modality is ordered).	Chronic care management services are provided when medical and/or psychosocial needs of the patient require establishing, implementing, revising, or monitoring the care plan. Code **99490** is reported when, during the calendar month, at least 20 minutes of clinical staff time is spent in care management activities. Complex CCM services (**99487, 99489**) are provided during a calendar month that includes criteria for CCM services as well as establishment or substantial revision of a comprehensive care plan; medical, functional, and/or psychosocial problems requiring medical decision-making of moderate or high complexity; and clinical staff care management services for at least 60 minutes, under the direction of a physician or other qualified health care professional.
Medical, functional, and/or psychosocial problems that require medical decision-making of moderate or high complexity and extensive clinical staff support are required for all complex chronic care coordination services.	Moderate- or high-complexity medical decision-making is required for codes **99487** and **99489**. The level of medical decision-making does not affect reporting of code **99490**.
The care coordination office/practice must have the following capabilities: ⊛ Provide 24/7 access to physicians or other qualified health care professionals or clinical staff. ⊛ Use a standardized methodology to identify patients who require chronic complex care coordination services. ⊛ Have an internal care coordination process/function whereby a patient identified as meeting the requirements for these services starts receiving them in a timely manner. ⊛ Use a form and format in the medical record that is standardized within the practice. ⊛ Be able to engage and educate patients and caregivers as well as coordinate care among all service professionals, as appropriate for each patient.	The care management office/practice must have the following capabilities (in addition to those listed for care coordination): ⊛ Provide 24/7 access to physicians or other qualified health care professionals or clinical staff, including providing patients/caregivers with a means to make contact with health care professionals in the practice to address urgent needs regardless of the time of day or day of week. ⊛ Provide continuity of care with a designated member of the care team with whom the patient is able to schedule successive routine appointments. ⊛ Provide timely access and management for follow-up after an emergency department visit or facility discharge. ⊛ Use an electronic health record system so that care providers have timely access to clinical information.

Chapter 11: Evolving Evaluation and Management and Nonphysician Services

Code	Description
Table 11-5. Chronic Care Management	
99487	Complex CCM services, with the following required elements: ⚙ multiple (two or more) chronic conditions expected to last at least 12 months, or until the death of the patient, ⚙ chronic conditions place the patient at significant risk of death, acute exacerbation/decompensation, or functional decline, ⚙ establishment or substantial revision of a comprehensive care plan, ⚙ moderate or high complexity medical decision making; ⚙ 60 minutes of clinical staff time directed by a physician or other qualified health care professional, per calendar month
+99489	each additional 30 minutes of clinical staff time directed by a physician or other qualified health care professional, per calendar month (List separately in addition to **99487**.)
99490	CCM services, at least 20 minutes of clinical staff time directed by a physician or other qualified health care professional, per calendar month, with the following required elements: ⚙ multiple (two or more) chronic conditions expected to last at least 12 months, or until the death of the patient, ⚙ chronic conditions place the patient at significant risk of death, acute exacerbation/decompensation, or functional decline, ⚙ comprehensive care plan established, implemented, revised, or monitored

Practices providing CCM services must have the ability to

⚙ Use an electronic health record system allowing care providers timely access to clinical information.

⚙ Use a medical record form and format that are standardized within the practice.

⚙ Identify patients who require care management using a standardized methodology.

⚙ Adopt an internal care management process to provide care management services in a timely manner following identification of need for these services.

⚙ Provide access to care providers or clinical staff 24 hours a day, 7 days a week, including providing patients and caregivers with a means to make contact with health care professionals in the practice to address urgent needs regardless of the time of day or day of the week.

⚙ Provide continuity of care through scheduling of the patient's successive routine appointments with a designated member of the care team.

⚙ Provide timely access and management for necessary follow-up when the patient is discharged from the ED or hospital.

⚙ Engage and educate patients and caregivers.

⚙ Coordinate care among all service providers, as appropriate for each patient. Reportable clinical staff time includes

⚙ Face-to-face and non–face-to-face time spent communicating with and engaging the patient and/or family, caregivers, other professionals, community services, and agencies

⚙ Developing, revising, documenting, communicating, and implementing a comprehensive care plan

⚙ Collecting health outcomes data and registry documentation

⚙ Teaching patient and/or family/caregiver patient self-management, independent living, and activities of daily living

⚙ Identifying community and health resources

⚙ Facilitating access to care and other services needed by the patient and/or family

⚙ Management of care transitions not reported as part of TCM (**99495, 99496**)

Chapter 11: Evolving Evaluation and Management and Nonphysician Services

- ☀ Ongoing review of patient status, including review of laboratory and other studies not reported as part of an E/M service
- ☀ Assessment and support for adherence to the care plan

Guidelines for reporting CCM services

- ☀ Codes **99487, 99489,** and **99490** are reported only once per calendar month.
- ☀ Services include all face-to-face and non–face-to-face clinical staff time spent in CCM activities on days other than a date when the physician or other qualified health care professional reporting care management services also provides a separately reportable E/M service (eg, office visit). Time spent on the date of an E/M service may not be included to meet requirements for reporting CCM.
- ☀ Includes care plan oversight services (**99339, 99340, 99374–99380**), prolonged services without direct patient contact (**99358, 99359**), anticoagulant management (**99363, 99364**), medical team conferences (**99366–99368**), education and training (**98960–98962, 99071, 99078**), telephone services (**98966–98968, 99441–99443**), online medical evaluation (**98969, 99444**), preparation of special reports (**99080**), analysis of data (**99090, 99091**), TCM services (**99495, 99496**), and medication therapy management services (**99605–99607**).
- ☀ Cannot be reported with end-stage renal disease (ESRD) services (**90951–90970**) during the same month.
- ☀ Cannot be reported if performed within the postoperative portion of the global period of a surgery or procedure reported by the same physician or other physician of the same specialty and same group practice.
- ☀ Cannot be reported for any post-discharge CCM services for any days within 30 days of discharge, if reporting **99495** or **99496** (TCM services).
- ☀ Are reported in any calendar month when the clinical staff time requirements are met. Only time spent by clinical staff of the reporting professional is included. If multiple clinical staff members meet about one patient, count the time for only one staff member.
- ☀ When care management resumes after a discharge in a new month, start a new period or report TCM services (**99495, 99496**) as appropriate.
- ☀ If discharge occurs in the same month, continue the reporting period or report TCM services.

Complex CCM services (**99487** and **99489**) require additional physician work and clinical staff time. Medical decision-making for the reporting period must be moderate or high complexity. Code **99487** is reported when at least 60 minutes of clinical staff time is spent in care management activities. Code **99489** is reported when at least 90 minutes are spent in complex CCM and for each additional 30 minutes of clinical staff time spent in care management activities during the calendar month. Do not report **99489** for care management services of less than 30 minutes beyond the first 60 minutes of complex CCM services during a calendar month

The reporting physician or other qualified health care professional must develop or substantially revise the plan of care for all health problems. (See the *CPT*® manual for description of a typical care plan.) Complex CCM is not reported when the care plan is unchanged or requires minimal change (eg, medication change, adjustment of a treatment modality).

In contrast, substantial revision of the care plan is not required for CCM (**99490**). Code **99490** may be reported for 20 minutes or more of clinical staff time spent in CCM activities in a calendar month even if no substantial revision to the care plan is required.

Examples

> ➤ **A 6-year-old has spastic quadriplegia, gastrostomy, gastroesophageal reflux with recurrent bouts of aspiration pneumonia and reactive airway disease, chronic seizure disorder, failure to thrive, and severe neurodevelopment delay.** He receives home occupational, physical, and speech therapy services. During the course of a calendar month, the care plan is substantially revised. Clinical staff time of CCM services is 110 minutes.
>
> Codes **99487** and **99489** (1 unit) are reported.

> ➤ **A 12-year-old has severe atopic disease and recurrent asthma, which has led to multiple ED visits, hospital admissions, lost school days, and behavioral adjustment reactions.** Clinical staff spend 30 minutes in the calendar month providing education, care plan monitoring, and facilitating access to community services.
>
> Code **99490** is reported.

Transitional Care Management Services (99495 and 99496)

Transitional care management includes services provided to a new or established patient whose medical and/or psychosocial problems require moderate- or high-complexity MDM during the transition from an inpatient hospital setting, observation care setting, or skilled nursing facility to the patient's home, domiciliary, rest home, or assisted living facility. See Table 11-6.

- The reporting physician or other qualified health care professional oversees the management and/or coordination of services.
- Only one physician or other qualified health care professional may report these services and only once per patient within 30 days of discharge.
- The TCM services begin on the date of discharge and continue for the next 29 days.
- One face-to-face visit is included, in addition to non–face-to-face services performed by the physician or other qualified health care professional and/or licensed clinical staff under the direction of the physician or other qualified health care professional.
- Non–face-to-face services provided by the physician or other qualified health care professional may include obtaining and reviewing the discharge information; reviewing, ordering, or following up on pending diagnostic tests and treatments; communication/interaction with or education provided to family, caregivers, or other qualified health care professionals; scheduling assistance for necessary follow-up services; and arranging referrals and community resources as necessary.
- Clinical staff time (under the direction of the physician or other qualified health care professional) may include
  - ❖ Face-to-face and non–face-to-face time spent communicating with the patient and/or family, caregivers, other professionals, and agencies
  - ❖ Revising, documenting, and implementing the care plan
  - ❖ Collecting health outcomes data and registry documentation
  - ❖ Teaching patient and/or family/caregiver patient self-management
  - ❖ Assessment and support for adherence to treatment plan and medication management
  - ❖ Facilitating access to care and other services needed by the patient and/or family, including identification of community and health resources

Table 11-6. Transitional Care Management

Code	Description
99495	Transitional care management services with the following required elements: ⚬ Communication (direct contact, telephone, electronic) with the patient and/or caregiver within 2 business days of discharge ⚬ Medical decision-making of at least moderate complexity during the service period ⚬ Face-to-face visit, within 14 calendar days of discharge
99496	Transitional care management services with the following required elements: ⚬ Communication (direct contact, telephone, electronic) with the patient and/or caregiver within 2 business days of discharge ⚬ Medical decision-making of high complexity during the service period ⚬ Face-to-face visit, within 7 calendar days of discharge

Codes **99495** and **99496**

⚬ Require a face-to-face visit, initial patient contact, and medication reconciliation within specified time frames.

⚬ Medication management must occur *no later than* the date of the face-to-face visit.

⚬ Code selection is based on the level of MDM and the date of the first face-to-face visit.

⚬ The first face-to-face visit is included in the TCM service and is not reported separately.

⚬ Additional E/M services on dates subsequent to that of the first face-to-face visit may be reported.

⚬ Another TCM service may not be reported by the same provider (or provider of the same group) for any subsequent discharge(s) within the 30 days.

⚬ Hospital or observation discharge services (**99238, 99239,** or **99217**) can be reported by the same physician reporting TCM services. Discharge services do not qualify as the required face-to-face visit for TCM.

⚬ The TCM services cannot be reported when provided during a postoperative portion of the global period of a service reported by the same physician or other physician of the same specialty and same group practice.

⚬ Services include care plan oversight services (**99339, 99340, 99374–99380**), prolonged services without direct patient contact (**99358, 99359**), anticoagulant management (**99363, 99364**), medical team conferences (**99366–99368**), education and training (**98960–98962, 99071, 99078**), telephone services (**98966–98968, 99441–99443**), ESRD services (**90951–90970**), online medical evaluation services (**98969, 99444**), preparation of special reports (**99080**), analysis of data (**99090, 99091**), CCM services (**99487–99490**), or medication therapy management services (**99605–99607**). These services may not be separately reported by the same physician or physicians of the same group practice during a period of TCM.

Selection of Code

Type of Medical Decision-making	Face-to-Face Visit Within 7 Days	Face-to-Face Visit Within 8 to 14 Days
Moderate complexity	99495	99495
High complexity	99496	99496

- Medical decision-making is defined by the E/M service guidelines. Medical decision-making over the service period reported is used to define the MDM of TCM. Documentation includes the timing of the initial post-discharge communication with the patient or caregivers, date of the face-to-face visit, and complexity of MDM.
- Only one individual may report these services and only once per patient within 30 days of discharge. Another TCM service may not be reported by the same individual or group for any subsequent discharge(s) within the 30 days.

Examples

> **A 6-year-old who is neurologically impaired and developmentally delayed and has a chronic seizure disorder is discharged from the hospital after an admission for breakthrough seizures.** Two days after discharge the physician speaks with the mother. Clinical staff assesses adherence with the treatment plan and educates the parents on management of the child. The child is seen by the physician in follow-up 10 days after discharge. Medical decision-making is moderately complex.
> Code **99495** is reported.

> **A 6-month-old born at 25 weeks' gestation with a diagnosis of chronic lung disease on home oxygen, diuretics, bronchodilators, and high-caloric formula is discharged from the hospital after admission for respiratory failure.** The physician speaks with the mother the day after discharge. Clinical staff assesses adherence with the treatment plan and educates the parents on management of the child. The child is seen by the physician in follow-up in 5 days. Medical decision-making is highly complex.
> Code **99496** is reported.

Medical Team Conferences (99366–99368)

Medical team conference codes are used to report participation by a minimum of 3 qualified health care professionals of different specialties in conferences to coordinate or manage care and services for established patients with chronic or multiple health conditions (eg, child who is ventilator dependent with developmental delays, seizures, and gastrostomy tube for nutrition). See Table 11-7 for the complete description of these codes.

- Codes differentiate provider (physician vs other qualified health care professional) and distinguish between face-to-face and non–face-to-face (patient and/or family is not present) patient team conference services.
- Medical team conferences may not be reported if the facility or organization is contractually obligated to provide the service, they are informal meetings or simple conversations between physicians and other qualified health care professionals (NPPs), and less than 30 minutes of conference time is spent in the team conferences.
- Code **99367** is the only code that may be reported by a physician, and it can only be reported when the patient and/or family is not present at the team conference.
- When the physician participates in a medical team conference with the patient and/or family present, the appropriate-level E/M code (eg, **99212–99215**) will be reported based on the place of service and total face-to-face time spent in counseling and/or coordination of care.
- Medical team conferences may be reported separately from other E/M services provided on the same day of service with modifier **25** appended to the appropriate-level E/M code. However, the time reported for these conferences may not be used in the determination of time for care plan oversight (**99339** and **99340;**

99374–99380), CCM services (**99487–99490**), TCM services (**99495** and **99496**), prolonged services (**99354–99359**), psychotherapy (**90832–90853**), or any E/M service.

Medical team conferences require

❋ Face-to-face participation by a minimum of 3 qualified health care professionals from different subspecialties or disciplines (eg, speech-language pathologists, dieticians, social workers), with or without the presence of the patient, family member(s), community agencies, surrogate decision-maker(s) (eg, legal guardian), and/or caregiver(s).

❋ Active involvement in the development, revision, coordination, and implementation of health care services needed by the patient by each participant.

❋ Face-to-face evaluations and/or treatments by the participant that are separate from any team conference within the previous 60 days.

❋ Only one individual from the same specialty may report codes **99366–99368** for the same encounter.

❋ Medical record documentation supporting the participation of the physician or other qualified health care professional, the time spent from the beginning of the review of an individual patient until the conclusion of the review, and the contributed information and subsequent treatment recommendations.

❋ If licensed NPPs (including clinical nurse specialists and clinical nurse practitioners) participated in the conference without direct physician supervision, they may report the service (**99367**) if it is within the state's scope of practice and they use their own NPI. State Medicaid and commercial payers may follow these Medicare requirements or may have their own specific rules.

Table 11-7. Medical Team Conferences

Code	Description
99366	Medical team conference with interdisciplinary team of health care professionals, face to face with patient and/or family, 30 minutes or more; participation by nonphysician qualified health care professional
99367	Medical team conference with interdisciplinary team of health care professionals, patient and/or family not present, 30 minutes or more; participation by physician
99368	Medical team conference with interdisciplinary team of health care professionals, patient and/or family not present, 30 minutes or more; participation by nonphysician qualified health care professional

Examples

➤ **A 14-year-old girl with spinal muscular atrophy is wheelchair bound and receives her education at home.** Over the past 6 months, her respiratory compromise has progressed and she has required 2 inpatient admissions for pneumonia. She is on oxygen at night. She receives physical and occupational therapy services at home and twice-weekly visits from a respiratory therapist. She sees a pediatric pulmonologist every 4 months and a pediatric physiatrist every 6 months. You have started discussions with her parents about how aggressive the family wishes to be if she were to require assisted ventilation. The pediatrician, pulmonologist, physiatrist, occupational and physical therapists, respiratory therapist, home care coordinator, home educator, and social worker attend the conference to discuss the child's current medical status, prognosis for the short and long term, and the child's and family's wishes as her condition deteriorates. The conference lasts 60 minutes.

Each participating physician (if they are different specialties and/or from different practices [ie, separate tax identification numbers]) } **99367**

ICD-9-CM
335.11 (spinal muscular atrophy, juvenile)

ICD-10-CM
G12.1 (other inherited spinal muscular atrophy)

Each NPP (eg, respiratory therapist, occupational therapist) } **99368**

➤ **A patient with cerebral palsy requires coordination with multiple health care professionals (eg, physical and occupational therapy, neurologist, pediatrician).** Each participant in the conference has completed his or her evaluation of the patient within 60 days prior to the conference, and a team conference of 40 minutes is held to assess the current plan of care and therapy. The patient's family is present at this conference.

Because the patient's family is present, the participating physicians must report an appropriate E/M service rather than team conference services. The appropriate E/M code for the site of service (eg, **99215**) and typical time would be reported by each participating physician if they are different specialties and/or from different practices (ie, separate tax identification numbers). Code **99368** would be reported by the physical and occupational therapists.

Care Plan Oversight Services (99339, 99340, 99374–99380)

Care plan oversight is recurrent physician supervision of a complex patient or a patient who requires multidisciplinary care and ongoing physician involvement. Chronic care management or TCM services would not be reported in conjunction with care plan oversight services. (When reporting criteria are met for CCM or TCM and payer policy allows payment, it may be beneficial to report these services in lieu of care plan oversight.) Care plan oversight services are not face-to-face and reflect the complexity and time required to supervise the care of the patient. The codes are reported separately from E/M office visits. See Table 11-8.

> |||||||| *Coding Pearl* ||||||||
>
> Care plan oversight services are reported by the physician who has the predominant supervisory role in the care of the patient.

Care plan oversight services

❖ Are reported only by the physician who has the predominant supervisory role in the care of the patient or is the sole provider of the services. A face-to-face service with the patient must have been provided by the physician prior to assuming care plan oversight.

❖ Include
  ❖ Regular physician development and/or revision of care plans
  ❖ Review of subsequent reports of the patient's status
  ❖ Review of related laboratory or other diagnostic studies
  ❖ Communication (including telephone calls) for purposes of assessment or care decisions with health care professionals, family members, surrogate decision-makers (eg, legal guardians), and/or key caregivers involved in the patient's care
  ❖ Integration of new information into the medical treatment plan or adjustment of medical therapy
  ❖ Team conferences
  ❖ Prolonged E/M service before and/or after direct patient care when the same time is attributed to care plan oversight

◉ Require recurrent supervision of therapy by the physician. Provision of very low-intensity or infrequent supervision services is considered part of the pre- and post-encounter work for home, office/outpatient, hospital, and nursing facility or domiciliary visit codes. For example, a child is discharged from the hospital and requires weekly laboratory tests for 2 weeks. The test results are called to the physician's office and the physician relays the findings to the mother. These low-intensity services would be included in the post-service work of the hospital services.

◉ Are reported once per month based on the amount of time spent by the physician during that calendar month.

◉ Cumulative time begins with the first day of the month and ends with the last day of the month.

◉ Are reported based on the patient's location (eg, home, hospice) and the total time spent by the physician within a calendar month. Less than 15 minutes' cumulative time within a calendar month cannot be reported.

◉ Are reported separately from other office/outpatient, hospital, home, nursing facility, or domiciliary E/M services.

◉ Time spent on the following activities *may not* be considered care plan oversight:

❖ Travel time to or from the facility or place of domicile

❖ Services furnished by ancillary or incident-to staff

❖ Very low-intensity or infrequent supervision services included in the pre- and post-encounter work for an E/M service

❖ Interpretation of laboratory or other diagnostic studies associated with a face-to-face E/M service

❖ Informal consultations with health professionals not involved in the patient's care

❖ Routine postoperative care provided during the global surgery period of a procedure

❖ Time spent on telephone calls, online medical evaluation, or in medical team conferences if they are separately reported with codes **99441–99443, 99444,** or **99367**

Table 11-8. Care Plan Oversight

99339	Individual physician supervision of a patient (patient not present) in home, domiciliary, or rest home (eg, assisted living facility) requiring complex and multidisciplinary care modalities involving regular physician development and/or revision of care plans; review of subsequent reports of patient status; review of related laboratory and other studies; communication (including telephone calls) for purposes of assessment or care decisions with health care professional(s), family member(s), surrogate decision-maker(s) (eg, legal guardian), and/or key caregiver(s) involved in patient's care; integration of new information into the medical treatment plan; and/or adjustment of medical therapy, within a calendar month; 15–29 minutes
99340	≥30 minutes
99374	Physician supervision of a patient under care of home health agency (patient not present) in home, domiciliary, or equivalent environment (eg, Alzheimer's facility) requiring complex and multidisciplinary care modalities involving regular physician development and/or revision of care plans; review of subsequent reports of patient status; review of related laboratory and other studies; communication (including telephone calls) for purposes of assessment or care decisions with health care professional(s), family member(s), surrogate decision-maker(s) (eg, legal guardian), and/or key caregiver(s) involved in patient's care; integration of new information into the medical treatment plan; and/or adjustment of medical therapy, within a calendar month; 15–29 minutes
99375	≥30 minutes

Table 11-8. Care Plan Oversight, continued

Code	Description
99377	Physician supervision of a hospice patient (patient not present) requiring complex and multidisciplinary care modalities involving regular physician development and/or revision of care plans; review of subsequent reports of patient status; review of related laboratory and other studies; communication (including telephone calls) for purposes of assessment or care decisions with health care professional(s), family member(s), surrogate decision-maker(s) (eg, legal guardian), and/or key caregiver(s) involved in patient's care; integration of new information into the medical treatment plan; and/or adjustment of medical therapy, within a calendar month; 15–29 minutes
99378	≥30 minutes
99379	Physician supervision of a nursing facility patient (patient not present) requiring complex and multidisciplinary care modalities involving regular physician development and/or revision of care plans; review of subsequent reports of patient status; review of related laboratory and other studies; communication (including telephone calls) for purposes of assessment or care decisions with health care professional(s), family member(s), surrogate decision-maker(s) (eg, legal guardian), and/or key caregiver(s) involved in patient's care; integration of new information into the medical treatment plan; and/or adjustment of medical therapy, within a calendar month; 15–29 minutes
99380	≥30 minutes

A care plan oversight log serves as medical record documentation and as an encounter form for reporting purposes. An example is found in Appendix B-8 and online at www.aap.org/cfp (access code AAPCFP20). A completed care plan oversight log follows:

Care Plan Oversight Provided to a Patient in the Home[a]

Total time for care plan oversight activities performed in August=37 minutes (code **99340**)

Date of Service	Special Services Provided A–F	Contact Name and Agency	Start Time	End Time	Total Minutes	Monthly Subtotal
August 4	C, D	Consultation with pediatric endocrinologist	12:00 pm	12:06 pm	6	6
August 4	D, A	Phone call to mother, change in medication	12:15 pm	12:21 pm	6	12
August 15	C	Review of individualized education program (IEP)	5:15 pm	5:25 pm	10	22
August 16	D	Phone calls to mother and teacher re: changes in IEP	5:30 pm	5:45 pm	15	37

[a]See worksheet in Appendix B-8 and online at www.aap.org/cfp; use access code AAPCFP20.

Medicare requires the use of Level II HCPCS codes for care plan oversight services provided to patients under the care of a home health agency (**G0181**) or hospice (**G0182**). To report these G codes, Medicare requires a minimum of 30 minutes of physician supervision per calendar month. Because some state Medicaid programs may follow suit, check with your payer to learn its requirements for reporting these services.

Reporting a Combination of Non–Face-to-Face Services

When CCM or TCM services do not apply or a payer does not provide benefits for these services, it may be necessary to report a combination of codes for non–face-to-face services provided to a child with special health care needs. These may include care plan oversight, online or telephone E/M services, prolonged services, and team conference services.

Example

➤ **On January 3, several days prior to performing a preventive medicine visit on a 4-year-old new patient with cerebral palsy, the physician reviews medical records that were brought in by the mother.** It takes the physician 30 minutes at noon and another 20 minutes after regular office hours to complete the review. The total time spent is documented.

On January 5, the child is seen by the pediatrician in the morning and a preventive medicine visit is performed and documented. During the visit the mother relates that the child has had wheezing for 1 day and increased gastroesophageal reflux. A detailed history is performed for the wheezing and reflux. Medications are prescribed and reflux precautions are reviewed in detail. Later that day, the physician spends 40 minutes developing a care plan and an emergency information form to summarize the medical condition(s), medications, and special health care needs that will be used to inform other health care professionals of the child's special health conditions and needs. The nurse (under direction of the physician) spends 35 minutes scheduling appointments with a neurologist, physical therapist, and social worker.

The next day, an additional 12 minutes is spent by the physician on the telephone with the patient's mother to discuss the care plan and coordination of care. All services and the time spent are documented on the care plan oversight log.

On January 16, the child's mother calls the physician because she is concerned that the child will have problems adjusting to his new school. The physician spends a total of 15 minutes on the telephone with the mother to discuss how she should handle the issue. The physician documents the time spent on the telephone call, the history, and issues discussed.

On January 24, the pediatrician attends a medical team conference with the child's neurologist, physical therapist, occupational therapist, and social worker to discuss the current plan of care and therapy and make appropriate revisions. The patient and family are not present at this conference. The conference lasts 35 minutes. Each participant documents the total time spent in conference and a summary of the treatment recommendations and plans.

Pediatrician reports		
January 3	**99358** Prolonged E/M service before and/or after direct patient care; first hour	*ICD-9-CM* **343.9** Infantile cerebral palsy, unspecified *ICD-10-CM* **G80.9** Infantile cerebral palsy, unspecified
January 5	**99382** Preventive medicine visit, 1–4 years of age, new patient **99214 25** Detailed history, moderate-level medical decision-making	*ICD-9-CM* **V20.2** Routine child health check **530.81** Gastroesophageal reflux **786.07** Wheezing **343.9** Infantile cerebral palsy, unspecified *ICD-10-CM* **Z00.129** Routine child health check with abnormal findings **K21.9** Gastroesophageal reflux without esophagitis **R06.2** Wheezing **G80.9** Infantile cerebral palsy, unspecified

Pediatrician reports, continued		
January 16	**99442** Telephone E/M service; 11–20 minutes of medical discussion Alternatively, the time spent on the telephone call could be included in the care plan oversight time.	*ICD-9-CM* **V65.49** Other specified counseling *ICD-10-CM* **Z71.89** Other specified counseling
January 24	**99367** Medical team conference	*ICD-9-CM* **343.9** *ICD-10-CM* **G80.9**
January 31	**99340** Care plan oversight, patient at home, ≥30 minutes) Total physician time spent was 52 minutes.	*ICD-9-CM* **343.9** *ICD-10-CM* **G80.9**

Nonphysician Codes

The use of nonphysician codes is based on state scope of practice laws and payer interpretation. When a qualified NPP in your office provides the following services, negotiate with payers for coverage for the services. See also a list of HCPCS codes that may be used to report nonphysician education services. Payers may recognize these services when they realize the overall cost savings (eg, decrease in physician or ED visits, decreased hospital care). The services are reported with the appropriate E/M codes when they are performed by the physician.

Medical Nutrition Assessments

|||||| *Coding Pearl* ||||||

When a physician performs medical nutrition therapy, the services will be reported with the appropriate E/M codes.

97802   Medical nutrition therapy, initial assessment and intervention, individual, face to face with the patient, each 15 minutes

99803   Reassessment and intervention, individual, face to face with the patient, each 15 minutes

97804   Group (2 or more individuals), each 30 minutes

⁜ Codes are reported when provided by a registered nutritionist or licensed nutritional professional who may report services under his or her individual state's scope of practice.

Health and Behavior Assessments/Interventions

96150   Health and behavior assessment, each 15 minutes face to face with the patient, initial assessment

96151   Reassessment

⁜ The initial assessment (**96150**) may include a health-focused clinical interview, behavioral observations, psychophysiological monitoring, and completion of health-oriented questionnaires.

⁜ Report the service based on each 15 minutes of face-to-face time with the patient and/or family.

⁜ Code **96151** is used to report the reassessment of a patient's condition by interview and behavioral health instruments.

96152   Health and behavior intervention, each 15 minutes, face to face

96153   Group (2 or more patients)

96154   Family (with patient present)

96155   Family (without patient present)

❂ Face-to-face health and behavior intervention services are reported per each 15 minutes of time spent. The total time must be documented in the medical record.

Codes **96150–96155**

❂ May be reported by psychologists, clinical social workers, licensed therapists, and other NPPs within their scope of practice who have specialty or subspecialty training in health and behavior assessment/intervention procedures. Physicians and other qualified health care professionals who may report E/M services are instructed to report E/M or preventive service codes.

❂ Are used when assessing or addressing psychosocial factors affecting patients who have an established medical illness or diagnosis and may benefit from assessments and interventions that focus on the biopsychosocial factors related to the patient's health status (eg, services differ from preventive medicine counseling and risk-factor reduction interventions).

❂ Are not used in conjunction with a primary diagnosis of mental disorder. (Payers may deny when a diagnosis code indicating mental disorder is included on the claim for these services.)

❂ Are used to identify the psychological, behavioral, emotional, cognitive, and/or social factors needed for the prevention, treatment, or management of physical health problems with a focus on treating the biopsychosocial factors contributing to physical problems.

❂ Do not require a standardized curriculum.

❂ Are not reported with psychiatric codes (**90791–90899**) when provided on the same day. Only the primary service is reported (eg, either **96150–96155** or **90791–90899**).

❂ Are not reported with an E/M code (eg, **99201–99215**, **99401**–**99412**) on the same day.

❂ Do not include neuropsychological testing (**96116**), which can be reported separately.

Examples

➤ **A 12-year-old girl undergoing treatment for acute lymphoblastic leukemia is referred to an advanced practice nurse trained in health and behavior assessment/intervention procedures for assessment of pain, behavioral distress, and combativeness associated with repeated procedures and treatment.** The patient is assessed using standardized questionnaires (eg, Pediatric Pain Questionnaire, Coping Strategies Inventory). The child's parents are also interviewed.

Code **96150** would be reported with, for example, *ICD-9-CM* code **204.00,** acute lymphoid leukemia without mention of having achieved remission or *ICD-10-CM*, code **C91.00,** acute lymphoblastic leukemia, without remission.

Transitioning to **10**

➤ **Results from the health and behavior assessment are used to develop a treatment plan.** Thirty minutes is spent with the patient discussing the behavior and suggested coping skills.

Code **96152** with 2 units of service would be reported with the same diagnosis as used in the initial assessment.

Chapter 11: Evolving Evaluation and Management and Nonphysician Services

Education and Training for Patient Self-management

❋ The purpose of these services is to teach the patient and caregivers how to self-manage the illness or disease or delay disease comorbidity(ies) in conjunction with the patient's professional health care team.

❋ Qualifications of the NPPs and the content of the program have to be consistent with guidelines or standards established or recognized by a physician or NPP society, association, or other appropriate source.

❋ Codes are used to report education and training services provided to patients with an established illness or disease. Code **98960** (education and training for patient self-management by a qualified NPP using a standardized curriculum, face to face with the patient [could include caregiver/family]; each 30 minutes) is reported when services are provided to an individual patient. Code **98961** is reported when services are provided to 2 to 4 patients, and **98962** is reported when 5 to 8 patients receive the education and training.

❋ A physician must prescribe services, and a standardized curriculum must be used.

Example

➤ **A 7-year-old patient was recently diagnosed with asthma and is referred to the asthma educator for therapy and training under an approved curriculum.** This includes review of protocols for prevention, including use of controller medications and treatment of potential exacerbations.

   The content, type, duration, and patient response to the training must be documented in the medical record. Because these are time-based services, the total time spent in education, counseling, or training must be documented in the medical record. One unit of service is reported for each 30 minutes of service.

Genetic Counseling Services

96040   Medical genetics and genetic counseling services, each 30 minutes face to face with patient/family

❋ Trained genetic counselors provide services that may include obtaining a structured family genetic history, pedigree construction, analysis for genetic risk assessment, and counseling of the patient and family.

❋ Services may be provided during one or more sessions and may include review of medical data and family information, face-to-face interviews, and counseling services.

❋ For genetic counseling by a nonphysician to a group, see codes **98961–98962.**

❋ Genetic counseling by physicians and other qualified health care professionals who may report E/M services are reported with the appropriate E/M service code.

Patient Education HCPCS Codes

HCPCS Level II codes may be reported when the narrative differs from the *CPT*® code. These codes are only reported when services are provided by NPPs.

S9441   Asthma education, NPP; per session
S9445   Patient education, not otherwise classified, NPP, individual, per session
S9446   group, per session
S9449   Weight management classes, NPP, per session
S9451   Exercise class, NPP, per session
S9452   Nutrition class, NPP, per session
S9454   Stress management class, NPP, per session

S9455   Diabetic management program, group session
S9460   nurse visit
S9465   dietitian visit
S9470   Nutritional counseling, dietitian visit

Home Health Procedures/Services

Codes **99502–99600** are used to report home health services (eg, home visit for new-born care and assessment) or procedures (eg, home visits for respiratory therapy, stoma care, administration of intramuscular injections). Refer to *CPT® 2015* for the description of home health services.

- ☀ Used to report services provided in a patient's residence (including assisted living apartments, group homes, nontraditional private homes, custodial care facilities, or schools).

- ☀ Physicians should report home E/M visits (**99341–99350**) and other codes for any additional procedure or service provided to a patient living in a residence.

- ☀ Health care professionals who are authorized to use E/M home visit codes (**99341–99350**) may also report codes **99500–99600** if both services are performed and the patient's condition requires a significant, separately identifiable service. Modifier **25** would be appended to codes **99341–99350.**

Chapter 11: Evolving Evaluation and Management and Nonphysician Services

Common Procedures and Non–Evaluation and Management Medical Services

Surgical Package Rules

Current Procedural Terminology (*CPT*®) surgical codes (**10021–69990**) are packaged or global codes.

- Surgical codes include certain anesthesia services and the associated preoperative and postoperative care.
- The *CPT* definition of a surgical package differs from the Centers for Medicare & Medicaid Services (CMS) definition of a global surgical period, as seen in Table 12-1.
- Most state Medicaid programs follow the CMS definition.
- Each commercial insurance company will have its own policy for billing and payment of global surgical care, and most will designate a specific number of follow-up days for surgical procedures.
- The CMS designated global periods for each *CPT* procedure code can be found on the Medicare Resource-Based Relative Value Scale (RBRVS) at www.cms.hhs.gov/physicianfeesched.

When determining the postoperative period, the day after surgery is day 1 of a 10- or 90-day period.

|||||||||| *Coding Pearl* ||||||||||

Most state Medicaid programs follow the CMS surgical package guidelines.

Table 12-1. Comparison of the *CPT* and CMS Surgical Packages

CPT Definition of Surgical Package	CMS Medicare Global Surgery
Anesthesia • Includes local infiltration, regional block, or topical anesthesia	• Same
Preoperative care • Includes E/M service(s) subsequent to the decision for surgery (eg, assessing the site and condition, explanation of procedure, obtaining informed consent) on the day before and/or on the date of the procedure (including history and physical). • When the initial decision to perform surgery is made on the day prior to or on the day of surgery, the appropriate-level E/M visit may be reported separately with modifier **57** (decision for surgery) appended. This modifier shows the payer that the E/M service was necessary to make the decision for surgery (ie, not the routine preoperative evaluation). • When an E/M service performed on the day of the procedure is unrelated to the decision to perform surgery and is significant and distinct from the usual preoperative care associated with the procedure, it may be reported with modifier **25** (significant, separately identifiable E/M service by the same physician on the same day of the procedure or other service) appended. • Medical record documentation must support that the service was significant, separately identifiable, and medically necessary or was performed prior to the decision to perform the procedure. • Different diagnoses are not required when reporting an E/M visit and procedure.	• Same with following exceptions: • For "minor" procedures (ie, procedures assigned a 0- or 10-day global period or endoscopies), the E/M visit on the date of the procedure is considered a routine part of the procedure regardless of whether it is prior or subsequent to the decision for surgery. In these cases, modifier **57** is not recognized. • An E/M code may be reported on the same day as a minor surgical procedure only when a significant, separately identifiable E/M service is performed with modifier **25** appended to the E/M code. • When the initial decision to perform a major surgical procedure (ie, procedures assigned a 90-day global period) is made on the day prior to or on the day of a procedure, the E/M service may be reported appended with modifier **57**. Medical record documentation should support that the decision for surgery was made during the encounter and that additional time was spent in performing counseling of the risks, benefits, and outcomes.

Table 12-1. Comparison of the *CPT* and CMS Surgical Packages, continued

CPT Definition of Surgical Package	CMS Medicare Global Surgery
Postoperative care ◈ Includes all associated typical postoperative care (dictation of progress notes; counseling with the patient, family, and/or other physicians; writing orders; evaluating the patient in the postanesthesia recovery area). ◈ Care for therapeutic surgical procedures includes only the care that is usually part of the surgical service. ◈ Care for diagnostic procedures (eg, endoscopies, arthroscopies, injection procedures for radiography) includes only the care that is related to the recovery from the diagnostic procedure. ◈ Care resulting from complications of surgery. ◈ Any complications, exacerbations, recurrence, treatment of unrelated diseases or injuries, or the presence of other diseases or injuries that require additional services may be reported separately.	◈ Same ◈ Guidelines are contradictory.
Postoperative days ◈ Does not include any specific number of postoperative days.	◈ All additional medical or surgical services performed by the surgeon that do not require an additional trip to the operating room are included, though underlying conditions or added courses or treatment that are not part of the normal recovery from the procedure are not included in the surgery package. ◈ Designates specific postoperative periods for certain procedure codes (0 days, 10 days, 90 days). Other codes are designated YYY, which means the postoperative period is set by the carrier. There are no associated postoperative days included in the payment for codes assigned with status codes XXX (the global concept does not apply) or ZZZ (code related to another service [ie, XXX base code] that is always included in the global period of the other service).

Abbreviations: CMS, Centers for Medicare & Medicaid Services; CPT, Current Procedural Terminology; E/M, evaluation and management.

Reporting Postoperative Care

◈ Report *CPT®* code **99024** (postoperative follow-up visit) for follow-up care provided during the global surgery period.

❖ Reporting code **99024** allows a practice to track the number of visits performed during the postoperative period of specific procedures, calculate office overhead expenses (eg, supplies, staff, physician time) associated with the procedure, and potentially use the data to negotiate higher payment rates.

❖ Payers track the postoperative care provided. If a physician is not providing or reporting the postoperative care typically performed for a procedure, payers may reduce payment for the surgical service because payment includes postoperative care as part of the procedure.

> ||||||| **Coding Pearl** |||||||
>
> Payers may reduce payment of a surgical procedure if the physician does not report code **99024**.

* When the physician who performed the procedure provides an unrelated evaluation and management (E/M) service during the postoperative period, modifier **24** (unrelated E/M service by the same physician during a postoperative period) should be appended to the E/M service code.

* When physicians from different practices perform part of a surgical package, the procedure should be reported with modifier **54** (surgical care only), **56** (preoperative management only), or **55** (postoperative management only). These situations require communication among the surgeon, the physician providing preoperative or postoperative care, and their respective billing personnel to ensure accurate reporting and payment. (See Chapter 3 for a more detailed description of modifiers.)

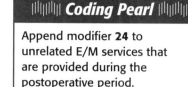

||||||||| *Coding Pearl* |||||||||

Append modifier **24** to unrelated E/M services that are provided during the postoperative period.

* When a physician other than the surgeon provides unrelated services to a patient during the postoperative period, the services are reported without a modifier. Despite the use of different provider numbers and diagnosis codes, some payers with assigned follow-up surgical periods will deny the service. The claim should be appealed for payment with a letter advising the payer that the service was unrelated to any surgery.

Physicians at Teaching Hospitals (PATH) Guidelines for Billing Procedures

Physicians at Teaching Hospitals (PATH) guidelines for billing procedures are less complex than those for billing E/M services. Guidelines specify that

* When a procedure is performed by a resident, teaching physician attendance and participation are required and must be documented.

* The level of participation required by the teaching physician depends on the type of procedure being performed.

* A resident, nurse, or teaching physician may document the teaching physician's attendance.

The rules for supervising physicians in teaching settings can be obtained on the CMS Web site at http://cms.hhs.gov/manuals/downloads/clm104c12.pdf, section 100.

Minor Procedures

* The CMS defines a *minor procedure* as one taking 5 minutes or less to complete with relatively little decision-making once the need for the procedure is determined.

* Minor procedures are usually assigned a 0- to 10-day global period.

* Teaching physicians may bill for a minor procedure when they personally perform the service or when a resident performs the service and they are present for the entire procedure.

* The resident may document the procedure but must attest to the teaching physician's presence.

Interpretation of Diagnostic Radiology and Other Diagnostic Tests

* The teaching physician may bill for the interpretation of the diagnostic service if he or she interprets tests or reviews the findings with the resident.

* Documentation must support a personal interpretation or a review of the resident's notes with indication of agreement with the resident's interpretation.

* Changes to the resident's interpretation must be documented.

Chapter 12: Common Procedures and Non–Evaluation and Management Medical Services

Coding Conundrum: Procedure or E/M and Procedure?

The differences in the CMS and *CPT®* surgical package guidelines are somewhat open to interpretation, often leading to confusion. Try to answer these questions when determining if you should report a procedure alone or a procedure with an E/M service.

Did you address a problem or condition prior to making a decision to perform the procedure (above and beyond the usual preoperative care associated with the procedure) or a significant and separately identifiable problem? If yes, report an E/M and procedure.

Does the medical record documentation clearly support the performance of a medically necessary E/M service (required key components), the procedure (procedure note), the medical necessity for both, and the decision to perform the surgery? If yes, report an E/M and procedure.

Was the purpose of the visit for the procedure only? If yes, do not report an E/M.

Does the payer follow the *CPT* or CMS guidelines with regard to reporting surgical procedures?

If the focus of an E/M service is related to the procedure, the history and physical examination are part of preoperative service and only the surgical procedure should be reported.

Endoscopy

- The teaching physician must be present for the entire viewing starting at the time of insertion and ending at the time of removal of the endoscope.
- Viewing the procedure through a monitor located in another room does not meet the requirements for billing.
- The presence of the teaching physician must be documented in the medical record. The teaching physician's presence must be stated.

Surgery Other Than Minor Procedures

- The teaching physician must assume the responsibility of preoperative, operative, and postoperative care of the patient. He or she must be present during all critical and key portions (as determined by the teaching physician) of the procedure. For example, if opening or closing is not considered to be key or critical, the teaching physician does not need to be present.
- The teaching physician must be immediately available to furnish services during the entire procedure.
- If circumstances prevent the physician from being immediately available, arrangements must be made with another qualified surgeon to be immediately available to assist with the procedure.
- The physician's presence for single surgical procedures may be demonstrated in notes made by the teaching physician, resident, or nurse.
- When the teaching physician is present for the entire procedure, only the written attestation of his or her presence is required.
- If the teaching physician is present during only the key or critical portions of the surgery, documentation must indicate his or her presence at those portions of the procedure (the resident may still document the operative report).
- When billing for 2 overlapping (concurrent) surgeries, the teaching physician must be present for the key or critical portions of both procedures and must so document his or her presence. The surgeon cannot be involved in a second case until all key or critical portions in the first case have been completed.

- Arrangements may be made with another qualified surgeon to be present at one of the surgeries. The name of the other surgeon who was immediately available during overlapping surgeries must be documented.

Complex or High-Risk Surgeries and Procedures

A complex procedure or surgery is usually assigned a 90-day global period or, in the case of diagnostic procedures (eg, transesophageal echocardiography), require the direct or personal supervision of a physician.

- A teaching physician must be present with a resident for the entire procedure when billing for a service identified by the CMS or local policy as complex and requiring personal supervision by a physician.
- Documentation must support that the teaching physician was present.

Postoperative Care

- The teaching physician determines which postoperative visits are considered key or critical and require his or her presence.
- If the teaching physician is not providing postoperative care included in the global surgery package, he or she will report the procedure(s) with modifiers **54** (surgical care only) and **56** (preoperative management only).
- Postoperative care is reported by another physician with the same surgical procedure code with modifier **55** (postoperative management only).
- The surgeon and physician providing postoperative care must keep a copy of a written transfer agreement in the patient's medical record.

PATH Guidelines: Examples of Appropriate Documentation	
Minor Procedures	*"Dr Teaching Physician was present during the entire procedure."* –Nurse *"Dr Teaching Physician observed me performing this procedure."* –Dr Resident
Interpretation of Diagnostic Radiology and Other Diagnostic Tests	*"I personally reviewed the MRI with Dr Resident and agree with his findings."* –Dr Teaching Physician *"I personally reviewed the CAT scan with Dr Resident. Findings are indicative of (insert)."* –Dr Teaching Physician
Endoscopy	*"I was present during the entire viewing of this endoscopy."* –Dr Teaching Physician
Surgery (except minor)	*"Dr Teaching Physician was present during entire surgery."* –Dr Resident *"I was present and observed Dr Resident perform the key portion of this procedure."* –Dr Teaching Physician
Complex or High-Risk Surgeries and Procedures	*"I was physically present during this entire procedure with the exception of the [opening and/or closing], as that overlapped with the key portion of another case."* –Dr Teaching Physician *"Dr Y was immediately available during the overlapping portions of this case, which included [cite specifics]."* –Dr Teaching Physician

Laceration Repairs

12001–12018   Simple repair

12031–12057   Intermediate repair

13100–13160   Complex repair

- Categories of difficulty of wound repairs are described as
  - *Simple:* Superficial wound and/or subcutaneous wound requiring a simple single-layer closure or tissue adhesives
  - *Intermediate:* Wound requiring layered closure of one or more of the deeper layers of subcutaneous tissue and non-muscle fascia in addition to skin closure or contaminated wound that requires extensive cleaning or removal of particulate matter
  - *Complex:* Wounds requiring reconstructive surgery, complicated closure, or grafting

> ||||||| **Coding Pearl** |||||||
>
> Wounds closed using adhesive strips alone are not reported with codes **12001–13160.**

- Codes **12001–13160** are used to report wound closure using sutures, staples, or tissue adhesives (Dermabond), singly or in combination with adhesive strips.
- Wound closure using adhesive strips (eg, Steri-Strips, butterfly bandages) only is considered inherent to the E/M service. However, the supplies (eg, Steri-Strips, butterfly bandages) may be reported separately using code **99070** (supplies and materials) or **A4450** (tape, non-waterproof, per 18 sq in). There is not a specific Healthcare Common Procedure Coding System (HCPCS) code for Steri-Strips or butterfly bandages. Some payers may accept HCPCS code **G0168** (wound closure using tissue adhesive[s]) in lieu of simple repair codes (eg, **12001, 12011**).
- Codes are reported based on the difficulty of the repair, measured length of the wound, and the location. To report wound repair, measure the length of the repaired wound(s) in centimeters.
  - If multiple wounds belong to the same category of difficulty and location, add the lengths and report with a single code.
  - If multiple wounds do not belong in the same category, report each repair separately with the more complicated repair reported as the primary procedure and the less complicated repair reported as the secondary procedure. Modifier **51** (multiple procedures) should be appended to the secondary code(s).
- Simple ligation of vessels is considered as part of the wound closure.
- Wound debridement and/or cleaning and the provision of topical or injected local anesthesia are considered to be included in the wound repair code. Debridement is considered a separate procedure only when gross contamination requires prolonged cleaning, excessive amounts of devitalized tissue are removed, or debridement is performed without immediate primary closure. To report extensive tissue debridement, see codes **11042–11047** or **97597, 97598.**

Transitioning to 10

External cause codes (eg, **W09.8XXA**) are assigned for each encounter for treatment with a seventh character indicating initial (A), subsequent (D), or sequela (S). Place of occurrence (eg, **Y92.838**) is reported only for the initial encounter for an injury and requires no seventh character.

Examples

➤ **A 10-year-old sustained a 1.5-cm laceration on his left knee requiring an intermediate repair after a fall from playground equipment.**

12031 (repair, intermediate, wounds of scalp, axillae, trunk, and/ or extremities; 2.5 cm or less)

International Classification of Diseases, Ninth Revision, Clinical Modification (ICD-9-CM)
891.0 (open wound of knee, leg, and ankle, without mention of complication)
E884.0 (fall from playground equipment)
E849.4 (place of recreation and sport)

International Classification of Diseases, 10th Revision, Clinical Modification (ICD-10-CM)
S81.012A (initial encounter, laceration without foreign body left knee)
W09.8XXA (initial encounter, fall on or from other playground equipment)
Y92.838 (other recreation area)

➤ **In addition to the laceration of the knee, the same patient has a 1.5-cm laceration on his left forearm that also requires an intermediate repair.**

12032
The measurement of both wounds is between 2.5 and 7.5 cm, both wounds are in the same family of anatomic sites, and they both require the same level of repair.

ICD-9-CM
891.0
881.00 (open wound of forearm without mention of complication)
E884.0
E849.4

ICD-10-CM
S81.012A (laceration without foreign body left knee)
S51.812A (laceration of left forearm without foreign body)
W09.8XXA
Y92.838

➤ **An 8-year-old sustained a 0.5-cm laceration on her forehead.** The wound on her face requires a simple repair. She is seen in follow-up 7 days later. The wound is clean and sutures are removed.

Initial visit
12011 (simple repair of the facial laceration 2.5 cm or less)

ICD-9-CM
873.42 (open wound forehead without mention of complication)

ICD-10-CM
S01.81XA (initial encounter for laceration without foreign body of other part of head)

Follow-up visit
99212 (problem-focused E/M visit, office or outpatient)

Z48.02 (encounter for removal of sutures)
S01.81XD (subsequent encounter for laceration of other part of head)

Transitioning to 10

The seventh character D (ie, **S01.81XD**) is reported for encounters after the patient has received active treatment of the condition and is receiving routine care for the condition during the healing or recovery phase.

Chapter 12: Common Procedures and Non–Evaluation and Management Medical Services

---

Coding Conundrum: Suture Removal

Suture removal can be coded in a variety of ways depending on the circumstances involved.

Sutures Placed by a Different Physician

When sutures are removed by another physician with a different tax identification number, an E/M office visit code may be reported for the suture removal. Some payers may allow reporting of HCPCS code **S0630**. Code **S0630** is for removal of sutures by a physician other than the physician who originally closed the wound. S codes are HCPCS Level II codes, designated by the CMS and recognized by national Blue Cross and Blue Shield payers, but coverage is on a payer-by-payer basis.

Sutures Placed by Same Physician or Physician of the Same Specialty in the Same Group (Same Tax Identification Number)

Simple Repair

The Medicare global surgery period for *CPT*® codes **12001–12018** (simple repair of superficial wound) is 0 days, meaning that payment includes the procedure or service plus any associated care provided on the same day of service. Therefore, practices may report a separate E/M service for removal of sutures placed in their office.

Intermediate or Complex Repair

The Medicare global surgery period for intermediate (**12031–12057**) and complex (**13100–13153**) wound repairs is 10 days. Payment includes the procedure or service plus any associated follow-up care for a period of 10 days. Therefore, the charge for the procedure already includes suture removal by the same physician or physician of the same group and specialty as part of the global surgical package.

Burn Care

- *Current Procedural Terminology* code **16000** (initial treatment, first-degree burn, where no more than local treatment is required) is reported when initial treatment is performed for the symptomatic relief of a first-degree burn that is characterized by erythema and tenderness.

  Codes **16020–16030**

  Dressings and/or debridement of partial-thickness burns, initial or subsequent

16020	small or less than 5% total body (eg, finger)
16025	medium or 5%–10% total body surface area (eg, whole face or whole extremity)
16030	large or greater than 10% total body surface area (eg, more than 1 extremity)

- Are used to report treatment of burns with dressings and/or debridement of small to large partial-thickness burns (second degree), whether initial or subsequent.

- Are reported based on the percentage of total body surface area (TBSA) affected.

- The percentage of TBSA involved must be calculated and documented when reporting care of second- or third-degree burns. Physicians will use what is referred to as the Rule of 9s (ie, dividing the TBSA into 9% or multiples of 9% segments). There are 2 sets of rules: one for infants and another for adults. (The Rule of 9s diagram is located in *CPT 2015 Professional Edition.*) As you can see from the diagram, the rules differ because of the large area of an infant or child's torso and head.

Transitioning to 10

It is advisable to use *ICD-10-CM* category **T31,** burns classified according to extent of body surface involved, as an additional code for reporting purposes when there is mention of a third-degree burn involving 20% or more of the body surface.

☀ An E/M visit with modifier **25** appended may be reported if a significant, separately identifiable E/M service is medically indicated, performed, and documented in addition to the burn care.

Examples

➤ **A 9-year-old is seen by the physician complaining of sunburn on her shoulders.** There is redness and tenderness but no blistering. Over-the-counter treatment for the first-degree burn is ordered.

16000 (first-degree burn requiring local treatment)

ICD-9-CM
692.71 (sunburn, local treatment)

ICD-10-CM
L55.0 (1st degree sunburn)

➤ **A 4-year-old is seen in the office after sustaining a burn on the first finger of her right hand.** The area is red and blistered. Following examination by the physician, the finger is treated with a topical cream and bandaged.

16020
ICD-9-CM
944.21 (burn, blisters, epidermal loss, finger)

ICD-10-CM
T23.221A (initial encounter for 2nd degree burn of single finger)
X19.XXXA (initial encounter for contact with other heat and hot substances)

Other Repairs

Code **11760** (repair of nail bed) is reported when part or all of the nail plate is lifted and a laceration of the nail bed is repaired.

Report code **40650** (repair of vermilion border of the lip) when a laceration of the full thickness of the lip and vermilion is repaired.

Laceration repairs of the tongue (**41250–41252**) are reported based on size and location (eg, repair of laceration 2.5 cm or less, anterior two-thirds of the tongue is reported using code **41250**).

Removal of Foreign Bodies

☀ Code **10120** (removal of a foreign body from subcutaneous tissue via simple incision) includes the removal of splinters when the physician has to go beneath the skin to retrieve the splinter.

Code **10121** is used to report the complicated removal of a foreign body by incision.

Example: The removal of an embedded earring requiring an incision would be reported with code **10120** or **10121,** depending on the complexity of the procedure required to remove it. If the earring is removed by wiggling it out or other method that does not require incision, this work is included in the E/M service.

||||||| *Coding Pearl* |||||||

Do not report code **10120** or **10121** when a foreign body is removed using forceps alone.

Chapter 12: Common Procedures and Non–Evaluation and Management Medical Services

- *Current Procedural Terminology* includes codes for reporting removal of foreign bodies from many different body sites. Musculoskeletal codes are reported when a foreign body is removed from *within the fascia, subfascial, or muscle.* Always check the CPT® index to direct you to the most accurate code.
- Foreign body in foot: Code **28190** is used to report the removal of a subcutaneous foreign body from the foot; code **28192** is used to report a complicated removal of a foreign body from the foot. If the removal of the foreign body does not involve the fascia, refer to codes **10120** or **10121** as appropriate. Code **24200** (subcutaneous) or **24201** (deep) is used to report removal of foreign bodies from the upper arm or elbow area.
- Intranasal foreign body: Removal of intranasal foreign bodies is reported using code **30300** (removal of intranasal foreign bodies when performed in the office) or **30310** (removal of intranasal foreign bodies under general anesthesia).
- Fecal impaction or anal foreign body: Code **45915** is used to report removal of fecal impaction or foreign body when performed under anesthesia. When digital removal of fecal impaction or anal foreign body is performed by a physician without anesthesia, code **45999** (unlisted procedure, rectum) may be reported.
- Foreign body in vagina: Report code **57415** when a vaginal foreign body is removed when the child is under anesthesia (not local anesthesia). Code **58999** (unlisted procedure, female genital system, non-obstetrical) may be reported for removal of a vaginal foreign body without anesthesia.
- Foreign body in eye: When removing a superficial conjunctival foreign body, report code **65205.** Removal of a corneal foreign body without the use of a slit lamp is reported with code **65220.**
- External auditory canal: Report code **69200** when the foreign body is removed without general anesthesia.

Note: If an unlisted procedure code is reported, a written report must be submitted with the claim. It is more appropriate to report these procedures using an appropriate E/M service code.

Table 12-2 emphasizes the increase in revenue that results from reporting the appropriate code (eg, procedure vs low-level E/M code).

Table 12-2. Comparing RVUs: 2014 Medicare RBRVS[a]

Code	Description	Total Non-facility RVUs
99201	Level 1 office visit, new patient	1.21
99202	Level 2 office visit, new patient	2.08
99212	Level 2 office visit, established patient	1.22
99213	Level 3 office visit, established patient	2.04
30300	Foreign body removal from nose	6.59
10120	Foreign body removal from subcutaneous tissue	4.26

Abbreviations: RBRVS, Resource-Based Relative Value Scale; RVUs, relative value units.

[a] The 2015 Medicare RBRVS was not available at the time this manual was printed. For an online copy of the pediatric-specific 2014 Medicare RBRVS, go to www.aap.org/cfp.

Removal of Cerumen (69210)

69210   Removal impacted cerumen requiring instrumentation, unilateral

Code **69210** is *only* reported when the physician, under direct visualization, removes impacted cerumen using, at a minimum, an otoscope and instruments such as wax curettes or by using an operating microscope and suction plus specific ear instruments (eg, cup forceps, right angles).

❋ Medical record documentation must support that the cerumen was impacted and removed by the physician and include a description of what equipment and method were used to perform the procedure.

❋ Report code **69210** with modifier **50** when bilateral procedures are performed.

❋ Removal of cerumen that is not impacted is included in an E/M code regardless of how it is removed.

> ||||||| **Coding Pearl** ||||||
>
> Removal of cerumen that is not impacted is included in an E/M code regardless of how it is removed.

Examples

➤ **A physician removes impacted cerumen by lavage.** Because the child is uncooperative, the procedure takes 10 minutes.

99201–99215 based on performance and documentation   Appropriate diagnosis
of required key components (See Chapter 6.)

➤ **Physician documents, "Impacted cerumen removed from both ears using an otoscope and curette."**

99201–99215 25   Appropriate diagnosis
Use modifier **25** if required by payer.
(See Chapter 3.)

69210 50   *ICD-9-CM*
                                                      380.4 (impacted cerumen)

                                                      ICD-10-CM
                                                      H61.23 (impacted cerumen, bilateral)

 Transitioning to **10**

Note: Medicare does not recognize modifier **50** when reported on code **69210** (impacted cerumen removal); therefore, those payers that follow Medicare payment policy will not recognize either and may deny the claim outright. Check with your payers.

Other Minor Procedures

11200   Removal of skin tags, multiple fibrocutaneous tags, any area; up to and including 15 lesions

Code **11200** is used to report the removal of a sixth digit from a newborn. It is equivalent to a skin tag and would not fall under the coding of an actual digit removal. The *ICD-9-CM* diagnosis code would be **755.00** (supernumerary digits). After transition to *ICD-10-CM*, the diagnosis code would be **Q69.0,**

> ||||||| **Coding Pearl** ||||||
>
> To report destruction of common or plantar warts, flat warts, or molluscum contagiosum, report only one code (**17110** or **17111**) with one unit of service, depending on the number of lesions removed.

accessory fingers; **Q69.1,** accessory thumb; **Q69.2,** accessory toes; or **Q69.9,** unspecified.

17110 Destruction (eg, laser surgery, electrosurgery, cryosurgery, chemosurgery, surgical curettement) of benign lesions other than skin tags or cutaneous vascular proliferative lesions; up to 14 lesions

17111 15 or more lesions

   ☯ To report destruction of common or plantar warts, flat warts, or molluscum contagiosum, report code **17110** or **17111** (with one unit of service), depending on the number of lesions removed. Do not report both **17110** and **17111** because they are mutually exclusive. Report the *ICD-9-CM* code appropriate to the type of warts treated (eg, **078.0** for molluscum contagiosum, **078.10** for common warts, **078.12** for plantar warts). After transition to *ICD-10-CM*, use code **B08.1** for molluscum contagiosum, **B07.8** for common warts, or **B07.0** for plantar warts.

17250 Chemocauterization of the umbilicus (chemical cauterization of granulation tissue [proud flesh, sinus, or fistula])

Example

➤ **A 2-month-old presents for her well-baby check.** On examination, a recently unseen umbilical granuloma is noted. The physician takes a very brief history and decides to cauterize. The routine well-baby check is completed and vaccines are given.

99391 25	*ICD-9-CM*
	V20.2 (routine infant/child health examination)
	ICD-10-CM
	Z00.121 (encounter for routine child health examination with abnormal findings)
17250	*ICD-9-CM*
Report vaccines as appropriate.	**686.1** (pyogenic granuloma)
	ICD-10-CM
	L92.8 (other granulomatous disorders of the skin and subcutaneous tissue)

30901 Cauterization of nosebleed (control nasal hemorrhage, anterior, simple [limited cautery and/or packing], any method)

    If the cauterization is performed bilaterally, report code **30901** with modifier **50.**

41010 Incision in the lingual frenulum to free the tongue

51701 Urinary catheterization, straight

    Report code **51701** when you insert a urinary catheter to collect a clean-catch urine specimen, after which the catheter is removed.

51702 Urinary catheterization, temporary

   ☯ Code **51701** is reported when a non-indwelling bladder catheter (straight catheterization) is inserted (eg, for residual urine, for a urine culture collection). Code **51702** is reported when a temporary indwelling bladder catheter is inserted (ie, Foley).

Table 12-3 details the number of global days for each of the commonly reported office procedures.

Table 12-3. Common Office Procedures and Global Days

CPT Code	Description	Global Days
10120–10121	FB removal, SQ	010
11200	Removal of skin tags	010
11760	Repair of nail bed	010
12001–12018	Laceration repair, simple	000
12031–12057	Laceration repair, intermediate	010
13100–13160	Laceration repair, complex	010
16000–16030	Burn care	000
17110–17111	Destruction benign lesions	010
17250	Chemical cautery	000
28190	FB removal, foot	010
28192	FB removal, foot, complex	090
30300	Removal intranasal FB, office	010
30310	Removal intranasal FB w/general anesthesia	010
30901	Nosebleed cautery/packing	000
40650	Repair of vermilion border of lip	090
41010	Incision in lingual frenulum	010
41250–41252	Laceration repairs of tongue	010
45915	Removal, fecal impaction or anal FB	010
51701–51702	Bladder catheterization	000
57415	Removal FB vagina, general anesthesia	010
65205	Removal, superficial conjunctival FB	000
65220	Removal of a corneal FB w/o slit lamp	000
69200	Removal FB, ear	000
69210	Removal impacted cerumen	000

Abbreviations: FB, foreign body; CPT, Current Procedural Terminology; SQ, subcutaneous.

Minor Procedures That Do Not Have a Code

Some minor procedures are considered inherent to an E/M code or do not have separate *CPT*® codes. However, any supplies used may be reported. The following procedures are included in an E/M service:

- Insertion or removal of an ear wick.
- Removal of non-impacted cerumen from the ear.
- Nasal aspiration.
- Nasogastric tube insertion without fluoroscopic guidance.
- Removal of an umbilical clamp.
- Removal of foreign bodies that do not require an incision.

||||||| **Coding Pearl** |||||||

Peak flow analysis is included in an E/M service.

Chapter 12: Common Procedures and Non-Evaluation and Management Medical Services

- Puncture of abscess without aspiration.
- The use of fluorescein dye and a Wood lamp to examine for a corneal abrasion or foreign body of the eye is included in the E/M service and is not reported separately. However, the work of a detailed eye examination and history may allow the reporting of a higher-level E/M code.

Fracture and/or Dislocation Care

Casts/Strapping/Splints

- Codes for the application of casts, splints, or strapping (**29000–29590**) cannot be reported for the initial (first) application when fracture or dislocation care is reported because they are included as part of the global surgery package.
- May be reported when they are replacements for the initial application or when they are performed as part of the initial E/M visit and fracture care is not reported.
- The following codes are commonly used when treating a fracture or dislocation:
    - ❖ Application of splints
        - — Short arm splint (forearm to hand): static (**29125**); dynamic (**29126**)
        - — Finger splint: static (**29130**); dynamic (**29131**)
        - — Short leg splint (calf to foot): **29515**
    - ❖ Strapping
        - — Shoulder: **29240**
        - — Elbow or wrist: **29260**

Supplies

- Supplies associated with fracture care may be billed with every application, including the initial casting, splinting, or strapping performed in association with the global surgery procedure code when the service is performed in the private office setting.
- Healthcare Common Procedure Coding System codes **A4580, A4590,** and **Q4001–Q4051** may be reported for cast supplies; codes **E1800–E1841** may be reported for splints. Check with your major payers and/or review their payment policies for reporting these supplies.
- The HCPCS codes are accepted by many Medicaid and commercial payers and are very specific to the age of the patient and the type of supply and/or material.
- A description of supplies may be required when reporting special supplies code **99070.**
- The following codes are commonly used:
    - ❖ Supplies and materials (except spectacles)
    - ❖ **A4565** Slings
    - ❖ **A4570** Splint
    - ❖ **L3650–L3678** Clavicle splints
    - ❖ **Q4001–Q4051** Cast and splint supplies
    - ❖ **S8450–S8452** Splint, prefabricated for finger, wrist, ankle, or elbow

Fracture and Dislocation Care Codes

Codes for fracture/dislocation care

- Are listed by anatomic location
- Are provided (in most cases) for closed or open treatment, with or without manipulation, and with or without internal fixation.
- Include a 90-day period of follow-up care under the Medicare global package.
- Include the initial casting, splinting, or strapping.
- Do not include radiographs.
- Fractures most commonly seen in a primary care pediatric practice include closed fractures (ie, fracture site is not surgically opened), and treatment is typically without manipulation (an exception is treatment of nursemaid elbow).
- Clavicular fracture: Report closed treatment without manipulation with code **23500.**
- Nursemaid elbow: Report closed treatment of radial head subluxation (nursemaid elbow) with manipulation with code **24640.**
- Radial fracture: Report code **25500** for closed treatment of radial shaft fracture without manipulation and **25600** for closed treatment of distal radius fracture without manipulation.
- Phalanx fracture: Closed treatment of a proximal or middle phalanx, finger, or thumb (each) without manipulation is reported with code **26720.** Closed treatment of a distal phalangeal fracture (each) without manipulation is reported with code **26750.**
- Great toe fracture: Code **28490** is reported for the closed treatment of a fracture of the great toe, phalanx, or phalanges without manipulation.
- Metatarsal fracture: Report code **28470** for closed treatment of a metatarsal fracture without manipulation.
- Lesser toe fracture: Closed treatment of fracture, phalanx, or phalanges, other than great toe without manipulation, **28510.**

Examples

➤ **A physician performs and documents a comprehensive evaluation on a child with multiple injuries, including a fracture of the shaft of the left clavicle and abrasions on the left upper arm and cheek, after a fall from the monkey bars.**

CPT	ICD-9-CM	ICD-10-CM
99201–99205 25	**912.0** (abrasion upper arm)	**S40.812A** (abrasion upper arm)
	910.0 (abrasion face)	**S00.81XA** (abrasion face)
	E884.0 (fall from playground equipment)	**W09.8XXA** (fall from playground equipment)
23500 (closed treatment of the clavicle fracture)	**810.00** (fracture clavicle, closed) **E884.0**	**S42.022A** (displaced fracture shaft of clavicle, closed) **W09.8XXA**

Transitioning to 10

Fractures not specified as displaced or non-displaced are reported with a code for a displaced fracture. Fractures not specified as open or closed are reported with a code for a closed fracture.

Chapter 12: Common Procedures and Non-Evaluation and Management Medical Services

➤ **A 9-year-old established patient is seen with complaints of left and right arm pain following a fall while snowboarding.** An expanded problem-focused history and physical examination are performed. The x-ray demonstrates a left Colles fracture (distal radius with dorsal [posterior] displacement of the wrist and hand). A fiberglass cast is applied and the patient is advised to return for follow-up.

The physician can elect to report the fracture care or the E/M services provided over the course of the global surgery period (see Coding Conundrum: Reporting Fracture Care below).

Coding Conundrum: Reporting Fracture Care

If a payer follows Medicare payment policy, the physician has the option of using the appropriate E/M codes and reporting each service separately in lieu of using procedure codes. The decision to use the global fracture code rather than E/M service codes requires an analysis of payment by payers for these codes.

Current Procedural Terminology code **25600** (closed treatment of distal radial fracture, closed treatment without manipulation) includes all associated preoperative care, application of the splint, and follow-up care for 90 days. If there was a significant, separately identifiable E/M service provided on the day of the fracture care (eg, child sustained sprain to other arm), an E/M service could also be reported with modifier **25** appended to the E/M service. Follow-up visits would be reported with code **99024** (postoperative follow-up visit included in surgical package). If a physician chooses not to bill fracture care, an E/M visit would be reported with code **29075** (application of short arm cast). You could also report code **Q4012** (cast supplies, short arm cast, pediatric, fiberglass). Any diagnostic procedures such as x-rays would be reported in either situation.

Before you decide how to bill the service, consider your total payments for the care associated with this fracture.

Tip: *Unrelated* services that are provided during the global surgery period by the same physician (or physician of the same group and specialty) may be reported. Modifier **24** would be appended to the unrelated E/M service. Refer to Chapter 3 for instructions for reporting modifiers.

Reporting Fracture Care Codes		Reporting E/M and Follow-up	
Code	**2014 Medicare Non-facility RBRVS**[a]	**Code**	**2014 Medicare Non-facility RBRVS**[a]
25600	9.25	**99213**	2.04
73100	0.90	**73100**	0.90
		29075	2.46
Q4012[b]	—	**Q4012**[b]	—
99024	0.00	**99212**	1.22
Total	10.15		6.62

Abbreviations: CPT, Current Procedural Terminology; *E/M, evaluation and management; RBRVS, Resource-Based Relative Value Scale.*

[a]*The 2015 Medicare RBRVS was not available at the time this manual was printed. For an online copy of the pediatric-specific 2014 Medicare RBRVS, go to www.aap.org/cfp.*
[b]*Supplies are not valued on the RBRVS.*

Intubation and Airway Management

31500   Intubation, endotracheal, emergency (and elective)

⁕ Moderate sedation (**94143–94150**) may be reported in addition to the intubation if reporting criteria are met.

31502   Tracheostomy tube change prior to establishment of fistula tract

⁕ Report code **31502** when an indwelling tracheostomy tube is replaced.

31505–31520

⁕ Indirect diagnostic laryngoscopy: Report code **31505**. If, while performing this procedure, a foreign body is removed, report code **31511** (laryngoscopy with removal of foreign body).

⁕ Direct laryngoscopy with or without tracheoscopy: Code **31515** is reported when it is performed for aspiration.

When a diagnostic direct laryngoscopy, with or without tracheoscopy, is performed on a newborn, report code **31520**.

31525   Laryngoscopy, direct, with or without tracheoscopy; diagnostic except newborn

Vascular Access

Blood Sampling for Diagnostic Study

⁕ Codes **36415** (collection of venous blood by venipuncture) and **36416** (collection of capillary blood specimen [eg, finger, heel, ear stick]) are used for any age child when the physician is not needed to perform the procedure.

⁕ When a physician's skill is required to perform venipuncture (eg, access is too difficult for other staff to attain) on a child younger than 3 years, codes **36400–36406** are reported based on the anatomic site of the venipuncture. Report code **36400** when performed on the femoral or jugular vein, code **36405** when on the scalp vein, or code **36406** when another vein is accessed.

|||||||| Coding Pearl ||||||||

Report **36415** when the physician performs a venipuncture as a convenience.

❖ When a physician's skill is required to perform venipuncture on a child 3 years and older, code **36410** (venipuncture, age >3 years necessitating physician's skill, for diagnostic or therapeutic purposes [not to be used for routine venipuncture]) is reported.

❖ If the physician performs the venipuncture as a convenience or because staff is not trained in the procedure, code **36415** is reported because the physician's skill was not required.

⁕ Although typically not required, some payers will require that modifier **25** be appended to the E/M code if an E/M service is reported on the same day of service.

⁕ It is not appropriate to report *CPT*® code **99211** along with code **36415** if the nurse only collects the blood specimen and no separately identified E/M service is provided.

⁕ Code **36591** (collection of blood specimen from a completely implantable venous access device) is reported only when in conjunction with a laboratory service.

Chapter 12: Common Procedures and Non-Evaluation and Management Medical Services

Specimen Handling

 **Coding Pearl** ‖‖‖‖

Code **99000** may be reported for each specimen when costs are incurred for handling and/or transportation.

99000　Handling and/or conveyance of specimen for transfer from the office to a laboratory

99001　Handling and/or conveyance of specimen for transfer from the patient in other than an office to a laboratory (distance may be indicated)

❀ Codes **99000** and **99001** are used to report packaging and sending medical specimens (eg, blood, throat swabs, urine specimens, stool samples) to an off-site laboratory.

❀ Code **99000** may be reported for each specimen for which the practice incurs costs in the handling and/or transportation.

Other Percutaneous Vessel

Catheterization for diagnosis or therapy; newborn

❀ Catheterization of the umbilical vein will be reported with code **36510;** catheterization of the umbilical artery is reported with code **36660.**

Insertion of central venous access device

❀ There is no distinction between venous access percutaneously or via cutdown.

❀ Report the code appropriate to the type of catheter (eg, non-tunneled vs tunneled), device (eg, with or without port), and age of child. See Table 12-4.

Table 12-4. Insertion of Central Venous Catheter

Insertion of Central Venous Catheter	Child <5 years	Child ≥5 years
Non-tunneled centrally inserted central venous catheter	36555	36556
Tunneled centrally inserted central venous catheter, without subcutaneous port or pump	36557	36558
Tunneled centrally inserted central venous access device, with subcutaneous port	36560	36561
Peripherally inserted central venous catheter, without subcutaneous port or pump	36568	36569
Peripherally inserted central venous access device, with subcutaneous port	36570	36571

Arterial access

❀ An arterial puncture for diagnosis is reported with code **36600.**

❀ Code **36620** is reported when a percutaneous peripheral arterial catheterization is performed.

❀ Code **36625** is reported when a cutdown is performed.

Removal of central venous access device

❀ Report repairs, partial catheter replacements, complete replacements, or removal of catheters with or without subcutaneous ports or pumps with codes **36578–36590.**

❖ Code **36589** is reported for removal of tunneled central venous catheter, without subcutaneous port or pump, and code **36590** for the removal of tunneled central venous catheter, with subcutaneous port or pump, central or peripheral.

❀ If a central venous access device is removed and replaced with a new one *through a separate venous access site,* the removal and insertion of the new device should be reported.

Transfusions

36430 Transfusion, blood or blood components

36440 Push transfusion; blood, 2 years or younger

* Indirect transfusion of blood or blood products (**36430**) should be used only if the physician personally infuses the substance, not if the blood is administered by nursing personnel and allowed to enter the vessel via gravity or meter flow. Push transfusion (**36440**) is used only for patients younger than 2 years. This code should be used only if the physician personally performs the transfusion.

36450 Exchange transfusion, blood, newborn

36455 other than newborn

* Exchange transfusions performed during the neonatal period are reported using code **36450;** exchange transfusions for all other age groups are reported using code **36455.** The assumption is that the exchange for the neonate is performed via the umbilical vein, while an exchange for an older child or adult is performed via a peripheral vessel.

* The actual placement of catheters to support the exchange transfusion may be reported separately with the appropriate vascular access codes.

* Partial exchange transfusions for hyperviscosity syndrome in the neonate should be reported using the code for therapeutic phlebotomy (**99195**). Placement of the catheter may be listed independently.

> ||||||||| **Coding Pearl** |||||||||
>
> The placement of catheters to support exchange transfusions may be reported separately with the appropriate vascular access codes.

Circumcision

54150 Circumcision, using clamp or other device with regional dorsal penile or ring block

* If the circumcision using a clamp or other device is performed without dorsal penile or ring block, append modifier **52** (reduced services) to **54150.**

* Medicare has a global period of 0 assigned to code **54150.** When performing a circumcision and a separately identifiable E/M service on the same day (eg, **99462** [subsequent normal newborn care] or **99238** [discharge services <30 minutes]), append modifier **25** to the E/M code. Link the appropriate *ICD-9-CM* code (eg, **V30.0**) or *ICD-10-CM* code (eg, **Z38.00**) to the E/M service and link *ICD-9-CM* code **V50.2** or *ICD-10-CM* code **Z41.2** to the circumcision code.

54160 Circumcision, surgical excision other than clamp, device, or dorsal slit; neonate (28 days of age or less)

54161 older than 28 days

Medicare has a global period of 10 assigned to codes **54160** and **54161.**

When circumcisions are performed in the office

* If a payer does not base payment on RBRVS, a supply code for the surgical tray can be reported with code **99070**. The description of the supply (circumcision tray) would need to be included on the claim form.

* Anesthetic creams (eutectic mixture of local anesthetics) are included in the circumcision code itself and should not be reported unless a third-party payer pays for topical anesthetic agents. In that case, it would be reported with code **99070**.

Coding Conundrum: Lysis/Excision of Labial or Penile Adhesions

Code **54450** (foreskin manipulation including lysis of preputial adhesions and stretching) does not require general anesthesia. It has a relative value unit (RVU) of 1.97 when performed in a non-facility setting (eg, office). Medicare has assigned it a 0-day global surgery period. This procedure is performed on the uncircumcised foreskin and the head of the penis. Adhesions are broken by stretching the foreskin back over the head of the penis onto the shaft or by inserting a clamp between the foreskin and the head of the penis and spreading the jaws of the clamp.

Code **54162** (lysis or excision of penile post-circumcision adhesions) is only reported when lysis is performed under general anesthesia or regional block, with an instrument, and under sterile conditions. This code has a RVU of 7.23 when performed in a non-facility setting (eg, office) and Medicare 10-day global surgery period, which your payer may or may not use. If post-circumcision adhesions are manually broken during the postoperative period by the physician or physician of the same group and specialty who performed the procedure, it would be considered as part of the global surgical package. Report the service with *ICD-9-CM* code **605** (redundant prepuce and phimosis) or, after transition to *ICD-10-CM*, code **N47.0,** adherent prepuce, newborn.

Code **56441** (lysis of labial adhesions) is performed by using a blunt instrument or scissors under general or local anesthesia. The total RVUs for this procedure in a non-facility setting are 4.1. This procedure also includes a Medicare 10-day global surgery period, which may or may not be used by your payer. *ICD-9-CM* code **752.49** (other anomalies of cervix, vagina, and external genitalia) or *ICD-10-CM* code **Q52.5** (fusion of labia) would be reported with *CPT*® code **56441.**

If lysis of labial or penile adhesions is performed by the application of manual pressure without the use of an instrument to cut the adhesions, it would be considered part of the E/M visit and would not be reported separately.

Sedation

Moderate Sedation

- ☀ Moderate sedation is a drug-induced depression of consciousness. No interventions are required to maintain a patent airway, and spontaneous ventilation is adequate. Moderate sedation does not include minimal sedation (anxiolysis), deep sedation, or monitored anesthesia care (**00100–01999**). Moderate sedation includes the following:
  - ❖ Assessment of the patient
  - ❖ Establishment of intravenous (IV) access and fluids
  - ❖ Administration of the agent
  - ❖ Maintenance of sedation
  - ❖ Monitoring oxygen saturation, heart rate, and blood pressure
  - ❖ Recovery
- ☀ The service time included in the code descriptions starts at the time of the administration of the sedation agent.
- ☀ Oxygen saturation (**94760–94762**) cannot be reported separately.
- ☀ Codes **99143–99150** are distinguished by service provider, patient age, and time spent (Table 12-5).
- ☀ Cannot be reported with codes listed in Appendix G of the *CPT*® manual. Those procedures include moderate sedation as an inherent part of the procedure.
- ☀ If a medically necessary, significant, and separately identifiable E/M service had

Coding Pearl

Codes listed in Appendix G of *CPT* may not be reported with codes **99143–99145**.

also been performed, an E/M visit with modifier **25** appended could be reported.

☀ The agent itself may also be reported.

Table 12-5. Moderate Sedation		
Moderate Sedation	**First 30 Minutes Intra-service Time**	**Each Additional 15 Minutes Intra-service Time**
Moderate sedation services (other than those services described by codes **00100–01999**) provided by the same physician performing the diagnostic or therapeutic service that the sedation supports, requiring the presence of an independent trained observer to assist in the monitoring of the patient's level of consciousness and physiological status; younger than 5 years	99143	+99145
5 years or older	99144	+99145
Moderate sedation services (other than those services described by codes **00100–01999**) provided by a physician other than the health care professional performing the diagnostic or therapeutic service that the sedation supports; younger than 5 years	99148	+99150
5 years or older	99149	+99150

Codes **99143–99145** are reported when

☀ The administration of moderate (conscious) sedation is provided by the physician who is simultaneously performing a procedure (eg, fracture reduction, vessel cutdown, central line placement, wound repair).

☀ An independent trained observer is present to assist the physician in the monitoring of the patient during the procedure or diagnostic service.

☀ The procedure performed is not listed in Appendix G of *CPT®* and does not include conscious sedation as an inherent part of the procedure.

Codes **99148–99150** are reported when

☀ A second physician other than the health care professional performing the diagnostic or therapeutic services provides moderate (conscious) sedation.

☀ Performed with the procedures identified in Appendix G in the *CPT®* manual only if provided in a facility setting (eg, hospital, outpatient hospital/ambulatory surgery center, skilled nursing facility) in cases requiring a higher intensity of work than normal. If one physician provides moderate sedation and another physician performs the procedure in a non-facility setting, codes **99148–99150** cannot be reported when the procedure has been identified in Appendix G in the *CPT* manual.

Note: Documentation must include the description of the procedure, name and dosages of the sedation agent(s), route of administration of the sedation agent(s), and who administered the agent (physician or independent observer); the ongoing assessment of the child's level of consciousness and physiological (eg, heart rate, oxygen saturation levels) status during and after the procedure; and the presence, name, and title of the independent observer and total time from administration of the sedation agent(s) (start time) until the physician's face-to-face service is no longer required (end time).

Chapter 12: Common Procedures and Non–Evaluation and Management Medical Services

Table 12-6 helps clarify the reporting guidelines.

Codes	May Report 99143–99145 in a Facility	May Report 99143–99145 in a Non-facility	May Report 99148–99150 in a Facility	May Report 99148–99150 in a Non-facility
Table 12-6. Moderate (Conscious) Sedation Reporting Guidelines				
Listed in Appendix G	No	No	Yes	No
All other *CPT* codes	Yes	Yes	Yes	Yes

Abbreviation: CPT, Current Procedural Terminology.

Examples

➤ **A 24-month-old requires a layered closure of a 2.5-cm laceration of the right knee.** Moderate sedation is required and is performed by the Pediatric Advanced Life Support–trained physician with an independent trained observer who has been trained in pediatric basic life support. The physician supervises the administration of the sedating agent and assesses the child until an effective, safe level of sedation is achieved and continues to assess the child's level of consciousness and physiological status while performing the laceration repair. The procedure, from the time of administration of the agent until the physician completes the repair and determines that the child is stable and face-to-face physician time is no longer required, takes a total of 30 minutes.

12031 (intermediate repair of wound of extremities, 2.5 cm or less)
99143 (moderate [conscious] sedation, patient younger than 5 years, 30 minutes)

ICD-9-CM
891.0 (open wound, knee, without mention of complication) or **891.1** (with complication)

ICD-10-CM
S81.011A (laceration without foreign body, right knee, initial encounter)

➤ **A 5-year-old hospitalized child needs insertion of a tunneled central venous catheter (36558).** A second physician will provide the moderate sedation while the first physician performs the procedure. The sedating physician administers the agent(s) and assesses the patient continuously until a safe level of moderate sedation is achieved. He or she monitors the child closely and administers additional doses of sedating and/or analgesic agent(s) as needed. The service, from the time of administration of the agent until determination that the child is stable and face-to-face physician time is no longer required, takes a total of 35 minutes. The physician providing the moderate sedation will report

99149 (moderate [conscious] sedation services, patient 5 years or older, 30 minutes)

Appropriate diagnosis code

Deep Sedation

Pediatricians who provide deep sedation services for procedures performed outside the operating suite should follow the same anesthesia policies and coding instructions as other providers of anesthesia services. *Current Procedural Terminology* codes for reporting anesthesia services, including deep sedation, monitored anesthesia care, or general anesthesia, are **00100–01999.** These codes are not as specific as codes for other services and generally identify a body area or type of procedure.

Examples

00102	Anesthesia for procedures involving plastic repair of cleft lip
01820	Anesthesia for all closed procedures on radius, ulna, wrist, or hand bones

      Add-on codes may be reported to identify special circumstances that increase the complexity of providing anesthesia care. Special circumstances include

99100	Patient under 1 year or older than 70 years (not reported in conjunction with codes **00326, 00561, 00834,** or **00836**)
99116	Anesthesia complicated by total body hypothermia
99135	Anesthesia complicated by controlled hypotension
99140	Emergency conditions

      Emergency is defined by *CPT* as a situation in which delay in treatment of the patient would lead to a significant increase in the threat to life or body part.

      Modifiers are reported in addition to anesthesia codes to indicate the physical status of the patient. The American Society of Anesthesiologists classification of the patient's physical status is represented by the following HCPCS modifiers:

P1	Normal healthy patient
P2	Patient with mild systemic disease
P3	Patient with severe systemic disease
P4	Patient with severe systemic disease that is a constant threat to life
P5	Moribund patient who is not expected to survive without the operation
P6	Declared brain-dead patient whose organs are being removed for donor purposes

      Other modifiers that may be required by payers for anesthesia services by pediatric physicians are those identifying the type of anesthesia or anesthesia provider.

AA	Anesthesia services performed personally by anesthesiologist

      Payers may require this modifier for services personally rendered by physicians other than anesthesiologists. This signifies that services were not rendered by a nonphysician provider such as a certified registered nurse anesthetist.

G8	Monitored anesthesia care for deep complex, complicated, or markedly invasive surgical procedure
G9	Monitored anesthesia care for patient who has history of severe cardio-pulmonary condition
QS	Monitored anesthesia care service

      Medicare considers deep sedation equivalent to monitored anesthesia care. Private payers may vary.

GC	This service has been performed in part by a resident under the direction of a teaching physician

      Base units for anesthesia services are published in the American Society of Anesthesiologists *Relative Value Guide* and by the CMS for each anesthesia procedure code. Payers typically do not require reporting of base units on the claim for services.

Chapter 12: Common Procedures and Non–Evaluation and Management Medical Services

- Many private payers will allow additional base units for physical status modifiers **P3** (1 unit), **P4** (2 units), and **P5** (3 units).

- Anesthesia time is reported in minutes unless a payer directs to report units (1 unit per 15 minutes). Start and stop times must be documented, including multiple start and stop times when anesthesia services are discontinuous.

For more information on coding for deep sedation services, please see articles in the April and May 2014 *AAP Pediatric Coding Newsletter*™ at www.coding.aap.org.

Example

> **A child requires placement of a peripherally inserted central catheter.** The pediatric intensivist is consulted to provide deep sedation for the procedure performed by another physician.

00532 Anesthesia for access to central venous circulation   Appropriate diagnosis code

Other Services and Procedures

99170   Anogenital examination, magnified, in childhood for suspected trauma including image recording when performed

Example

> **A 6-year-old girl is brought to the emergency department (ED) by her mother after the mother noted blood in the child's underpants and was concerned about sexual molestation.** The physician performs a comprehensive history and physical examination. Because of the findings on general examination, the physician elects to further examine the child's genitalia with magnification to document findings that may be consistent with abuse or trauma.

99285 (comprehensive ED examination)
99170 (anogenital examination)
If the same physician performs moderate (conscious) sedation, also report code **99144.**

ICD-9-CM
Diagnosis code appropriate to findings after the examination (eg, **959.14,** other injury of external genitals). If the cause of an injury is verified as child abuse, report code **995.53** (child sexual abuse). The first E code reported will be taken from categories **E960.0–E966** or **E968.9** (homicide and injury purposely inflicted by other persons). would be reported. If the perpetrator is known, a code from category **E967** (child and adult battering and other maltreatment) should be reported as an

ICD-10-CM
Report confirmed abuse with an appropriate injury code such as **S39.848A,** initial encounter for other specified injuries of external genitals; **T74.22XA,** child sexual abuse, confirmed; a code from categories **X92–Y06** or **Y08** for assault; and a code from category **Y07** to identify the perpetrator of assault. If abuse is suspected but not confirmed, report a code for injury and **T76.22XA,** child sexual abuse, suspected. If there are no findings, report **Z04.42,** encounter for examination

Transitioning to **10**

additional code. If abuse cannot be confirmed, code **V71.81** (observation and evaluation for suspected abuse and neglect) would be reported. If there are no findings, code **V71.5** (observation and evaluation for alleged rape or seduction, not found) would be reported.

and observation following alleged child rape or sexual abuse.

Gastric Intubation and Aspiration

43753   Gastric intubation and aspiration(s), therapeutic (eg, for ingested poisons), including lavage if performed

Example

➤ **A 10-year-old is brought to the ED after having ingested drugs.** Gastric intubation and lavage are performed.

Code **43753** would be reported in addition to the appropriate E/M service but is not separately reported when performed in conjunction with critical care (eg, **99291–99292, 99468–99476**) or when performed by a physician during pediatric patient transport (**99466–99467**).

Immune Globulins

When reporting codes **90281–90399,** remember that they are only for the cost of the immunoglobulin (Ig) and the appropriate separate administration code should also be reported (eg, **96372, 96374**). A significant, separately identifiable E/M service performed during the same visit may also be billed if indicated. Most Igs are reported with *ICD-9-CM* code **V07.2.** However, respiratory syncytial virus monoclonal antibody (**90378**), for example, is reported with **V04.82.** *ICD-10-CM* diagnosis codes to support Ig services include codes from categories **D80–D84** for certain disorders involving the immune mechanism or codes for specific conditions such as mucocutaneous lymph node syndrome (**M30.3**). Code **Z23** is used to report an encounter for immunization.

Hearing Screening and Ear, Nose, and Throat Screening/Assessment and Procedure Codes

(*For central auditory function evaluation, see* **92620, 92621.**)
Audiometric tests require the use of calibrated electronic equipment, recording of results, and a written report with interpretation. Services include testing of both ears. If the test is applied to one ear only, modifier **52** (reduced services) must be appended to the code.

☀ Code **92551** (screening test, pure tone, air only) is used when earphones are placed on the patient and the patient is asked to respond to tones of different pitches and intensities. This is a limited study.

> ‖|‖|‖ *Coding Pearl* ‖|‖|‖
>
> Automated audiometry testing is reported with Category III codes **0208T–0212T**. See Chapter 13 for a listing of these codes.

- Code **92552** (full pure tone audiometric assessment) is used when earphones are placed on the patient and the patient is asked to respond to tones of different pitches and intensities. The threshold, which is the lowest intensity of the tone that the patient can hear 50% of the time, is recorded for a number of frequencies. Bone thresholds are obtained in a similar manner (**92553**). Air and bone thresholds are compared to differentiate among conductive, sensorineural, or mixed hearing losses.

- Code **92558** is reported for evoked otoacoustic emissions, screening (qualitative measurement of distortion product or transient evoked otoacoustic emissions), automated analysis. This is a screening procedure typically done by audiologists. Coverage for this is typically limited to newborn screening, including follow-up newborn screening from a failed screen in the hospital and screening on younger children. Check with your payers.

- Code **92583** (select picture audiometry) is typically used for younger children. The patient is asked to identify different pictures with the instructions given at different intensity levels.

- Auditory evoked potentials for evoked response audiometry and/or testing of the central nervous system, comprehensive, is reported with code **92585.** A limited study is reported with code **92586.**

- Distortion product evoked otoacoustic emissions codes are reported based on the number of frequencies used. Code **92587** is used to report testing for confirmation of the presence or absence of a hearing disorder, 3 to 6 frequencies. Code **92588** is reported when a comprehensive (quantitative analysis of outer hair cell function by cochlear mapping) diagnostic evaluation with a minimum of 12 frequencies is performed. A written interpretation and report are required.

- Other commonly performed procedures include codes **92567** (tympanometry [impedance testing]) and **92568** (acoustic reflex testing, threshold portion).

Ear, Nose, and Throat Procedures

30901   Central nasal hemorrhage, anterior, simple (cautery or packing)
   If performing cautery or packing on both sides, report **30901** with modifier **50.**

69420   Myringotomy

92511   Nasopharyngoscopy with endoscope (separate procedure)
- Code **92511** is designated as a "separate procedure" and should not be reported in addition to the code for the total procedure or service of which it is considered an integral component. However, if carried out independently or considered to be unrelated or distinct from other procedures/services provided at that time, it may be reported by itself or in addition to other procedures/services by appending modifier **59** to the specific separate procedure code.

Respiratory Tests and Treatments

- Ventilation assist and management, with initiation of pressure or volume preset ventilators for assisted or controlled breathing, is reported based on the location of the service and whether performed on an initial or subsequent day of service.

- When performed in the hospital or observation setting, report code **94002** for the initial day of care and code **94003** for subsequent day of care.

- Report code **94004** for the initial or subsequent daily care provided in the nursing home.
- Services include determining ventilator settings, establishing a plan of care, and providing ongoing monitoring.
- Ventilator management includes all of the E/M services (physical examination, review of the medical record or diagnostic tests performed, counseling the patient and/or parents, coordinating care with other health care professionals, and documenting the medical record) performed by the physician responsible for providing the ventilation management.

> ||||||||| **Coding Pearl** |||||||||
>
> Ventilator management includes all of the E/M services performed by the responsible physician.

- Codes **94002–94004** are not reported when performed in conjunction with an E/M service (**99201–99499**).
  - ❖ Initiation and management of continuous positive airway pressure (CPAP) is reported with code **94660** (CPAP ventilation, initiation and management); initiation and management of continuous negative pressure ventilation is reported with code **94662,** not codes **94002–94005.**
  - ❖ Ventilation assist and management is a bundled component of all critical care and neonatal and pediatric intensive care services (codes **99291** and **99292, 99466–99476,** and **99477–99480**).
  - ❖ Endotracheal intubation (**31500**) may be reported separately when performed in addition to ventilation assist and management.
- Concurrent care may be reported by physicians from different practices (usually, but not always, different specialties) when services are medically necessary. Each physician should only submit the diagnosis(es) for which he or she is managing the patient. The diagnosis code reported should reflect the need for the services and the physician's role in the care and management of the patient.
- Code **94005** (home ventilator management care plan oversight of patient [patient not present] in home, domiciliary, or rest home) is used to report home ventilator management care plan oversight. It may only be reported when 30 or more minutes of care plan oversight is provided within a calendar month. See Chapter 11 for a full description of requirements for reporting care plan oversight services.

Examples

> **A 4-year-old is admitted in acute respiratory distress.** The pediatric pulmonologist is called and performs a history and physical examination, reviews the diagnostic study results, counsels the parents, discusses the case with the pediatrician, and initiates ventilator support.

94002 (initial ventilator management)

ICD-9-CM
518.82 (acute respiratory distress)

ICD-10-CM
J80 (acute respiratory distress syndrome)

Transitioning to **10**

> **A pediatric pulmonologist is providing ventilator management care plan oversight of a 2-year-old with spinal muscular atrophy who is cared for at home.** The patient's pediatrician also provides care plan oversight services to manage the patient. Each physician maintains a care plan oversight service log that includes documentation of the activities performed and time spent on each activity. The pulmonologist spent 35 minutes providing ventilator management oversight in December. The pediatrician spent 25 minutes providing home care plan oversight services.

Chapter 12: Common Procedures and Non-Evaluation and Management Medical Services

The pediatric pulmonologist would report code **94005** for his 35 minutes of oversight services. The pediatrician would report code **99339** (care plan oversight, home, 15–29 minutes). Each physician would report the appropriate *ICD-9-CM* or *ICD-10-CM* code(s) for the diagnosis and/or conditions that were treated.

Pulmonary Function Tests

The National Correct Coding Initiative (NCCI) edit file was updated January 1, 2014. Edits now exist between office-based E/M services and all pulmonology services (**94010–94799**). Append modifier **25** to the E/M service as appropriate when also reporting a pulmonology service on the same claim. Refer to Chapter 3 for more information on coding edits.

There is no code for peak flow analysis. It is considered part of the E/M service and/or a component of pulmonary function testing.

> ||||||| **Coding Pearl** |||||||
>
> *CPT* code **94060** includes spirometry and pre- and post-bronchodilation. Do not report code **94060** with **94010** or **94640** when they are a component of code **94060**.

- Codes include laboratory procedure(s) and interpretation of test results. If a separately identifiable E/M service is performed, the appropriate E/M service code may also be reported.
- When spirometry is performed before and after administration of a bronchodilator, report **94060** (bronchodilation responsiveness, spirometry as in **94010,** pre- and post-bronchodilator administration) only. Code **94640** (nebulizer treatment) is inherent to (ie, included as part of) code **94060**.
- Measurement of vital capacity (**94150**) is a component of spirometry and is only reported when performed alone.
- Measurement of spirometric forced expiratory flows in an infant or child through 2 years of age is reported with code **94011.**
- Code **94012** is used to report measurement of bronchodilation spirometric forced expiratory flows (before and after bronchodilator) in an infant or child.
- Code **94013** is used to report measurement of lung volumes (eg, functional residual capacity, expiratory reserve volume, forced vital capacity) in an infant or child through 2 years of age.
- Report pulse oximetry (**94760** [noninvasive ear or pulse oximetry for oxygen saturation; single determination] and **94761** [multiple determinations]) because *CPT*® guidelines allow reporting the services, services may be paid if they are the only service received (according to the NCCI), some payers do allow payment, and a practice needs to be aware of all services that are performed and monitor associated costs. See Chapter 3 for a detailed explanation of NCCI edits.

Neonatal Car Seat/Bed Testing for Airway Integrity

94780   Car seat/bed testing for airway integrity, neonate, with continual nursing observation and continuous recording of pulse oximetry, heart rate, and respiratory rate, with interpretation and report; 60 minutes

+94781   each additional full 30 minutes (List separately in addition to code for primary procedure.)

See Chapter 10 for reporting instructions.

Inhalation

Report code **94640** (pressurized or non-pressurized inhalation treatment for acute airway obstruction or for sputum induction for diagnostic service [nebulizer, metered-dose inhaler (MDI), or intermittent positive-pressure breathing (IPPB)])

☀ When treatment such as aerosol generator, nebulizer, MDI, or IPPB device is administered.

☀ With modifier **76** (repeat procedure) with the number of units when more than one treatment is given on a date of service. Some payers require reporting with the number of units only and no modifier. Follow payer guidelines for reporting these services.

☀ When any treatment of less than 30 minutes is performed.

At the time of publication, NCCI edit policy does not allow for code **94640** to be reported more than once per patient encounter. The American Academy of Pediatrics (AAP) is working with NCCI edit staff to change this policy.

Report code **94644** (continuous inhalation treatment with aerosol medication for acute airway obstruction; first hour) and **94645** (each additional hour) when

☀ A treatment lasts 31 minutes or longer.

☀ The total time spent in the provision of continuous inhalation treatments is documented in the medical record.

Codes **94644** and **94645** are not reported by physicians when services are provided in a facility setting because no physician work value is assigned to these codes.

Report code **94664** (demonstration and/or evaluation of patient utilization of an aerosol generator, nebulizer, MDI, or IPPB device) when an initial or subsequent demonstration and/or evaluation is performed and documented. This code is intended to be reported only once per day.

Note that peak flow analysis and administration of oxygen do not have *CPT* codes. They are inherent to E/M services.

Coding Conundrum: Reporting 94664 With 94640

When the physician or nurse (of the same group and specialty) performs demonstration and/or evaluation of patient use of a nebulizer (**94664**) on the same day as a nebulizer treatment (**94640**), modifier **59** (distinct procedural service) should be appended to code **94664** to indicate to the payer that the services were separate and distinct and that both were clinically indicated. Per the 2014 Medicaid NCCI manual, the demonstration and/or evaluation described by code **94664** is included in code **94640** if it utilizes the same device (eg, aerosol generator) that is used in the performance of *CPT* code **94640.** The NCCI edits pair code **94664** with **94640** but allow an override of the edit with modifier **59** when the services are indicated. However, as currently written, some payers may not allow the use of modifier **59** in this instance because the 2 services did not occur at separate encounters. Check with your Medicaid providers.

Modifier **25** should be appended to the E/M service to signify a separately identifiable service. All services must be documented in the medical record as significant, separately identifiable, and medically necessary.

Chapter 12: Common Procedures and Non–Evaluation and Management Medical Services

Examples

➤ **A 6-year-old established patient with asthma arrives in acute exacerbation.** Pulse oximetry is performed and one nebulizer treatment given via a small volume nebulizer (SVN); physical examination after first treatment shows decreased wheezing and work of breathing. The nurse documents her evaluation of use and education for home use of the MDI. An order is written for continuing treatments at home, evaluation and education in use of MDI, and return to the office as needed. Later the same day, the patient returns again in acute exacerbation. A second nebulizer treatment is given by SVN. Physical examination after the second treatment shows no improvement and the patient is hypoxic. He is sent to the hospital to be admitted to observation by the hospitalist. Diagnosis is acute exacerbation of mild persistent asthma with hypoxemia.

99212–99215 25 (office/outpatient E/M, established patient)

94640 76 × 2 units or **94640** × 2 (nebulizer treatments × 2)

94664 59 (MDI demonstration) Medication (See HCPCS codes listed in this chapter.)

94760 (pulse oximetry)

ICD-9-CM

493.02 (extrinsic asthma with acute exacerbation)

799.02 (hypoxemia)

ICD-10-CM

J45.31 (mild persistent asthma with acute exacerbation)

R09.02 (hypoxemia)

Transitioning to 10

Teaching Point: Modifier **59** appended to **94664** indicates that the MDI demonstration is reported in addition to nebulizer treatments provided via a different device.

➤ **A 12-year-old with severe exacerbation of mild persistent asthma is seen in the physician's office.** The patient is placed on continuous bronchodilator therapy for an hour and a half. The patient is monitored closely during the procedure. Medical record documentation supports the total time of the treatment and frequent assessments.

99212–99215 25 (office/outpatient E/M, established patient)

94644

94645

Medication (See HCPCS codes listed in this chapter.)

ICD-9-CM

493.02

ICD-10-CM

J45.31

Transitioning to 10

Pediatric Home Apnea Monitoring

❋ Report code **94772** when circadian respiratory pattern recording (pediatric pneumogram), 12- to 24-hour continuous recording, is performed on an infant.

❋ Codes **94774–94777** are reported once per 30-day period.

❋ Codes **94774** and **94777** are reported by the physician.

❖ Code **94774** (pediatric home apnea monitoring event recording including respiratory rate, pattern, and heart rate per 30-day period; includes monitor attachment, download of data, physician review and interpretation, and preparation of a report) is reported by the physician when he or she orders home monitoring, chooses the monitor limits, and arranges for a home health care provider to teach the parents. It includes reviewing and interpreting data and preparation of the report.

❖ Code **94777** (physician review, interpretation, and preparation of report only) is reported when the physician receives the downloaded information on disc or hard copy, reviews the patterns and periods of abnormal respiratory or heart rate, and summarizes in a written report the findings and recommendations for continuation or discontinuation of monitoring. This information is provided to the primary care physician and/or the family.

☀ Codes **94775** (monitor attachment only including hookup, initiation of recording, and disconnection) and **94776** (monitoring, download of information, receipt of transmission[s], and analyses by computer only) are reported by the home health agency because there is no physician work involved.

  ❖ Code **94775** is reported by the home health agency and includes connecting the child to the monitoring equipment, teaching the family how to connect and disconnect the leads, checking the proper function of the equipment, responding to alarms, and resetting the monitor.

  ❖ Code **94776** is reported when the monitor is downloaded by the home health care agency and converted to a hard copy or CD-ROM and provided to the interpreting physician.

  ❖ Codes **94774–94777** are not reported in conjunction with codes **93224–93272** (electrocardiographic monitoring). The apnea recording device cannot be reported separately. When oxygen saturation monitoring is used in addition to heart rate and respiratory monitoring, it is not reported separately.

Example

➤ **An infant born at 23 weeks' gestation, now 2 months old, has chronic lung disease and requires prolonged low-flow oxygen.** She continues to have occasional episodes of self-stimulated apnea lasting less than 15 seconds. Her physicians and parents are concerned about the possibility of unwitnessed prolonged apnea requiring intervention but agree to have her go home with heart rate and respiratory monitoring during unattended periods and sleep. The physician orders the monitor, contacts the home health agency for its provision, and instructs the home health agency to teach the parents about cardiopulmonary resuscitation, proper attachment of the monitor leads, and resetting of the monitor. The home health agency provides the physician with the downloaded recordings. The first month's data are interpreted by the physician and a written report generated. The physician counsels the parents about the need to continue monitoring.

Report code **94774** and the appropriate *ICD-9-CM* (eg, **327.25** for congenital central alveolar hypoventilation/hypoxemia) or *ICD-10-CM* (eg, **G47.35** for congenital central alveolar hypoventilation/hypoxemia) code.

In subsequent months, the physician receives the downloaded recordings, interprets them, and generates reports with recommendations for continued or discontinuation of monitoring. These services are reported with code **94777.**

Transitioning to **10**

Chapter 12: Common Procedures and Non–Evaluation and Management Medical Services

Allergy and Clinical Immunology

Allergy Testing

- Allergy testing is coded by type of test (percutaneous, immediate type reaction [**95004**], or any combination of percutaneous and intracutaneous, sequential and incremental tests with venoms [**95017**] or with drugs or biologicals [**95018**]) and requires specification of the number of tests applied.

- Codes **95004, 95017, 95018, 95024,** and **95027** include test interpretation and report.

  - Patch and photo patch testing are reported with code **95044–95056.**

  - Specific challenge testing (**95060–95079**) is coded according to target organ (eg, ophthalmic mucous membrane, nasal, inhalation bronchial challenges without pulmonary function testing, ingestion).

  - An E/M service should not be reported for interpretation and report. However, if a significant, separately identifiable E/M service is performed and documented, it may be reported with modifier **25** appended to the appropriate E/M code.

  - Nasal cytology, a test for allergy-type cells (eosinophils) or infection-type cells (neutrophils) on a nasal scraping, is reported with code **89190.**

  - Nitric oxide expired gas determination is reported with *CPT*® code **95012.** Nitric oxide determination by spectroscopy should be reported with code **94799.**

Allergen Immunotherapy

Allergen Immunotherapy, Extract Provided

Immunotherapy administered by the prescribing physician is listed by number of antigens or venoms and by antigen or venom type.

Administration of Extract Only

- Codes **95115** (professional services for allergen immunotherapy not including provision of allergenic extracts; single injection) and **95117** (professional services for allergen immunotherapy not including provision of allergenic extracts; 2 or more injections) are used to report administration of the allergenic extract only.

  - Code **95115** or **95117** (not both) is reported when another health care professional (eg, the patient's allergist) prepares and supplies the allergenic extract or when a physician (usually an allergist) administers the prospectively prepared extract (ie, prepared with the intent to administer on a planned schedule).

- Codes **95144–95170** are used to report preparation and provision of antigens for allergen immunotherapy without administration of the allergenic extract.

  95144   Professional services for the supervision of preparation and provision of antigens for allergen immunotherapy, single-dose vials(s) (specify number of vials)

  95145   Professional services for the supervision of the preparation and provision of antigens for allergy immunotherapy (specify number of doses); single stinging insect venom

||||||| Coding Pearl |||||||

Code **95115** or **95117** is used to report administration of the allergenic extract when it is prepared and supplied by another health care professional; these codes cannot be reported together on the same day for the same patient.

- Codes **95146–95149** are reported for more than one single stinging venom (eg, code **95146** is reported for 2, **95147** for 3).
  - ❖ Codes **95144–95170** describe the preparation of the antigen, the antigen extract itself, the physician's assessment and determination of the concentration and volume to use based on the patient's history and results of previous skin testing, and the prospective planned schedule of administration of the extract.
  - ❖ The number of doses/vials must be specified when reporting these codes.
  - ❖ Services may be reported at the time the allergenic extract is prepared because injections occur on later dates (prospectively planned) or may not occur at all.
  - ❖ Administration of the allergenic extract is not included.
- Codes **95120–95134** are used to report professional services for the preparation and provision of the extract with administration.

95120	Professional services for allergen immunotherapy in the office or institution of the prescribing physician or other qualified health care professional, including provision of allergenic extract; single injection
95125	2 or more injections
95130	single stinging insect venom

- Codes **95131–95134** are reported for more than one single stinging venom (eg, code **95131** is reported for 2, **95132** for 3).

95131	2 stinging insect venoms
95132	3 stinging insect venoms
95133	4 stinging insect venoms
95134	5 stinging insect venoms

  - ❖ Codes **95120–95134** are reported when the entire service of preparing, providing, and administering (injection) allergenic extract are performed at one patient encounter.
  - ❖ Codes **95115** and **95117** *cannot* be reported with codes **95120–95134**.
  - ❖ *Current Procedural Terminology* recommends codes **95120–95134** be reported only when specifically required by the payer.
  - ❖ Codes **95120** and **95125** are reported based on the number of injections administered (ie, a single injection or ≥2 injections). Codes **95130–95134** are reported per injection. Therefore, if 2 separate injections of 2 stinging insect venoms (eg, wasp and bee) are provided, code **95131** would be reported 2 times.
- An appropriate office/outpatient code may be reported with allergen immunotherapy codes. Modifier **25** is appended to the E/M service when it is performed and documented.
- For rapid desensitization per hour, see code **95180**.

Coding Conundrum: CMS Allergen Immunotherapy Guidelines

The CMS Medicare program will only accept codes **95115, 95117,** and **95144–95170** and will not allow payment for codes **95120–95134**. State Medicaid and commercial payers may follow the CMS Medicare guidelines or may have their own established guidelines. Therefore, before reporting these services, research the reporting policies of your major payers.

Examples

➤ **An allergist prepares a 10-dose vial of allergen extract and administers one dose at the time of the visit (allergenic extract was prepared with the intent to administer on a planned schedule).**

The allergist will report code **95165** with 10 units of service and **95115** with 1 unit of service and the specific diagnosis code. Using *ICD-9-CM*, allergic rhinitis due to pollen would be reported with code **477.0;** if due to food, report code **477.1.** Allergic rhinitis due to pollen would be reported with *ICD-10-CM* code **J30.1** or, if due to food, code **J30.5.**

➤ **The pediatrician administers 3 injections of allergen extract for a patient with allergic rhinitis due to pollen.** The extract was prepared and supplied by the allergist.

The pediatrician will report code **95117** with *ICD-9-CM* code **477.0** or with *ICD-10-CM* code **J30.1.**

> **Transitioning to 10**
>
> Allergic rhinitis may also be classified as other seasonal allergic rhinitis (**J30.2**), allergic rhinitis due to animal hair and dander (**J30.81**), or other allergic rhinitis (**J30.89**) that includes perennial allergic rhinitis.

Central Nervous System

Assessment Tests/Developmental Services Codes

These codes are used to report services provided during testing of the cognitive function of the central nervous system. They include use of standardized instruments to screen for and/or assess cognitive, mental status, speech/language, and other areas of development. A written report is required (or written documentation that is made available to other health care professionals). Although any qualified health care professional may report these codes, payers may restrict payment to psychiatrists or other mental health specialists based on the code descriptor and their payment policy for mental health–related services when reported using mental health diagnosis codes.

Codes **96101** (psychological testing [includes psychodiagnostic assessment of emotionality, intellectual abilities, personality, and psychopathology (eg, Minnesota Multiphasic Personality Inventory, Rorschach, Wechsler Adult Intelligence Scale)], per hour of the psychologist's or physician's time, both face-to-face time administering tests to the patient and time interpreting these test results and preparing the report) and **96118** (neuropsychological testing [eg, Halstead-Reitan Neuropsychological Battery, Wechsler Memory Scales, and Wisconsin Card Sorting Test], per hour of the psychologist's or physician's time, both face-to-face time administering tests to the patient and time interpreting test results and preparing the report)

- Are used in those circumstances when additional time is necessary to integrate other sources of clinical data, including previously completed and reported technician- and computer-administered tests, with psychologist/physician testing done as described by **96101/96118.**
- Should not be reported for interpreting or reporting tests administered by a technician (**96102** and **96119**) or computer (**96103** and **96120**) when the psychologist/physician does not perform separate testing. Services reported with codes **96102, 96103, 96119,** and **96120** include any additional necessary time for integration of the test data acquired from the computer or technician testing or other data into the report.

❋ Are reported based on time spent in the provision of the service. Additional units of the code may be reported when time exceeds the average time listed for the service.

Code **96110** (developmental screening/brief assessment with scoring and documentation, per standardized instrument)

❋ Is reported for standardized developmental screening instruments. It is not reported when the pediatrician conducts an informal survey or surveillance of development as part of a comprehensive preventive medicine service (which is considered to be part of the history and is not separately billed).

❋ May be reported for each standardized developmental screening instrument administered.

❋ Includes standardized screening tools such as the Ages & Stages Questionnaire, Australian Scale for Asperger's Syndrome, Modified Checklist for Autism in Toddlers, or Parents' Evaluation of Developmental Status (PEDS). Other tools are also used for developmental screening.

❋ Is not reported for brief emotional or behavioral assessment; see code **96127.**

Code **96111** (developmental testing [includes assessment of motor, language, social, adaptive, and/or cognitive functioning by standardized developmental instruments], with interpretation and report)

❋ Is used by pediatricians with a special interest or special training in developmental and behavioral pediatrics.

❋ Allows reporting of developmental testing in which the child is observed doing standardized tasks that are then scored, with interpretation and report.

❋ Includes assessment of motor, language, social, adaptive, and/or cognitive function by standardized developmental instruments, such as the Bayley Scales of Infant Development.

❋ When reported in conjunction with an E/M service, the time and effort to perform the developmental testing itself should not count toward the key components (history, physical examination, and medical decision-making) or time for selecting the accompanying E/M code level.

❋ Medicare NCCI edits pair code **96111** with E/M services but allow both services when modifier **25** is appended to the medically necessary E/M service. See Chapter 3 for more information on NCCI edits.

❋ For more information on reporting codes **96110** and **96111,** refer to the Developmental Screening/Testing Coding Fact Sheet for Primary Care Pediatricians at www.aap.org/cfp.

Code **96116** (neurobehavioral status examination [clinical assessment of thinking, reasoning, and judgment (eg, acquired knowledge, attention, language, memory, planning, and problem solving), and visual-spatial abilities], per hour of the psychologist's or physician's time, both face-to-face time with the patient and time interpreting test results and preparing the report)

❋ Is used to report a neurobehavioral status examination. This might also include assessment for serious communication/social developmental disorders such as autism spectrum disorder (ASD) through the use of the Autism Diagnostic Observation Schedule.

❋ Mini-mental status examination performed by a physician would be included as part of the nervous system physical examination of an E/M service and not separately reportable.

❋ Documentation of these services includes scoring, observation of behavior, and interpretation and report. It should include the date and time of testing, reason for the test, and titles of all instruments used.

Code **96125** (standardized cognitive performance testing [eg, Ross Information Processing Assessment] per hour of a qualified health care professional's time, both face-to-face time administering tests to the patient and time interpreting these test results and preparing the report)

- Includes standardized cognitive performance testing performed by a qualified health care professional (eg, speech-language pathologists, occupational therapists).

Note that a minimum of 31 minutes must be provided when reporting the per-hour codes (ie, **96101, 96116, 96118,** and **96125**). Services of 30 minutes or less may be reported with modifier **52.** The time reported includes face-to-face time with the patient and time spent interpreting and preparing the report.

Code **96120** (neuropsychological testing [eg, Wisconsin Card Sorting Test], administered by a computer, with qualified health care professional interpretation and report)

- May be reported for computerized testing requiring a technician's oversight (instructs patient on test procedures, provides access to each ordered test, administers pretest trials, and periodically monitors patient progress)
- Includes physician or other qualified health care professional interpretation and report
- Is reported once per session regardless of the number of tests administered

Code **96127** (brief emotional/behavioral assessment [eg, depression inventory, attention-deficit/hyperactivity disorder (ADHD) scale], with scoring and documentation, per standardized instrument)

- Like developmental screening (**96110**), code **96127** represents the practice expense of administering, scoring, and documentation of each standardized instrument. No physician work value is included. Physician interpretation is included in a related E/M service.
- Not reported in conjunction with **99401–99404, 96101–96103,** or **96118–96120.**
- Two separate completions (eg, by teacher and parent) of the same form may be separately reported (ie, 2 units of service).

Examples

▶ **The mother of a 5-year-old expresses her concern about her child's language delay.** The PEDS (a standardized developmental screening instrument) is ordered, completed by the mother, and scored by the nurse. Results indicate concerns only limited to expressive language delay.

The appropriate E/M service code (preventive medicine visit, new or established patient office visit, or consultation) would be reported in addition to code **96110.** The diagnosis, expressive language disorder, would be reported with *ICD-9-CM* code **315.31** or *ICD-10-CM* code **F80.1.**

▶ **The mother of an 8-year-old girl expresses concerns about the child daydreaming and not paying attention at school.** The parent version of a behavior assessment system for children is administered to the mother and scored for the physician's review. The physician recommends that an additional behavioral assessment be completed by the girl's teacher to confirm or rule out predominantly inattentive ADHD.

The appropriate E/M service code (preventive medicine visit, new or established patient office visit, or consultation) would be reported in addition to code **96127.** Because the physician did not diagnose ADHD, assign *ICD-9-CM* code **799.51** or *ICD-10-CM* code **R41.840** for symptoms of attention and concentration deficit.

➤ **A 4-year-old boy is being evaluated for possible autism.** The Autism Diagnostic Observation Schedule is administered, scored, and interpreted in a written report. The diagnosis is autism. The total time for testing, scoring, and report writing is 3 hours.

This service is reported with code **96116** (neurobehavioral status examination).

The diagnosis code would be *ICD-9-CM* code **299.01** (autistic disorder, residual state) or *ICD-10-CM* code **F84.0** (autistic disorder). Depending on payer requirements, the service may be reported as **96116** with 3 units of service or on 3 service lines with modifier **59** appended.

96116

96116 59

96116 59

Transitioning to 10

ICD-10-CM does not differentiate active and residual states of autism.

➤ **A 10-year-old established patient has shown a progressive pattern of academic struggles since the first grade.** He says the fourth-grade work is "too hard." His parents wonder if he is "lazy" or if he may not be "smart enough." His school psychologist says there is no reason for her to do any psychoeducational testing. The physician administers a Kaufman Brief Intelligence Test, Second Edition, and a Wide Range Achievement Test 4 to briefly assess overall cognitive level and academic achievement levels. The tests are scored, interpreted, and discussed with the family in a 40-minute discussion. A concise written report is created for them to take to the school psychologist.

This service is reported with code **99215** (office/outpatient E/M, established patient, based on 40 minutes of counseling time) and **96111** (developmental testing, extended). Modifier **25** is appended to the E/M code to signify that it was significant and separately identifiable.

➤ **A 15-year-old girl is seen in follow-up for a concussion caused by hitting her head against another player's during a soccer match 5 days ago.** The patient requested a release to participate in soccer. Her physician has ordered computerized neuropsychologic testing for comparison to a baseline performed at the start of the school year. A technician instructs the patient about the test program, conducts pretest trials for each test, and monitors the patient's progress as she completes the series of tests. After the tests are completed, the physician interprets the test results and creates a report. Results are discussed with the patient and her caregivers as part of an E/M service that takes place later that day.

This service is reported with code **96120** (neuropsychological testing administered by a computer) and an appropriate E/M code (eg, **99213**). Modifier **25** indicates the E/M was a significant, separately identifiable service from the physician interpretation and report of the neuropsychologic testing.

Chapter 12: Common Procedures and Non–Evaluation and Management Medical Services

Hydration, IV Infusions

Services included as inherent to an infusion or injection are the use of local anesthesia, starting the IV, access to indwelling IV lines or a subcutaneous catheter or port, flushing lines at the conclusion of an infusion or between infusions, standard tubing, syringes and supplies, and preparation of chemotherapy agents.

These codes are intended for reporting by the physician or other qualified health care professional in an office setting. They are not reported by a physician or other qualified health care professional when performed in a facility setting because the physician work associated with these procedures involves only affirmation of the treatment plan and direct supervision of the staff performing the services. If a significant, separately identifiable E/M service is performed, the appropriate code may be reported with modifier **25** appended. The diagnosis may be the same for the E/M service and codes **96360–96379**.

Hydration

Codes **96360** (IV infusion, hydration; initial, 31 minutes to 1 hour) and **96361** (each additional hour)

- Are intended to report IV hydration infusion using prepackaged fluid and/or electrolyte solutions (eg, normal saline, D5-1/2 normal saline with potassium).
- Typically require direct physician supervision for purposes of consent, safety oversight, or supervision of staff with little special handling for preparation or disposal of materials.
- Do not typically require advanced training of staff because there usually is little risk involved with little patient monitoring required.
- Are reported based on the actual time over which the infusion is administered and do not include the time spent starting the IV and monitoring the patient after infusion. Medical record documentation must support the service reported.
- Code **96360** may be reported for hydration infusion lasting more than 31 minutes and up to 1 hour. Code **96361** is reported for each additional hour of hydration infusion and for a final interval of greater than 30 minutes beyond the last hour reported.
- Are not reported when IV infusions are 30 minutes or less.
- Are not used to report infusion of drugs or other substances; nor are they reported when it is incidental to non-chemotherapeutic/diagnostic or chemotherapeutic services.
- Code **96361** is reported if an IV hydration infusion is provided secondary or subsequent to a therapeutic, prophylactic, or diagnostic infusion and administered through the same IV access.

Therapeutic, Prophylactic, and Diagnostic Infusions

96365	Intravenous infusion, for therapy, prophylaxis, or diagnosis (specify substance or drug); initial, up to 1 hour
+96366	each additional hour (List separately in addition to code for primary procedure.)
+96367	additional sequential infusion of a new drug/substance, up to 1 hour (List separately in addition to code for primary procedure.)
+96368	concurrent infusion (List separately in addition to code for primary procedure.)

Codes **96365–96368**

☀ Are for infusions for the purpose of administering drugs or substances.

☀ Typically require direct physician supervision and special attention to prepare, calculate dose, and dispose of materials.

☀ If fluid infusions are used to administer the drug(s), they are considered incidental hydration and are not reported.

☀ Each drug administered is reported separately with the appropriate infusion code.

> **|||||||| Coding Pearl |||||||||**
>
> Short infusions of less than 15 minutes should be reported with code **96374**.

Table 12-7. Hydration, Injection, and IV Codes to Be Reported as Primary and Additional Codes

Primary Code	Additional Codes
96360	96361
96365	96366, 96367, 96368, 96375, 96376[a]
96367	96366
96366	96368
96369	96370, 96371
96374	96367, 96375, 96376[a]
96409	96367, 96375, 96376[a]
96413	96367, 96368, 96375, 96376[a]
96415	96368
96416	96368

Abbreviation: IV, intravenous.

[a]Code is only to be reported in the facility setting.

Coding Conundrum: Multiple and Concurrent Infusions or Injections

When administering multiple infusions, injections, or combinations, only one "initial" service code should be reported for a given date, unless protocol requires that 2 separate IV sites must be used. Do not report a second initial service on the same date due to an IV line requiring a restart, an IV rate not being able to be reached without 2 lines, or accessing a port of a multi-lumen catheter. If an injection or infusion is of a subsequent or concurrent nature, even if it is the first such service within that group of services, a subsequent or concurrent code from the appropriate section should be reported. For example, the first IV push given subsequent to an initial 1-hour infusion is reported using a subsequent IV push code.

When services are performed in the physician's office, report as follows:

Initial Infusion

Physician reporting: Report the code that best describes the *key* or *primary* reason for the service regardless of the order in which the infusions or injections occur. Only one initial service code (eg, **96365**) should be reported unless the protocol or patient condition requires using 2 separate IV sites. The difference in time and effort in providing this second IV site access is also reported using the *initial* service code with modifier **59**, distinct procedural service, appended (eg, **96365, 96365 59**).

Facility reporting: An initial infusion is based on the hierarchy. Only one initial service code (eg, **96365**) should be reported unless the protocol or patient condition requires using 2 separate IV sites. The difference in time and effort in providing this second

Chapter 12: Common Procedures and Non–Evaluation and Management Medical Services

Coding Conundrum: Multiple and Concurrent Infusions or Injections, continued

IV site access is also reported using the *initial* service code with modifier **59**, distinct procedural service, appended (eg, **96365, 96365 59**).

Sequential Infusion

This is an infusion or IV push of a new substance or drug following a primary or initial service. For example, if an IV push was performed through the same IV access subsequent to an IV infusion for therapy, the appropriate codes to report would be **96365** and **96375**. If an IV push was performed through a different IV access route, the services would be reported using codes **96365** and **96374**. Sequential infusions are reported only one time for the same infusate. However, if additional hours were required for the infusion, the appropriate "each additional hour" add-on code would be reported. Different infusates can be reported using the same code as the original sequential code. Hydration may not be reported concurrently with any other service. All sequential services require that there be a new substance or drug, except that facilities may report a sequential IV push of the same drug using **96376**.

Concurrent Infusion

This is an infusion of a new substance or drug infused at the same time as another drug or substance. This is not time-based and is only reported once per day regardless of whether a new drug or substance is administered concurrently. Hydration may not be reported concurrently with any other service. A separate subsequent concurrent administration of another new drug or substance (the third substance or drug) is not reported.

If IV hydration (**96360, 96361**) is given from 11:00 pm to 2:00 am, code **96360** would be reported once and **96361** with 2 units of service. However, if instead of a continuous infusion, a medication were given by IV push at 10:00 pm and 2:00 am, both administrations would be reported as initial (**96374**) because the services are not continuous. For continuous services that last beyond midnight, use the date in which the service began and report the total units of time provided continuously. Although in conflict with *CPT®* guidelines, some payers may require that the primary infusion code be reported for each day of service. See Table 12-7.

Therapeutic, Prophylactic, and Diagnostic Injections

Codes **96374** (therapeutic, prophylactic, or diagnostic injection [specify substance or drug]; IV push, single or initial substance/drug) and **96375** (each additional sequential IV push of a new substance/drug)

- Are only used when the health care professional administering the substance/drug is in constant attendance during the administration *and* must observe the patient. The IV push must be less than 15 minutes.
- Short infusions of less than 15 minutes are reported as a push (eg, **96374**).

Codes **96372–96374**

- Report code **96372** for the administration of a diagnostic, prophylactic or therapeutic (eg, antibiotic) subcutaneous or intramuscular injection. Do not report for the administration of a purified protein derivative (PPD) test.
- Report code **96373** for an initial intra-arterial injection and **96374** for an initial injection administered by IV push. Sequential IV push of a new substance or drug is reported with add-on code **96375**. Code **96375** may be reported in addition to codes for IV infusion (**93635**), initial IV push (**96374**), or chemotherapy administration (**96409, 96413**). Additional sequential IV push of the same substance or drug (**96376**) is reported only by a facility.

Each drug administered is reported separately with the appropriate infusion code.

Example

➤ **A 3-year-old established patient is seen with a complaint of vomiting and fever for the past 24 hours.** She has refused all food and liquids and last voided 12 hours prior to the visit. A detailed history and physical examination with moderate-level medical decision-making are performed. Her diagnosis is bilateral acute suppurative otitis media and dehydration. Intravenous fluids are initiated with normal saline, and IV ceftriaxone (750 mg) is infused over 30 minutes for her otitis media. After 1 hour and 45 minutes of IV hydration, she urinates, begins tolerating liquids, and is released to home.

99214 25 (established patient office E/M)
96365 (IV infusion, for therapy)
96361 (IV infusion, hydration, each additional hour)
J0696 (ceftriaxone sodium, per 250 mg); 3 units
J7030 (infusion, normal saline solution, 1,000 cc)

ICD-9-CM
276.51 (dehydration)
382.9 (otitis media unspecified)

ICD-10-CM
E86.0 (dehydration)
H66.003 (acute suppurative otitis media without spontaneous rupture of ear drum, bilateral)

> **Transitioning to 10**
>
> When reporting otitis media with *ICD-10-CM*, documentation elements include laterality, incidence (ie, acute or chronic), type (eg, serous, allergic, suppurative), and tympanic membrane status (ie, with or without spontaneous rupture).

Link the appropriate diagnosis code to each procedure (eg, code **382.9** is linked to code **J0696**). The medication and infusion solution may need to be reported with the National Drug Code (NDC) if required by the payer.

The fluid used to administer ceftriaxone is not reported because it is considered incidental hydration.

Other Injection and Infusion Services

96523   Irrigation of implanted venous access device for drug delivery systems

Code **96523** is used to report irrigation required for implanted venous access devices for drug delivery systems when services are provided on a separate day from the injection or infusion service. Do not report **96523** in conjunction with other services.

Miscellaneous Services

Hospital Mandated On-Call Services

99026   Hospital mandated on-call service; in-hospital, each hour
99027   out of hospital, each hour

- ☀ Codes **99026** and **99027** describe services provided by a physician who is on call per hospital mandate as a condition of medical staff privileges.
- ☀ Used to report on-call time spent by the physician when he or she is not providing other services.
- ☀ Time spent performing separately reportable services should not be included in time reported as mandated on-call services.
- ☀ Most payers do not cover these services because they consider this a contract issue between the hospital and physician.

Chapter 12: Common Procedures and Non–Evaluation and Management Medical Services

Administrative Services

Codes in this section cover some of the administrative aspects of medical practice.

Codes **99071–99075** are for administrative services.

☀ Code **99071** may be reported when the physician incurs costs for educational supplies and provides them to the patient at his or her cost.

☀ Code **99075** may be reported when a physician presents medical testimony before a court or other administrative body.

Physician group education services

☀ Code **99078** is used to report physician educational services provided to established patients in group settings (eg, obesity classes, diabetes classes).

❖ There are no time requirements.

❖ Modifier **25** (significant, separately identifiable E/M service) should *not* be appended to the E/M service because **99078** is an adjunct service.

❖ Documentation in each medical record includes the education and training provided, follow-up for ongoing education, and total time of the education.

❖ Services are reported on each participating child.

❖ Payers may require that these services be reported differently.

Other administrative services

99082   Unusual travel (eg, transportation and escort of patient)

99090   Analysis of clinical data stored in computers (eg, electrocardiogram [ECG], blood pressure, hematologic data)

99091   Collection and interpretation of physiological data (eg, ECG, blood pressure, glucose monitoring) digitally stored and/or transmitted by the patient and/or caregiver to the physician or other qualified health care professional, requiring a minimum of 30 minutes of time (Do not report more than once in a 30-day period.)

☀ With the exception of code **99091,** none of these services are assigned Medicare RVUs.

☀ Healthcare Common Procedure Coding System code **S9981** (medical records copying fee, administrative) or **S9982** (medical record copying fee, per page) may be reported in lieu of code **99080** (insurance forms or other medical reports above and beyond the information conveyed in the usual insurance form). Commercial payers and some Medicaid programs may accept S codes.

☀ State medical insurance departments or medical associations determine the amount that a practice can charge for copying medical records. Be sure to know the state charge limitations and do not overcharge.

Supplies and Materials

99070   Supplies and materials provided by the physician over and above those usually included with the office visit or other services rendered

☀ Items such as elastic wraps, clavicle splints, or circumcision and suturing trays may be reported with this code. Remember that some supplies (eg, suturing trays, circumcision trays) may be included with the surgical procedure if the payer uses RBRVS as its basis for payment.

☀ Only the supplies purchased in an office-based practice may be reported.

||||||| **Coding Pearl** |||||||

If reporting code **99070**, identify the supplies or materials on the claim form and be prepared to submit an invoice.

❋ Some payers will require the use of HCPCS codes. More specific HCPCS codes are available for a number of supplies (eg, codes **Q4001–Q4051** for cast and splint supplies). Use HCPCS codes when they are more specific.

HCPCS Codes

Medications

A9150	Nonprescription drugs
J8498	Antiemetic drug, rectal/suppository (not otherwise specified [NOS])
J8499	Prescription drug, oral, non-chemotherapeutic (NOS)
J7030–J7120	Infusions (eg, normal saline solution)
J8540	Dexamethasone, oral, 0.25 mg
J8597	Oral antiemetic drug (NOS)

||||||||| **Coding Pearl** |||||||||

You can find a list of NDCs at www.accessdata.fda.gov/scripts/cder/ndc/default.cfm.

See Table 12-8 for a list of the most commonly used J codes.

❋ The practice must have incurred a cost for the medication reported.

❋ Most payers do not cover services reported with nonspecific codes.

❋ Check with payers to determine if they accept these HCPCS codes or if they require reporting with code **99070.**

❋ Drugs are listed with a base dosage. When the dosage exceeds the amount listed, report additional units for the total dosage administered.

❋ Some payers require use of the NDC instead of or in addition to J codes.

❖ The NDCs are universal product identifiers for prescription drugs and insulin products. Codes are 10-digit, 3-segment numbers that identify the product, labeler, and trade package size. The Health Insurance Portability and Accountability Act of 1996 standards require an 11-digit code. If you are not currently reporting injectables with NDCs, be sure to coordinate the requirements with your billing software company. For more information on NDC codes, visit www.fda.gov/Drugs/InformationOnDrugs/ucm142438.htm or link through www.aap.org/cfp.

Table 12-8. Common J Codes[a]

Inhalation Solution		J Code	Administration
Albuterol, inhalation solution, FDA-approved final product, noncompounded, administered through DME, concentrated form, 1 mg	Proventil, Ventolin	J7611	**94640** or **94644** (for first hour)
Levalbuterol, inhalation solution, FDA-approved final product, noncompounded, administered through DME, concentrated form, 0.5 mg	Xopenex	J7612	**94640** or **94644** (for first hour)
Albuterol, inhalation solution, FDA-approved final product, noncompounded, administered through DME, unit dose, 1 mg	AccuNeb, Proventil, Ventolin	J7613	**94640** or **94644** (for first hour)
Levalbuterol, inhalation solution, FDA-approved final product, noncompounded, administered through DME, unit dose, 0.5 mg	Xopenex	J7614	**94640** or **94644** (for first hour)

Table 12-8. Common J Codes[a], continued

Inhalation Solution, continued		J Code	Administration
Levalbuterol, inhalation solution, compounded, administered through DME, unit dose, 0.5 mg	Levalbuterol HCl	J7615	**94640** or **94644** (for first hour)
Albuterol, up to 2.5 mg, and ipratropium bromide, up to 0.5 mg, FDA-approved final product, noncompounded, administered through DME	Albuterol, DuoNeb, Ipratropium bromide	J7620	**94640** or **94644** (for first hour)
Budesonide, inhalation solution, FDA-approved final product, noncompounded, administered through DME, unit dose form, up to 0.5 mg	Pulmicort	J7626	**94640** or **94644** (for first hour)
Budesonide, inhalation solution, compounded product, administered through DME, unit dose form, up to 0.5 mg	Pulmicort Respules	J7627	**94640** or **94644** (for first hour)
Injection		**J Code**	**Administration**
Epinephrine, 0.1 mg	Adrenalin chloride Sus-Phrine	J0171	**96372**
Ampicillin, 500 mg	Omnipen-N Totacillin-N	J0290	(IV)[b] **96372** (IM)
Atropine sulfate, 0.01 mg	AtroPen	J0461	**96372**
Penicillin G benzathine and penicillin G procaine, 100,000 units	Bicillin CR	J0558	**96372**
Penicillin G benzathine, 100,000 units	Bicillin LA	J0561	**96372**
Ceftriaxone, per 250 mg	Rocephin	J0696	**96372** (IM) (IV)[b]
Cefotaxime, per gram	Claforan	J0698	**96372** (IM) (IV)[b]
Betamethasone acetate, 3 mg, and betamethasone sodium phosphate, 3 mg	Celestone Soluspan	J0702	**96372**
Dexamethasone acetate, 1 mg	Decadron LA	J1094	**96372**
Dexamethasone sodium phosphate, 1 mg	Decadron	J1100	**96372** (IM) (IV)[b]
Phenytoin sodium, per 50 mg	Dilantin	J1165	**96374**
Diphenhydramine HCl, up to 50 mg	Benadryl	J1200	**96372**
Gamma globulin, IM, 1 cc Gamma globulin, IM, over 10 cc	Gammar Gamastan	J1460 J1560	**96372**
Immunoglobulin, 500 mg	Gammar-IV	J1566	**96374**
Gentamicin, up to 80 mg	Garamycin	J1580	**96372** (IM) (IV)[b]
Glucagon, per 1 mg		J1610	**96374**
Heparin sodium (heparin lock flush), per 10 units	Hep-Lock	J1642	**96374**
Hydrocortisone sodium succinate, up to 100 mg	Solu-Cortef	J1720	**96374**
Promethazine HCl, up to 50 mg	Phenergan	J2550	**96372**

Table 12-8. Common J Codes^a, continued

Other		J Code	Administration
Dexamethasone, oral, 0.25 mg	Decadron	J8540	None
Antiemetic drug, rectal/suppository, not otherwise specified	Phenergan	J8498	None

Abbreviations: DME, durable medical equipment; FDA, US Food and Drug Administration; HCPCS, Healthcare Common Procedure Coding System; IM, intramuscular; IV, intravenous.

^aBrand names are furnished for identification purposes only. No endorsement of the manufacturers or products is implied.

^bFor IV administration codes, please see pages 308–311.

The 2015 HCPCS codes were released subsequent to the publication of this book. Refer to www.aap.org/cfp for HCPCS updates.

Pathology and Laboratory Procedures

Current Procedural Terminology laboratory codes may be generic for a particular analyte that is independent of testing method or else have a specific *CPT*® code, depending on the method used for the particular analysis.

- Reporting guidelines
    - ❖ A test performed in the office's laboratory should be billed using the appropriate laboratory code and, if performed, the appropriate blood collection code (**36400–36416**).
    - ❖ If the specimen (eg, blood, urine, stool, cerebrospinal fluid) is collected in the office and sent to an outside laboratory, the office visit (if applicable) plus any specimen acquisition procedure code (eg, venipuncture, capillary blood collection, spinal tap) and a handling fee (**99000**) should be billed.
    - ❖ If the laboratory bills the pediatrician for the test, bill the patient using the appropriate laboratory analysis code with modifier **90** to indicate that the procedure was performed in an outside laboratory.
    - ❖ Link the appropriate diagnosis code to the laboratory procedure and/or venipuncture and handling fee. The diagnosis must support the medical necessity or reason for the test or service.
    - ❖ If the only service provided is a urinalysis or obtaining a blood specimen, only the laboratory test and/or venipuncture or capillary stick is reported. It is not appropriate to report a nurse visit (**99211**) in these cases.
    - ❖ Do not report any laboratory test that is not performed in the office (eg, thyroid, laboratory panels, phenylketonuria). Instead, report the appropriate blood-drawing code (**36415** or **36416**).
    - ❖ For example, the physician orders a lead test and the nurse obtains the blood via venipuncture. The specimen is sent to an outside laboratory for processing. Only the venipuncture (**36415**) and handling fee (**99000**) would be reported in addition to the E/M service and other procedures performed on that day.

CLIA-Waived Tests

The Clinical Laboratory Improvement Amendments (CLIA) establish quality standards for all laboratory testing to ensure the accuracy, reliability, and timeliness of patient test results regardless of where the test was performed.

A *laboratory* is defined as any facility that performs laboratory testing on specimens derived from humans for the purpose of providing information for the diagnosis, prevention, and treatment of disease or impairment, or assessment of health.

❋ The term *CLIA-waived* refers to tests commonly done in a laboratory or office. One typical test in the *CPT®* **80000** series that is CLIA-waived includes the rapid streptococcus group B test (**87802**).

❋ Laboratories and physician offices performing waived tests may need to append modifier **QW** to the *CPT* code for CLIA-waived procedures. Some of the CLIA-waived tests are exempt from the use of modifier **QW** (eg, **81002, 82272**). The use of modifier **QW** is payer specific. To review the list of CLIA-waived procedures, go to www.cms.hhs.gov/CLIA.

Urinalysis

81000   Urinalysis, by dipstick or tablet reagent for bilirubin, glucose, hemoglobin, ketones, leukocytes, nitrite, pH, protein, specific gravity, urobilinogen, any number of these constituents; nonautomated, with microscopy

81001   as per **81000** but automated

81002   as per **81000** but without microscopy

81003   as per **81000** but automated, without microscopy

For urinalysis, infectious agent detection, semiquantitative analysis of volatile compounds, use **81099.**

> ||||||||| **Coding Pearl** |||||||||
>
> Urinalysis, by dipstick or tablet reagent, nonautomated with microscopy, is reported with code **81000.**

Urine Pregnancy Test

81025   Urine pregnancy test, by visual color comparison method

Report code **81025** with *ICD-9-CM* codes **V72.40–V74.42** or *ICD-10-CM* codes **Z32.00–Z32.02,** depending on the findings of the test (ie, positive result, negative result, or unconfirmed result).

Glucose Tests

82947   Glucose, quantitative, blood (without a reagent strip)

82948   Blood, reagent strip

82951   Glucose tolerance test (GTT), 3 specimens

82952   GTT, each additional beyond 3 specimens

❋ Continuous glucose monitoring of interstitial tissue fluid via a subcutaneous sensor with sensor placement, hookup, calibration of monitor, patient training, removal of the sensor, and printout of the recording is reported with code **95250.** Monitoring must be a minimum of 72 hours. Physician interpretation and report of the continuous glucose monitoring is reported with code **95251.**

Cultures

❋ Use code **87088** (culture, bacterial; quantitative colony count, urine with isolation and presumptive identification of each isolate) if performed with a commercial kit or code; use **87086** (culture, bacterial; quantitative colony count, urine) if done by another method.

❋ Code **81007** (urinalysis; bacteriuria screen, except by culture or dipstick) can be used for a bacteriuria screen by non-culture technique using a commercial kit. The type of commercial kit must be specified.

❋ Code **87070** (culture, bacterial; any other source except urine, blood, or stool) is reported for throat cultures.

❋ Use code **87045** to report culture, bacteria of the stool, aerobic, with isolation and preliminary examination (eg, KIA, LIA) for *Salmonella* and *Shigella* species. Additional pathogens are reported with code **87046** with one unit per plate.

❋ Report services with the symptoms (eg, microscopic hematuria) or the confirmed diagnosis (eg, urinary tract infection).

Streptococcal Test

87081   Culture, presumptive pathogenic organisms, screening only

87430   Enzyme immunoassay, qualitative, streptococcus, group A

    ❋ Report the code based on the test method rather than on the site of specimen collection.

    ❋ Culture plates using sheep blood agar with bacitracin disks should be coded with **87081** (culture, screening only).

Infectious Agent Detection by Immunoassay With Direct Optical Observation (ie, Rapid Tests)

87802   Streptococcus group B

87804   Influenza

    ❋ If tests performed separately detect the influenza A and B antigen providing 2 distinct results, report code **87804** twice with modifier **59** appended to the second service. This applies whether the test kit uses 1 or 2 analytic chambers to deliver 2 distinct results. Check with your payers because some do not recognize modifier **59** and may require reporting with 2 units of service and no modifier.

87807   Respiratory syncytial virus

87880   Streptococcus, group A

Tuberculosis (TB) Skin Test (Mantoux)

86580   Tuberculosis, intradermal

    ❋ The tuberculosis (TB) skin test (Mantoux) using the intradermal administration of PPD is the recommended diagnostic skin test for TB. This is not the bacille Calmette-Guérin TB vaccine. The AAP supports the use of the Mantoux test (TB, intradermal) for TB screening when appropriate.

    ❋ Code **99211** is the appropriate code to report the reading of a PPD test when that is the only reason for the encounter. The appropriate *ICD-9-CM* diagnosis code is **V74.1** (special screening examination for bacterial and spirochetal diseases); the appropriate *ICD-10-CM* code is **Z11.1** (encounter for screening for respiratory tuberculosis). In the case of a positive test result when the physician sees the patient, the complexity may lead to a higher-level code.

    ❋ There is not a separate administration code reported when the TB test is performed.

|||||||| *Coding Pearl* ||||||||

Code **99211** is the appropriate code to report the reading of a PPD test.

Transitioning to **10**

Chapter 12: Common Procedures and Non-Evaluation and Management Medical Services

Lead Testing

83655   Lead, quantitative analysis

     ◉ This test does not specify the specimen source or the method of testing. Alternative tests sometimes (though now rarely) used for lead screening are **82135** (aminolevulinic acid, delta), **84202** (protoporphyrin, red blood cell count, quantitative), and **84203** (protoporphyrin, red blood cell count, screen).

     ◉ Some states provide the lead testing at no cost to patients covered under the Medicaid Early Periodic Screening, Diagnosis, and Treatment program. Check your state Medicaid requirements for reporting this service.

     ◉ Report *ICD-9-CM* code **V82.5** (special screening for chemical poisoning and other contamination) or *ICD-10-CM* code **Z13.88** (encounter for screening for disorder due to exposure to contaminants) when performing lead screening.

Testing Stool for Occult Blood

82272   Blood, occult, by peroxidase activity (eg, guaiac), qualitative, feces, 1–3 simultaneous determinations, performed for other than colorectal neoplasm screening

     ◉ Reported when a single sample is obtained from a digital rectal examination or a multi-test card is returned from the patient and is tested for blood.

> ||||||| **Coding Pearl** |||||||
>
> Report code **82272** when a single sample or multi-test card is tested for occult blood.

Hematology

85013   Spun microhematocrit

85018   Hemoglobin

85025–85027   Complete blood cell count, automated

     ◉ If using a complete blood cell count (CBC) machine to perform only a hemoglobin test, follow these guidelines.

         ❖ If the CBC is normal, only the hemoglobin may be reported because that was the medically necessary test ordered.

         ❖ If the CBC reveals an abnormality and it is addressed during the course of the visit, the CBC may be reported. The abnormality would be linked to the procedure, and the medical record would need to include documentation for the ordering of the test and to support the medical necessity of the procedure.

Laboratory Panel Coding

All laboratory test panels in *CPT®* were specifically developed for coding purposes only and should not be interpreted as clinical parameters. (See codes **80047–80076** for a component listing of these panels.) For example, the lipid panel (**80061**) includes total cholesterol (**82465**), high-density lipoprotein cholesterol (**83718**), and triglycerides (**84478**). Any additional tests performed can be coded separately from the panel code. Do not unbundle individual laboratory tests if a laboratory panel code is available.

Serum and Transcutaneous Bilirubin Testing

82247   Total bilirubin

82248   Direct bilirubin

88720   Transcutaneous total bilirubin

Papanicolaou Tests

- The laboratory performing the cytology and interpretation reports Papanicolaou (Pap) tests with codes **88141–88155, 88164–88167,** or **88174–88175.**

- Obtaining a Pap test is inherent to the physical examination performed during a preventive medicine visit or a problem-oriented office visit.

- Medicare does require reporting HCPCS code **Q0091** (screening Papanicolaou, obtaining, preparing, and conveyance of cervical and vaginal smear to laboratory) in addition to the E/M service for preventive medicine and problem-oriented office visits.

  - Some state Medicaid programs and commercial payers may also recognize obtaining a Pap test as a separate service.

  - Code **Q0091** cannot be reported when a patient must return for a repeat Pap test due to inadequate initial sampling.

  - If not reporting **Q0091,** a handling fee (**99000**) can be reported in addition to an E/M service if the Pap test was obtained.

- The appropriate *ICD-9-CM* code to link to the E/M code or code **Q0091** is code **V76.2** (special screening, malignant neoplasm, cervix); for high-risk patients you may also use code **V15.89.** *ICD-10-CM* codes are **Z01.411** (encounter for gynecological examination [general] [routine] with abnormal findings) or **Z01.419** (encounter for gynecological examination [general] [routine] without abnormal findings). For screening cervical Pap test not part of a gynecologic examination, report *ICD-10-CM* code **Z12.4** (encounter for screening for malignant neoplasm of cervix). For high-risk patients, you may also use code **Z92.89** or **Z77.9.** These diagnosis codes may be used as secondary when linked with a routine preventive medicine code or problem-oriented sick visit.

> ||||||| **Coding Pearl** ||||||
>
> The CMS Web site (www. cms.hhs.gov/clia) lists current CLIA-waived tests and CLIA edit exempt tests.

Transitioning to **10**

Professional and Technical Components

Certain procedures (eg, ECGs, radiographs, surgical diagnostic tests, laboratory tests) include a professional and technical component. The professional component includes the physician work (eg, interpretation of the test, written report). The technical component includes the costs associated with providing the service (eg, equipment, salaries of technical personnel, supplies, facility expense). Some codes were developed to distinguish between the technical and professional components (eg, routine ECG codes **93000–93010**); however, many are not. If a physician is performing a service or procedure with equipment owned by a facility or another entity and the codes are written as a global service, services are reported with modifier **26** (professional component). *Current Procedural Terminology* does not include a modifier for reporting the technical component. However, most payers recognize HCPCS modifier **TC** (technical component). Facilities or an office providing use of its equipment only would report the same service using modifier **TC.** When the physician owns the equipment and is performing the technical and professional services, a modifier should not be appended to the code.

Chapter 12: Common Procedures and Non-Evaluation and Management Medical Services

Examples

> **A pediatrician orders a 2-view chest x-ray on a child.** The child is sent to a neighboring physician's office (or outpatient department) for the x-ray. The films are then brought back to the office and the pediatrician interprets them.
>
> Pediatrician: **71020 26,** radiologic examination, chest, 2 views: frontal and lateral
> Other office or outpatient department: **71020 TC**

> **A pediatrician orders a 12-lead ECG on an adolescent patient.** The patient is sent to another office with the ECG machine to perform the ECG. The tracings are taken back to the pediatrician for review and written interpretation and report.
>
> Pediatrician: **93010,** routine ECG with at least 12 leads; interpretation and report only
>
> Other office: **93005,** routine ECG with at least 12 leads; tracing only, without interpretation and report

‖‖‖‖

Category II *CPT*® Codes—
Pay for Performance Measures

and

Category III *CPT*® Codes—
Emerging Technologies

‖‖‖‖

Category II *CPT*® Codes—Pay for Performance Measures

Category II codes were developed and are used by physicians and hospitals to report performance measures and certain aspects of care not yet included in performance measures. The performance measures are developed by national organizations including the National Committee for Quality Assurance and the American Medical Association (AMA) Physician Consortium for Performance Improvement (PCPI) based on quality indicators currently accepted and used in the health care industry. As a member of the AMA PCPI, the American Academy of Pediatrics (AAP) is involved with the development of performance measures for pediatric diseases or conditions. The AAP policy statement, "Principles for the Development and Use of Quality Measures," which includes guidance on pay for performance, can be found at http://pediatrics.aappublications.org/content/121/2/411.full. Any updated information on quality improvement can be found at www2.aap.org/visit/qualityimppublic.htm.

The Centers for Medicare & Medicaid Services (CMS) is collecting data on evidence-based quality measures for the Medicare population through the use and reporting of a specific set of Healthcare Common Procedure Coding System Level II G and Category II *Current Procedural Terminology* (*CPT*®) codes.

Reporting Category II codes allows internal monitoring of performance, patient compliance, and outcomes.

Performance Measure Codes

* Are intended for reporting purposes only.
* Describe clinical conditions (including complete performance measurements sets) and screening measures.
* Have no relative values on the Medicare Physician Fee Schedule (Resource-Based Relative Value Scale).
* Are reported on a voluntary basis.
* Are reported in addition to, *not in place of,* Category I *CPT* codes.
* Describe the performance of a clinical service typically included in an evaluation and management (E/M) code or the result that is part of a laboratory procedure/test.

Category II code development and maintenance take place on an as-needed basis. Category II code changes since the printing of the last *CPT* manual are posted to www.ama-assn.org/ama/pub/physician-resources/solutions-managing-your-practice/coding-billing-insurance/cpt/about-cpt/category-ii-codes.page. The online document, "CPT Category II Codes Alphabetical Clinical Topics Listing" (ACTL), includes the latest code changes with revision, implementation, and publication dates.

Codes are grouped within categories based on established clinical documentation methods (ie, history, physical findings, assessment, and plan). Each code identifies the specific clinical condition and performance measured.

Categories are defined in the following ways:

Chapter 13: Category II *CPT*® Codes—Pay for Performance Measures and Category III *CPT*® Codes—Emerging Technologies

Performance Measure Codes

Category of Codes	Examples
Composite Measures—0000F Series Codes in the **0000F** range comprise several measures that are grouped to facilitate reporting of a clinical condition when all included components are performed.	Code **0012F** is reported when the assessment on an 18-year-old with community-acquired bacterial pneumonia includes all of the following components: **1026F** Comorbid conditions assessed **2010F** Vital signs recorded **2014F** Mental status assessed **2018F** Hydration status assessed
Patient Management—0500F Series Codes in the **0500F** range are used to describe utilization measures or measures of patient care provided for specific clinical purposes (eg, prenatal care, presurgical and postsurgical care, referrals).	Code **0505F** is used to report that a hemodialysis plan of care was documented on a patient with end-stage renal disease (ESRD) who is receiving dialysis.
Patient History—1000F Series Codes in the **1000F** range are used to describe measures for aspects of patient history and review of systems.	Code **1031F** is used to report that the smoking status and exposure to secondhand smoke in the home was assessed in patients with asthma. Code **1050F** is used to report a patient history of new or changing moles.
Physical Examination—2000F Series Codes in the **2000F** range describe aspects of the physical examination or clinical assessment.	Code **2030F** is reported when the hydration status is documented as normally hydrated on a 2-month-old with acute gastroenteritis.
Diagnostic/Screening Processes or Results—3006F Codes in the **3006F** range are used to report results of clinical laboratory tests and radiologic or other procedural examinations.	When the most recent hemoglobin A_{1c} (HbA_{1c}) level is less than 7.0% on an 18-year-old with diabetes mellitus, code **3044F** is reported.
Therapeutic, Preventive, or Other Interventions—4000F Codes in the **4000F** range are used to report pharmacologic, procedural, or behavioral therapies, including preventive services such as patient education and counseling.	Code **4058F** is reported when gastroenteritis education is provided to the mother of a 6-month-old with acute gastroenteritis and documented in the medical record.
Follow-up or Other Outcomes—5005F Codes in the **5005F** range are used to describe the review and communication of test results to patients, patient satisfaction and experience with care, patient functional status, and patient morbidity and mortality.	Code **5050F** is reported when a treatment plan is communicated to the provider(s) managing continuing care within 1 month of the diagnosis of melanoma.
Patient Safety—6005F Codes in the **6005F** range are used to describe patient safety practices.	Code **6005F** is used to report the rationale (eg, severity of illness and safety) for the recommended level of care (eg, home, hospital) for a patient with community-acquired bacterial pneumonia.

Performance Measure Codes, continued

Category of Codes	Examples
Structural Measures—7010F Codes in the **7010F** range are used to identify measures that address the setting or system of the delivered care and address aspects of the capabilities of the organization or health care professionals providing the care.	Code **7010F** is reported when patient information is entered into a recall system that includes a specified target date for the next examination of a patient with melanoma and a process to follow up with patients about missed or unscheduled appointments.
Non-measure Claims-Based Reporting—9001F Codes in the **9001F** range are used to identify certain aspects of care not currently represented by recognized performance measures but which may later be associated with measures approved by an appropriate quality improvement organization.	Code **9001F** is reported to identify the size of an abdominal aortic aneurysm less than 5.0 cm maximum diameter on centerline-formatted computed tomography (CT) or minor diameter on axial- formatted CT.

Category II Modifiers

Category II modifiers (**1P, 2P, 3P,** and **8P**) are used to report services that were considered but not provided because of a medical reason(s), patient choice, or system reason. Modifier **8P** is equivalent to "action not performed, reason not otherwise specified."

Category II modifiers

- Are used only when allowed based on the specific reporting instructions for each performance measure
- Are appended only to Category II *CPT®* codes
- Serve as a denominator exclusion from a performance measure (when measure allows)

The medical record should include written documentation of the reason that the service was ultimately not provided. Category II modifiers are only appended to Category II codes.

Category II Modifiers

Category II Modifier	Examples
Modifier 1P (performance measure exclusion modifier due to medical reasons) Used to report that one of the performance measures was not performed because it was not indicated (eg, already performed) or was contraindicated (eg, due to a patient's allergy).	Modifier **1P** is appended to code **6070F** (documentation that patient was queried and counseled about antiepileptic drug [AED] side effects) because the patient is not receiving an AED.
Modifier 2P (performance measure exclusion modifier due to patient choice) Used to report that the performance measure was not performed due to a patient's religious, social, or economic reasons; the patient declined (eg, noncompliance with treatment); or other specific reasons.	Modifier **2P** is appended to code **3210F** (group A streptococcus test performed) when a physician considered the testing for strep but the parent refused testing.

Category II Modifiers, continued

Category II Modifier	Examples
Modifier 3P (performance measure exclusion modifier due to system reasons) Used to report that the performance measure was not performed because the payer does not cover the service, the resources to perform the service are not available, or other reasons attributable to the health care delivery system. Keep in mind that in the emergency department setting, appropriate medical screening and stabilization must be provided regardless of any consideration of payment. Providers are prohibited by federal statute from making treatment decisions in these circumstances based on payer coverage.	Modifier **3P** is appended to code **4062F** (patient referral for psychotherapy documented) when a 15-year-old with a diagnosis of major depressive disorder is not referred for psychotherapy because it is not available.
Modifier 8P (performance measure reporting modifier—action not performed, not otherwise specified) Used to allow the reporting of circumstances when an action described in a measure's numerator is not performed and the reason is not otherwise specified.	Modifier **8P** would be appended to code **2001F** (weight recorded) when a 2-year-old with acute gastroenteritis is not weighed and therefore does not meet the performance measurement requirement.

Performance Measures Applicable to Pediatrics

Many performance measures apply to the pediatric population. In addition, pediatric practices caring for patients 18 years or older may report Category II codes for conditions such as hypertension, diabetes mellitus, chronic kidney disease, gastroesophageal reflux disease, and community-acquired bacterial pneumonia and screening codes for tobacco use and cessation. Refer to the ACTL at www.ama-assn.org/resources/doc/cpt/cpt-cat2-codes-alpha-listing-clinical-topics.pdf (account set-up required).

Acute Otitis Externa (AOE)

These codes apply to patients aged 2 years and older with a diagnosis of acute otitis externa (AOE). Clinical components are reported to denote if the pain was assessed, if topical therapy was prescribed, and if systemic antimicrobial therapy was avoided.

Category II Codes—AOE		Guidelines
1116F	Auricular or periauricular pain assessed	Report at each encounter. Append modifier **1P** when the appropriate performance exclusion exists.
4130F	Topical preparations (including over the counter) prescribed for AOE	If topical preparations are not prescribed, medical record documentation must indicate the medical and/or patient reasons, and modifier **1P** or **2P** or drug allergy or other adverse effects indicated by diagnosis codes would be appended to code **4130F**.
4131F 4132F	Systemic antimicrobial therapy prescribed Systemic antimicrobial therapy not prescribed	Report code **4132F** when systemic antimicrobial therapy is not prescribed. Report code **4131F** with modifier **1P** when there is a valid medical reason for prescribing systemic antimicrobial therapy. Exclusion modifiers cannot be reported with code **4132F**.

Acute Otitis Media With Effusion (OME)

These codes apply to patients aged 2 months through 12 years with a diagnosis of acute otitis media with effusion (OME). Clinical components reported as part of this measure signify that an assessment of tympanic membrane mobility was performed using pneumatic otoscopy or tympanometry, that hearing testing was performed within 6 months prior to a tympanostomy tube insertion, and whether or not antihistamines, decongestants, or systemic steroids were avoided.

Category II Codes—OME		Guidelines
2035F	Tympanic membrane mobility assessed with pneumatic otoscopy or tympanometry	Reported at each encounter. Modifier **1P** or **2P** is appended when appropriate.
3230F	Documentation that hearing test was performed within 6 months prior to a tympanostomy tube insertion	Reported at the time the tympanostomy tube insertion is performed. Medical record documentation must reflect the performance and results of the test or, if the test is performed by another physician or provider, documentation should include a copy of the test results. Modifiers **1P** or **3P** may be appended to code **3230F** as appropriate.
4131F	Systemic antimicrobial therapy prescribed	Used to report the absence or overuse of medications for each patient. Modifier **1P** is used with codes **4131F**, **4133F**, and **4135F** when appropriate. Modifiers **1P**, **2P**, and **3P** may not be reported with codes **4132F**, **4134F**, or **4136F**.
4132F	Systemic antimicrobial therapy not prescribed	
4133F	Antihistamines or decongestants prescribed or recommended	
4134F	Antihistamines or decongestants neither prescribed nor recommended	
4135F	Systemic corticosteroids prescribed	
4136F	Systemic corticosteroids not prescribed	

Asthma

This measure is applicable to all patients 5 to 50 years of age with a diagnosis of asthma.

Assessment of Asthma Control

Category II Codes—Asthma		Guidelines
2015F	Asthma impairment assessed	Used for each patient who was evaluated at least once for asthma control. Evaluation of asthma impairment and asthma risk must occur during the same medical encounter. There are no exclusions to the measures. Code **2016F** is also reported independently for each emergency department encounter or inpatient admission (with a diagnosis of acute asthma exacerbation). There are no performance exclusions for this measure.
2016F	Asthma risk assessed	
1031F	Smoking status and exposure to secondhand smoke in the home assessed	Report for each patient whose smoking status and exposure to secondhand smoke in the home was assessed. There are no performance exclusions.
1032F	Current tobacco smoker OR currently exposed to secondhand smoke	Report code **1032F** or **1033F** to indicate tobacco use status. If reporting code **1032F**, report **4000F** OR **4001F** to indicate type of tobacco use cessation intervention. There are no performance exclusions for this measure.
1033F	Current tobacco nonsmoker AND not currently exposed to secondhand smoke	
4000F	Tobacco use cessation intervention, counseling	
4001F	Tobacco use cessation intervention, pharmacologic therapy	

Chapter 13: Category II *CPT*® Codes—Pay for Performance Measures and Category III *CPT*® Codes—Emerging Technologies

Category II Codes–Asthma, continued	Guidelines
1038F Persistent asthma, mild, moderate, or severe **1039F** Intermittent asthma **4140F** Inhaled corticosteroids prescribed **4144F** Alternative long-term control medication prescribed	Report code **1038F** or **1039F** to indicate asthma severity. For patients with persistent asthma (**1038F**), report code **4140F**, **4144F**, or both. For patients with appropriate exclusion criteria, report code **4140F** or **4144F** with modifier **1P** or **2P**.
5250F Asthma discharge plan provided to patient	Report for each emergency department encounter or inpatient admission (with a diagnosis of acute asthma exacerbation) when an asthma discharge plan is provided to patient at time of discharge. There are no performance exclusions for this measure.

Pediatric Acute Gastroenteritis (PAG)

The pediatric acute gastroenteritis (PAG) measure applies to patients aged 1 month through 5 years with a diagnosis of acute gastroenteritis.

Category II Codes–PAG	Guidelines
4056F Appropriate oral rehydration solution recommended **4058F** Pediatric gastroenteritis education provided to caregiver	Used to report that the patient's caregiver was given a recommendation on an appropriate oral rehydration solution, diet education was performed, and the patient's caregiver was advised when to contact the physician. There are no performance exclusions.
2030F Hydration status documented, normally hydrated **2031F** Hydration status documented, dehydrated	Report when hydration status is documented in the medical record. When the patient is dehydrated and appropriate oral rehydration solution is recommended, report codes **4056F** and **2031F**. There are no performance exclusions.
2001F Weight recorded	Report when weight measurement is documented in the medical record. Modifiers **1P**, **2P**, and **3P** may not be reported. Modifier **8P** may be reported.

Pediatric Pharyngitis (PHAR) and Upper Respiratory Infections (URIs)

The pediatric pharyngitis (PHAR) measure applies to patients 2 through 18 years of age (inclusive) with a diagnosis of pharyngitis who were dispensed or prescribed antibiotic treatment and/or received a group A streptococcus test.

The upper respiratory infection (URI) measure applies to patients 3 months through 18 years of age (inclusive) who were seen with a diagnosis of only URI and were appropriately not prescribed or dispensed an antibiotic.

Category II Codes–PHAR and URI	Guidelines
3210F Group A streptococcus test performed	Report when a patient is diagnosed with pharyngitis, is dispensed or prescribed an antibiotic, and received a group A streptococcus test. Modifier **1P** for medical exclusions or **2P** for patient exclusions may be used.
4120F Antibiotic prescribed or dispensed **4124F** Antibiotic neither prescribed nor dispensed	Report as appropriate for both performance measures (PHAR and URI). Modifier **1P**, **2P**, or **3P** may not be reported with code **4120F** or **4124F** for pharyngitis. Modifier **1P** is reported with code **4124F** when appropriate for URI. If a patient was dispensed or prescribed an antibiotic and received the group A streptococcus test, codes **3210F** and **4120F** would be reported.

Pediatric End-Stage Renal Disease (ESRD)

Applies to patients aged 17 years and younger with a diagnosis of ESRD receiving hemodialysis, having clearance of urea/volume (Kt/V) measurements as per the criteria listed in the codes, having received an influenza vaccine, and having a plan of care documented. This measure is reported during each calendar month that the patient is receiving hemodialysis.

Category II Codes—ESRD		Guidelines
0505F	Hemodialysis plan of care documented	Report when the hemodialysis plan of care is documented in the medical record on a patient aged 17 years or younger.
3082F	Kt/V less than 1.2	Report code applicable to the corresponding Kt/V measurement. If the Kt/V is less than 1.2 (**3082F**) and the patient has a plan of care for inadequate hemodialysis, also report code **0505F**. There are no performance exclusions for this measure.
3083F	Kt/V greater than or equal to 1.2 and less than 1.7	
3084F	Kt/V greater than or equal to 1.7	
4274F	Influenza immunization administered or previously received	Report when a patient aged 6 months through 17 years (with a diagnosis of ESRD and receiving dialysis) is seen between November 1 and February 15 and receives the influenza immunization or has received the influenza immunization from another provider. The medical record must support that the vaccine was administered. Modifier **1P, 2P,** or **3P** may be used when appropriate.

Epilepsy

This measure will be reported by the physician providing care to children and adults with a diagnosis of epilepsy.

Category II Codes—Epilepsy		Guidelines
1200F	Seizure type(s) and current seizure frequency(ies) documented	Report when the seizure type(s) and current seizure frequency for each seizure type are documented in the medical record. Modifier **1P** or **2P** may be reported if appropriate.
1205F	Etiology of epilepsy or epilepsy syndrome(s) reviewed and documented	When the medical record documentation includes the etiology of epilepsy or the epilepsy syndrome(s) is reviewed and documented (if known) or documented as unknown or cryptogenic, code **1205F** is reported. There are no performance exclusions for code **1205F**.
3650F	Electroencephalogram (EEG) ordered, reviewed, or requested	Code **3650F** is used to report whether or not the patient with a diagnosis of epilepsy seen for an initial evaluation had at least one EEG ordered or, if an EEG was performed previously, results were reviewed or requested. If code **3650F** is reported on the same day as a new patient E/M service (**99201–99205**), neither code **1119F** nor **1121F** is reported. If code **3650F** is reported on the same day as an established patient E/M visit (**99211–99215**) or office/outpatient consultation (**99241–99245**), code **1119F** is also reported to denote an initial evaluation for the condition or code **1121F** is reported to denote a subsequent evaluation. Modifier **1P, 2P,** or **3P** may be reported with code **3650F** when appropriate.
1119F	Initial evaluation for condition	
1121F	Subsequent evaluation for condition	

Category II Codes— Epilepsy, continued	Guidelines
3324F Magnetic resonance imaging (MRI) or CT scan ordered, reviewed, or requested **1119F** Initial evaluation for condition **1121F** Subsequent evaluation for condition	When a patient with the diagnosis of epilepsy has MRI (preferred imaging) or CT ordered or if results are reviewed or requested of an MRI or CT previously obtained, code **3324F** is reported. If code **3324F** is reported on the same day as a new patient E/M service (**99201–99205**), neither code **1119F** nor **1121F** is reported. If code **3324F** is reported on the same day as an established patient E/M visit (**99211–99215**) or office/outpatient consultation (**99241–99245**), code **1119F** is also reported to denote an initial evaluation for the condition or code **1121F** is reported to denote a subsequent evaluation. Modifier **1P, 2P,** or **3P** may be reported with code **3324F.**
6070F Patient queried and counseled about AED side effects	Report when the patient is queried and counseled about AED side effects and the counseling is documented in the medical record. Modifier **1P** may be reported. This includes patients who are not taking an AED.
5200F Consideration of referral for a neurologic evaluation of appropriateness for surgical therapy for intractable epilepsy within the past 3 years	Report when a patient with a diagnosis of intractable epilepsy was considered for referral for a neurologic evaluation of appropriateness for surgical therapy within the past 3 years. There are no performance exclusions applicable.
4330F Counseling about epilepsy-specific safety issues provided to patient (or caregiver[s])	Report when counseling is provided to a patient and/or their caregiver(s) about context-specific safety issues, appropriate to the patient's age, seizure type(s) and frequency(ies), and occupation and leisure activities (eg, injury prevention, burns, appropriate driving restrictions, bathing), at least once a year and is documented in the medical record. Modifier **3P** may be reported when appropriate.
4340F Counseling for women of childbearing potential with epilepsy	Report whether or not a female of childbearing potential (12–44 years old) was counseled about how epilepsy and its treatment may affect contraception and pregnancy and the counseling is documented in the medical record. Modifier **1P** may be reported.

Major Depressive Disorder (MDD)—Child and Adolescent

Applicable for reporting care to all patients aged 6 through 17 years with a diagnosis of major depressive disorder (MDD).

Category II Codes—MDD	Guidelines
2060F Patient interviewed directly by evaluating clinician on or before date of diagnosis of MDD **1040F** *Diagnostic and Statistical Manual of Mental Disorders, Fifth Edition (DSM-5)* criteria for MDD documented at the initial evaluation **3085F** Suicide risk assessed	Report code **2060F** when a patient is interviewed directly by the evaluating clinician on or before the date of diagnosis. Report code **1040F** when there is documented evidence that the patient met the *DSM-5* criteria—at least 5 elements with symptom duration of 2 weeks or longer, including depressed mood (can be irritable mood in children and adolescents) or loss of interest or pleasure—during the visit in which the new diagnosis or recurrent episode was identified. Code **3085F** is reported when an assessment for suicide risk is performed and documented. Modifiers **1P, 2P, 3P,** and **8P** may not be reported.

Category II Codes—MDD, continued	Guidelines
4060F Psychotherapy services provided **4062F** Patient referral for psychotherapy documented	Report code **4060F** when a patient receives psychotherapy during an episode of MDD and the service is documented in the medical record. Report code **4062F** when a patient is referred for psychotherapy and the referral is documented in the medical record. Modifier **1P, 2P,** or **3P** may be reported.
4064F Antidepressant pharmacotherapy prescribed **4063F** Antidepressant pharmacotherapy considered and not prescribed	Used to report whether the patient was considered or prescribed an antidepressant medication during an episode of MDD. Modifier **1P, 2P,** or **3P** may not be reported.
0545F Plan for follow-up care for MDD, documented	Report when a plan for follow-up care is documented in the medical record. There are no performance exclusions for this measure.

HIV/AIDS

This measure is reported by the physician providing ongoing HIV care to children and adults. There are 29 Category II codes used in this measure. Each measure has a different denominator that is specific to the patient's age. Measures include reporting cell counts, use of antiretroviral therapy, screening for opportunistic infections and high-risk behaviors, administration of vaccines, and use of *Pneumocystis jiroveci* pneumonia prophylaxis. Refer to the ACTL at www.ama-assn.org/resources/doc/cpt/cpt-cat2-codes-alpha-listing-clinical-topics.pdf (account set-up required) for details on the requirements for reporting these codes.

Reporting Category II Codes

The ACTL should be used in coordination with the Category II section in *CPT®*.

Alphabetical Clinical Topics Listing (ACTL)

- ⊛ Includes an alphabetic index of performance measures by clinical condition or topic
- ⊛ Includes the measure developer (eg, PCPI), the performance measure, a description of the measure, and the associated Category II code
- ⊛ Directs the reader to the measure developer's Web site to access the complete description of the measure (eg, specifications and requirements for reporting performance measures for asthma are located at www.physicianconsortium.org)

Access the measure developer's Web site for the specification documents (ie, clinical measurement set, measurement set numerators and denominators, measure specifications, specifications for paper and electronic medical records, an algorithm for measure calculation, data abstraction definitions, a medication table, and a retrospective data abstraction tool) of the performance measure.

The following Web sites provide information and resources:

www.ahrq.gov/child

www.qualitymeasures.ahrq.gov

www.ama-assn.org/go/quality

www.ama-assn.org/go/CPT

www.physicianconsortium.org

> ⫿⫿⫿⫿ **Coding Pearl** ⫿⫿⫿⫿
>
> A patient must meet the criteria specified in the denominator (diagnosis code) to be included in the numerator (Category II code) for a particular performance measure. Only the diagnosis code for the condition or disease will be linked to Category II *CPT* codes.

Each performance measure includes a symptom or activity assessment, numerator, denominator, percentage, and reporting instructions. A patient must meet the criteria specified in the denominator (diagnosis code) to be included in the numerator (Category II code) for a particular performance measure.

Reporting measures to a payer (electronically or with a CMS-1500 claim form) is done the same way as reporting any *CPT*® code. Report the appropriate E/M code (eg, **99201–99215, 99241–99245**) based on the level of service performed and documented with all of the appropriate *diagnosis* codes that were addressed during the course of the visit. Report the Category II *CPT* code that relates to the performance measure with any applicable Category II modifier. Only the diagnosis code for the condition or disease will be linked to Category II *CPT* codes.

Examples

➤ **A 4-year-old presents with acute onset of right ear pain.** An expanded-level history and physical examination are performed. The diagnosis is AOE. The patient is sent home on topical antimicrobial and anti-inflammatory medication. All of the criteria in the AOE measurement set as specified by the developer of the performance measurement are met. The applicable codes identified under the Category II *CPT* code section are reviewed and the ACTL is consulted for current measure criteria.

99213	(established patient; expanded history and physical examination with low-complexity medical decision-making)	*ICD-9-CM* **380.22** (other acute otitis externa)
1116F	(auricular or periauricular pain assessed)	
4130F	(topical preparations [including over the counter] prescribed for AOE)	*ICD-10-CM* **H60.501** (AOE non-infective right ear)
4132F	(systemic antimicrobial therapy not prescribed)	

➤ **A 15-year-old new patient is seen with complaints of sleep disturbance and depressed mood.** The adolescent has not been eating well and has been increasingly irritable. A comprehensive history and detailed physical examination are performed. The patient is determined to meet *DSM-5* criteria for moderate MDD. Treatment options, including psychotherapy and antidepressant medications, are discussed. The patient chooses to pursue psychotherapy and a referral is provided. The patient is scheduled for follow-up in 6 weeks.

99203	(new patient; comprehensive history, detailed physical examination with moderate-complexity medical decision-making)	*ICD-9-CM* **296.22** (major depressive disorder, single episode, moderate)
2060F	(patient interviewed directly by evaluating clinician on or before date of diagnosis of MDD)	
1040F	(criteria for MDD documented at the initial evaluation)	*ICD-10-CM* **F32.1** (MDD single episode, moderate)
3085F	(suicide risk assessed)	
4062F	(patient referral for psychotherapy documented)	

➤ **A 10-year-old is seen with exacerbation of asthma.** His last exacerbation was 3 months ago. An expanded history and detailed physical examination are performed. A nebulizer treatment with albuterol is ordered and administered. Examination following treatment shows decreased wheezing. He is sent home on albuterol and steroids administered by MDI with plan to follow up as necessary. Assessment of asthma status is documented as mild persistent. Category II codes for evaluation of asthma symptoms, persistent asthma, assessment of asthma status, and prescription of inhaled corticosteroids are reported. If documentation supports asthma risk (**2016F**), smoking status and exposure to secondhand smoke in the home (**1031F–1033F**), or tobacco use cessation intervention (**4000F–4001F**), these may be additionally reported.

99214 25	(established patient; expanded history, detailed physical examination with moderate-complexity medical decision-making)	} *ICD-9-CM* **493.92** (asthma, unspecified, with [acute] exacerbation)
94640	(aerosol treatment)	
J7611	(albuterol, inhalation solution, US Food and Drug Administration–approved final product, non-compounded, administered through durable medical equipment concentrated form, 1 mg)	*ICD-10-CM* **J45.31** (mild persistent asthma with exacerbation)
1005F	(asthma symptoms evaluated)	
1038F	(persistent asthma, mild, moderate, or severe)	
2015F	(assessment of asthma status)	
4140F	(inhaled corticosteroids prescribed)	

Category III *CPT*® Codes

Category III *CPT* codes are temporary codes used for data collection purposes to substantiate the usage of emerging technologies, services, and procedures. Category III *CPT* codes are not assigned relative value units, and payment for these services is based strictly on payer policies. If you are performing any procedure or service identified with a Category III *CPT* code, work with your payers to determine their coverage and payment policies.

Category III codes are released biannually with an implementation date 6 months following the release date. For instance, code **0341T** (described later) was released on July 1, 2013, and implemented January 1, 2014. The most recent Category III code listing is found online at www.ama-assn.org/ama/pub/physician-resources/solutions-managing-your-practice/coding-billing-insurance/cpt/about-cpt/category-iii-codes.page.

In general, Category III codes must be replaced for reporting by Category I codes or approved for continued Category III status within 5 years following the Category III code assignment. Category III codes that are not renewed for continued utilization are archived and the codes are not reused.

Current Category III codes include

0188T, +0189T Remote real-time interactive videoconferenced critical care, E/M of the critically ill or critically injured patient

Chapter 13: Category II *CPT*® Codes—Pay for Performance Measures and Category III *CPT*® Codes—Emerging Technologies

(See Chapter 10 for specific *CPT®* reporting guidelines when reporting remote critical care.)

0208T Pure tone audiometry (threshold), automated; air only

0209T air and bone

0210T Speech audiometry threshold, automated

0211T with speech recognition

0212T Comprehensive audiometry threshold evaluation and speech recognition (**0209T, 0211T** combined), automated

(For audiometric testing using audiometers performed manually by a qualified health care professional, see **92551–92557.**)

0240T Esophageal motility (manometric study of the esophagus and/or gastro-esophageal junction) study with interpretation and report; with high-resolution esophageal pressure topography

+0241T with stimulation or perfusion during high-resolution esophageal pressure topography study (eg, stimulant, acid, or alkali perfusion) (List separately in addition to code for primary procedure.)

(Report **0241T** in conjunction with **0240T.**)

(Do not report **0240T** in conjunction with **91010** or **91013.**)

(Do not report **0241T** more than once per session.)

(To report esophageal motility studies without high-resolution esophageal pressure topography, use **91010;** with stimulant or perfusion, use **91013.**)

0333T Visual evoked potential, screening of visual acuity, automated

(See Chapter 5 for more information on screening of visual acuity by automated visual evoked potential.)

0341T Quantitative pupillometry with interpretation and report, unilateral or bilateral

●0359T Behavior identification assessment, by the physician or other qualified health care professional, face-to-face with patient and caregiver(s), includes administration of standardized and non-standardized tests, detailed behavioral history, patient observation and caregiver interview, interpretation of test results, discussion of findings and recommendations with the primary guardian(s)/caregiver(s), and preparation of report

●0360T Observational behavioral follow-up assessment, includes physician or other qualified health care professional direction with interpretation and report, administered by one technician; first 30 minutes of technician time, face-to-face with the patient

●0361T each additional 30 minutes of technician time, face-to-face with the patient (List separately in addition to code for primary service.)

●0362T Exposure behavioral follow-up assessment, includes physician or other qualified health care professional direction with interpretation and report, administered by physician or other qualified health care professional with the assistance of one or more technicians; first 30 minutes of technician(s) time, face-to-face with the patient

+●0363T each additional 30 minutes of technician(s) time, face-to-face with the patient (List separately in addition to code for primary procedure.)

●0364T Adaptive behavior treatment by protocol, administered by technician, face-to-face with one patient; first 30 minutes of technician time

+●0365T each additional 30 minutes of technician time (List separately in addition to code for primary procedure.)

●0366T Group adaptive behavior treatment by protocol, administered by technician, face-to-face with two or more patients; first 30 minutes of technician time

+●0367T each additional 30 minutes of technician time (List separately in addition to code for primary procedure.)

●0368T Adaptive behavior treatment with protocol modification administered by physician or other qualified health care professional with one patient; first 30 minutes of patient face-to-face time

+●0369T each additional 30 minutes of patient face-to-face time (List separately in addition to code for primary procedure.)

●0370T Family adaptive behavior treatment guidance, administered by physician or other qualified health care professional (without the patient present)

●0371T Multiple-family group adaptive behavior treatment guidance, administered by physician or other qualified health care professional (without the patient present)

●0372T Adaptive behavior treatment social skills group, administered by physician or other qualified health care professional face-to-face with multiple patients

●0373T Exposure adaptive behavior treatment with protocol modification requiring two or more technicians for severe maladaptive behavior(s); first 60 minutes of technicians' time, face-to-face with patient

+●0374T each additional 30 minutes of technicians' time face-to-face with patient (List separately in addition to code for primary procedure.)

●0381T External heart rate and 3-axis accelerometer data recording up to 14 days to assess changes in heart rate and to monitor motion analysis for the purposes of diagnosing nocturnal epilepsy seizure events; includes report, scanning analysis with report, review and interpretation by a physician or other qualified health care professional

●0382T review and interpretation only
(Do not report **0381T, 0382T** in conjunction with **0383T, 0384T, 0385T, 0386T**)

●0383T External heart rate and 3-axis accelerometer data recording from 15 to 30 days to assess changes in heart rate to monitor motion analysis for the purposes of diagnosing nocturnal epilepsy seizure events; includes report, scanning analysis with report, review and interpretation by a physician or other qualified health care professional.

●0384T review and interpretation only
(Do not report **0383T, 0384T** in conjunction with **0381T, 0382T, 0385T, 0386T**)

●0385T External heart rate and 3-axis accelerometer data recording more than 30 days to assess changes in heart rate to monitor motion analysis for the purposes of diagnosing nocturnal epilepsy seizure events; includes report, scanning analysis with report, review and interpretation by a physician or other qualified health care professional

●0386T review and interpretation only
(Do not report **0385T, 0386T** in conjunction with **0381T, 0382T, 0383T, 0384T**)

‖‖‖‖‖

Preventing Fraud and Abuse:
Compliance, Audits, and Paybacks

‖‖‖‖‖

Chapter 14: Preventing Fraud and Abuse: Compliance, Audits, and Paybacks

This chapter was contributed by the American Academy of Pediatrics (AAP) Committee on Medical Liability and Risk Management.

Although most physicians work ethically, provide high-quality care, and submit appropriate claims for payment, unfortunately there are a few dishonest people who exploit the health care system for personal gain. These few have necessitated an array of laws to combat fraud and abuse and protect the integrity of the health care system. Just as patients put enormous trust in physicians, so do payers. Medicare, Medicaid, other federal health care programs and private payers rely on physicians' medical judgment to treat patients with appropriate services. They depend on physicians to submit accurate and truthful claims for the services provided to their enrollees. And the majority of physicians intend to do just that. However, it is easier said than done, given the complex and dynamic nature of payer coding and billing procedures which, despite efforts to standardize variations, persist from carrier to carrier, policy to policy, state to state, and month to month.

This chapter outlines the importance of safeguarding the health care system from fraud and abuse, describes how compliance programs can protect medical practices from unintentional and intentional billing errors, and provides general considerations on how to respond to overpayment notices and inquiries from auditors.

Defining Medical Fraud and Abuse

According to reports from Attorney General Eric Holder and US Department of Health and Human Services (HHS), for every dollar spent on health care–related fraud and abuse investigations from 2010 to 2013, the federal government recovered $8.10. This was the highest 3-year average return on investment in the 17-year history of the health care fraud and abuse control program. With that kind of success, it's no wonder that public and private health care payers are investing more in fraud and abuse.

The federal government has more than a dozen laws in its antifraud and abuse arsenal. But the 5 most important that apply to physicians are the False Claims Act, the Anti-Kickback Statute, the Physician Self-Referral Law, the Exclusion Authorities, and the Civil Monetary Penalties Law. Abiding by these laws is not only the right thing to do; violating them, even (for some) unwittingly, could result in criminal penalties, civil fines, exclusion from federal health care programs, or loss of medical license from a state medical board. It all begins with understanding the definition of *fraud and abuse* in health care.

Fraud

Fraud is obtaining something of value through intentional misrepresentation or concealment of material facts.

Examples of fraud in the physician's office may include

- Requiring that a patient return for a procedure that could have been performed on the same day
- Billing Medicare or Medicaid for services not provided, including no-shows
- Billing one member for services provided to another (non-covered) member
- Billing more than one party for the same service
- Taking a kickback in money, in-kind, or other valuable compensation for referrals
- Completing a certificate of medical necessity for a patient who does not need the service or who is not professionally known by the provider

Abuse

Abuse includes any practice that is not consistent with the goals of providing patients with services that

- Are medically necessary
- Meet professionally recognized standards
- Are fairly priced

Some examples of actions that will likely be considered to be abuse are

- Charging in excess for services or supplies
- Billing Medicare or Medicaid based on a higher fee schedule than for other patients
- Providing medically unnecessary services
- Submitting bills to Medicare or Medicaid that are the responsibility of another insurance plan
- Routinely waiving co-payments or deductibles
- Advertising for free services
- Coding all visits at the same level
- Unbundling claims—billing separately for services that are correctly billed under one code
- Billing claims under the wrong provider number

Antifraud and Anti-abuse Activities

The battle against health care fraud and abuse is being waged on many fronts—federal and state governments as well as private payers. More and more, these groups are sharing information, so that a provider under investigation by one government health care program will likely be contacted by another and possibly by private payers. The HHS Office of Inspector General (OIG) has several antifraud campaigns underway. Most are Medicare focused, but these are often models for future Medicaid programs. In addition to the federal antifraud and abuse laws, many states have enacted antifraud and anti-abuse legislation, and state Medicaid programs have established Medicaid fraud control units. That means that physician practices are subject to several levels of scrutiny for possible fraudulent activity. The Patient Protection and Affordable Care Act (PPACA) introduced new Medicaid program integrity provisions such as increased fraud detection methods, terminating providers previously terminated from other government health care programs, suspending future payments based on credible allegations of fraud, and adopting the National Correct Coding Initiative edits (see Chapter 3 for more information on edits). All of this means that the momentum and resources for rooting out fraud and abuse at the federal and state level have intensified.

In addition, Medicaid auditors have a financial incentive to find fraud. The Medicaid Recovery Audit Contractors (RAC) program allows states to hire private contractors to audit Medicaid payments and keep a percentage of what they collect. Because it is Medicaid, pediatricians may be included in RAC audits. The RAC was established in provisions of the PPACA and modeled on a similar successful Medicare program. So far, the Medicare and Medicaid RAC programs have gone after larger organizations, but it is not inconceivable that they will eventually turn their attention to physician practices. It's always better to be prepared. Information on the status of state Medicaid RAC programs is available through the Centers for Medicare & Medicaid (CMS) at http://w2.dehpg.net/RACSS/Map.aspx. This site includes the name and contact information for each state's RAC contractors and medical directors and look-back period for audits.

Office of Inspector General (OIG) Antifraud Program

A sign that physician billing is taking a more prominent role in OIG fraud investigations can be found in its current initiatives. The following OIG antifraud programs demonstrate a shift in focus to physician billings and the need for good documentation and proper coding.

OIG Antifraud Program	
OIG Initiative	**Description**
Physicians at Teaching Hospitals—IL372	Monitors the involvement of attending physicians in teaching hospitals in patient care and verifies that bills reflect the correct level of service provided to the patient
Physician relationships on Medicare health maintenance organizations	Studies provider payment methods to see how they affect quality of care (eg, do capitation plans hinder patient access?)
Physician certification of durable medical equipment	Looks at how well the equipment needs of patients are documented
Hospital ownership of physician practices	Monitors the referral relationships between hospitals and their owned physician practices to detect possible overutilization
Accuracy and carrier monitoring of coding	Measures how accurately physicians perform evaluation and management (E/M) coding in the nonhospital setting and whether carriers are also monitoring this
Use of modifiers	Verifies that a separate service was performed and documented
Use of diagnosis codes	Compares claims against medical records to see if diagnosis codes match reasons for ordering and providing various services
Physician credit balances	Monitors physicians' handling of Medicare credit balances (eg, overpayments, duplicate payments) and refunds to patients or carriers
Multiple discharges	Looks at duplicate billing for inpatient or observation discharge management
Anesthesia services	Monitors compliance with Medicare rules for supervising and billing for residents and nurse anesthetists
Critical care services	Gauges adherence to guidelines for reporting critical care services
Billing service companies	Verifies that agreements between physicians and billing companies meet Medicare standards
Improper billing of psychiatric services	Monitors whether or not service reporting is accurate and complies with guidelines (eg, billing for psychotherapy instead of using inpatient hospital codes, billing for psychologic tests by the test performed and not by the hour, billing for individual psychotherapy when the service was performed in a group setting, providing this service to patients who are not able to receive services because of their mental status)

The OIG Work Plan

Another clue that physician billing will be on the OIG antifraud radar can be found in its Medicare and Medicaid program annual work plan. Looking at the OIG antifraud priorities for physicians for the coming year can help practices anticipate the coding or

Chapter 14: Preventing Fraud and Abuse: Compliance, Audits, and Paybacks

billing activities that may attract an auditor's attention simply because it falls within the parameters of the work plan.

Here are some of the activities identified in the OIG Work Plan targeting physicians and other health professionals:

- Coding of E/M services—electronic health record (EHR) documentation practices associated with potentially improper payments
- Assessing the effectiveness of security controls over networked medical devices in securing electronic protected health information
- Reviewing claims from the top error-prone providers as identified by program audit contractors
- Identifying atypical antipsychotic drugs prescribed for children in Medicaid
- Identifying questionable billing patterns for outpatient mental health services
- Assessing the completeness of Medicaid Early Periodic Screening, Diagnosis, and Treatment screenings (medical, vision, and hearing)
- Detecting the error rate for incident-to services performed by nonphysicians
- Finding Medicaid payments resulting in credit balances (overpayment or coordination of benefits error)
- Conducting state rescreening or revalidation of all Medicaid-enrolled providers by 2016
- Terminating Medicaid providers that have been terminated by Medicare or another state Medicaid plan

While knowing what the OIG is looking for may be helpful, making sure the practice is doing everything possible to comply with coding and billing requirements is essential.

Compliance Programs

Does your practice have a fraud and abuse prevention compliance program? You should. For many years, compliance programs for small practices were voluntary but a good idea. This is no longer the case; they are now required even for small practices, but they can be scalable.

What is a compliance program? A compliance program establishes strategies to prevent, detect, and resolve conduct that does not conform to

- Federal and state law
- Federal, state, and private payer health care program requirements
- The practice's own ethical and business policies

Pediatric practices benefit from having compliance initiatives because they tighten billing and coding operations and documentation. Practices with written compliance programs report having better control on internal procedures, improved medical record documentation, and streamlined practice operations.

Section 6401(a) of the PPACA requires physicians and other providers and suppliers who enroll in Medicare, Medicaid, or Children's Health Insurance Program to establish a compliance program with certain "core elements."

The 7 Elements of the OIG Compliance Program

Although the OIG has yet to publish the official guidance for required compliance programs, it's helpful to look at the 7 core elements described in the OIG guidance on voluntary compliance program for small physician practices published in 2000.

- Conduct internal monitoring and auditing.
- Implement compliance and practice standards.

- Designate a compliance officer or contact.
- Conduct appropriate training and education.
- Respond appropriately to detected offenses and develop corrective action.
- Develop open lines of communication.
- Enforce disciplinary standards through well-publicized guideline.

It's also useful to consult the *United States Sentencing Commission Guidelines Manual*, which makes it clear that an organization under investigation may be given more sympathetic treatment if a good compliance program is in place. Compliance programs not only help to prevent fraudulent or erroneous claims, but they also show that the physician practice is making a good-faith effort to submit claims appropriately. However, that would require the program to be integrated into the daily operations of the practice. It cannot be a set of policies and procedures merely kept in a binder or on a computer unrelated to actual business operations.

Here are some reasons the *United States Sentencing Commission Guidelines Manual* identifies to implement an effective compliance program.

- It may save the practice money if it prevents costly civil suits and criminal investigations.
- It sends an unambiguous message to employees: Fraud and abuse will not be tolerated.
- It decreases the risk of employees bringing suit against the practice under the False Claims Act because employees will have an internal communication system for reporting questionable activities and resolving problems.
- It helps if an investigation occurs. Investigators may be more inclined to resolve the problem as a civil rather than a criminal matter, or it may lead to an administrative resolution rather than a formal false claim action.
- It may help reduce the range used for imposing fines under federal sentencing guidelines.
- It may influence an OIG decision whether to exclude a provider from participation in federal health care programs.
- It frequently results in improved medical record documentation.
- It improves coding accuracy, reduces denials, and makes claims and payment processes more effective.
- It educates physicians and employees on their responsibilities for preventing, detecting, and reporting fraud and abuse.
- It should meet governmental requirements for practices to have a formal compliance plan.

Steps to Developing a Compliance Program

The CMS has described the steps to create an effective compliance and ethics program. A key aspect is that the organization exercise due diligence to prevent and detect criminal conduct and promote a culture that encourages ethical conduct and a commitment to compliance with the law.

The CMS specifies that in creating the compliance program, the practice

1. Develop and distribute written policies, procedures, and standards of conduct to prevent and detect inappropriate behavior.
2. Designate a chief compliance officer and other appropriate bodies (eg, a corporate compliance committee) charged with the responsibility of operating and monitoring the compliance program and who report directly to high-level personnel and the governing body.

Chapter 14: Preventing Fraud and Abuse: Compliance, Audits, and Paybacks

3. Use reasonable efforts not to include any individual in the substantial authority personnel whom the organization knew, or should have known, has engaged in illegal activities or other conduct inconsistent with an effective compliance and ethics program.

4. Develop and implement regular, effective education and training programs for the governing body, all employees, including high-level personnel and, as appropriate, the organization's agents.

5. Maintain a process, such as a hotline, to receive complaints and the adoption of procedures to protect the anonymity of complainants and to protect whistle-blowers from retaliation. (In a small practice, a hotline could be replaced with an "anonymous fraud report box.")

6. Develop a system to respond to allegations of improper conduct and the enforcement of appropriate disciplinary action against employees who have violated internal compliance policies, applicable statutes, regulations, or federal health care program requirements.

7. Use audits and/or other evaluation techniques to monitor compliance and assist in the reduction of identified problem areas.

8. Investigate and remediate identified systemic problems, including making any necessary modifications to the organization's compliance and ethics program.

Written Policies and Procedures

Any effective compliance program should have written compliance standards and procedures that the practice follows. They should specifically describe the lines of responsibility for implementing the compliance program. Those standards and procedures should reduce the likelihood of fraudulent activity while also helping to identify any incorrect billing practices. Policies and procedures should be updated periodically to address newly identified areas of risk, new regulations, or process changes in the practice.

Coding and Billing

The following billing risk areas have been frequent areas of investigations and audits by the OIG and should be addressed in a good compliance program:

- Billing for items or services not provided or not provided as claimed
- Submitting claims for equipment, medical supplies, and services that are not reasonable and necessary
- Double billing
- Billing for non-covered services as if covered
- Known misuse of National Provider Identifiers, which results in improper billing
- Billing separately for bundled services
- Misuse of modifiers
- Consistently under-coding or over-coding services
- Using only one E/M service code within a category of service

  Other areas that may trigger an audit include
  - Profile of services reported differs from payer profiles of physicians of your specialty.
  - Repeated use of unspecified diagnosis codes or use of codes that are not consistent with the service or your specialty.
  - Surgical services not consistent with claims submitted by a facility.
  - Number of procedures or services reported exceed the hours in a day.
  - High numbers of denials.

||||||| Coding Pearl |||||||

Place of service errors are a targeted area of review for the OIG.

Medical Record Documentation

One of the most important physician practice compliance issues is the appropriate documentation of diagnosis and treatment. The written compliance plan should specify that medical record documentation should comply with the following documentation principles and guidelines:

- The medical record should be complete and legible.
- Documentation should be completed at the time of service or as soon as possible afterward.
- The documentation of each patient encounter should include the reason for the encounter; any relevant history; physical examination findings; prior diagnostic test results; assessment, clinical impression, or diagnosis; plan of care; and date and legible identity of the observer.
- If not documented, the rationale for ordering diagnostic and other ancillary services should be easily inferred by an independent reviewer or third party. Past and present diagnoses should be accessible to the treating and/or consulting physician.
- Appropriate health risk factors should be identified. The patient's progress, patient's response to and any changes in treatment, and any revision in diagnosis should be documented.
- All pages in the medical record should include the patient name and an identifying number or birth date.
- Prescription drug management should include the name of the medication, dosage, and instructions.
- Clinically important telephone calls should be documented, including date, time, and instructions.
- Anticipatory guidance, patient education, and counseling must be documented when performed.
- Any addenda should be dated, initialed, and signed.
- Consent forms should be dated, the procedure documented, and the form signed by the patient or his or her legal representative. Documentation should include a summary of the discussion of the procedure and risks.
- All abbreviations used should be explicit.
- Patient noncompliance should be documented as well as discussion of the risks and adverse consequences of noncompliance.
- Allergies and adverse reactions should be prominently displayed.
- Immunization and growth charts must be maintained.
- Problem and medication lists should be completed and current.

Please see Coding Conundrum: Pitfalls of EHR Coding on page 346 for considerations specific to EHR documentation.

> ||||||| **Coding Pearl** |||||||
>
> An important physician practice compliance issue is the appropriate documentation of diagnosis and treatment to support that care was medically necessary and within recognized standards of care and codes submitted are accurate.

Chapter 14: Preventing Fraud and Abuse: Compliance, Audits, and Paybacks

Coding Conundrum: Pitfalls of EHR Coding

One of the advantages of using EHRs is enhanced documentation of services. Documentation of an E/M service may be easier because of the use of templates or drop-down options, and legibility is not an issue. However, there are disadvantages to EHRs when it comes to documentation. When completing an audit, be aware of

- The use of templates may not accurately describe pertinent patient history or abnormal findings on examination. Some EHR systems do not allow free texting, thereby prohibiting more detailed, appropriate documentation. If a system does not allow free texting, work with the vendor to add this capability, or add any and all abnormal findings that might be pertinent in the template so that documentation can be complete and accurate.
- Users should be familiar with the manner in which the EHR constructs a note from the data entered into each field and how the system may be customized to enhance the final note.
- Only the history and physical examination that are pertinent to the problem or condition should be used in selection of an E/M code. Therefore, physicians should code each E/M service and override the EHR-assigned E/M code when appropriate.
- The physician must document history of present illness (HPI). The EHR will usually capture all documentation, whether performed by ancillary staff or the provider. Make certain that it is clear who documented each portion of the service. For example, if HPI is documented by a nurse or medical assistant, the physician *must* document his or her HPI. (Electronic health record systems include audit trails that may be used to prove who entered specific elements of documentation. It is important to understand how the practice's EHR system creates and produces an audit trail.)
- The use of a scribe to enter information relayed by a physician or provider must be clearly entered in each record, when applicable. Most payers require identification of the scribe that includes a statement such as "acting as a scribe for Dr X." The physician or provider must review the note for accuracy and cosign indicating his or her words and actions were accurately recorded.
- If an EHR system automatically transfers the documented review of systems (ROS) and past, family, and social history from one encounter to the next or lists every medication that has been prescribed in the past, make certain that the physician reviews the information to be certain it is still accurate and documents his or her review of the pertinent copied information to support the level of history that was necessary and performed.
- Physicians may document the same comment in the ROS that was obtained and documented in the HPI (eg, HPI, "fever of 102"; ROS, "fever"). The repeated comment should only be used as HPI or ROS, not both, based on the context for which it was obtained (eg, description of problem, question to better define problem). The EHR system may not differentiate and will count the redundant information twice (or more), leading to a higher level of history.
- Most EHR systems have integrated an E/M coding system using the CMS 1995 or 1997 *Documentation Guidelines for Evaluation and Management Services.* Systems measure or count the elements of each of the required key components (ie, history, physical examination, and medical decision-making) without regard to the nature of the presenting problem, severity of illness, or medical necessity. Therefore, if a physician elects to perform a detailed or comprehensive-level history and physical examination on every established patient, the reported E/M code will always be a higher-level E/M service.

Coding Conundrum: Pitfalls of EHR Coding, continued

- If previous diagnoses are carried over from one encounter to the next, make sure that only those that are pertinent to the current visit are considered when determining the complexity of the service provided.
- List the primary diagnosis first because the EHR system may report the diagnoses in the order in which they are documented.
- To support management options, it may be necessary to document the diagnoses being considered. These suspected or ruled-out diagnoses should not be reported by the EHR system in the outpatient setting.
- Make certain that any separately reportable procedure or service has documentation to support that it was performed.
- Don't depend on the software vendor to add *Current Procedural Terminology* (*CPT*®); *International Classification of Diseases, Ninth Revision, Clinical Modification* or *International Classification of Diseases, 10th Revision, Clinical Modification;* or Healthcare Common Procedure Coding System codes to the system. Review all new, deleted, and revised codes each year. Notify the vendor if codes have not been revised and educate physicians and billing staff on their appropriate use.

Kickbacks, Inducements, and Self-referrals

Business arrangements in which physician practices refer business to an outside entity (eg, hospitals, hospices, nursing facilities, home health agencies, durable medical equipment suppliers, vendors) should be on a fair market value basis. Whenever a physician practice intends to enter into a business arrangement that involves making referrals, legal counsel familiar with antikickback and physician self-referral laws should review the arrangement.

> ||||||||| **Coding Pearl** |||||||||
>
> Use experienced health care lawyers. To possibly locate one, contact your state bar association or the American Health Lawyers Association (www.healthlawyers.org).

Risk areas that may need to be addressed in policies and procedures include

- Offering inappropriate inducements to patients (eg, waiving coinsurance or deductible amounts without a good-faith determination that the patient is in financial need, failing to make reasonable efforts to collect the cost-sharing amount)
- Financial arrangements with outside entities to which the practice may refer federal health care program business
- Joint ventures with entities supplying goods or services to the physician practice or its patients
- Consulting contracts or medical directorships
- Office and equipment leases with entities to which the physician refers business
- Soliciting, accepting, or offering any gift or gratuity of more than nominal value to or from those who may benefit from a physician practice's referral of federal health care program business

When considering whether to engage in a particular billing practice, enter into a particular business venture, or pursue an employment, consulting, or other personal services relationship, it is prudent to evaluate the arrangement for potential compliance problems. Use experienced health care lawyers to analyze the issues and provide a legal evaluation and risk analysis of the proposed venture, relationship, or arrangement. The state bar association may have a directory of local attorneys who practice in the health care field. The American Health Lawyers Association is another resource (www.healthlawyers.org).

Retention of Records

Policies and procedures should be written to include the creation, distribution, retention, and destruction of documents. In designing a record-retention system, privacy concerns and federal and state regulatory requirements should be taken into consideration. In addition to maintaining appropriate and thorough medical records on each patient, the OIG recommends that the system include the following types of documents:

- All records and documentation (eg, billing and claims documentation) required for participation in federal, state, and private-payer health care programs
- All records necessary to demonstrate the integrity of the physician practice's compliance process and to confirm the effectiveness of the program
  The following record-retention guidelines should be used:
- The length of time that a physician's medical record documentation is to be retained should be specified. Federal and state statutes should be consulted for specific time frames.
  - ❖ Consulting with an attorney or risk management department of a medical liability insurer is prudent to determine the appropriate retention period. At a minimum, pediatricians may want to retain records until patients obtain the age of majority plus the statute of limitations in their jurisdiction. Longer retention periods may be prudent depending on the circumstances.
- Medical records should be secured against loss, destruction, unauthorized access, unauthorized reproduction, corruption, and damage.
- Policies and procedures should stipulate the disposition of medical records in the event the practice is sold or closed.

The AAP provides free Health Insurance Portability and Accountability Act of 1996 (HIPAA) privacy and security manuals with downloadable templates, policies, and procedures at www.aap.org/en-us/professional-resources/practice-support/practice-management/HIPAA/Pages/HIPAA-and-HITECH.aspx.

Document Advice From Payers

A physician practice should document its efforts to comply with applicable federal, state, and private health care program requirements. For example

- When requesting advice from a government agency charged with administering a federal or state health care program or from a private payer, document and retain a record of the request and of all written or oral responses.
- Maintain a log of oral inquiries between the practice and third parties.
- Keep copies of all provider manuals, provider bulletins, and communications from payers about coding and submission of claims.

Designate a Compliance Officer

> ||||||| **Coding Pearl** |||||||
>
> The compliance officer should establish methods to improve the practice's efficiency and quality of services and reduce the practice's vulnerability to fraud and abuse.

To administer the compliance program, the practice should designate an individual responsible for overseeing the compliance program. More than one employee may be designated with the responsibility of compliance monitoring, or a practice may outsource all or part of the functions of a compliance officer to a third party. Attributes and qualifications of a compliance officer include

- Independent position to protect against any conflicts of interest from "regular" position responsibilities and compliance officer duties
- Attention to detail
- Experience in billing and coding

- Effective communication skills (oral and written) with employees, physicians, and carriers

The primary responsibilities of a compliance officer include

- Overseeing and monitoring the implementation of the compliance program.
- Establishing methods, such as periodic audits, to improve the practice's efficiency and quality of services and reduce the practice's vulnerability to fraud and abuse.
- Revising the compliance program in response to changes in the needs of the practice or changes in the law and in the policies and procedures of government and private payer health plans.
- Developing, coordinating, and participating in a training program that focuses on the elements of the compliance program and seeks to ensure that training materials are appropriate.
- Checking the HHS OIG List of Excluded Individuals/Entities and the federal System for Award Management to ascertain whether any potential new hires, current employees, medical staff, or independent contractors are listed, advising management, and seeing that appropriate action is taken as described in the compliance program.
- Informing employees and physicians of pertinent federal and state statutes, regulations, and standards and monitoring their compliance.
- Investigating any report or allegation concerning suspected unethical or improper business practices and monitoring subsequent corrective action, compliance, or both.
- Assessing the practice's situation and determining what best suits the practice in terms of compliance oversight.
- Maintaining records of compliance-related activities, including meetings, educational activities, and internal audits. Particular attention should be given to documenting violations found by the compliance program and documenting the remedial actions.

Don't Get Caught Without a Plan

Most practices will never have to deal with demands for paybacks or fraud audits. Nevertheless, all practices should have a plan just in case they occur. Because time is of the essence in responding to these communications, it would be a calamity to have a letter sit on someone's desk while precious days tick away. Often, a response must be received within 30 days of the date of the request, and the paperwork demanded is not insignificant.

The first communication may be a request for repayment based on payer software analysis of claims history to detect claims paid in conflict with payment policies. It is important for all staff to be trained to recognize these requests and know to get them to the compliance officer immediately. Then qualified staff tasked with receiving all requests for paybacks can determine the veracity of the request and, if inaccurate, act in accordance with the payer's rebuttal and appeal processes in a timely manner. Likewise, requests for records must be handled carefully and expeditiously.

Responding to Repayment Demands

In an effort to control costs and stamp out fraud, carrier claims processing and special investigative units use sophisticated software programs to identify providers with atypical coding patterns that could indicate erroneous coding and potential overpayments. For example, some carriers may flag providers considered outliers in frequently reporting high-level E/M codes or frequent use of modifiers. They then extrapolate the alleged over-payments over several years and demand across-the-board repayments. Worse, carriers will reduce payments on future claims to correct alleged overpayments on past claims. These requests require a swift and skilled response. Usually several thousand dollars are involved. Given the compressed timeline and dollars at stake, seeking legal advice is invaluable in these situations.

Here are some general guidance for your consideration.

- If it is truly due to a billing error by the practice, take action to correct the problem and demonstrate to the carrier how it has or will be corrected and the measures implemented to avoid the problem in the future.
- Reply in writing to inform the carrier you are willing to work with it, and ask that it identify each of the claims in question as well as the specific criteria or standards it is applying to the audit.
- Make sure the practice and the carrier consistently apply current *CPT*® guidelines. Reference *CPT* coding guidelines and have appropriate documentation for support. The AAP Coding Hotline can be a resource to you as well; inquiries can be made to aapcodinghotline@aap.org.
- Review your carrier contract's clauses on audits and dispute resolution as well as applicable state laws on audits and repayments with your attorney.
- Focus any overpayment recovery efforts on a case-by-case basis. Avoid unilateral take-backs by not allowing the carrier to extrapolate repayments on any or all future claims.
- Have the carrier provide documentation as proof of overpayment for each contested claim.
- Obtain and secure written documentation of all contacts with the carrier on this issue. Should a carrier payment policy require reporting that varies from *CPT* guidelines, obtain written, dated documentation from the carrier to verify that is the case. Keep this documentation permanently.
- Use legal counsel skilled in carrier contracting when negotiating contracts and confronted with repayment demands.

The AAP Private Payer Advocacy Advisory Committee has a resource for AAP members on responding to retrospective audit and carrier take-back. To access it, go to www.aap.org/cfp (use access code AAPCFP20).

What if Your Practice Is Audited?

- Contact legal counsel as soon as possible. Make sure the attorney or legal practice has experience with audits. If it is a Medicaid audit, it is preferable to have an attorney with Medicaid audit experience. An audit is a complex legal process with significant consequences. It is unwise to attempt to maneuver through this process without sound legal advice.
- Designate one physician or staff member to serve as the primary contact with the attorney and auditors. However, keep in mind that all physicians and staff members may need to work with auditors to some extent.
- Request that the auditor provide you with an opening and closing conference. At the initial meeting, ask for the individual's credentials and job title and ask him or her to summarize the purpose of the review or audit.
- Know how far back auditors may conduct reviews, the number of records a contractor may request, the amount of time allowed to respond to each request, any rebuttal process in place, and steps necessary to appeal adverse findings.
- If the time requirements for producing copies or gathering medical records are unmanageable, contact the auditing entity to request an extension. Provide a clear justification for the extension request.

- Keep copies of all written communication (eg, letters, directives, memos, e-mails). Keep the postmarked envelopes of all letters, including the original notice.
- Fully document all verbal communication, including time, date, persons involved, substance of the discussion, and conclusions and agreements.
- In response to requests for information, provide only the information requested and maintain copies of what you provide auditors. Before providing files, remove any information unrelated to the audit. For example, in a Medicaid audit, you could exclude information related to services provided when the patient was covered under a commercial plan or was uninsured.
- Do not alter any documents or medical records.
- Respond only to questions from the auditors; do not try to engage them in any conversations. If the auditors are conducting the review in your office, try to place them in a separate office away from patients, staff, and business operations.
- Be prepared to respond promptly to each request received. Keep a log of requests received by date, response due date, requesting party, any communication with the requestor, date of response, and outcome.
- Know HIPAA privacy regulations, documentation principles, coding guidelines, and payment policies, and verify that all supporting documentation is included in each response.
- If legibility of the record is questionable, include a transcribed copy with attestation by the author of the original document stating that the transcription is accurate and provided to ensure legibility. Any unsigned entry should also be accompanied by a separate attestation by its author.
- Copied or scanned medical records should be carefully reviewed to be sure that all pages were legibly copied (front and back, if applicable) and are straight and within the margins on the page.
- Any questions about the sufficiency of medical record documentation should be addressed with the physician or provider who ordered or documented the service prior to responding to the request for records. Any corrections to an entry should be performed in a manner that maintains legibility of the original content (eg, single-line strike-through) and should be signed and dated. A summary of the service provided may be included to provide further information but should be distinctly labeled as such and not as part of the original record.
- Include any policy or correspondence from the payer that was used to guide your billing and coding practices related to the service. (Archived payer manuals supportive of claims from previous years may be available on state Medicaid Web sites.) Clinical practice guidelines, policy statements, textbooks, and manuals may also be supportive of medical necessity.
- Send records in a manner that allows for confirmation of receipt.
- Secure a copy of auditors' contact information in case you need to follow up.
- Obtain, in writing, the expected date of a written summary of findings.

Can This Really Happen?

Conventional wisdom says that auditors will probably go after big organizations when it comes to investigating fraud and abuse, but the OIG has said repeatedly that it has zero tolerance for fraud, so technically everyone is at risk. Because most of the software programs used to detect unusual coding and billing patterns are based on adult services, pediatricians may be identified as outliers because their coding does not conform to adult-based parameters. Unfortunately, valid pediatric coding may be tagged as improper and honest providers may have to respond to inappropriate recoupment requests or audits. The AAP works hard to minimize these problems and help chapters respond when state Medicaid programs target pediatric coding as inappropriate. This is an ongoing challenge.

Sadly, there are instances of fraud involving pediatricians. A review of past OIG reports to Congress revealed the following cases:

* A pediatrician pleaded guilty to a misdemeanor count of health care fraud as part of a global resolution of criminal and civil violations of the False Claims Act. The pediatrician said that from about January 2007 through November 2012, he knowingly up-coded billings for infant auditory screening examinations to Medicaid and commercial insurance programs—specifically, billing for comprehensive auditory examinations even though only less-expensive auditory screens had been performed. The investigation revealed that the pediatrician did not even have equipment capable of performing the comprehensive tests for which he billed. According to the plea agreement, he admitted that through numerous clinics, he systemically billed for urinalysis testing as though its office had performed a microscopic examination of the sample despite the fact that no microscopy had been performed. He up-coded the billings in this manner even though his clinics did not possess the microscopes necessary to conduct such examinations.

* A pediatrician was sentenced to 8 years' incarceration and ordered to pay $7,116,423 in restitution after pleading guilty to charges of health care fraud, mail fraud, and forfeiture. From 2003 through 2009, the pediatrician submitted fraudulent claims to Medicaid, Tricare, and private insurance companies for services not rendered. The investigation involved OIG, the US Postal Inspection Service, the Defense Criminal Investigative Service, the Attorney General Medical Fraud Control Unit and Insurance Fraud Section, the state insurance fraud division, and the county district attorney's office.

* Operation Free Shot focuses on health care providers who bill Medicaid and other insurance programs for childhood vaccines the providers received free of charge from the Vaccines for Children (VFC) program, a joint federal and state program that provides childhood immunizations. Under the VFC program, doctors and other health care providers receive free vaccines distributed by the US Department of Public Health and agree not to bill Medicaid or any other third party for the cost of the vaccines. The provider may recover a minimal fee for administrative costs associated with inoculating a child. Overall, there have been 7 civil settlements and 2 criminal convictions, with a total recovery in excess of $2 million; in fiscal year 2006, there were 2 civil settlements against a physician and practice in the amount of $430,000.

* In another state, an investigation of the VFC program resulted in 4 settlements against a pediatrician in the amount of $53,000 over a 3-year period.

* A pediatrician who operated an immunization program utilizing federal VFC program funds agreed to pay the government $65,000. The pediatrician allegedly administered 3,851 vaccine doses to children who were not eligible to receive the free immunizations. He also allegedly administered expired vaccines to children in at least 2 cases.

Explore the Need for Additional Insurance

Many medical liability insurers and insurance brokers offer products to provide additional coverage for the consequences of billing errors and omissions. Pediatric practices may want to contact their insurers to see whether their current medical liability policies cover any of the following problems. If they don't, it might be worthwhile to explore insurance options for obtaining that additional protection.

- Defense coverage for a Medicaid audit
- Qui tam action (False Claims Act)
- Unintentional billing errors and omissions
- Stark violations
- Unintentional release of medical or financial data
- Breach of computers or network security
- Data recovery

Summary

These are interesting times for pediatric practices that require thoughtful preparation and ongoing concern. Learn about the fraud and abuse enforcement climate in your state. Implement an effective compliance program and follow it. Be sure your staff knows what a demand for repayment or audit notice looks like and what they need to do with it just on the off chance that something should happen. Have a response plan in place should an auditor knock on your door or a recoupment letter come in the mail. Consult with an attorney when needed. Think about the need for insurance for billing errors and omissions. Keep current with coding and billing updates.

Chapter 14: Preventing Fraud and Abuse: Compliance, Audits, and Paybacks

The Business of Medicine:
From Clean Claims to Correct Payment
and
Emerging Payment Methodologies

Physicians and their staff need to continually refine their practice management skills to be able to respond to changing payment systems to maintain a viable practice. The first section of this chapter provides an overview of guidelines and tools that may be used to monitor and manage charge accumulation, claims filing, review of payments, the appeals process, and guidelines for conducting baseline and subsequent documentation and coding reviews. The second section provides an introduction to newer payment methodologies such as accountable care organizations (ACOs).

Clean Claims to Correct Payment

An effective charge accumulation system, reporting appropriate codes, and a timely claims filing system will result in clean claims. Ongoing payment review and an efficient appeals process and collections policy will result in appropriate payments. An effective accounts receivable system requires

> ||||||||| **Coding Pearl** |||||||||
>
> Regular practice performance assessments benefit physician practices by increasing the number of correctly submitted claims, resulting in faster and more appropriate payments.

- ☀ Development and use of management tools.
  - ❖ Consider incorporating claims processing tools for analysis of your claims processing procedures. Examples of these tools can be found at www.aap.org/en-us/professional-resources/practice-support/financing-and-payment/Pages/Private-Payer-Advocacy-Resources-on-Coding-and-Payment.aspx.
- ☀ Continuing staff education with constant oversight and communication with staff, payers, and patients.
  - ❖ Policies and procedures should be adopted to support continuous monitoring of payer communications and to disseminate information on benefit policy changes that affect coding and payment.
  - ❖ Ensure that staff assigned with responsibilities related to correct coding and billing have access to authoritative resources on coding and documentation (eg, current Medicaid National Correct Coding Initiative [NCCI] edits and manual). Please see chapters 3 and 14 for more information on code edits and compliant coding and billing.
- ☀ Regular audits with any necessary corrective action to be compliant with billing standards, coding guidelines, and federal rules and regulations (eg, Health Insurance Portability and Accountability Act of 1996, Anti-Kickback Act, False Claims Act). Audits benefit the practice by identifying
  - ❖ The number of timely and correctly submitted claims, resulting in faster and more appropriate payments
  - ❖ The need for physician and staff education on coding and documentation
  - ❖ Inappropriate carrier denials and reductions requiring appeals, thus decreasing practice costs
  - ❖ Issues for payer contract negotiations
  - ❖ The chances of incorrect coding and potential charges of fraud
  - ❖ Areas in need of written office policies and procedures (eg, pre-authorizations and referrals processes, claims follow-up processes, control systems)

Chapter 15: The Business of Medicine: From Clean Claims to Correct Payment and Emerging Payment Methodologies

The Encounter Form

Designing and Reviewing the Encounter Form

The encounter form, whether computer generated or printed, should be reviewed periodically and updated at the time of the *Current Procedural Terminology (CPT®)*; *International Classification of Diseases, Ninth Revision, Clinical Modification (ICD-9-CM)* or, when adopted, *International Classification of Diseases, 10th Revision, Clinical Modification (ICD-10-CM)*; and Healthcare Common Procedure Coding System (HCPCS) updates (ie, January, April, July, and October) to be certain that it includes most, if not all, of the services and procedures that are commonly performed in the practice and that the codes are accurate.

If using electronic health records (EHRs), make sure that codes in the system are accurate and updated in accordance with code set updates.

Practices Generating Charges From a Printed Encounter Form (Superbill)

Consider the following when developing the encounter form:

- Include all levels of service for each category of evaluation and management (E/M) services (eg, **99201–99205**, **99221–99223**).
- List procedures (eg, laboratory) in alphabetic order within the category of service. For example, group vaccine administration codes and vaccine product codes together.
- Allow space on the printed encounter form to write in specific details of a procedure when required. For example
  Code **120**_____ Laceration repair; loc _____; size_____
- Include the most commonly reported diagnosis codes. Consider grouping diagnosis codes by organ system, then alphabetically within the system.
- When an *ICD-9-CM* code requires a fourth or fifth digit and when *ICD-10-CM* is implemented, leave space on the printed form to allow the reporting of the specific diagnosis. For example
  ICD-9-CM: **719.4**_____ Joint pain; loc _____
  ICD-10-CM: **M25.0**___ Joint pain; loc _____
- Include the most frequently used modifiers.
- Include add-on codes for prolonged and special services. For example
  99354   Prolonged service in the office or outpatient, first hour
  99058   Services provided on an emergency basis in the office, disrupting other scheduled services
- Develop a separate encounter form for hospital and outpatient hospital services. Make sure that it includes all of the services most commonly performed in the hospital setting.
- Leave space on the printed form to write in any services or diagnoses that are not included.

Completing the Printed Encounter Form

Every practice should develop a written policy for the requirements for completion of the form. Some points that should be part of the policy include

- The encounter form is *not* part of the medical record. Information such as the need for follow-up care, diagnostic tests, or referrals must always be documented in the medical record even if written on the encounter form.

- Services must be clearly identified (eg, circle procedure, use check mark).
- The person providing the service (eg, physician, laboratory technologist, medical assistant) should note that service on the encounter form to ensure that only the procedures performed are reported.
  - ❖ For example, it is common for a physician to mark a urinalysis on the encounter form when he or she orders the test. However, if a specimen could not be obtained, the procedure would have been billed inappropriately. If the nurse (under supervision of the physician) had been responsible for reporting the service when performed, it would not have been reported because the urine was not obtained.
- The physician is ultimately responsible for the services reported and billed.
- The physician should identify the diagnosis as, for example, primary or secondary.
- Diagnoses and services/procedures must be numbered and linked to each other.
- For example, an E/M service and removal of impacted cerumen from the right ear (**69210**) is performed. The physician reports the primary diagnosis (acute suppurative otitis media without spontaneous rupture of eardrum [**382.00**]) (1) and the secondary diagnosis (impacted cerumen [**380.4**]) (2). *ICD-9-CM* diagnosis code **382.00** is linked to the office visit and the secondary diagnosis code (**380.4,** impacted cerumen) is linked to the procedure.

  99213 25 (1)   **382.00** (1)
  69210 (2)   **380.4** (2)

  - ❖ Following transition to *ICD-10-CM*
    99213 25 (1)   **H66.001** (1) (acute suppurative otitis media without spontaneous rupture of ear drum, right ear)
    69210 (2)   **H61.21** (2) (impacted cerumen, right ear)

- Procedures or diagnoses must be written, if not preprinted, on the form.
- A billing manager or clerk should never independently add or change a service or diagnosis.
- A system should be instituted to monitor and ensure capture of all of the day's patient encounter forms (eg, cross-reference to the patient sign-in records).

Reviewing the Encounter Form

A staff member who understands correct coding and reporting guidelines should always review the completed encounter form before charges are posted and the claim is submitted to ensure that all procedures and services are captured and accurate.

For example, the reviewer should look to see that

- An administration code is reported with vaccines and/or injections.
- A venipuncture or finger stick is reported with a laboratory test.
- A handling fee is reported when the specimen is prepared and sent to an outside laboratory.
- A modifier is appended when appropriate (eg, modifier **76** for repeat procedures or services).
- The office visit is reported using the appropriate new or established patient category of service.
- The diagnoses reported as primary and secondary are appropriate and are linked to the appropriate services or procedures.
- The documentation to support each service has been completed with appropriate dates and signatures.

Chapter 15: The Business of Medicine: From Clean Claims to Correct Payment and Emerging Payment Methodologies

Submitting Clean Claims

Many states have enacted laws that require prompt payment of "clean claims." In general, clean claims are those that contain sufficient and correct information for processing without further investigation or development by the payer (definitions may vary by state). Submitted claims must be accurate and in accordance with the process as outlined in the executed carrier or health plan agreement. Knowing a payer's claim requirements will decrease chances of denied claims. Make sure the practice understands payer rules for billing for nonphysician services, incident-to billing, etc. (See Chapter 4 for more information on billing for nonphysician services.) Be aware of any updates issued by the carrier that affect billing and claims submission. Generally, a clean claim should have the following information:

> ||||||||| **Coding Pearl** |||||||||
>
> The optimum time for filing claims is on the day of or the day following the service but no more than 2 to 3 days from the date of service.

- Practice information (name, address, phone, National Provider Identifier [NPI], group tax identification number)
- Patient information (patient name, birth date, policyholder, policy number, patient identification number, address)
- Codes (*CPT*®, *ICD-9-CM* and *ICD-10-CM*, HCPCS, place of service), modifiers, and service dates
- Carrier information
- Secondary insurance information
- Referring physician name and NPI, if applicable
- Facility name and address as appropriate

If additional information is necessary to support a service or explain an unusual circumstance (eg, unlisted procedure code, unusual procedure, complicated procedure)

- Send a "hard copy" claim with a cover letter and a narrative report or copy of the appropriate part of the medical record (eg, progress note, procedure note) to facilitate the claim's processing.
- Any documentation (coordination of benefits information, letter of medical necessity, clinical reports) should include the patient's name, service date, and policy number on each page in case the papers become separated.
- Keep a copy of the claim and supporting information for follow-up of payment.
- When filing claims for patients with coordination of benefits, make certain that all required information (ie, primary and secondary insurance information) has been obtained from the patient and that the claims are filed with the supporting information (eg, explanation of benefits [EOB]) according to the plan requirements.

Claims should be submitted for payment as soon as possible and before the agreed-on deadline as specified in the agreement. The optimum time for filing claims is on the day of or the day following the service but no more than 2 to 3 days from the date of service.

Special Consideration for Medicare Claims

Many health plans receive Medicare claims automatically when they are the secondary payer. In this case, the explanation of Medicare benefits will indicate that the claim has been automatically crossed over for secondary consideration. Physicians and providers should look for this indication on their EOBs and should not submit a paper claim to the secondary payer.

Monitoring Payments

Develop a process to monitor the timeliness of all payments. Tips for monitoring payments include

- Identify payers who do not pay clean claims within the time frame agreed on in your contract and follow up on all late payments with the payer. Check the provisions of your state's prompt pay law and know the provisions for clean claims, timely filing, and penalties. Report the payer's practice of late or delinquent payments to the proper agency because your practice may be entitled to payment plus interest payments.
- Review each EOB and/or remittance advice carefully to determine if the payment is correct.
- Compare the EOBs and/or remittance advice to a spreadsheet listing your top 40 codes and their allowable payments by carrier to monitor contract compliance. Practice management software may also include the ability to add contractual allowances by payer.
- Identify any discrepancies such as changes to codes, reduced payment, or denials.
- Review all payer explanations, particularly reasons for denials or down-coding. If the service provided is not a benefit covered by the plan, the patient should be billed directly (may need a signed waiver form).
- Make certain that any denials or reductions in payment are not due to practice billing errors (eg, incorrect modifiers, obsolete codes). If so, correct the errors immediately and educate staff members as appropriate to ensure correct future claim submissions. The American Academy of Pediatrics (AAP) has developed a Claim Correction Form that may be completed and submitted with a corrected claim. (See Appendix B-10 online at www.aap.org/cfp, access code AAPCFP20.)
- Make certain that the payment is consistent with the fee schedule, write-offs, and discounts agreed to by the practice and payer. Follow up with the payer on any discrepancies.
- Maintain a log of all denials or payment reductions. This can be used as a basis for future negotiations or education of the payer. (Identify one individual who has billing and coding expertise to monitor as well as accept or reject denials.)
- Review your fee schedule to see if your practice is paid at 100% of the billed charges because this is an indication that your fees are below the maximum amount established by the carrier.
- Review your fees annually and understand the Medicare Resource-Based Relative Value Scale (RBRVS), using it to value the services you provide. (For details on using the RBRVS, see "2014 RBRVS: What Is It and How Does It Affect Pediatrics?" at www.aap.org/coding.)

> **|||||||| Coding Pearl ||||||||**
> Review all payer explanations, particularly reasons for denials or down-coding, and appeal when appropriate.

Filing Appeals

Do not assume that the carrier's denials or audits are accurate. Be prepared to challenge the carrier. If you are coding correctly and in compliance with coding conventions, you should appeal all inappropriately denied claims and carrier misapplication of CPT® coding principles. Develop a system to monitor payer updates and any changes to the provider agreement so that you are aware of the current payment policies and coding edits used by the payer.

- By accepting inappropriate claim denials, a practice may be setting itself up to charges of billing fraud.

> **|||||||| Coding Pearl ||||||||**
> If a practice recodes claims as a result of inappropriate carrier denials, the resubmitted claim may not actually reflect the treatment the patient received.

- If a practice recodes claims as a result of inappropriate carrier denials, the resubmitted claim may not actually reflect the treatment the patient received.

Here is a summary of basic guidelines and tips for appealing payments.

- When in contact with the payer, always document the date, name, and title of the payer representative with whom you have talked and a summary of the details of the conversation.
  - Address issues with the person who has the authority to make decisions to overturn denials or reductions in payment.
  - Keep an updated file with names and contact information of the appropriate personnel with each of your contracted payers.
  - Request an e-mail or letter verifying the information provided and archive written correspondence containing payer representative advice and payer policies. If the carrier does not provide written documentation, prepare a summary and send it to your contact stating that this will constitute the documentation of the discussion.
- Make all appeals in writing.
  - Understand the payer's appeals process and appeal within its timeliness guidelines.
  - Format the letter to include the name of the patient, policy number, claim control number, and date of service(s) in question on each page of the letter.
  - The body of the letter should state the reason for the appeal and why you are in disagreement with the payer's adjudication of the claim.
  - Specify a date by which you expect the carrier to respond.
  - Support your case by providing medical justification and referencing *CPT*® coding guidelines. If necessary, consult with the AAP Coding Hotline for clarification of correct coding. It may be helpful to hire a certified coding expert with knowledge in pediatric coding to review your claims. (If hiring a full-time certified coding expert is not practical for a small practice, part-time employment or periodic consultation may be options for access to coding and compliance expertise.)
  - Consider sending correspondence to the carrier by certified mail to verify receipt.
- Maintain an appeals pending file.
  - If there is no response from the payer within 4 weeks of the date of the letter, send a copy of the appeal letter stamped "Second Request."
  - If there is no response within 2 weeks or if the matter continues to remain unresolved, contact the state department of insurance (or other appropriate agency in your state) to file a complaint or engage its assistance.
  - Contact your AAP chapter and pediatric council, if your chapter has one, to make them aware of the situation with the payer. American Academy of Pediatrics chapter pediatric councils meet with health plans to discuss carrier policies and practices affecting pediatrics and pediatricians.

The AAP has developed several sample appeal letters that may be used as templates in appealing payer decisions. The appeal letter templates can be found on MyAAP at www.aap.org/en-us/professional-resources/practice-support/financing-and-payment/Pages/Private-Payer-Advocacy-Templates-for-Appeal-Letters.aspx. Template topics include

- Bundling of services (eg, obesity services)
- Immunization administration services (**90460–90461; 90471–90474**)
- Inappropriate linking of *CPT* and diagnosis (*ICD-9-CM/ICD-10-CM*) codes
- Modifier **25**
- Vision screen (**99173**)

✸ Well-child care (**99381–99397**) and sick visit (**99201–99215**) reported on the same calendar day

In addition, the AAP has posted a narrative that explains the appropriateness of reporting certain circumstances based on NCCI edits.

When the AAP recognizes systemic issues with payer policies, it sends letters to payers on specific issues that need resolution or for information. These letters and carrier responses are posted on MyAAP on the Private Payer Advocacy page (www.aap. org/en-us/professional-resources/practice-support/financing-and-payment/Pages/Private-Payer-Advocacy.aspx).

Knowing when to appeal a payer denial is just as important as knowing how to properly appeal. Writing an effective appeal letter to payers requires knowledge of *CPT®* guidelines, Centers for Medicare & Medicaid Services (CMS) policy, and payer policy. The AAP Private Payer Advocacy Advisory Committee has developed a resource to effectively respond to inappropriate claim denials, Effective Health Plan Appeals: The Ins and Outs, which can be used as a guide for appealing inappropriate health plan claim denials and is found in Appendix B-12 and online at www.aap.org/cfp (access code AAPCFP20).

Negotiating With Payers

Payers need to be made aware and held accountable when their payment policies negatively affect the physician-carrier contractual arrangement. Recent class-action lawsuits against national carriers in response to payers' inappropriate down-coding and bundling of services have strengthened the position of physicians appropriately following *CPT* guidelines.

The following suggestions can facilitate negotiations:

✸ Know a health plan's policies and procedures and their effect on pediatric services. Develop a system to monitor all updates and changes to the physician contract.

✸ Know *CPT* codes, modifiers, and guidelines for their use.

✸ Understand and be able to describe the scope of services provided and the time requirements for the service.

✸ Be prepared to demonstrate cost savings that may be recognized by the plan as well as the value that the practice brings to the plan in terms of savings, quality, and/or patient satisfaction. This is your leverage.

✸ Monitor and know the use (distribution) of codes by each physician and, if in a group practice, for the practice as a whole.

✸ Identify your payer mix. Know how many patients you have in each plan and what percent of your total patients that represents. In addition, know what percentage of relative value units (RVUs) each payer pays for your most frequently used codes and how they compare in payment to each other.

✸ Know and understand the payment basis and process.

✸ Have specific codes or issues to discuss, not generalities (agreement with general ideas may not address specific issues).

✸ Try to negotiate for coverage and payment of services or, if payers refuse to cover services, get your contract amended to state that you can bill the service as non-covered. If the plan will allow for billing the patient for non-covered services, you must then advise your patients of this policy.

✸ If the plan does agree to provide coverage for a particular service, make certain you understand how the carrier will cover and pay for the service and if there will be any restrictions or limitations.

> |||||||| **Coding Pearl** ||||||||
>
> When negotiating for coverage of a service, be prepared to demonstrate cost savings that may be recognized by the plan.

- Keep notes during the discussion and be certain that you understand answers to any of your questions. Any specific agreements should be in writing and signed by both parties.
- Engage parents or employers to work in partnership to help you negotiate with a plan. Encourage parents to work through their human resources department to communicate and appeal with payers. Petition from them can be very effective.
- Many AAP chapters have developed pediatric councils, which meet with payers to address pediatric issues. Advise your chapter pediatric council of specific issues you have experienced and see how it can work with the plan. If your chapter does not have a pediatric council, this may be the right time to work with your chapter to begin developing one. To see if your state has a pediatric council or for more information, visit www.aap.org/en-us/professional-resources/practice-support/financing-and-payment/Pages/Private-Payer-Advocacy-Pediatric-Councils.aspx (AAP members only).
- If the insurance company is not addressing your concerns satisfactorily, you should be willing to withdraw from its plan. Inform the payer (a formal notification process may be outlined in your contract), patients' families, and even the state insurance commission why continued participation is impossible. Some reasons for withdrawal might be slow payment, excessive documentation requirements, and substandard payment compared with other plans. Many times negotiation begins when you walk away from the table.

> **|||||||| Coding Pearl ||||||||**
>
> Practices should conduct a prospective documentation and coding review so that corrections can be made before a claim is filed.

Documentation and Coding Audits

Medicare, state Medicaid programs, and commercial payers will audit claims as well as monitor E/M coding profiles. While the specialty-specific E/M profiles published by the CMS provide helpful information, keep in mind that these distributions only reflect code use and not code accuracy. An atypical distribution of codes may be the result of care for a more complex patient population than average, including patients with chronic diseases and with social and economic challenges. Correct coding appropriately identifies the risk stratification for your patients and may directly affect your payments.

Also, just because you got paid does not mean that payers can't go back and demand repayment, particularly if claims were processed incorrectly or it was in error according to your contract. Practices are advised to become familiar with state laws addressing retrospective audits and repayments and with payer procedures for repayment.

> **|||||||| Coding Pearl ||||||||**
>
> If a physician is not actually performing the audit or medical record reviews, one should be available to assist as necessary.

- Focus audits on documentation and coding of the most commonly performed services, adherence to medical record standards, appropriate reporting of diagnosis codes, use of modifiers, and adherence to coding and federal guidelines (eg, teaching physician guidelines, physician self-referral laws). Please see Chapter 14 for more information on compliance with federal guidelines such as physician self-referral laws.
- Make certain that all physicians in the practice are in agreement with how any review will be conducted and how results will be used.
- The person performing the audit (eg, physician, physician extender, coder or other administrative employee, outside consultant, a combination thereof) must be proficient at coding, understand payer guidelines and requirements, and know medical terminology. Consider a team approach (eg, nurse and coder). If a physician is not actually performing record reviews, one should be available to assist as necessary.

- Determine if audits should be performed under the direction of a health care attorney who may offer assistance with developing an audit process and provide guidance on any internal compliance concerns discovered in the process. Attorney/client privilege may apply when audits are directed by an attorney.

- Determine if your review will be retrospective (ie, performed on paid claims and services) or prospective (ie, performed on services and claims that have not yet been billed). It is recommended that practices conduct a prospective review because any necessary corrections can be made before a claim is filed. However, be aware that a prospective review will delay claims submission.

- Select the types of services or procedures that will be included in the review. For example, if the review will include only office or outpatient services, include those services most frequently reported (eg, a sampling of new and established patient problem-oriented and preventive medicine visits, documentation of nebulizer treatments). When performing a review of hospital services, include newborn care, critical care, initial and subsequent observation, and inpatient services.

- Determine the number of records or encounters that will be included in the audit. Most coding consultants recommend that a minimum of 10 records per physician or provider be reviewed in a baseline or subsequent review. However, if a more focused review is required, the sample size may need to be increased. Medical records should be randomly selected for each E/M level of service and selected from different dates of service.

- Determine the frequency of audits. Large practices might consider conducting audits on one physician or provider per week during a quarter or one physician or provider per month throughout the year.

- Make certain that the reviewer has all appropriate and necessary tools, including

    - The CMS *Documentation Guidelines for Evaluation and Management Services* (1995 and/or 1997) that are used by the practice or physician.

    - Current *CPT®*, *ICD-9-CM* (and after adoption, *ICD-10-CM*), and HCPCS manuals.

    - Access to or copies of all payer newsletters or information bulletins that outline their coding and/or payment policies.

    - An audit worksheet. This may be one designed by your practice, or one of many published templates may be used. Note that the CMS has never endorsed any specific audit form or coding template. Make certain that the audit form used includes appropriate requirements for selection of an E/M service. One example of an audit tool (Marshfield Audit Tool) is found in Appendix B-14 at www.aap.org/cfp (use access code AAPCFP20). The inclusion of this tool is not an official AAP endorsement but an example of a widely used and recognized audit tool.

    - A log to document findings for each provider. This log should include a summary detail of findings for each encounter reviewed. The log and E/M audit worksheets can be used as teaching tools at the conclusion of the audit.

Chapter 15: The Business of Medicine: From Clean Claims to Correct Payment and Emerging Payment Methodologies

Sample Audit Log[a]

Physician:		Date:		Auditor:	
Patient Name	**Patient ID/ DOB**	**Date of Service**	**Reported Code**	**Audited Code**	**Comments**
Jane	5/1/09	6/3/13	99214	99213	Total and counseling time not documented; key components = **99213**; plan for return not documented
			493.02; 786.07 or in *ICD-10-CM*, **J45.31**; R06.2	493.02 J45.31	Wheezing is inherent to asthma **493.02**, or in *ICD-10-CM*, **J45.31**
Zach	2/4/10	6/4/13	69210	0	Cerumen not documented as impacted
Gracie	11/12/08	6/4/13	99213	99214	Key components = **99214**

Abbreviations: DOB, date of birth; ID, identification.

[a]Also available at www.aap.org/cfp; use access code AAPCFP20.

The Audit/Review Process

1. Obtain and review a productivity report from your billing system.
2. Calculate the percentage distribution of E/M codes within each category of service (new and established office/outpatient visits, initial observation or inpatient services, use of modifier **25**) for each physician in the practice. (Most billing software provides these calculations.) You might also use the AAP Coding Calculator found at www.aap.org/coding to help you profile your E/M code use and distribution.
3. Use data from a 12-month period because they include seasonal trends and are more reflective of practice patterns.

> ||||||||| **Coding Pearl** |||||||||
>
> Use data from a 12-month period in your audit/review because they include seasonal trends and are more reflective of practice patterns.

4. Perform a comparative analysis of the distribution with each physician in the practice. Remember that data only reflect the billing patterns, not if one is more correct than another. More frequent oversight and monitoring is necessary for services provided by physicians who are new to the practice and may use documentation or coding guidance that conflicts with practice policy.
5. Review the report to ensure that all procedures performed are being captured and reported appropriately. For example, are discharge visits (**99238** and **99239**) being billed and is the number proportionate to the number of newborn and other hospital admissions performed?
6. Review the practice encounter form to ensure that *CPT®* and *ICD-9-CM/ICD-10-CM* codes are correct and match the corresponding description.
7. Review the actual encounter and claim form with the medical record to ensure that the claim is submitted with the appropriate codes and/or modifiers.
8. Review medical records to ensure that they are compliant with national standards and office policies. Standards for maintenance of medical records can be found on the National Committee for Quality Assurance Web site (www.ncqa.org).
9. Review each medical record and encounter form for
   ❖ Are the patient's name, identification number, and/or date of birth on every page in the medical record?
   ❖ Is updated demographic information in the medical record?
   ❖ Are allergies noted and prominently displayed?
   ❖ Is the date of service documented?

❖ Was the service medically necessary?

❖ Does the documentation support the level of E/M service based on the required key components and/or type of service (eg, consultation, preventive medicine service)?

❖ Are all of the services and/or procedures documented captured on the encounter form?

❖ Does the documentation for the preventive medicine visit meet the requirements of the Medicaid Early Periodic Screening, Diagnosis, and Treatment program?

❖ Does the documentation support the procedure billed (eg, administration of injection, catheterization, impacted cerumen removal)?

❖ Does the documentation support the diagnosis code(s) billed?

❖ If using EHRs, does the documentation support physician review and personal documentation? For example, if the EHR always brings up the patient's history, is there a notation that the physician reviewed it? If not, it should not be counted as part of the service.

❖ Is there a completed growth chart and immunization record?

❖ Is the documentation legible?

❖ Does any order for medication include the specific dosage and use?

❖ Is there documentation of a follow-up plan?

❖ Are diagnostic reports (eg, laboratory, x-ray) signed and dated to reflect review?

❖ Did the physician or provider sign the documentation including his or her credentials?

❖ Was an appropriate modifier reported with sufficient documentation?

❖ Is the documentation in compliance with Physicians at Teaching Hospitals guidelines and/or incident-to provisions as appropriate?

Following the audit

❖ Discuss audit findings with each provider.

❖ Educate providers and staff as necessary.

❖ If a problem is encountered (eg, inappropriate use of modifiers, miscoding), a more focused retrospective review should be conducted to determine how long the error has been occurring and its effect. This is especially important when reviewing claims for physicians new to the practice or when a particular coding guideline or code has changed.

❖ If overpayments have occurred due to miscoding or billing error(s), the error(s) should be corrected and education of appropriate staff performed. The error(s) may need to be disclosed and incorrect payments refunded. Always refer to payer contracts and agreements to understand their requirements and policies for overpayments and disclosure. Always seek advice from the practice's attorney prior to disclosure or repayment.

❖ Schedule follow-up audits if indicated to determine if problems have been resolved (eg, improved documentation, capturing procedures, correct use of modifiers).

❖ Determine if audits need to be performed on a quarterly or annual basis and follow through with audits on a routine basis.

❖ If changes need to be made to the EHR system, contact the vendor and discuss how these might be accomplished. Educate physicians and providers on the changes made or need for additional physician documentation.

❖ Establish or update written policies and procedures.

❖ Maintain records of your compliance efforts and training.

Tools for the Pediatric Practice

Working with third-party payers on coding and payment issues can be a difficult task because there is little uniformity between carriers and frequently great inconsistencies within the same umbrella organization of carriers. The AAP Private Payer Advocacy Advisory Committee is charged with enhancing systems for members and chapters to identify and respond to issues with private carriers.

To assist the pediatric practice, the AAP has several available resources to consider.

* American Academy of Pediatrics staff is available to provide clarification on coding issues. The Coding Hotline can be accessed online through the AAP Web site at www.aap.org/en-us/professional-resources/practice-support/Coding-at-the-AAP/Pages/Coding-Inquiry-Form.aspx (AAP members only) as well as by e-mail at aapcodinghotline@aap.org.

* Claims processing tools, a collection of template letters practices can use in appealing inappropriate carrier claims denials, and other claims processing tools are available through the AAP Private Payer Advocacy page at www.aap.org/en-us/professional-resources/practice-support/financing-and-payment/Pages/Private-Payer-Advocacy.aspx (AAP members only). Also, the AAP Coding Calculator allows physician practices to compare their actual E/M code use distribution to statistical norms and assess the potential effect on payment. It can be accessed at www.aap.org/en-us/professional-resources/practice-support/coding-resources/Pages/Coding-Calculator.aspx.

* Many AAP state chapters have developed pediatric councils to meet regularly with carriers to discuss pediatric issues related to access, coverage, and quality. Pediatric councils have the potential to facilitate better working relationships between pediatricians and carriers by identifying, informing, and educating payers on issues affecting pediatrics and pediatricians. The AAP chapter pediatric councils are not forums for contract negotiation, setting fees, or discussing payments. For information on pediatric councils, go to www.aap.org/en-us/professional-resources/practice-support/financing-and-payment/Pages/Private-Payer-Advocacy-Pediatric-Councils.aspx (AAP members only).

* The AAP has created tools to assist practices with managed care contracting. These resources are available at www.aap.org/en-us/professional-resources/practice-support/financing-and-payment/Pages/Private-Payer-Advocacy.aspx under "Managed Care Contracts."

* Members of the AAP are encouraged to access the AAP Hassle Factor Form online to report health plan issues. The information submitted is used to assist the AAP and chapters in identifying issues and facilitating public and private payer advocacy related to health plans, including discussion topics with national carriers and at chapter pediatric council meetings with regional carriers. The Hassle Factor Form can be accessed at www.aap.org/en-us/professional-resources/practice-support/financing-and-payment/Pages/Hassle-Factor-Form-Concerns-with-Payers.aspx (AAP members only) and can be submitted electronically.

* American Academy of Pediatrics members and their staff are encouraged to attend AAP Pediatric Coding Webinars, presented by pediatric coding experts. To obtain a list of scheduled webinars and to register, visit www.aap.org/webinars/coding.

Appendix D of this manual lists published coding resources available from the AAP.

Emerging Payment Methodologies

There is a movement by payers away from volume-based payments such as fee-for-service (FFS) to value-based payment models that incentivize providers on quality, outcomes, and cost containment. The intent is to promote patient value and efficiency, but one consequence is to shift some risk to physician practices. Under these emerging payment models, practice viability will be dependent on how well quality, cost, and efficiency are managed. Examples of some of these newer payment models include bundled payments, shared savings, and pay for performance. Physician payments may be based on a combination of FFS and newer payment methodology. Emerging forms of health care financing and delivery models include ACOs and integrated delivery systems.

- *Bundled payments:* These are a type of prospective payment in which health care providers (hospitals, physicians, and other health care professionals) share one payment for a specified range of services as opposed to paying each provider individually. The intent of bundled payment is to foster collaboration among the multiple providers to coordinate services and control costs, thereby reducing unnecessary utilization.
- *Shared savings:* Under a shared savings arrangement, providers and payers look to deliver care at a cost that is below current budgeted amounts, and the resulting savings are shared between the payer(s) and providers. The contractual arrangement between the payer(s) and providers will specify how the savings are calculated and distributed. Shared savings models may include upside risk exclusively or upside and downside risk. In an upside risk arrangement, the provider only shares in any savings and not the risk of loss. Under downside risk, the practice would be responsible for a portion of the difference between actual total costs that exceed budgeted costs, in addition to any shared savings.
- *Pay for performance:* In this arrangement, physician payments are based on an agreed-on evaluation of the provider's performance according to acknowledged benchmarks. If the provider meets those benchmarks, an enhanced payment or bonus is provided.

In considering whether to participate in one of these newer payment models, the practice needs to determine expected costs and utilization and assess whether the practice can deliver services under the projected budget. Using *CPT* codes and their RVUs will aid in this assessment. Projections can be made using RVUs of the services currently provided and projected to be provided. With these types of data, the practice can assess the effect of new payment methodologies to the practice's bottom line.

For more information on ACOs and alternative payment models, go to www.aap.org/en-us/professional-resources/practice-support/Pages/Accountable-Care-Organizations.aspx.

Accountable Care Organizations (ACOs)

Most of the content about ACOs is adapted with permission from the January 2011 *AAP News*. The information provided herein has been updated since publication of that article.

The Patient Protection and Affordable Care Act of 2010 (PPACA) included a number of provisions that establish ACOs in Medicare, Medicaid, and the Children's Health Insurance Program. In October 2011, the CMS issued final regulations to assist physicians, hospitals, and other health care professionals in coordinating care through ACOs.

Interest in ACOs is accelerating, and the market continues to witness a growth in their numbers. As of January 2014, the CMS has documented 343 Medicare Shared Savings Program (MSSP) ACOs. In addition, there are currently 35 ACOs participating in the Advanced Payment ACO Model, which is designed for physician-based and rural providers who have come together voluntarily to provide coordinated care to the Medicare patients they serve. Participants in this model will receive up-front and monthly payments, which they can use to make critical investments in their care coordination infrastructure. Finally, there are 23 Pioneer ACO Models starting their third year in demonstration. This approach will evaluate the effectiveness of various payment models and how their approach can provide better care, work in conjunction with private payers, and reduce Medicare cost growth.

Beyond the federal government's push toward ACOs, commercial health insurers are also actively exploring the development of ACOs. One of the special features of commercially driven ACOs is their flexibility in implementing accountable care contracts. Many private ACOs emulate the CMS MSSP approach; however, the flexibility provided by market-driven ACOs permits them to undertake more creative approaches in modeling payment methodologies. Estimates suggest that there were more than 200 private sector ACOs in operation in early 2014.

In early 2014, the CMS posted results for the MSSP and Pioneer ACO models. Nearly half of the hospitals and provider groups that formed in 2012 under the MSSP reduced costs in their first year. Among those, 29 saved enough to share the savings with the CMS, resulting in $128 million net savings to the Medicare trust fund. In addition, an independent evaluation of 23 Pioneer ACO Models shows that they saved the Medicare program $147 million in their first year of operation, even though not all saved money. While evaluation of the program's overall effect is ongoing, the interim results are within the range originally projected for the program's first year. A significant majority of the program's overall net effect was projected to phase in over the program's ensuing performance years, according to the CMS.

Pediatricians must be in a position to assess the ACO transition locally. More importantly, pediatricians need to be actively engaged in this transition to a new care model to ensure that it best serves the needs of children and families and the pediatric health care delivery system.

Background

As defined by the CMS, an ACO is an organization of health care professionals that agrees to be accountable for the quality, cost, and overall care of beneficiaries. In return, the ACO will receive incentive payments based on quality and cost containment instead of volume and intensity. Eligible providers are likely to be individual and group practices, hospitals, integrated delivery systems, and others who create a legal entity with a management structure able to deliver and report on evidence-based and informed care to a defined population, effectively engage patients, and receive and distribute shared savings.

The growing interest in ACOs as a principal driver in the reconfiguration of the US health care delivery system aligns with the "Triple Aim" espoused by former CMS administrator Don Berwick, MD. In the aggregate, the Triple Aim is designed to improve the individual experience of care, improve the health of populations, and reduce per capita costs of care for populations.

The Pediatric ACO Demonstration Project, legislated as part of the PPACA but unfunded, calls for participating state Medicaid programs to allow pediatric medical professionals to form ACOs and receive incentive payments. The US Department of Health and Human Services (HHS) will develop quality guidelines that must be met. The applicant state and ACO must meet a certain level of savings or slow the rate of growth in health care costs to receive an incentive payment. However, if funded, it is anticipated that CMS will derive many of the ACO requirements on the basis of its MSSP.

In response to growing interest in the development of ACOs, in 2011 the AAP ACO Workgroup produced guidance for members on factors to consider in evaluating an opportunity to participate in an ACO. The guidance was reevaluated in 2013 by a group of pediatrician experts in financing and economics and deemed to still be timely.

Key Considerations in Ensuring Pediatric Representation in an ACO

The goal of an ACO is to increase access to care and improve the quality and outcomes of care while at the same time restraining growth in the cost of care, making the care more efficient. The following considerations will need to be addressed by pediatricians when evaluating the organizational attributes of a pediatric-specific or a pediatric-adult or mixed population–based ACO. The following enumerated points can be used to measure the commitment of any ACO to a strong and enduring pediatric base:

Organizational and Legal Structure

- The family-centered medical home is the foundation of a primary care–based integrated delivery system that should anchor the ACO. There must be sufficient pediatric primary and specialty care pediatricians for the number of children managed by the ACO. In addition, the ACO must understand, encourage, and support family-centered care, recognizing that maintaining a child's health is a family responsibility. Integrating oral (dental) and mental health care into ACO delivery and payment structure is essential because they are some of the most common major chronic care conditions children and adolescents experience. Moreover, the future payment system should fully incorporate behavioral health into ACOs by requiring that the ACO has sufficient providers of inpatient and outpatient care and the entire array of services necessary to provide comprehensive services.

- Although the ACO is an integrated system of care (eg, hospitals, physician practices), governance and leadership of any ACO should be physician-driven, and its design must encourage collaboration among physicians. Primary care physicians must occupy key positions in leadership during all formative stages of the development of an ACO, and leadership should be elected or chosen by physicians participating in the ACO. The governing leadership should be equally balanced with primary care and specialty physicians.

- There is an explicit commitment to equal representation on all governance and clinical committees between primary care and specialty physicians. Clinical professionals from the oral and mental health disciplines also should be considered to be part of the governance structure and committees of the ACO. Equity in representation extends to pediatric primary, pediatric medical subspecialty, and pediatric surgical specialty care. More specifically, the following should be adopted:

  - ❖ The ACO should be guided by a board of directors that is elected by ACO physicians. Any physician entity (medical group, independent practice association) that contracts with the ACO should be physician (and not hospital) controlled and governed by an elected board of directors.

  - ❖ The ACO physicians should be licensed in the state in which an ACO operates and in the active practice of medicine in the ACO service area.

  - ❖ Where a hospital is part of an ACO, the governing board of the ACO should be separate and independent of the hospital board.

- The ACO has systems in place to provide direct and indirect support to primary care practices that are committed to transforming to a family-centered medical home. This includes but is not limited to practice management support, technical assistance (including health information technology), and resources for clinical and nonclinical (eg, community, social, educational) care. Practices should be rewarded for achieving medical home recognition by agencies deemed to provide such recognition.

Chapter 15: The Business of Medicine: From Clean Claims to Correct Payment and Emerging Payment Methodologies

- The ACO should interface with all health-related operations in the state where it operates. This may include state Title V programs; early intervention programs; Head Start offices; Special Supplemental Nutrition Program for Women, Infants, and Children; immunization information systems; and public education entities as needed to ensure children achieve optimal growth, development, and healthy outcomes.

- Medical management committees should be established to assist the ACO with analysis of clinical data to identify specific interventions where value and cost can be affected, with resulting efficiencies stimulating payer and employer support. All participants in an ACO should have ready access to real-time data to evaluate care processes and support analysis of creative interventions designed to promote improved quality and effectiveness of care.

- The ACO leadership should establish a family advisory council to help guide the ACO in developing a family-centered health care system.

- The ACO should form strong dedicated links to key community resources to support care coordination and the delivery of primary and specialty care to its constituency, particularly children with complex conditions.

- Legal structures should be in place to ensure all payment and managerial policies are in compliance with existing state and federal laws. Antitrust, federal and state antikickback and self-referral laws, and the federal Civil Monetary Penalties Law (which prohibits payments by hospitals to physicians to reduce or limit care) should be sufficiently flexible to allow pediatricians and other physicians to collaborate with hospitals in forming ACOs without being employed by the hospitals or ACOs. This is particularly important for physicians in small- and medium-sized practices who may want to remain independent but otherwise integrate and collaborate with other physicians (eg, so-called virtual integration) for purposes of participating in an ACO.

- The ACOs should be prohibited from imposing exclusive arrangements with pediatricians. Pediatricians should be able to exercise independence and align themselves with multiple ACOs.

Structure of Clinical and Financial Performance Metrics and Monitoring

- The ACO should have essential clinical and organizational elements in place to ensure the successful performance of all clinical care activities. However, the primary responsibility for care coordination should be maintained jointly with the medical home and ACO.

- Quality performance metrics that pertain to children should be developed with robust input from primary care and subspecialty care physicians using AAP quality improvement measurement methodology.

- Systems should be in place to permit the sharing of performance data with all members of the care team.

- There is a method of attributing patients to providers for purposes of reporting, and the ACO should accommodate multiple methods if dictated by different payers.

- There should be leadership support for the development of practice teams to support primary care pediatricians, including appropriate funding for other health care professionals participating in their care.

- Provider satisfaction should be monitored at least annually for all members of the care teams.

- Patient and family satisfaction measures should be elements of a performance metric portfolio for the ACO.

◉ Interoperable health information technology and EHR systems are keys to ACO success. Pediatricians and hospitals must have effective communication processes in place to ensure information is shared on a timely basis and that are designed to ensure effective and efficient coordination of care and reporting on all dimensions of quality improvement.

Payment Methodologies

◉ Compensation systems and incentives are aligned internally and externally among providers and payers. The formula must be designed to ensure adequate supports for primary care, the backbone of the ACO, but should not compromise participation of subspecialty physicians. Values developed within the medical home, such as e-mail and telephone support and advice services, coordination of care, and teleconferencing, need to be recognized for the important contribution that they have in the efficient delivery of health care services.

◉ Systems should be in place to ensure appropriate payment methodologies (eg, bundled payments, full or partial capitation, shared savings, episodes of care payments, enhanced primary care coordination payments) that recognize the special elements of pediatric care, including appropriate and fair payment for the administration of vaccines, and are distributed to participating providers of care in an equitable manner.

◉ A pediatric risk-adjustment methodology should be in place to ensure adequate and appropriate payment for the delivery of care to children with special health care needs. Pediatric practices should be adequately paid for the additional effort required to involve family, community and educational resources, and other pertinent entities and activities in care management and coordination.

◉ The quality performance standards required to be established by the HHS secretary must be consistent with AAP policy on the development of and reporting out of quality measures. The ACO quality reporting program must meet AAP principles for quality reporting, including the use of clinically validated measures developed by leading organizations, such as the American Medical Association Physician Consortium for Performance Improvement; the inclusion of a sufficient number of patients to produce statistically valid quality information; appropriate attribution methodology; and the right of pediatricians to appeal inaccurate quality reports and have them corrected. There must also be timely notification and feedback provided to physicians on quality measures and results.

◉ Savings and revenues from ACO operations should be retained for patient care services as well as sharing with participating pediatricians and other health care professionals in a fair and equitable manner.

In addition, the CMS has published fact sheets that provide general information about ACOs and their operational and financial characteristics. They can be accessed at http://innovations.cms.gov/initiatives/ACO/index.html. The *AAP Pediatric Coding Newsletter*™ will also continue to address ACOs as they progress.

There are many unanswered questions that will need to be addressed as ACOs evolve. For more information about ACOs, contact Ed Zimmerman, director of the AAP Department of Practice, at 800/433-9016, ext 7917.

Continuing Education Units (CEUs) for American Academy of Professional Coders Accreditation

This publication has prior approval of the American Academy of Professional Coders (AAPC) for 4.0 continuing education units (CEUs). Granting of this approval in no way constitutes endorsement by the AAPC of the publication, content, or publication sponsor.

Complete the 40-question quiz online (www.aap.org/pcorss/pcnoquiz). The access code for the quiz is AAPCFP20.

You will only need the current Coding for Pediatrics 2015 *publication and* Current Procedural Terminology; International Classification of Diseases, Ninth Revision, Clinical Modification; *and* International Classification of Diseases, 10th Revision, Clinical Modification *manuals to answer the questions. You will require a 70% or better to earn the CEUs. If you pass the test, you will also receive a CEU certificate. If you do not receive a passing score, you may retake it. This quiz will expire on October 1, 2015.*

E-mail aapcodinghotline@aap.org *if you have any questions.*

4.0 CEUs

1. Which of the following may be considered abuse but is not an example of health care fraud?
    A. Billing for services not provided
    B. Billing more than one party for the same service
    C. Routinely waiving co-payments and deductibles
    D. Taking a kickback for referrals

2. In *International Classification of Diseases, 10th Revision, Clinical Modification (ICD-10-CM)*, "Use additional code" is an instruction found in the tabular listing of a code that directs to do which of the following?
    A. Do not report this code and report another code.
    B. Sequence an additional code for a manifestation after this code.
    C. Report this code and another code sequenced in order of clinical significance.
    D. Use a combination code rather than this code.

3. According to the Vaccines for Children Web site, providers are encouraged to use what *Current Procedural Terminology (CPT®)* code for an immunization administration?
    A. **90471**
    B. **90461**
    C. Report only the vaccine product code with an **SL** modifier.
    D. **90460**

4. Which key component is required by some payers as 1 of the 2 components met to support the level of subsequent evaluation and management (E/M) service reported?
    A. Risk
    B. History
    C. Medical decision-making (MDM)
    D. Chief complaint

5. For coding and reporting purposes, the perinatal period is defined as
    A. The period from beginning of mother's labor to delivery
    B. Birth through the 28th day following birth
    C. Birth through hospital discharge
    D. Conception through 28 days following birth

6. A 15-year-old new patient is seen in the office for a preventive medicine service. The physician notes that the patient smokes cigarettes. Approximately 5 minutes are spent counseling the patient about the known health effects of tobacco use and encouraging the patient to quit using tobacco. How is the time spent in counseling the patient about the effects of tobacco use and cessation reported?
    A. Risk-factor reduction is a component of the preventive medicine service and not separately reported.
    B. The preventive medicine service is reported based on time spent counseling and coordinating care.
    C. Code **99406** is reported in addition to code **99384**.
    D. Code **99406 25** is reported in addition to code **99384.**

7. When a procedural service is performed at the same encounter as a significant, separately identifiable E/M service, modifier **59** may be appended to the E/M service code.
    A. True
    B. False

8. Which elements of the history component may be documented by the patient, family, or ancillary staff?
   A. History of present illness (HPI) and review of systems (ROS)
   B. None
   C. HPI, ROS, and past, family, and social history (PFSH)
   D. ROS and PFSH

9. When reporting otitis media with *ICD-10-CM*, what is required to support reporting of recurrent otitis media?
   A. The condition is documented as having been diagnosed more than once in the last 3 months.
   B. The physicians refers the patient for an otolaryngology consultation.
   C. The physician documents recurrence based on clinical judgment.
   D. The condition is documented as chronic.

10. What is the appropriate *CPT*® code to report for a follow-up visit during the global surgical period with the physician who performed the procedure?
    A. **99024**
    B. An E/M service code with modifier **24** appended
    C. The appropriate code for the procedure appended with modifier **55**
    D. No service can be reported.

11. Which of the following are true of *ICD-10-CM*?
    A. *ICD-10-CM* guidelines for reporting diagnoses related to a physician's professional services allow reporting of a condition documented as "suspected" or "probable."
    B. All sections of the *ICD-10-CM* guidelines apply to physician services.
    C. *ICD-10-CM* guidelines that apply to physician services are found in sections I and IV.
    D. *ICD-10-CM* codes for suspected or probable conditions are reported by physicians only when reporting inpatient care.

12. Payment for services represented by *CPT* Category III code(s) is based on which of the following?
    A. Each individual payer may determine an allowed amount.
    B. No payment is allowed for Category III codes because they are for tracking purposes only.
    C. The assigned relative value units
    D. The Centers for Medicare & Medicaid Services determines the payment.

13. A procedure that is assigned a 90-day global period is performed. On what day does the postoperative period begin?
    A. The day before surgery
    B. The day of surgery
    C. The day after the day of surgery
    D. None of the above

14. Which of the following is *not* true regarding a teaching physician's reporting of interpretation and report of a diagnostic test?
    A. The teaching physician may report his or her personal interpretation of test results.
    B. The teaching physician may report the service when the findings were reviewed with the resident.
    C. Documentation supports review and agreement with the resident's interpretation and report.
    D. The teaching physician must be present during the resident's review and interpretation.

15. A physician provides continuous inhalation treatment with aerosol medication for acute airway obstruction for a total of 40 minutes in her office. What is the appropriate code for reporting this service?

    A. Report the appropriate E/M service and a code for prolonged services in the outpatient setting.

    B. **94640**

    C. **94644**

    D. **94645**

16. *ICD-10-CM* does not differentiate active and residual states of autism.

    A. True

    B. False

17. A physician counsels the parents of a 13-month-old patient about the risks and benefits of the measles, mumps, rubella, varicella; inactivated poliovirus; and *Haemophilus influenzae* type b vaccines and administers each vaccine. Which of the following is a correct way of reporting these services?

    A. **90460** × 3, **90461** × 3

    B. **90471, 90472** × 2

    C. **90460** × 4, **90461** × 1

    D. None of the above

18. A child is hospitalized for severe exacerbation of asthma. The child is evaluated in the morning by a physician assistant who provides initial hospital care. Later the same day, a physician of the same group practice reviews the patient history, examines the patient, and makes changes to the treatment plan based on the patient's current condition. Is this a split or shared visit?

    A. Yes, because the physician assistant cannot report initial hospital care.

    B. No, because incident-to requirements were not met.

    C. Yes, but only if each provider documents the portion of the service he or she personally performed.

    D. No, the concept of split or shared visit does not apply.

19. If a payer refuses to cover services, what action can your practice take to protect against lost revenue for that service?

    A. Get your contract amended to state that you can bill the service as non-covered.

    B. File a claim and get a remittance showing the denial.

    C. Notify the patient or caregiver that he or she needs to contact the payer.

    D. Post a sign in the waiting area stating the service is non-covered.

20. When the nature of the presenting problem is moderate, which of the following is true?

    A. Full recovery without functional impairment is expected.

    B. High probability of severe, prolonged functional impairment

    C. Risk of morbidity or mortality without treatment is low.

    D. There is uncertain prognosis or increased probability of prolonged functional impairment.

21. Which of the following is one of the criteria of critical care services?

    A. Illness or injury acutely impairs one or more vital organs.

    B. The patient is receiving care in an area designated for intensive and critical care.

    C. The patient requires frequent assessments by the health care team.

    D. The patient requires frequent physiological monitoring.

22. Which of the following is not included in unit/floor time?
    A. Time spent at the patient's bedside
    B. Time spent on the floor documenting care, performing the history and examination, and reviewing diagnostic tests
    C. Time spent coordinating care with care team members
    D. Time spent in the radiology department viewing the patient's x-rays

23. When determining MDM, what level is supported when the number of diagnoses is extensive, amount and complexity of data is moderate, and risk is low?
    A. High complexity
    B. Moderate complexity
    C. More information is needed to determine the level of MDM.
    D. Low complexity

24. A 15-year-old girl is seen for a new patient well-child visit. The physician conducts a comprehensive physical examination, including routine breast and pelvic examination, and obtains a Papanicolaou test. Which *CPT* code(s) may be reported?
    A. **99384**
    B. **99394 33, 99000 33**
    C. **99394, Q0091, 99000**
    D. **99394, 99000**

25. A hematologist is consulted by another physician for an opinion on management of a patient's chronic anemia and spends 10 cumulative minutes communicating on the telephone, 5 minutes reviewing medical records, and 5 minutes preparing a written report. The physician has not seen this patient face-to-face and no transfer of care takes place. Which code may be reported for the physician's services?
    A. **99252**
    B. **99447**
    C. **99358**
    D. **99442**

26. Which of the following components represent a comprehensive history for an inpatient hospital visit?
    A. Chief complaint (CC), HPI for 2–9 systems, complete ROS, at least 2 elements of PFSH
    B. CC, HPI with status of 3 chronic conditions, ROS for 2–9 systems, at least 2 elements of PFSH
    C. CC, 4 elements of HPI, ROS for 2–9 systems, 1 item each of PFSH
    D. CC, 4 elements of HPI, complete ROS, and 1 item each of PFSH

27. What code may be reported for closure of a 1.3-cm wound of the leg using adhesive strips?
    A. **12001**
    B. **12020**
    C. This service is included in an E/M service.
    D. None of the above

28. When reporting a fracture with *ICD-10-CM,* what is the default if documentation does not specify that the fracture is displaced or non-displaced?
    A. Open
    B. Closed
    C. Displaced
    D. Non-displaced

29. A critically ill 30-month-old requires venipuncture, but the phlebotomist is unable to successfully access the child's veins. A physician performs the venipuncture on the femoral vein. What code will the physician report for this service?
    A. **36415**
    B. **36405**
    C. **36400**
    D. **36425**

30. A physician performs a circumcision using a clamp or other device on a 6-week-old male. The same physician performs a ring block as anesthesia for the procedure. What *CPT* code(s) will be reported?
    A. **54150**
    B. **54161**
    C. **54161 47**
    D. **54150, 00920**

31. A neonate is born at 11:30 pm on Monday night without the presence of the pediatrician, who is notified of the birth by a phone call from nursing staff at the facility. The physician instructs the nurse to follow his standing orders for newborn care and contact him if the neonate develops any problems. On Tuesday morning, the pediatrician examines the healthy newborn boy and performs circumcision (**54150**). Which code(s) will the physician report?
    A. **99460** on Monday, **54150** on Tuesday
    B. **54150** on Tuesday only
    C. **99460 25, 54150** on Tuesday only
    D. **99462 25, 54150** on Tuesday only

32. What is the appropriate order of *International Classification of Diseases, Ninth Revision, Clinical Modification* codes when reporting services provided during the birth admission?
    A. Birth outcome (**V30–V39**), codes for perinatal conditions, codes for congenital anomalies
    B. The reason most responsible for the physician's service should be listed first, followed by codes for other conditions that were clinically significant.
    C. Conditions due to birth process are reported first, followed by codes for other conditions.
    D. None of the above

33. A pediatrician is caring for a 10-year-old patient with multiple chronic health conditions. The patient lives 1 hour away from the pediatrician's clinic. Between regularly scheduled follow-up visits, the physician and her clinical staff provide care management services to the patient by providing access through a secure communications portal of their electronic health record and by telephone. Over a calendar month, the physician and clinical staff document 25 minutes of time monitoring the care plan and communicating with the patient, caregivers, and other health care professionals involved in the patient's care. What code may the physician report for these services?
    A. **99495**
    B. **99496**
    C. **99490**
    D. **99339**

34. A new patient is seen in the office for exacerbation of asthma. The physician performs and documents a comprehensive history, detailed physical examination, moderate MDM, and nebulizer treatment with albuterol. Which of the following codes will be reported for the care provided at this encounter?
    A. **99214**
    B. **99203, 94640, J7611**
    C. **99204 25, 94640, J7611**
    D. **99203 25, 94640, J7611**

35. A 3-year-old critically ill child is admitted for suspected bacterial meningitis. The admitting physician provides initial critical care services, including a diagnostic lumbar puncture. Which *CPT*® code(s) will the physician report for care on this date?
    A. **99475 25, 62270**
    B. **99475**
    C. The information provided is not sufficient for code selection.
    D. **62270**

36. A child is seen in the physician's office for follow-up of attention-deficit/hyperactivity disorder. The parent and 2 teachers have completed behavioral rating instruments. The physician reviews each instrument in addition to providing an established patient office visit with more than 50% of the 30-minute face-to-face visit spent in counseling. What *CPT* code(s) would be reported for this service?
    A. **99214, 96110** × 3
    B. **99214, 96127**
    C. **99214, 96127** × 3
    D. **99214**

37. A follow-up visit is performed on a child whose otitis media has resolved. Which of the following *ICD-10-CM* codes will be reported?
    A. **Z09**
    B. **Z71.1**
    C. **Z71.2**
    D. **Z86.19**

38. What documentation is necessary to select a specific *ICD-10-CM* code for asthma?
    A. Asthma type—intrinsic or extrinsic
    B. Classification as intermittent, mild persistent, moderate persistent, or severe persistent
    C. Status of uncomplicated, with exacerbation, or status asthmaticus
    D. Both B and C

39. When *ICD-10-CM* is implemented, which code(s) will be used to report recurrent acute purulent otitis media with acute myringitis and spontaneous rupture of the eardrum in the left ear?
    A. **H66.005**
    B. **H66.012**
    C. **H66.015**
    D. **H67.2, H73.002, H72.92**

40. What code would be reported to a payer who does not cover consultation services (ie, follows Medicare policy) when the consulting physician documents a new patient service in the office with a comprehensive history and examination and moderate MDM?
    A. **99244**
    B. **99204**
    C. **99254**
    D. More information is needed for code assignment.

||||||||||

All online documents **e** can be accessed at www.aap.org/cfp. Use access code AAPCFP20.

||||||||||

1995 Documentation Guidelines for Evaluation and Management Services

I. Introduction

What is documentation and why is it important?

Medical record documentation is required to record pertinent facts, findings, and observations about an individual's health history including past and present illnesses, examinations, tests, treatments, and outcomes. The medical record chronologically documents the care of the patient and is an important element contributing to high-quality care. The medical record facilitates

- ☀ The ability of the physician and other health care professionals to evaluate and plan the patient's immediate treatment, and to monitor his/her health care over time
- ☀ Communication and continuity of care among physicians and other health care professionals involved in the patient's care
- ☀ Accurate and timely claims review and payment
- ☀ Appropriate utilization review and quality of care evaluations
- ☀ Collection of data that may be useful for research and education
  An appropriately documented medical record can reduce many of the "hassles" associated with claims processing and may serve as a legal document to verify the care provided, if necessary.

What do payers want and why?

Because payers have a contractual obligation to enrollees, they may require reasonable documentation that services are consistent with the insurance coverage provided. They may request information to validate

- ☀ The site of service
- ☀ The medical necessity and appropriateness of the diagnostic and/or therapeutic services provided
- ☀ That services provided have been accurately reported

II. General Principles of Medical Record Documentation

The principles of documentation listed below are applicable to all types of medical and surgical services in all settings. For E/M services, the nature and amount of physician work and documentation varies by type of service, place of service, and the patient's status. The general principles listed below may be modified to account for these variable circumstances in providing E/M services.

1. The medical record should be complete and legible.
2. The documentation of each patient encounter should include
   - ☀ Reason for the encounter and relevant history, physical examination findings, and prior diagnostic test results
   - ☀ Assessment, clinical impression, or diagnosis
   - ☀ Plan for care
   - ☀ Date and legible identity of the observer
3. If not documented, the rationale for ordering diagnostic and other ancillary services should be easily inferred.

Appendix A

4. Past and present diagnoses should be accessible to the treating and/or consulting physician.
5. Appropriate health risk factors should be identified.
6. The patient's progress, response to and changes in treatment, and revision of diagnosis should be documented.
7. The *CPT* and *ICD-10-CM* codes reported on the health insurance claim form or billing statement should be supported by the documentation in the medical record.

III. Documentation of E/M Services

This publication provides definitions and documentation guidelines for the three key components of E/M services and for visits that consist predominantly of counseling or coordination of care. The three key components—history, examination, and medical decision making—appear in the descriptors for office and other outpatient services, hospital observation services, hospital inpatient services, consultations, emergency department services, nursing facility services, domiciliary care services, and home services. While some of the text of *CPT* has been repeated in this publication, the reader should refer to *CPT* for the complete descriptors for E/M services and instructions for selecting a level of service. **Documentation guidelines are identified by the symbol •DG.**

The descriptors for the levels of E/M services recognize seven components that are used in defining the levels of E/M services. These components are

- ◉ History
- ◉ Examination
- ◉ Medical decision making
- ◉ Counseling
- ◉ Coordination of care
- ◉ Nature of presenting problem
- ◉ Time

The first three of these components (ie, history, examination, and medical decision making) are the **key** components in selecting the level of E/M services. An exception to this rule is the case of visits that consist predominantly of counseling or coordination of care; for these services time is the key or controlling factor to qualify for a particular level of E/M service.

For certain groups of patients, the recorded information may vary slightly from that described here. Specifically, the medical records of infants, children, adolescents, and pregnant women may have additional or modified information recorded in each history and examination area.

As an example, newborn records may include under history of the present illness (HPI) the details of mother's pregnancy and the infant's status at birth; social history will focus on family structure; family history will focus on congenital anomalies and hereditary disorders in the family. In addition, information on growth and development and/or nutrition will be recorded. Although not specifically defined in these documentation guidelines, these patient group variations on history and examination are appropriate.

A. Documentation of History

The levels of E/M services are based on four types of history (problem focused, expanded problem focused, detailed, and comprehensive.) Each type of history includes some or all of the following elements:

- Chief complaint (CC)
- History of present illness (HPI)
- Review of systems (ROS)
- Past, family, and/or social history (PFSH)

The extent of history of present illness; review of systems; and past, family, and/or social history that is obtained and documented is dependent upon clinical judgment and the nature of the presenting problem(s).

History of Present Illness (HPI)	Review of Systems (ROS)	Past, Family, and/or Social History (PFSH)	Type of History
Brief	N/A	N/A	Problem focused
Brief	Problem pertinent	N/A	Expanded problem focused
Extended	Extended	Pertinent	Detailed
Extended	Complete	Complete	Comprehensive

The chart below shows the progression of the elements required for each type of history. To qualify for a given type of history, **all three elements in the table must be met.** (A chief complaint is indicated at all levels.)

•**DG:** *The CC, ROS, and PFSH may be listed as separate elements of history, or they may be included in the description of the history of the present illness.*

•**DG:** *A ROS and/or a PFSH obtained during an earlier encounter does not need to be rerecorded if there is evidence that the physician reviewed and updated the previous information. This may occur when a physician updates his or her own record or in an institutional setting or group practice where many physicians use a common record. The review and update may be documented by*

- *Describing any new ROS and/or PFSH information or noting there has been no change in the information*
- *Noting the date and location of the earlier ROS and/or PFSH*

•**DG:** *The ROS and/or PFSH may be recorded by ancillary staff or on a form completed by the patient. To document that the physician reviewed the information, there must be a notation supplementing or confirming the information recorded by others.*

•**DG:** *If the physician is unable to obtain a history from the patient or other source, the record should describe the patient's condition or other circumstance that precludes obtaining a history.*

Definitions and specific documentation guidelines for each of the elements of history are listed below.

Chief Complaint (CC)

The CC is a concise statement describing the symptom, problem, condition, diagnosis, physician-recommended return, or other factor that is the reason for the encounter.

•**DG:** *The medical record should clearly reflect the chief complaint.*

History of Present Illness (HPI)

The HPI is a chronological description of the development of the patient's present illness from the first sign and/or symptom or from the previous encounter to the present. It includes the following elements:

- Location
- Quality

Appendix A

- Severity
- Duration
- Timing
- Context
- Modifying factors
- Associated signs and symptoms

Brief and **extended** HPIs are distinguished by the amount of detail needed to accurately characterize the clinical problem(s).

A **brief** HPI consists of one to three elements of the HPI.

•DG: *The medical record should describe one to three elements of the present illness (HPI).*

An **extended** HPI consists of four or more elements of the HPI.

•DG: *The medical record should describe four or more elements of the present illness (HPI) or associated co-morbidities.*

Review of Systems (ROS)

A ROS is an inventory of body systems obtained through a series of questions seeking to identify signs and/or symptoms that the patient may be experiencing or has experienced.

For purposes of ROS, the following systems are recognized:

- Constitutional symptoms (eg, fever, weight loss)
- Eyes
- Ears, nose, mouth, throat
- Cardiovascular
- Respiratory
- Gastrointestinal
- Genitourinary
- Musculoskeletal
- Integumentary (skin and/or breast)
- Neurological
- Psychiatric
- Endocrine
- Hematologic/lymphatic
- Allergic/immunologic

A **problem-pertinent** ROS inquires about the system directly related to the problem(s) identified in the HPI.

•DG: *The patient's positive responses and pertinent negatives for the system related to the problem should be documented.*

An **extended** ROS inquires about the system directly related to the problem(s) identified in the HPI and a limited number of additional systems.

•DG: *The patient's positive responses and pertinent negatives for two to nine systems should be documented.*

A **complete** ROS inquires about the system(s) directly related to the problem(s) identified in the HPI plus all additional body systems.

•DG: *At least 10 organ systems must be reviewed. Those systems with positive or pertinent negative responses must be individually documented. For the remaining systems, a notation indicating all other systems are negative is permissible. In the absence of such a notation, at least 10 systems must be individually documented.*

Appendix A

Past, Family, and/or Social History (PFSH)

The PFSH consists of a review of three areas

* Past history (the patient's past experiences with illnesses, operations, injuries, and treatments)
* Family history (a review of medical events in the patient's family, including diseases that may be hereditary or place the patient at risk)
* Social history (an age-appropriate review of past and current activities)

For the categories of subsequent hospital care, follow-up inpatient consultations and subsequent nursing facility care, *CPT* requires only an "interval" history. It is not necessary to record information about the PFSH.

A **pertinent** PFSH is a review of the history area(s) directly related to the problem(s) identified in the HPI.

•DG: *At least one specific item from **any** of the three history areas must be documented for a pertinent PFSH.*

A *complete* PFSH is a review of two or all three of the PFSH history areas, depending on the category of the E/M service. A review of all three history areas is required for services that by their nature include a comprehensive assessment or reassessment of the patient. A review of two of the three history areas is sufficient for other services.

•DG: *At least one specific item from **two** of the three history areas must be documented for a complete PFSH for the following categories of E/M services: office or other outpatient services, established patient; emergency department; subsequent nursing facility care; domiciliary care, established patient; and home care, established patient.*

•DG: *At least one specific item from **each** of the three history areas must be documented for a complete PFSH for the following categories of E/M services: office or other outpatient services, new patient; hospital observation services; hospital inpatient services, initial care; consultations; comprehensive nursing facility assessments; domiciliary care, new patient; and home care, new patient.*

B. Documentation of Examination

The levels of E/M services are based on four types of examination that are defined as follows:

* **Problem Focused**—a limited examination of the affected body area or organ system.
* **Expanded Problem Focused**—a limited examination of the affected body area or organ system and other symptomatic or related organ system(s).
* **Detailed**—an extended examination of the affected body area(s) and other symptomatic or related organ system(s).
* **Comprehensive**—a general multisystem examination or complete examination of a single organ system.

For purposes of examination, the following **body areas** are recognized:

* Head, including face
* Neck
* Chest, including breasts and axillae
* Abdomen
* Genitalia, groin, buttocks
* Back, including spine
* Each extremity

Appendix A

For purposes of examination, the following **organ systems** are recognized:

- Constitutional (eg, vital signs, general appearance)
- Eyes
- Ears, nose, mouth, throat
- Cardiovascular
- Respiratory
- Gastrointestinal
- Genitourinary
- Musculoskeletal
- Skin
- Neurological
- Psychiatric
- Hematologic/lymphatic/immunologic

The extent of examinations performed and documented is dependent upon clinical judgment and the nature of the presenting problem(s). They range from limited examinations of single body areas to general multisystem or complete single organ system examinations.

•DG: *Specific abnormal and relevant negative findings of the examination of the affected or symptomatic body area(s) or organ system(s) should be documented. A notation of "abnormal" without elaboration is insufficient.*

•DG: *Abnormal or unexpected findings of the examination of the unaffected or asymptomatic body area(s) or organ system(s) should be described.*

•DG: *A brief statement or notation indicating "negative" or "normal" is sufficient to document normal findings related to unaffected area(s) or asymptomatic organ system(s).*

•DG: *The medical record for a general multisystem examination should include findings about eight or more of the 12 organ systems.*

C. Documentation of the Complexity of Medical Decision Making

The levels of E/M services recognize four types of medical decision making (straightforward, low complexity, moderate complexity, and high complexity). Medical decision making refers to the complexity of establishing a diagnosis and/or selecting a management option as measured by

- The number of possible diagnoses and/or the number of management options that must be considered
- The amount and/or complexity of medical records, diagnostic tests, and/or other information that must be obtained, reviewed, and analyzed
- The risk of significant complications, morbidity, and/or mortality, as well as co-morbidities, associated with the patient's presenting problem(s), the diagnostic procedure(s), and/or the possible management options.

The chart on page 391 shows the progression of the elements required for each level of medical decision making. To qualify for a given type of decision making, **two of the three elements in the table must be either met or exceeded.**

Each of the elements of medical decision making is described below.

Number of Diagnoses or Management Options	Amount and/or Complexity of Data to Be Reviewed	Risk of Significant Complications, Morbidity, and/or Mortality	Type of Decision Making
Minimal	Minimal or none	Minimal	Straightforward
Limited	Limited	Low	Low complexity
Multiple	Moderate	Moderate	Moderate complexity
Extensive	Extensive	High	High complexity

Number of Diagnoses or Management Options

The number of possible diagnoses and/or the number of management options that must be considered is based on the number and types of problems addressed during the encounter, the complexity of establishing a diagnosis, and the management decisions that are made by the physician.

Generally, decision making with respect to a diagnosed problem is easier than that for an identified but undiagnosed problem. The number and type of diagnostic tests employed may be an indicator of the number of possible diagnoses. Problems that are improving or resolving are less complex than those that are worsening or failing to change as expected. The need to seek advice from others is another indicator of complexity of diagnostic or management problems.

•*DG:* *For each encounter, an assessment, clinical impression, or diagnosis should be documented. It may be explicitly stated or implied in documented decisions regarding management plans and/or further evaluation.*

    ❖ *For a presenting problem with an established diagnosis the record should reflect whether the problem is: (a) improved, well controlled, resolving, or resolved; or (b) inadequately controlled, worsening, or failing to change as expected.*

    ❖ *For a presenting problem without an established diagnosis, the assessment or clinical impression may be stated in the form of a differential diagnoses or as "possible," "probable," or "rule out" (R/O) diagnoses.*

•*DG:* *The initiation of, or changes in, treatment should be documented. Treatment includes a wide range of management options including patient instructions, nursing instructions, therapies, and medications.*

•*DG:* *If referrals are made, consultations requested, or advice sought, the record should indicate to whom or where the referral or consultation is made or from whom the advice is requested.*

Amount and/or Complexity of Data to Be Reviewed

The amount and/or complexity of data to be reviewed is based on the types of diagnostic testing ordered or reviewed. A decision to obtain and review old medical records and/or obtain history from sources other than the patient increases the amount and complexity of data to be reviewed.

Discussion of contradictory or unexpected test results with the physician who performed or interpreted the test is an indication of the complexity of data being reviewed. On occasion the physician who ordered a test may personally review the image, tracing, or specimen to supplement information from the physician who prepared the test report or interpretation; this is another indication of the complexity of data being reviewed.

Appendix A

•DG: *If a diagnostic service (test or procedure) is ordered, planned, scheduled, or performed at the time of the E/M encounter, the type of service (eg, lab or x-ray) should be documented.*

•DG: *The review of lab, radiology, and/or other diagnostic tests should be documented. An entry in a progress note such as "WBC elevated" or "chest x-ray unremarkable" is acceptable. Alternatively, the review may be documented by initialing and dating the report containing the test results.*

•DG: *A decision to obtain old records or to obtain additional history from the family, caretaker, or other source to supplement that obtained from the patient should be documented.*

•DG: *Relevant findings from the review of old records and/or the receipt of additional history from the family, caretaker, or other source should be documented. If there is no relevant information beyond that already obtained, that fact should be documented. A notation of "old records reviewed" or "additional history obtained from family" without elaboration is insufficient.*

•DG: *The results of discussion of laboratory, radiology, or other diagnostic tests with the physician who performed or interpreted the study should be documented.*

•DG: *The direct visualization and independent interpretation of an image, tracing, or specimen previously or subsequently interpreted by another physician should be documented.*

Risk of Significant Complications, Morbidity, and/or Mortality

The risk of significant complications, morbidity, and/or mortality is based on the risks associated with the presenting problem(s), the diagnostic procedure(s), and the possible management options.

•DG: *Co-morbidities/underlying diseases or other factors that increase the complexity of medical decision making by increasing the risk of complications, morbidity, and/or mortality should be documented.*

•DG: *If a surgical or invasive diagnostic procedure is ordered, planned, or scheduled at the time of the E/M encounter, the type of procedure (eg, laparoscopy) should be documented.*

•DG: *If a surgical or invasive diagnostic procedure is performed at the time of the E/M encounter, the specific procedure should be documented.*

•DG: *The referral for or decision to perform a surgical or invasive diagnostic procedure on an urgent basis should be documented or implied.*

The following table may be used to help determine whether the risk of significant complications, morbidity, and/or mortality is **minimal, low, moderate,** or **high.** Because the determination of risk is complex and not readily quantifiable, the table includes common clinical examples rather than absolute measures of risk. The assessment of risk of the presenting problem(s) is based on the risk related to the disease process anticipated between the present encounter and the next one. The assessment of risk of selecting diagnostic procedures and management options is based on the risk during and immediately following any procedures or treatment. The highest level of risk in any one category (presenting problem(s), diagnostic procedure(s), or management options) determines the overall risk.

D. Documentation of an Encounter Dominated by Counseling or Coordination of Care

In the case where counseling and/or coordination of care dominates (more than 50%) the physician/patient and/or family encounter (face-to-face time in the office or other outpatient setting or floor/unit time in the hospital or nursing facility), time is considered the key or controlling factor to qualify for a particular level of E/M services.

> •**DG:** *If the physician elects to report the level of service based on counseling and/ or coordination of care, the total length of time of the encounter (face-to-face or floor time, as appropriate) should be documented and the record should describe the counseling and/or activities to coordinate care.*

Table of Risk		
Level of Risk	**Presenting Problem(s)**	**Diagnostic Procedure(s) Ordered** · **Management Options Selected**

Level of Risk	**Presenting Problem(s)**	**Diagnostic Procedure(s) Ordered**	**Management Options Selected**
Minimal	⚬ One self-limited or minor problem, eg, cold, insect bite, tinea corporis	⚬ Laboratory tests requiring venipuncture ⚬ Chest x-rays ⚬ EKG/EEG ⚬ Urinalysis ⚬ Ultrasound, eg, echocardiography ⚬ KOH prep	⚬ Rest ⚬ Gargles ⚬ Elastic bandages ⚬ Superficial dressings
Low	⚬ Two or more self-limited or minor problems ⚬ One stable chronic illness, eg, well-controlled hypertension or non–insulin-dependent diabetes, cataract, BPH ⚬ Acute uncomplicated illness or injury, eg, cystitis, allergic rhinitis, simple sprain	⚬ Physiologic tests not under stress, eg, pulmonary function tests ⚬ Non-cardiovascular imaging studies with contrast, eg, barium enema ⚬ Superficial needle biopsies ⚬ Clinical laboratory tests requiring arterial puncture ⚬ Skin biopsies	⚬ Over-the-counter drugs ⚬ Minor surgery with no identified risk factors ⚬ Physical therapy ⚬ Occupational therapy ⚬ IV fluids without additives
Moderate	⚬ One or more chronic illnesses with mild exacerbation, progression, or side effects of treatment ⚬ Two or more stable chronic illnesses ⚬ Undiagnosed new problem with uncertain prognosis, eg, lump in breast ⚬ Acute illness with systemic symptoms, eg, pyelonephritis, pneumonitis, colitis ⚬ Acute complicated injury, eg, head injury with brief loss of consciousness	⚬ Physiologic tests under stress, eg, cardiac stress test, fetal contraction stress test ⚬ Diagnostic endoscopies with no identified risk factors ⚬ Deep needle or incisional biopsy ⚬ Cardiovascular imaging studies with contrast and no identified risk factors, eg, arteriogram, cardiac catheterization ⚬ Obtain fluid from body cavity, eg, lumbar puncture, thoracentesis, culdocentesis	⚬ Minor surgery with identified risk factors ⚬ Elective major surgery (open, percutaneous, or endoscopic) with no identified risk factors ⚬ Prescription drug management ⚬ Therapeutic nuclear medicine ⚬ IV fluids with additives ⚬ Closed treatment of fracture or dislocation without manipulation

Appendix A

Table of Risk, continued

Level of Risk	Presenting Problem(s)	Diagnostic Procedure(s) Ordered	Management Options Selected
High	◉ One or more chronic illnesses with severe exacerbation, progression, or side effects of treatment ◉ Acute or chronic illnesses or injuries that pose a threat to life or bodily function, eg, multiple trauma, acute MI, pulmonary embolus, severe respiratory distress, progressive severe rheumatoid arthritis, psychiatric illness with potential threat to self or others, peritonitis, acute renal failure ◉ An abrupt change in neurologic status, eg, seizure, TIA, weakness, or sensory loss	◉ Cardiovascular imaging studies with contrast with identified risk factors ◉ Cardiac electrophysiological tests ◉ Diagnostic endoscopies with identified risk factors ◉ Discography	◉ Elective major surgery (open, percutaneous, or endoscopic) with identified risk factors ◉ Emergency major surgery (open, percutaneous, or endoscopic) ◉ Parenteral controlled substances ◉ Drug therapy requiring intensive monitoring for toxicity ◉ Decision not to resuscitate or to de-escalate care because of poor prognosis

1997 Documentation Guidelines for Evaluation and Management Services

I. Introduction

What Is Documentation and Why Is It Important?

Medical record documentation is required to record pertinent facts, findings, and observations about an individual's health history including past and present illnesses, examinations, tests, treatments, and outcomes. The medical record chronologically documents the care of the patient and is an important element contributing to high-quality care. The medical record facilitates

- The ability of the physician and other health care professionals to evaluate and plan the patient's immediate treatment and to monitor his/her health care over time
- Communication and continuity of care among physicians and other health care professionals involved in the patient's care
- Accurate and timely claims review and payment
- Appropriate utilization review and quality of care evaluations
- Collection of data that may be useful for research and education

An appropriately documented medical record can reduce many of the "hassles" associated with claims processing and may serve as a legal document to verify the care provided, if necessary.

What Do Payers Want and Why?

Because payers have a contractual obligation to enrollees, they may require reasonable documentation that services are consistent with the insurance coverage provided. They may request information to validate

- The site of service
- The medical necessity and appropriateness of the diagnostic and/or therapeutic services provided
- That services provided have been accurately reported

II. General Principles of Medical Record Documentation

The principles of documentation listed below are applicable to all types of medical and surgical services in all settings. For Evaluation and Management (E/M) services, the nature and amount of physician work and documentation varies by type of service, place of service, and the patient's status. The general principles listed below may be modified to account for these variable circumstances in providing E/M services.

1. The medical record should be complete and legible.
2. The documentation of each patient encounter should include
   - Reason for the encounter and relevant history, physical examination findings, and prior diagnostic test results
   - Assessment, clinical impression, or diagnosis
   - Plan for care
   - Date and legible identity of the observer
3. If not documented, the rationale for ordering diagnostic and other ancillary services should be easily inferred.

4. Past and present diagnoses should be accessible to the treating and/or consulting physician.
5. Appropriate health risk factors should be identified.
6. The patient's progress, response to and changes in treatment, and revision of diagnosis should be documented.
7. The *CPT* and *ICD-10-CM* codes reported on the health insurance claim form or billing statement should be supported by the documentation in the medical record.

III. *Documentation of E/M Services*

This publication provides definitions and documentation guidelines for the three key components of E/M services and for visits that consist predominantly of counseling or coordination of care. The three key components—history, examination, and medical decision making—appear in the descriptors for office and other outpatient services, hospital observation services, hospital inpatient services, consultations, emergency department services, nursing facility services, domiciliary care services, and home services. While some of the text of *CPT* has been repeated in this publication, the reader should refer to *CPT* for the complete descriptors for E/M services and instructions for selecting a level of service. Documentation guidelines are identified by the symbol •*DG.*

The descriptors for the levels of E/M services recognize seven components that are used in defining the levels of E/M services. These components are

- History
- Examination
- Medical decision making
- Counseling
- Coordination of care
- Nature of presenting problem
- Time

The first three of these components (ie, history, examination, and medical decision making) are the key components in selecting the level of E/M services. In the case of visits that consist *predominantly* of counseling or coordination of care, time is the key or controlling factor to qualify for a particular level of E/M service.

Because the level of E/M service is dependent on two or three key components, performance and documentation of one component (eg, examination) at the highest level does not necessarily mean that the encounter in its entirety qualifies for the highest level of E/M service.

These Documentation Guidelines for E/M services reflect the needs of the typical adult population. For certain groups of patients, the recorded information may vary slightly from that described here. Specifically, the medical records of infants, children, adolescents, and pregnant women may have additional or modified information recorded in each history and examination area.

As an example, newborn records may include under history of the present illness (HPI) the details of mother's pregnancy, and the infant's status at birth; social history will focus on family structure; family history will focus on congenital anomalies and hereditary disorders in the family. In addition, the content of a pediatric examination will vary with the age and development of the child. Although not specifically defined in these documentation guidelines, these patient group variations on history and examination are appropriate.

A. Documentation of History

The levels of E/M services are based on four types of history (problem focused, expanded problem focused, detailed, and comprehensive). Each type of history includes some or all of the following elements:

- ☀ Chief complaint (CC)
- ☀ History of present illness (HPI)
- ☀ Review of systems (ROS)
- ☀ Past, family, and/or social history (PFSH)

The extent of history of present illness; review of systems; and past, family, and/or social history that is obtained and documented is dependent upon clinical judgment and the nature of the presenting problem(s).

The chart below shows the progression of the elements required for each type of history. To qualify for a given type of history all three elements in the table must be met. (A chief complaint is indicated at all levels.)

History of Present Illness	Review of Systems	Past, Family, and/or Social History	Type of History
Brief	N/A	N/A	Problem focused
Brief	Problem pertinent	N/A	Expanded problem focused
Extended	Extended	Pertinent	Detailed
Extended	Complete	Complete	Comprehensive

•*DG:* *The CC, ROS, and PFSH may be listed as separate elements of history or they may be included in the description of the history of the present illness.*

•*DG:* *A ROS and/or a PFSH obtained during an earlier encounter does not need to be rerecorded if there is evidence that the physician reviewed and updated the previous information. This may occur when a physician updates his or her own record or in an institutional setting or group practice where many physicians use a common record. The review and update may be documented by*

- ☀ *Describing any new ROS and/or PFSH information or noting there has been no change in the information*
- ☀ *Noting the date and location of the earlier ROS and/or PFSH*

•*DG:* *The ROS and/or PFSH may be recorded by ancillary staff or on a form completed by the patient. To document that the physician reviewed the information, there must be a notation supplementing or confirming the information recorded by others.*

•*DG:* *If the physician is unable to obtain a history from the patient or other source, the record should describe the patient's condition or other circumstance that precludes obtaining a history.*

Definitions and specific documentation guidelines for each of the elements of history are listed below.

Chief Complaint (CC)

The CC is a concise statement describing the symptom, problem, condition, diagnosis, physician recommended return, or other factor that is the reason for the encounter, usually stated in the patient's words.

•*DG:* *The medical record should clearly reflect the chief complaint.*

History of Present Illness (HPI)

The HPI is a chronological description of the development of the patient's present illness from the first sign and/or symptom or from the previous encounter to the present. It includes the following elements:

- Location
- Quality
- Severity
- Duration
- Timing
- Context
- Modifying factors
- Associated signs and symptoms

Brief and *extended* HPIs are distinguished by the amount of detail needed to accurately characterize the clinical problem(s).

A *brief* HPI consists of one to three elements of the HPI.

•**DG:** *The medical record should describe one to three elements of the present illness (HPI).*

An *extended* HPI consists of at least four elements of the HPI or the status of at least three chronic or inactive conditions.

•**DG:** *The medical record should describe at least four elements of the present illness (HPI), or the status of at least three chronic or inactive conditions.*

Review of Systems (ROS)

A ROS is an inventory of body systems obtained through a series of questions seeking to identify signs and/or symptoms that the patient may be experiencing or has experienced.

For purposes of ROS, the following systems are recognized:

- Constitutional symptoms (eg, fever, weight loss)
- Eyes
- Ears, nose, mouth, throat
- Cardiovascular
- Respiratory
- Gastrointestinal
- Genitourinary
- Musculoskeletal
- Integumentary (skin and/or breast)
- Neurological
- Psychiatric
- Endocrine
- Hematologic/lymphatic
- Allergic/immunologic

A *problem-pertinent* ROS inquires about the system directly related to the problem(s) identified in the HPI.

•**DG:** *The patient's positive responses and pertinent negatives for the system related to the problem should be documented.*

An *extended* ROS inquires about the system directly related to the problem(s) identified in the HPI and a limited number of additional systems.

•**DG:** *The patient's positive responses and pertinent negatives for two to nine systems should be documented.*

A *complete* ROS inquires about the system(s) directly related to the problem(s) identified in the HPI plus all additional body systems.

•DG: *At least 10 organ systems must be reviewed. Those systems with positive or pertinent negative responses must be individually documented. For the remaining systems, a notation indicating all other systems are negative is permissible. In the absence of such a notation, at least 10 systems must be individually documented.*

Past, Family, and/or Social History (PFSH)

The PFSH consists of a review of three areas

* Past history (the patient's past experiences with illnesses, operations, injuries, and treatments)
* Family history (a review of medical events in the patient's family, including diseases that may be hereditary or place the patient at risk)
* Social history (an age-appropriate review of past and current activities)

For certain categories of E/M services that include only an interval history, it is not necessary to record information about the PFSH. Those categories are subsequent hospital care, follow-up inpatient consultations, and subsequent nursing facility care.

A *pertinent* PFSH is a review of the history area(s) directly related to the problem(s) identified in the HPI.

•DG: *At least one specific item from any of the three history areas must be documented for a pertinent PFSH.*

A *complete* PFSH is of a review of two or all three of the PFSH history areas, depending on the category of the E/M service. A review of all three history areas is required for services that by their nature include a comprehensive assessment or reassessment of the patient. A review of two of the three history areas is sufficient for other services.

•DG: *At least one specific item from two of the three history areas must be documented for a complete PFSH for the following categories of E/M services: office or other outpatient services, established patient; emergency department; domiciliary care, established patient; and home care, established patient.*

•DG: *At least one specific item from each of the three history areas must be documented for a complete PFSH for the following categories of E/M services: office or other outpatient services, new patient; hospital observation services; hospital inpatient services, initial care; consultations; comprehensive nursing facility assessments; domiciliary care, new patient; and home care, new patient.*

B. Documentation of Examination

The levels of E/M services are based on four types of examination

* **Problem Focused**—a limited examination of the affected body area or organ system.
* **Expanded Problem Focused**—a limited examination of the affected body area or organ system and any other symptomatic or related body area(s) or organ system(s).
* **Detailed**—an extended examination of the affected body area(s) or organ system(s) and any other symptomatic or related body area(s) or organ system(s).
* **Comprehensive**—a general multisystem examination or complete examination of a single organ system and other symptomatic or related body area(s) or organ system(s).

These types of examinations have been defined for general multisystem and the following single organ systems:

- Cardiovascular
- Ears, nose, mouth, throat
- Eyes
- Genitourinary (female)
- Genitourinary (male)
- Hematologic/lymphatic/immunologic
- Musculoskeletal
- Neurological
- Psychiatric
- Respiratory
- Skin

A general multisystem examination or a single organ system examination may be performed by any physician regardless of specialty. The type (general multisystem or single organ system) and content of examination are selected by the examining physician and are based upon clinical judgment, the patient's history, and the nature of the presenting problem(s).

The content and documentation requirements for each type and level of examination are summarized below and described in detail in tables beginning on page 402. In the tables, organ systems and body areas recognized by *CPT* for purposes of describing examinations are shown in the left column. The content, or individual elements, of the examination pertaining to that body area or organ system are identified by bullets (•) in the right column.

Parenthetical examples, "(eg, ...)", have been used for clarification and to provide guidance regarding documentation. Documentation for each element must satisfy any numeric requirements (such as "Measurement of *any three of the following seven...*") included in the description of the element. Elements with multiple components but with no specific numeric requirement (such as "Examination of *liver* and *spleen*") require documentation of at least one component. It is possible for a given examination to be expanded beyond what is defined here. When that occurs, findings related to the additional systems and/or areas should be documented.

- **•DG:** *Specific abnormal and relevant negative findings of the examination of the affected or symptomatic body area(s) or organ system(s) should be documented. A notation of "abnormal" without elaboration is insufficient.*
- **•DG:** *Abnormal or unexpected findings of the examination of any asymptomatic body area(s) or organ system(s) should be described.*
- **•DG:** *A brief statement or notation indicating "negative" or "normal" is sufficient to document normal findings related to unaffected area(s) or asymptomatic organ system(s).*

General Multisystem Examinations

General multisystem examinations are described in detail beginning on page 402. To qualify for a given level of multisystem examination, the following content and documentation requirements should be met:

- **Problem-Focused Examination**—should include performance and documentation of one to five elements identified by a bullet (•) in one or more organ system(s) or body area(s).

- **Expanded Problem-Focused Examination**—should include performance and documentation of at least six elements identified by a bullet in one or more organ system(s) or body area(s).
- **Detailed Examination**—should include at least six organ systems or body areas. For each system/area selected, performance and documentation of at least two elements identified by a bullet is expected. Alternatively, a detailed examination may include performance and documentation of at least 12 elements identified by a bullet in two or more organ systems or body areas.
- **Comprehensive Examination**—should include at least nine organ systems or body areas. For each system/area selected, all elements of the examination identified by a bullet should be performed, unless specific directions limit the content of the examination. For each area/system, documentation of at least two elements identified by a bullet is expected.

Single Organ System Examinations

The single organ system examinations recognized by *CPT* are described in detail in the tables starting on page 405. Variations among these examinations in the organ systems and body areas identified in the left columns and in the elements of the examinations described in the right columns reflect differing emphases among specialties. To qualify for a given level of single organ system examination, the following content and documentation requirements should be met:

- **Problem-Focused Examination**—should include performance and documentation of one to five elements identified by a bullet, whether in a shaded or unshaded area.
- **Expanded Problem-Focused Examination**—should include performance and documentation of at least six elements identified by a bullet, whether in a shaded or unshaded area.
- **Detailed Examination**—examinations other than the eye and psychiatric examinations should include performance and documentation of at least 12 elements identified by a bullet, whether in a shaded or unshaded area.
- Eye and psychiatric examinations should include the performance and documentation of at least nine elements identified by a bullet, whether in a shaded or unshaded area.
- **Comprehensive Examination**—should include performance of all elements identified by a bullet, whether in a shaded or unshaded area. Documentation of every element in a shaded area and at least one element in each category in each unshaded area is expected.

Appendix A

General Multisystem Examination

System/Body Area	Elements of Examination
Constitutional	• Measurement of **any three of the following seven** vital signs: 1) sitting or standing blood pressure, 2) supine blood pressure, 3) pulse rate and regularity, 4) respiration, 5) temperature, 6) height, 7) weight (may be measured and recorded by ancillary staff) • General appearance of patient (eg, development, nutrition, body habitus, deformities, attention to grooming)
Eyes	• Inspection of conjunctivae and lids • Examination of pupils and irises (eg, reaction to light and accommodation, size and symmetry) • Ophthalmoscopic examination of optic discs (eg, size, C/D ratio, appearance) and posterior segments (eg, vessel changes, exudates, hemorrhages)
Ears, Nose, Mouth, and Throat	• External inspection of ears and nose (eg, overall appearance, scars, lesions, masses) • Otoscopic examination of external auditory canals and tympanic membranes • Assessment of hearing (eg, whispered voice, finger rub, tuning fork) • Inspection of nasal mucosa, septum, and turbinates • Inspection of lips, teeth, and gums • Examination of oropharynx: oral mucosa, salivary glands, hard and soft palates, tongue, tonsils, and posterior pharynx
Neck	• Examination of neck (eg, masses, overall appearance, symmetry, tracheal position, crepitus) • Examination of thyroid (eg, enlargement, tenderness, mass)
Respiratory	• Assessment of respiratory effort (eg, intercostal retractions, use of accessory muscles, diaphragmatic movement) • Percussion of chest (eg, dullness, flatness, hyperresonance) • Palpation of chest (eg, tactile fremitus) • Auscultation of lungs (eg, breath sounds, adventitious sounds, rubs)

Cardiovascular	• Palpation of heart (eg, location, size, thrills)
	• Auscultation of heart with notation of abnormal sounds and murmurs
	Examination of:
	  • Carotid arteries (eg, pulse amplitude, bruits)
	  • Abdominal aorta (eg, size, bruits)
	  • Femoral arteries (eg, pulse amplitude, bruits)
	  • Pedal pulses (eg, pulse amplitude)
	  • Extremities for edema and/or varicosities

Chest (Breasts)	• Inspection of breasts (eg, symmetry, nipple discharge) • Palpation of breasts and axillae (eg, masses or lumps, tenderness)

General Multisystem Examination, continued

System/Body Area	Elements of Examination
Gastrointestinal (Abdomen)	• Examination of abdomen with notation of presence of masses or tenderness • Examination of liver and spleen • Examination for presence or absence of hernia • Examination (when indicated) of anus, perineum, and rectum, including sphincter tone, presence of hemorrhoids, rectal masses • Obtain stool sample for occult blood test when indicated
Genitourinary	*Male* • Examination of the scrotal contents (eg, hydrocele, sperma-tocele, tenderness of cord, testicular mass) • Examination of the penis • Digital rectal examination of prostate gland (eg, size, symmetry, nodularity, tenderness) *Female* • Pelvic examination (with or without specimen collection for smears and cultures) including • Examination of external genitalia (eg, general appearance, hair distribution, lesions) and vagina (eg, general appearance, estrogen effect, discharge, lesions, pelvic support, cystocele, rectocele) • Examination of urethra (eg, masses, tenderness, scarring) • Examination of bladder (eg, fullness, masses, tenderness) • Cervix (eg, general appearance, lesions, discharge) • Uterus (eg, size, contour, position, mobility, tenderness, consistency, descent, or support) • Adnexa/parametria (eg, masses, tenderness, organomegaly, nodularity)
Lymphatic	Palpation of lymph nodes in **two or more** areas: • Neck • Axillae • Groin • Other
Musculoskeletal	• Examination of gait and station • Inspection and/or palpation of digits and nails (eg, clubbing, cyanosis, inflammatory conditions, petechiae, ischemia, infections, nodes) Examination of joints, bones, and muscles of **one or more of the following six areas:** 1) head and neck; 2) spine, ribs, and pelvis; 3) right upper extremity; 4) left upper extremity; 5) right lower extremity; and 6) left lower extremity. The examination of a given area includes: • Inspection and/or palpation with notation of presence of any misalignment, asymmetry, crepitation, defects, tenderness, masses, effusions • Assessment of range of motion with notation of any pain, crepitation, or contracture

Appendix A

General Multisystem Examination, continued

System/Body Area	Elements of Examination
Musculoskeletal, continued	• Assessment of stability with notation of any dislocation (luxation), subluxation, or laxity • Assessment of muscle strength and tone (eg, flaccid, cog wheel, spastic) with notation of any atrophy or abnormal movements
Skin	• Inspection of skin and subcutaneous tissue (eg, rashes, lesions, ulcers) • Palpation of skin and subcutaneous tissue (eg, induration, subcutaneous nodules, tightening)
Neurological	• Test cranial nerves with notation of any deficits • Examination of deep tendon reflexes with notation of pathological reflexes (eg, Babinski) • Examination of sensation (eg, by touch, pin, vibration, proprioception)

Psychiatric	• Description of patient's judgment and insight
	Brief assessment of mental status including:
	  • Orientation to time, place, and person
	  • Recent and remote memory
	  • Mood and affect (eg, depression, anxiety, agitation)

Content and Documentation Requirements

Level of Exam	Perform and Document
Problem Focused	**One to five** elements identified by a bullet.
Expanded Problem Focused	**At least six** elements identified by a bullet.
Detailed	**At least two** elements identified by a bullet **from each of six areas/systems** OR **at least 12** elements identified by a bullet **in two or more areas/systems.**
Comprehensive	Perform **all** elements identified by a bullet in **at least nine** organ systems or body areas and document **at least two** elements identified by a bullet **from each of nine areas/systems.**

Cardiovascular Examination

System/Body Area	Elements of Examination
Constitutional	• Measurement of any three of the following seven vital signs: 1) sitting or standing blood pressure, 2) supine blood pressure, 3) pulse rate and regularity, 4) respiration, 5) temperature, 6) height, 7) weight (may be measured and recorded by ancillary staff) • General appearance of patient (eg, development, nutrition, body habitus, deformities, attention to grooming)
Head and Face	
Eyes	• Inspection of conjunctivae and lids (eg, xanthelasma)
Ears, Nose, Mouth, and Throat	• Inspection of teeth, gums, and palate • Inspection of oral mucosa with notation of presence of pallor or cyanosis
Neck	• Examination of jugular veins (eg, distension; a, v, or cannon a waves) • Examination of thyroid (eg, enlargement, tenderness, mass)
Respiratory	• Assessment of respiratory effort (eg, intercostal retractions, use of accessory muscles, diaphragmatic movement) • Auscultation of lungs (eg, breath sounds, adventitious sounds, rubs)
Cardiovascular	• Palpation of heart (eg, location, size, and forcefulness of the point of maximal impact; thrills; lifts; palpable S3 or S4) • Auscultation of heart including sounds, abnormal sounds, and murmurs • Measurement of blood pressure in two or more extremities when indicated (eg, aortic dissection, coarctation) Examination of • Carotid arteries (eg, waveform, pulse amplitude, bruits, apical-carotid delay) • Abdominal aorta (eg, size, bruits) • Femoral arteries (eg, pulse amplitude, bruits) • Pedal pulses (eg, pulse amplitude) • Extremities for peripheral edema and/or varicosities
Chest (Breasts)	
Gastrointestinal (Abdomen)	• Examination of abdomen with notation of presence of masses or tenderness • Examination of liver and spleen • Obtain stool sample for occult blood from patients who are being considered for thrombolytic or anti-coagulant therapy
Genitourinary (Abdomen)	
Lymphatic	

Appendix A

Cardiovascular Examination, continued

System/Body Area	Elements of Examination
Musculoskeletal	• Examination of the back with notation of kyphosis or scoliosis • Examination of gait with notation of ability to undergo exercise testing and/or participation in exercise programs • Assessment of muscle strength and tone (eg, flaccid, cog wheel, spastic) with notation of any atrophy and abnormal movements
Extremities	• Inspection and palpation of digits and nails (eg, clubbing, cyanosis, inflammation, petechiae, ischemia, infections, Osler's nodes)
Skin	• Inspection and/or palpation of skin and subcutaneous tissue (eg, stasis dermatitis, ulcers, scars, xanthomas)
Neurological/ Psychiatric	Brief assessment of mental status including: • Orientation to time, place, and person • Mood and affect (eg, depression, anxiety, agitation)

Content and Documentation Requirements

Level of Exam	Perform and Document
Problem Focused	**One to five** elements identified by a bullet.
Expanded Problem Focused	**At least six** elements identified by a bullet.
Detailed	**At least 12** elements identified by a bullet.
Comprehensive	Perform **all** elements identified by a bullet; document every element in each shaded area and at least one element in each category in each unshaded area.

Ear, Nose, and Throat Examination

System/Body Area	Elements of Examination
Constitutional	• Measurement of **any three of the following seven** vital signs: 1) sitting or standing blood pressure, 2) supine blood pressure, 3) pulse rate and regularity, 4) respiration, 5) temperature, 6) height, 7) weight (may be measured and recorded by ancillary staff) • General appearance of patient (eg, development, nutrition, body habitus, deformities, attention to grooming) • Assessment of ability to communicate (eg, use of sign language or other communication aids) and quality of voice
Head and Face	• Inspection of head and face (eg, overall appearance, scars, lesions, and masses) • Palpation and/or percussion of face with notation of presence or absence of sinus tenderness • Examination of salivary glands • Assessment of facial strength
Eyes	• Test ocular motility including primary gaze alignment
Ears, Nose, Mouth, and Throat	• Otoscopic examination of external auditory canals and tympanic membranes including pneumo-otoscopy with notation of mobility of membranes • Assessment of hearing with tuning forks and clinical speech reception thresholds (eg, whispered voice, finger rub) • External inspection of ears and nose (eg, overall appearance, scars, lesions, and masses) • Inspection of nasal mucosa, septum, and turbinates • Inspection of lips, teeth, and gums • Examination of oropharynx: oral mucosa, hard and soft palates, tongue, tonsils, and posterior pharynx (eg, asymmetry, lesions, hydration of mucosal surfaces) • Inspection of pharyngeal walls and pyriform sinuses (eg, pooling of saliva, asymmetry, lesions) • Examination by mirror of larynx including the condition of the epiglottis, false vocal cords, true vocal cords, and mobility of larynx (use of mirror not required in children) • Examination by mirror of nasopharynx including appearance of the mucosa, adenoids, posterior choanae, and eustachian tubes (use of mirror not required in children)
Neck	• Examination of neck (eg, masses, overall appearance, symmetry, tracheal position, crepitus) • Examination of thyroid (eg, enlargement, tenderness, mass)
Respiratory	• Inspection of chest including symmetry, expansion, and/or assessment of respiratory effort (eg, intercostal retractions, use of accessory muscles, diaphragmatic movement) • Auscultation of lungs (eg, breath sounds, adventitious sounds, rubs)
Cardiovascular	• Auscultation of heart with notation of abnormal sounds and murmurs • Examination of peripheral vascular system by observation(eg, swelling, varicosities) and palpation (eg, pulses, temperature, edema, tenderness)

Appendix A

Ear, Nose, and Throat Examination, continued

System/Body Area	Elements of Examination
Chest (Breasts)	
Gastrointestinal (Abdomen)	
Genitourinary	
Lymphatic	• Palpation of lymph nodes in neck, axillae, groin, and/or other location
Musculoskeletal	
Extremities	
Skin	
Neurological/ Psychiatric	• Test cranial nerves with notation of any deficits Brief assessment of mental status including: • Orientation to time, place, and person • Mood and affect (eg, depression, anxiety, agitation)

Content and Documentation Requirements

Level of Exam	Perform and Document
Problem Focused	**One to five** elements identified by a bullet.
Expanded Problem Focused	**At least six** elements identified by a bullet.
Detailed	**At least 12** elements identified by a bullet.
Comprehensive	Perform **all** elements identified by a bullet; document every element in each shaded area and at least one element in each category in each unshaded area.

Appendix A

Eye Examination

System/Body Area	Elements of Examination
Constitutional	
Head and Face	

Eyes	• Test visual acuity (does not include determination of refractive error)
	• Gross visual field testing by confrontation
	• Test ocular motility including primary gaze alignment
	• Inspection of bulbar and palpebral conjunctivae
	• Examination of ocular adnexae including lids (eg, ptosis or lagophthalmos), lacrimal glands, lacrimal drainage, orbits, and preauricular lymph nodes
	• Examination of pupils and irises including shape, direct and consensual reaction (afferent pupil), size (eg, anisocoria), and morphology
	• Slit lamp examination of the corneas including epithelium, stroma, endothelium, and tear film
	• Slit lamp examination of the anterior chambers including depth, cells, and flare
	• Slit lamp examination of the lenses including clarity, anterior and posterior capsule, cortex, and nucleus
	• Measurement of intraocular pressures (except in children and patients with trauma or infectious disease)
	Ophthalmoscopic examination through dilated pupils (unless contraindicated) of:
	  • Optic discs including size, C/D ratio, appearance (eg, atrophy, cupping, tumor elevation), and nerve fiber layer
	  • Posterior segments including retina and vessels (eg, exudates and hemorrhages)

Ears, Nose, Mouth, and Throat	
Neck	
Respiratory	• Inspection of chest including symmetry, expansion, and/or assessment of respiratory effort (eg, intercostal retractions, use of accessory muscles, diaphragmatic movement) • Auscultation of lungs (eg, breath sounds, adventitious sounds, rubs)
Cardiovascular	
Chest (Breasts)	
Genitourinary	
Lymphatic	
Musculoskeletal	
Extremities	
Skin	

Appendix A

Eye Examination, continued	
System/Body Area	**Elements of Examination**
Neurological/ Psychiatric	Brief assessment of mental status including: • Orientation to time, place, and person • Mood and affect (eg, depression, anxiety, agitation)

Content and Documentation Requirements	
Level of Exam	**Perform and Document**
Problem Focused	**One to five** elements identified by a bullet.
Expanded Problem Focused	**At least six** elements identified by a bullet.
Detailed	**At least nine** elements identified by a bullet.
Comprehensive	Perform **all** elements identified by a bullet; document every element in each shaded area and at least one element in each category in each unshaded area.

Appendix A

Genitourinary Examination

System/Body Area	Elements of Examination
Constitutional	• Measurement of **any three of the following seven** vital signs: 1) sitting or standing blood pressure, 2) supine blood pressure, 3) pulse rate and regularity, 4) respiration, 5) temperature, 6) height, 7) weight (may be measured and recorded by ancillary staff) • General appearance of patient (eg, development, nutrition, body habitus, deformities, attention to grooming)
Head and Face	
Eyes	
Ears, Nose, Mouth, and Throat	
Neck	• Examination of neck (eg, masses, overall appearance, symmetry, tracheal position, crepitus) • Examination of thyroid (eg, enlargement, tenderness, mass)
Respiratory	• Assessment of respiratory effort (eg, intercostal retractions, use of accessory muscles, diaphragmatic movement) • Auscultation of lungs (eg, breath sounds, adventitious sounds, rubs)
Cardiovascular	• Auscultation of heart with notation of abnormal sounds and murmurs • Examination of peripheral vascular system by observation (eg, swelling, varicosities) and palpation (eg, pulses, temperature, edema, tenderness)
Chest (Breasts)	[See Genitourinary (female)]
Gastrointestinal (Abdomen)	• Examination of abdomen with notation of presence of masses or tenderness • Examination for presence or absence of hernia • Examination of liver and spleen • Obtain stool sample for occult blood test when indicated
Genitourinary	*Male* • Inspection of anus and perineum Examination (with or without specimen collection for smears and cultures) of genitalia including: • Scrotum (eg, lesions, cysts, rashes) • Epididymides (eg, size, symmetry, masses) • Testes (eg, size, symmetry, masses) • Urethral meatus (eg, size, location, lesions, discharge) • Penis (eg, lesions, presence or absence of foreskin, foreskin retractability, plaque, masses, scarring, deformities) Digital rectal examination including: • Prostate gland (eg, size, symmetry, nodularity, tenderness) • Seminal vesicles (eg, symmetry, tenderness, masses, enlargement) • Sphincter tone, presence of hemorrhoids, rectal masses

Appendix A

Genitourinary Examination, continued

System/Body Area	Elements of Examination
Genitourinary, continued	*Female* Includes **at least seven of the following 11** elements identified by bullets: • Inspection and palpation of breasts (eg, masses or lumps, tenderness, symmetry, nipple discharge) • Digital rectal examination including sphincter tone, presence of hemorrhoids, rectal masses Pelvic examination (with or without specimen collection for smears and cultures) including: • External genitalia (eg, general appearance, hair distribution, lesions) • Urethral meatus (eg, size, location, lesions, prolapse) • Urethra (eg, masses, tenderness, scarring) • Bladder (eg, fullness, masses, tenderness) • Vagina (eg, general appearance, estrogen effect, discharge, lesions, pelvic support, cystocele, rectocele) • Cervix (eg, general appearance, lesions, discharge) • Uterus (eg, size, contour, position, mobility, tenderness, consistency, descent, or support) • Adnexa/parametria (eg, masses, tenderness, organomegaly, nodularity) • Anus and perineum
Lymphatic	• Palpation of lymph nodes in neck, axillae, groin, and/or other location
Musculoskeletal	
Extremities	
Skin	• Inspection and/or palpation of skin and subcutaneous tissue (eg, rashes, lesions, ulcers)
Neurological/ Psychiatric	Brief assessment of mental status including: • Orientation (eg, time, place, and person) • Mood and affect (eg, depression, anxiety, agitation)

Content and Documentation Requirements

Level of Exam	Perform and Document
Problem Focused	**One to five** elements identified by a bullet.
Expanded Problem Focused	**At least six** elements identified by a bullet.
Detailed	**At least 12** elements identified by a bullet.
Comprehensive	Perform **all** elements identified by a bullet; document every element in each shaded area and at least one element in each category in each unshaded area.

Hematologic/Lymphatic/Immunologic Examination

System/Body Area	Elements of Examination
Constitutional	• Measurement of **any three of the following seven** vital signs: 1) sitting or standing blood pressure, 2) supine blood pressure, 3) pulse rate and regularity, 4) respiration, 5) temperature, 6) height, 7) weight (may be measured and recorded by ancillary staff) • General appearance of patient (eg, development, nutrition, body habitus, deformities, attention to grooming)
Head and Face	• Palpation and/or percussion of face with notation of presence or absence of sinus tenderness
Eyes	• Inspection of conjunctivae and lids
Ears, Nose, Mouth, and Throat	• Otoscopic examination of external auditory canals and tympanic membranes • Inspection of nasal mucosa, septum, and turbinates • Inspection of teeth and gums • Examination of oropharynx (eg, oral mucosa, hard and soft palates, tongue, tonsils, posterior pharynx)
Neck	• Examination of neck (eg, masses, overall appearance, symmetry, tracheal position, crepitus) • Examination of thyroid (eg, enlargement, tenderness, mass)
Respiratory	• Assessment of respiratory effort (eg, intercostal retractions, use of accessory muscles, diaphragmatic movement) • Auscultation of lungs (eg, breath sounds, adventitious sounds, rubs)
Cardiovascular	• Auscultation of heart with notation of abnormal sounds and murmurs • Examination of peripheral vascular system by observation (eg, swelling, varicosities) and palpation (eg, pulses, temperature, edema, tenderness)
Chest (Breasts)	
Gastrointestinal (Abdomen)	• Examination of abdomen with notation of presence of masses or tenderness • Examination of liver and spleen
Genitourinary	
Lymphatic	• Palpation of lymph nodes in neck, axillae, groin, and/or other location
Musculoskeletal	
Extremities	• Inspection and palpation of digits and nails (eg, clubbing, cyanosis, inflammation, petechiae, ischemia, infections, nodes)
Skin	• Inspection and/or palpation of skin and subcutaneous tissue (eg, rashes, lesions, ulcers, ecchymoses, bruises)
Neurological/ Psychiatric	Brief assessment of mental status including: • Orientation to time, place, and person • Mood and affect (eg, depression, anxiety, agitation)

Appendix A

Hematologic/Lymphatic/Immunologic Examination, continued

Content and Documentation Requirements

Level of Exam	Perform and Document
Problem Focused	**One to five** elements identified by a bullet.
Expanded Problem Focused	**At least six** elements identified by a bullet.
Detailed	**At least 12** elements identified by a bullet.
Comprehensive	Perform **all** elements identified by a bullet; document every element in each shaded area and at least one element in each category in each unshaded area.

Musculoskeletal Examination

System/Body Area	Elements of Examination
Constitutional	• Measurement of **any three of the following seven** vital signs: 1) sitting or standing blood pressure, 2) supine blood pressure, 3) pulse rate and regularity, 4) respiration, 5) temperature, 6) height, 7) weight (may be measured and recorded by ancillary staff) • General appearance of patient (eg, development, nutrition, body habitus, deformities, attention to grooming)
Head and Face	
Eyes	
Ears, Nose, Mouth, and Throat	
Neck	
Respiratory	
Cardiovascular	• Examination of peripheral vascular system by observation (eg, swelling, varicosities) and palpation (eg, pulses, temperature, edema, tenderness)
Chest (Breasts)	
Gastrointestinal (Abdomen)	
Genitourinary	
Lymphatic	• Palpation of lymph nodes in neck, axillae, groin, and/or other location
Musculoskeletal	• Examination of gait and station Examination of joint(s), bone(s), and muscle(s)/tendon(s) of **four of the following six** areas: 1) head and neck; 2) spine, ribs, and pelvis; 3) right upper extremity; 4) left upper extremity; 5) right lower extremity; and 6) left lower extremity. The examination of a given area includes: • Inspection, percussion, and/or palpation with notation of any misalignment, asymmetry, crepitation, defects, tenderness, masses, or effusions • Assessment of range of motion with notation of any pain (eg, straight leg raising), crepitation, or contracture • Assessment of stability with notation of any dislocation (luxation), subluxation, or laxity • Assessment of muscle strength and tone (eg, flaccid, cog wheel, spastic) with notation of any atrophy or abnormal movements Note: For the comprehensive level of examination, all four of the elements identified by a bullet must be performed and documented for each of four anatomic areas. For the three lower levels of examination, each element is counted separately for each body area. For example, assessing range of motion in two extremities constitutes two elements.
Extremities	[See Musculoskeletal and Skin]

Appendix A

Musculoskeletal Examination, continued

System/Body Area	Elements of Examination
Skin	• Inspection and/or palpation of skin and subcutaneous tissue (eg, scars, rashes, lesions, cafe-au-lait spots, ulcers) in **four of the following six** areas: 1) head and neck, 2) trunk, 3) right upper extremity, 4) left upper extremity, 5) right lower extremity, and 6) left lower extremity. Note: For the comprehensive level, the examination of all four anatomic areas must be performed and documented. For the three lower levels of examination, each body area is counted separately. For example, inspection and/or palpation of the skin and subcutaneous tissue of two extremities constitutes two elements.
Neurological/ Psychiatric	• Test coordination (eg, finger/nose, heel/knee/shin, rapid alternating movements in the upper and lower extremities, evaluation of fine motor coordination in young children) • Examination of deep tendon reflexes and/or nerve stretch test with notation of pathological reflexes (eg, Babinski) • Examination of sensation (eg, by touch, pin, vibration, proprioception) Brief assessment of mental status including: • Orientation to time, place, and person • Mood and affect (eg, depression, anxiety, agitation)

Content and Documentation Requirements

Level of Exam	Perform and Document
Problem Focused	**One to five** elements identified by a bullet.
Expanded Problem Focused	**At least six** elements identified by a bullet.
Detailed	**At least 12** elements identified by a bullet.
Comprehensive	Perform **all** elements identified by a bullet; document every element in each shaded area and at least one element in each category in each unshaded area.

Neurological Examination

System/Body Area	Elements of Examination
Constitutional	• Measurement of **any three of the following seven** vital signs: 1) sitting or standing blood pressure, 2) supine blood pressure, 3) pulse rate and regularity, 4) respiration, 5) temperature, 6) height, 7) weight (may be measured and recorded by ancillary staff) • General appearance of patient (eg, development, nutrition, body habitus, deformities, attention to grooming)
Head and Face	
Eyes	• Ophthalmoscopic examination of optic discs (eg, size, C/D ratio, appearance) and posterior segments (eg, vessel changes, exudates, hemorrhages)
Ears, Nose, Mouth, and Throat	
Neck	
Respiratory	
Cardiovascular	• Examination of carotid arteries (eg, pulse amplitude, bruits) • Auscultation of heart with notation of abnormal sounds and murmurs • Examination of peripheral vascular system by observation (eg, swelling, varicosities) and palpation (eg, pulses, temperature, edema, tenderness)
Chest (Breasts)	
Gastrointestinal (Abdomen)	
Genitourinary	
Lymphatic	

Musculoskeletal	• Examination of gait and station
	Assessment of motor function including:
	  • Muscle strength in upper and lower extremities
	  • Muscle tone in upper and lower extremities (eg, flaccid, cog wheel, spastic) with notation of any atrophy or abnormal movements (eg, fasciculation, tardive dyskinesia)

Extremities	[See Musculoskeletal]
Skin	

Neurological	Evaluation of higher integrative functions including:
	  • Orientation to time, place, and person
	  • Recent and remote memory
	  • Attention span and concentration
	  • Language (eg, naming objects, repeating phrases, spontaneous speech)
	  • Fund of knowledge (eg, awareness of current events, past history, vocabulary)

Appendix A

Neurological Examination, continued

System/Body Area	Elements of Examination
Neurological, continued	Test the following cranial nerves: • 2nd cranial nerve (eg, visual acuity, visual fields, fundi) • 3rd, 4th, and 6th cranial nerves (eg, pupils, eye movements) • 5th cranial nerve (eg, facial sensation, corneal reflexes) • 7th cranial nerve (eg, facial symmetry, strength) • 8th cranial nerve (eg, hearing with tuning fork, whispered voice, and/or finger rub) • 9th cranial nerve (eg, spontaneous or reflex palate movement) • 11th cranial nerve (eg, shoulder shrug strength) • 12th cranial nerve (eg, tongue protrusion) • Examination of sensation (eg, by touch, pin, vibration, proprioception) • Examination of deep tendon reflexes in upper and lower extremities with notation of pathological reflexes (eg, Babinski) • Test coordination (eg, finger/nose, heel/knee/shin, rapid alternating movements in the upper and lower extremities, evaluation of fine motor coordination in young children)
Psychiatric	

Content and Documentation Requirements

Level of Exam	Perform and Document
Problem Focused	**One to five** elements identified by a bullet.
Expanded Problem Focused	**At least six** elements identified by a bullet.
Detailed	**At least 12** elements identified by a bullet.
Comprehensive	Perform **all** elements identified by a bullet; document every element in each shaded area and at least one element in each category in each unshaded area.

Appendix A

Psychiatric Examination

System/Body Area	Elements of Examination
Constitutional	• Measurement of **any three of the following seven** vital signs: 1) sitting or standing blood pressure, 2) supine blood pressure, 3) pulse rate and regularity, 4) respiration, 5) temperature, 6) height, 7) weight (may be measured and recorded by ancillary staff) • General appearance of patient (eg, development, nutrition, body habitus, deformities, attention to grooming)
Head and Face	
Eyes	
Ears, Nose, Mouth, and Throat	
Neck	
Respiratory	
Cardiovascular	
Chest (Breasts)	
Gastrointestinal (Abdomen)	
Genitourinary	
Lymphatic	
Musculoskeletal	• Assessment of muscle strength and tone (eg, flaccid, cog wheel, spastic) with notation of any atrophy and abnormal movements • Examination of gait and station
Extremities	
Skin	
Neurological	
Psychiatric	• Description of speech including: rate, volume, articulation, coherence, and spontaneity with notation of abnormalities (eg, perseveration, paucity of language) • Description of thought processes including: rate of thoughts (eg, logical vs. illogical, tangential), abstract reasoning, and computation • Description of associations (eg, loose, tangential, circumstantial, intact) • Description of abnormal or psychotic thoughts including hallucinations, delusions, preoccupation with violence, homicidal or suicidal ideation, and obsessions • Description of the patient's judgment (eg, concerning everyday activities and social situations) and insight (eg, concerning psychiatric condition)

Appendix A

Psychiatric Examination, continued

System/Body Area	Elements of Examination
Psychiatric, continued	Complete mental status examination including: • Orientation to time, place, and person • Recent and remote memory • Attention span and concentration • Language (eg, naming objects, repeating phrases) • Fund of knowledge (eg, awareness of current events, past history, vocabulary) • Mood and affect (eg, depression, anxiety, agitation, hypomania, lability)

Content and Documentation Requirements

Level of Exam	Perform and Document
Problem Focused	**One to five** elements identified by a bullet.
Expanded Problem Focused	**At least six** elements identified by a bullet.
Detailed	**At least nine** elements identified by a bullet.
Comprehensive	Perform **all** elements identified by a bullet; document every element in each shaded area and at least one element in each category in each unshaded area.

Respiratory Examination

System/Body Area	Elements of Examination
Constitutional	• Measurement of **any three of the following seven** vital signs: 1) sitting or standing blood pressure, 2) supine blood pressure, 3) pulse rate and regularity, 4) respiration, 5) temperature, 6) height, 7) weight (may be measured and recorded by ancillary staff) • General appearance of patient (eg, development, nutrition, body habitus, deformities, attention to grooming)
Head and Face	
Eyes	
Ears, Nose, Mouth, and Throat	• Inspection of nasal mucosa, septum, and turbinates • Inspection of teeth and gums • Examination of oropharynx (eg, oral mucosa, hard and soft palates, tongue, tonsils, and posterior pharynx)
Neck	• Examination of neck (eg, masses, overall appearance, symmetry, tracheal position, crepitus) • Examination of thyroid (eg, enlargement, tenderness, mass) • Examination of jugular veins (eg, distension; a, v, or cannon a waves)
Respiratory	• Inspection of chest with notation of symmetry and expansion • Assessment of respiratory effort (eg, intercostal retractions, use of accessory muscles, diaphragmatic movement) • Percussion of chest (eg, dullness, flatness, hyper-resonance) • Palpation of chest (eg, tactile fremitus) • Auscultation of lungs (eg, breath sounds, adventitious sounds, rubs)
Cardiovascular	• Auscultation of heart including sounds, abnormal sounds, and murmurs • Examination of peripheral vascular system by observation (eg, swelling, varicosities) and palpation (eg, pulses, temperature, edema, tenderness)
Chest (Breasts)	
Gastrointestinal (Abdomen)	• Examination of abdomen with notation of presence of masses or tenderness • Examination of liver and spleen
Genitourinary	
Lymphatic	• Palpation of lymph nodes in neck, axillae, groin, and/or other location
Musculoskeletal	• Assessment of muscle strength and tone (eg, flaccid, cog wheel, spastic) with notation of any atrophy and abnormal movements • Examination of gait and station
Extremities	• Inspection and palpation of digits and nails (eg, clubbing, cyanosis, inflammation, petechiae, ischemia, infections, nodes)

Appendix A

Respiratory Examination, continued

System/Body Area	Elements of Examination
Skin	• Inspection and/or palpation of skin and subcutaneous tissue (eg, rashes, lesions, ulcers)
Neurological/ Psychiatric	Brief assessment of mental status including: • Orientation to time, place, and person • Mood and affect (eg, depression, anxiety, agitation)

Content and Documentation Requirements

Level of Exam	Perform and Document
Problem Focused	**One to five** elements identified by a bullet.
Expanded Problem Focused	**At least six** elements identified by a bullet.
Detailed	**At least 12** elements identified by a bullet.
Comprehensive	Perform **all** elements identified by a bullet; document every element in each shaded area and at least one element in each category in each unshaded area.

Skin Examination	
System/Body Area	**Elements of Examination**
Constitutional	• Measurement of **any three of the following seven** vital signs: 1) sitting or standing blood pressure, 2) supine blood pressure, 3) pulse rate and regularity, 4) respiration, 5) temperature, 6) height, 7) weight (may be measured and recorded by ancillary staff) • General appearance of patient (eg, development, nutrition, body habitus, deformities, attention to grooming)
Head and Face	
Eyes	• Inspection of conjunctivae and lids
Ears, Nose, Mouth, and Throat	• Inspection of lips, teeth, and gums • Examination of oropharynx (eg, oral mucosa, hard and soft palates, tongue, tonsils, posterior pharynx)
Neck	• Examination of thyroid (eg, enlargement, tenderness, mass)
Respiratory	
Cardiovascular	• Examination of peripheral vascular system by observation (eg, swelling, varicosities) and palpation (eg, pulses, temperature, edema, tenderness)
Chest (Breasts)	
Gastrointestinal (Abdomen)	• Examination of liver and spleen • Examination of anus for condyloma and other lesions
Genitourinary	
Lymphatic	• Palpation of lymph nodes in neck, axillae, groin, and/or other location
Musculoskeletal	
Extremities	• Inspection and palpation of digits and nails (eg, clubbing, cyanosis, inflammation, petechiae, ischemia, infections, nodes)
Skin	• Palpation of scalp and inspection of hair of scalp, eyebrows, face, chest, pubic area (when indicated), and extremities Inspection and/or palpation of skin and subcutaneous tissue (eg, rashes, lesions, ulcers, susceptibility to and presence of photo damage) in **eight of the following 10** areas: • Head, including face • Neck • Chest, including breasts and axillae • Abdomen • Genitalia, groin, buttocks • Back • Right upper extremity • Left upper extremity • Right lower extremity • Left lower extremity

Appendix A

Skin Examination, continued	
System/Body Area	**Elements of Examination**
Skin, continued	*Note:* For the comprehensive level, the examination of at least eight anatomic areas must be performed and documented. For the three lower levels of examination, each body area is counted separately. For example, inspection and/or palpation of the skin and subcutaneous tissue of the right upper extremity and the left upper extremity constitutes two elements. • Inspection of eccrine and apocrine glands of skin and subcutaneous tissue with identification and location of any hyperhidrosis, chromhidroses, or bromhidrosis
Neurological/ Psychiatric	Brief assessment of mental status including: • Orientation to time, place, and person • Mood and affect (eg, depression, anxiety, agitation)

Content and Documentation Requirements	
Level of Exam	**Perform and Document**
Problem Focused	**One to five** elements identified by a bullet.
Expanded Problem Focused	**At least six** elements identified by a bullet.
Detailed	**At least 12** elements identified by a bullet.
Comprehensive	Perform **all** elements identified by a bullet; document every element in each shaded area and at least one element in each category in each unshaded area.

C. Documentation of the Complexity of Medical Decision Making

The levels of E/M services recognize four types of medical decision making (straightforward, low complexity, moderate complexity, and high complexity). Medical decision making refers to the complexity of establishing a diagnosis and/or selecting a management option as measured by

- The number of possible diagnoses and/or the number of management options that must be considered
- The amount and/or complexity of medical records, diagnostic tests, and/or other information that must be obtained, reviewed, and analyzed
- The risk of significant complications, morbidity, and/or mortality, as well as co-morbidities associated with the patient's presenting problem(s), the diagnostic procedure(s), and/or the possible management options

The chart on page 425 shows the progression of the elements required for each level of medical decision making. To qualify for a given type of decision making, two of the three elements in the table must be either met or exceeded.

Number of Diagnoses or Management Options	Amount and/or Complexity of Data to Be Reviewed	Risk of Significant Complications, Morbidity, and/ or Mortality	Type of Decision Making
Minimal	Minimal or none	Minimal	Straightforward
Limited	Limited	Low	Low complexity
Multiple	Moderate	Moderate	Moderate complexity
Extensive	Extensive	High	High complexity

Each of the elements of medical decision making is described below.

Number of Diagnoses or Management Options

The number of possible diagnoses and/or the number of management options that must be considered is based on the number and types of problems addressed during the encounter, the complexity of establishing a diagnosis, and the management decisions that are made by the physician.

Generally, decision making with respect to a diagnosed problem is easier than that for an identified but undiagnosed problem. The number and type of diagnostic tests employed may be an indicator of the number of possible diagnoses. Problems that are improving or resolving are less complex than those that are worsening or failing to change as expected. The need to seek advice from others is another indicator of complexity of diagnostic or management problems.

- **•DG:** *For each encounter, an assessment, clinical impression, or diagnosis should be documented. It may be explicitly stated or implied in documented decisions regarding management plans and/or further evaluation.*
  - ☀ *For a presenting problem with an established diagnosis, the record should reflect whether the problem is: a) improved, well controlled, resolving, or resolved or b) inadequately controlled, worsening, or failing to change as expected.*
  - ☀ *For a presenting problem without an established diagnosis, the assessment or clinical impression may be stated in the form of differential diagnoses or as a "possible," "probable," or "rule out" (R/O) diagnosis.*
- **•DG:** *The initiation of, or changes in, treatment should be documented. Treatment includes a wide range of management options including patient instructions, nursing instructions, therapies, and medications.*
- **•DG:** *If referrals are made, consultations requested, or advice sought, the record should indicate to whom or where the referral or consultation is made or from whom the advice is requested.*

Amount and/or Complexity of Data to Be Reviewed

The amount and complexity of data to be reviewed is based on the types of diagnostic testing ordered or reviewed. A decision to obtain and review old medical records and/or obtain history from sources other than the patient increases the amount and complexity of data to be reviewed.

Discussion of contradictory or unexpected test results with the physician who performed or interpreted the test is an indication of the complexity of data being reviewed. On occasion the physician who ordered a test may personally review the image, tracing, or specimen to supplement information from the

Appendix A

physician who prepared the test report or interpretation; this is another indication of the complexity of data being reviewed.

•DG: *If a diagnostic service (test or procedure) is ordered, planned, scheduled, or performed at the time of the E/M encounter, the type of service (eg, lab or x-ray) should be documented.*

•DG: *The review of lab, radiology, and/or other diagnostic tests should be documented. A simple notation such as "WBC elevated" or "chest x-ray unremarkable" is acceptable. Alternatively, the review may be documented by initialing and dating the report containing the test results.*

•DG: *A decision to obtain old records or to obtain additional history from the family, caretaker, or other source to supplement that obtained from the patient should be documented.*

•DG: *Relevant findings from the review of old records and/or the receipt of additional history from the family, caretaker, or other source to supplement that obtained from the patient should be documented. If there is no relevant information beyond that already obtained, that fact should be documented. A notation of "old records reviewed" or "additional history obtained from family" without elaboration is insufficient.*

•DG: *The results of discussion of laboratory, radiology, or other diagnostic tests with the physician who performed or interpreted the study should be documented.*

•DG: *The direct visualization and independent interpretation of an image, tracing, or specimen previously or subsequently interpreted by another physician should be documented.*

Risk of Significant Complications, Morbidity, and/or Mortality

The risk of significant complications, morbidity, and/or mortality is based on the risks associated with the presenting problem(s), the diagnostic procedure(s), and the possible management options.

•DG: *Co-morbidities/underlying diseases or other factors that increase the complexity of medical decision making by increasing the risk of complications, morbidity, and/ or mortality should be documented.*

•DG: *If a surgical or invasive diagnostic procedure is ordered, planned, or scheduled at the time of the E/M encounter, the type of procedure (eg, laparoscopy) should be documented.*

•DG: *If a surgical or invasive diagnostic procedure is performed at the time of the E/M encounter, the specific procedure should be documented.*

•DG: *The referral for or decision to perform a surgical or invasive diagnostic procedure on an urgent basis should be documented or implied.*

The following table may be used to help determine whether the risk of significant complications, morbidity, and/or mortality is minimal, low, moderate, or high. Because the determination of risk is complex and not readily quantifiable, the table includes common clinical examples rather than absolute measures of risk. The assessment of risk of the presenting problem(s) is based on the risk related to the disease process anticipated between the present encounter and the next one. The assessment of risk of selecting diagnostic procedures and management options is based on the risk during and immediately following any procedures or treatment. **The highest level of risk in any one category (presenting problem(s), diagnostic procedure(s), or management options) determines the overall risk.**

D. Documentation of an Encounter Dominated by Counseling or Coordination of Care

In the case where counseling and/or coordination of care dominates (more than 50%) the physician/patient and/or family encounter (face-to-face time in the office or other outpatient setting, floor/unit time in the hospital or nursing facility), time is considered the key or controlling factor to qualify for a particular level of E/M services.

•*DG:* *If the physician elects to report the level of service based on counseling and/ or coordination of care, the total length of time of the encounter (face-to-face or floor time, as appropriate) should be documented and the record should describe the counseling and/or activities to coordinate care.*

Table of Risk

Level of Risk	Presenting Problem(s)	Diagnostic Procedure(s) Ordered	Management Options Selected
Minimal	◉ One self-limited or minor problem, eg, cold, insect bite, tinea corporis	◉ Laboratory tests requiring venipuncture ◉ Chest x-rays ◉ EKG/EEG ◉ Urinalysis ◉ Ultrasound, eg, echo-cardiography ◉ KOH prep	◉ Rest ◉ Gargles ◉ Elastic bandages ◉ Superficial dressings
Low	◉ Two or more self-limited or minor problems ◉ One stable chronic illness, eg, well controlled hypertension, non–insulin-dependent diabetes, cataract, BPH ◉ Acute uncomplicated illness or injury, eg, cystitis, allergic rhinitis, simple sprain	◉ Physiologic tests not under stress, eg, pulmonary function tests ◉ Non-cardiovascular imaging studies with contrast, eg, barium enema ◉ Superficial needle biopsies ◉ Clinical laboratory tests requiring arterial puncture ◉ Skin biopsies	◉ Over-the-counter drugs ◉ Minor surgery with no identified risk factors ◉ Physical therapy ◉ Occupational therapy ◉ IV fluids without additives
Moderate	◉ One or more chronic illnesses with mild exacerbation, progression, or side effects of treatment ◉ Two or more stable chronic illnesses ◉ Undiagnosed new problem with uncertain prognosis, eg, lump in breast	◉ Physiologic tests under stress, eg, cardiac stress test, fetal contraction stress test ◉ Diagnostic endoscopies with no identified risk factors ◉ Deep needle or incisional biopsy	◉ Minor surgery with identified risk factors ◉ Elective major surgery (open, percutaneous, or endoscopic) with no identified risk factors ◉ Prescription drug management

Table of Risk

Level of Risk	Presenting Problem(s)	Diagnostic Procedure(s) Ordered	Management Options Selected
Moderate, continued	• Acute illness with systemic symptoms, eg, pyelonephritis, pneumonitis, colitis • Acute complicated injury, eg, head injury with brief loss of consciousness	• Cardiovascular imaging studies with contrast and no identified risk factors, eg, arteriogram, cardiac catheterization • Obtain fluid from body cavity, eg, lumbar puncture, thoracentesis, culdocentesis	• Therapeutic nuclear medicine • IV fluids with additives • Closed treatment of fracture or dislocation without manipulation
High	• One or more chronic illnesses with severe exacerbation, progression, or side effects of treatment • Acute or chronic illnesses or injuries that pose a threat to life or bodily function, eg, multiple trauma, acute MI, pulmonary embolus, severe respiratory distress, progressive severe rheumatoid arthritis, psychiatric illness with potential threat to self or others, peritonitis, acute renal failure • An abrupt change in neurological status, eg, seizure, TIA, weakness, sensory loss	• Cardiovascular imaging studies with contrast with identified risk factor • Cardiac electrophysiological tests • Diagnostic endoscopies with identified risk factors • Discography	• Elective major surgery (open, percutaneous, or endoscopic) with identified risk factors • Emergency major surgery (open, percutaneous, or endoscopic) • Parenteral controlled substances • Drug therapy requiring intensive monitoring for toxicity • Decision not to resuscitate or to de-escalate are because of poor prognosis

Physicians at Teaching Hospitals (PATH) Guidelines (online only)

Found at www.aap.org/cfp, access code AAPCFP20

MLN Matters SE0441—CMS Incident-To Requirements (online only)

Found at www.aap.org/cfp, access code AAPCFP20

Appendix A

Appendix B. Your Coding Toolkit

Figure B-1. *CPT*® Coding Change Request Form (online only)

Found at www.aap.org/cfp, access code AAPCFP20

Figure B-2. Commonly Used *ICD-9-CM* Codes Crosswalked to *ICD-10-CM* Codes
See online at www.aap.org/cfp, access code AAPCFP20.

Condition	*ICD-9-CM* Codes	*ICD-10-CM* Codes
Abdominal pain, loc _____	789.0__	R10.___
Abnormal neonatal screen	796.6	P09
Acne	706.1	L70.9
ADD w/o hyperactivity	314.00	F90.0
ADD w/ hyperactivity	314.01	F90.1
Allergic rhinitis	477.9	J30.9
Anal fissure	565.0	K60.2
Anemia (NOS)	285.9	D64.9
Anemia—iron deficiency	280.9	D50.8
Anxiety	300.00	F41.9
Apnea (neonate)	770.81	P29.3
Apnea, sleep	780.57	G47.30
Asthma, acute exacerbation	493.02	J45.21 (mild intermittent) J45.31 (mild persistent) J45.41 (moderate persistent) J45.51 (severe persistent)
Asthma, uncomplicated	493.00	J45.20 (mild intermittent) J45.30 (mild persistent) J45.40 (moderate persistent) J45.50 (severe persistent)
Atopic dermatitis/eczema	691.8	L20.89
Back pain (unspecified)	724.5	M54.9
Behavior problems, NOS	312.9	F91.9
Body mass index, specify	V85.__	Z68.___
Bronchiolitis, other organism	466.19	J21.8
Bronchitis	466.0	J20.9
Bullous myringitis	384.01	H73.011 (R) H73.012 (L) H73.013 (B)
Candidiasis (skin/nails)	112.3	B37.2
Chest pain (NOS)	786.50	R07.9
Colic (NOS)	789.7	R10.83
Conjunctivitis (NOS)	372.00	H10.31 (R) H10.32 (L) H10.33 (B)
Constipation	564.00	K59.00
Contact dermatitis, spec _____	692.9	L23.9

Appendix B

Figure B-2. Commonly Used *ICD-9-CM* Codes Crosswalked to *ICD-10-CM* Codes, continued
See online at www.aap.org/cfp, access code AAPCFP20.

Condition	*ICD-9-CM* Codes	*ICD-10-CM* Codes
Corneal abrasion, loc	918.1	S05.01X√ (R) S05.02X√ (L)
Costochondritis	733.6	M94.0
Cough	786.2	R05
Coxsackievirus (herpangina)	074.0	B08.5
Croup	464.4	J05.0
Dacryocystitis, neonatal	771.6	P39.1
Dacryostenosis, neonatal	375.55	H04.531 (R) H04.532 (L) H04.533 (B)
Dehydration	276.51	E86.0
Dehydration, neonatal	775.5	P74.1
Delayed milestones	783.42	R62.0
Dermatitis (NOS)	692.9	L23.9
Diabetes—type 1 (controlled)	250.01	E10.9
Diabetes—type 1 (uncontrolled)	250.03	E10.65
Diaper dermatitis	691.0	L22
Diarrhea (NOS)	787.91	R19.7
Dysuria	788.1	R30.0
Encopresis, nonorganic	307.7	F98.1
Enuresis, nonorganic	307.6	F98.0
Enuresis (nocturnal)	788.36	N39.44
Epistaxis	784.7	R04.0
Erythema infectiosum (fifth disease)	057.0	B08.3
Erythema multiforme, spec_____	695.1__	L51.8__
Eustachian tube dysfunction	381.81	H69.91 (R) H69.92 (L) H69.93 (B)
Excessive crying infant	780.92	R68.11
Exposure to strep	V01.89	Z20.89
Failure to thrive, neonatal	779.34	P92.6
Failure to thrive	783.41	R62.51
Fatigue	780.79	R53.83
Fecal impaction	560.32	K56.41
Feeding disorder	307.59	F98.29

Figure B-2. Commonly Used *ICD-9-CM* Codes Crosswalked to *ICD-10-CM* Codes, continued

See online at www.aap.org/cfp, access code AAPCFP20.

Condition	*ICD-9-CM* Codes	*ICD-10-CM* Codes
Feeding problem, neonatal	779.31	P92.8
Fever, unspecified	780.60	R50.9
Fever, postvaccination	780.63	R50.83
Fracture	By site_____	√te site_____
Fussy infant	780.91	R68.12
Gastroenteritis, presumed infectious	009.1	No code
Gastroenteritis, noninfectious	558.9	K52.9
GE reflux	530.81	K21.9 w/o esophagitis
Giardiasis	007.1	A07.1
Gingivostomatitis (herpetic)	054.2	B00.2
Hand, foot, mouth disease	074.3	B08.4
Headache, NOS	784.0	R51
Heart murmur	785.2	R01.1
Hematochezia	578.1	K92.1
Hematuria, unspecified	599.70	R31.9
Hematuria, gross	599.71	R31.0
Hematuria, microscopic	599.72	R31.2
Hordeolum (sty)	373.11	H00.01- site_____
Hyperbilirubinemia, neonatal	774.6	P59.9
Hypercholesterolemia	272.0	E78.0
Impacted cerumen	380.4	H61.21 (R) H61.22 (L) H61.23 (B)
Impetigo	684	L01.00
Influenza (NOS)	487.1	J11.1
Ingrown nail	703.0	L60.0
Inguinal hernia, unilateral	550.90	K40.90 K40.91 (recurrent)
Insect bite, noninfectious	By site_____	√By site_____
Jaw pain	784.92	R68.84
Kawasaki disease	446.1	M30.3
Learning disability	315.2	F81.89
Leukocytosis	288.60	D72.829
Lice (head)	132.0	B85.0

Appendix B

Figure B-2. Commonly Used *ICD-9-CM* Codes Crosswalked to *ICD-10-CM* Codes, continued

See online at www.aap.org/cfp, access code AAPCFP20.

Condition	ICD-9-CM Codes	ICD-10-CM Codes
Lymphadenitis, acute	683	L04.9
Lymphadenopathy	785.6	R59.1
Migraine spec ___	346.__	G43.10- w/ aura G43.00- w/o aura
Molluscum contagiosum	078.0	B08.1
Mononucleosis, infectious	075	B27.90
MRSA	038.12	A41.02
Nausea	787.02	R11.0
Nursemaid elbow	832.2	S53.031√ (R) S53.032√ (L)
Obesity	278.00	E66.9
Otalgia	388.70	H92.01 (R) H92.02 (L) H92.03 (B)
Otitis externa, infective, loc_____	380.10	H60.91 (R) H60.92 (L) H60.93 (B)
Otitis media, acute, purulent	382.00	H66.001 (R) H66.002 (L) H66.003 (B) H66.004 (recurrent—R) H66.005 (recurrent—L) H66.006 (recurrent—B)
Otitis media, purulent, perforated	382.01	H66.011 (R) H66.012 (L) H66.013 (B) H66.014 (recurrent—R) H66.015 (recurrent—L) H66.016 (recurrent—B)
Otitis media, chronic, purulent	382.3	H66.3X1 (R) H66.3X2 (L) H66.3X3 (B)
Otitis media w/ effusion	381. 4	H65.91 (R) H65.92 (L) H65.93 (B)
Otitis serous, acute	381.01	H65.01 (R) H65.02 (L) H65.03 (B) H65.04 (recurrent—R) H65.05 (recurrent—L) H65.06 (recurrent—B)

Appendix B

Figure B-2. Commonly Used *ICD-9-CM* Codes Crosswalked to *ICD-10-CM* Codes, continued

See online at www.aap.org/cfp, access code AAPCFP20.

Condition	*ICD-9-CM* Codes	*ICD-10-CM* Codes
Otitis serous, chronic	381.10	H65.21 (R) H65.22 (L) H65.23 (B)
Overweight	278.02	E66.3
Pharyngitis (NOS)	462	J02.9
Pneumonia	486	J18.9
Poison ivy	692.6	L23.7
Prematurity, birth weight__	765.__	P07.___
Preoperative exam, type __	V72.8__	Z01.818
Rhinitis, chronic	472.0	J31.0
RSV	079.6	B97.4
RSV bronchiolitis	466.11	J21.0
Scabies	133.0	B86
Scarlatina	034.1	A38.9
Scoliosis, spec region _____	737.30	M41.0- (infantile) M41.11- (juvenile) M41.12- (adolescent)
Screen for lead poisoning	V82.5	Z13.88
Seborrhea capitis (infant)	690.11	L21.0
Seborrheic dermatitis (infant)	690.12	L21.1
Seizure (epileptic), spec___	345.9__	G40.9___
Seizure (febrile)	780.31	R56.00
Seizure (posttraumatic)	780.33	R56.1
Seizure (NOS)	780.39	R56.9
Sinusitis (NOS)	461.9	J01.90
Speech disorder, spec_____	315.3__	F80.___
Strabismus	378.9	H50.9
Strep pharyngitis/Strep sore throat	034.0	J02.0 J03.00 strep tonsillitis
Stuttering	315.35	F80.81
Suture removal	V58.32	Z48.02
Teething syndrome	520.7	K00.7
Thrush	112.0	B37.0
Thrush, neonatal	771.7	P37.5
Tinea capitis	110.0	B35.0

Appendix B

Figure B-2. Commonly Used *ICD-9-CM* Codes Crosswalked to *ICD-10-CM* Codes, continued

See online at www.aap.org/cfp, access code AAPCFP20.

Condition	*ICD-9-CM* Codes	*ICD-10-CM* Codes
Tinea corporis	110.5	B35.4
Tonsillitis, unspecified	463	J03.90 acute J03.91 acute recurrent
Umbilical granuloma (neonatal)	771.4	P38.9
Umbilical hernia	553.1	K42.9
URI	465.9	J06.9
Urinary frequency	788.41	R35.0
Urticaria (NOS)	708.9	L50.9
UTI	599.0	N39.0
Vaginitis (NOS)	616.10	N76.0
Varicella	052.9	B01.9
Vertigo/dizziness	780.4	R42
Viral exanthem (NOS)	057.9	B09
Vomiting (neonatal)	779.33	P92.09
Vomiting	787.03	R11.11
Wart	078.10	B07.9

For ICD-10-CM codes: Do not report before October 1, 2015.

Abbreviations: √, insert encounter type (**A**: initial encounter; **D**: subsequent encounter; **S**: sequel); –, refer to ICD-10-CM for more specific code; ADD, attention-deficit disorder; (B), bilateral; GE, gastroesophageal; ICD-9-CM, International Classification of Diseases, Ninth Revision, Clinical Modification; ICD-10-CM, International Classification of Diseases, 10th Revision, Clinical Modification; (L), left side; loc, location; MRSA, methicillin-resistant Staphylococcus aureus; NOS, no other symptoms; (R), right side; recur, recurrent; RSV, respiratory syncytial virus; spec, specify; w/, with; w/o, without; URI, upper respiratory infection; UTI, urinary tract infection; X, placeholder (be sure to use the X as placed in code).

Appendix B

Figure B-3. AAP Documentation Forms (online only)

For AAP documentation forms for a variety of visit types, see www.aap.org/cfp, access code AAPCFP20.

Figure B-4. FAQ: Immunization Administration (online only)

Found at www.aap.org/cfp, access code AAPCFP20

Figure B-5. Vaccine Products (online only)

Found at www.aap.org/cfp, access code AAPCFP20

Appendix B

Figure B-6. Global Per Diem Critical Care Codes: Direct Supervision and Reporting Guidelines

The delivery of neonatal and pediatric critical care has undergone significant changes in the last 2 decades, incorporating expanded technology and services and new patterns of delivery of care. Neonatal intensive care units (NICUs) have grown dramatically as improvements in perinatal care have led to markedly improved survival rates of the small preterm neonate. There has also been a growing national population with major socioeconomic shifts. These changes have led to a large increase in NICU beds. Simultaneous to these demographic and epidemiologic changes, serious Accreditation Council for Graduate Medical Education and Residency Review Committee limitations in resident and fellow work hours and, more specifically, to those hours allocated to clinical care in the NICU, have reduced the number of house officers providing neonatal critical care. There has been a rapid expansion of other neonatal providers working as a team in partnership with an attending physician to meet expanding bedside patient care needs. These nonphysician providers (NPPs by Centers for Medicare & Medicaid Services nomenclature) are primarily neonatal nurse practitioners (NNPs). They have assumed a critical role in assisting the attending physician in caring for this expanding population of patients.

Neither NNPs nor resident/fellows are substitutes for the attending physician, who continues to remain fully in charge of these patients and directly supervises NNPs and resident/fellow physicians as well as other ancillary providers (eg, registered nurses, respiratory therapists, nutritionists, social workers, physical therapists, occupational therapists), who all play important contributory roles in the care of these critical patients. Unlike the supervision for residents/fellows enrolled in graduate medical education programs, the attending physician's supervision and documentation of care provided by NNPs is not covered by Physicians at Teaching Hospitals (PATH) guidelines. The attending physician is not "sharing services" with the NNP or resident/fellow. The attending physician (the physician responsible for the patient's care and reporting the service for that date) remains solely responsible for the supervision of the team and development of the patient's plan of care. In developing that plan, the attending physician will use the information acquired by and discussed with other members of the care team, including that of the resident/fellow and NNP.

When supervising residents/fellows, the attending physician will use this collective information as part of his or her own documentation of care. The attending physician must demonstrate in his or her own note that he or she has reviewed this information, performed his or her own focused examination of the patient, documented any additional findings or disagreements with the resident's/fellow's findings, and discussed the plan of care with the resident/fellow to meet PATH guideline requirements. These rules allow the attending physician to use the resident/fellow note as a major component of his or her own note and in determining the level of care the attending physician will report for that patient on that date.

Physicians at Teaching Hospitals guidelines do not apply to patients cared for by NNPs because NNPs are not enrolled in postgraduate education. This is true whether the NNP is employed by the hospital, medical group, or independent contractor. Centers for Medicare & Medicaid Services rules prohibit NPPs (in this case NNPs) and the reporting physician from reporting "shared or split services" when critical care services are provided. The reporting physician may certainly review and use the important information and observation of the NNPs, but the physician also provides his or her own evaluation along with documentation of the services he or she personally provided. Documentation expectations for the reporting physician include review of the notes and observations of other members of the care team; an independent-focused, medically appropriate bedside examination of the patient; and documentation that he or she has directed the plan of care for each patient whose services the physician reports. In many critically ill but stable patients, this requirement can be met by a single daily note. In situations in which the patient is very unstable and dramatic changes and major additional interventions are required to maintain stability, more extensive or frequent documentations are likely and may be entered by any qualified member of the care team.

In some states NNPs, through expanded state licenses, are permitted to independently report their services. If these NNPs are credentialed by the hospital and health plan to provide critical care services and procedures and possess their own National Provider Identifier (NPI), they may independently report the services they provide. In these states they can function as independent contractors or as employees of the hospital or a medical group, reporting their services under their own NPI. It is important to emphasize again that the NNP and the physician do not report a shared critical care service. Critical care services are reported under the NNP or physician NPI,

Figure B-6. Global Per Diem Critical Care Codes: Direct Supervision and Reporting Guidelines, continued

dependent on who was primarily providing the patient service and directing the care of the patient. Two providers may not report a global per diem critical care code (eg, **99468, 99469**) on the same date of service. In most situations the physician is serving as responsible and supervising provider and the NNP (employed by the group or hospital) is acting as a member of the team of providers the physician supervises.

Physician Supervision

Current Procedural Terminology (CPT®) states that codes **99468–99476** (initial and subsequent inpatient neonatal and pediatric critical care, per day, for the evaluation and management of a critically ill neonate or child through 5 years of age) are used to report services provided by a physician directing the inpatient care of a critically ill neonate or young child. *Current Procedural Terminology* makes clear that the reporting provider is not required to maintain 24-hour, in-hospital physical presence. *Current Procedural Terminology* notes that the physician or other reporting provider must be physically present and at bedside at some time during the 24-hour period to examine the patient and review and direct the patient's care with the health care team. The physician must be readily available to the health care team if needed but does not have to provide 24-hour, in-house coverage. One provider reports the appropriate code only once per day, even though multiple providers may have interacted with the patient during the 24-hour global period (eg, on-call physician, NNP).

Medical Record Documentation

The medical record serves the dual purpose of communicating the medical status and progress of the patient and documenting the work of the reporting provider.

Based on the information presented previously, it is the suggestion of the American Academy of Pediatrics Committee on Coding and Nomenclature that the medical record documentation by the reporting physician or NPP supporting critical care codes should contain at a minimum

- Documentation of the critical status of the infant or child (This is not to be inferred.)
- Documentation of the **bedside** direction and supervision of all aspects of care
- Review of pertinent historical information and verification of significant physical findings through a medically indicated, focused patient examination
- Documentation of all services provided by members of the care team and discussion and direction of the ongoing therapy and plan of care for the patient
- Additional documentation of any major change in patient course requiring significant hands-on intervention by the reporting provider

The following are *not* required of the reporting physician or NPP:

- Twenty-four–hour presence in the facility or bedside
- Two or more documented notes a day
- Personally ordering all tests, medications, and therapies
- Performing all or any of the bundled procedures
- Documenting a daily comprehensive physical examination
- Documenting stable or unstable status so long as the infant or child meets critical care criteria

Each patient has a different level of illness(es), grouping of diagnoses, and medical and socioeconomic problems. The following are only examples of notes and should not be interpreted as requirements in every note for each patient:

A. The following note represents a sample attestation that could be appended to a resident or fellow's progress note:

"I have reviewed the resident's progress note and the baby has been seen and examined by me. He continues to be critically ill with respiratory failure requiring mechanical ventilation. I concur with the resident's evaluation and findings, though I did not appreciate abdominal tenderness on examination. I have discussed and agreed on a plan of care with the resident."

B. The following 2 paragraphs represent a single sample documentation that a reporting physician might write when care is delivered by an NNP and physician team. This note could be appended by the reporting physician to the NNP documentation or written as separate physician documentation.

Figure B-6. Global Per Diem Critical Care Codes: Direct Supervision and Reporting Guidelines, continued

"(Name) has been seen and examined by me on bedside rounds. The interval history, laboratory findings, and physical examination of the patient have been reviewed with members of the neonatal team. The notes have been reviewed. All aspects of care have been discussed, and I have agreed on an assessment and plan for the day with the care team.

"(Name) continues to be critically ill, requiring high-frequency jet ventilation. On examination, her breath sounds are coarse but equal, there is no heart murmur, and the abdomen is soft and non-tender. Her oxygen requirements have been at 100% for the past 12 hours. She remains on antibiotics for *Proteus* sepsis. At the recommendation of infectious disease, we have changed her antibiotic coverage to cefotaxime and gentamicin. Her blood pressure is acceptable today, but her urine output is only at 1 mL/kg/hour. We are watching this closely and may need to restart dopamine. She remains NPO and is on total parenteral nutrition."

Approach to Documentation

This information deals largely with neonatal care. However, the same coding and documentation principles apply for critical care services provided to all children through the age of 5 years. The guidelines provided in this statement represent clarification of documentation recommendations for this unique code set. They are intended to create clarity going forward for physicians and other parties as they incorporate this new guidance into their documentation processes. Physicians should structure their documentation such that on review of a medical record representing a physician-rendered per-day neonatal or pediatric critical care service, one should be able to discern the reporting physician's unique documentation in support of the physician's role in that patient's care. It is especially important that an electronic health record used in documenting these services be configured to uniquely identify the author of each entry and allow for timely response to requests for documentation substantiating billed services. It is equally as important to log out of the record when your documentation is complete.

Figure B-7. Chronic Care Management Worksheet

Reporting month/year _____

Patient _____

DOB _____ MR# _____

Type of residence[1] _____

Chronic condition(s): _____

_____

_____

Other medical conditions: _____

_____

_____

Other needs (social, access to care): _____

_____

_____

Date initial plan of care developed by physician/QHCP ___

_____

Date plan of care provided to patient/caregiver _____

_____

Clinical staff activities may include

- ✷ Communication (with patient, family members, guardian/caregiver, surrogate decision-makers, or other professionals) about aspects of care
- ✷ Communication with home health agencies and other community services used by the patient
- ✷ Collection of health outcomes data and registry documentation
- ✷ Patient or family/caregiver education to support self-management, independent living, and activities of daily living
- ✷ Assessment of and support for treatment regimen adherence and medication management
- ✷ Identification of available community and health resources
- ✷ Facilitating access to care and services needed by the patient/family
- ✷ Management of care transitions not reported as part of transitional care management
- ✷ Ongoing review of patient status, including review of laboratory and other studies not reported as part of E/M
- ✷ Development and maintenance of a comprehensive care plan

Activity Documentation Table

In the following table, include date, activity description, time spent, and location of any associated documentation (eg, plan of care, call notes).

Date	Activity (Include reference to other documentation when indicated.)	Time (start and stop)	Total Time	Clinical Staff Signature (legible/credentials)
		Total Time	min	

_____ **99487** first hour of clinical staff time with establishment or substantial revision of care plan, per calendar month

_____ **99489** <u>each additional 30 minutes</u> of clinical staff time per calendar month **(Enter number of units.)**

_____ **99490** <u>at least 20 minutes</u> of clinical staff time per calendar month

Supervising physician/QHCP signature_____ **Date**_____

Abbreviations: DOB, date of birth; E/M, evaluation and management; MR, medical record; QHCP, qualified health care professional.

[1]*Specify if patient lives in a private residence, group home, or other type of domiciliary. Do not report complex chronic care coordination services for patients residing in a facility that provides more than minimal medical care (eg, nursing facility).*

Appendix B

Figure B-8. Care Plan Oversight Encounter Worksheet

See www.aap.org/cfp for an online version of this worksheet, access code AAPCFP20.

Physician: _____   Patient Name: _____

Services Provided:
The letter that corresponds with each service provided should be placed in column #2.
A. Regular physician development and/or revision of care plans
B. Review of subsequent reports of patient status
C. Review of related laboratory or other studies
D. Communication (including telephone calls not separately reported with codes **99441–99443**) with other health care professionals involved in patient's care
E. Integration of new information into the medical treatment plan and/or adjustment of medical therapy
F. Other (Attach additional explanatory materials on the services provided.)

Date of Service XX/XX/XXXX	Services Provided	Contact Name and Agency	Start Time	End Time	Total Minutes	Monthly Subtotal

Explanation for additional services provided:

Date:_____/_____

_____

Date:_____/_____

_____

Date:_____/_____

Time Requirements Per Calendar Month	Patient in Home, Domiciliary, or Rest Home (eg, Assisted Living Facility)	Patient Under the Care of a Home Health Care Agency	Hospice Patient	Nursing Facility Patient
15–29 min	99339	99374	99377	99379
≥30 min	99340	99375	99378	99380
≥30 min Medicare code		G0181	G0182	

Monthly Total: _____ *CPT* Code: _____

Appendix B

Figure B-9. Sample Denial Tracking Tool

See www.aap.org/cfp for an online version of this tool, access code AAPCFP20.

Codes Paid When Submitted as a Clean Claim	Payer Name	Payer Name	Payer Name	Payer Name	Payer Name	Payer Name	Payer Name	Payer Name
Example: **90460/90461; 90471/90472:** Immunization admin codes	Yes							
Example: **992__** with preventive medicine visit (**9938_/9939_**) on same DOS	No							
Example: Normal newborn care or hospital visits/discharges when billed with circumcision								
Example: **92551** Hearing screen		No, adj off						

Key: Yes = paid; No = no payment, appealed; Varies = payment is specific to employer's benefit plan; No, adj off = billed, denied, NO APPEAL, based on contract, adjust off.

Figure B-10. Claim Correction Form (online only)
Found at www.aap.org/cfp, access code AAPCFP20

Figure B-11. Sample Appeal Letter (online only)
Found at www.aap.org/cfp, access code AAPCFP20

Appendix B

Figure B-12. Effective Health Plan Appeals: The Ins and Outs

I. Know How and Why to Appeal Inappropriate Health Plan Claim Denials

It is estimated that physicians are losing billions of dollars in revenue each year by not appealing inappropriate claim denials.

There are many reasons why physician practices do not appeal denied claims; the most common is that they believe appealing claims will create an increased administrative burden on the practice. However, not appealing denied or partially paid claims can be quite costly to your practice and can often result in decreased revenue. Since health plans have introduced claims editing software into their claims processing systems, they have generated an increased number of inappropriate claim denials and reductions in payment. An effective way for your practice to combat these erroneous payment reductions and denials is to be diligent in submitting appeals.

Why Appeal?

When your practice increases its appeals for wrongfully underpaid or denied claims, the health plan may correct its claims editing software and processes. This, in turn, may result in improved claim processes and appropriate payment to your practice for the provision of health care services. The 12 steps under How to Simplify the Claim Auditing and Appeals Process below simplify the claim auditing and appeals processes and can help to reduce your administrative burden. These processes make it easy for your practice to identify and appeal health plan claim denials when the health plan misapplies the American Medical Association *Current Procedural Terminology (CPT®)* codes, guidelines, and conventions or the health plan's contracted policies. When a physician performs a procedure or service and then reports according to *CPT* codes, guidelines, and conventions, the health plan should recognize the physician work involved in providing this patient care. To ensure that your work is recognized, your practice should identify all inappropriate claim denials and communicate with the appropriate health plan representatives through each plan's claim appeals processes.

What Is Lost When Your Practice Does Not Appeal?

When your practice does not audit and appeal inappropriately paid or denied health plan claims, you may lose revenue. You also may lose the opportunity to recover overhead expenses by not implementing a claims management process. This process is your practice's internal designated work flow for accurately preparing, submitting, and collecting on claims. When you challenge inappropriate claim payments, you demonstrate that your practice has made an effort to correct the plan's inaccuracy. This could lead to a positive change in the health plan's business practices. Appealing claims that are inappropriately denied by health plans can make a difference in your practice by reducing future denials.

For additional information, there are 2 easy ways to contact the American Academy of Pediatrics (AAP) Private Payer Advocacy Advisory Committee.

1.   Go to www.aap.org/en-us/professional-resources/practice-support/financing-and-payment/Pages/Private-Payer-Advocacy.aspx (AAP members only).
2.   Contact the AAP Coding Hotline at aapcodinghotline@aap.org.

How to Simplify the Claim Auditing and Appeals Processes

1.   Know the health plan's claim appeals processes before you need to submit a claim appeal. Understanding these processes will allow you to acquire the health plan information (eg, supporting documentation, health plan language) required to prepare a claim appeal.
2.   Know where to locate the following health plan policies and, if possible, include them in the health plan contract:
     • Claim adjudication procedures (ie, definitions of complete or clean claims and medical necessity)
     • Rates and payment methodology, including a comprehensive fee schedule
     • Claim appeals processes
3.   Document, document, document. The supporting documentation of a claim submitted to a health plan must substantiate the performance of a service by the treating physician or health care professional. If a service is not documented, it didn't happen in the eyes of the health plan, and the claim may not be paid.
4.   Review and monitor all claims before submitting them to the health plan to ensure that you are filing complete and accurate claims. One way to avoid a claim denial is to correctly code the original claim. Implement a checks-and-balances system between physicians and the coding and billing professionals in your practice to determine whether claims are being coded appropriately.
5.   Maintain a coding reference sheet in your practice with a list of commonly used *International Classification of Diseases, Ninth Revision, Clinical Modification* codes; when implemented, *International Classification of Diseases, 10th Revision, Clinical Modification* codes; and *CPT* codes, as well as any other commonly reported codes on the standard claim form.

I. Know How and Why to Appeal Inappropriate Health Plan Claim Denials, continued

6. Evaluate the health plan's explanation of benefits (EOB) for accuracy (eg, potential processing errors, lack of recognition of a *CPT* modifier, incorrect Physician Fee Schedule).

7. Know your contracted fee schedule rate with each health plan for procedures and services commonly performed in your practice. Review each EOB you receive to ensure the negotiated payment and discount rate with each health plan is calculated appropriately.

8. Maintain a health plan follow-up log that contains the reason that the claim was partially paid, delayed, or denied by the health plan and also the internal follow-up action by practice staff to reduce future health plan underpayments and denials.

9. When submitting a formal claim appeal letter to a health plan, thoroughly explain your rationale for challenging the health plan's claim denial. Additionally, include the appropriate documentation to support your request to reverse the denial.

10. Streamline your practice's claim auditing and appeals processes by maintaining an appeals resource file with appeal template letters, rationales, and supporting documentation of previously submitted claim appeal letters that resulted in overturning the denial.

11. Keep on appealing. It may take more than one appeal to reverse a health plan's incorrect denial. When a procedure or service has been appropriately performed, documented, and reported, be persistent to ensure your practice obtains the proper compensation based on the negotiated health plan contracted rate.

12. If the appeal is not overturned by the health plan after appeals are exhausted, file for an external review if available through the appropriate state or federal regulatory agency.

II. Supporting Your Appeals for Payment

Filing appeals using these suggestions makes the payer aware that the physician is knowledgeable of coding guidelines and adheres to coding conventions.

- Include a quote from the current coding guidelines that is applicable to the billed service. Example: "According to *Current Procedural Terminology (CPT®)*, modifier **25** is used to identify a 'significant, separately identifiable evaluation and management (E/M) service by the same physician or other qualified health care professional on the same day of the procedure or other service.' See the American Medical Association publication *CPT® 2015, Professional Edition.*"

- Note where a denial is in conflict with the payer's written policy, quoting from its policies and procedures manual. Example: "According to Section xxx.x of your Professional Services Manual dated July 1, 2013, your policy is to follow National Correct Coding Initiative (NCCI) edits in your claim adjudication process."

- Quote NCCI edits reflecting correct coding and/or use of modifiers. Example: "According to Version xxx of the Centers for Medicare & Medicaid Services NCCI edits, there is no edit that pairs *CPT* code **69210** (removal of cerumen) with an E/M service. The E/M service was necessary to diagnose otitis media, and the removal of cerumen was medically indicated because the patient had impacted cerumen. The reported diagnoses were linked to the appropriate service performed and billed."

- Include as appropriate any operative and/or procedure notes. Highlight the procedures that relate to the codes.

   If a problem is recurring, suggest to the insurer ways it can be avoided in the future. Frame the proposed resolution in a way that enhances quality, access, value, and cost-effectiveness to patients, the payer, and the practice.

III. Elements of an Effective Appeal Letter

Generally, an appeal letter should contain the following:

Date:
Carrier Address:

Address the letter to one having the authority to make a decision on the claim, such as the Carrier Claims Review Department Director or Carrier Medical Director.

Dear:
RE: Claim #:
I am writing regarding the aforementioned claim and (Insurance Carrier Name)'s practice of

List the offending carrier practice (eg, bundling codes, not recognizing codes).

Provide rationale as to why this practice is unacceptable to the pediatrician, the patient, and fair business practice. Reference appropriate *CPT* guidelines, contract language, fee schedule, and state or federal law.

State how the situation is to be rectified and what you expect the carrier to do. Specify a time frame for a response and how the carrier may reach you should it have any questions.

Enclosed is a copy of the original claim that was submitted with a request that you process payment as indicated on the claim. I look forward to receiving your response by (date).
If you have any questions, please feel free to contact me at _____.

Sincerely,

Also available at www.aap.org/cfp, access code AAPCFP20.

IV. Sample Appeal Letter: Well/Sick Same Day

Date:

Insurance Carrier Claims Review Department and address or
Insurance Carrier Medical Director and address

Dear:

RE: Claim #:

I am writing regarding the aforementioned claim and <u>(Insurance Carrier Name)'s</u> practice of bundling preventive medicine service codes and office/outpatient service codes. *Current Procedural Terminology (CPT®)* guidelines indicate that in certain cases, it is appropriate to report a preventive medicine service code (**99381–99397**) in conjunction with an office/outpatient service code (**99201–99215**) on the same date of service.

According to the American Medical Association *CPT* guidelines, "If an abnormality(ies) is encountered or a preexisting problem is addressed in the process of performing a preventive medicine evaluation and management service, and if the problem/abnormality(ies) is significant enough to require additional work to perform the key components of a problem-oriented service, then the appropriate office/outpatient code should also be reported. Modifier **25** should be added to the office/outpatient code to indicate that a significant, separately identifiable evaluation and management service was provided by the same physician on the same day as the preventive medicine service. The appropriate preventive medicine service is additionally reported" (page 35, *CPT 2013 Professional Edition*). These statements clearly indicate that a "well" and a "sick" visit should be recognized as separate services when reported on the same day.

Unfortunately, many carriers are not familiar with the *CPT* guidelines that allow for the reporting of 2 visits on the same day of service by use of modifier **25.** Further, there are no diagnosis *(International Classification of Diseases, 10th Revision, Clinical Modification [ICD-10-CM])* requirements tied to the use of modifier **25.** In fact, "The descriptor for modifier **25** was revised to clarify that since the E/M service may be prompted by the symptom or condition for which the procedure and/or service was provided, different diagnoses are not required to report the E/M services on the same date" *(CPT Assistant.* May 2000;10[5]). This basic tenet of *CPT* coding underscores the fact that it is *inherently incorrect for carriers to place restrictions on the number, type, or order of diagnoses associated with the reporting of 2 visits on the same day.*

There are also some carriers that, through failure to recognize all services provided during a single patient session, <u>potentially increase the number of visits necessary to address a patient's concerns.</u> If a patient is seen for a preventive medicine visit and the physician discovers that the patient has symptoms of otitis media during the examination, clinical protocol and common sense would dictate that the physician take care of the well-child examination and the treatment of the otitis media during that single patient visit. Unfortunately, the fact that some carriers fail to fairly pay the physician for providing both services will motivate providers to address only the acute problem and have the patient/parent return at a later date for the preventive medicine visit. This situation is frustrating for everyone involved, especially for the insureds.

While there is no legal mandate requiring private carriers to adhere to the aforementioned *CPT* guidelines, it is considered a good-faith gesture for them to do so, given that the guidelines are the current standard within organized medicine. Because providers are clearly instructed that an office/outpatient "sick" visit cannot be reported unless it represents a significant, separately identifiable service beyond the preventive medicine service, carriers should feel confident that the reporting of 2 visits on a single date of service *will not occur unless it is justified.*

Enclosed is a copy of the original claim that was submitted with a request that you process payment as indicated on the claim. I look forward to receiving your response.

If you have any questions, please feel free to contact me at _____.

Sincerely,

Appendix B

Figure B-13. FAQ: Alternative Payment Methodologies (online only)

Found at www.aap.org/cfp, access code AAPCFP20

Figure B-14. Marshfield Audit Tool (online only)

Found at www.aap.org/cfp, access code AAPCFP20

Figure B-15. Coding Fact Sheets (online only)

Found at www.aap.org/cfp, access code AAPCFP20

Appendix C. Asthma Clinical Performance Measures (online only)

Found at www.aap.org/cfp, access code AAPCFP20

Appendix D. 2015 Pediatric Coding Resources Exclusively From the AAP

2015 Pediatric Coding Resources

Pediatric-Specific, Peer-Reviewed, and Newly Updated for 2015

AAP Pediatric Coding Newsletter™—Practice-tested coding and compliance guidelines from the AAP! Month after month, *AAP Pediatric Coding Newsletter™* helps you maximize payment, save time, and implement best business practices to support quality patient care. Included in this annual subscription product is **print and online access** to broad coverage of coding for pediatric primary care and subspecialty services. Subscribers have priority access to the AAP Coding Hotline, timely updates and alerts on coding changes and evolving compliance guidelines, convenient continuing education, and much more. Visit http://coding.aap.org to preview a complete issue.

Principles of Pediatric ICD-10-CM Coding—Pediatric-specific guidelines to help ease the transition to 10! Start preparing your practice for migration to *ICD-10-CM* with this all-new AAP guidebook. Designed to complement the complete *ICD-10-CM* code set, it provides the pediatric-specific knowledge your staff will need to successfully implement the new code set. Chapters devoted to individual disease categories and organ systems offer expert guidance for appropriate *ICD-10-CM* code selection and much more.

Pediatric ICD-10-CM: A Manual for Provider-Based Coding—Forthcoming in early 2015! A pediatric-specific, condensed version of the *ICD-10-CM* manual! Only pediatric-relevant codes and provider-based guidelines will be included in this manual. With the expansion of codes from *ICD-9-CM* to *ICD-10-CM*, the size of the *ICD-10-CM* manual will grow, making its use only more difficult over time. By removing the codes and guidelines that do not pertain to pediatrics and placing those relevant guidelines right alongside the corresponding codes in the tabular portion of the manual, this version will be the go-to manual for daily use and ease of navigation.

Pediatric Code Crosswalk: ICD-9-CM to ICD-10-CM—Simplify *ICD-9-CM* coding AND prepare for *ICD-10-CM* transition! This handy time-saving resource will be used again and again as you start integrating the *ICD-10-CM* nomenclature and code set into your practice. *And* it continues to include all *ICD-9-CM* codes for easy identification and reference. This spiral-bound quick reference guide simplifies the transition process by listing *ICD-9-CM* codes for the most common pediatric diagnoses right alongside their *ICD-10-CM* counterparts.

Quick Reference Card for Pediatric Immunization Coding and Guidance 2015—Newly updated for 2015! This 8½" × 11" laminated card includes immunization administration codes, code usage guidelines, and access to codes, manufacturers, and brands for all current pediatric immunizations.

Pediatric Evaluation and Management (E/M) Coding Card 2015—Newly updated for 2015! This handy 8½" × 11" card is used for quicker, more accurate E/M reporting. It provides documentation guidelines for each level of service—including typical times.

The AAP Pediatric Coding Webinar series includes 1-hour live events with pediatric-specific insights, tips, and strategies from experienced coding professionals that you can't afford to miss. For more information on scheduled 2014–2015 events or to register today, visit www.aap.org/webinars/coding.

To order these and other pediatric resources, visit shopAAP at http://shop.aap.org/books or **call toll-free 888/227-1770.**

‖‖‖‖

Subject Index
Code Index

‖‖‖‖

CODE INDEX

Code Index